Library of Congress Cataloging-in-Publication Data

Troiano, Edna M.
    The contemporary writer / Edna M. Troiano, Julia D. Scott.
        p.   cm.
    Includes bibliographical references and index.
    1. English language—Rhetoric.   2. English language—Grammar.   3. Report writing. I.
Scott, Julia D. II. Title.
PE1408.T6954 2000
808'.042—dc21
ISBN 0-13-090930-0

00-062325

Editor-in-Chief: Leah Jewell
Acquisitions Editor: Corey Good
VP, Director of Production and Manufacturing:
  Barbara Kittle
Managing Editor: Mary Rottino
Production Editor: Randy Pettit
Prepress and Manufacturing Manager: Nick Sklitsis
Prepress and Manufacturing Buyer:
  Mary Ann Gloriande

Marketing Director: Beth Gillett Mejia
Marketing Manager: Brandy Dawson
Creative Design Director: Leslie Osher
Interior Art Director and Designer: Kathryn Foot
Cover Design Director: Kathryn Foot
Cover Design: Kathryn Foot
Cover Art: Theo Rudnak

For permission to use copyrighted material, grateful
acknowledgment is made to the copyright holders listed
on page 557–559, which is considered an extension of this
copyright page.

This book was set by TSI Graphics and printed and bound by
R.R. Donnelley & Sons Company.
The cover was printed by Phoenix Color Corp.

Pearson Education Limited (UK)
Pearson Education Australia Pty. Ltd.
Prentice Hall Canada Ltd
Pearson Educacion de Mexico, S.A. de C.V.
Pearson Education Japan KK
Pearson Education China Ltd.
Pearson Education Asia Pte. Ltd.

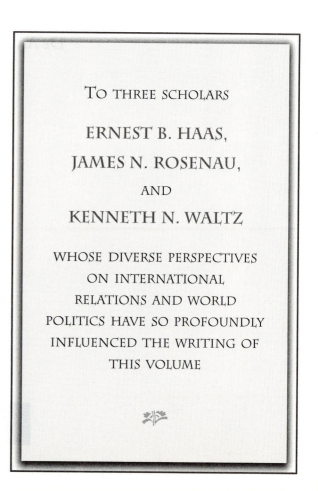

TO THREE SCHOLARS

ERNEST B. HAAS,

JAMES N. ROSENAU,

AND

KENNETH N. WALTZ

WHOSE DIVERSE PERSPECTIVES
ON INTERNATIONAL
RELATIONS AND WORLD
POLITICS HAVE SO PROFOUNDLY
INFLUENCED THE WRITING OF
THIS VOLUME

BRIEF CONTENTS

CONTENTS

CHAPTER 2   *Effective Reading*

CHAPTER 3   *Purpose and Thesis*

CHAPTER 4   *Information Gathering*

CHAPTER 5   *Paragraphs and Essays*

CHAPTER 6   *Supporting Evidence*

CHAPTER 8 *Revision*

PART II: Using Rhetorical Strategies and Argument to Develop Academic and Workplace Texts

CHAPTER 9   *Rhetorical Strategies*

CHAPTER 10   *Narration*

CHAPTER 14   *Causal Analysis*

CHAPTER 15   *Comparison and Contrast*

CHAPTER 16   *Classification*

CHAPTER 20   *Internet and Library Research*

CHAPTER 21   *Documentation*

PART IV: Special Topics

CHAPTER 22   *Essay Exams*

CHAPTER 23   *Document Design*

CHAPTER 24   *Oral Presentations*

PART V: Handbook

I. *Sentence Structure*

II. *Usage*

III. *Punctuation*

IV. *Guidelines for Speakers of Other Languages*

PREFACE

TO THE INSTRUCTOR

Effective writing, whether academic, workplace, or personal, shares the same process and the same characteristics. Whether writing a research paper for an economics course, a report on office absenteeism, or a letter about a billing error to a credit card company, writers must consider their purpose and audience, gather information, organize ideas, express themselves clearly, revise, edit, and proofread their work.

College composition courses have traditionally limited their content to academic reading and writing, as if the demands of college composition were unrelated to the reading and writing students do in their professional and personal lives. Traditional rhetorics assume either that composition instruction is relevant only to the academic realm, or that students will instinctively apply what they learn in their composition courses to the writing they do at work and in their personal lives. Students, however, frequently view their composition courses as isolated both from the typical demands of their college curricula and from the writing tasks they do at work or at home. Because this text is intended for use in college composition courses, it focuses on instruction and practice in the conventions of academic writing. However, each chapter also demonstrates, through examples, exercises, and assignments, that the techniques effective in academic writing are equally effective in workplace and personal writing.

During recent years, the demographics of current college students have shifted: In two-year colleges the average student is about twenty-seven years old, has a job, and attends college part time; in four-year colleges, the average age is approaching twenty-one years old, and an increasing number of students work, are married, and have children. The instruction, examples, and assignments in this text are designed to be both useful and relevant to contemporary students.

Each chapter focuses on one trait of effective writing and demonstrates its applicability to academic, professional, and personal writing. In every chapter, discussions, examples, exercises, and assignments reflect workplace and personal as well as academic writing. Readings are tied to the chapter's topic; for example, the chapter on purpose contains readings intended to record, inform, and persuade, and the chapter on research contains readings about research. Each chapter concludes with five writing assignments—three academic assignments drawn from various disciplines, one workplace writing assignment, and one personal assignment. These assignments reinforce the composition instruction and reflect the readings. Although the topic of constructing essays is not discussed thoroughly until Chapter 5, guided assignments allow students to begin writing well-constructed essays in the first chapter. Because the needs, interests, and skill levels of students vary widely, the text provides abundant choices of readings, writing assignments, and collaborative and computer exercises. No professor would expect students to undertake all of the assignments or exercises; however, every professor should find ample material suitable for any class.

Because students cannot write well unless they think clearly, *The Contemporary Writer* promotes clear thinking in two ways. First, students cannot be passive learners because the text provides activities that require them to manipulate the information they read. Second, the text's assignments require that students think critically and creatively and gather fresh information before writing.

Finally, *The Contemporary Writer* reflects real writing in two additional ways: The incorporation of technology and the presence of collaborative writing. Almost all writers today rely on computers for research and writing. This text assumes that students use computers to draft and revise papers and that they seek information online. To help them use computers as something other than electronic typewriters, the text contains computer strategies for writing and computer-based assignments. Most writers also rely on the advice and support of colleagues, friends, and family. This text encourages students to work collaboratively and provides discussion topics, exercises, and writing assignments for students to work on in groups.

Students take seriously the studies they deem relevant and useful. *The Contemporary Writer* is designed to make composition instruction useful and relevant in students' academic, professional, and personal lives.

SUPPLEMENTARY MATERIAL
FOR INSTRUCTORS AND STUDENTS

Unique Online Study Resource…the *Companion Website*™
www.prenhall.com/troiano

This website provides additional reinforcement of the text's content while providing a collection of supplementary resources to guide the student through the process of writing in academic, personal, and workplace settings.

Each chapter contains:

- **Writing Workshop** activities guide students through the writing process.
- **Self-graded** questions reinforce the chapter content and test comprehension.
- **Working Together** modules reinforce collaborative learning through various activities.
- **Reading comprehension questions** for in text and additional on-line readings.
- **Timed essay exams.**
- **Links** throughout the website to provide topics for writing, help with research, and key resources for writing.
- Additional modules on **documenting sources, oral presentations, and document design.**

Daedalus® Online   DAEDALUS

Prentice Hall is proud to offer a customized version of Daedalus Online designed around the structure and organization of ***The Contemporary Writer*** offering you consistency in your writing program. Developed *by* writing teachers *for* writing teachers, this web-based program focuses on teaching and learning by means of interactive, written discourse-encouraging exploration of the writing process, collaborative work, peer review, critical thinking, and communication.

This program features:

- Invent
- Interchange
- Reference Links
- Discussion Board
- E-Mail
- Respond
- Document Manager

Access to Daedalus Online is available at a discounted price when packaged with *The Contemporary Writer.* Learn more about Daedalus Online at *www.prenhall.com/english*

WEB CT and Blackboard courses for *The Contemporary Writer*

These complete online courses include all of the functionality and content from the companion website along with additional material for students and instructors. The site includes lecture notes, self-check quizzes, additional writing models, bulletin board/chat topics, and more. These courses are available at a discounted price when you adopt the Troiano text.

FREE when packaged with any Prentice Hall English textbook. Contact your local representative for details.

- *The New American Webster Handy College Dictionary,* **Third Edition**

    An updated and expanded edition contains more than 115,000 definitions, covering current phrases, slang, and scientific terms, and including advice on usage and grammar, notes on etymology, foreign words and phrases, and a world gazetteer. It is a brief paperback dictionary that is available FREE when packaged with any Prentice Hall English textbook.
    ISBN: 0-13-032870-7

- *English on the Internet 2001: Evaluating online sources*

    Contains information on how to get online, popular search engines, the most useful English sites, a glossary of terms and, of course the latest MLA documentation guidelines for electronic sources.
    ISBN: 0-13-022073-6

- **Guide to Research and Documentation: Prentice Hall Resources for Writing by Kirk G. Rasmussen—Newly Updated With 2000 MLA Guidelines!**

    This useful booklet provides students with research and documentation in a paperback format designed for ease of use and portability. A handy guide, it

features the most recent information on MLA, APA, CBE, and CM formats, and covers the research process.
ISBN: 0-13-081627-2

- **Model Student Essays by Mark Gallaher**

  This anthology features 25 student essays collected from around the country which are organized into three broad categories: personal experience, explain and inform, and argue a position.
  ISBN: 0-13-645516-6

- **New! The Writer's Guide Series**

  Provides students and instructor's in-depth coverage on contemporary topics, allowing instructors to cover relevant information based on their course structure and students' needs.
  Writer's Guide to Document & Web Design ISBN: 0-13-018929-4
  Writer's Guide to WAC & Oral Presentations ISBN: 0-13-018931-6
  Writer's Guide to Public Writing ISBN: 0-13-018932-4

- **Model Research Papers for Writers 2/E by Janette Lewis**

  Nine (9) additional, reproducible model research papers are contained in this supplement. They range from 10 to 12 pages and come from the following disciplines: English, Philosophy, Biology, Psychology, Sociology, Chemistry, History/Classics, and Political Science.
  ISBN: 0-13-238296-2

- **The Prentice Hall/New York Times "Themes of the Times" Program**

  The "Themes of the Times" program is co-sponsored by Prentice Hall and *The New York Times*. It is a newspaper supplement that contains current articles designed to inspire students to write.
  ISBN: 0-13-022221-6

Available to Qualified Adopters: Prentice Hall Resources for Composition

- **ABC News/Prentice Hall Video Library: Composition, Volume 2**
  ISBN: 0-13-149030-3

- **"Profiles of a Writer" Video Series**

- **Computers and Writing, 2E, by Dawn Rodrigues**—University of Texas at Brownsville.
  ISBN: 0-13-084034-3

- **The Prentice Hall/Simon & Schuster Transparencies for Writers**
  ISBN: 0-13-703209-9

- **Classroom Strategies by Wendy Bishop**—Florida State University
  ISBN: 0-13-572355-8

- **Portfolios by Pat Belanoff**—SUNY Stonybrook
  ISBN: 0-13-572322-1

- Journals by Chris Burnham—New Mexico State University
  ISBN: 0-13-572348-5
- Collaborative Learning by Harvey Kail—University of Maine & John Trimbur—Worcester Polytechnic Institute
  ISBN: 0-13-572371-X
- English as a Second Language by Ruth Spack—Tufts University
  ISBN: 0-13-572389-2
- Distance Education by W. Dees Stallings—University of Maryland, University College
  ISBN: 0-13-572314-0
- Teaching Writing Across the Curriculum 2E by Art Young—Clemson University
  ISBN: 0-13-081650-7

Special Offers

- Takenote!

  A complete information management tool for people who write research papers. TakeNote! integrates note taking, outlining and bibliographic reference management software into one easy-to-use CD-ROM package. Just $6 net when packaged with any text or $24 standalone. ISBN 0-13-022209-7

- Writer's Helper, Version 4.0 (*Microsoft® Windows and Macintosh®*)

  Based on the notion that software tools can be attributed to imaginative and well-organized writing, WRITER'S HELPER offers a collection of unique nineteen prewriting activities and 18 revising tools to help students through the writing process. Available for $10 when packaged with this text.

TO THE STUDENT

College composition does not typically rank high among students' favorite courses. Many students approach college composition courses with emotions ranging from indifference to anxiety or even dread. One reason for students' negative attitude toward composition courses is that writing is difficult. No composition text can make writing easy; however, *The Contemporary Writer* does provide clear, helpful information and useful strategies for writing.

A second reason that many students dislike composition courses is that the courses appear to have few practical benefits. The goal of *The Contemporary Writer* is to improve students' writing in their academic, professional, and personal lives. The text reflects the real writing that people do, not only in their college courses, but also on their jobs and in their personal lives, and provides information, guidelines, and practice for the writing people do in college, at work, and at home.

Sometimes students' reluctance stems from qualms they have about themselves as writers as well as doubts they have about the purpose and usefulness of composition courses. Dispelling a few myths is a good starting point.

ELIMINATING MYTHS ABOUT WRITERS AND WRITING

MYTHS ABOUT WRITERS

Myth #1: Writers are born, not made.

No one is born a pianist, a golfer, a mechanic, a chef, or a writer. As people grow and learn, they develop different abilities, but people become experts only at the skills they spend time practicing. Just as no one can be a talented golfer without spending endless hours on the links, no one can become a talented writer without writing. Writers are not special people; they are merely people who write often and who, like pianists or golfers, strive to improve their skills.

Myth #2: Journalists, novelists, and poets are writers—not ordinary college students or working people.

Everyone who writes is a writer, whether they write books for publication, papers for college courses, memos at work, or e-mail messages to friends. Writing well is a key to success in college courses and on the job; furthermore, as people progress in college or their careers, the more writing they do, and the more their success depends on their ability to write effectively and efficiently. Since most people who are successful in college and on the job are effective writers, developing expertise now will contribute to your long-term academic and profesional success.

Myth #3: To write well, a person must be inspired.

Inspiration would be nice. It would make writing more exciting and easier. However, you've probably heard the expression that genius is 1% inspiration and 99% perspiration. On rare occasions, a writer may suddenly be seized by an idea and dash off an inspired and excellent piece of writing. However, 99% of the time writers—even seasoned professional writers—think, plan, worry, write, change their minds and plan again, write again, and finally, after a difficult and messy process, finish a piece of writing—and then wish they'd written it slightly differently.

MYTHS ABOUT COMPOSITION COURSES

Myth #1: College composition courses are irrelevant to other college courses.

In your college composition course, you will probably be asked to keep a writer's log, respond in writing essays you read, work in groups to generate ideas and evaluate each other's writing, and revise your initial drafts. You may never be asked to repeat many of these tasks in another college course. However, the skills you gain through the writing activities in your composition course should produce major benefits in your other college courses. You will approach writing assignments with increased confidence because you'll know how to generate ideas, how to locate and incorporate supporting information, how to organize ideas effectively, and how to produce a final assignment efficiently. Composition courses not only improve your writing skills, but they also improve your reading skills, your thinking skills, and your communication skills—not a bad profit for your investment in one course.

Myth #2: College composition courses are unrelated to jobs and personal life.

Entry level jobs typically do not require much writing. However, the further people rise in their career fields, the more important communication skills are. Even people in career fields that may seem divorced from writing, such as computer technology, often find that their career success is closely linked to their ability to write effective documents such as grant proposals or project reports.

The same skills you need to succeed in college courses will also help you in your professional and personal life. For example, in your composition course, you may be asked to write a paper justifying your opinion on a topic; in a job application letter, you may use the same strategies to convince a prospective employer of the reasons you should be hired. Because composition courses enhance your ability to read and to think critically as well as to write effectively, they can lead to surprising benefits in your personal and professional life.

Myth #3: If teachers don't agree with a student's ideas, the student won't receive a good grade.

Teachers function as editors, not as judges. If you submit a poorly organized paper with limited evidence, then your editor/teacher will undoubtedly give the paper a poor grade, whether or not your opinions coincide with those of your teacher. However, if the paper contains ample evidence for your opinion, is well organized, and clearly written, your editor/teacher will undoubtedly give the paper a good grade, even if your opinions do not echo those of your teacher. Composition teachers do not want you to parrot their ideas: they do want you to develop your own ideas and express them in your own voice.

Myth #4: Once you master the writing process, you'll know how to write well.

Writing isn't simple, and it isn't easy: if it were, then composition courses would be unnecessary. Even professional writers get bouts of anxiety about their ability to meet an assignment, and even successful, prolific writers sometimes stare helplessly at a blank page or a blinking cursor.

The good news is that a composition course will give you insights, practice, and experience in writing effectively in college, on the job, and in your personal life. The bad news is that there's no magic formula. Learning to write is not like solving a simple algebraic formula. Solving for X in a formula is an easy, straightforward process; solving the problem of what to say in an essay and how to say it is trickier. Furthermore, everyone in the math class should come to the same conclusion about the value of X in a given formula, but on a writing assignment, every paper in a composition course will differ. Although the writing process is not a foolproof formula, it will lead you to discover processes, techniques, and strategies that work well for you.

USING THE TEXTBOOK AS A TOOL

The goal of this textbook is to help you become a more effective, more efficient writer in your academic, professional, and personal life. As you progress through the chapters, you will discuss and practice the skills used by most accomplished writers. Since writing is closely linked to personality and experiences, you will also develop your own voice and discover strategies that work well for you individually. A composition textbook cannot provide you with a template or a flowchart for good writing: writing is too complex a process. A textbook can, however, offer solid advice and demonstrate established strategies; it can be the tool you use as you develop as a writer.

USING THE WRITER'S LOG AS A TOOL

Most writers keep a journal or notebook where they record their thoughts, write passages for future use, or questions they want to explore. This textbook asks you to keep a writer's log as a place to record practice writing, prewriting exercises, prereading prompt responses and reflections on the chapter. The best format for this writer's log would be a binder with loose leaf pages. You could then write your responses in class, at home or on computer, then transfer them to your binder.

Throughout the text are assignments for your Writer's Log. These assignments are designed to get you thinking about the issues raised in the chapter, to generate material you can use in later papers, and to provide a base for collaborative assignments. Each chapter ends with Postscript questions which ask you to reflect on what you've learned, read, and written in the chapter. These will go in your log. The reading section in each chapter begins with prereading questions; these should also be answered in your log.

The first six chapters contain assignments under the heading "Building an Essay." As you do these assignments in each of the chapters, you will be practicing the steps in the writing process as you construct one complete essay. These "Building an Essay" assignments can also be kept in your writer's log binder.

USING COMPUTERS AS A TOOL

Having briefly discussed the nature of writers, composition courses, and textbooks, let's look briefly at the writer's best tool—a computer. Most of you will use computers to produce the papers required in your academic, professional, and personal life. Computers are an enormous asset to writers; they check your spelling, locate hard-to-spot typos, and advise you about possible grammatical errors. More importantly, computers allow you to rethink your material, reorganize ideas, and add or delete material with a few keystrokes. Throughout this book, we'll show you how to improve your writing and make research more efficient by using a computer as an aid to composition.

For those writers' who have not had much experience using the computer as a tool for writing, here are some tips to start you out:

✓ **Learn about the computer you'll be using at home or at school before you begin an assignment** You might want to spend a half hour or so during the first week of classes familiarizing yourself with the following computer tools:

- **word processing software**—learn to type in text, delete words and sections, move words, lines or sections, use highlighting devices such as boldface, italics and underlining, save to a disk, and print.
- **Internet browser**—learn to access the browser, connect to the Internet, go to a URL address, and search using a keyword.

✓ **Begin the habit of saving your work as you compose.** To avoid losing your work, save frequently to your disk.

✓ **Save important files on two disks.** Because accidents happen and disks get lost, important files should be copied to two disks. Keep copies of each disk in different places—one in your backpack and one at home, for example.

✓ **Print hard copies frequently.** Print a hard copy after each draft. A hard copy is insurance. You can use it even if your computer dies.

✓ **Revise final drafts in hard copy.** Because reading a hard copy gives you a different perspective on your work than reading the same text on the screen, most writer's read their final draft in the printed page, make final revisions and proofread, then enter those changes into their onscreen text and print out a clean copy.

WORKING WITH OTHERS

In addition to your textbook and computer, the other students in your composition class are a valuable writing resource. Professional writers discuss their ideas and share their drafts with other writers, and workplace writers discuss their projects and share their drafts with colleagues. Students should consult with professors, classmates, friends, or family. To help you gain skills in working productively with others, this text includes discussion topics, exercises, and writing assignments designed to be done collaboratively.

When working collaboratively with other students keep the following guidelines in mind:

✓ **Respect others' points of view.** In school, at work and in the community, team work is valued because, as the saying goes, two heads are better than one. There would be no benefit to working collaboratively if everyone thought the same way. The differences which make working with other people frustrating or annoying also make collaboration dynamic and productive.

✓ **Read others' drafts carefully.** Others in the class are counting on you to be an intelligent and careful editor of their work. If you don't read thoughtfully and thoroughly, you will be missing opportunities to help other students improve their papers.

✔ **Prepare for collaborative assignments.**   If you need to do work as an individual to bring to the group, come prepared to contribute your share. If you don't pull your weight, others will have to take up the slack.

ACKNOWLEDGMENTS

Though our names are on the cover, this book is the creation of many people who have shared their ideas and talents with us. We are grateful for their contributions. The staff at Prentice Hall guided us through the editing and production process. Alice Barr started us on our way by encouraging us to submit our manuscript for consideration. Many thanks to Leah Jewell, Editor in Chief of English who saw potential in our manuscript and had a vision for its development. Joyce Perkins and Corey Good provided much assistance and support. The production editor, Randy Pettit, handled the book—and us—with care and patience. We are grateful for Janet Masterson's careful and thorough copy editing. Finally, thanks to Brandy Dawson for the attention she's given our text through the marketing process.

Our developmental editors, Trish Taylor and Bronwyn Becker, were invaluable partners in making of this book. Their creative and insightful suggestions about our manuscript resulted in a coherent, complete, and accessible text. We appreciated their enthusiasm, persistence and sensitivity.

We would also like to thank the following reviewers, whose comments and criticisms helped us focus and refine the text: Cathryn M. Amdahl, Harrisburg Area Community College; Robert W. Barnett, University of Michigan—Flint; Michel de Benedictis, Miami Dade Community College; Brenda Bilodeau, Mesa Community College; T. A. Fishman, Purdue University; Philip T. Greenfield, Eastern Michigan University; Shari Hammond, South West Virginia Community College; Sarah H. Harrison, Tyler Junior College; Lori Kanitz, Oral Roberts University; Ilka Luyt, Jefferson Community College; Richard N. Matzen, Jr., Indiana University of Pennsylvania; Miles S. McCrimmon, J. Sargeant Reynolds Community College; Adelle Mery, University of Texas Pan American; Margaret P. Morgan, University of North Carolina Charlotte; Amy J. Paul, Washington University; Lee Smith, University of Houston; Linda E. Smith, Fort Hays State University; Wayne Wooten, Catawba Valley Community College.

Finally, we thank our family and friends who have supported and encouraged us through the long process of bringing this book to print.

Edna Troiano
Julie Scott

THE
CONTEMPORARY
WRITER

WRITERS, ROLES, AND READERS

1

P R E V I E W

This chapter's explanations about exploring your role as a writer, discovering workable writing topics, and understanding your readers and their expectations will help answer these questions:

- Why do people think writing is so important?
- How can you decide what to write about?
- What is the relationship between your college writing and the "real world"?
- What do professors and supervisors expect from your writing?

LEARNING ABOUT TEXTS

Understanding Texts

What do the lab report you write in chemistry class, William Shakespeare's play *Romeo and Juliet*, the instructions for adjusting the brakes on a bicycle, the letter you receive from an old friend, an income tax form, and this book have in common? They are all written texts. A text is not merely a book used in a college class. In fact, not all texts are written; a text can be any work—whether in words, images, or actions—that conveys a meaning to someone. So a text could be a photograph, an advertisement, a short story, an editorial, a television program, a computer program, or a rock concert.

However, college courses focus primarily on written texts. Students must read and write texts especially suited in style, format, and content to their professors' interests and expectations. Although you are already fairly accomplished at reading and writing, this book will help you become a better reader and writer of academic texts.

Because all written texts have many features in common, improving your ability to read and write college texts will also help you become a more successful writer in your personal life and on the job.

Despite their obvious differences—a college essay and song lyrics do not seem to have many common features—written texts share certain characteristics. These traits apply to all the texts you read. They are equally true of the texts that you write in college, at work, and in your personal life:

1. Texts have power. They can alter readers' expectations and beliefs, spark controversy, sway public opinion, and move people to action. Consider, for example, how the Declaration of Independence started the American Revolution or how Nike advertisements persuade millions of people around the world to buy Nike shoes. The texts you produce might convince your professor to give you an A, an employer to give you a job, or your landlord to give you a refund on your security deposit.

2. All writers make choices, including how to organize their texts, what information to include, and what formats to use. Students who write business letters in one class and essay exams in another automatically change the form, content, and style of their papers. They would not write "Dear Teacher" at the top of the essays, nor would they include title pages on the business letters.

3. Writers' choices about their texts are influenced by many factors, including historical events, social and personal circumstances, time, distance, and other texts. For example, during a hurricane in Florida, local newspapers would report specific information about shelter locations, evacuation routes, and damage to roads and public buildings, whereas articles in *The New York Times* or *USA Today* would report more general information about the hurricane's effects on the area.

4. Texts are completed by readers who interpret the meaning according to their own information, experience, and expectations. Consider three readers of a newsmagazine article on an experimental treatment for lung cancer:

   - A physician might analyze the information for scientific validity.
   - A patient with lung cancer looking for treatment options might react with hope.
   - A biology student gathering information for a college research paper might see the article as more evidence to support his thesis.

Because the three readers have different backgrounds, experiences, and needs, they react differently to the article and use the information for different purposes. Because readers play such an important role in completing a text's meaning, all texts are open to multiple interpretations and criticism. Almost everyone, at one time or another, has disputed the meaning of a report, a letter, or a poem. If you discuss almost any popular song with a group of your classmates, you will find they have different opinions about its meaning and different reactions to its message.

Activity: WORKING TOGETHER

Read the letter of recommendation for Martin Luther King written by Morton Enslin, one of King's professors at Crozer Seminary, on p. 34. In small groups, discuss the questions below. Select one group member to jot down the group's responses. Remember that texts are open to interpretation, so your group members may have varied and even contradictory insights and reactions.

1. **Texts have power.**
   A. Who will be reading this letter of recommendation? What would you guess to be their age, race, gender, social class, or concerns? What might the readers have in common with the writer of the letter?
   B. What effect does the writer hope to have on the reader?
   C. Why would this letter influence readers' opinions about King?

2. **All writers make choices.**
   A. How did the writer choose which information to include about King?
   B. Why did the writer put the information in the order he did? What information came first, last, in the middle? Why?
   C. What other choices did the writer make?

3. **Writers' choices about their texts are influenced by many factors.**
   A. How might the writer's characteristics such as gender, age, financial status, ethnic background, or special interests affect his choices?
   B. How might a letter of recommendation for a student like King be different if it were written today? What might have been omitted or changed?

4. **Texts are completed by readers who interpret the meaning.**
   A. How might readers' reactions vary depending on their gender, age, financial status, ethnicity, or special interests?
   B. Would a reader of today react differently to the letter than a reader of King's time?
   C. Can you think of two readers who would have opposite reactions to the letter of recommendation? Who might react positively, and who might react negatively?
   D. How do you think King himself would have reacted to the letter if he had read it?

Present the group's interpretation of the letter to the class and compare responses with other groups.

Understanding Context

The term *context* combines the prefix *con*, which means *with*, and the word *text*, so *context* refers to all the circumstances that go with a text. To understand any text, written or unwritten, we often need to know more about the context. Because our interpretation of an event depends on many circumstances, we are likely to react in different ways, depending on factors such as the people involved, their motives, and the results of the event.

For example, imagine that you are in a vehicle that has stopped at a traffic signal. The light has just turned green when a vehicle races across the highway in front of you, running the red light and narrowly missing you. You are likely to interpret the event and to respond differently if

- the vehicle running the red light is an ambulance with the siren wailing
- the vehicle running the red light is a station wagon driven by a woman in her thirties. There are three children moving around in the car, none of whom seems to be wearing a seat belt
- the vehicle running the red light is an expensive sports car driven by a sixteen-year-old male
- the vehicle running the red light is a police car in pursuit of an obviously reckless driver.

Clearly, this list could continue, and each change in context would create a change in your interpretation and response to the event.

Context in Written Texts

When we respond to written texts, whether we are aware of it or not, we also respond to context. To understand the meaning of specific words, we consider the context—the surrounding words or sentences—of the passage. Consider this sentence: "Your assets should be liquid in times of personal crisis when you may need fast access to cash." The sentence provides clues to indicate to readers that "liquid," a word with numerous meanings, in this case means "cash or easily convertible to cash." However, when we speak of the context of a written text, we are frequently talking about more than the surrounding words in the passage.

Cultural context

Unconscious cultural expectations influence us as readers and writers of texts. Consider, for example, the simple sentence, "The woman entered the room." Each student in a class would imagine a different person, a different room, and different circumstances. But, to the degree that people come from a similar culture, they bring similar expectations to the text. For example, in a classroom in Japan, students would automatically imagine the person to be Japanese. They would assume she enters the room through a door, and most readers would picture a rectangular room. If they imagine the woman carrying something, they would probably imagine her carrying the items in her hands or arms, and not, say, on her head. But suppose the person reading the sentence is from Swaziland, Lapland, or Nepal. Everything the sentence evokes would change. The reader would supply a different image of the woman, the room, and the act of entering.

Cultural assumptions also shape your choices when you create a text. If you write, "I was approaching the intersection when the light turned red," you assume that the reader understands the cultural implications: the writer was probably in a vehicle, most likely a car; the light is a traffic signal; red indicates the driver should stop; not stopping would violate a law and might be dangerous to the driver and to others.

Historical context

When you read and write, you also automatically bring to the text expectations that vary with time. Consider George Orwell's novel *1984*. Before the historical year 1984, it was read as a futuristic novel predicting the evolution of an eerie new society; after the historical year 1984, it became a historical document depicting how the future was once imagined. Obviously, none of the words in the novel changed. Time, however, changes how readers react to texts. Time also affects the texts you write. Think of a minor incident within the last year that you felt strongly about at the time, perhaps a frustration in a college class, an irritation at work, a quarrel with a friend or family member. Try to imagine what you might have written in a diary or journal the day the incident occurred; then think about how you might write about the incident today. Although the event is unchanged, time has undoubtedly changed your reaction to the event, which would in turn change your written response.

Conventions and context

In addition, readers and writers have expectations about formats based on the conventions of the situation—whether workplace, academic, or personal. For example, someone asking for a job application expects to fill in blanks with information. No one would expect a job application to look like a poem, nor would anyone expect a poem to contain blanks in which writers would supply their names and addresses. When writers begin a personal letter, a memo at work, or a paper for a college course, they choose the format appropriate to the task. In fact, no matter what text you decide to read or write, you bring to it many expectations about what it should look like on the page, what it should contain, and what style it should be written in.

FYI: For more on workplace writing conventions see p. 12.

The context of a written text, then, includes—among many other interwoven elements—the culture of the writer and reader, the historical time in which the document is created and read, and the conventions of the writing situation.

Activity: WORKING TOGETHER

DAEDALUS ONLINE

Working in small groups, reexamine Enslin's letter of recommendation for King. Now list as much contextual information as your group can think of. Include the considerations listed below. When the groups have finished, share the responses with the class.

1. What format do you expect a letter of recommendation to use? Does the letter meet your expectations or vary from them?
2. For what institution did the writer work? Where did the readers work? Might they have written or read the letter differently if they had worked at other schools or other organizations such as churches or corporations?
3. How does this letter reflect the American culture and values of its time?

Understanding the Writer

All written texts have to be created by a writer. Just as no two people are alike, no two writers make exactly the same choices. Both what writers say (content) and how they say it (style) depend on who they are. The *Talmud*, a Jewish holy book, says, "We see things not as they are, but as we are." Who we are—our gender, race, age, religion, social class, aspirations, experiences—determines both what and how we write. Writing well, then, requires discovering and developing personal viewpoints and expressing them clearly and effectively.

Discovering Roles for Writing

Although our individual personalities depend on many variables, examining a few factors can help us understand ourselves as writers. Focusing on our roles, background, stage of life, interests, and knowledge can help us have a clearer sense of ourselves as writers.

Each of us functions in several roles. Everyone is, inescapably, someone's son or daughter. In addition, you are currently a student. However, your roles go far beyond the classroom and family. You are further defined by your job, your activities, your affiliations. A thirty-year-old woman in a writing class listed these roles:

daughter	divorced woman
mother of a kindergartner	African-American
part-time college student	member of the PTA
receptionist in a dentist's office	Methodist

Each of these roles—and she could have added many more—determines what she has to say as a writer. In her role of daughter, she might have a different viewpoint of privacy than she has in her role as mother. In her role as office worker, she might have a different message about time management than she has in her role as college student. When you write, you need to consider your role: are you writing as a student, an employee, a Democrat, a father, a Latino? Focusing on your role will help you clarify what you want to say.

Writers' backgrounds and ages also have a profound effect on their ideas, writing styles, and methods. For example, someone who grew up in Puerto Rico would write about the country differently than someone who vacationed there. Even the same person views events differently at different periods. For example, think of how you felt about going to school when you were five and when you were fifteen; your current viewpoint is unlikely to resemble either of your former attitudes. Because we are growing, changing, and maturing throughout our lives, our perspectives and viewpoints, even of the same event, are constantly changing. Being aware of our background, experiences, and stage of life can help us understand ourselves and our viewpoints more clearly and can help us interact with our readers more effectively.

Discovering Topics for Writing

To be an effective writer, you must also consider both your knowledge and your interests. "Write about what you know" is an old, but true, adage. A topic that is excellent for the person sitting next to you in class may be no good at all for you. As a writer, you will be more convincing and more accurate if you write about a familiar subject. Furthermore, you are more likely to have a personal viewpoint on a topic familiar to you, so you are more likely to write an interesting, convincing paper.

In addition to choosing a topic you know about, finding one that interests you is important. Writing a good paper involves spending time thinking as well as writing. Thinking about a topic that interests you is relatively easy to do; thinking about a topic that bores you is easy to avoid.

Even when your professor or supervisor assigns a topic you have little knowledge about or interest in, you can still write well if you can find an angle that interests you and about which you can find information. For example, in an introductory economics course, instead of tackling a complicated area of economics about which you know little, perhaps you could find information about salary increases at your workplace over the last five years. Then you could find the rate of inflation in your area over the same period. By comparing salary increases with cost of living, you could write a convincing paper about the change in purchasing power in your workplace.

FYI: For more on discovering writing topics, see Chapter 3.

Remember that as a writer you bring to the text your culture, your background, your personality. Although you may be writing a paper about the decline in purchasing power in your workplace, you are simultaneously revealing a great deal about yourself. If you create a text that seems vague and indifferent, your readers may sense that you do not have much interest in or commitment to your ideas and may conclude that the issue is insignificant. On the other hand, if you are extremely emotional about the issue, your readers may be distracted from the material you present and may conclude that you are overreacting and perhaps not to be trusted. Although you cannot entirely control the readers' response, you should be aware that while you are conveying information about a topic, you are also revealing information about yourself.

Understanding the Audience

All the writing we do—whether a grocery list, a memo on the job, or a research paper in a college course—has an audience, i.e., a reader. Some texts, such as newspapers, have large, diverse audiences; other texts, such as letters, often have just one reader. All readers approach written texts with certain expectations; however, these expectations differ. For instance, the readers of grocery lists are usually satisfied if they can decipher the lists so they will know what to buy, but a supervisor or a college professor will have more complex expectations of writing. Being an effective writer, then, involves thinking about your audience and making choices with an understanding of their needs. Before you begin to write, you should decide what information your readers require, what format they expect (e.g., a letter, a report, a summary), and what style they think appropriate.

Understanding Readers' Expectations

Even if you are writing for yourself, you have certain expectations. For example, if you are making a list of chores and errands for the week, you will be exasperated if you read the list two days later and cannot decipher some of the items. You expect

Activity: BUILDING AN ESSAY

In each chapter of this textbook, you will do assignments that you will keep in a notebook—a writer's log. The *Building an Essay* assignments in Chapters 1 through 8 build on each other so that step-by-step you will go through the process of writing one complete essay. Keep these assignments in your Writer's Log. This first assignment helps you generate topics for an essay.

1. Make two lists about yourself. In the first list, write the roles you think are most significant. Choose the aspects about you that influence much of your life, for example, college student, son, brother. In the second list, include interests, experiences, character traits, hobbies, skills, anything that helps define you. Be specific; for example, you may not know world geography, but you may know four great places to fish in your county.

2. Considering both lists, what papers could you write? Brainstorm for five minutes, and list all the personal, academic, or professional texts you might write in any of your roles. For example, a parent who pays household bills monthly, works as a secretary, is taking a sociology class, and enjoys soap operas might generate these texts:

   A. A letter to a credit card company asking for an increase in the credit limit.
   B. A research paper written for her sociology professor about how soap operas have evolved over the past fifty years.
   C. A letter to her child's teacher about her son's special health needs.
   D. A memo to her supervisor outlining a new office filing system.

3. Finally, keeping the lists of your roles and interests in mind, generate a list of at least ten potential topics that you might be able to use for papers in college classes. Try to list topics for papers in various disciplines, e.g., history, psychology, business, science. For example, a parent of a preschooler might be interested in writing a psychology paper about childhood fears; as a secretary, she might be interested in writing a sociology paper about the status of clerical workers. Keep these lists handy and add items as you think of new topics.

FYI: For more on brainstorming, see p. 126.

and need clarity, even in simple lists. However, if you write in a diary or journal, you will not be satisfied if you reread your entry later only to find that you merely listed activities such as washing your car, your hair, or your dog instead of expressing insights, plans, hopes, and reactions to people and events.

When someone else reads your writing, which is what usually happens, the expectations become more complicated. To write effectively, you must analyze what the audience wants. By becoming familiar with some of the expectations common to readers of texts in your personal, academic, and professional life, you can avoid inadvertently annoying or confusing your readers. Of course, you may choose to ignore or contradict your readers' expectations, but at least you will be better prepared as a writer if you know what they are.

Expectations of readers in your personal life

If your writing is personal, the expectations are usually fairly simple. If you are writing a note to the telephone company or to your child's teacher, all the reader usually expects are a few relevant facts about your topic and a clear point to your message. However, if you are writing a personal letter to a friend, the reader will want to know not only the relevant facts, but also your reactions to the circumstances. Your readers will probably expect a friendly, informal style and might well be puzzled if you sound as if you were writing a term paper for a college course or a memo for work. In addition, the readers of personal letters are likely to want you to express some curiosity or concern about their lives. These expectations, that your writing would sound friendly and informal and that you would be curious or concerned about the lives of your readers, are ones that supervisors or professors are unlikely to share.

FYI: For more on style, see Chapter 7.

Expectations of readers in your working and academic life

When you are writing at work or in the classroom, your readers will share certain expectations. A supervisor or professor will have these expectations:

- What you say will be clear and easy to understand.
- Your information will be correct.
- You will provide any necessary background information or explanations.
- You will provide supporting evidence for your assertions.
- Your paper will be in an appropriate form (e.g., letter, report, position paper, proposal, essay, summary).
- Your ideas will be organized clearly and logically so that they are easy to follow.
- Your paper will not include irrelevant or unnecessary information.
- Your paper will be in Standard English, with very few mechanical errors.

Additional expectations of readers of academic writing

If your paper is written for a college course, your professor will have all of the expectations listed above. In addition, your professor may expect your paper to contain original ideas and insights. Usually, a professor will not expect you merely to repeat information found in lectures, textbooks, or other sources. Finally, an effective college paper must match the assignment. If the assignment is to react to an editorial, and instead a student summarizes the editorial, the writing—no matter how mechanically flawless or accurate the summary—is ineffective.

Additional expectations of readers of workplace writing

If your paper is written on the job, your readers will have the eight expectations listed above. Furthermore, readers will expect your information to be feasible, useful, and helpful. For example, if you propose a new filing system for documents in your office, your readers will want your system to solve a problem or improve a situation, to be accurate and efficient, and to be less complicated than the current system. If your idea cannot be used or will not improve the current situation, it is not helpful, and your proposal, regardless of how mechanically correct it may be, will not be effective writing.

The Workplace

WRITING THAT WORKS

This chapter distinguishes among the differing expectations readers have of academic, workplace, and personal writing. In general, business and professional readers expect writing to be:

- **Complete**—Answer all questions readers may have. Make sure they know who, what, where, when, and why.
- **Concise**—Include only relevant information, omit wordy phrases, and avoid unnecessary repetition.
- **Reader-Oriented**—Keep the focus on readers and information that benefits or interests them. Use "you" instead of "I" or "we." Emphasize the positive, and be honest.
- **Specific**—Include specific facts and figures. Choose words and images that create pictures in the readers' minds. Prefer verbs that show action.
- **Clear**—Choose familiar words and construct readable sentences and paragraphs.
- **Polite**—Maintain a pleasant tone, showing thoughtfulness and avoiding offensive or angry expressions.
- **Correct**—Use Standard English and follow the conventions of writing. Make sure your facts are accurate. Use nondiscriminatory language.

Analyzing the Audience

As you can see, depending on the writing task, audiences and their expectations vary. When you begin a writing project, answer the following questions about your readers. Use your answers to make decisions about your paper, such as how formal or informal your writing should be, what information you should include, and how you should organize your ideas.

1. Is the audience personal, professional, or academic? What expectations do your intended readers have of your paper?
2. How much do the readers already know about the topic? Do the readers need any background information? What other types of information about the topic do they need?
3. Are the readers likely to agree or disagree with the point you are making? If they are likely to disagree, what kind of information might persuade them to change their minds? How much factual evidence will you need to include?
4. What characteristics do your readers share? Are you writing for coworkers, classmates, or another group with whom you share many traits? Do your read-

ers share other traits, such as age, gender, social status, ethnic group, religious or political affiliations? If so, how might these common characteristics affect their expectations?

Activity: COMPUTER WORKSHOP

Create a file on your word processor named "letter1." In this file, type a letter to a friend or family member justifying or defending some action you took that was criticized by others. For example, if one of your professors criticized you for leaving class early every day, you might write a letter to your parents explaining why you feel that leaving class early is justified and why the professor is wrong for criticizing you; or if your friends criticized you for not spending enough time with them, you might write to your sister explaining your reasons and venting your frustration with your friends.

After you have written the letter, save it, and create a new file named "letter2." Copy the file named "letter1" into this new file, "letter2." Now revise the text, making all the changes necessary to make it acceptable as a letter to the person who criticized you. In this case, a change in the reader means a change in the purpose. Instead of defending yourself to a friendly audience, you will be apologizing to a critical audience. Your goal is to smooth things over and get on better terms with the reader while explaining your actions.

Finally, create a third file named "list." Look at the two letters and record in this file a list of all the ways that changing the reader affected your choices of content and style. What differences are there in the information you included, the language you used, the way you organized your ideas, or your attitude toward the reader? Are different aspects of your personality revealed in the two letters because your role has changed?

Print the letters and the list.

Working in small groups, compare the letters and the lists. Did most group members make similar changes when the reader of the letters or the role of the writer changed? Compare the group lists to compile a class list.

Writing with Integrity

When you write at work or in college, your name is on your papers, and your readers can identify you as the author of the work. In college and at work, you automatically present information and opinions rationally and avoid offending your readers. Writing online, however, can provide a different writing context. Since much online writing is anonymous, writers sometimes yield to the temptation to insult or demean readers, to present outrageous opinions, or to falsify information. The same guidelines apply to college, workplace, and online writing: You should be able to stand behind what you write, whether you are online, at work, or in class. When you are writing anonymously online, check yourself by asking whether you would write differently if the reader were a colleague, a classmate, or anyone who knew you personally.

READING AND WRITING TEXTS

Readings

Most of the readings in this section are by the Rev. Dr. Martin Luther King, Jr. (1929-1968), one of America's greatest civil rights leaders. As you read the three letters written by King, the "Autobiography of Religious Development" that King wrote in the seminary, and the "Letter from Birmingham Jail," think about the context in which the texts were originally written and read, how King's writing developed as he grew and changed, and how your responses to the texts might compare to the responses of the original readers. The one reading not by King, a letter of recommendation from one of his seminary professors, allows us to see what others of his time may have seen in this man destined to become a leader of our country.

　　To understand these texts, it's important to know something about their author. A black Baptist minister, King led the Southern Christian Leadership Conference (SCLC), a group that struggled for racial equality through nonviolent means. Despite being jailed, threatened, and attacked, King never wavered from his belief that justice and equality could be attained without violence. Through boycotts, sit-ins, marches, and other nonviolent means, King and the SCLC brought about massive improvements in civil rights in America. An eloquent writer and speaker, King is most widely known for his "I Have a Dream" speech, delivered at the Lincoln Memorial during the famous 1963 March on Washington, an event attended by more than 200,000 Americans. The following year, King won the Nobel Peace Prize. Four years later, on April 4, 1968, the day before a march in Memphis, Tennessee, King, aged thirty-nine, was assassinated. Since 1983, King's birthday has been a national holiday, celebrated on the third Monday in January.

Go For It!

"The Martin Luther King, Jr. Papers Project," which includes a biography of King and works written by and about him, can be accessed at this address:

☞　　http://www.stanford.edu/group/King

To learn more about nonviolent social change, access

☞　　http://www.thekingcenter.com

Activity: PREREADING

In your Writer's Log

1. List characteristics, interests, or experiences that might affect your individual reaction to King's readings.

2. Write a few questions you would like to have answered about King's life and work.

In small discussion groups

1. List all the facts you already know about King.
2. List everything you know about the political, cultural, and social situation during the period King wrote these letters.

To Martin Luther King, Sr.

Martin Luther King, Jr.

King, at fifteen, wrote this letter to his father during the summer he was working on a tobacco farm in Connecticut. What impresses King most about the North is the lack of discrimination.

Dear father:

I am very sorry I am so long about writing but I having been working most of the time. We are really having a fine time here and the work is very easy. We have to get up every day at 6:00. We have very good food. And I am working kitchen so you see I get better food.

   We have service here every Sunday about 8:00 and I am the religious leader we have a Boys choir here and we are going to sing on the air soon. Sunday I went to church in Simsbury it was a white church. I could not get to Hartford [to church] but I am going next week. On our way here we saw some things I had never antiscipated to see. After we passed Washington the was no discrimination at all the white people here are very nice. We go to any place we want to and sit any where we want to.

   Tell everybody I said hello and I am still thinking of the church and reading my bible. And I am not doing any thing that I would not doing front of you.

Your Son
[*signed*] M. L. Jr.

Activity: RESPONDING TO THE TEXT

1. What can you infer about King at fifteen from his letter to his father? What were his interests, values, activities?

2. What points is he trying to make to his father? What can you infer about his father?
3. What do you learn indirectly about civil rights in the 1940s?
4. Do you, as a modern reader, find any significance in the letter that his father, the original reader, might not have?

Letter to *The Atlanta Constitution*
Martin Luther King, Jr.

At age seventeen, two years after he had written the letter to his father, King had completed his sophomore year at Morehouse College. In this letter to the editor of The Atlanta Constitution, *one of the South's largest newspapers, King argues for equal opportunity and decent treatment.*

Editor Constitution:

I often find when decent treatment for the Negro is urged, a certain class of people hurry to raise the scarecrow of social mingling and intermarriage. These questions have nothing to do with the case. And most people who kick up this kind of dust know that it is simple dust to obscure the real question of rights and opportunities. It is fair to remember that almost the total of race mixture in America has come, not at Negro initiative, but by the acts of those very white men who talk loudest of race purity. We aren't eager to marry white girls, and we would like to have our own girls left alone by both white toughs and white aristocrats.

We want and are entitled to the basic rights and opportunities of American citizens: The right to earn a living at work for which we are fitted by training and ability; equal opportunities in education, health, recreation, and similar public services; the right to vote; equality before the law; some of the same courtesy and good manners that we ourselves bring to all human relations.

M. L. KING, JR.
Morehouse College.
PD. *Atlanta Constitution*, 6 August 1946.

Activity: RESPONDING TO THE TEXT

1. Who do you think would have been King's audience when he wrote to *The Atlanta Constitution*? How might they have reacted to his letter?

2. How do you think writing to a newspaper affected King's choices as he wrote? What would King be concerned about that he might not have worried about in his letter to his father?
3. In what ways do you think King had grown as a writer after two years at Morehouse College?

An Autobiography of Religious Development
Martin Luther King, Jr.

In 1950, King, now in seminary, wrote this essay for a course titled "Religious Development of Personality." In the essay, King explores the influences of his family, church, and college on his personality and concludes that "Religion for me is life."

[12 September–22 November 1950]
[*Chester, Pa.*]

My birthplace was Atlanta Georgia, the capital of the state and the so-called "gate-way to the south." I was born in the late twenties on the verge of the great depression, which was to spread its disastrous arms into every corner of this nation for over a decade. I was much too young to remember the beginning of this depression, but I do recall how I questioned my parent about the numerous people standing in bread lines when I was about five years of age. I can see the effects of this early childhood experience on my present anti capitalistic feelings.

I was the second child of a family of three children, having one brother and one sister. Because of {our} relative closeness of ages we all grew up together, and to this day there still exist that intimate relationship which existed between us in childhood. Our parents themselves were very intimate, and they always maintained an intimate relationship with us. In our immediate family there was also a saintly grandmother (my mother's mother) whose husband had died when I was one years old. She was [very] dear to each of us, but especially to me. I sometimes think that I was his favorite grandchild. I can remember very vividly how she spent many evenings telling us interesting stories.

From the very beginning I was an extraordinarily healthy child. It is said that at my birth the doctors pronounced me a one hundred percent perfect child, from a physical point of view. Even today this physical harmony still abides, in that I hardly know how an ill moment feels. I guess the same thing would apply to my mental life. I have always been ~~somewh~~ somewhat precocious, both physically and mentally. My I.Q. stands somewhat above the average. So it seems that from a hereditary point of view nature was very kind to me.

The same applies to my environment. I was born in a very congenial home situation. My parents have always lived together very intimately, and I can hardly remember a time that they ever argued (My father happens to be the kind who just wont argue), or had any great fall out. I have never experienced the feeling of not having the basic necessities of life. These things were always provided by a father who always put his family first. My father has always been a real father. This is not to say that I was born with a silver spoon in my mouth; far from it. My father has never made more than an ordinary salary, but the secret is that he knows the art of saving and budgeting. He never wastes his money at the expense of his family. He has always had sense enough not to live beyond his means. So for this reason He has been able to provide us with the basic necessities of life with little strain. For the past three years he has had the tremendous responsibility of keeping all of us in school, (my brother in college, my sister in graduate school, and me in the Seminary) and although it has been somewhat a burden from a financial angle, he has done it with a smile. Our mother has also been behind the scene setting forth those motherly cares, the lack of which leaves a missing link in life.

The community in which I was born was quite ordinary in terms of social status. No one in our community had attained any great wealth. Most of the Negroes in my home town who had attained wealth lived in a section of town known as "Hunter Hills." The community in which I was born was characterized with a sought of unsophisticated simplicity. No one in our community was in the extremely poor class. This community was not the slum district. It is probably fair to class the people of this community as those of average income. Yet I insist that this was a wholesome community, notwithstanding the fact that none of us were ever considered member of the "upper upper class." Crime was at a minimum in our community, and most of our neighbors were deeply religious. I can well remember that all of my childhood playmates were regular Sunday School goers, not that I chose them on that basis, but because it was very difficult to find playmates in my community who did not attend Sunday School.

I was exposed to the best educational conditions in my childhood. At three I entered nursery school. This great childhood contact had a tremendous effect on the development of my personality. At five I entered kindergarten and there I remained for one year until I entered the first grade.

One may ask at this point, why discuss such factors as the above in a paper dealing with ones religious development? The answer to this question lies in the fact that the above factors were highly significant in determining my religious attitudes. It is quite easy for me to think of a God of love mainly because I grew up in a family where love was central and where lovely relationships were ever present. It is quite easy for me to think of the universe as basically friendly mainly because of my uplifting hereditary and environmental circumstances. It is quite easy for me to lean more toward optimism than pessimism about human nature mainly because of my childhood experiences. It is impossible to get at the roots of ones religious attitudes without taking in account the psychological and historical factors that play upon the individual. So that the above biographical factors are absolutely necessary in understanding my religious development.

Now for a more specific phase of my religious development. It was at the age of five that I joined the church. I well remember how this event occurred. Our church was in the midst of the spring revival, and a guest evangelist had come down from Virginia. On Sunday morning the guest evangelist came into our Sunday School to talk to us about salvation, and after a short talk on this point he extended an invitation to any of us who wanted to join the church. My sister was the first one to join the church that morning, and after seeing her join I decided that I would not let her get ahead of me, so I was the next. I had never given this matter a thought, and even at the time of {my} baptism I was unaware of what was taking place. From this it seems quite clear that I joined the church not out of any dynamic conviction, but out of a childhood desire to keep up with my sister.

Conversion for me was never an abrupt something. I have never experienced the so called "crisis moment." Religion has just been something that I grew up in. Conversion for me has been the gradual intaking of the noble {ideals} set forth in my family and my environment, and I must admit that this intaking has been largely unconscious.

The church has always been a second home for me. As far back as I can remember I was in church every Sunday. I guess this was inevitable since my father was the pastor of my church, but I never regretted going to church until I passed through a state of scepticism in my second year of college. My best friends were in Sunday School, and it was the Sunday School that helped me to build the capacity for getting along with people.

The lessons which I was taught in Sunday School were quite in the fundamentalist line. None of my teachers ever doubted the infallibility of the Scriptures. Most of them were unlettered and had never heard of Biblical criticism. Naturally I accepted the teachings as they were being given to me. I never felt any need to doubt them, at least at that time I didn't. I guess I accepted Biblical studies uncritically until I was about twelve years old. But this uncritical attitude could not last long, for it was contrary to the very nature of my being. I had always been the questioning and precocious type. At the age of 13 I shocked my Sunday School class by denying the bodily resurrection of Jesus. From the age of thirteen on doubts began to spring forth unrelentingly. At the age of fifteen I entered college and more and more could I see a gap between what I had learned in Sunday School and what I was learning in college. This conflict continued until I studied a course in Bible in which I came to see that behind the legends and myths of the Book were many profound truths which one could not escape.

One or two incidents happened in my late childhood and early adolescence that had tremendous effect on my religious development. The First was the death of my grandmother when I was about nine years old. I was particularly hurt by this incident mainly because of the extreme love I had for her. As stated above, she assisted greatly in raising all of us. It was after this incident for the first time that I talked at length on the doctrine of immortality. My parents attempted to explain it to me and I was assured that somehow my grandmother still lived. I guess this is why today I am such a strong believer in personal immortality.

The second incident happened when I was about six years of age. From about the age of three up until this time I had had a white playmate who was about my age. We always felt free to play our childhood games together. He did not live in our community, but he was usually around every day until about 6:00; his father owned a store just across the streets from our home. At the age of six we both entered school—separate schools of course. I remember how our friendship began to break as soon as we entered school, of course this was not my desire but his. The climax came when he told me one day that his father had demanded that he would play with me no more. I never will forget what a great shock this was to me. I immediately asked my parents about the motive behind such a statement. We were at the dinner table when the situation was discussed, and here for the first time I was made aware of the existence of a race problem. I had never been conscious of it before. As my parents discussed some of the tragedies that had resulted from this problem and some of the insults they themselves had confronted on account of it I was greatly shocked, and from that moment on I was determined to hate every white person. As I grew older and older this feeling continued to grow. My parents would always tell me that I should not hate the white [man], but that it was my duty as a Christian to love him. At this point the religious element came in. The question arose in my mind, how could I love a race of people [who] hated me and who had been responsible for breaking me up with one of my best childhood friends? This was a great question in my mind for a number of years. I did not conquer this anti White feeling until I entered college and came in contact with white students through working in interracial organizations.

My days in college were very exciting ones. As stated above, my college training, especially the first two years, brought many doubts into my mind. It was at this period that the shackles of fundamentalism were removed from my body. This is why, when I came to Crozer, I could accept the liberal interpretation with relative ease.

It was in my senior year of college that I entered the ministry. I had felt the urge to enter the the ministry from my latter high school days, but accumulated doubts had somewhat blocked the urge. Now it appeared again with an inescapable drive. My call to the ministry was not a miraculous or supernatural something, on the contrary it was an inner urge calling me to serve humanity. I guess the influence of my father also had a great deal to do with my going in the ministry. This is not to say that he ever spoke to me in terms of being a minister, but that my admiration for him was the great moving factor; He set forth a noble example that I didn't mine following. Today I differ a great deal with my father theologically, but that admiration for a real father still remains.

At the age of 19 I finished college and was ready to enter the seminary. On coming to the seminary I found it quite easy to fall in line with the liberal tradition there found, mainly because I had been prepared for it before coming.

At present I still feel the affects of the noble moral and ethical ideals that I grew up under. They have been real and precious to me, and even in moments of theological doubt I could never turn away from them. Even though

I have never had an abrupt conversion experience, religion has been real to me and closely knitted to life. In fact the two cannot be separated: religion for me is life.

Activity: RESPONDING TO THE TEXT

1. Who was the audience for this "Autobiography of Religious Development"? Do you think King's original audience looked at this essay differently than you and other modern readers would? What affects your reading of this? What would you be thinking about that his professor would not have?
2. Considering that King was training to be a minister, his religious "autobiography" is fairly short. What influences on his spiritual development does he focus on? Why do you think those influences were the ones he included rather than other possibilities such as books he read, teachers or preachers he listened to? Does his focus reflect his own values and concerns or those of his audience?

To Charles E. Batten

Martin Luther King, Jr.

King, a senior at Crozer Theological Seminary, wrote this letter of recommendation for Worth Barbour, who was applying to Crozer in 1950.

30 October 1950
Chester, Pa.

Dean Charles E. Batten
Crozer Theological Seminary
Chester, Pennsylvania

I have known Worth L. Barbour for a number of years, but for the last three years our relationship has been much more intimate than in previous years. In my dealings with him I have been greatly impressed with his sincerity of purpose, his conscientiousness, and his enthusiasm for the Christian ministry. I feel that he knows what he wants to do and he is settled enough to attempt to do it. He has a very [*mark illegible*] approach to life, and one which I think beneficial to any young man entering the ministry.

I am not in a position to give quite an objective statement of Littlejohn's academic because of my limited contact with him in that area, however I might say that in ordinary conversational dealings I have found him to be mentally alert and quite open-minded. He confronts issues on quite a mature level. While I have not received the impression that Littlejohn is of superior intelligence, I feel that he can do the work at Crozer on the level of an average student.

Activity: RESPONDING TO THE TEXT

1. What do you know about the audience for this letter?
2. In his letter of recommendation for Worth L. Barbour, King chooses to emphasize certain positive qualities of his friend. Why do you think he chose those particular qualities? Was he thinking of his audience?
3. Why do you think he included the somewhat negative final sentence?

Letter from Birmingham Jail, April 16, 1963
Martin Luther King, Jr.

The "Letter from Birmingham Jail" was written to his fellow clergy in 1963, when King was thirty-four. President of the Southern Christian Leadership Conference, King was jailed for leading protests against racial injustice in Birmingham, Alabama. In this now famous letter, King explains his motives and justifies the breaking of unjust laws.

*AUTHOR'S NOTE: This response to a published statement by eight fellow clergymen from Alabama (Bishop C. C. J. Carpenter, Bishop Joseph A. Durick, Rabbi Hilton L. Grafman, Bishop Paul Hardin, Bishop Holan B. Harmon, the Reverend George M. Murray, the Reverend Edward V. Ramage and the Reverend Earl Stallings) was composed under somewhat constricting circumstance. Begun on the margins of the newspaper in which the statement appeared while I was in jail, the letter was continued on scraps of writing paper supplied by a friendly Negro trusty, and concluded on a pad my attorneys were eventually permitted to leave me. Although the text remains in substance unaltered, I have indulged in the author's prerogative of polishing it for publication.

MY DEAR FELLOW CLERGYMEN:

While confined here in the Birmingham city jail, I came across your recent statement calling my present activities "unwise and untimely." Seldom do I pause to answer criticism of my work and ideas. If I sought to answer all the criticisms that cross my desk, my secretaries would have little time for anything other than such correspondence in the course of the day, and I would have no time for constructive work. But since I feel that you are men of genuine good will and that your criticisms are sincerely set forth, I want to try to answer your statements in what I hope will be patient and reasonable terms.

I think I should indicate why I am here in Birmingham, since you have been influenced by the view which argues against "outsiders coming in." I have the honor of serving as president of the Southern Christian Leadership Conference, an organization operating in every southern state, with headquarters in Atlanta, Georgia. We have some eighty-five affiliated organizations across the South, and one of them is the Alabama Christian Movement for Human Rights. Frequently we share staff, educational and financial resources with our affiliates. Several months ago the affiliate here in Birmingham asked us to be on call to engage in a nonviolent direct-action program if such were deemed necessary. We readily consented, and when the hour came we lived up to our promise. So I, along with several members of my staff, am here because I was invited here. I am here because I have organizational ties here.

But more basically, I am in Birmingham because injustice is here. Just as the prophets of the eighth century B.C. left their villages and carried their "thus saith the Lord" far beyond the boundaries of their home towns, and just as the Apostle Paul left his village of Tarsus and carried the gospel of Jesus Christ to the far corners of the Greco-Roman world, so am I compelled to carry the gospel of freedom beyond my own home town. Like Paul, I must constantly respond to the Macedonian call for aid.

Moreover, I am cognizant of the interrelatedness of all communities and states. I cannot sit idly by in Atlanta and not be concerned about what happens in Birmingham. Injustice anywhere is a threat to justice everywhere. We are caught in an inescapable network of mutuality, tied in a single garment of destiny. Whatever affects one directly, affects all indirectly. Never again can we afford to live with the narrow, provincial "outside agitator" idea. Anyone who lives inside the United States can never be considered an outsider anymore within its bounds.

You deplore the demonstrations taking place in Birmingham. But your statement, I am sorry to say, fails to express a similar concern for the conditions that brought about the demonstrations. I am sure that none of you would want to rest content with the superficial kind of social analysis that deals merely with effects and does not grapple with underlying causes. It is unfortunate that demonstrations are taking place in Birmingham, but it is even more unfortunate that the city's white power structure left the Negro community with no alternative.

In any nonviolent campaign there are four basic steps: collection of the facts to determine whether injustices exist; negotiation; self-purification; and direct action. We have gone through all of these steps in Birmingham. There can be no gainsaying the fact that racial injustice engulfs this community. Birmingham is probably the most thoroughly segregated city in the United States. Its ugly record of brutality is widely known. Negroes have experienced grossly unjust treatment in the courts. There have been more unsolved bombings of Negro homes and churches in Birmingham than in any other city in the nation. These are the hard, brutal facts of the case. On the basis of these conditions, Negro leaders sought to negotiate with the city fathers. But the latter consistently refused to engage in good-faith negotiation.

Then, last September, came the opportunity to talk with leaders of Birmingham's economic community. In the course of the negotiations, certain promises were made by the merchants—for example, to remove the stores' humiliating racial signs. On the basis of these promises, the Reverend Fred Shuttlesworth and the leaders of the Alabama Christian Movement for Human Rights agreed to a moratorium on all demonstrations. As the weeks and months went by, we realized that we were the victims of a broken promise. A few signs, briefly removed, returned; the others remained.

As in so many past experiences, our hopes had been blasted, and the shadow of deep disappointment settled upon us. We had no alternative except to prepare for direct action, whereby we would present our very bodies as a means of laying our case before the conscience of the local and the national community. Mindful of the difficulties involved, we decided to undertake a process of self-purification. We began a series of workshops on nonviolence, and we repeatedly asked ourselves: "Are you able to accept blows without retaliating?" "Are you able to endure the ordeal of jail?" We decided to schedule our direct-action program for the Easter season, realizing that except for Christmas, this is the main shopping period of the year. Knowing that a strong economic withdrawal program would be the by-product of direct action, we felt that this would be the best time to bring pressure to bear on the merchants for the needed change.

Then it occurred to us that Birmingham's mayoralty election was coming up in March, and we speedily decided to postpone action until after election day. When we discovered that the Commissioner of Public Safety, Eugene "Bull" Connor, had piled up enough votes to be in the run-off we decided again to postpone action until the day after the run-off so that the demonstrations could not be used to cloud the issues. Like many others, we waited to see Mr. Connor defeated, and to this end we endured postponement after postponement. Having aided in this community need, we felt that our direct-action program could be delayed no longer.

You may well ask: "Why direct action? Why sit-ins, marches, and so forth? Isn't negotiation a better path?" You are quite right in calling for negotiation. Indeed, this is the very purpose of direct action. Nonviolent direct action seeks to create such a crisis and foster such a tension that a community which has constantly refused to negotiate is forced to confront the issue. It seeks to so dramatize the issue that it can no longer be ignored. My citing the creation of tension as part of the work of the nonviolent resister may sound rather shocking. But I must confess that I am not afraid of the word "tension." I have earnestly opposed violent tension, but there is a type of constructive, nonviolent tension which is necessary for growth. Just as Socrates felt that it was necessary to create a tension in the mind so that individuals could rise from the bondage of myths and half-truths to the unfettered realm of creative analysis and objective appraisal, so must we see the need for nonviolent gadflies to create the kind of tension in society that will help men rise from the dark depths of prejudice and racism to the majestic heights of understanding and brotherhood.

The purpose of our direct-action program is to create a situation so crisis-packed that it will inevitably open the door to negotiation. I therefore concur with you in your call for negotiation. Too long has our beloved Southland been bogged down in a tragic effort to live in monologue rather than dialogue.

One of the basic points in your statement is that the action that I and my associates have taken in Birmingham is untimely. Some have asked: "Why didn't you give the new city administration time to act?" The only answer that I can give to this query is that the new Birmingham administration must be prodded about as much as the outgoing one, before it will act. We are sadly mistaken if we feel that the election of Albert Boutwell as mayor will bring the millennium to Birmingham. While Mr. Boutwell is a much more gentle person than Mr. Connor, they are both segregationists, dedicated to maintenance of the status quo. I have hope that Mr. Boutwell will be reasonable enough to see the futility of massive resistance to desegregation. But he will not see this without pressure from devotees of civil rights. My friends, I must say to you that we have not made a single gain in civil rights without determined legal and nonviolent pressure. Lamentably, it is an historical fact that privileged groups seldom give up their privileges voluntarily. Individuals may see the moral light and voluntarily give up their unjust posture; but, as Reinhold Niebuhr has reminded us, groups tend to be more immoral than individuals.

We know through painful experience that freedom is never voluntarily given by the oppressor; it must be demanded by the oppressed. Frankly, I have yet to engage in a direct-action campaign that was "well timed" in the view of those who have not suffered unduly from the disease of segregation. For years now I have heard the word "Wait!" It rings in the ear of every Negro with piercing familiarity. This "Wait" has almost always meant "Never." We must come to see, with one of our distinguished jurists, that "justice too long delayed is justice denied."

We have waited for more than 340 years for our constitutional and God-given rights. The nations of Asia and Africa are moving with jetlike speed toward gaining political independence, but we still creep at horse-and-buggy pace toward gaining a cup of coffee at a lunch counter. Perhaps it is easy for those who have never felt the stinging darts of segregation to say, "Wait." But when you have seen vicious mobs lynch your mothers and fathers at will and drown your sisters and brothers at whim; when you have seen hate-filled policemen curse, kick, and even kill your black brothers and sisters; when you see the vast majority of your twenty million Negro brothers smothering in an airtight cage of poverty in the midst of an affluent society; when you suddenly find your tongue twisted and your speech stammering as you seek to explain to your six-year-old daughter why she can't go to the public amusement park that has just been advertised on television, and see tears welling up in her eyes when she is told that Funtown is closed to colored children, and see ominous clouds of inferiority beginning to form in her little mental sky, and see her beginning to distort her personality by developing an unconscious bitterness toward white people; when you have to concoct an answer for a five-year-old son who is asking: "Daddy, why do white people treat colored people so mean?"; when you take a cross-country drive and find it necessary to sleep night after night in the uncomfortable corners of your automobile because no motel will accept you; when you are humiliated day in and day out by nagging signs reading "white" and "colored," when your first name becomes "nigger," your middle name becomes "boy" (however old you are) and your last name becomes "John," and your wife and mother are never given the respected title "Mrs."; when you are harried by day and haunted by night by the fact that you are a Negro, living constantly at tiptoe stance, never quite knowing what to expect next, and are plagued with inner fears and outer resentments; when you are forever fighting a degenerating sense of "nobodiness"—then you will understand why we find it difficult to wait. There comes a time when the cup of endurance runs over, and men are no longer willing to be plunged into the abyss of despair. I hope, sirs, you can understand our legitimate and unavoidable impatience.

You express a great deal of anxiety over our willingness to break laws. This is certainly a legitimate concern. Since we so diligently urge people to obey the Supreme Court's decision of 1954 outlawing segregation in the public schools, at first glance it may seem rather paradoxical for us consciously to break laws. One may want to ask: "How can you advocate breaking some laws and obeying others?" The answer lies in the fact that there are two types of laws: just and unjust. I would be the first to advocate obeying just laws. One has not only a legal but a moral responsibility to obey just laws. Conversely, one has a moral responsibility to disobey unjust laws. I would agree with St. Augustine that "an unjust law is no law at all."

Now, what is the difference between the two? How does one determine whether a law is just or unjust? A just law is a man-made code that squares with the moral law or the law of God. An unjust law is a code that is out of harmony with the moral law. To put it in the terms of St. Thomas Aquinas: An unjust law is a human law that is not rooted in eternal law and natural law. Any law that uplifts human personality is just. Any law that degrades human personality is unjust. All segregation statutes are unjust because segregation distorts the soul and damages the personality. It gives the segregator a false sense of superiority and the segregated a false sense of inferiority. Segregation, to use the terminology of the Jewish philosopher Martin Buber, substitutes an "I-it" relationship for an "I-thou" relationship and ends up relegating persons to the status of things. Hence segregation is not only politically, economically, and sociologically unsound, it is morally wrong and awful. Paul Tillich said that sin is separation. Is not segregation an existential expression of man's tragic separation, his awful estrangement, his terrible sinfulness? Thus it is that I can urge men to obey the 1954 decision of the Supreme Court, for it is morally right; and I can urge them to disobey segregation ordinances, for they are morally wrong.

Let us consider a more concrete example of just and unjust laws. An unjust law is a code that a numerical or power majority group compels a minority group to obey but does not make binding on itself. This is *difference* made legal. By the same token, a just law is a code that a majority compels a minority to follow and that it is willing to follow itself. This is *sameness* made legal.

Let me give another explanation. A law is unjust if it is inflicted on a minority that, as a result of being denied the right to vote, had no part in enacting or devising the law. Who can say that the legislature of Alabama which set up that state's segregation laws was democratically elected? Throughout Alabama all sorts of devious methods are used to prevent Negroes from becoming registered voters, and there are some counties in which, even though Negroes constitute a majority of the population, not a single Negro is registered. Can any law enacted under such circumstances be considered democratically structured?

Sometimes a law is just on its face and unjust in its application. For instance, I have been arrested on a charge of parading without a permit. Now, there is nothing wrong in having an ordinance which requires a permit for a parade. But such an ordinance becomes unjust when it is used to maintain segregation and to deny citizens the First Amendment privilege of peaceful assembly and protest.

I hope you are able to see the distinction I am trying to point out. In no sense do I advocate evading or defying the law, as would the rabid segregationist. That would lead to anarchy. One who breaks an unjust law must do so openly, lovingly, and with a willingness to accept the penalty. I submit that an individual who breaks a law that conscience tells him is unjust and who willingly accepts the penalty of imprisonment in order to arouse the conscience of the community over its injustice, is in reality expressing the highest respect for law.

Of course, there is nothing new about this kind of civil disobedience. It was evidenced sublimely in the refusal of Shadrach, Meshach, and Abednego to obey the laws of Nebuchadnezzar, on the ground that a higher moral law was at stake. It was practiced superbly by the early Christians, who were willing to face hungry lions and the excruciating pain of chopping blocks rather than submit to certain unjust laws of the Roman Empire. To a degree, academic freedom is a reality today because Socrates practiced civil disobedience. In our own nation, the Boston Tea Party represented a massive act of civil disobedience.

We should never forget that everything Adolf Hitler did in Germany was "legal" and everything the Hungarian freedom fighters did in Hungary was "illegal." It was "illegal" to aid and comfort a Jew in Hitler's Germany. Even so, I am sure that, had I lived in Germany at the time, I would have aided and comforted my Jewish brothers. If today I lived in a Communist country where certain principles dear to the Christian faith are suppressed, I would openly advocate disobeying that country's antireligious laws.

I must make two honest confessions to you, my Christian and Jewish brothers. First, I must confess that over the past few years I have been gravely disappointed with the white moderate. I have almost reached the regrettable conclusion that the Negro's great stumbling block in his stride toward freedom is not the White Citizen's Counciler or the Ku Klux Klanner, but the white moderate, who is more devoted to "order" than to justice; who prefers a negative peace which is the absence of tension to a positive peace which is the presence of justice; who constantly says: "I agree with you in the goal you seek, but I cannot agree with your methods of direct action";

who paternalistically believes he can set the timetable for another man's freedom; who lives by a mythical concept of time and who constantly advises the Negro to wait for a "more convenient season." Shallow understanding from people of good will is more frustrating than absolute misunderstanding from people of ill will. Lukewarm acceptance is much more bewildering than outright rejection.

I had hoped that the white moderate would understand that law and order exist for the purpose of establishing justice and that when they fail in this purpose they become the dangerously structured dams that block the flow of social progress. I had hoped that the white moderate would understand that the present tension in the South is a necessary phase of the transition from an obnoxious negative peace, in which the Negro passively accepted his unjust plight, to a substantive and positive peace, in which all men will respect the dignity and worth of human personality. Actually, we who engage in nonviolent direct action are not the creators of tension. We merely bring to the surface the hidden tension that is already alive. We bring it out in the open, where it can be seen and dealt with. Like a boil that can never be cured so long as it is covered up but must be opened with all its ugliness to the natural medicines of air and light, injustice must be exposed, with all the tension its exposure creates, to the light of human conscience and the air of natural opinion, before it can be cured.

In your statement you assert that our actions, even though peaceful, must be condemned because they precipitate violence. But is this a logical assertion? Isn't this like condemning a robbed man because his possession of money precipitated the evil act of robbery? Isn't this like condemning Socrates because his unswerving commitment to truth and his philosophical inquiries precipitated the act by the misguided populace in which they made him drink hemlock? Isn't this like condemning Jesus because his unique God-consciousness and never-ceasing devotion to God's will precipitated the evil act of crucifixion? We must come to see that, as the federal courts have consistently affirmed, it is wrong to urge an individual to cease his efforts to gain his basic constitutional rights because the quest may precipitate violence. Society must protect the robbed and punish the robber.

I had also hoped that the white moderate would reject the myth concerning time in relation to the struggle for freedom. I have just received a letter from a white brother in Texas. He writes: "All Christians know that the colored people will receive equal rights eventually, but it is possible that you are in too great a religious hurry. It has taken Christianity almost two thousand years to accomplish what it has. The teachings of Christ take time to come to earth." Such an attitude stems from a tragic misconception of time, from the strangely rational notion that there is something in the very flow of time that will inevitably cure all ills. Actually, time itself is neutral; it can be used either destructively or constructively. More and more I feel that the people of ill will have used time much more effectively than have the people of good will. We will have to repent in this generation not merely for the hateful words and actions of the bad people but for the appalling silence of the good people. Human progress never rolls in on wheels of inevitability; it comes through the tireless efforts of men willing to be co-workers with

God, and without this hard work, time itself becomes an ally of the forces of social stagnation. We must use time creatively, in the knowledge that the time is always ripe to do right. Now is the time to make real the promise of democracy and transform our pending national elegy into a creative psalm of brotherhood. Now is the time to lift our national policy from the quicksand of racial injustice to the solid rock of human dignity.

You speak of our activity in Birmingham as extreme. At first I was rather disappointed that fellow clergymen would see my nonviolent efforts as those of an extremist. I began thinking about the fact that I stand in the middle of two opposing forces in the Negro community. One is a force of complacency, made up in part of Negroes who, as a result of long years of oppression, are so drained of self-respect and a sense of "somebodiness" that they have adjusted to segregation; and in part of a few middle-class Negroes who, because of a degree of academic and economic security and because in some ways they profit by segregation, have become insensitive to the problems of the masses. The other force is one of bitterness and hatred, and it comes perilously close to advocating violence. It is expressed in the various black nationalist groups that are springing up across the nation, the largest and best-known being Elijah Muhammad's Muslim movement. Nourished by the Negro's frustration over the continued existence of racial discrimination, this movement is made up of people who have lost faith in America, who have absolutely repudiated Christianity, and who have concluded that the white man is an incorrigible "devil."

I have tried to stand between these two forces, saying that we need emulate neither the "do-nothingism" of the complacent nor the hatred and despair of the black nationalist. For there is the more excellent way of love and nonviolent protest. I am grateful to God that, through the influence of the Negro church, the way of nonviolence became an integral part of our struggle.

If this philosophy had not emerged, by now many streets of the South would, I am convinced, be flowing with blood. And I am further convinced that if our white brothers dismiss as "rabble-rousers" and "outside agitators" those of us who employ nonviolent direct action, and if they refuse to support our nonviolent efforts, millions of Negroes will, out of frustration and despair, seek solace and security in black-nationalist ideologies—a development that would inevitably lead to a frightening racial nightmare.

Oppressed people cannot remain oppressed forever. The yearning for freedom eventually manifests itself, and that is what has happened to the American Negro. Something within has reminded him of his birthright of freedom, and something without has reminded him that it can be gained. Consciously or unconsciously, he has been caught up by the *Zeitgeist*, and with his black brothers of Africa and his brown and yellow brothers of Asia, South America, and the Caribbean, the United States Negro is moving with a sense of great urgency toward the promised land of racial justice. If one recognizes this vital urge that has engulfed the Negro community, one should readily understand why public demonstrations are taking place. The Negro has many pent-up resentments and latent frustrations, and he must release them. So let him march; let him make prayer pilgrimages to the city hall; let him go on freedom rides—and try to understand why he must do so. If his repressed emotions are not released in nonviolent ways, they will seek expression through violence; this is not a threat but a fact of history. So I have not said to my people: "Get rid of your discontent." Rather, I have tried to say that this normal and healthy discontent can be channeled into the creative outlet of nonviolent direct action. And now this approach is being termed extremist.

But though I was initially disappointed at being categorized as an extremist, as I continued to think about the matter I gradually gained a measure of satisfaction from the label. Was not Jesus an extremist for love: "Love your enemies, bless them that curse you, do good to them that hate you, and pray for them which despitefully use you, and persecute you." Was not Amos an extremist for justice: "Let justice roll down like waters and righteousness like an ever-flowing stream." Was not Paul an extremist for the Christian gospel: "I bear in my body the marks of the Lord Jesus." Was not Martin Luther an extremist: "Here I stand; I cannot do otherwise, so help me God." And John Bunyan: "I will stay in jail to the end of my days before I make a butchery of my conscience." And Abraham Lincoln: "This nation cannot survive half slave and half free." And Thomas Jefferson: "We hold these truths to be self-evident, that all men are created equal. . . ." So the question is not whether we will be extremists, but what kind of extremists we will be. Will we be extremists for hate or for love? Will we be extremists for the preservation of injustice or for the extension of justice? In that dramatic scene on Calvary's hill three men were crucified. We must never forget that all three were crucified for the same crime—the crime of extremism. Two were extremists for immortality, and thus fell below their environment. The other, Jesus Christ, was an extremist for love, truth, and goodness, and thereby rose above his environment. Perhaps the South, the nation, and the world are in dire need of creative extremists.

I had hoped that the white moderate would see this need. Perhaps I was too optimistic; perhaps I expected too much. I suppose I should have realized that few members of the oppressor race can understand the deep groans and passionate yearnings of the oppressed race, and still fewer have the vision to see that injustice must be rooted out by strong, persistent, and determined action. I am thankful, however, that some of our white brothers in the South have grasped the meaning of this social revolution and committed themselves to it. They are still too few in quantity, but they are big in quality. Some—such as Ralph McGill, Lillian Smith, Harry Golden, James McBride Dabbs, Ann Braden and Sarah Patton Boyle—have written about our struggle in eloquent and prophetic terms. Others have marched with us down nameless streets of the South. They have languished in filthy, roach-infested jails, suffering the abuse and brutality of policemen who view them as "dirty nigger-lovers." Unlike so many of their moderate brothers and sisters, they have recognized the urgency of the moment and sensed the need for powerful "action" antidotes to combat the disease of segregation.

Let me take note of my other major disappointment. I have been so greatly disappointed with the white church and its leadership. Of course, there are some notable exceptions. I am not unmindful of the fact that each of you has taken some significant stands on this issue. I commend you, Reverend Stallings, for your Christian stand on this past Sunday, in welcoming Negroes to your worship service on a nonsegregated basis. I commend the Catholic leaders of this state for integrating Spring Hill College several years ago.

But despite these notable exceptions, I must honestly reiterate that I have been disappointed with the church. I do not say this as one of those negative critics who can always find something wrong with the church. I say this as a minister of the gospel, who loves the church; who was nurtured in its bosom; who has been sustained by its spiritual blessings and who will remain true to it as long as the cord of life shall lengthen.

When I was suddenly catapulted into the leadership of the bus protest in Montgomery, Alabama, a few years ago, I felt we would be supported by the white church. I felt that the white ministers, priests, and rabbis of the South would be among our strongest allies. Instead, some have been outright opponents, refusing to understand the freedom movement and misrepresenting its leaders; all too many others have been more cautious than courageous and have remained silent behind the anesthetizing security of stained-glass windows.

In spite of my shattered dreams, I came to Birmingham with the hope that the white religious leadership of this community would see the justice of our cause and, with deep moral concern, would serve as the channel through which our just grievances could reach the power structure. I had hoped that each of you would understand. But again I have been disappointed.

I have heard numerous southern religious leaders admonish their worshipers to comply with a desegregation decision because it is the *law*, but I have longed to hear white ministers declare: "Follow this decree because integration is morally *right* and because the Negro is your brother." In the midst of blatant injustices inflicted upon the Negro, I have watched white churchmen stand on the sideline and mouth pious irrelevancies and sanctimonious trivialities. In the midst of a mighty struggle to rid our nation of racial and economic injustice, I have heard many ministers say: "Those are social issues, with which the gospel has no real concern." And I have watched many churches commit themselves to a completely other-worldly religion which makes a strange, un-Biblical distinction between body and soul, between the sacred and the secular.

I have traveled the length and breadth of Alabama, Mississippi, and all the other southern states. On sweltering summer days and crisp autumn mornings I have looked at the South's beautiful churches with their lofty spires pointing heavenward. I have beheld the impressive outlines of her massive religious-education buildings. Over and over I have found myself asking: "What kind of people worship here? Who is their God? Where were their voices when the lips of Governor Barnett dripped with words of interposition and nullification? Where were they when Governor Wallace gave a clarion call for defiance and hatred? Where were their voices of support when bruised and weary Negro men and women decided to rise from the dark dungeons of complacency to the bright hills of creative protest?"

Yes, these questions are still in my mind. In deep disappointment I have wept over the laxity of the church. But be assured that my tears have been tears of love. There can be no deep disappointment where there is not deep love. Yes, I love the church. How could I do otherwise? I am in the rather unique position of being the son, the grandson, and the great-grandson of preachers. Yes, I see the church as the body of Christ. But, oh! How we have blemished and scarred that body through social neglect and through fear of being nonconformists.

There was a time when the church was very powerful—in the time when the early Christians rejoiced at being deemed worthy to suffer for what they believed. In those days the church was not merely a thermometer that recorded the ideas and principles of popular opinion; it was a thermostat that transformed the mores of society. Whenever the early Christians entered a town, the people in power became disturbed and immediately sought to convict the Christians for being "disturbers of the peace" and "outside agitators." But the Christians pressed on, in the conviction that they were "a colony of heaven," called to obey God rather than man. Small in number, they were big in commitment. They were too God intoxicated to be "astronomically intimidated." By their effort and example they brought an end to such ancient evils as infanticide and gladiatorial contests.

Things are different now. So often the contemporary church is a weak, ineffectual voice with an uncertain sound. So often it is an archdefender of the status quo. Far from being disturbed by the presence of the church, the power structure of the average community is consoled by the church's silent—and often even vocal—sanction of things as they are.

But the judgment of God is upon the church as never before. If today's church does not recapture the sacrificial spirit of the early church, it will lose its authenticity, forfeit the loyalty of millions, and be dismissed as an irrelevant social club with no meaning for the twentieth century. Every day I meet young people whose disappointment with the church has turned into outright disgust.

Perhaps I have once again been too optimistic. Is organized religion too inextricably bound to the status quo to save our nation and the world? Perhaps I must turn my faith to the inner spiritual church, the church within the church, as the true *ekklesia* and the hope of the world. But again I am thankful to God that some noble souls from the ranks of organized religion have broken loose from the paralyzing chains of conformity and joined us as active partners in the struggle for freedom. They have left their secure congregations and walked the streets of Albany, Georgia, with us. They have gone down the highways of the South on torturous rides for freedom. Yes, they have gone to jail with us. Some have been dismissed from their churches, have lost the support of their bishops and fellow ministers. But they have acted in the faith that right defeated is stronger than evil triumphant. Their witness has been the spiritual salt that has preserved the true meaning of the gospel in these troubled times. They have carved a tunnel of hope through the dark mountain of disappointment.

I hope the church as a whole will meet the challenge of this decisive hour. But even if the church does not come to the aid of justice, I have no despair about the future. I have no fear about the outcome of our struggle in Birmingham, even if our motives are at present misunderstood. We will reach the goal of freedom in Birmingham, and all over the nation, because the goal of America is freedom. Abused and scorned though we may be, our destiny is tied up with America's destiny. Before the pilgrims landed at Plymouth, we were here. Before the pen of Jefferson etched the majestic words of the Declaration of Independence across the pages of history, we were here. For more than two centuries our forefathers labored in this country without wages; they made cotton king; they built the homes of their masters while suffering gross injustice and shameful humiliation—and yet out of a bottomless vitality they continued to thrive and develop. If the inexpressible cruelties of slavery could not stop us, the opposition we now face will surely fail. We will win our freedom because the sacred heritage of our nation and the eternal will of God are embodied in our echoing demands.

Before closing I feel impelled to mention one other point in your statement that has troubled me profoundly. You warmly commended the Birmingham police force for keeping "order" and "preventing violence." I doubt that you would have so warmly commended the police force if you had seen its dogs sinking their teeth into unarmed, nonviolent Negroes. I doubt that you would so quickly commend the policemen if you were to observe their ugly and inhumane treatment of Negroes here in the city jail; if you were to watch them push and curse old Negro women and young Negro girls; if you were to see them slap and kick old Negro men and young boys; if you were to observe them, as they did on two occasions, refuse to give us food because we wanted to sing our grace together. I cannot join you in your praise of the Birmingham police department.

It is true that the police have exercised a degree of discipline in handling the demonstrators. In this sense they have conducted themselves rather "nonviolently" in public. But for what purpose? To preserve the evil system of segregation. Over the past few years I have consistently preached that nonviolence demands that the means we use must be as pure as the ends we seek. I have tried to make clear that it is wrong to use immoral means to attain moral ends. But now I must affirm that it is just as wrong, or perhaps even more so, to use moral means to preserve immoral ends. Perhaps Mr. Connor and his policemen have been rather nonviolent in public, as was Chief Pritchett in Albany, Georgia, but they have used the moral means of nonviolence to maintain the immoral end of racial injustice. As T. S. Eliot has said: "The last temptation is the greatest treason: To do the right deed for the wrong reason."

I wish you had commended the Negro sit-inners and demonstrators of Birmingham for their sublime courage, their willingness to suffer, and their amazing discipline in the midst of great provocation. One day the South will recognize its real heroes. There will be the James Merediths, with the noble sense of purpose that enables them to face jeering and hostile mobs, and with the agonizing loneliness that characterizes the life of the pioneer. There will be the old, oppressed, battered Negro women, symbolized in a seventy-two-year-old woman in Montgomery, Alabama, who rose up with a sense of dignity and with her people decided not to ride segregated buses, and who responded with ungrammatical profundity to one who inquired about her weariness: "My feets is tired, but my soul is at rest." They will be the young high school and college students, the young ministers of the gospel and a host of their elders, courageously and nonviolently sitting in at lunch counters and willingly going to jail for conscience' sake. One day the South will know that when these disinherited children of God sat down at lunch counters, they were in reality standing up for what is best in the American dream and for the most sacred values in our Judaeo-Christian heritage, thereby bringing our nation back to those great wells of democracy which were dug deep by the founding fathers in their formulation of the Constitution and the Declaration of Independence.

Never before have I written so long a letter. I'm afraid it is much too long to take your precious time. I can assure you that it would have been much shorter if I had been writing from a comfortable desk, but what else can one do when he is alone in a narrow jail cell, other than write long letters, think long thoughts, and pray long prayers?

If I have said anything in this letter that overstates the truth and indicates an unreasonable impatience, I beg you to forgive me. If I have said anything that understates the truth and indicates my having a patience that allows me to settle for anything less than brotherhood, I beg God to forgive me.

I hope this letter finds you strong in the faith. I also hope that circumstances will soon make it possible for me to meet each of you, not as an integrationist or a civil rights leader but as a fellow clergyman and a Christian brother. Let us all hope that the dark clouds of racial prejudice will soon pass away and the deep fog of misunderstanding will be lifted from our fear-drenched communities, and in some not too distant tomorrow the radiant stars of love and brotherhood will shine over our great nation with all their scintillating beauty.

Yours for the cause of Peace and Brotherhood,
Martin Luther King, Jr.

Activity: RESPONDING TO THE TEXT

1. What would King's clerical audience consider important? What would impress them? How does King appeal to their values and interests?
2. How do you think they might have reacted to the letter? Do you react differently than the clergy might have?
3. How does King's background affect his writing choices?

Morton Scott Enslin to Chester M. Alter

Morton Scott Enslin

Morton Enslin was one of King's professors at Crozer. He wrote this recommendation in support of King's application to the School of Theology at Boston University.

14 December 1950

Dean Chester M. Alter
Boston University Graduate School
725 Commonwealth Avenue
Boston 15, Massachusetts

Dear Dean Alter:

One of our seniors, Martin L. King, Jr., tells me that he has made application for admission to Boston University for graduate work upon completion of his work and the reception of his B.D. from Crozer. He also intimated that a letter from me to your office would be appreciated. I am very glad to be able to recommend Mr. King without qualification for admission to graduate work with an eye to an eventual doctorate. He has proved himself to be a very competent student, conscientious, industrious, and with more than usual insight. He has had several courses with me and in each of them has done able work. He is president of the Student Government and has conducted himself well in this position. The fact that with our student body largely Southern in constitution a colored man should be elected to and be popular [in] such a position is in itself no mean recommendation. Unless I am greatly in error, he will go far in his profession. The comparatively small number of forward-looking and thoroughly trained negro leaders is, as I am sure you will agree, still so small that it is more than an even chance that one as adequately trained as King will find ample opportunity for useful service. He is entirely free from those somewhat annoying qualities which some men of his race acquire when they find themselves in the distinctly higher percent of their group. So far as his moral character is concerned there is no need of any qualification, at least so far as I know, and I think that very few details of that sort escape me. Accordingly I recommend him with distinct pleasure to you for serious consideration for admission to Boston University.

Very sincerely,
Morton S. Enslin

Activity: RESPONDING TO THE TEXT

1. What does this letter reveal about its writer? About its reader?
2. What does this letter reveal about the culture of the time in which it was written? How would the letter differ if it were written today?

Activity: SYNTHESIZING THE TEXTS

1. The first letter you read was written when King was fifteen; the last letter you read was written when he was thirty-four. How had his writing evolved?

2. Compare the letter of recommendation King wrote for Barbour to the one Enslin wrote for King. What are the similarities and differences in content, organization, and style? What role did historical, cultural, and conventional context play in creating these similarities and differences?

Writing Assignments

Academic Essays

1. History

Imagine that you are a historian. You and your colleagues have never heard of Martin Luther King, Jr., and the only information you have about him is contained in the six texts reprinted in this book. What facts could you determine about his life, his family, and his ideas from these readings? Make a list of facts that can be found in the documents. You may want to work with a group of students to create an extensive list. Organize the facts into categories; for example, all the facts about his family might go into one category. Write a paper to your fellow historians reporting what you have "discovered" about King.

2. Psychology

In King's "Autobiography of Religious Development" he explains, "It is quite easy for me to lean more toward optimism than pessimism about human nature mainly because of my childhood experiences." Do you believe, as King claims, that childhood experiences help determine whether a person is optimistic or pessimistic? Discuss King's idea, explain your point of view, and give evidence from your own life, the lives of people you know, or the lives of famous people such as King to support your opinion.

3. Political Science

In "Letter from Birmingham Jail," King states that people have a responsibility to disobey unjust laws. Decide whether or not you agree with King's opinions on this topic. Then write a letter to the editor stating your opinion and explaining your reasons. You may want to look at King's letter to the editor of *The Atlanta Constitution* for an example of appropriate tone and format. Your letter to the editor may be longer than King's with an introduction stating your opinion and supporting paragraphs giving specific examples.

Workplace Writing

One of your favorite high school or college teachers has been nominated as teacher of the year. The nominees must submit letters of recommendation from former students, and your teacher has asked you to write one. The selection committee included the following guidelines for writing the recommendation:

- Use standard business letter format.
- Address the letter to: Teacher-of-the-Year Selection Committee
  1111 Best Street
  Outstanding, TN 11111.

- Include information about your relationship to the teacher: when you were a student, what class(es) you took with this teacher, and whether you worked with this teacher in any other activities.
- Be as specific as possible about the teacher's abilities, accomplishments, and character. The committee wants to get a sense of what it was like to be a student in this teacher's class.
- Limit your letter to one page.
- Use Standard English, free from grammar, punctuation, and spelling errors.

You want your teacher to win the award, so write the best possible letter. As with any formal piece of business writing, you should have at least one, and preferably two or three, people proofread your letter before you send it.

Personal Writing

Using King's "Autobiography of Religious Development" as a model, write an "Autobiography of Educational Development" or "Autobiography of Career Development." Describe the influences and incidents that shaped you as a student or a worker. Think about the influences of family, friends, teachers, bosses, coworkers, or others who have made you the kind of student or worker you are. Think about incidents that were crucial in shaping your feelings, behavior, or beliefs about your education or your work. Try to focus your paper, as King did, around a few major ideas. Organize your ideas so that there are smooth transitions between sections, a logical beginning, and a satisfying ending.

POLISHING AND REFLECTING ON TEXTS

Learning from Other Student Writers

Autobiography of Educational Development
Otis Berry

Otis Berry, an African-American student in his early fifties who was profoundly influenced by Martin Luther King, Jr., wrote an educational autobiography modeled on King's "Autobiography of Religious Development," the personal writing assignment above. Because Berry's educational experiences are numerous and varied, his biography is several pages long. As you read the following excerpts from Berry's biography, consider his role as writer and your response as reader.

I was born in Waco, Texas, on November 2, 1948, the fifth child out of nine. I can remember the railroad tracks and the cow pens across the dirt road on which we lived. My father was a construction worker and my mother did ironing. Later on, I found out that he was also going to night school for nursing. After my father completed the tenth grade, he dropped out of school to join a work camp in Melbourne, Australia. After a short time there he joined the U.S. Army, served in World War II, and received the Bronze Star and a Purple Heart. My mother made it to the eighth grade. She always told us that schoolwork did not feed her family. Everyone had to work or starve. At the age of four, I can remember pulling a wagon with pecans, peaches, and plums to sell at the market. The money we made went into the brown basket next to my mother's ironing board.

When I was five, my father became a nurse's aid at the Veterans Hospital. We moved to a bigger house with a back yard and a paved street in front. Also, at the age of five I attended school. My mother made sure that my older sister taught me to write my name, count to ten, and say my ABCs. I was fortunate. There were other kids that did not fare as well.

*****

In 1964, my parents bought a farm and we moved to the country. I was fourteen years of age. That move put me in another school district. This school was quite different. There was no discipline. The teacher would award a passing grade of "D" if a student would just sit there and be quiet. The only satisfaction I received was going to band practice. In one school year, my grades had dropped from all As to barely passing. My attendance suffered also. I had never missed a day in school until that year. I just did not want to go.

In 1965, integration began. Because we lived in the new school district, I had to go to the new white school. Although it was a relief to get away from the school of hell, I felt like I was being pushed farther and farther away from the happiness I had known as a child. My tenth grade at the new white school was a nightmare. Fights occurred throughout the day between the black and white students. A few white teachers would not recognize or respond to a black hand raised in class. In one particular class, the teacher put the Negroes in the back of the classroom in alphabetical order. In another class, a teacher said, "It doesn't matter whether or not ya'll sit in alphabet order because ya'll are all niggers."

My first band rehearsal was different. I had been placed in the third trumpet section, last chair. The band was playing a song that I had performed at the school of hell. No one could play the solo. On the band's third attempt I stood up and played the solo. I did not notice that the band had stopped playing. The band director immediately told me to move to the first chair. The news of a Negro playing first chair trumpet spread like wild fire. The next day a few students threatened me, but the teachers looked at me differently and treated me with respect. My grades were improving and I began to feel a sense of belonging. I played football in the fall and baseball in the spring. I also played in the concert band and performed with the stage band on weekends.

*****

I finished my junior year with a B average. I received an A+ plus in band. At the beginning of the senior year, it was mandatory to talk with the school counselor and discuss education after high school. The school counselor told all blacks that the only college we could attend was a city vocational school that offered refrigeration and air condition repair, mechanics, plumbing, butchering, and of course nursing aid for the girls. He suggested that if we wanted to go to college we would have to transfer to an all-Negro school before beginning the senior year. That was the first time I had seen so many black parents in school since the May Fair celebration years before. The counselor was fired the following week.

At the beginning of the senior year, faces were missing in the crowd. Some kids just didn't come back to school. Others falsified documents to show proof of new residency in an all-black school district. Although there were band directors at the black schools offering me musical scholarships to college if I would transfer, my mother was against it. It was a thousand-dollar fine if students were caught fabricating their residence. My father assured me that he would send me to college. He had been saving funds for several years.

In the middle of the fall semester, my two older brothers were arrested for burglary and assault. My father used the funds for my college tuition on lawyers defending my brothers. They went to prison. I felt that my world had ended. I knew that the money spent was my education going down the drain, and there was no other way I would be going to college. I quit school and enlisted in the Marine Corps. Nine months later, I was in Vietnam.

In Vietnam, I had a lot of time to reflect on my past life and where I wanted to be in the future. In my wonder years, I had received a quality education. In my teen life, it seemed as though teachers stopped teaching and students stopped learning.

After Vietnam, I dropped in on my fifth-grade teacher. I told her of my experiences in high school and Vietnam. She responded by saying that education and death know no color, and to go through life not learning is to die. She said that school is a tool, and the real education is in living life and learning from experiences. She added that in order to live the life they want, people need the tools that schooling provides.

When I returned to my duty station, I enrolled in a general education development course. Years have passed and I am still seeking education. I own my own business, and I am actively enrolled in a computer program. I did become an entertainer, and I performed in many cities and countries. My two brothers served their time in prison. One brother is an ordained minister, and the other owns a trucking company. They learned from life, and they also sought the education to improve their lives.

Activity: RESPONDING TO THE TEXT

1. In reading excerpts from Berry's essay, you learn many facts about his life. Based on these facts, what conclusions can you draw about the writer?
2. How do you respond to Berry's essay? How does the cultural and historical context in which you are reading the essay shape your response to it?
3. What aspects of Berry's education are still reflected in schools today?

Activity: PEER WORKSHOP

DAEDALUS
ONLINE

Using an essay you have drafted, work in pairs or small groups to review your paper. For this workshop, the writer and the reader answer the same questions about the writer's role and the audience's expectations and compare their answers. When answering these questions, be as specific and complete as possible.

About the Writer

1. What is the writer's role in this paper?
2. Put a **W** next to places in the paper where the writer's values, character, personality, age, race, gender, religion, or social class is revealed. Are these revelations appropriate for this kind of paper?
3. Put a ★ next to sections of the paper where the author impresses you as being particularly knowledgeable or credible. What about the sentence or passage gives that impression?

About the Audience

1. Who is the audience for this paper? Briefly describe their knowledge about the topic, their interests, values, and expectations. Are they likely to agree or disagree with the writer on the topic?
2. Put an **A** next to passages where the writer has accounted for the audience's knowledge (or lack of knowledge), interests, values, and expectations.
3. Put **X**s next to passages where the writer has not given the audience information or evidence they need, has offended or bored them, or has failed to meet expectations. Explain the problem in the margin.

General Responses

1. What did you like best about this paper?
2. What one thing should be worked on before submitting this paper?

Activity: PROOFREADING YOUR WORK

Do one of the following for two paragraphs of your paper:
1. Find sentences beginning with "there is," "there are," or "it is." Rewrite the sentences, eliminating those phrases. You will probably need to change the structure of each sentence significantly. If you like the new sentence better, use it in the final draft of your paper.
2. Find one or two sentences that sound awkward to you, or that gave you trouble when you were writing the drafts of your paper. Try rewriting the sentences one more time to see if you can come up with a clearer, simpler version.

POSTSCRIPT

1. Can you give an example of how awareness of the writer's role and readers' expectations affected your writing?
2. What do you and Martin Luther King have in common as writers? What can he do as a writer that you would like to learn how to do?
3. If someone twenty years from now read your paper, what do you think he or she would conclude about you as a writer?
4. What part of the writing process did you enjoy most? Which did you enjoy least? Can you think of a way to make that part of writing easier or more enjoyable?

EFFECTIVE READING

P R E V I E W

This chapter's explanations of the importance of reading, the relationship between reading and writing, and strategies for reading carefully and critically will help answer these questions:

- Why do teachers emphasize reading?
- How does reading improve your writing?
- How do you read effectively and efficiently?

LEARNING ABOUT TEXTS

Understanding Reading and Writing

Musicians usually like listening to music, chefs enjoy eating, and athletes often watch sports events. People who perform certain skills well also enjoy seeing those skills used by others. Painters view the work of other artists to compare techniques and get ideas. Scientists review the work of colleagues to maintain current knowledge of the field. Teachers observe each other's classes to learn new strategies for communicating with students. In the same way, people who wish to write well usually begin by reading avidly, and professional writers devote significant time to reading the work of others. You may have heard teachers say that the most important thing you can do to become a good writer is to read. By reading, you can

- generate topics for writing
- increase your stockpile of information to support your ideas
- draw relationships between your ideas and the subjects you study in college
- become familiar with grammatical structures and organizational patterns
- increase your ability to evaluate sources, use evidence, and argue persuasively.

Although you may not become a voracious reader overnight, you can increase the time you devote to reading. You can also improve your ability to read carefully and critically, thereby gaining more from the material you read.

Reading Widely

Francis Bacon, a seventeenth-century British philosopher and essayist, proclaimed in his essay "Of Heresies" that "knowledge itself is power." This aphorism is frequently echoed in a modern phrase more suited to our "info-age": "Information is power." Even the video games in the *Mortal Kombat* series open with the line, "There is no knowledge that is not power." In any situation—at work, in college courses, or in social interactions—the people with the broadest knowledge or the most information usually gain the most respect, and others consult them the most frequently. In short, knowledgeable people are likely to have power within their academic, workplace, or personal spheres.

How do we accumulate this knowledge? One important avenue, of course, is through college courses and on-the-job training. However, while college courses and job training may give you an "information" edge over those who receive no such education or training, they do not distinguish you from all the others who take courses, pursue degrees, or participate in workshops and seminars at work. The exceptional students and employees are those who go beyond the classroom and pursue information from outside sources.

We accrue information in various ways—talking with others, watching television, observing people and situations, and practicing skills. However, almost all highly educated people possess one common trait: They read widely. By reading widely, we mean they read many different types of texts on many different subjects. For example, during a typical week, wide readers are likely to read numerous articles in different sections of a major daily newspaper, portions of a weekly newsmagazine such as *Time* or *Newsweek*, job-related articles, information about their special interests, and contemporary fiction or nonfiction.

Few people today can devote long periods of time to reading, but almost everyone can still read widely. By devoting only fifteen minutes a day to reading a major newspaper, newsmagazine, or new website, you could read seven to twenty articles, depending on their length and your speed. If you read only seven articles in one week, you could learn about a breakthrough in genetics, a new campaign to help the homeless, a change in public school curricula, the frustrations faced by the space program, conflict in Eastern Europe, a controversy about nutrition, and the employment prospects for new college graduates—all valuable information that would not be in your college textbooks.

What effect would reading widely have on your writing? You've heard the adage, "Write about what you know." Because you would increase your general knowledge, you would have more topics to write about. If, for example, your sociology teacher assigned a term paper about changing family structures in the United States, you would probably be able to think of several potential topics from your reading, and you would also be aware of the prevailing viewpoints and the most important experts on the topic. In the most practical terms, you would be weeks ahead of students who had to browse through the library for an overview of the subject before discovering a specific topic suitable for the assignment.

READING IN THE WORKPLACE

Busy, successful people usually read widely. In fact, there is probably a correlation between their broad knowledge and their success. John Seng, the president of SPECTRUM Science Public Relations, Inc., reads the following in a typical week:

- **E-mail and print messages** all day, including

    Internal business memos and reports

    Correspondence from clients

    Contracts, proposals, and other business documents

    News clips relating to client issues and products retrieved online by staff

- **Online sources,** including

    cnn.com and washingtonpost.com websites (once a day)

    Profnet journalist information (request service once a day)

    Amazon.com (browse music and book reviews once a week)

    Primary search engine, AltaVista.com (to reach specific sites of interest)

- **Newspapers**

    The Wall Street Journal (twice weekly)

    The Washington Post (four times weekly, cover-to-cover)

- **Magazines and journals**

    New England Journal of Medicine (scan headlines, read 3-4 articles)

    Journal of the American Medical Association (scan headlines, read 2-3 articles)

    Journal of the National Cancer Institute (scan headlines, read 1-2 articles)

    The Pink Sheet (Food, Drug, and Cosmetic Reports) (scan headlines, read 1-2 articles)

    The Economist (browse weekly, read 1-2 articles)

    SmartMoney (read cover-to-cover monthly)

    Inc. Magazine (read cover-to-cover monthly)

    National Geographic (read two articles last week in dentist's office)

- **Religious texts**

    The Catholic Standard, newspaper (browse, read one article weekly)

    Resurrection Church bulletin (browse weekly)

- **Books**

    Blind Man's Bluff: The Untold Story of American Submarine Espionage (two chapters weekly)

- **Children's homework**

    Book report about Dr. Florence Sabin, prepared by ten-year-old daughter

    Two homework packets (review and sign off on weekly)

A second effect of wide reading would be a growing stockpile of information, much of which could at some point become supporting evidence in the papers you write. Perhaps the greatest benefit of wide reading, however, would come when you began to see connections between academic areas. Wide readers frequently develop the ability to see the relationships between ideas and to forge new links between them. Having read widely, you may suddenly see that the principles of ethics you studied in your philosophy class can be applied to the issue of using animal organs for transplants, or you may be able to see how conflict-resolution techniques you read about in your company's newsletter could be applied to a neighborhood dispute you read about in the local newspaper. This ability to synthesize, that is, to combine seemingly separate elements to produce a new idea, is the highest level of thinking and—not coincidentally—the one most valued by employers and professors.

Activity: COMPUTER WORKSHOP

Access your college's website and look through the catalog or schedule of classes. List ten major academic areas. Now go online and look through one issue of a major urban newspaper and one issue of a weekly newsmagazine. Try to find at least one article on each academic area on your list. Consider the content of the article, not just its title. For example, articles in the food section of a newspaper might contain information on nutrition which could be appropriate for courses in food service, health, or science.

Activity: WRITER'S LOG

"You are what you eat" is a widely accepted statement about the relationship of nutrition to physical well-being. Would the expression "You are what you read" be an accurate reflection of the relationship between reading and personality? Review John Seng's reading list on p. 45. What does it reveal about his interests? His professional life? His personal life? To investigate the relationship between your reading and your personality, keep a log of everything you read for five days. In addition to obvious texts,

Activity: BUILDING AN ESSAY

Using either print or electronic sources, read at least fifteen minutes a day for one week from various newspapers, magazines, and other texts. Keep a record of your time and of the title or content of your daily reading. At the end of the week, explore these topics in your Writer's Log:

- the relationships between your reading and the lists you made in your Writer's Log of your roles and interests in Chapter 1
- possible topics for papers suggested by your reading

Several websites offer information about books and magazines. Bookbrowser, which offers reading lists, book reviews, author information and interviews, and links to other book-related sites, can be accessed at

☞   http://www.bookbrowser.com.

The two online bookstores below offer synopses, excerpts, and reviews of books as well as interviews with authors:

☞   http://www.amazon.com

☞   http://www.barnesandnoble.com

US News and World Report provides a free news service:

☞   http://www.usnews.com

such as newspapers, magazines, or books, record less obvious texts, such as unit prices on grocery store shelves, software instructions, memos at work, personal letters, and junk mail you receive at home. At the end of five days, review your reading log and decide what your reading reveals about your interests, activities, and personality. Record your responses in your Writer's Log.

Reading Carefully

Reading carefully will affect your writing more significantly than the study of grammar and mechanics will. You will probably write more varied and more sophisticated sentences, increase your vocabulary, and make fewer grammatical errors. While these improvements can also stem from a formal study of language, reading widely and carefully will help you painlessly assimilate effective language and organizational patterns. Although the benefits will not be apparent immediately, over a period of time your writing will reflect your reading.

Almost all of us have read a text and discovered that, although we looked at every word, we reached the end with no idea of what we read. Occasionally we fail to understand a text because the material is complex, but usually the problem is that we have not concentrated on reading. Using strategies for careful reading helps us read more efficiently and effectively.

Strategies for Reading Carefully

No effective writer begins by typing the first word of a paper and concludes by typing the final word. Writing involves planning, drafting, and revising. Reading is a similarly complex process, involving previewing, reading, and reviewing. Clearly you would use different strategies to read a memo at work, a chapter in an economics textbook, a poem, and a recipe. Nevertheless, the following techniques, which will help you read college texts, apply to many types of reading, including work-related documents.

Previewing

Previewing, the process of examining elements of a text before beginning to read it, provides an overview of the text's contents. Previewing makes reading more efficient: Because readers anticipate the contents of the text, they can better understand and recall the information. To preview a text, use the following guidelines:

1. <u>Clarify your purpose</u>. Before beginning to read, clarify your purpose for reading. Be specific—are you looking for the main ideas, searching for data to use in your writing, exploring information relevant to your personal life? Once you know why you are reading, continue with these other steps to establish an overview of the text.
2. <u>Check the title</u>. The title will indicate the text's topic, but it may also reveal the material's organization, the author's attitude, or the relation of the material to other information.
3. <u>Check the table of contents</u>. If you are reading a chapter of a book, skim through the book's table of contents so you will understand the relationship between the part you're reading and the whole book. If the table of contents includes an outline of each chapter, focus closely on the contents of the chapter you will read to orient yourself to the author's organizational strategy.
4. <u>Look for introductions and summaries</u>. If you're reading an entire book, skim the preface or introduction to get an overview. If you're reading an article or a chapter, the first few paragraphs will probably provide a general introduction. Many textbooks conclude each chapter with a summary. Reading the summary first is an excellent way to preview the material.
5. <u>Read the headings</u>. Skim the headings and subheadings in an article or chapter to preview the contents and the organization. If you are looking for specific information, the headings will also alert you to the sections of the text most pertinent to your research.
6. <u>Look for other visual clues</u>. Some texts include bold print, italics, numbered or bulleted lists, boxes, or other visual devices to call attention to special elements of the text. These visual effects are worth noting, as they might indicate key terms, significant data, or summaries.
7. <u>Be curious</u>. If you are curious, you begin to generate questions about the topic and the author's point of view during your previewing. Approaching a text with curiosity will help you focus on your reading, respond to the text more actively, and increase your enjoyment of the process.

Although these previewing techniques might seem to slow down your reading, the seven steps usually take only a few minutes. More significantly, previewing material will increase your understanding and retention, making your reading time more productive.

Reading

If you are reading material that you will need to remember or use at a later date, you will have to organize the information that you read. The two common strategies you can use are annotation and notetaking. By actively engaging you in the reading process, both strategies help you to recall information and to respond actively to the text. Neither strategy is inherently better than the other, so your choice should depend on your preferences and your reading material.

Annotation.   Annotation simply means marking information directly on the pages you're reading. Your purpose for reading should be your guide to annotation. For example, if you were reading a chapter of a biology text in preparation for a midterm exam, you would want to note the main ideas, supporting evidence, key terms, and any topic or data your instructor stressed. If the test were going to include essay questions, you might also want to mark issues appropriate for essays. On the other hand, if you were reading the same chapter to find supporting information to include in a research paper, you would mark only the data relevant to your paper—which might not include any of the main ideas.

To annotate effectively, avoid making any marks as you first read the material because the first time through, nearly every piece of information will seem significant. After you have finished reading a segment of the text, recall your purpose for reading, and then go back and mark the information you need to fulfill your purpose.

You can annotate a text in several ways. Some people prefer to use colored highlighters, perhaps one color for main ideas, another for supporting evidence, a third for key terms and definitions. Others underline information, circle terms, or draw arrows to show the relationships between ideas. In either case, the margins should be used for jotting down definitions, insights, and reactions to your reading.

The following illustrates an annotation of the first three paragraphs of Holtzman's article "Don't Look Back":

> For centuries, the book has been the primary vehicle for record- ¶ 1–Books
> ing, storing, and transferring knowledge. But it's hard to imagine that
> paper will be the preferred format in a hundred years. (Digital media
> will marginalize this earlier form of communication), relegating it to a
> (niche) just as music CDs have replaced LPs. The book will be forced   main
> to redefine itself, just as TV forced radio to redefine itself, and radio   points
> and TV together transformed the newspaper's role. The process is sur-
> vival of the fittest—competition in the market to be a useful medium.
> Whatever the book's future is, clearly its role will never be the same.
> (The book has lost its preeminence.)
>
> The print medium of newspaper is also fading. Almost every major   ¶ 2–Newspapers
> newspaper in the United States is experiencing significant declines in cir-
> culation. (The exception is *USA Today*—characterized by itself as "TV on
> paper.") More than 70 percent of Americans under the age of thirty don't
> read newspapers. And this trend isn't about to change.
>
> The powers of the media business today understand this. As part of   ¶ 3–New Media
> the frenzied convergence of media, communications, and the digital
> world, we're witnessing a dizzying tangle of corporate alliances and mega-
> mergers. Companies are jockeying for position for this epochal change.
> The list includes many multibillion-dollar companies—AT&T, Bertels-
> mann, Disney, Microsoft, Time Warner, Viacom—and many, many more
> small startup technology companies. They all want to position themselves
> as preeminent new media companies.

definitions—
   niche–small place for putting something
   preeminence–having highest rank

Annotation has one main advantage: It's quick. For many people, however, the speed is offset by a disadvantage. Annotating a text is a fairly passive activity, so annotated information is not always easy to remember. To recall and understand more of the material you annotate, you may want to make an informal "backward" outline like the one on p. 51. If you still find, after annotating a text, that you don't remember much of what you read, then notetaking may be a more productive method for you.

Notetaking.   If annotating your reading is not effective for you or if you are using a library book or other text you cannot write on, you will need to take notes. Four effective notetaking strategies are outlines, backward outlines, maps, and double-entry logs. Since the goal in notetaking is to organize material so you can understand, remember, or use it, you should use the method that works best for you.

1. <u>Outlining</u>. If you are focusing on only one segment of a text or looking through the text only for specific information, then outlining would not be an efficient strategy. Outlining is most useful when you want an overview of a text's organization and contents. It helps you discover the main ideas and recognize the relationships between main ideas and supporting evidence. If you are asked to prepare a formal outline of your reading, you will need to adhere to the following traditional format, which uses numbers, letters, and indentations.

   I. First Main idea
      A. Supporting evidence
         1. Supporting detail
         2. Supporting detail
            a. Minor detail
            b. Minor detail
      B. Supporting evidence
   II. Second Main idea

   The outline continues until all the main ideas and their supporting evidence are included. Notice that one convention of the formal outline is that every level contains at least two entries; there should be no letter **A** without a **B**, no number **1** without a **2**.

   The following is an outline of "Clinging to the Past," the second section of Holtzman's article "Don't Look Back" (p. 73):

   II. Writers and critics of literature are not enthusiastic about digital media.
      A. Sven Birkerts
         1. Contemporary students can't enjoy literature.
         2. Contemporary students don't value literary culture.
      B. Sarah Lyall
         1. CD-ROMs aren't as satisfying as reading books.
         2. Books result from centuries of development.
      C. William Irwin Thompson
         1. This new digital culture doesn't come from established literary sources.
         2. The new culture is anti-intellectual and doesn't appreciate the greatness of European civilization.

If you are outlining for your own purposes, you can be less formal and find a method of outlining that suits you. Just be sure you don't discard so many of the conventions of the formal outline that you end up with a list of contents that ignores the relationships between ideas.

2. <u>Backward Outlining</u>. The backward outline, in which you create an outline from the annotations you make as you read, is simple to create:
   A. As you annotate, identify the key point of each paragraph in the margin.
   B. After reading, use those key points to form an informal outline.
   C. Review the reading to find the relationships between the key points.
   D. Add supporting evidence from the reading to your outline.

The following is a backward outline created from the annotated excerpt (p. 49) of Holtzman's article "Don't Look Back":

Main point: Digital media will make books and newspapers far less important than they have been in the past.
  I. Books have been the major source of information for centuries.
     A. New technology always makes old technology less important.
        1. TV changed the role of radio.
        2. CDs have replaced records.
     B. Books are no longer the primary source of information.
 II. Newspapers are losing importance.
     A. Circulation is decreasing for almost all major newspapers.
     B. The majority of readers under age thirty don't read newspapers.
III. Media companies are gaining power.
     A. Large corporations are merging and competing to gain power.
        1. Disney
        2. Time-Warner
        3. Viacom
        4. AT&T
     B. Many small startup technology companies are getting into the business.

3. <u>Mapping</u>. Mapping, like outlining, highlights the main ideas and illustrates the relationships between the main ideas and the supporting evidence. Mapping, however, replaces numbers, letters, and indentations with a visual pattern. If you absorb information easily from flowcharts, diagrams, or charts, then mapping may be an effective strategy for you. Although there is no one correct way to map, you can follow these guidelines, using circles, boxes, lines, or even colors to link items on the map.
   A. First, label the topic of your reading, either at the top of the page or in the center.
   B. Place each main idea in a circle or box. If your topic is at the top of the page, you can line the main ideas up underneath, creating a flowchart. If your topic is in the center, the main ideas can radiate out

from the center. In either case, use lines or arrows to connect the main ideas to the topic.

    C. Write the supporting evidence for each main idea and attach it with a line or arrow. You can continue to add supporting details by creating other levels of circles or boxes.

Your map will be most helpful if you restrict it to one page. Try to keep all writing facing the same direction, so you won't have to turn the page sideways or upside-down to read the map.

    The following is a map based on the portion of Holtzman's article in the sample annotation and backward outline:

FYI: For more on using maps to gather ideas, see p. 127.

DIGITAL MEDIA OVERTAKING BOOKS AND NEWSPAPERS

⇓   ⇓

DECREASING IMPORTANCE	INCREASING IMPORTANCE
Books = Have been major source of information	Digital Media = Big corporations merging Lots of new companies
Old technology always replaced by new	
Newspapers = Losing circulation nationwide	
Under 30s don't read newspapers	

⇓

CONCLUSION: Print media will be less important than digital media in the future.

  4. Making a <u>double-entry reader's log</u>. A double-entry reader's log allows you to take two types of notes simultaneously. On one segment of the log you will jot down information that you may need to recall, such as definitions, facts, and lists; on the other segment you will respond to the text by recording reactions, questions, and ideas for writing. To create a double-entry log, follow these guidelines:

    A. Using standard 8½-by-11-inch paper, draw a line down the center of the page. The right side of the page will be used for taking notes, and the left side will be used for recording your response to the text.

    B. On the right side, write notes on your reading material. You may need to jot down key words and phrases, list main ideas, or define unfamiliar terms. When you have finished taking notes on the right side, go back to the beginning and decide whether you've briefly captured the key information.

    C. Return once more to the beginning of your notes. On the left side of the page, jot down your reaction to the reading. You may question the author's viewpoint or the contents, compare the text to others you've read, tie the reading to your own experience, or record any other response you have.

    D. When you review your notes, keep in mind your purpose for reading. If you are reviewing information that you need to know, focus primarily on the information on the right side of the log. If your purpose for reading is to appreciate or react to the text or to generate ideas for writing, then you should focus primarily on the left side of the log.

The double-entry log is undoubtedly a more time-consuming notetaking strategy than outlining or mapping, but if you have difficulty remembering or reacting to the material you've read, it may be the most effective strategy for you.

The following example of a double-entry log is based on "Clinging to the Past," the portion of Holtzman's article printed on p. 73 and outlined on p. 50.

Reactions	Notes
* I like reading books for relaxation, but when I want some quick information, I don't want to read a book! The Web lets me find information on any topic quickly.	Reactions of 3 critics: <u>Birkerts</u>—thinks students don't enjoy or value literature
* CD-ROMs and books—why does it have to be one or the other?	<u>Lyall</u>—thinks books are more pleasant to read and result from centuries of development
* Anti-intellectual? Maybe the new form for new intellectual ideas? Maybe books will become "unintellectual"?	<u>Thompson</u>—thinks digital technology is anti-intellectual and that "cyberpunks" don't value greatness of European civilization.

Reviewing

Having previewed the material and read actively by annotating or taking notes, you may think that you have completed the reading process. There is still one more step: reviewing. These three strategies will help you benefit most from reviewing:

1. *Paraphrase the text.* To recall information, paraphrase the text by stating the key ideas in your own words. If you get stuck, review your notes. Repeat the process until you can easily summarize the information.

2. *Create a dialogue with the author.* To increase your understanding of the material, create a dialogue with the author. Write down questions about portions of the material that you do not understand. Then search the text for answers and explain the material as if you were the author.

3. *Respond to questions.* To understand the relevance of your reading, jot down responses to questions such as these:
   - How does what you've read relate to other course material?
   - How does it relate to your previous knowledge?
   - What use might you make of the information?
   - What kinds of essay questions might a professor pose about the material?

Spending a few minutes reviewing your reading and thinking about its implications will significantly increase both the amount of information you remember later and your ability to use that information.

Reading with Integrity

In college you may sometimes be asked to read texts that you find boring, time-consuming, difficult, or even impenetrable. The difficulty you have reading these texts may result from the complexity of the material, the unfamiliar cultural or historical context, or even from your relative inexperience with the particular type of text. Instead of abandoning the text or resorting to published summaries, persevere. The ability to struggle with complex, difficult material is an asset both in college and in the workplace. Furthermore, the more you read difficult texts, the less difficult they become.

Activity: WRITER'S LOG

1. Preview the next section of this chapter, "Reading Critically." Read the material and use each of the four methods listed above—annotation, outlining, mapping, and the double-entry log.
2. In your writer's log, freewrite about using the four methods. Decide which method seems most effective for you. Which seems simplest? Which seems to make material clearest? Which seems to make material easiest to recall?

Reading Critically

When you were first learning to read as a child, you were expected merely to recognize letters and then words. Later you were expected to understand and remember what you read. As an adult, you are expected not only to understand and remember what you read, but also to evaluate and react critically to your reading. When you evaluate a text, you assess its significance, effectiveness, or merits.

The ability to read critically will strengthen your writing in several ways. You will become more aware of the need for clear, convincing ideas and more adept at choosing solid evidence. When you edit your own writing, you will be better able to spot weaknesses, such as inadequate evidence, inconsistent ideas, or personal biases.

Strategies for Reading Critically

To determine how critically to read a text, review your purpose for reading: A grant proposal must be evaluated much more critically than a letter from a friend, and an anonymous article on the Internet more critically than an article on the same topic by a noted authority on the subject.

To become a more critical reader, follow these guidelines:

1. Approach the text with an open mind. You bring to your reading a complex set of opinions, attitudes, values, and biases. Recognizing your own point of view can help you maintain an open mind and avoid automatic or rigid reactions to your reading.

2. <u>Consider your prior knowledge on the topic</u>. Keep in mind everything you have read, heard, or thought about the topic. Use this prior knowledge to help you evaluate your reading.

3. <u>Identify the historical and cultural context</u>. Ask yourself when, where, and why the author wrote the text, because as context changes, your understanding of and reaction to text changes. For example, a text about marriage that advised women to have dinner on the table when their husbands came home from work would seem amusing or infuriating if it were written today, but if the text had been written in the 1950s, you might regard the advice as a quaint example of the attitudes of that historical period.

FYI: For more on context, see pp. 5–7.

4. <u>Evaluate the author's expertise</u>. Being an expert on a topic doesn't necessarily make someone right. Still, a person educated and experienced in a particular subject is more likely to offer reliable information and form defensible opinions than someone untrained or inexperienced. Because websites rarely note their authors' credentials (or even the authors' names), you will have to be more cautious when using Internet sources than when using print sources.

FYI: For more on evaluating electronic sources, see pp. 416–418.

5. <u>Distinguish between facts, inferences, and judgments</u>. A fact is a statement based on evidence that can be verified, an inference is a reasoned opinion or conclusion, and a judgment is a statement of value, opinion, or personal belief. For example, when we see someone smiling broadly, we assume the person is happy. The smile is a fact that other people could verify; the person's state of mind is an inference we arrive at based on the fact. If we believe that the person's happiness is deserved, we're making a judgment.

An inference is a conclusion based on evidence. A belief is a claim that cannot be argued using evidence. Academic and workplace writing require reasoned inferences; unsupported claims and statements of belief find little respect in college or workplace writing.

A writer's point of view usually reflects both facts and opinions. Since people using the same set of facts can sometimes arrive at different opinions, a critical reader distinguishes between the factual evidence a writer supplies and the opinions a writer expresses.

6. <u>Make inferences about the author's point of view</u>. Every text is written by a person—someone who has knowledge, opinions, theories, and biases. Being aware of the author's attitude and beliefs can help you evaluate the information. Sometimes writers will state their opinions and conclusions clearly; other times, they will present data and expect the readers to make inferences and arrive at conclusions. For example, we might infer that a writer who extols the beauty, biodiversity, and fragility of a tract of wetlands is probably opposed to development in that area. When we become actively engaged in the text and make careful inferences, we will be less likely to misinterpret the author's intentions.

7. <u>Recognize incorrect thinking or manipulative language</u>. In order to be convincing, writers must support their assertions with evidence. As a reader, you should be cautious about any generalization a writer does not support with specific data. Also be alert for any attempts to distort the issue or manipulate the reader.

FYI: For more on generalizations and logical fallacies, see pp. 379–381.

8. <u>Analyze and reassess your position on a topic</u>. Reading critically ensures that you can evaluate what you have read. You may conclude that an author's theory is based on solid evidence and is persuasive, or you may conclude that the data

are inadequate to support the conclusions, or that the author's approach is biased. Reading critically will enable you to decide whether to reassess your own ideas because of the information you have read.

Activity: WORKING TOGETHER

Using the strategies for critical reading listed above, read Steven Holtzman's article "Don't Look Back." In groups of three or four, discuss your reaction to the points he makes. Is the evidence he gives persuasive? Does he give adequate evidence for his arguments? Does he attempt to manipulate readers in any way? What arguments might a reader who disagrees with Holtzman make? Did your reaction to Holtzman's ideas change as a result of your group discussion?

READING AND WRITING TEXTS

Readings

In this chapter four writers reveal their thoughts on reading—its value, its effect on them and on other readers, its place in culture. As you read the articles, think about what you typically read, how you react to the texts you read, and how your reading does or does not reflect contemporary American culture.

Activity: PREREADING

In small discussion groups

- Glance at the titles of the four readings in this chapter, but do not read beyond the titles.
- Select the reading that looks most interesting.
- Write for two minutes, jotting down your expectations and one question based on the title. Share these with the other group members.
- Read the first paragraph. Write for two to three minutes: Revise your expectations and ask another question. Share these with the other group members.
- Read for five minutes. Stop and write for three minutes: how is the text fulfilling or disappointing your expectations? Ask more questions, and note any personal reactions to the text's ideas or descriptions. Share your responses with the other group members.
- Discuss with your group how engaging actively with the text alters your reading experience.

Discovering Books
Richard Wright

"Discovering Books," by Richard Wright, is an excerpt from Black Boy, *Wright's autobiographical account of his childhood. Wright, probably best known for the novel* Native Son, *wrote many works that shaped readers' understanding of African-American life, history, and culture. In this excerpt Wright describes how African-Americans in the South were denied the use of libraries and how he managed to overcome the barriers to gain access to the knowledge and power that books had to offer.*

One morning I arrived early at work and went into the bank lobby where the Negro porter was mopping. I stood at a counter and picked up the Memphis *Commercial Appeal* and began my free reading of the press. I came finally to the editorial page and saw an article dealing with one H. L. Mencken. I knew by hearsay that he was the editor of the *American Mercury*, but aside from that I knew nothing about him. The article was a furious denunciation of Mencken, concluding with one, hot, short sentence: Mencken is a fool.

I wondered what on earth this Mencken had done to call down upon him the scorn of the South. The only people I had ever heard denounced in the South were Negroes, and this man was not a Negro. Then what ideas did Mencken hold that made a newspaper like the *Commercial Appeal* castigate him publicly? Undoubtedly he must be advocating ideas that the South did not like. Were there, then, people other than Negroes who criticized the South? I knew that during the Civil War the South had hated northern whites, but I had not encountered such hate during my life. Knowing no more of Mencken than I did at that moment, I felt a vague sympathy for him. Had not the South, which had assigned me the role of a nonman, cast at him its hardest words?

Now, how could I find out about this Mencken? There was a huge library near the riverfront, but I knew that Negroes were not allowed to patronize its shelves any more than they were the parks and playgrounds of the city. I had gone into the library several times to get books for the white men on the job. Which of them would now help me to get books? And how could I read them without causing concern to the white men with whom I worked? I had so far been successful in hiding my thoughts and feelings from them, but I knew that I would create hostility if I went about this business of reading in a clumsy way.

I weighed the personalities of the men on the job. There was Don, a Jew; but I distrusted him. His position was not much better than mine and I knew that he was uneasy and insecure; he had always treated me in an offhand, bantering way that barely concealed his contempt. I was afraid to ask him to help me to get books; his frantic desire to demonstrate a racial solidarity with the whites against Negroes might make him betray me.

Then how about the boss? No, he was a Baptist and I had the suspicion that he would not be quite able to comprehend why a black boy would want to read Mencken. There were other white men on the job whose attitudes showed clearly that they were Kluxers or sympathizers, and they were out of the question.

There remained only one man whose attitude did not fit into an anti-Negro category, for I had heard the white men refer to him as a "Pope lover." He was an Irish Catholic and was hated by the white Southerners. I knew that he read books, because I had got him volumes from the library several times. Since he, too, was an object of hatred, I felt that he might refuse me but would hardly betray me. I hesitated, weighing and balancing the imponderable realities.

One morning I paused before the Catholic fellow's desk.

"I want to ask you a favor," I whispered to him.

"What is it?"

"I want to read. I can't get books from the library. I wonder if you'd let me use your card?"

He looked at me suspiciously.

"My card is full most of the time," he said.

"I see," I said and waited, posing my question silently.

"You're not trying to get me into trouble, are you, boy?" he asked, staring at me.

"Oh, no, sir."

"What book do you want?"

"A book by H. L. Mencken."

"Which one?"

"I don't know. Has he written more than one?"

"He has written several."

"I didn't know that."

"What makes you want to read Mencken?"

"Oh, I just saw his name in the newspaper." I said.

"It's good of you to want to read," he said. "But you ought to read the right things."

I said nothing. Would he want to supervise my reading?

"Let me think," he said. "I'll figure out something."

I turned from him and he called me back. He stared at me quizzically.

"Richard, don't mention this to the other white men," he said.

"I understand," I said. "I won't say a word."

A few days later he called me to him.

"I've got a card in my wife's name," he said. "Here's mine."

"Thank you, sir."

"Do you think you can manage it?"

"I'll manage fine." I said.

"If they suspect you, you'll get in trouble," he said.

"I'll write the same kind of notes to the library that you wrote when you sent me for books," I told him. "I'll sign your name."

He laughed.

"Go ahead. Let me see what you get," he said.

That afternoon I addressed myself to forging a note. Now, what were the names of books written by H. L. Mencken? I did not know any of them. I finally wrote what I thought would be a foolproof note: *Dear Madam: Will you please let this nigger boy*—I used the word "nigger" to make the librarian feel that I could not possibly be the author of the note—*have some books by H. L. Mencken?* I forged the white man's name.

I entered the library as I had always done when on errands for whites, but I felt that I would somehow slip up and betray myself. I doffed my hat, stood a respectful distance from the desk, looked as unbookish as possible, and waited for the white patrons to be taken care of. When the desk was clear of people, I still waited. The white librarian looked at me.

"What do you want, boy?"

As though I did not possess the power of speech, I stepped forward and simply handed her the forged note, not parting my lips.

"What books by Mencken does he want?" she asked.

"I don't know, ma'am," I said, avoiding her eyes.

"Who gave you this card?"

"Mr. Falk," I said.

"Where is he?"

"He's at work, at the M—— Optical Company," I said. "I've been in here for him before."

"I remember," the woman said. "But he never wrote notes like this."

Oh, God, she's suspicious. Perhaps she would not let me have the books? If she had turned her back at that moment, I would have ducked out the door and never gone back. Then I thought of a bold idea.

"You can call him up, ma'am," I said, my heart pounding.

"You're not using these books, are you?" she asked pointedly.

"Oh, no, ma'am. I can't read."

"I don't know what he wants by Mencken," she said under her breath.

I knew now that I had won; she was thinking of other things and the race question had gone out of her mind. She went to the shelves. Once or twice she looked over her shoulder at me, as though she was still doubtful. Finally she came forward with two books in her hand.

"I'm sending him two books," she said. "But tell Mr. Falk to come in next time, or send me the names of the books he wants. I don't know what he wants to read."

I said nothing. She stamped the card and handed me the books. Not daring to glance at them, I went out of the library, fearing that the woman would call me back for further questioning. A block away from the library I opened one of the books and read a title: *A Book of Prefaces*. I was nearing my nineteenth birthday and I did not know how to pronounce the word *preface*. I thumbed the pages and saw strange words and strange names. I shook my head, disappointed. I looked at the other book; it was called *Prejudices*. I knew what that word meant; I had heard it all my life. And right off I was on guard against Mencken's books. Why would a man want to call a book *Prejudices*? The word was so stained with all my memories of racial hate that I could not conceive of anybody using it for a title. Perhaps I had made a mistake about Mencken? A man who had prejudices must be wrong.

When I showed the books to Mr. Falk, he looked at me and frowned.

"That librarian might telephone you," I warned him.

"That's all right," he said. "But when you're through reading those books, I want you to tell me what you get out of them."

That night in my rented room, while letting the hot water run over my can of pork and beans in the sink, I opened *A Book of Prefaces* and began to read. I was jarred and shocked by the style, the clear, clean, sweeping sentences. Why did he write like that? And how did one write like that? I pictured the man as a raging demon, slashing with his pen, consumed with hate, denouncing everything American, extolling everything European or German, laughing at the weaknesses of people, mocking God, authority. What was this? I stood up, trying to realize what reality lay behind the meaning of the words. . . . Yes, this man was fighting, fighting with words. He was using words as a weapon, using them as one would use a club. Could words be weapons? Well, yes, for here they were. Then, maybe, perhaps, I could use them as a weapon? No. It frightened me. I read on and what amazed me was not what he said, but how on earth anybody had the courage to say it.

Occasionally I glanced up to reassure myself that I was alone in the room. Who were these men about whom Mencken was talking so passionately? Who was Anatole France? Joseph Conrad? Sinclair Lewis, Sherwood Anderson, Dostoevski, George Moore, Gustave Flaubert, Maupassant, Tolstoy, Frank Harris, Mark Twain, Thomas Hardy, Arnold Bennett, Stephen Crane, Zola, Norris, Gorky, Bergson, Ibsen, Balzac, Bernard Shaw, Dumas, Poe, Thomas Mann, O. Henry, Dreiser, H. G. Wells, Gogol, T. S. Eliot, Gide, Baudelaire, Edgar Lee Masters, Stendhal, Turgenev, Huneker, Nietzsche, and scores of others? Were these men real? Did they exist or had they existed? And how did one pronounce their names?

I ran across many words whose meanings I did not know, and I either looked them up in a dictionary or, before I had a chance to do that, encountered the word in a context that made its meaning clear. But what strange world was this? I concluded the book with the conviction that I had somehow overlooked something terribly important in life. I had once tried to write, had once reveled in feeling, had let my crude imagination roam, but the impulse to dream had been slowly beaten out of me by experience. Now it surged up again and I hungered for books, new ways of looking and seeing. It was not a matter of believing or disbelieving what I read, but of feeling something new, of being affected by something that made the look of the world different.

As dawn broke I ate my pork and beans, feeling dopey, sleepy. I went to work, but the mood of the book would not die: it lingered, coloring everything I saw, heard, did. I now felt that I knew what the white men were feeling. Merely because I had read a book that had spoken of how they lived and thought, I identified myself with that book. I felt vaguely guilty. Would I, filled with bookish notions, act in a manner that would make the whites dislike me?

I forged more notes and my trips to the library became more frequent. Reading grew into a passion. My first serious novel was Sinclair Lewis's *Main Street*. It made me see my boss, Mr. Gerald, and identify him as an

American type. I would smile when I saw him lugging his golf bags into the office. I had always felt a vast distance separating me from the boss, and now I felt closer to him, though still distant. I felt now that I knew him, that I could feel the very limits of his narrow life. And this had happened because I had read a novel about a mythical man called George F. Babbitt.

The plots and stories in the novels did not interest me so much as the point of view revealed. I gave myself over to each novel without reserve, without trying to criticize it; it was enough for me to see and feel something different. And for me, everything was something different. Reading was like a drug, a dope. The novels created moods in which I lived for days. But I could not conquer my sense of guilt, my feeling that the white men around me knew that I was changing, that I had begun to regard them differently.

Whenever I brought a book to the job, I wrapped it in newspaper—a habit that was to persist for years in other cities and under other circumstances. But some of the white men pried into my packages when I was absent and they questioned me.

"Boy, what are you reading those books for?"

"Oh, I don't know, sir."

"That's deep stuff you're reading, boy."

"I'm just killing time, sir."

"You'll addle your brains if you don't watch out."

I read Dreiser's *Jennie Gerhardt* and *Sister Carrie* and they revived in me a vivid sense of my mother's suffering; I was overwhelmed, I grew silent, wondering about the life around me. It would have been impossible for me to have told anyone what I derived from these novels, for it was nothing less than a sense of life itself. All my life had shaped me for the realism, the naturalism of the modern novel, and I could not read enough of them.

Steeped in new moods and ideas, I bought a ream of paper and tried to write; but nothing would come, or what did come was flat beyond telling. I discovered that more than desire and feeling were necessary to write and I dropped the idea. Yet I still wondered how it was possible to know people sufficiently to write about them? Could I ever learn about life and people? To me, with my vast ignorance, my Jim Crow[1] station in life, it seemed a task impossible of achievement. I now knew what being a Negro meant. I could endure the hunger. I had learned to live with hate. But to feel that there were feelings denied me, that the very breath of life itself was beyond my reach, that more than anything else hurt, wounded me. I had a new hunger.

In buoying me up, reading also cast me down, made me see what was possible, what I had missed. My tension returned, new, terrible, bitter, surging, almost too great to be contained. I no longer felt that the world about me was hostile, killing; I *knew* it. A million times I asked myself what I could do to save myself, and there were no answers. I seemed forever condemned, ringed by walls.

---

[1]Segregation and suppression of African-Americans in public places such as buses, restaurants, and educational institutions.

I did not discuss my reading with Mr. Falk, who had lent me his library card; it would have meant talking about myself and that would have been too painful. I smiled each day, fighting desperately to maintain my old behavior, to keep my disposition seemingly sunny. But some of the white men discerned that I had begun to brood.

"Wake up there, boy!" Mr. Olin said one day.

"Sir!" I answered for the lack of a better word.

"You act like you've stolen something," he said.

I laughed in the way I knew he expected me to laugh, but I resolved to be more conscious of myself, to watch my every act, to guard and hide the new knowledge that was dawning within me.

If I went north, would it be possible for me to build a new life then? But how could a man build a life upon vague, unformed yearnings? I wanted to write and I did not even know the English language. I bought English grammars and found them dull. I felt that I was getting a better sense of the language from novels than grammars. I read hard, discarding a writer as soon as I felt that I had grasped his point of view. At night the printed page stood before my eyes in sleep.

Mrs. Moss, my landlady, asked me one Sunday morning:

"Son, what is this you keep on reading?"

"Oh, nothing, just novels."

"What you get out of 'em?"

"I'm just killing time," I said.

"I hope you know your own mind," she said in a tone which implied that she doubted if I had a mind.

I knew of no Negroes who read the books I liked and I wondered if any Negroes ever thought of them. I knew that there were Negro doctors, lawyers, newspapermen, but I never saw any of them. When I read a Negro newspaper I never caught the faintest echo of my preoccupation in its pages. I felt trapped and occasionally, for a few days, I would stop reading. But a vague hunger would come over me for books, books that opened up new avenues of feeling and seeing, and again I would forge another note to the white librarian. Again I would read and wonder as only the naive and unlettered can read and wonder, feeling that I carried a secret, criminal burden about with me each day.

That winter my mother and brother came and we set up housekeeping, buying furniture on the installment plan, being cheated and yet knowing no way to avoid it. I began to eat warm food and to my surprise found the regular meals enabled me to read faster. I may have lived through many illnesses and survived them, never suspecting that I was ill. My brother obtained a job and we began to save toward the trip north, plotting our time, setting tentative dates for departure. I told none of the white men on the job that I was planning to go north; I knew that the moment they felt I was thinking of the North they would change toward me. It would have made them feel that I did not like the life I was living, and because my life was completely conditioned by what they said or did, it would have been tantamount to challenging them.

I could calculate my chances for life in the South as a Negro fairly clearly now.

I could fight the southern whites by organizing with other Negroes, as my grandfather had done. But I knew that I could never win that way; there were many whites and there were but few blacks. They were strong and we were weak. Outright black rebellion could never win. If I fought openly I would die and I did not want to die. News of lynchings were frequent.

I could submit and live the life of a genial slave, but that was impossible. All of my life had shaped me to live by my own feelings and thoughts. I could make up to Bess and marry her and inherit the house. But that, too, would be the life of a slave; if I did that, I would crush to death something within me, and I would hate myself as much as I knew the whites already hated those who had submitted. Neither could I ever willingly present myself to be kicked, as Shorty had done. I would rather have died than do that.

I could drain off my restlessness by fighting with Shorty and Harrison. I had seen many Negroes solve the problem of being black by transferring their hatred of themselves to others with a black skin and fighting them. I would have to be cold to do that, and I was not cold and I could never be.

I could, of course, forget what I had read, thrust the whites out of my mind, forget them; and find release from anxiety and longing in sex and alcohol. But the memory of how my father had conducted himself made that course repugnant. If I did not want others to violate my life, how could I voluntarily violate it myself?

I had no hope whatever of being a professional man. Not only had I been so conditioned that I did not desire it, but the fulfillment of such an ambition was beyond my capabilities. Well-to-do Negroes lived in a world that was almost as alien to me as the world inhabited by whites.

What, then, was there? I held my life in my mind, in my consciousness each day, feeling at times that I would stumble and drop it, spill it forever. My reading had created a vast sense of distance between me and the world in which I lived and tried to make a living, and that sense of distance was increasing each day. My days and nights were one long, quiet, continuously contained dream of terror, tension, and anxiety. I wondered how long I could bear it.

Activity: RESPONDING TO THE TEXT

1. In "Discovering Books" Wright says, "my reading had created a vast sense of distance between me and the world in which I lived and tried to make a living." Why does reading give him this sense of distance? Have you ever felt the same way? Could reading have the opposite effect by making the reader feel more connected to the world?

2. The strategy Wright used to gain access to the library was not only inconvenient but also dangerous. He risked arrest or physical harm each time he used the library. Are there any clues to why Wright was willing to risk so much for books when others were not? What motivated Wright and gave him the courage to proceed with his reading?

No Snapshots in the Attic:
A Granddaughter's Search for a Cherokee Past

Connie May Fowler

"No Snapshots in the Attic" describes Fowler's struggle to learn about the past, particularly that of her grandmother and her Cherokee ancestors. Fowler looks for the "truth" about her grandmother in written records, but she rejects these sources after judging them biased and incomplete. Turning to storytelling and imagination, Fowler reconstructs her grandmother's past in fiction, which she says is "truer" than nonfiction.

For as long as anyone can remember, poverty has crawled all over the hearts of my family, contributing to a long tradition of premature deaths and a lifetime of stories stymied behind the mute lips of the dead. The survivors have been left without any tangible signs that evoke the past: no photographs or diaries, no wedding bands or wooden nickels.

This absence of a record seems remarkable to me since our bloodline is diverse: Cherokee, Irish, German, French; you would think that at least a few people would have had the impulse to offer future generations a few concrete clues as to who they were. But no; our attics are empty. Up among the cobwebs and dormer-filtered light you will find not a single homemade quilt, not one musty packet of love letters.

Lack of hard evidence of a familial past seems unnatural to me, but I have developed a theory. I believe that my relatives, Indians and Europeans alike, couldn't waste free time on preserving a baby's first bootee. There were simply too many tales to tell about each other, living and dead, for them to be bothered by objects that would only clutter our homes and our minds.

The first time I noticed this compulsion to rid ourselves of handed-down possessions was in the summer of my eighth year when my mother decided to fix the front screen door, which was coming off its hinges. As she rummaged through a junk drawer for a screwdriver, she came upon a dog-eared photograph of her father. He stood in front of a shack, staring into the camera as though he could see through the lens and into the eyes of the photographer. "Oh, that old picture," my mother said disdainfully. "Nothing but a dust catcher." She tossed the photo in the trash, pulled up a chair, lit a cigarette and told me about how her Appalachian-born daddy could charm wild animals out of the woods by standing on his front porch and singing to them.

The idea that my family had time only for survival and storytelling takes on special significance when I think of my grandmother, my father's mother, Oneida Hunter May, a Cherokee who married a white man. Hers was a life cloaked in irony and sadness, yet 30 years after she died her personal history continues to suggest that spinning tales is a particularly honest and noble activity.

Throughout her adult life, the only time Oneida Hunter May felt free enough to claim her own heritage was in the stories she told her children. At all other times, publicly and privately, she declared herself white. As both a writer and a granddaughter, I have been haunted by her decision to excise her Indian heart and I have struggled to understand it. Of course, her story would work its way into my fiction, but how it did and what I would learn about the truth of cultural and familial rumors when they contradict the truth of our official histories would change the way I see the world, the way I write, and how and whom I trust.

Until I became an adult this is what I accepted as true about my grandmother: She was a Cherokee Indian who married a South Carolinian named John May. Early in the marriage they moved to St. Augustine, Fla. They had three children, two boys and a girl. Shortly after moving to Florida, John May abandoned his wife and children. The family believed he joined the circus. (When I was a child my family's yearly pilgrimage to the Greatest Show on Earth took on special significance as I imagined that my grandfather was the lion tamer or the high-wire artist.) Grandmama May was short and round. While she was straightforward with the family about her Indian ancestry, she avoided instilling in us a shred of Native American culture or custom. Through the use of pale powder and rouge, she lightened her skin. Her cracker-box house on the wrong side of the tracks was filled with colorful miniature glass animals and hats and boots, all stolen from tourist shops downtown. According to my father, she was "run out of town on a rail" more than once because of the stealing, and she even spent time in the city jail. Her laughter was raucous. She tended to pick me up by putting her hands under my armpits, which hurt, and it seemed as if every time I saw her she pinched my cheeks, which also hurt. My grandmother mispronounced words and her syntax was jumbled. I've since realized that her strange grammar patterns and elocution were the results of having no formal education and of speaking in a language that was not her native tongue.

For me, growing up was marked not only by a gradual loss of innocence but by the loss of the storytellers in my life: grandparents, aunts and uncles, parents. With them went my ability to believe and know simple truths, to accept the face value of things without needless wrestling. As the cynicism of adulthood took hold, I began to doubt the family stories about my grandmother and I even decided my recollections were warped by time and the fuzzy judgment of childhood, and that the stories were based on oral tradition rooted in hearsay. What is this ephemeral recitation of our lives anyway? A hodgepodge of alleged fact, myth and legend made all the more unreliable because it goes unchecked by impartial inquiry. After all, don't scholars dismiss oral histories as anecdotal evidence?

I told myself I was far too smart to put much stock in my family's Homeric impulses. In choosing to use my grandmother's life as a stepping-off point for a new novel, I decided that everything I knew as a child was probably exaggerated at best and false at worst. I craved empirical evidence, irrefutable facts; I turned to government archives.

I began my inquiry by obtaining a copy of my grandmother's death certificate. I hoped it would provide me with details that would lead to a trail back to her early life and even to her birth. The document contained the following data: Oneida Marie Hunter May was born Aug. 14, 1901, in Dillon, S.C. She died June 8, 1963, of diabetes. But from there her history was reduced to no comment. Line 13, father's name: five black dashes. Line 14, mother's maiden name: five dashes. Line 16, Social Security number: none. The most chilling, however, because it was a lie, was line 6, color or race: white.

Her son, my uncle J. W., was listed as the "informant." Perhaps he thought he was honoring her by perpetuating her longstanding public falsehood. Perhaps, despite what he knew, he considered himself white—and therefore so was she. Perhaps in this small Southern town he was embarrassed or frightened to admit his true bloodline. Did he really not know his grandparents' names? Or did he fear the names would suggest his Indian lineage? Whether his answers were prompted by lack of knowledge or a desire to be evasive, the result was that the "facts" of the death certificate were suspect. The information recorded for posterity amounted to a whitewash. The son gave answers he could live with, which is what his mother had done, answers that satisfied a xenophobic society.

Thinking that perhaps I had started at the wrong end of the quest, I went in search of her birth certificate. I contacted the proper office in South Carolina and gave the clerk what meager information I had. I realized that without a Social Security number, my chances of locating such a document were slim, but I thought that in its thirst for data the government might have tracked Indian births. "No, I'm sorry," I was told over the phone by the clerk who had been kind enough to try an alphabetical search. "South Carolina didn't keep detailed files on Indians back then. You could try the Cherokees, but I don't think it will help. In those days they weren't keeping good records either."

I was beginning to understand how thoroughly a person can vanish and how—without money and folklore—one can be doomed to oblivion. But I pursued history, and I changed my focus to Florida. I began reading accounts of St. Augustine's Indian population in the last century, hoping to gain insight into my grandmother's experience. There is not a great amount of documentation, and most of what does exist was written by long-dead Roman Catholic missionaries and Army generals, sources whose objectivity was compromised by their theological and military mandates. Nevertheless, I stumbled on an 1877 report by Harriet Beecher Stowe about the incarceration of Plains Indians at Castillo de San Marcos (then called Fort Marion) at the mouth of the St. Augustine harbor.

During their imprisonment, which lasted from 1875 to 1878, the Indians were forced to abandon their homes, religions, languages, their dress and all other cultural elements that white society deemed "savage"—a term used with alarming frequency in writings of the time. Calling the Indians in their pre-Christian state "untamable," "wild" and "more like grim goblins than human beings," Stowe apparently approved of what they became in the fort: Scripture-citing, broken-spirited Indians dressed like their tormentors,

United States soldiers. She writes, "Might not the money now constantly spent on armies, forts and frontiers be better invested in educating young men who shall return and teach their people to live like civilized beings?"

The written record, I was discovering, was fabulous in its distortion, and helpful in its unabashedness. It reflected not so much truth or historical accuracy as the attitudes of the writers.

The most obvious evidence of the unreliable nature of history is the cultural litany set down in tourist brochures and abstracted onto brass plaques in parks and on roadsides across America. My family has lived for three generations in St. Augustine, "The Oldest Continuously Inhabited City in America. Founded in 1565." What this proclamation leaves out is everything that preceded the town's European founding. Like my uncle's carefully edited account of my grandmother's life, St. Augustine's official version amounts to historical genocide because it wipes away all traces of the activities and contributions of a specific race. For hundreds of years this spit of land between two rivers and the sea was the thriving village of Seloy, home to the Timucuan Indians. But while still aboard a ship, before ever stepping onto the white and coral-colored shores of the "New World," Pedro Menéndez renamed Seloy in honor of the patron saint of his birthplace. Then he claimed this new St. Augustine and all of "La Florida" to be the property of Spain; the Timucuans and their culture had been obliterated by a man at sea gazing at their land.

These distinctions between European facts and Indian facts are not trivial. The manipulation of our past is an attempt, unconscious or not, to stomp out evidence of the success and value of other cultures. My grandmother's decision to deny her heritage was fueled by the fear of what would happen to her if she admitted to being an Indian and by the belief that there was something inherently inferior about her people. And the falsehoods and omissions she lived by affected not just her; her descendants face a personal and historical incompleteness.

But when the official chronicles are composed of dashes and distortions and you still hunger for the truth, what do you do? For me, the answer was to let my writer's instincts take over. I slipped inside my grandmother's skin and tried to sort out her motives and her pain. I imagined her birth and what her mother and father might have looked like. I gave them names, Nightwater and Billy. I called the character inspired by my grandmother Sparrow Hunter. She would bear a daughter, Oneida. And it would be Oneida's offspring, Sadie Hunter, who would uncover the stories that revealed the truth.

But I needed to know how a young Indian woman with three babies to feed survives after she's been abandoned in a 1920's tourist town that promoted as its main attraction an ancient and massive fort that had served as a prison for Commanches, Kiowas, Seminoles, Apaches, Cheyennes, Arapaho, Caddos and others. The writer-granddaughter listened to her blood-born voices and heard the answers. Her grandmother made up a birthplace and tried to forget her native tongue. She stayed out of the sun because she tanned easily and she bought the palest foundations and powders available.

She re-created herself. For her children and grandchildren never to be called "Injun" or "savage" must have been one of her most persistent hopes. And what bitter irony it must have been that her children obeyed and took on the heritage of the man who had deserted them. I was discovering that my novel would be far better served if I stopped digging for dates and numbers and instead strove to understand my grandmother's pain.

My research had another effect, one far more important than causing me to question our written record. It pushed me forward along the circle, inching me back to where I had started: the oral history. My family has relentlessly nurtured its oral tradition as though instinctively each of us knew that our attics would be empty for generations but our memory-fed imaginations could be filled to overbrimming with our tales of each other. And certainly, while the stories are grandiose and often tall, I decided they are no more slanted than what is fed to us in textbooks.

I have come to view my family's oral history as beautifully double-edged, for in fiction—oral or written—there is a desire to reveal the truth, and that desire betrays my grandmother's public lie. It is in the stories shared on our beloved windy porches and at our wide-planked pine tables, under the glare of naked moth-swept light bulbs, that the truth and the betrayal reside. Had my grandmother not felt compelled to remember her life before John May stepped into it and to relate to little Henry and J. W. and Mary Alice what times were like in South Carolina in the early 1900's for a dirt-poor Indian girl, then a precious link to her past and ours would have been lost forever. And while she raised her children to think of themselves as solely white, she couldn't keep secret who she really was.

Those must have been wondrous moments when she tossed aside the mask of the liar to take up the cloak of the storyteller. It was a transformation rooted in our deepest past, for she transcended her ordinary state and for a brief time became a shaman, a holy person who through reflection, confession and interpretation offered to her children an opportunity to become members of the family of humankind, the family that traces its history not through DNA and documents but through the follies and triumphs, the struggles and desires of one another. So I turn to where the greatest measure of truth exists: the stories shared between mother and child, sister and brother, passed around the table like a platter of hot biscuits and gravy and consumed with hungry fervor.

My attempt to write about my grandmother's life was slow and often agonizing. But turning a tangle of information and inspiration into a novel and into a facet of the truth that would shine was the process of becoming a child again, of rediscovering the innocence of faith, of accepting as true what I have always known. I had to believe in the storyteller and her stories again.

The novel my grandmother inspired is fiction, for sure, but it reinforces the paradox that most writers, editors and readers know: fiction is often truer than nonfiction. A society knows itself most clearly not through the allegedly neutral news media or government propaganda or historical records but through the biased eyes of the artist, the writer. When that vision is tempered by heaven and hell, by an honesty of the intellect and gut, it allows the reader and viewer to safely enter worlds of brutal truth, confrontation and redemption. It allows the public as both voyeur and safely distanced participant to say, "Aha! I know that man. I know that woman. Their struggles, their temptations, their betrayals, their triumphs are mine."

One of my favorite relatives was Aunt Emily, J. W.'s wife. I saw her the night of my father's death in 1966 and—because my aunt and uncle divorced and because my father's death was a catastrophic event that blew my family apart—I did not see her again until 1992. She was first in line for the hometown book signing of my debut novel, "Sugar Cage." We had a tearful and happy reunion, and before she left she said, "I remember the day you were born and how happy I was that you were named for your Grandmother Oneida."

I looked at her stupidly for a moment, not understanding what she was saying. Then it dawned on me that she misunderstood my middle name because we pronounced Oneida as though it rhymed with Anita. "Oh, no," I told her. "My name is Connie Anita." Aunt Emily smiled and said, "Sweetheart, the nurse wrote it down wrong on your birth certificate. All of us except for your grandmother got a big laugh out of the mistake. But believe me, it's what your parents said: you're Connie Oneida."

I loved that moment, for it was a confirmation of the integrity of our oral histories and the frailties of our official ones. As I go forward with a writing life, I accept that my creative umbilical cord is attached to my ancestors. And to their stories. I've decided to allow their reflective revelations to define me in some measure. And I have decided not to bemoan my family's bare attics and photo albums, because as long as we can find the time to sit on our porches or in front of our word processors and continue the tradition of handing down stories, I believe we will flourish as Indians, high-wire artists, animal charmers and writers all. And the truth will survive. It may be obscured occasionally by the overblown or sublime, but at least it will still be there, giving form to our words and fueling our compulsion to tell the tale.

Activity: RESPONDING TO THE TEXT

1. What does Fowler discover about the written records and descriptions of her grandmother's life and history? How do the written records differ from the oral history and stories? How are they the same?

2. Fowler discovers that the written word has been destructive to her Native American ancestors. In what ways did reading and writing undermine their lives, culture, and history?

3. Fowler writes about "the paradox that most writers, editors, and readers know: fiction is often truer than nonfiction." In what ways can fiction be "truer" than nonfiction?

Letter One: The City of Invention

Fay Weldon

This reading is an excerpt from Letters to Alice on First Reading Jane Austen, *an epistolary novel by Fay Weldon which deftly blends fiction, literary criticism, and social history. Weldon offers another view on the effects and value of literacy: She urges readers to delve into books, promising many rewards from immersion into literature. A contemporary British novelist, Weldon is the author of numerous novels which merge a comic vision, fantasy, and an examination of the complexities of contemporary relationships and family life.*

My dear Alice,

It was good to get your letter. I am a long way from home here; almost in exile. And you ask me for advice, which is warming, and makes me believe I must know something; or at any rate more than you. The impression of knowing less and less, the older one gets, is daunting. The last time I saw you, you were two, blonde and cherubic. Now, I gather, you are eighteen, you dye your hair black and green with vegetable dye, and your mother, my sister, is perturbed. Perhaps your writing to me is a step towards your and her eventual reconciliation? I shall not interfere between the two of you: I shall confine myself to the matters you raise.

Namely, Jane Austen and her books. You tell me, in passing, that you are doing a college course in English Literature, and are obliged to read Jane Austen; that you find her boring, petty and irrelevant and, that as the world is in crisis, and the future catastrophic, you cannot imagine what purpose there can be in your reading her.

My dear child! My dear pretty little Alice, now with black and green hair.

How can I hope to explain Literature to you, with its capital 'L'? You are bright enough. You could read when you were four. But then, sensibly, you turned to television for your window on the world: you slaked your appetite for information, for stories, for beginnings, middles and ends, with the easy tasty substances of the screen in the living room, and (if I remember your mother rightly) no doubt in your bedroom too. You lulled yourself to sleep with visions of violence, and the cruder strokes of human action and reaction; stories in which every simple action has a simple motive, nothing is inexplicable, and even God moves in an un-mysterious way. And now you realize this is not enough: you have an inkling there is something more, that your own feelings and responses are a thousand times more complex than this tinny televisual representation of reality has ever suggested: you have, I suspect and hope, intimations of infinity, of the romance of creation, of the wonder of love, of the glory of existence; you look around for companions in your wild new comprehension, your sudden vision, and you see the same zonked-out stares, the same pale faces and dyed cotton-wool hair, and you turn, at last, to education, to literature, and books—and find them closed to you.

Do not despair, little Alice. Only persist, and thou shalt see, Jane Austen's all in all to thee. A coconut fell from a tree just now, narrowly missing the head of a fellow guest, here at this hotel at the edge of a bright blue tropical sea, where sea-stingers in the mating season (which cannot be clearly defined) and at paddling depth, grow invisible tentacles forty feet long, the merest touch of which will kill a child; and any easily shockable adult too, no doubt. Stay out of the sea, and the coconuts get you!

But there is a copy of Jane Austen's *Emma* here, in the small bookshelf, and it's well-thumbed. The other books are yet more tattered; they are thrillers and romances, temporary things. These books open a little square window on the world and set the puppets parading outside for you to observe. They bear little resemblance to human beings, to anyone you ever met or are likely to meet. These characters exist for purposes of plot, and the books they appear in do not threaten the reader in any way; they do not suggest that he or she should reflect, let alone *change*. But then, of course, being so safe, they defeat themselves, they can never enlighten. And because they don't enlighten, they are unimportant. (Unless, of course, they are believed, when they become dangerous. To *believe* a Mills & Boon novel reflects real life, is to life in perpetual disappointment. You are meant to believe while the reading lasts, and not a moment longer.) These books, the tattered ones, the thrillers and romances, are interchangeable. They get used to light the barbecues, when the sun goes down over the wild hills, and there's a hunger in the air—not just for steak and chilli sauce, but a real human demand for living, sex, experience, change. The pages flare up, turn red, turn black, finish. The steak crackles, thanks to a copy of *Gorky Park*. Everyone eats. Imperial Caesar, dead and turned to clay, would stop a hole to keep the wind away!

But no one burns *Emma*. No one would dare. There is too much concentrated here: too much history, too much respect, too much of the very essence of civilization, which is, I must tell you, connected to its Literature. It's Literature, with a capital 'L', as opposed to just books. Hitler, of course, managed to burn Literature as well as Just Books at the Reichstag fire, and his nation's cultural past with it, and no one has ever forgiven or forgotten. You have to be really *bad* to burn Literature.

How can I explain this phenomenon to you? How can I convince you of the pleasures of a good book, when you have McDonald's around one corner and *An American Werewolf in London* around the next? I suffer myself from the common nervous dread of literature. When I go on holiday, I read first the thrillers, then the sci-fi, then the instructional books, then *War and Peace*, or whatever book it is I know I ought to read, ought to have read, half want to read and only when reading want to fully. Of course one dreads it: of course it is overwhelming: one both anticipates and fears the kind of swooning, almost erotic pleasure that a good passage in a good book gives; as something nameless *happens*. I don't know what it is that happens: is it the pleasure of mind meeting mind, untrammelled by flesh? Of

flat-paneled handheld computers to an "electronic book." We need to develop a new aesthetic—a digital aesthetic. And the emerging backlash from the literati makes clear to me how urgently we need it.

When we've mastered digital media, we won't be talking about anything that has much to do with the antiquated form of the book. I imagine myself curled up in bed with laser images projected on my retinas, allowing me to view and travel through an imaginary three-dimensional virtual world. A story about the distant past flashes a quaint image of a young woman sitting and reading a book, which seems just as remote as the idea of a cluster of Navajo Indians sitting around a campfire and listening to a master of the long-lost tradition of storytelling. In a hundred years, we'll think of the book as we do the storyteller today.

Will we lose a part of our cultural heritage as we assimilate new media? No doubt. Is this disturbing? Absolutely. Today's traditional media will be further marginalized. Is there much value in decrying an inevitable future? Probably not. The music of *today* is written on electric instruments. Hollywood creates our theater. And soon digital media will be *our* media. Digital technology and new digital media—for better or worse—are here to stay.

That's not to say that all things digital are good. Perhaps, like the Luddites in Britain during the first half of the nineteenth century, the literati raise a flag of warning, raise awareness, and create debate, debunking some of the myths of a utopian digital future. But in the end, for better or for worse, the efforts of the Luddites were futile when it came to stopping the industrial revolution.

Likewise, today you can't turn off the Internet. Digital technology isn't going away. There are already thousands of multimedia CD-ROMs and hundreds of thousands of sites on the World Wide Web; soon there will be thousands of channels of on-demand digital worlds.

Digital technology is part of our lives, a part of our lives that we know will only continue to grow. We can't afford to dismiss it. Rather we must embrace it—not indiscriminately, but thoughtfully. We must seize the opportunities generated by the birth of a new medium to do things we've never been able to do before. Don't look back.

Activity: **RESPONDING TO THE TEXT**

1. If Steven Holtzman is correct and printed texts are replaced by digital media, what aspects of culture might be lost? What cultural advantages might be gained?
2. Identify statements of fact in Holtzman's article. Then identify a few statements that contain inferences and a few that state his judgments or beliefs. What kind of statement is most common in Holtzman's writing?
3. Make some inferences about Holtzman's beliefs and biases based on what he says in this article. How do your inferences about him affect your evaluation of his credibility?

Activity: SYNTHESIZING THE TEXTS

1. Compare the viewpoints of Fowler and Wright on the effects and value of reading and writing on a marginalized minority. How do each of these writers' views compare to Weldon's view on the value of reading? What might a typical college professor or employer think about the value of reading?

2. From the time that Gutenberg's printing press allowed for the proliferation of books until television became commonplace in the mid-twentieth century, people turned to the printed page for information. Now most of our information comes to us through electronic media—especially television and computers. In what ways do you think reading electronic and print information differ? Are the two sources likely to contain different types of information? Are they read in different contexts? What are the relative advantages of each? Is one "truer" than the other? In what ways?

Writing Assignments

Academic Essays

1. Literature

Fay Weldon contends that reading literature will help you make sense of your own experience. Think of a work of literature that has given you some insight into your own life. You may have read a story or novel that gave you insights into the turmoil of adolescence or into coping with the death of a friend. The connection between the literary work and your life may be indirect. For example, you might have read *Hamlet* and recognized the pain and confusion remarriage sometimes causes for sons and daughters. You might have read *Moby Dick* and learned something about obsession (and more than you ever wanted to know about whaling). Write a two- or three-page paper explaining how the literary work helped you gain personal understanding.

2. Education

As a student, you read many textbooks. Choose one you are using or have used in the past and write an evaluation of it. The critique should be similar to a book or movie review you might read in a newspaper: it should both describe and evaluate the text. Use the previewing, reviewing, and critical reading strategies you learned about in this chapter to examine the book. First, determine the text's purpose. Is it meant to be a comprehensive treatment of the subject, a general overview, an auxiliary to a more substantial text? While previewing the text, brainstorm a list of the topics you will cover in your critique. List anything you might want to include about the text's content, organization, visual features, or style. You might want to talk to other students who have used the text to gather more information about what is appealing or unappealing to them. Your review of the text should give students and instructors a good idea about the text's strengths and weaknesses in fulfilling its purpose.

3. Political Science

Although literacy is generally considered an education issue, Wright's account demonstrates that literacy and access to information are also political issues: Limiting a group's literacy or their access to information limits their power. Fowler, on the other hand, demonstrates how reading and writing can render a minority group politically powerless by alienating them from their native culture, assimilating them into the majority culture, and eliminating them from history. What and how people read and write affects their place and power in the community; similarly, the political community is shaped by what and how people read and write. Two issues currently being debated in the public arena revolve around this relationship between literacy and the political community: bilingual education and censorship.

Choose one of these issues to read more about. The articles listed below, which you can find at most libraries, are representative of the kinds of arguments presented on both sides:

Bilingual Education

Porter, Rosalie Pedalino. "The Case Against Bilingual Education." *The Atlantic Monthly* May 1998: 28–31.

Revira, Lourdes. "Let's Not Say Adios to Bilingual Education." *U.S. Catholic* Nov. 1998: 22–26.

Rothstein, Richard. "Bilingual Education: The Controversy." *Phi Delta Kappan* May 1998: 672–678.

Censorship of the Internet

Berry, John N. III. "Choosing Sides." *Library Journal* 1 Mar. 1998: 6.

Carr, John. "It's Time to Tackle Cyberporn." *New Statesman* 20 Feb. 1998: 24.

Kirchner, Jake. "When It Comes to the Web, the ACLU Is Clueless." *PC Magazine* 7 Oct. 1997: 30.

After reading all the articles on the subject you chose, focus on one to read more critically. As you read, take notes using annotation or a double-entry reader's log. Then try to outline the author's main arguments and evidence. Review the arguments and evidence critically. What is the writer's expertise? Can you make inferences about the writer's bias? Is the supporting evidence factual? Are there any errors in logic? Finally, consider your own response to the writing. Were you convinced of the writer's position? Why or why not? Did the writer change your point of view or just confirm it?

Write an analysis of the article which includes the following elements:

- an overview of the arguments on both sides of the issue
- a summary of the article's arguments and evidence
- an evaluation of the argument's effectiveness in convincing the audience

Workplace Writing

You are looking for employment and need to do some research to determine which job you want or which company you want to work for. Follow these steps to gather information:

1. Identify what you want to know. Brainstorm in a group or by yourself to come up with a list of information you need before you can make a decision. Try to make your list as inclusive as possible.

2. Identify ways you could find the information you need. What could you read that might have the information you want? Magazines? Newspapers? Books? Company publications? Whom could you interview? Could you contact professional or governmental organizations? What could you observe? Could you find information on the Internet? What search terms might you use to find the information? Make a plan for gathering the information you need.

3. Review the information you have gathered to determine whether you can answer the questions from Step 1. You may have two or three sources that answer one question. For example, you may have wanted to know what kinds of people you would be working with, and you might have found answers in an interview with someone who currently has the job you want and in a description in a book you read. Organize your research so that you can group related information together.

4. Write a letter to a parent or friend explaining why you chose a particular company or job. Use the facts you found in your research to explain your decision.

Personal Writing

Fowler makes fiction out of her family history: You can do the same. Write a story about your family's past. Before you begin, think about why people like to read stories about other people's lives. How does it benefit them to know what has happened to others? Write your story so that it satisfies the readers' desire for entertainment, education, enlightenment, or community.

POLISHING AND REFLECTING ON TEXTS

Learning from Other Student Writers

My Aunt's Stuffing
Brendt Uebel

"My Aunt's Stuffing (A Tale of Terror)," written by Brendt Uebel, tells a story that reveals much about his family's traditions and values. His story illustrates how his ideas and actions are different from his family's and how one individual can change a family tradition.

PURPOSE AND THESIS

LEARNING ABOUT TEXTS

Understanding Purpose

Everybody who puts pen to paper or sits down at a keyboard has a reason for doing so. The reason for writing, called **purpose**, is determined by context. Writers create texts to accomplish goals that reflect their circumstances, their own ideas and attitudes, and their audience's needs and interests.

For example, a group of scientists examining the relationship between diet and heart disease would have different purposes for writing depending on the context. When they wrote a lab report, their goal would be to accurately record the process of the experiment so the results and procedures could be examined and repeated. When they wrote an article for a professional journal to present their findings to colleagues for comment and criticism, their goal would be to clearly explain the experiment's design and their conclusions about the results. If they wrote an article for a newsmagazine like *Time* or *Newsweek*, their purpose might be to persuade readers to change their diet.

Because the purpose of a piece of writing affects many of the writer's choices about content, organization, form, length, and style, a clear purpose makes both writing and reading any text easier. The scientists' lab report would include detailed information about the procedures used in their experiment but probably would not be written in complete sentences. The article for *Newsweek*, on the other hand, would leave out much of the detailed information about experimental procedures, focusing instead on the results of the experiment and its importance to the readers' health. Not only would the magazine article be written in complete sentences, but it might also use persuasive techniques to convince readers to change their diets.

Activity: **WORKING TOGETHER**

In almost any situation, a variety of texts with different purposes may be produced by participants and observers. For example, the decision to discontinue a computer technician program at a college might generate:

- a study of the program's increasing expense, declining enrollment, and job placement rates
- reports to the state department of education, other colleges, or licensing agencies
- letters to students enrolled in the program
- changes in the next college catalog
- a press release in a local newspaper
- letters of protest to the college administration from students or regional employers
- letters to the editor of the local newspaper
- letters or articles in higher-education publications, such as *The Chronicle of Higher Education.*

For each of the four situations below, answer: (a) What kind of texts might be created? (b) Who would probably write each of those texts? (c) What would be the purpose of each text?

1. The daily operations of a fast-food restaurant
2. A person's hospital stay
3. A high-school graduation
4. A local election

How Purpose Affects Text

Like the writer's role and the audience's expectations, purpose affects a writer's decisions about form, content, organization, and style. Suppose, for example, that you decide to ask your supervisor to promote you. That purpose, to request a promotion, will trigger these decisions:

FORM:	Memorandum
CONTENT:	Statement of purpose
	Reasons for request
	List of qualifications and accomplishments

ORGANIZATION:	Initial paragraph explaining your purpose
	One paragraph for each piece of evidence supporting the request
	Paragraphs probably arranged from least to most significant
STYLE:	Clear, competent, professional

Being aware of the interrelationship of purpose with other elements of the text can make writing faster, easier, and more effective.

Format and length

Your purpose will be the major factor in determining the format and length of your text. For example, if your purpose is to inform employees about company policies and procedures, you are more likely to write a twenty-page booklet than a two-page memo. If your purpose is to persuade your classmates to go on an upcoming field trip, you will probably produce a one-page flyer rather than a two-page essay. In ideal circumstances, the length and format are adjusted to fit your purpose.

However, sometimes the writing context specifies a certain length or format. For example, your instructor might ask you to write a three-page essay about your academic major, or your supervisor might ask you to produce a brief memo about company policies. In these instances, you must adjust your purpose to fit the specifications. For example, instead of writing a lengthy explanation of all the program requirements for your major, you could argue that one requirement, such as an internship, should be added or eliminated. A two-page memo would not allow a thorough explanation of the company's policies; however, you might narrow the purpose and write a clarification of one or two that seem most confusing or create the most problems.

Content

Texts about similar topics might contain significantly different information if they have different purposes. For example, an advertisement to sell your car describes the appealing qualities of your vehicle, but a note to the mechanics at your repair shop describes all the difficulties you are having with your car. If you were informing college students in a nutrition class about the nutrients found in fruit, you would include different information than you would if you were convincing students in a health class that they should include more fruit in their diets. The text written for the nutrition class would report facts about the vitamins, minerals, and fiber in different fruits; it might include a chart listing several fruits, the vitamins, minerals, and fiber in each, and the quantities of the nutrients in each fruit. The text written for the health class might mention some facts about nutrients in fruits, but a list of those nutrients would not be the primary focus; instead, the text would focus on the benefits of eating more fruit. Clearly, awareness of your purpose will not only help you decide what information to include, but it will also prevent you from adding unnecessary information or omitting crucial information.

Organization

Writers organize information differently depending on their purpose. For example, students in an American history class taking notes for a research paper on the events leading to the outbreak of the Civil War will probably record the

FYI: For more on conventional organizational patterns in workplace writing, see pp. 467–476 in Chapter 23.

major incidents in chronological order. However, if they are analyzing the political, economic, and social causes of the Civil War, they will probably group the events by the category into which they fit rather than the order in which they occurred.

FYI: For more on traditional patterns of organization, see Chapters 9–18.

Once you know your purpose, deciding how to organize your writing is often not too difficult. For example, if you are writing to persuade your supervisor to buy new software for your office, you will need to compare the software you recommend to the one you currently use and show that the new software would be a better product for your purposes. If you are writing a paper for a literature course on the characteristics of Romantic poetry, you will probably list several characteristics of Romanticism and give examples showing how various poems fit those categories. If you are writing to a family member to explain a difficult decision you recently made, you will probably want to explain the causes of your decision. All three of these patterns for organizing ideas—comparison and contrast, classification, and cause and effect—are conventional ones. Knowing your purpose and your reader will usually be enough to help you organize your writing; however, as you write, you may decide that your purpose has changed, so you may need to shift your organizational pattern as well.

Style

Your choice of style will also be governed by your purpose. Someone creating an advertisement for this season's new fashions wants to sell the product by gaining the readers' immediate attention and will therefore probably choose a lively, informal style, selecting language that seems as contemporary as the new designs. Someone writing a letter to the editor about the need to improve the local recycling program wants to gain community understanding and support and will probably adopt a more serious, formal style.

The purposes for writing in your personal life will probably vary widely, and so will the styles of the texts you write. In college and at work, your writing style will also vary according to your purpose; however, in general, academic and professional writing usually adopt a formal style and emphasize the conventions of Standard English, such as sentence structure, spelling, and punctuation.

Activity: WORKING TOGETHER   DAEDALUS ONLINE

Working in small groups, examine each of the following writing assignments. First decide what the purpose of each assignment is. Then make a chart or a list showing the probable (a) length, (b) format, (c) content, (d) organization, and (e) style of each assignment.

1. A review of a current movie for a college newspaper
2. A resumé
3. A campaign speech for a local school board election
4. Instructions on using a rug shampooer
5. A letter protesting an unfair grade

ORGANIZING RESUMÉS

The
Workplace

The pupose of a resumé—highlighting a job candidate's qualifications—affects the content, organization, format, and style of the document. Most resumés cluster related qualifications together and put the strongest qualifications at the beginning. Headings, typeface, and spacing are used to emphasize the most impressive qualifications. A resumé should use specific details and action words when describing work experience to create a dynamic impression of the candidate.

All resumés include these categories of information:

- contact information (name, address, phone number, e-mail)
- career objectives
- work experience
- education
- skills (e.g., foreign languages, software expertise)
- honors, awards, achievements, relevant activities

Depending on its purpose, a resumé can be organized by chronology, function, or target:

- A **chronological** resumé organizes information from most recent to earliest, starting with work experience, and includes responsibilities and achievements under each work entry. A recent college graduate with limited work experience should begin with education instead of work.
- A **functional** resumé begins with a list of relevant job skills and achievements and lists education and work experience in subsequent sections. College students with limited experience or who are changing career fields can use the functional resumé to highlight their abilities and downplay their lack of experience.
- A **targeted** resumé resembles the functional resumé in its organization. However, the purpose of a targeted resumé is to focus on a specific job or workplace, so the information in the first category—skills and achievements—will be tailored to a specific job or workplace.

FYI: For samples of chronological, functional, and targeted resumés, see Chapter 23.

Importance of Identifying Your Purpose

In daily life, you often write without being conscious that you have chosen a purpose because the writing context provides you with one. When filling out a credit card application, you do not say to yourself, "My purpose is to record my personal information and credit history accurately and completely so that the company can check my record easily." You don't need to be aware of your purpose because the format of the application insures that your purpose is fulfilled. Likewise, when you write an e-mail message to a friend, you do not formulate a purpose consciously ("My purpose is to give news of my life.") because the goal of the message is inherent in your desire to communicate with your friend.

However, the purpose of a piece of writing is not always immediately clear. If you are unsure of your purpose, you may have difficulty thinking of something to write, organizing your thoughts, or finding the right words to express your ideas. Therefore, awareness of your purpose is one of your most important writing tools. Sometimes you will know your purpose before you begin writing; other times, you will discover your purpose as you draft and revise your ideas. In the final version of your writing, all the elements should work together to accomplish your goal.

Identifying your purpose can be especially difficult when you are writing at someone else's command, as you might at work or school. In these situations, you may not be sure who your audience is, what format is required, or what information is most appropriate, because you do not have a clear picture of the writing situation. If, for example, your supervisor asks you to write a report about copier use in the office, you may be left wondering whether you are supposed to record the number of copies made per day, analyze usage patterns, or persuade the company to purchase a new machine. Because it was not your idea to write the report, you may not be sure of its purpose. As a result, you may be confused about what information to include or what style to use.

Similarly, if your music appreciation instructor asks you to write a review of a concert you attended, you may be unsure about what information to include. Should you describe how each piece sounded? Should you give your personal reaction to the concert as a whole? Should you evaluate the performers' competence? Or should you make a judgment about the concert's value to the audience? To write well in a situation where you did not initiate the process, you need to discover as much as possible about the supervisor's or the instructor's goals for your project so the writing you produce fulfills their needs.

Even when the idea to write is entirely your own, you may find yourself running into difficulties because your purpose is vague. For example, you might decide to write a letter of complaint to an airline about discourteous treatment you received at check-in. You write the letter but are dissatisfied with it because your description of the incident seems hysterical and silly and because you were not able to come up with a good ending that would persuade the airline to take action on your complaint. In this example, the problem may be that you are uncertain about your purpose. Are you trying to convey your anger or to rationally describe the incident? Do you want compensation or do you want the discourteous employee disciplined? By deciding what you want to accomplish, you simplify the process of writing and strengthen the final letter.

Activity: WORKING TOGETHER

Working in small groups, discuss the following situations. List some questions you would need to answer to clarify your purpose. What could result if you misunderstood the purpose?

1. Your instructor asks you to write about a movie you saw.
2. Your supervisor asks you to write a memo giving your opinion of a coworker.
3. A college organization asks you to write an article for the school paper about a group you belong to.

How to Identify Your Purpose

If you are having trouble identifying your purpose in a particular text, begin by asking yourself two questions:

1. **What** is the subject of my writing?
2. **Why** am I writing about this subject?

When you answer these questions, be as clear and specific as possible.

Suppose your political science professor asks you to write a paper taking a stand on a local political issue. If you decide to write a paper against a local landfill, you might think that you have answered the question about your paper's subject. However, you need to be much more specific. To be really clear about your purpose, you have to state more precisely what you want to say about the landfill. Are you going to describe the landfill's history, its procedures for processing waste, its financial difficulties, or its damaging effects on the surrounding neighborhood? Your understanding of your purpose will be stronger if you can state the topic of your paper as not just "the landfill" or even "the problems of the landfill" but, more specifically, "dangers of the landfill accepting hazardous waste" or "water contamination caused by the landfill." The more specific you can be about your paper's topic, the clearer your purpose will be, and the easier your paper will be to write.

Once you have selected a specific topic, you should further refine your understanding of your purpose by asking yourself why you are writing about this particular subject. What do you hope to accomplish by writing? What is your goal? If you are writing about water contamination caused by the landfill, why do you want to describe that contamination? Are you writing a report to record results of tests on local groundwater affected by the landfill? Are you writing a letter to the general public informing them about the groundwater contamination? Are you writing a letter to the owners of the landfill persuading them to stop the contamination? Each of these different reasons for writing about the subject reflects a slightly different purpose. The more specifically you can determine what you are writing about and why, the easier it will be to write a paper that fulfills your purpose.

Three Major Types of Purpose

Writers' purposes for creating texts are many: People write to express themselves, to entertain others, to discover or explore ideas, to elicit emotional responses. Often, writers have more than one purpose, for example, entertainment and self-expression. Even though purposes often overlap, most writers at home, on the job, or at school have one of three major reasons for writing: **to record**, **to inform**, or **to persuade**.

Writing to Record

When you write to record observations and ideas, answering the following questions will focus your efforts:

1. Why am I recording this information?
2. How much of my observations or ideas should I record?
3. Who will use this record?
4. How will they use this record?

By answering the first question, you prepare yourself to record the necessary information, no more and no less. If you know why you are recording, who will use the information, and how it will be used, you will be able to select the appropriate information to include in your record.

Many times you write to record your own thoughts or information that will be used by you alone. For instance, when you take notes in your chemistry class, you are recording information that you will review when you study. Because your record will be read by you alone, you do not need to worry about a standard format; you can choose whatever works best for you. You also will not write down everything the instructor says because you will want to review only the important concepts. Class notes, diaries, grocery or to-do lists, notes from brainstorming sessions, and research notes are all records for your own eyes and use, so format, content, organization, and style are not standardized.

However, some writing that records will be read by other people, so it requires more attention to format, content, and style. If, for example, your psychology instructor assigned a report on students' behavior during exams, you would need to keep your record in some standard format, since someone else would be reading it, and you would need to record events completely and specifically. You probably would not be fulfilling your purpose if you wrote, "The student paused repeatedly and looked out the window." An accurate, complete record would require that you record how many times the student paused and for how long: "The student wrote for three minutes, paused and looked away from the paper for one minute, still holding his pen in his hand." The more specific description is necessary to fulfill your purpose in this record of events.

When you write to record for an audience, you must keep their needs in mind. The format, content, and style should be appropriate for their use. Minutes of meetings, transcripts of interviews, charts, tables of data, and eyewitness accounts of events would all be examples of writing that records. In these kinds of writings, you usually follow standardized formats.

Writing to Inform

FYI: For more on audience analysis, see p. 12 in Chapter 1.

If you have decided that your purpose in writing is to inform the readers about your subject, you can further clarify that purpose by asking yourself two questions:

1. Why do I want to give readers this information?
2. Why do the readers want this information?

Knowing why you want to inform readers or why they might want to be informed helps you choose relevant information and organize that information in the most effective way.

Once you have clarified your purpose for informing your readers, you should ask some additional questions to help you decide on the content:

3. What general or background information do the readers already know? What general or background information must I provide?
4. What terms, expressions, or acronyms special to my subject do I need to define for the readers?

Suppose your supervisor asks you to write an informative memo about copier use in your office. Answering the first question about why you want to inform the reader will not help you much in this case, since your goal in informing the supervisor is to satisfy a job requirement—pleasing your boss. However, if in answering the second question you discover that the supervisor wants the information about the copier to justify the purchase of a better machine, you will be able to limit your purpose. Your memo will include information about only those aspects of copier usage relating to the need for a new copier. You will not need to worry about finding or including information about other aspects of copier usage, such as the problem of people using the copier for personal documents. Answering the third and fourth questions about the readers' familiarity with background information and terminology will help you avoid boring or confusing your readers by providing too much or too little information on the topic. By clarifying your purpose and focusing on your readers' needs, you eliminate unnecessary work for yourself and ensure that the memo will fulfill your goal—writing a report that meets your supervisor's needs.

Almost all writing is, to some degree, informative. Personal letters inform families and friends about your life. Memos inform workers, colleagues, and supervisors about policies, changes, problems, or opportunities within the company. Textbooks, journal articles, essays, and reports inform their readers about what is known or newly discovered in academic fields. Newspapers, magazines, and newsletters inform the public about what is happening in the world around them.

Writing to Persuade

When writing to persuade, you can clarify your purpose by asking the following questions:

1. What do you want your audience to do as a result of reading your persuasive paper?
2. Why do you want the readers to be persuaded? What do you have to gain?
3. How do you think readers will benefit by following your recommendations?

You might want your readers to reconsider their opinions, change their minds, or even take some action. Knowing the answers to these three questions will enable you to choose arguments that will accomplish your purpose.

Suppose the phone company charged you on last month's bill for calls you didn't make. When writing to the company, you might think that your purpose is to convince them of their error. But to make your purpose clearer, you should also decide what action you want them to take: Do you want them to admit they are wrong, to credit your bill for the amount in error, or to send you a check for that amount immediately? If you know what you want them to do, there is more likelihood that you will persuade them to do it.

If you are writing an essay persuading people of the value of economic sanctions against countries violating international law, you must determine exactly why you are trying to convince them. Do you want your readers to participate in economic boycotts, to encourage politicians to support economic sanctions, or to discourage more violent solutions to international conflict? The effectiveness of your argument will increase if you have a clear conception of your purpose.

In writing persuasive texts, remember that you are unlikely to be persuasive if your readers sense you are indifferent to your topic. On the other hand, if readers sense you react too emotionally to your subject or overstate your case, they may feel you are biased or even untrustworthy.

Essays, editorials, proposals, applications, and many letters, memos, and magazine articles are all persuasive texts. Persuasive texts are usually also informative since writers could not effectively convince readers to change their opinions or spur them to action without first providing them with the necessary information.

The following three excerpts from the September 14, 1995, edition of *The New England Journal of Medicine*, a journal aimed at physicians, are examples of texts written to record, inform, and persuade. Excerpts one and two are from an article titled "Body Weight and Mortality Among Women"; excerpt three is from an editorial in the same issue of the journal.

The first excerpt **records** the data collected in a study of the relationship of women's weight to their likelihood of dying at a younger age than might be expected. Because the writers are trying to convey a large amount of information in a brief form, they use a graph.

Excerpt 1:

Women Who Never Smoked and Had Stable Weight, 1980–1992 (531 deaths)

Chi for trend=4.67
P<0.001

Multivariate Relative Risk

Body=Mass Index

3.2   3.4

FYI: For more on effective argumentation, see Chapter 18.

The second excerpt **informs** readers about the results of the study. Although wording such as "optimal analyses" and "predictor of mortality in this cohort" might be intimidating to the average readers, and concepts such as "J-shaped curve" or "body-mass index" might be foreign to them, physicians reading the journal expect and can comprehend this scientific style and content.

Excerpt 2:

>   These prospective data support a direct association between body-mass index and mortality among women, after cigarette smoking and disease-related weight loss were taken into account. In the optimal analyses—limited to women who had never smoked and had recently had stable weight—the lowest mortality was among the leanest women (those with a body-mass index below 19.0), weighing at least 15 percent below average U.S. weights for middle-aged women. We observed no evidence of a J-shaped curve or of increased mortality in the leanest group of women. Mortality among the obese women (body-mass index 29.0) was more than twice that among the leanest women. Although mortality did not increase substantially until the body-mass index reached 27.0, a trend toward higher mortality due to coronary heart disease and other cardiovascular diseases, as well as cancer, was apparent even among women at average weights and those who were mildly overweight. Furthermore, body-mass indexes of 22.0 or higher at 18 years of age were associated with a significant elevation in subsequent mortality from cardiovascular disease; a weight gain of 10 kg or more since the age of 18 predicted increased mortality due to cardiovascular disease, cancer, and all causes. The body-mass index was a stronger predictor of mortality in this cohort than was the waist-to-hip ratio.

The third excerpt attempts to **persuade** physicians to alter their approach in dealing with overweight patients. Its style is much clearer and more conversational because in an editorial, the writer is conveying a personal point of view rather than presenting facts and information. However, the writer's organization of the material according to a logical progression of ideas shows his understanding that physicians trained to think in scientific terms are likely to be persuaded by reason and clarity.

Excerpt 3:

>   One thing is clear from the hundreds of studies of weight control conducted in the past twenty years. Without regular physical activity, weight control can usually not be achieved. Conversely, regular physical activity can improve longevity, even for those with body-mass indexes in the "overweight" range. Therefore, both in future research and in health education, we would do well to focus less on body weight as such and more on the primary factor that increases body weight: inadequate physical activity for the amount of food we eat. We have pushed the limits of epidemiology to provide answers to the easy questions about body weight and mortality. We must now do more to overcome the harder behavioral and cultural barriers to healthier food choices, increased physical activity, and lifetime weight control.

Activity: BUILDING AN ESSAY

Refer to the potential paper topics you generated in the "Building an Essay" assignments in Chapters 1 and 2. Select five topics from the lists, and then answer these questions for each to identify and clarify your purpose:

1. What is my subject?
2. Why might I be writing about this subject?

Make your answers to these questions specific and complete. Write statements of purpose for each topic for use in a subsequent assignment.

Next, decide whether the topics will result in texts that record, inform, or persuade. For each of the topics, further define the purpose by answering the questions listed in the sections on writing to record, inform, or persuade.

Activity: WORKING TOGETHER

Find three print or online texts—one that records, one that informs, and one that persuades. You can find the texts at home, school, or work; think about magazine and newspaper articles, books, advertisements, warranties, instructions, packaging, or your own notes, papers, and letters. The list of possible texts is almost endless. In small groups, analyze the purposes of these three texts, using the questions presented in this chapter as guidelines for writing to record, inform, and persuade.

Recording, Informing, and Persuading with Integrity

Whether you are writing to record, inform, or persuade, you usually discover information that supports your point of view and information that opposes your point of view. When you are recording or informing, you must consider all the data, whether or not they bolster your opinions. When you are writing to persuade, you must acknowledge opposing viewpoints. To omit significant data or ignore opposing viewpoints biases your writing and is unfair to your reader.

Working Thesis Statements

The thesis is a statement that declares the main point you want your readers to understand, believe, or act on. Because the thesis states the opinion or conclusion you have reached about your topic, it reflects the decision you made about purpose. If you have identified a specific, focused purpose, you can construct a clear thesis. All you need to do is to turn your statement of purpose into a sentence which summarizes the main point you intend to make. If, for example, you are writing a persuasive paper about the local landfill, your thesis might say, "The landfill should be permanently closed," or "No hazardous waste should be accepted by the landfill." If you are writing an informative paper about the nutritional benefits of fruit for a health class, your thesis might say, "Adding fruit to your daily diet will help improve your health." You can write strong thesis statements by carefully thinking through your purpose before formulating the sentence.

Although many writers develop a thesis before they begin to write by thinking creatively and critically about their topic and purpose, for others, a thesis emerges as they draft and redraft material on their topic. The thesis that a writer composes during the initial stages of writing is called a "working thesis" because it may change or be refined during the drafting process. Whether you begin writing with a thesis clearly in mind or discover your thesis in the writing process, remember that formulating a thesis is a crucial phase of effective writing. A clear working thesis keeps you, as writer, focused on fulfilling your purpose.

Activity: COMPUTER WORKSHOP

Write five thesis statements about changes you would like to see at your job or school, in your home, in your relationships, or in your community. Before you write your thesis statement, clarify your purpose by considering the two basic questions about purpose: What is your subject, and why are you writing about it? You should also consider the questions about purpose listed on p. 93 in the section on writing to persuade.

Then follow these steps:

1. E-mail the five thesis statements to all the students in the class.
2. When you receive each classmate's list, reply with your choice of the two strongest thesis statements.
3. After you have received others' responses, decide which is your strongest thesis.
4. Compile a class list of the strongest thesis statements by e-mailing your best thesis statement to the teacher, who will then send the compiled list to each student.
5. What are the common characteristics of the strongest thesis statements?

Activity: BUILDING AN ESSAY

Review the topics and statements of purpose you wrote in the Building an Essay assignment on p. 96. Choose one of the topics and its purpose and create three different working thesis statements that you think would be appropriate for a college essay. In small groups, discuss each working thesis statement.

READING AND WRITING TEXTS

Readings

The four readings in this chapter illustrate former and present practices and attitudes regarding sexuality, marriage, and out-of-wedlock births. They also illustrate various purposes—to record, inform, and persuade. As you read the selections, consider each author's purpose. Notice how the author's choice of format, organization, content, and style fits the purpose. When you have finished reading each piece, decide whether you think the author achieved the purpose.

Activity: PREREADING

In your Writer's Log
1. How do you think people's attitudes and practices regarding sexuality, marriage, and out-of-wedlock births have changed since the 1700s?
2. Do these sound like readings that would interest you? Why or why not?

In small discussion groups
1. List all the problems out-of-wedlock births cause for the child, the parents, and the community. Then list all the ways that out-of-wedlock births may result in benefits for the child, the parents, and the community.
2. List ways the government or society encourages the formation of traditional families with a mother, father, and children. List ways the government and society put up obstacles to the formation of traditional families.

From *A Midwife's Tale: The Life of Martha Ballard, Based on Her Diary, 1785–1812*
Laurel Thatcher Ulrich

A Midwife's Tale contains a series of entries from a diary by an eighteenth-century midwife, accompanied by a commentary by Laurel Thatcher Ulrich, a historian specializing in the lives of colonial American women. In the excerpt you will read, Ballard records information about her work as a midwife and events in her family and community. Ulrich uses this information as historical evidence for conclusions about eighteenth-century life.

November 1792

"Matrimonial writes"

OCTOBER

28 G *At home. A Marriage in my Family.*
Cloudy fornoon, a little rain & Thunder, Clear before night. Cyrus was not at home. Thee Matrimonial writes were cellibrated between Mr Moses Pollard off this Town and my daughter Hannah this Evening. Esquire Cony performed the ceremony. My son & his wife & son tarry here.

29 2 *At home. We killd three young Turkeys.*
Cloudy. Dolly went to Mr Densmores, Mr Ballard to the hook. I have been at home. Sally here helping the girls. Mr Pollard & Savage supt here.

30 3 *At home. Roasted a Turkey.*
Clear & pleasant. Mr Ballard been to Colonel Sewalls & the Hook. I have been at home. Sally & the girls put a Bed quilt in to the fraim for Parthenia. Sarah Densmore & Dolly here the Evng.

31 4 *At home.*
Clear. Mr Ballard went to Pittston. Polly Pollard, Mrs Damrin, & my daughter Dolly quilted all day. Mrs Livermore afternoon. I have been at home. Mr Town sleeps here.

NOVEMBER

1 5 *At Mr Hodges Birth 38th. Son Town went home.*
Cloudy & some rain. Mr Town left here after breakfast. The girls had the Ladies to help them quilt. I was Calld to see Mrs Hodges at 4 h pm. Shee was safe delivered at 11 h Evening off a very fine son her sixth child. Mr Ballard came home.
Birth Ezra Hodges Son X X

2 6 *At dittoes & Mr Burtuns & Magr Stickneys. Birth 39. Bizer Benjamins wife delivered of 2 sons Both dead.* *
Clear forenoon, Cloudy afternoon, rain at Evening. I received 6/ of Mr Hodges & returnd home at noon. Left my patient cleverly. Calld at Mr Burtuns. His Lady is cleverly. I Bot off him 2 iron kettles which cost 7/, 1 spider at 3/6, 2 pepper boxes & 2 dippirs at /6 each, 2/, 1 yd binding /1, ginn 2/6, total 15/1.† I went to Magr Stickneys at 9 h Evn. His wife delivered at 11 h 5 m off a daughter. I tarried all night.
Birth Benjamin Stickneys daughter X X

---

*Here Martha is reporting a delivery she did not attend.
†In eighteenth-century accounting, a virgule (/) divided shillings and pence. "7/" therefore means 7 shillings, "/6" means 6 pence.

3 7 *At Mr Stickneys & Mr Devenports.*
Rainy forenoon. I tarried at the Magrs till after dineing. Recevd 6/ as a reward. Mrs Conry came with me to Mr Devenports where we spent the remainder of the afternoon. Returned home at dusk. I left my patients Cleverly.

4 G *At home*
Clear. I have been at home. Dolly here. Dolly not [sentence incomplete]

5 2 *At home. J Jones here.*
Clear. Mr Ballard at Pittston. Mr John Jones & a Mr Dutten here. My girls washt. I at home.

6 3 *At Mr Burtuns.*
Clear. I went to see Mrs Burtun who has had an ill turn & is Better. Dolly sleeps here.

7 4 *At home. Ephraim was Banking the house.*
Clear. Cyrus Came here. I have been at home. Helpt quillt on Hannahs Bed quilt. We got it out late in the Evening.

8 5 *At home. Mr Jones here, Son Cyrus allso.*
Foggy morn. Sun shone at 10 h. Cyrus went to his Brothers. Mr J Jones here. I have been at home. Mrs Edson here to warp a web of Mrs Densmores. Mr Pollard & Pitt here the night.

9 6 *At home. Cyrus went to Pittston. Mrs Parker returned home.*
Cloudy morn. Cyrus went to Pittston afternoon. It rained before night. A sever N E Storm in the night. I have been at home. Mrs Bradbury & Betsy Champny here.

10 7 *At home*
Cloudy & some rain. I have been at home. Stript Turkey feathers.

11 G *At home. Mr Pages & Jones here.*
Clear part the day. Mr Ballard returnd from Pittston. Mr J Jones & Mr Page & son Jonathan dind here. Mr Pollard & Pitt supt. I have been at home. Mr Ballard paid John Jones 21 dollars in part of a note he had against him.

12 2 *At home. Cyrus came up here.*
Clear part of the day. Mr Ballard at the hook & to Joness mill. Cyrus came here at 6 hour pm. I have been at home.

13 3 *At home. Cyrus sleeps here.*
The sun rose clear. Cloudy some part the day. Mr Ballard in gone to Varsalboro. Cyrus up to Mr Savages 2 hour pm Clearing a wood road.

14 4 *At Savage Boltons & others.*
Cloudy & a very Chilly air. I went up as far as Savage Boltons. He paid me
8/ at Mr Burtuns for attending his wife the 19th of January last. I Bot 2
puter dishes weight 5 lb at 2/, 1 coffee pot 3/6, six table spoons 1/8, total
15/2. I paid 7/2 cash. Mr Bolton answers 8/ of it.

15 5 *At home. Cyrus & Dolly returned home.*
Clear. Mr Ballard workt at the Bridg over the gully. I have been at home.
Mrs Densmore dind & took Tea. Mr Seth Williams & his wife here. Cyrus
came home. Has quit thee grist mill he has tended. Dolly returnd from her
apprentiship with Mr Densmore. Cyrus tended Mr Hollowells mill 14
months. Capt Nichols has hired it now.

16 6 *At home. Finisht a pair of hos for Dolly.*
Snowd the most off the day. I have been at home. We killd 2 Turkeys. Mr
Ballard went to Mr Pollards. Bot 5 1/2 lb flax at /9, 5 lb Butter at /10.

17 7 *At home*
Clear. Mr Ballard been up to Jonathans & to the hook. Cyrus went to
Pittston and brot his chest & things home. I have been at home. Have not
been so well as I could wish.

18 G *At home. Mr Shubal Pitt and Parthenia Barton joind in Marriage.*
Rainy. Mr Pollard & Pitt dind here. Thee latter was joind in the Bands of
wedlock with Parthenia Barton. The ceremony performd by Samuel Dut-
tun Esq. I have been at home. We had no Company Except our famely attend. Thee Justice gave the fee to the Bride.

There were three marriages in the Ballard family in 1792, two of them
described in the diary segment that opens this chapter. The other occurred in February, when Jonathan reluctantly married Sally Pierce, who
had initiated a paternity suit against him. Martha's descriptions of the
three weddings and the events surrounding them—one so dramatic, the
others so placidly domestic—illuminate little-known marriage customs
in rural New England.

Some historians see the mid-eighteenth century as a transitional time
in the history of the family, an era when young people began to exercise
greater freedom in choosing marriage partners, when romantic and sexual attraction between couples became more important than economic negotiations between parents. Others argue that romantic love and economic
calculation had long coexisted in the English-speaking world, that well before the eighteenth century, marriages were primarily contracts between
individuals rather than alliances of families. Martha's diary supports the
notion that children chose their own spouses; there is no evidence of
parental negotiation, and little hint of parental supervision in any of the
courtships she describes. The diary also confirms the prevalence of premarital sex. Yet there is little evidence of romance and much to suggest
that economic concerns remained central. The weddings in the Ballard

family were distinctly unglamorous affairs, almost nonevents. For the women, they were surrounded by an intense productivity, a gathering of resources that defined their meaning and purpose.

It snowed on October 23, 1791, the day Martha was summoned to Sally Pierce. Because this was going to be an illegitimate birth, she knew what she had to ask. She also knew what Sally would say.

> Shee was safe delivered at 1 hour pm of a fine son, her illness very severe but I left her cleverly & returnd . . . about sun sett. Sally declard that my son Jonathan was the father of her child.

In the margin Martha wrote simply, "Sally Pierce's son. Birth 27th."

Before we can understand the full import of that entry, we need to know something about the legal position of unwed mothers in eighteenth-century New England. Massachusetts law had always defined sexual intercourse between unmarried persons as a crime. In the seventeenth and early eighteenth centuries, courts had punished men who fathered children out of wedlock as rigorously as the women concerned, often relying on testimony taken from mothers during delivery to establish the fathers' identity, but by the middle of the eighteenth century, most historians argue, fornication had become a woman's crime.

William Nelson has shown that while fornication prosecutions still accounted for more than a third of criminal actions in Massachusetts between 1760 and 1774, in only one case was the *father* of an illegitimate child prosecuted—a black man suspected of cohabiting with a white woman. By the end of the century, actions against women had also disappeared from court dockets. Prosecutions dropped from seventy-two per year in the years 1760–1774 to fifty-eight during the revolutionary years and finally to fewer than five after 1786. Nelson found only four prosecutions after 1790 in the entire Commonwealth. Lincoln County records show the same decline. Between 1761 and 1785, seventy-three women but only ten men were presented for fornication or related crimes. No women were presented after 1785.

Historians are still debating the significance of such changes. Some stress liberalization, arguing that as courts became more concerned with mediating property disputes than enforcing Puritan standards of moral behavior, sex became a private affair. Others perceive the decline in fornication prosecutions as reflecting generational tensions in a society that had given up the legalism of the Puritans but had not yet developed the repressive individualism of the Victorians. More recent studies have emphasized gender issues, arguing that changes in fornication proceedings reflected a larger argument over female sexuality, an argument vividly displayed in eighteenth-century novels of seduction, some of which openly challenged the prevailing double standard.

Against such evidence, Sally Pierce's declaration appears a quaint and inexplicable throwback to an earlier era. It was not. Evidence from Martha's diary and from supporting legal documents casts doubt on the notion that sexual behavior had in fact become a private concern. The diary suggests that even in a newly settled lumbering town like Hallowell, sexual norms (though neither Puritan nor Victorian) were clearly defined and communally enforced, that courts seldom prosecuted sexual deviance because informal mechanisms of control were so powerful. It also casts doubt on the use of General Sessions records or elite literature to define the double standard. There were certainly inequities in the way male and female culpability was defined in this period, yet there is no evidence that in rural communities women who bore children out of wedlock were either ruined or abandoned as early novels would suggest.

The prosecutorial double standard originated in a 1668 Massachusetts law that introduced the English practice of asking unwed mothers to name the father of their child during delivery. At first glance, questioning a woman in labor seems a form of harassment. In practice, it was a formality allowing the woman, her relatives, or in some cases the selectmen of her town to claim child support. The man she accused could not be convicted of fornication (confession or witnesses were needed for that), but unless there was overwhelming evidence to the contrary, he would be judged the "reputed father" of her child and required to pay for its support. The assumption was that a woman asked to testify at the height of travail would not lie.

In fact, early courts showed a remarkable reluctance to question such testimony. Although Alice Metherell of Kittery, Maine, had been convicted of a false oath in an earlier case of bastardy (she had delivered a black child after accusing a white man), she was able in 1695 to get maintenance from John Thompson and even to defend herself against a slander suit from him. As late as 1724 Bathsheba Lyston's accusation of Daniel Paul stood, even though a witness testified that the summer before, "she was a telling what a great Liberty a Young woman has to what a young man hath for, said She, I will Let any Young man get me with child and then, Said She, I can lay it to who I please because a woman has that Liberty granted to them." Courts were obviously less concerned about the possibility of a false accusation than about the problem of having to provide public support for fatherless children. Yet one need not interpret the law cynically. It formalized a common assumption in English society, evident in the Chesapeake as well as in New England, that women were guardians of the sexual values of the community. In this regard, the witnesses in the procedure were as important as the mother herself.

A 1786 "Act for the Punishment of Fornication, and for the Maintenance of Bastard Children" confirmed the old laws, but made one important change. A new clause made it possible for women to avoid appearing at the Court of General Sessions to answer a fornication charge by voluntarily confessing to the crime before a single justice of the peace and paying a fine (six shillings for the first offense and twelve shillings for any later ones). William Nelson has assumed this was a first step in the decriminalization of sexual behavior. Possibly—though he fails to notice that the procedure made it easier for a woman to initiate a paternity action. If a woman named a man at the time of her initial confession, and then "being put upon the discovery of truth respecting the same accusation in the time of her travail, shall thereupon accuse the same person," *he* would be tried before the Sessions and, if convicted, be required to provide for the child. In fact, the two actions were typically combined on one form, suggesting that confessing to fornication was simply a preliminary step to suing for the maintenance of one's child.

This was the procedure Sally Pierce followed. On July 19, 1791, Martha wrote that Mrs. Savage had come to the house to inform her "that Sally Peirce swore a Child on my son Jonathan & he was taken with a warrent. Mr Abisha Cowen is his Bondsman for appearance at Coart." In October, just as the law required, Sally confirmed her accusation before Martha Ballard. She was not the only unwed mother to do so. For thirteen of the twenty out-of-wedlock births in the diary, Martha recorded the name of the father, using stylized language that suggests she had indeed "taken testimony" as the law instructed. Lucy Shaw, for example, "declared that David Edwards was the True Father of the Child." In five of the cases in which Martha made no record of the father's name, there were unusual circumstances. Two babies were stillborn, one of the mothers being in convulsions at delivery. In another case, Martha wrote, "Called at the rising of the sun to Sarah White, she being in travail with her forth Child, & is yet unmarried."

Fornication actions in the country courts were the apex of a broad, community-based system of enforcement. Since the procedure began with individual judges and midwives, very few of whom left records, formal court documents provide at best a glimpse of the process. That women are overrepresented on county court dockets may have less to do with a decline of interest in prosecuting men for fornication than with the voluntary nature of paternity proceedings. The very structure of the process required an admission of fornication on a woman's part in order to establish an action for paternity against a man. At the initial stages—the examination before the justice of the peace, the testimony in travail—both parties were visible, but if the man chose to settle out of court rather than to contest the accusation or if the woman for some reason decided to drop charges, the man's name disappeared, though her conviction for fornication would remain.

So it was in the case of Sally Pierce. In official documents there is no evidence whatsoever that she sued Jonathan Ballard for the maintenance of her child, though the diary tells us that she did. The record of Sally's action disappeared because it was successful: Jonathan married her in February, four months after the child was born and a month before his scheduled trial at the Sessions.

Though trials for fornication were unusual, fornication was not. Between 1785 and 1797 Martha delivered 106 women of their first babies. Of these infants, forty, or 38 percent, were conceived out of wedlock. The great majority of the women concerned (thirty-one of the forty) had already married the fathers of their children. For these mothers, the average interval between marriage and delivery was 5.6 months, though these were enough "near-misses" to blur the distinction between legitimacy and illegitimacy. "Was calld by Mr Young to go and see the wife of John Dunn who was in Labour," Martha wrote on August 25, 1799, a Sunday. "She was safe delivered at 7 hour 30 Evening of a fine son. . . . Mr. Dunn was married last Thursday. He was 20 years old last July."

There were surely differences in attitudes toward sexuality in Hallowell just as there were differences over politics or theology. Some families probably condoned premarital sex. Others encouraged formal and decorous behavior. Yet nearly everyone in the town agreed with certain fundamental propositions. One was that marriage should certainly follow, if it did not always precede, conception. Another was that fathers as well as mothers were responsible for children born out of wedlock. In courtship, sexual activity was connected with a comprehensive transition to adulthood, to good citizenship and economic productivity. The communal rituals of birth marked women as well as men as sexual beings, and affirmed the obligations as well as rights of fatherhood.

If one did not know about Sally's confession to Martha in October, it would be easy to miss the suppressed anxiety, the suspense, the tension of the entries regarding Jonathan through the early winter of 1792. "Jonathan stayed from home last night," Martha wrote on December 29, and on January 6, "Jonathan has not been at home since yesterday." The same entry reappeared on January 11, January 29, and in slightly different form on February 20: "Jonathan has not been here this day till morning." He was missing again on February 26, but three days later his mother wrote, "My son Jonathan Brot his wife & little son here."

Henry Sewall's records show that Jonathan and Sally had been published on February 11, which means they could have been legally married on February 24 or sometime thereafter. Like the Pollards, the Ballards were not present at their son's wedding, though Martha made the new bride welcome as soon as she could. "Helpt Sally nurs her Babe," she wrote on March 2. Soon she was referring to the "Babe" as "Jack." Jonathan and Sally stayed alternately at the Ballards' and at the Pierces' for the next four weeks, and on April 4, 1792, "went to housekeeping."

For Jonathan, only one wedding ritual remained. At the Hallowell town meeting in June he, along with six other newly married men, was elected a "hog reeve," a humorous acknowledgment by the town fathers that another roving stag had been yoked.

Activity: RESPONDING TO THE TEXT

1. What was Ballard's purpose in writing her diary? How does her purpose affect the form, content, organization, and style of the writing?
2. What kind of information does she include? What important or interesting information did she exclude? Why do you think that Ballard selected certain information for inclusion and omitted other information?
3. In Laurel Thatcher Ulrich's interpretation of the information found in Ballard's diary, is the purpose to record, inform, or persuade? How does her purpose affect the form, content, organization, and style of the writing?
4. Write a sentence that specifically and completely states the purpose of Ulrich's writing. Where in the writing does Ulrich summarize the points she is making?

Unwed Motherhood: Insights from the Colonial Era
Abigail Trafford

In this column, published in the January 8, 1991, issue of The Washington Post, *Trafford uses information from* A Midwife's Tale, *written two centuries prior, to make comparisons with the plight of contemporary unwed mothers.*

Once again, the unwed mother has become a symbol of what is wrong with society.

Secretary of Health and Human Services Louis W. Sullivan calls out-of-wedlock births a reflection of the "ugly underbelly of American culture"—the environment of poverty, illness and violence that is decimating inner-city America. He points to the fact that 62 percent of black children are born into fatherless households.

For centuries, the plight of the single woman who gets pregnant has been the stuff of novelists and the staple of preachers. Today, the escalation of births to unmarried women is one of the most troubling health statistics, because of its correlation with lifelong poverty. One million babies in the U.S. are now born to single women every year—one quarter of all births. Since 1980, there has been a 50 percent increase in births to unmarried mothers.

Despite publicity about single professional superwomen who elect to have children without husbands, most unmarried mothers are poor and have little education. They are disproportionately black. But as Joel Kleinman, director of analysis at the National Center for Health Statistics, notes: "Class is the real issue. Among college-educated black mothers, 90 percent of births are to married women."

Overall, being born into a fatherless household is associated with higher infant mortality rates and lower social and economic status.

In the face of these grim statistics, it's tempting to call in the medical moralists and resurrect some virtuous bygone era when nice girls didn't have sex or get pregnant outside the boundaries of marriage. But a closer look at the past quickly shatters that myth.

"A Midwife's Tale—the Life of Martha Ballard, Based on Her Diary, 1785–1812" provides a fascinating chronicle of the most intimate social patterns of a rural community in Maine two centuries ago. What is striking in Martha Ballard's diary is the high rate of pregnancies among unmarried women—and the acceptance of sex before marriage and pregnancy out of wedlock.

Of 106 babies born to first-time mothers between 1785 and 1797, nearly 40 percent were conceived by single women.

For the community, unmarried pregnancy was less a moral issue than a practical one of arranging support for the child. Most of these women married the father before the child was born, but for those who remained single, the process of establishing paternity was straightforward: The woman told the midwife the name of the father during delivery. The courts, on the assumption that a woman would not lie at such a time, then held the man responsible for the economic support of the child.

"There is no evidence that in rural communities women who bore children out of wedlock were either ruined or abandoned," writes the author, Laurel Thatcher Ulrich, a history professor at the University of New Hampshire. A fundamental tenet of the community was that "fathers as well as mothers were responsible for children out of wedlock."

Two hundred years later, health officials are only beginning to bring unwed fathers into the equation of parenting. Most government programs such as Medicaid and Aid to Families with Dependent Children do not involve the father but focus solely on the mother and child, or children.

Meanwhile, the status of the unmarried pregnant woman has plummeted. In Martha Ballard's Maine, all the leading families had unwed pregnancies. Ballard, whose husband was a selectman, the New England equivalent of a city council member, delivered one baby born to an unwed mother who confessed that the father was Ballard's own son. "Sally declared that my son Jonathan was the father of her child," she recorded in her diary.

Another change is society's attitude toward marriage. For the pregnant single woman in 1791, marriage to the father was clearly seen as a solution. In 1991, it is not.

"There's much less stigma associated with having a child outside of marriage," says Kristin Moore of Child Trends, a private Washington-based research organization. "Why form a marriage solely to legitimize a birth if the marriage is likely to fall apart?"

Twenty years ago, nearly half of the newborns conceived out of wedlock were legitimized by marriage before birth; in the 1980s, that figure dropped to 25 percent.

Besides, not getting married makes good health sense for pregnant teenagers. Statistics show that under age 18, mothers—and their children—do better if they do not marry the father but live with their parents and stay in school. In this way, they are like the unwed mothers of 200 years ago who kept their babies, stayed with their parents and often married someone other than the child's father several years later.

But the main message from Martha Ballard's diary to modern health officials is not about the morals of marriage but the realities of sex. "In courtship, sexual activity was connected with a comprehensive transition to adulthood, to good citizenship and economic productivity," writes Ulrich. It was a social and legal system that "required an acceptance of female sexuality and an acknowledgment of fleshly sin." At the same time, continues Ulrich, "it did hold men responsible for their behavior."

That's not a bad framework for building an effective public health policy to deal with unmarried parents and their children.

Activity: RESPONDING TO THE TEXT

1. What is the purpose (or purposes) of Abigail Trafford's essay? What point does she want to make about the problem of unwed mothers?
2. Why does Trafford include information from *A Midwife's Tale* to talk about a modern problem?

A Second Chance

Kathleen Sylvester

"A Second Chance," published in the September/October 1995 issue of The New Democrat *offers a method of helping unwed teenage mothers complete their education or job training while learning parenting skills in a safe environment: group homes.*

There is a knock on Frances Santiago's door and a 17-year-old Hispanic woman with a grin bursts in to announce that she's expecting an important phone call. The job interview went well, says Sarah, and she expects to get an offer tomorrow. Frances doesn't wait for the next day's phone call to give Sarah a hug.

A moment later, the phone rings. Cynthia is calling to see if she has any mail. Yes, says Frances. "I can read it to you, but first tell me about the baby. Is she walking yet? Wonderful!" Next comes Rhonda with round-faced toddler Camilia in tow, bragging to Frances that "Camilia grabbed the spoon away this morning and started feeding herself." The tiny living room, cluttered with cast-off furniture and children's books and toys, is getting crowded. Then Myra brings in shy, dark-eyed Albert, who has a secret to share with Frances about his day at preschool. Santiago, a tiny and energetic woman who rarely stops moving, is forced to sit down: Albert needs a lap to sit on.

By dinnertime, nearly all the members of Santiago's "family" have checked in. Altogether, there are 10 teenage women who favor short skirts, bright lipstick, and big earrings. Santiago calls each of them *mijita*, the familiar term for daughter in Spanish. Their children are her *nietas*, her grandchildren.

In fact, none of these young mothers—nor any of their eight children—is related to Santiago. This family is made up of young women and children who live together in a "second-chance home": the Teen Parent Residence in Albuquerque. The residence, opened in 1990, is actually a cluster of two- and three-bedroom apartments in a low-income housing project. It was created by state officials who recognized that many teen mothers need the intensive support of a residential program in order to complete their education and get off welfare while trying to raise children.

In 1994, the federally funded Job Corps program, which provides job training to disadvantaged young adults, began administering the residential program, and all the young mothers are Job Corps participants.

All of them came to the residence for one reason: They needed a new home and a new family.

Some have come from unstable homes. Many have alcoholic or drug-addicted parents. For others, home was a dangerous place; one young mother was thrown through a plate glass window. Most of these young women report early histories of sexual abuse, often by fathers, brothers, or other relatives. Few come from intact two-parent families; many report that one parent is in jail or dead. Some, says Santiago, have been on their own since age 11 or 12. And some have no place to call home: One young woman was living in a car when she came to the residence.

Santiago and the other adults who work with these teens do not dwell on such horrors. Nor do they make excuses for the young women because of their troubled backgrounds. In the social contract between the mothers and the staff of the Teen Parent Residence, much is expected of these young women.

They must stay in school or job training, learn to be responsible parents, and learn how to live in the larger society—a society with vastly different rules and expectations from those of the neighborhoods from which most come. But in return for their efforts, the teen mothers get the help they need to succeed: the constant support of caring adults, the lessons of everyday living they did not get from their own families, and models for how they are expected to live.

This experiment with young mothers now taking place in Albuquerque—and many other communities across the country—is worth replicating.

Such community-based institutions will begin to remedy one of the unintended consequences of the New Deal. When government became the primary safety net for fatherless families, the importance of community values and community institutions was diminished and the notion of reciprocal responsibility disappeared.

And when government assumed primary responsibility for women and children in the welfare system, communities were relieved of responsibility to care for their own citizens. For too long, government has been a wedge between communities and individuals, providing each with excuses to ignore its obligations to the other.

There is another compelling reason to replicate the experiment. By creating these homes and requiring many teen mothers to live in them, society would send a very strong message to younger teens—those not yet pregnant. That message would be simple: Society no longer offers unconditional, open-ended financial support for young women who bear children out of wedlock. Government will help unmarried mothers, but only if they meet mutual obligations: learning to be good parents, finishing school, and joining the workforce.

Motherly Advice

In the Albuquerque program, education is the first priority. Contrary to popular belief, most teen mothers do not drop out of school after becoming pregnant; most leave earlier because they have experienced little success and see no advantage in obtaining a diploma. Because the Teen Parent Residence is run by the local Jobs Corps program and all the residents are Job Corps participants, all must either pursue a General Educational Development diploma or enroll in Job Corps skills training programs, such as welding or computer classes.

To make the task of juggling classes and small children possible, the young mothers have easy access to day care. Also, their education and training programs are structured to accommodate their children's schedules. The teens are surrounded by adults who constantly remind them to do their homework—and provide help with it if necessary. When one teen whose first language was Spanish couldn't understand mathematics taught in English, Judy Cintrone of the state's Teen Family Services program tutored her in Spanish until her English improved.

The residence's next priority is maintaining a sense of order. New residents are quickly introduced to rules and regulations. They must remain drug-free, abide by curfews, and agree to limits on male visitation. They sign agreements to follow house rules and share in household chores. These tasks, in fact, are designed to teach them to shoulder responsibilities—in other words, to help them grow up.

The teen mothers are eager to be good parents, but those whose own parents were troubled or absent need to learn how to nurture and discipline their children. They get plenty of advice, formal and informal. A local clinic provides "development assessments" of the babies. The U.S. Department of Agriculture's Cooperative Extension Service offers nutrition classes. There are many experienced adults around to offer "motherly advice" on everything from diaper rash to discouraging a child who bites. And because the mothers frequently care for each other's children, the children benefit by having many adults to watch over them.

The young mothers need watching over too. At night, the residence is supervised by Keith Holtzclaw, a male nurse who stays in the counselor's apartment. He is there for the middle-of-the-night crises: an unwelcome boyfriend who shows up, a child with a fever, or a young mother shaken by a bad dream. Often, their nightmares are about men.

Studies show that as many as two-thirds of teen mothers nationally were victims of rape or sexual abuse at an early age. These young women are no exception: Their histories of abuse have harmed them in powerful, lasting ways. Left untreated, they may suffer from bouts of depression, suicidal tendencies, drug addiction, and alcoholism. Thus, professional mental health counseling is a critical part of the program.

Teens who have been sexually abused develop emotional patterns that make them especially vulnerable to the attentions of older men. So, protecting them from controlling and abusive boyfriends is essential to the program's success. The home, with its strict schedules and rules about male visitation, gives young women an "out." They have an excuse to say no when they are most vulnerable. And when they can't say no, they have someone to do it for them. When Sharlene asks Santiago for permission to go out, Santiago asks the questions a mother would: "Where did you meet him? What do you know about him? Does he have a job?" The answers don't satisfy her, so she insists that Sharlene take along one of the other residents.

Someone To Look After Me

Santiago is not the only one who looks after these young women. Time after time, studies show that disadvantaged children who are "resilient" and overcome their backgrounds have benefitted from the presence of a strong, positive adult in their lives. These young women are exposed to many such adults. Rose Walsh and Bernadette Buhr are their counselors and friends, too. In addition to residence staff members and volunteers, they have a chance to interact with caring individuals from the greater community. Families from local churches invite the mothers and children home for Sunday dinner. One Presbyterian congregation puts on an annual Mother's Day picnic; the Civitan youth group helps with baby-sitting.

And long after they graduate, the teen mothers maintain their connections to the people who have cared for them. They send pictures of their children and call to report on successes—good report cards, new jobs, better apartments. They show up on holidays to be with their "family."

Barbara R. Otto, director of the state's Teen Family Services and founder of the residence, says that for all its successes, the program also has had its share of failures. Many mothers drop out or are expelled because they cannot abide by the rigid rules and requirements. Others cannot conquer drug abuse or mental health problems. Some are "reclaimed" by families eager to cash in on their welfare checks. Many cannot resist the power of old boyfriends who make new promises.

Perhaps most sadly, some of these young mothers are so damaged by their childhoods that they are emotionally incapable of bonding with their children or putting their children's needs ahead of their own. In those instances, the program makes sure that the children's well-being comes first. Of 117 teens who have passed through the Teen Parent Residence, 14 have had their parental rights terminated and their children have been placed for adoption. Otto says three of the mothers did so voluntarily, acknowledging they were unable to care for their children. The cases of the other 11, who had been given every opportunity to become good mothers, were referred to child protective services and their children were removed from their custody. As difficult as those decisions were, says Otto, they were made easier because of the program's sheltered, highly structured nature. At the residence, not only were the mothers distanced from the social pressures of their own families and neighborhoods, they had also seen examples of responsible parenting and better understood their own limitations.

But by and large, the program's young mothers have defied most expectations. Only six of 117 participants became pregnant with another child while enrolled. In terms of education, 74 obtained job training through the Job Corps, 14 completed requirements for a high school diploma, 19 earned their GEDs, and 20 completed postsecondary training either through the Job Corps or private vocational education schools.

Notable Results

Similar homes scattered across the country have produced some notable results: fewer second pregnancies, dramatically increased school completion rates for mothers, reduced incidence of child abuse, better maternal and child health, higher employment rates, and reduced welfare dependency.

The Albuquerque program defies expectations in another way. It is not solely a government-funded institution, and its costs are not so high as to preclude replication. The reason? The Teen Parent Residence is a community-supported institution. The program costs just $67,500 for services to 14 teen mothers for one year, and operates in government-subsidized low-income apartment units. The mothers pay below-market rent for the apartments they share and the state picks up the cost of an apartment for the resident "house mother," a night-duty nurse, and professional counseling services. Everything else comes from the community.

Local groups hold fundraisers for the residence; for example, a youth group collects cans and bottles for recycling and donates the proceeds to the program. Stores offer product discounts and often throw in extra groceries and diapers. The manager of a local furniture store gave the residents a discount on furniture, then provided them with a truck and a driver to pick up furniture donated from other sources. Albuquerque's Hispano Chamber of Commerce not only donates money to the program but also hires graduates. Otto says these are rarely one-time benevolent gestures. The residence has become a part of the community.

The Albuquerque experiment bears close attention, perhaps most importantly, because of its potential to change the lives of children. The sons and daughters of these teen mothers are happy and healthy, well loved and well cared for. And while it will take a generation to assess how living in Frances Santiago's home has affected their lives, the early results are too promising to ignore.

BUILDING SECOND-CHANCE HOMES: A BLUEPRINT

In 1993, about 296,000 unmarried teen mothers were on welfare in the United States. Only 67,000 of these mothers, however, were under age 18. Efforts to stem teen pregnancy should focus on these young women because they need the most help, their number is small, and the "community" with the potential to take them in is large. The federal government should set aside $20 million a year for three years as seed money to create a national network of second-chance homes like that described in the accompanying article. This network could be created with three implementing devices:

• *Leveraging the federal social welfare system.* A large portion of continuing support could be funded by fees paid from participants' welfare or foster care support, and by "cashing out" their food stamps and housing subsidies. In addition, the Department of Housing and Urban Development and other government agencies can make surplus property available for second-chance homes.

• *Using limited federal funds for seed money and evaluation.* In creating a national network of these homes, the federal role could be limited to two functions: a) offering seed money and guidance about how existing models are structured, and b) evaluating the effectiveness of the programs. Federal dollars for start-up costs, which would have to be matched by communities, could be designated from the Title XX Social Services Block

Grant or from Sen. Nancy Kassebaum's proposed Youth Development Block Grant. States and communities whose homes produce measurable results should be allowed to retain a portion of the savings from reductions in projected welfare caseloads. Thus, federal funds could provide seed money for more homes. As capacity in the system builds, teen mothers might use their welfare support as "vouchers" to choose homes that meet their needs.

• *Catalyzing community support: "Stone Soup."* The model for these second-chance homes comes from a children's story—the story of stone soup. When a traveler came into a very poor village whose residents had little food, he went to the village square and began to stir up a pot of stone soup. His pot contained only water and a large stone. As people gathered in curiosity, he suggested that with a little bit of salt, the soup might be better. A bystander offered some salt. Next, the traveler suggested a snip of parsley, and again, a villager came forward. After that, the traveler asked for potatoes, and then beans, and then carrots. Within a short time, he had convinced all of the poor villagers to share, and they had pooled their meager resources to create a fine meal. Government's role is to provide the stone for the soup: to be a catalyst for gathering together religious congregations, colleges, YMCAs, Rotary Clubs, and other community institutions to solve a problem that begins in their communities and affects the lives of their citizens.—KS

Activity: RESPONDING TO THE TEXT

1. What is the purpose of Sylvester's article, "A Second Chance"?
2. How does that purpose affect content, organization, and style?
3. Which sentence states the article's thesis?
4. Do you think Sylvester fulfilled her purpose?

Fighting Teen Pregnancy
Doug Bates

In this article, "Fighting Teen Pregnancy," which appeared in the San Jose Mercury News *on July 6, 1996, Doug Bates describes the attempt made by Gem County, Idaho, to cope with teen pregnancies: charging the couple with fornication.*

A note arrived from the principal's office as Amanda Smisek, great with child, sat in class this spring at her high school here. The message: A detective at the city police station wanted to speak with her.

"I thought someone must have got into trouble and they were going to question me to see if I knew anything about it," Smisek says. "So after school I went down there and talked to him, and he asked if I was pregnant.

"I said, 'Yeah,' and he goes, 'Who's the father? Where did it happen?' I told him and then I left."

Smisek, 17, says the detective then called in her 16-year-old boyfriend and questioned him, too. A couple of weeks later, both young people received summonses to appear in Gem County Court.

The formal charge: fornication.

Nearly forgotten statute

The pair joined a handful of other Emmett juveniles recently brought up on charges under a 75-year-old Idaho law banning sex by unmarried people. Virtually forgotten and ignored elsewhere in Idaho, the 1921 statute has been hauled out of mothballs by Gem County authorities appalled at the rise in teen pregnancy.

Their use of the fornication law has divided this conservative, heavily Mormon community of loggers and ranchers in southwestern Idaho and touched off a debate reaching all the way to the state capital.

"Prosecuting a 17-year-old for fornication, over her mother's objections, represents the worst kind of government interference in the family," says Jack Van Valkenburgh, executive director of the American Civil Liberties Union of Idaho. "This prosecution impinges on rights of privacy (and) drives a wedge into the mother-daughter relationship."

Nonsense, says Douglas Varie, the Gem County prosecutor who is the driving force behind the fornication cases.

"It is absolutely inarguable," Varie says, "that the state has a compelling interest in preventing the transmission and spread of sexually transmitted diseases as well as preventing teen pregnancies."

Figures not available

Noting that his fornication cases involve juveniles, Varie declines to discuss specifics or even disclose the number of prosecutions. Others, however, say a small number of fornication cases have been filed.

Nancy Callahan, Gem County public defender, said she thinks that "six to 10 kids" have been prosecuted for fornication.

Smisek's boyfriend pleaded guilty before Gem County Magistrate Gordon Petrie and received a 30-day suspended jail sentence, three years' probation and 40 hours of community service.

The case against the young couple might have gone unnoticed if Smisek—supported by her mother, Jody—hadn't decided to fight it and go public. Amanda pleaded not guilty and went to trial, where she was convicted by Petrie.

About 50 noisy demonstrators—many of them young mothers and pregnant girls—showed up for her sentencing last month at the courthouse. Smisek, by then nine months pregnant, says the judge lectured her behind closed doors about teenage pregnancy and its high cost to society.

"He said my case wasn't about sex," Smisek says. "He said it was about welfare and how much it cost taxpayers, and then he gave me a sentence like my boyfriend's, except that I've got parenting classes instead of community services."

Petrie declines to discuss juvenile cases such as Smisek's, but Varie, the prosecutor, issued a statement defending her prosecution.

"It was never the intention of the prosecutor's office or the court to punish the juvenile as much as to help her and her unborn child to become productive members of society," Varie says. "What Amanda Smisek received was a 30-day suspended detention time and three years' probation," during which she must finish high school and stay off drugs, alcohol, and cigarettes, among other conditions. "That's it. It's not much of a story."

But Smisek's conviction made headlines all over Idaho, and Varie found himself under fire.

"Yes, teen pregnancy is a problem," says Jeanette Germain, communications coordinator for Planned Parenthood of Idaho. "But charging a pregnant teenage girl with fornication is an ineffective means of prevention. We suggest comprehensive education and health services."

"Bringing kids up on charges is not the way to get a handle on the situation," says Wendy Brown, managing editor of Emmett's newspaper, the Messenger Index. "The problem is a family problem and should be dealt with as such. Big Brother should mind his own business."

Civil libertarians upset

Idaho lawyers, along with the ACLU, questioned the legality of the fornication cases. Not only did they invade family privacy, critics say, but the charges appeared to violate constitutional equal-protection guarantees.

"I know what me and my boyfriend did was wrong, but we didn't mean for this to happen," says Smisek, who gave birth May 28 to a healthy boy, Tyler. "What makes me mad is that if they're going to charge people with fornication, they should charge it equally—to adults, too—and they don't do that."

Varie acknowledges that he hasn't brought such charges against any unmarried adults.

Smisek and others accuse Varie of bringing fornication charges only against teenagers who—like Smisek—apply for Medicaid benefits covering their childbirth expenses. Varie denies singling out any group.

In the Smisek case, Varie says, he was only doing his job after receiving a report of a pregnancy that was "the result of a consensual act between two minors." Technically, according to Idaho law, the boy involved was guilty of statutory rape, and the girl of fornication.

Varie points out that he prosecutes boys just as vigorously as girls under the old law.

"The goal is to not only make them (boys) financially responsible for those children, but to encourage and do everything possible to ensure that they have contact with the child," Varie says. "It's a sad thing for a child to only know his or her natural father as someone who had a good time with his mother in the back seat of a car."

Activity: **RESPONDING TO THE TEXT**

1. What is the purpose of Doug Bates' article, "Fighting Teen Pregnancy"?
2. Which sentence identifies the author's main focus in the article?
3. Does this sentence take a stand on the issue of prosecuting unwed teenage parents? Why or why not?

Activity: **SYNTHESIZING THE TEXTS**

1. How do the attitudes toward unmarried mothers in the communities described by Ballard, Sylvester, and Bates differ?
2. Compare the attitude toward unwed mothers in your community to the attitudes described by Ballard, Sylvester, and Bates.
3. Should communities interfere with private issues such as unwed motherhood? Why or why not?

Writing Assignments

Academic Essays

1. Sociology/Anthropology

Ulrich uses evidence from the record of the daily life of one eighteenth-century New England woman to draw conclusions about the beliefs and values of colonial society. For a week, keep a complete and accurate record of one aspect of your own life. Choose one of the following:

the places you go

the things you spend money on

the people you speak to

Read your record, and draw some conclusions about your own values and beliefs. Do you think that your daily experiences and the conclusions you came to about your values and beliefs are typical? Do they reflect what most people in our society would do? If historians from another culture or time looked at your record, would they be able to draw valid conclusions about life at the end of the twentieth century in the United States? Write a paper of two or three pages that informs your readers about your conclusions.

2. Economics

Ulrich claims that Martha Ballard's diary contains "little evidence of romance and much to suggest that economic concerns remained central" to eighteenth-century marriage. Ulrich sees the economic aspects of marriage—gathering material goods like cookware and linens, settling into housekeeping, finding property, establishing financial stability through work or investments—as a central concern of the couples described in Ballard's diary. She comes to this conclusion because Ballard's records of her family members' marriages seem to be matter-of-fact notations about dates and purchases rather than sentimental or descriptive accounts of courtships and weddings.

Write a paper examining the role of economics in contemporary marriages. What role do you think economic concerns play in a modern person's decision to marry? Because this topic is so large, you will have to narrow it before you arrive at a thesis. You might focus on a particular group of people, for example, an age group, ethnic group, or social class. Or you might examine a particular aspect of marriage and determine how it is affected by economics. There are many possibilities for focusing your topic. Try to find an approach to the topic that intersects with your interests and experiences. First decide whether you are writing to record, inform, or persuade. Remember to clarify your purpose before formulating a thesis.

3. Education

Most public middle and high schools have sex education programs of some sort. The purposes of these programs vary, but most probably have several broad goals:

- educational—learning about reproduction
- health—preventing sexually transmitted diseases
- social—preventing unplanned pregnancies

Think about the sex education program in your school system. What form did the program take? What were the program's primary purposes? To what extent do you think the program accomplished its purposes?

Write a brief paper discussing the program's purposes and outcomes. If you feel the program is not effective, you could discuss why the purpose or curriculum is inappropriate for the audience or how the program could be improved.

Workplace Writing

Review the three types of resumés discussed on pp. 467–472. Decide which type of resumé would best suit your purposes:

- If you are seeking a specific job or want to work with a specific company, use a targeted resumé to stress why you would be a good job candidate.
- If you have limited job experience or are changing career fields, use a functional resumé to highlight your skills.
- If you have recent relevant job experience, education, or training, use a chronological resumé.

To draft your resumé, use the samples in Chapter 23 as models. Because the appearance of business communication is important, choose fonts and styles that give your resumé an appealing, professional appearance. Describe your qualifications using specific nouns and numbers and active verbs. For example, "Trained 30 new employees in customer service" clearly communicates exactly what you did. Because business communication is much more effective if it is free of grammatical and mechanical errors, proofread your resumé carefully.

Hundreds of websites offer tips on writing effective resumés and searching for jobs. Many job placement services are also available on the Web. To investigate some of these sites, simply type "job search" or a similar phrase in the "search" field of any search engine.

Personal Writing

Think about the problems unwed teenage mothers faced in your high school. What were their most serious difficulties? Were the problems they faced primarily economic, social, physical, or educational? If you have friends who became mothers while in high school, you might discuss with them the difficulties of being a mother while still in high school.

Now think of ways that your high school could help unwed mothers. Could they add support systems, special classes, counseling, connections with community services?

Write a letter to the principal of your high school recommending one specific action the school could take to support unwed teenage mothers. Decide first whether your purpose is to inform the principal about your idea or to persuade the principal to adopt your recommendation. Your introductory paragraph should first acknowledge the problem and then present your thesis: a statement of your recommendation. The body of your letter will contain reasons the action you recommend will benefit unwed mothers and specific suggestions for implementing your idea.

POLISHING AND REFLECTING ON TEXTS

Learning from Other Student Writers

Responsibilities Come First

Laura Fadeley

As part of the Sociology/Anthropology writing assignment on p. 116 of this chapter, Laura Fadeley kept a log of every place she went during one week. She discovered that almost all her activities are generated by the two most important aspects of her life: her son and her college courses. As a college student and mother, Laura's life is not typical of most seventeen-year-olds.

I've come to realize that my life no longer centers on my needs and myself, which makes life stressful at times. If I'm not at school, I'm either at home watching my son, grocery shopping, or taking my son somewhere. Although occasionally I go out alone or with friends to do something I want to do, being a full-time college student and a full-time mom leaves little room for myself.

During the week, the majority of my time is spent at home. Monday through Thursday I'm at school by four o'clock. My classes end around eight o'clock, and I head home to take care of my son. Sometimes my son is in bed when I get home, but I can't go out because I have homework to do. Since my boyfriend works, I stay home to watch our four-month-old son. If I get up early, I have time to go to the gym to work out before my boyfriend leaves for work. If I do go somewhere during the day, it's usually to the grocery store to buy baby food, formula, or diapers. Once in a while, I take my son to the doctor, or we run errands together. That's about the extent of my weekdays. If all else fails, my boyfriend might rent a movie from Blockbuster. Don't get me wrong. I do go to a lot of places. It's just that the places I go are uncommon for my age group. I go to the same places that my mom would go. I have to do the grocery shopping, run out to pay bills, and get all other outside chores done. If I want to go out to have fun, I can't just get up and go. I have to find a sitter first. This makes it difficult to be able to go a lot of places. Sometimes it's even hard to get out and run errands. It takes me a long time to get ready with the baby. It always seems that as soon as the baby and I reach our destination, he gets fussy. That's why I don't get out much. I don't even get a chance to run simple errands.

Most people my age would probably think that my life is boring because I don't go to parties or clubs like many people my age do. If anyone tried to explain the normal life of someone my age, I would not be a good example because many of the people I know are into drugs, alcohol, and partying all night. I'm the exact opposite. I like to go to dinner or a movie and get home at a decent time. Waking up with a baby in the middle of the night isn't fun if I've stayed up too late. For some reasons, I'm very happy with my life. I have a "Been there, done that" attitude. I've already had my fun going to parties and clubs. I'm a mother. This means my first priority is my son and my family. If that means all my outings revolve around my son and his needs, then that's how it has to be. Being a full-time student and mother may take time away from myself, but my life can't revolve around me anymore. It has to revolve around my responsibilities.

Activity: RESPONDING TO THE TEXT

1. In what ways were recording, informing, and persuading involved in the writing of this essay?
2. Where is the thesis located?
3. Fadeley might have divided the central paragraph into two and discussed the demands of college and the demands of motherhood separately. Why do you think she chose to mingle these two topics?

Activity: PEER WORKSHOP

Essays with a clear purpose and thesis statement are easier to read and write. In the activities below, you will examine one essay you have written in this class, making sure the content matches the purpose and thesis.

Readers:

1. Underline the thesis statement.
2. After identifying the thesis statement, pause in your reading and make a list of all the information the writer should include to support the thesis. As you read through the essay, put a check mark next to places where the writer is supplying necessary information and also check off the item on your list. At the end of the reading, notice which items are not checked. Should they be added to the draft in revision?

Writers and Readers answer the following questions:

1. What is the subject of the writing?
2. Why is the writer writing about this subject? (to record, inform, persuade)

If the paper's purpose is to record, answer the questions on p. 92 of the text about writing to record; if the paper's purpose is to inform, answer the questions on p. 92; if the paper's purpose is to persuade, answer the questions on p. 93. After completing these responses, writers and readers should compare their answers and discuss any differences. Do the differences reveal a problem that needs to be addressed by revision?

Activity: PROOFREADING YOUR WORK

In all sentences, subjects and verbs must agree in person and number. Most writers make their subjects and verbs agree automatically; however, there are some situations where the rules for subject-verb agreement are tricky, especially for non-native speakers. Review the rules for subject-verb agreement by finding answers to the following questions:

- What does it mean to say a subject and verb "agree in person and number"?
- When the subject is third-person singular, what form of the verb is used?
- When the subject is third-person plural, what form of the verb is used?
- What form of the verb is used with indefinite pronouns?
- What form of the verb is used with compound subjects?

Once you understand the rules for subject-verb agreement, do the following proofreading activities:

1. In the first paragraph of your paper, underline subjects once and verbs twice for each sentence. Do the subjects and verbs all agree in number?

2. Read through the entire paper, underlining all indefinite pronouns. If the indefinite pronoun is a subject of a clause, identify the verb and make sure it is singular.
3. Read through your entire paper, underlining all compound subjects of sentences and clauses. Have you used the correct verb form?

Activity: POSTSCRIPT

1. Do you usually focus on a purpose and thesis before you begin drafting, or do your purpose and thesis emerge as you write?
2. If you know an article or essay is trying to persuade you about something, do you read it differently than you would if its purpose were to record or inform? What is different about the way you read a persuasive text?
3. When you write in your personal and professional life, which purpose do you think you use most often? What do you write? Why? What did you learn in this chapter that might be useful for this kind of writing? What questions do you still have about this kind of writing?

INFORMATION GATHERING

P R E V I E W

This chapter's discussion of gathering ideas from your own head, from others, from observation, and from written sources will help answer these questions:

- How can you come up with good ideas for papers?
- How can you get the good ideas in your head onto your paper?
- How do you find evidence and information to support your ideas?

L E A R N I N G   A B O U T   T E X T S

Gathering Your Own Ideas

When you cook or bake, you usually gather your ingredients in one place before you begin. When you make a repair on your house or car, you usually make sure you have the right tools before you begin the project. In the same way, gathering the materials for your paper before you begin writing makes drafting much easier. Once you have determined your purpose, you have a general idea of what must be included in your text. However, you will need to spend some time finding the exact facts, arguments, examples, and details necessary to write the paper. Writers often find the information they need in their own heads because people usually write about what they know. Memories, opinions, observations, and feelings are the basis of many of the papers, letters, memos, and reports you read and write at home, at school, and at work.

It might seem that gathering ideas from your own brain would be easy because all the information you need is instantly available to you. However, most of us do not have neatly organized file cabinets in our brains. Most of our brains are more like attics full of great stuff that we just cannot put our hands on right away. Our thoughts and memories are jumbled up in piles that tumble down on us when we pull out one relevant piece of information. In our disordered brains, ideas about our parents might overlap with ideas about our teachers. Memories of our grandmother might be linked to memories of our childhood. The sometimes illogical connections in our minds can lead us to valuable insights that we might want to include in our writing, but frequently they lead us away from our purpose, making it difficult for the readers to understand our ideas at all. Before we can decide which information from our brains we want to include in our writing, we need to discover what we remember, feel, think, and know.

Writers use many different information-gathering techniques for unlocking their attic brains and getting their thoughts on paper where they can see them, evaluate them, and organize them. In this chapter you will find several methods that writers find effective. None of these methods is inherently better than another, and it is not important to master all of these techniques. However, finding one or two techniques that work well for you will make writing easier and more efficient because you will be able to explore interesting connections that would be harder to confront in the middle of writing a paper or memo. If you gather your ideas before you begin writing a first draft, you will have fewer problems as you go along. If you encounter writer's block as you draft, using these techniques may help you unblock the flow of ideas.

Freewriting

To get your thoughts flowing, sit down for a set period of time (five or ten minutes is fine) and write about your topic without stopping. When you write, do not worry about details like spelling or punctuating. If you cannot think of the correct word or cannot think of something that sounds good, just do the best you can and keep writing. Keep your pen or pencil moving, even if you just keep repeating the last few words you wrote. You are not producing a finished paper; you are just freeing yourself to get all the great stuff in your head onto paper. It is often best to repeat this process a few times to explore the topic completely. Once you have finished freewriting, you will be able to look over your work and discover your thoughts and feelings about the topic. You may be surprised to find out that you have mixed feelings about a topic you thought you were sure of. You might remember experiences and information you thought you had forgotten. The following is an example of freewriting:

> Who has influenced my life? Parents, grandparents, teachers, friends. Which ones? Maybe Kai Ling or Jason. They were big influences at a certain time in my life, but I guess my parent were the biggest influence for the longest time. They still are. But I guess thats true for everybody. Who else? Who else? Who else who else. Famous people? Like who? Like musicians? Did the music I listen to really influence me much? How did I get to be who I am today? I guess I wouldn't be here if it weren't for my grandmother. Shes significant in many ways. What about other people? I guess some people influence me to not want to be like them. Like my cousin. Hes a looser.

Notice that the writer has not stopped to correct errors in spelling or punctuation because such proofreading would slow down the flow of ideas. In this freewriting, the writer never really develops any one idea in much detail but does collect many possible ideas to explore later. The freewriting has allowed the writer to see some possibilities and begin to make decisions about how the paper will develop. The writer might decide to narrow the focus and freewrite again about a friend who was a major influence at a "certain time of my life" or her grandmother who was significant in "many ways."

Freewriting in the Dark

Sometimes freewriting may be unproductive because incorrect spellings, missing words, or awkward sentences distract you from the ideas you're expressing. To tune out distractions, freewrite at your computer with the monitor turned off. Because you can't see your writing, you are unable to edit as you type, and you are likely to write more productively. Begin by setting a time limit, usually five to ten minutes, and type without stopping. If you're a touch-typist, be sure your fingers are positioned correctly on the keyboard before you begin to type. When you've finished freewriting, you can review your writing on the monitor or print out the results.

Focused Freewriting: Looping

Once you've discovered some general ideas for writing, you can quickly and efficiently narrow and explore your topic through a process of focused freewriting called looping. To create a loop, follow these steps:

- Begin by choosing a topic, perhaps one that emerged from an earlier freewriting.
- Focusing on your topic, freewrite for five to ten minutes. Remember you must write continuously and uncritically.
- When you have finished, review what you've written, looking for interesting, significant ideas.
- Select what you see as the key idea and express it in one sentence.
- Focusing on the new sentence, begin to freewrite again.

In the example below, the writer has focused on the topic of negative influences that emerged at the end of her freewriting on p. 124.

> Its funny, when somebody asks you who influenced you, they assume you'll name somebody who was a positive influence—somebody like parents or grandparents, or somebody supposed to be very good, like your minister at church. I guess parents do influence us, but I know a lot of teenagers who don't want to be anything like there parents. And what about people who have lousy parents? I guess parents are still usually the biggest influence because their with you the most when your growing up. But their not that interesting, what's interesting? What influences influences influences. Other lousy influences? What about the shock you get when your around someone you don't like or who does awful things. Maybe negative influences are more important than people think—like when you see a mother slap her

little kid just cause the kid is tired and whiney, and you think I will NEVER do that! Who do I know who was a bad influence in my life? My cousin Barry. Better example than the mother & kid in K-Mart, because growing up I've had to be around him a lot. But a lot of the time when I'm with him, I think, "no, I won't be like him."

The key idea that emerges from this freewriting, the first "loop," is that her cousin Barry was an important negative influence. The looping process then begins again. In the next freewriting, the writer might explore all of the ways Barry's influenced her, or it might focus on one or two at a time, such as his attitude toward work or education. The looping process continues until the writer is satisfied that she has thoroughly explored her topic.

Looping can be an efficient method of discovering both topics and content for writing. In the example above, three or four loops of about five minutes each would provide enough specific material for a paper. Using looping, a student could discover a topic, a thesis, and supporting evidence in less than half an hour.

Brainstorming

Brainstorming, as the name implies, is an attempt to produce ideas quickly with no attempt to make thoughts complete or logical. When you brainstorm, jot down as many random ideas as you can generate. Since you are trying to capture ideas quickly, use words, phrases, or even symbols instead of bothering to write complete sentences. For once, chaos and disorganization are good. Include as many ideas as possible; you can always eliminate weak ideas later. In fact, sometimes writers get their best ideas when rethinking what seem to be their least valuable ideas. You may prefer to brainstorm alone, so you can concentrate on finding a topic to write about or information to include in your paper. On the other hand, you may find it useful to brainstorm with a small group of people, all of whom throw out ideas, insights, or information about a topic. Either way, you need to reexamine your jottings soon after your brainstorming session, or else you are likely to forget what you originally meant by some of the notes you have taken.

If the writer who produced the freewriting above decided to explore her grandmother's influence, she might brainstorm and produce a list such as this:

    came to America from China
    worked to support my father
    was widowed when she was young
    connects me to my Chinese heritage
    cooked for me
    always gave me treats
    taught me Chinese
    is always cheerful

This list is just a beginning, so many of the entries are unclear, some seem irrelevant, and they aren't in any particular order. However, now the writer has a place to start.

Grouping

After brainstorming, you will need to expand and organize the items on the list. If any of the items on the list look intriguing, you can brainstorm again, focusing attention on one item to explore the topic more thoroughly. Once the list is complete, you can then organize the items by grouping them. Use arrows to show the relationships between items, colored highlighters to create visual groups, numbers or symbols to label similar items, or any other system that helps you recognize the relationships between the items.

Mapping

A map is a visual, spatial arrangement of information. Spreading information on a sheet of paper may help you discover relationships between ideas. Although maps can take many forms, writers find these two mapping strategies—clustering and branching—helpful.

Clustering

Clustering is one mapping technique for exploring your topic and organizing information visually. To create a cluster, follow these steps:

- Begin by placing your topic in the center of a page.
- If you know the main divisions of your topic, write them in various portions of the paper and connect them with lines to the central topic.
- Next, focus on one of the subtopics and jot down as much related information as you can—details, examples, ideas, or facts. Connect them to the subtopic.

If you are unsure about the main divisions of your topic, begin by scattering your ideas, information, and reactions randomly on a page. Then draw arrows between ideas you would like to connect when you write. When you are unsure about the relationships between your ideas on a topic, clustering may help you see connections. Jotting your ideas down in some pattern helps you know what you think and then allows you to look at those ideas to see what needs to be added, subtracted, reorganized, or rethought. If your topic is large, you might draw a second cluster, in which you focus more intently on one of the secondary ideas in your first cluster.

Branching

Another mapping technique is called branching. Branching, like clustering, is a method of visualizing your topic and the relationships between pieces of information. To use branching, follow these steps:

- Place a sheet of paper sideways, and write your topic across the center.
- Underneath the topic, write your subtopics.
- Focusing on one subtopic at a time, form a list of information; include ideas, details, facts, or examples.

The following maps illustrate clustering and branching that the writer from the previous freewriting and brainstorming might have generated about her grandmother. They contain additional information because more details occurred to the writer during the mapping process.

Clustering

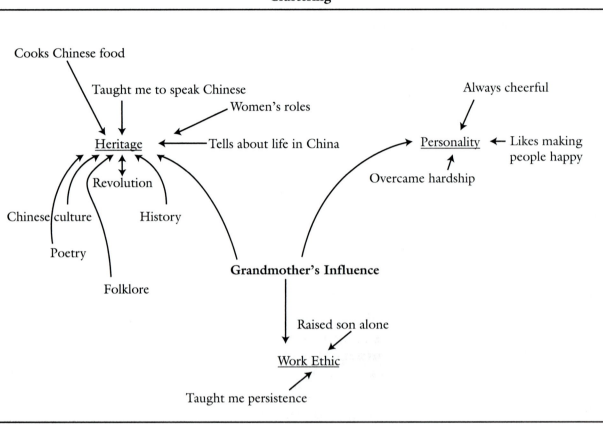

Branching

Grandmother's Influence

Chinese heritage
Taught me to speak Chinese
Tells me about her life in China
Tells me about Chinese culture—
     history
     revolution
     poetry
     folklore
     women's roles
Cooks Chinese food for me

Work ethic
Raised son alone
Taught me persistence
Overcame hardship

Personality
Always cheerful
Gave me treats (likes
     making people happy)

Organizing Ideas on the Computer

Whether you've created a cluster or a brainstormed list, you can use your computer to organize your ideas. Highlight an item and then click and drag that item next
to a similar item. Move the items on the page until they're all in similar groups. If

you decide to exclude a group from your paper, delete it. In case you change your mind, it's always a good idea to move the items that you no longer want to include to a file of "leftovers." If you change your mind, you can always recover your deletions with a few keystrokes.

Save your freewriting, brainstormed lists, and maps in one "invention" file. When you write, you can open that file to review, and you can transfer information from the "invention" file to the paper.

Conversation

When people have problems or ideas, they talk about them with friends or colleagues. These conversations help them discover and clarify their thoughts and feelings. In the same way, many writers find it very useful to talk about their ideas with others. You may find that by talking you are able to free ideas that you cannot free when you are facing a blank page. When using conversation to help gather ideas, find someone who is willing to spend time exploring the topic with you. Ask a friend, parent, teacher, coworker, or classmate to help you think through your ideas. Sometimes it's useful to talk to someone who is particularly interested in the topic, but usually, all you need is someone with time. Sometimes you might want your conversation partner to be fairly passive, just letting you talk through your ideas, maybe asking some questions at the end. At other times, you may prefer a listener who challenges your ideas as you present them. If you find that you have good ideas when you talk over your topic but cannot remember all of them later, you can use a tape recorder to preserve your own thoughts on a topic or your conversations with others about your topic. You will probably find that when you listen to your tape, you will be able to expand or refine your ideas further.

Questioning

If having a conversation about your topic isn't practical, you can have a conversation with yourself by posing and answering questions. One systematic approach to exploring a topic and gathering information is asking yourself the questions journalists ask. Reporters learn to investigate a story by asking six questions—who? what? where? when? why? and how? The answers to these questions help explore a topic from several perspectives.

You can, of course, formulate your own questions. The questions you ask yourself will vary according to your topic and your purpose. However, here are some general questions you might start with:

- Why is my subject significant?
- How can I define my subject?
- How can I describe my subject?
- Can my subject be divided into subtopics?
- What uses might my subject have?
- What significant causes or effects does my subject have?
- What is my subject similar to? Different from?

Activity: WRITER'S LOG

Gather information about an event or a person that influenced your life. Your purpose is to explain how that event or person influenced you. Use several of the invention strategies described so far in this chapter to explore your memories. Try to remember as much as possible about the event or person. For example, if you are gathering information about your father, and your freewriting contains a memory about a time you went to the beach with him, you might want to freewrite again to explore other activities you shared with your father. You might want to create a map or have a conversation with a friend to explore all the associations you have with your trip to the beach with your father.

Gathering Ideas from Others

Many writers gather ideas from other people. Sometimes just by conversing with another person or group of people, you can think of ideas or make connections that you would not have made on your own. Suppose your sociology professor wants you to write a paper about child-rearing practices in the United States. You, the writer, are a nineteen-year-old-female with two brothers, raised in the suburbs by a single mother. Based on your own experience and interests, you would be able to come up with many good ideas on your own: You might investigate child rearing in single-parent families, child rearing in the mid-1980s, how girls are raised differently from boys. You could use your own experience for all these topics, but by discussing your ideas with others who have different experiences or perspectives, you may gather more interesting or more comprehensive material. Talking to your

Activity: BUILDING AN ESSAY

In Chapter 2 you generated a list of possible topics based on the roles and interests you identified in Chapter 1. Choose one of the topics that interests you most and gather some information about it by using three or four of the techniques described in this chapter. Begin by freewriting or brainstorming to gather some initial ideas. Clustering or branching will help you begin organizing your thoughts. Try using questioning or conversation to generate a more specific and complete overview of the topic. Try any or all of the techniques to produce as much material about the topic as you can. After generating this new material, you should reconsider the thesis statement you developed in Chapter 3. Do you need to change it or refine it to suit some newly generated information you now want to include in your essay? Have you changed your point of view entirely so that you need to construct a new thesis?

brothers or your mother may give you a different angle on your memories and impressions of the way you were raised. Talking to friends or classmates who were also raised in single-parent families might supplement the observations you made on your own. The more people you can talk to and the more you discuss your own ideas, the more likely you will be to generate an insightful, complete paper.

Interviews

Interviews are a more formal way of gathering information from other people. You might interview one person who has a special knowledge of your subject. For instance, if you were writing a family history, you would want to interview your oldest living relative to find information about your family that others might be unaware of. Sometimes you might interview a number of experts to find out what different people think about a particular topic. For example, if you were writing a paper about gangs, you would want to talk to various people who had seen the problem from different perspectives: social workers, local politicians, teachers, and teenagers might all have different views of the problem.

Before you interview someone, make a list of the information you need. Then use these two guidelines to write questions that will prompt the person to recall and relate information.

- <u>Write more than one version of each question</u>. People sometimes react differently depending on how the question is phrased. For example, if you want to find out what kind of relationship your grandfather had with his father, you might ask, "Were you close to your father?" or "Did you and your father do things together?" or "Was your father someone you confided in?" These questions all aim at the same information, but the different wording may prompt different responses from your grandfather.
- <u>Make your questions specific</u>. If you were interviewing a school board member and you asked, "What plans does the board have to improve education in the district?" you might get a vague response. To get more specific information, ask a series of more specific questions such as "Does the district plan to increase expenditures for computer training of teachers? How much more money will be spent on literacy tutoring for bilingual elementary school students?" Writing more specific questions requires you to do more thinking and planning before the interview, but will result in less work in writing and revision because you will have more specific, complete information to write about.

Surveys

There might be a time when you need to gather information from a large group of people. In that case, you would probably want to design a survey that would yield very specific responses about a particular topic. For example, if you worked at a music store and wanted to know what kind of tapes and CDs to order, you might survey your customers to find out what music most interested them. Although a survey can be quite formal, using conventional methods and statistical analysis, you probably would use a more informal survey method for most college or work projects.

The Workplace

INFORMATIONAL JOB INTERVIEWING

Gathering information is a critical part of writing; it is also an important aspect of searching for a job. You may think that when you look for a job, you will be the person interviewed by an employer. However, another kind of job interview is called the informational interview, in which you gather information about a job or a company.

In informational interviews, your goal is to discover what kind of work you want to do or what kind of company you want to work for. To find out more about the job or company you're interested in, interview people who are currently working at your targeted job or company. Talk to them briefly (less than 15 minutes), asking a few questions you've prepared in advance. When preparing questions, consider asking questions about:

- How the worker prepared for and obtained the job
- What the worker likes or dislikes about the job
- What you particularly want to know about the job
- Other workers who might have similar kinds of jobs

As you interview people, you may revise or refine your ideas about what job or company you want to consider. Being knowledgeable enough to narrow your job search makes you a better job candidate. Knowing the job is right for you and you are right for the job will improve your confidence when you are interviewed for a particular position. Additionally, your knowledge about the job or company will impress your prospective employers.

If you do a survey to gather information from others, first determine what you want to find out. If you are writing a paper about student drinking, decide whether you want to know how much students drink, which students are more likely to drink, what settings encourage drinking, or any of the numerous other interesting areas that might be explored. Limiting your survey to one or two things you want to find out will help you stay focused as you gather information and write your paper.

Choose a few questions that can be answered quickly and easily. If you want to find out which settings encourage drinking, you might be able to ask one question such as "Where are you most likely to drink?" However, if you are trying to find out which students are more likely to drink, you will first have to ask "Do you drink?" You will then also include some follow-up questions such as "How old are you?" "Where do you live?" "What is your grade average?" or similar questions that will help you characterize students who drink.

Next, decide which group of people you are going to survey. It might seem obvious that in the example about student drinking you would survey students, but which students? If you hand out questionnaires only in a dormitory, you might not get a representative group. If you survey only students in 8:00 A.M. classes, you might also find that your results are inaccurate.

Surveying an adequate number of people will make your survey more useful and credible. If you surveyed only twenty students about their drinking habits, would your sample be large enough to represent the whole student body? Could you draw any valid generalizations based on such a small sample? In a formal survey, the minimum number of respondents is determined by sampling formulas; for your informal surveys, you will need to make reasonable judgments about the number of respondents necessary to yield meaningful results.

Also, you need to decide how to conduct the survey. Will you question people face to face? Will you hand out anonymous questionnaires? Different methods might yield different results. For example, students might not admit the extent of their own drinking (or might exaggerate it) if you asked them in person. Once you have collected your information, you can organize the results and interpret them for use as evidence in your paper.

Activity: WRITER'S LOG

Refer to the information you gathered about a significant event or person in your life in the previous Writer's Log. You are going to gather more information about the event or person by talking to other people.

1. First, talk to an individual or a group of people who have no connection to the person or event. Discuss your memories and thoughts with this person or group to see how they react to your explanations. Encourage them to ask you questions about the person or event to stimulate your thinking.
2. Next, interview someone who shared the event or knew the person you are gathering information about. Ask questions that will help fill in blanks in your memories and that will give you another perspective on your recollections.

Activity: WORKING TOGETHER   DAEDALUS ONLINE

Organize into groups of three or four to gather some information about what makes a college class popular with students. First, each member of the group will prepare to interview another member in the group about a favorite class by creating five to ten interview questions. Think about what information you need to determine what makes a class popular, and design questions that will elicit useful responses. Conduct the interview, then compare your questions and results with those of everyone in the group. Which questions seemed to get the best responses?

As a group, design a survey that will be given to the whole class. Use the questions from the interview as a basis, but you might want to add some or adapt the questions for the purposes of the survey. You are trying to determine what characteristics popular classes have in common, so your questions should help you gather that information.

Each group will then distribute its set of survey questions to the rest of the class. After the questionnaires have been completed and collected, the group will read them and evaluate the responses and the effectiveness of the questions.

Finally, each group will report to the whole class. What were your results? Which were good questions? Which were not? Why? After all the groups have reported, discuss the survey process itself. Do you think it would yield an accurate picture of what makes classes popular?

Gathering Information Through Observation

Gathering information often requires that you observe people, events, performances, objects, or natural phenomena. To write a movie review, you view the movie carefully. To write a lab report, you need to observe the experiment closely. To write a character sketch, you need to watch the person intently. As you observe, use all your senses and try to record your perceptions as completely and accurately as possible. It is best to record the useful data as you observe it. Take notes as you watch the movie or as you do the experiment. To ensure that your notetaking reflects your purpose, design a framework for recording your observations. For example, if you are writing a restaurant review for a local newspaper, you may know that you are interested in observing the service, atmosphere, food, and price. If you have your notes set up with these categories already outlined, it will be easier to record the relevant information during your visit.

When you are gathering information from observation, you usually have only one opportunity to get the data you need, so you must be thorough. A sports reporter who did not record details about a key play at the high-school football game cannot go back and ask the team to redo the play. Record any information that might possibly be useful; you can always eliminate unnecessary information later.

Activity: WRITER'S LOG

Prepare to observe a conversation between two strangers who are close enough for you to see them clearly but not close enough to overhear them. What might you be observing? What categories might you create to help organize your observations? Set up a piece of paper with these categories and take notes as you observe the conversation. After you have finished the observation, evaluate your choices of categories. Did they work well? Would you rearrange them if you were writing a description of your observation? Just for fun, you might write down any speculations about the content and tone of the conversation and the relationship of the participants.

Gathering Information by Doing Research

If you do not have the information you need stored in your memory and you cannot gain it through observation, interviews, or surveys, you must gather the information from sources such as books, movies, videos, CDs, pamphlets, magazines, newspapers, archives, or the Internet.

In some cases, you will turn to these sources to help you narrow a topic or determine a purpose. For example, a professor may assign a very broad research paper topic without clear guidelines about which particular information to include. In such a situation, you may not have a clear enough idea about your topic or purpose, so you will explore various sources to help trigger or shape your own ideas. For example, if your biology professor asks you to write a paper explaining the evolution of a species, your first task will be to identify which species you will research. Though you might have one species in mind—canines, for example—as your first choice, you will probably need to do some preliminary investigation on several species before you choose the one that best suits your interests and about which you can find adequate information. Perhaps you cannot find much material about the evolution of dogs or perhaps as you research that topic, you find yourself more interested in the evolution of birds. Being open to changing and narrowing your topic makes your research more interesting and productive. As you continue your research, you will consult a wide variety of sources in order to familiarize yourself with different scientists' work and conclusions. You may discover that there is some controversy about the descent of the modern domestic dog and that this controversy would make a great focus for your paper. After you have a more extensive knowledge of your topic, you can more clearly define the purpose and content of your paper. This kind of extensive preliminary research provides the basis for the more specific research you will need to do to find supporting information for your paper.

If you are looking to support or explain your ideas, you will want to turn to source material that provides you with the specific information necessary to fulfill your clearly defined purpose. For example, if you are writing a letter to your city council protesting a proposed tax increase, you might want to gather data about past tax increases, current expenditures, and tax rates in neighboring towns. Finding this information in public records or newspapers allows you to argue against the proposed tax more effectively. This kind of search is very limited because you know what information you want.

Whatever kind of research you are doing, you will probably use a library. Card or computerized catalogs, indexes, bibliographies, and other reference guides can direct you to the material you need. The reference librarian is your best resource for using the library. You should also investigate material available outside of libraries. Museums, for example, may contain information you can use. Most organizations have informational pamphlets they will send on request. Government publications and records may give you information you need.

In addition to print sources, you will also want to consult electronic sources. Reference librarians may refer you to CD-ROMs containing databases or other information. You may want to contact experts via e-mail. Because so much current information is available online, you will also want to investigate Internet sources.

When you gather information through research, just as when you gather information from your memory, from other people, or from observation, you need to make a record of what you learn. Take notes on your research, making sure you know where each piece of information comes from. If the material is from a book, note the title, author, publisher, place and date of publication, and the pages the material is on. If the material is from a periodical, note the title of the article, the author's name, the name of the magazine, newspaper, or journal, the volume and date of the publication, and the page numbers. If the material is from the Internet,

FYI: For more on using the library for research, see Chapter 20.

FYI: For more on using electronic sources, see Chapter 20.

FYI: For more on notetaking and documentation of sources, see Chapters 20 and 21.

note the author, document title, title of the document to which your file is linked, publication date, date you accessed the file, and Internet address. If you are writing a formal research paper, you will need more detailed information about research strategies and documentation.

Activity: WRITER'S LOG

Investigate what was going on in the world during the significant event you described or during the childhood of the person you described. Find newspapers and magazines from that period. Try to discover as much as you can about what was happening in the fields of politics, economics, entertainment, science and technology, and sports. Do you think these events influenced the event or person you described?

Gathering Information with Integrity

Whenever you use the information you've gathered from sources, whether you are expressing another's ideas, quoting exact words, or reporting data, you must give credit to the source. Failure to acknowledge and document the source of information, called plagiarism, is a form of academic dishonesty. Because it fails to give due credit for ideas and information, plagiarism is unfair to the source of the information; because it prevents the reader's access to the original information, plagiarism is also unfair to the reader.

Go For It!

Many sites are available for Web searches. These search engines and directories let you type in words to identify what you are searching for. They then return a list of results which are the names of websites that might contain relevant information. All the sites work in similar ways, but they often return different results, so try a number of different search sites to do a thorough Internet search. Here is a list of some you might try:

☞ GOOGLE	•	www.google.com
☞ YAHOO	•	www.yahoo.com
☞ HOTBOT	•	www.hotbot.com
☞ ALTA VISTA	•	www.altavista.com
☞ EXCITE	•	www.excite.com
☞ INFOSEEK	•	www.go.com
☞ LYCOS	•	www.lycos.com
☞ METACRAWLER	•	www.metacrawler.com
☞ DOGPILE	•	www.dogpile.com
☞ ASK JEEVES	•	www.askjeeves.com

READING AND WRITING TEXTS

Readings

The four readings in this chapter discuss or demonstrate gathering information, formulating ideas, and doing research. As you read the selections by Charles Darwin, Lewis Thomas, and Joan Didion, notice how their methods of observation fit their purposes. As you read Cynthia Crossen's discussion of bias in the polling process, think of how the information you gather from print and nonprint sources may be inaccurate or biased.

Activity: PREREADING

Respond briefly in your Writer's Log

1. Do you think that you're an observant person? What kind of information or insights do you gain from observations?
2. Did you ever keep any kind of diary, journal, or notebook? What was its purpose? If you never have, why haven't you?
3. If you read a poll saying 70 percent of people intended to vote for a particular presidential candidate, would you believe the poll? Would the poll results influence your voting decision? What if the poll showed that your favorite candidate had only 20 percent of the votes? Would your voting decision be influenced?

From Darwin's *Notebooks*
Charles Darwin

In a series of notebooks, Darwin jotted down ideas, plans, speculations, and observations that he might want to refer to or investigate further. These notes were not intended to be read by others, so they are disconnected thoughts expressed without concern for correctness or completeness. Darwin is most famous for his development of the theory of evolution, so the list of possible questions and experiments involving the breeding of animals may not be surprising. However, most people don't know that Darwin was also interested in the source of emotions. Many entries in Notebook N *are filled with fragments of ideas and anecdotes about various emotions, memory, and insanity. Some of these ideas were later incorporated in two of his books,* The Descent of Man *and* The Expression of the Emotions in Man and Animals.

4   Experiment in crossing animals.—&c

(1)   To cross some artificial male with <old> female of old breed & see result.—According to Mr Walker the form of male ought to preponderate; according to Mr Yarrell the latter ought: either in first breed or permanently.—

———

(2)   Cross two half-bred animals. which are exactly alike & see result.—

———

(3)   Cross the Esquimaux dog. with the hairless Brazilian or Persian animals of different heredetary constitution, to see whether offspring infertile.—

———

(4)   Does the number of pulse, Respiration, period of gestation differ in different breeds of dogs. Cattle, (Indian & Common) &c: length of life.

———

(5)   Does my Father know any case of quick or slow pulse being heredetary.

———

(6)   In the last 1000 years how many generations of man have there been.—on what principles calculated.—in order to guess how many generations in Mammalia. in group effect of crossing.—

———

(7)   Are the Eggs of the Penguin Duck quite similar to those of another Duck. ⸮ *in Pidgeon?*—**M^r. Miller said yes with regard to former**

4a

(8)   Is form of globule of blood in allied species similar.—if not how is it in <allied> varieties

(9)   Cross largest Malay with Bantam—will egg kill Hen Bantam.—Cross common Fowl with Dorking

(10)   Statistics of breeding in Zoolog. Gardens—with respect to conditions of animals & their general healthiness.—Fox's, Bears Badgers,—How few wild animals are propagated,, though valuable as show. & curiosities!! What is price of fox. otter. Badger &c &c &c.—

(11)   Keep. Tumbling pigeons. cross them with other breed.—

(12)   About the blended instincts

13   My F. says there is perfect gradation between sound people and insane.—that everybody is insane. at some time. Mania is quite distinct, different also from delirium, a peculiar complaint stomach not acted upon by Emetics.—people recognized,—sudden changes of disposition, like people in violent intoxication, often ends in insanity or delirium.— In Mania all idea of decency & affection are lost.—most delicate people do most indelicate actions,—as if «these emotions» acquired.—this may be doubted, whether rather not going against natural instincts.—

_____

My Grand F. thought the feeling of anger, which rises almost

14 involuntarily when a person is *tired* is akin to insanity.—«I know the feeling also of depression, & both these give strength & comfort to the body» I know the feeling, thinking over somebody who has, perhaps, slightly injured me, plotting speeches, yet with a sort of consciousness not just.—From habit the feeling of anger must be directed against somebody.—Have insane people any misgivings of the injustice of their hatreds, as <if> in my case.—It must be so from the curious story of the Birmingham Doctor praising his sister who confined him. & yet disinheriting her.—This

15 «N B. I have read paper somewhere on horse being insane at the sight of anything scarlet.—dogs ideotic.—dotage.—»

_____

Doctor communicated to my grandfather his feeling of consciousness of insanity coming on.—his struggles against it, his knowledge of the untruth of the idea, namely his poverty.—his manner of curing it. by keeping the sum-total of his accounts in his pocket, & studying mathematics.—My Father says after insanity is over people often think no more about it than of a dream.—

_____

16 Insanity is produced by moral causes (ideotcy by fear. Chile earth quakes). in people, who, probably otherwise would not have been so.—In Mr Hardinge. was caused by thinking over the misery of an illness at Rome. when by *accidental* <was> delay of money, he was «only» NEARLY thrown into a hospital.—My father was nearly drowned at High Ercall. the thoughts of it, for some years after, was far more painful than the thing itself.

17 Asked my F. whether insanity is not distinguished from whims passion &c by coming on suddenly. Ans no.—because often, if not generally, does not really come on suddenly.—Case of Mrs. C.O. who threw herself out of the window to kill herself from jealousy of husband connection with housemaid two years before. to prove she was not insane, answered she had known it at time & had bought arsenic for that purpose.—this found to be true.—Her Husband never suspected during these two years that she had been insane all the time.—

18 There are numberless people insane of particular ideas, «Case of Shrewsbury gentleman, unnatural union with turkey cock,—was *restrained* by remonstrances on him» which are never generally, if at all discovered.—<Sup> Sometimes comes on suddenly from <I> (in one case ipecacuhan—not acting) in others from drinking cold drink.—then brain affected like getting suddenly into passion.—There seems no distinction between enthusiasm passion & madness.—ira furor brevis est.—My father quite believe my grand F doctrine is true, that the only cure for madness is forgetfulness.—

19   which does appear a real difference, between oddity & madness.—but then people do not well recollect what they have done in passion.—

———

People are constantly well aware that they are insane & that their idea is wrong.—(Dr Ashe, the Birmingham Doctor), in this precisely like the passion, ill-humour & depression, which comes on from bodily causes.—

———

It is an argument for materialism. that cold water brings on suddenly in head, a frame of mind, analogous to those feelings. which may be considered as truly spritual.—

Activity: RESPONDING TO THE TEXT

1. What are your expectations for scientific notebooks? How do Darwin's notes meet or stray from your expectations?
2. What would Darwin have had to do to shape these notes into a piece of writing that would be clear and coherent to another reader?
3. Is there some benefit to having random thoughts jumbled together in a notebook?

The Tucson Zoo

Lewis Thomas

In "The Tucson Zoo," an essay from The Medusa and the Snail, *Lewis Thomas, a prominent science writer, describes an experience he had while observing an exhibit of beavers and otters. In his description of his observations, we see how an observer can choose to focus attention on one particular aspect of a subject or in one particular way. By observing in a way that diverges from his normal way of looking at things, Thomas develops new conclusions about familiar creatures.*

Science gets most of its information by the process of reductionism, exploring the details, then the details of the details, until all the smallest bits of the structure, or the smallest parts of the mechanisms, are laid out for counting and scrutiny. Only when this is done can the investigation be extended to encompass the whole organism or the entire system. So we say.

Sometimes it seems that we take a loss, working this way. Much of today's public anxiety about science is the apprehension that we may forever be overlooking the whole by an endless, obsessive preoccupation with the parts. I had a brief, personal experience of this misgiving one afternoon in Tucson, where I had time on my hands and visited the zoo, just outside the city. The designers there have cut a deep pathway between two small artificial ponds, walled by clear glass, so when you stand in the center of the path you can look into the depths of each pool, and at the same time you can regard the surface. In one pool, on the right side of the path, is a family of otters; on the other side, a family of beavers. Within just a few feet from your face, on either side, beavers and otters are at play, underwater and on the surface, swimming toward your face and then away, more filled with life than any creatures I have ever seen before, in all my days. Except for the glass, you could reach across and touch them.

I was transfixed. As I now recall it, there was only one sensation in my head: pure elation mixed with amazement at such perfection. Swept off my feet, I floated from one side to the other, swiveling my brain, staring astounded at the beavers, then at the otters. I could hear shouts across my corpus callosum, from one hemisphere to the other. I remember thinking, with what was left in charge of my consciousness, that I wanted no part of the science of beavers and otters; I wanted never to know how they performed their marvels; I wished for no news about the physiology of their breathing, the coordination of their muscles, their vision, their endocrine systems, their digestive tracts. I hoped never to have to think of them as collections of cells. All I asked for was the full hairy complexity, then in front of my eyes, of whole, intact beavers and otters in motion.

It lasted, I regret to say, for only a few minutes, and then I was back in the late twentieth century, reductionist as ever, wondering about the details by force of habit, but not, this time, the details of otters and beavers. Instead, me. Something worth remembering had happened in my mind, I was certain of that; I would have put it somewhere in the brain stem; maybe this was my limbic system at work. I became a behavioral scientist, an experimental psychologist, an ethologist, and in the instant I lost all the wonder and the sense of being overwhelmed. I was flattened.

But I came away from the zoo with something, a piece of news about myself: I am coded, somehow, for otters and beavers. I exhibit instinctive behavior in their presence, when they are displayed close at hand behind glass, simultaneously below water and at the surface. I have receptors for this display. Beavers and otters possess a "releaser" for me, in the terminology of ethology, and the releasing was my experience. What was released? Behavior. What behavior? Standing, swiveling flabbergasted, feeling exultation and a rush of friendship. I could not, as the result of the transaction, tell you anything more about beavers and otters than you already know. I learned nothing new about them. Only about me, and I suspect also about you, maybe about human beings at large: we are endowed with genes which code out our reaction to beavers and otters, maybe our reaction to each other as well. We are stamped with stereotyped, unalterable patterns of response, ready to be released. And the behavior released in us, by such confrontations, is, essentially, a surprised affection. It is compulsory behavior and we can avoid it only by straining with the full power of our conscious minds, making up conscious excuses all the way. Left to ourselves, mechanistic and autonomic, we hanker for friends.

Everyone says, stay away from ants. They have no lessons for us; they are crazy little instruments, inhuman, incapable of controlling themselves, lacking manners, lacking souls. When they are massed together, all touching, exchanging bits of information held in their jaws like memoranda, they become a single animal. Look out for that. It is a debasement, a loss of individuality, a violation of human nature, an unnatural act.

Sometimes people argue this point of view seriously and with deep thought. Be individuals, solitary and selfish, is the message. Altruism, a jargon word for what used to be called love, is worse than weakness, it is sin, a violation of nature. Be separate. Do not be a social animal. But this is a hard argument to make convincingly when you have to depend on language to make it. You have to print up leaflets or publish books and get them bought and sent around, you have to turn up on television and catch the attention of millions of other human beings all at once, and then you have to say to all of them, all at once, all collected and paying attention: be solitary; do not depend on each other. You can't do this and keep a straight face.

Maybe altruism is our most primitive attribute, out of reach, beyond our control. Or perhaps it is immediately at hand, waiting to be released, disguised now, in our kind of civilization, as affection or friendship or attachment. I don't see why it should be unreasonable for all human beings to have strands of DNA coiled up in chromosomes, coding out instincts for usefulness and helpfulness. Usefulness may turn out to be the hardest test of fitness for survival, more important than aggression, more effective, in the long run, than grabbiness. If this is the sort of information biological science holds for the future, applying to us as well as to ants, then I am all for science.

One thing I'd like to know most of all: when those ants have made the Hill, and are all there, touching and exchanging, and the whole mass begins to behave like a single huge creature, and *thinks*, what on earth is that thought? And while you're at it, I'd like to know a second thing: when it happens, does any single ant know about it? Does his hair stand on end?

Activity: RESPONDING TO THE TEXT

1. What is the difference between observing in a scientific reductionist way and observing with the intention of seeing "complexity"?
2. What is the insight Thomas comes to based on the observation of beavers and otters? Do you think his conclusion would have been different if he had observed them "scientifically" rather than more holistically?

On Keeping a Notebook

Joan Didion

In "On Keeping a Notebook" Joan Didion, a noted novelist and essayist, distinguishes between keeping a diary and keeping a notebook. Didion explains that recording observations and recording facts may be unrelated activities, and that, for the purposes of a writer, facts may be less relevant than reactions, memories, and insights.

"'That woman Estelle,'" the note reads, "'is partly the reason why George Sharp and I are separated today.' *Dirty crepe-de-Chine wrapper, hotel bar, Wilmington RR, 9:45 a.m. August Monday morning.*"

Since the note is in my notebook, it presumably has some meaning to me. I study it for a long while. At first I have only the most general notion of what I was doing on an August Monday morning in the bar of the hotel across from the Pennsylvania Railroad station in Wilmington, Delaware (waiting for a train? missing one? 1960? 1961? why Wilmington?), but I do remember being there. The woman in the dirty-crepe-de-Chine wrapper had come down from her room for a beer, and the bartender had heard before the reason why George Sharp and she were separated today. "Sure," he said, and went on mopping the floor. "You told me." At the other end of the bar is a girl. She is talking, pointedly, not to the man beside her but to a cat lying in the triangle of sunlight cast through the open door. She is wearing a plaid silk dress from Peck & Peck, and the hem is coming down.

Here is what it is: the girl has been on the Eastern Shore, and now she is going back to the city, leaving the man beside her, and all she can see ahead are the viscous summer sidewalks and the 3 a.m. long-distance calls that will make her lie awake and then sleep drugged through all the steaming mornings left in August (1960? 1961?). Because she must go directly from the train to lunch in New York, she wishes that she had a safety pin for the hem of the plaid silk dress, and she also wishes that she could forget about the hem and the lunch and stay in the cool bar that smells of disinfectant and malt and make friends with the woman in the crepe-de-Chine wrapper. She is afflicted by a little self-pity, and she wants to compare Estelles. That is what that was all about.

Why did I write it down? In order to remember, of course, but exactly what was it I wanted to remember? How much of it actually happened? Did any of it? Why do I keep a notebook at all? It is easy to deceive oneself on all those scores. The impulse to write things down is a peculiarly compulsive one, inexplicable to those who do not share it, useful only accidentally, only secondarily, in the way that any compulsion tries to justify itself. I suppose that it begins or does not begin in the cradle. Although I have felt compelled to write things down since I was five years old, I doubt that my

years—the man with the seeing-eye dog, the spinster who read the classified pages every day, the fat girl who always got off with me at Grand Central—looked older than they once had.

It all comes back. Even that recipe for sauerkraut: even that brings it back. I was on Fire Island when I first made that sauerkraut, and it was raining, and we drank a lot of bourbon and ate the sauerkraut and went to bed at ten, and I listened to the rain and the Atlantic and felt safe. I made the sauerkraut again last night and it did not make me feel any safer, but that is, as they say, another story.

Activity: RESPONDING TO THE TEXT

1. According to Didion, what is the difference between a diary and a notebook? What kinds of truths does each contain? What is missing in each?
2. Didion wonders why she keeps a notebook rather than a diary. What answer does she come up with?

From *Tainted Truth: The Manipulation of Truth in America*

Cynthia Crossen

This excerpt from Tainted Truth *by Cynthia Crossen, explores the polling process that is often used to gather information about people's opinions and attitudes. Crossen points out that gathering information through polling inevitably yields biased results.*

People know how to discount some kinds of information. We usually would not take too seriously a claim by the maker of Quick 'n Crispy Crinkle Cut Fries that "In a nationwide taste test, you preferred the crispiness of Quick 'n Crispy Crinkle Cut Fries, 3 to 1." Similarly, when the *National Examiner* publishes a story saying, "You can slash your cholesterol level [as much as 30 percent], strengthen your heart and add years to your life with a daily can of 7UP," many people would, rightly, not stop taking their cholesterol medication. We tend to give more weight to surveys, studies and polls reported in the *New England Journal of Medicine*, *Time* magazine, the *New York Times*, the network news shows or the *Wall Street Journal*. Yet even forums like these have been slow to recognize how dubious is much of the research they publish.

People know enough to be suspicious of some numbers in some contexts, but we are at the mercy of others. We have little personal experience or knowledge of the topics of much modern research, and the methodologies are incomprehensibly arcane. Nevertheless, we respect numbers, and we cannot help believing them. Numbers bring a sense of rationality to complex decisions—the ones we once made with common sense, experience and intelligence.

Yet more and more of the information we use to buy, elect, advise, acquit and heal has been created not to expand our knowledge but to sell a product or advance a cause. If the results of the research contradict the sponsor's agenda, they will routinely be suppressed. Researchers have become secretive and their sponsors greedy. The media, which can usually get the raw numbers if they want them, are stingy with data because data are boring, and so many journalists are themselves innumerate.

Behind the explosion of corrupted information is, first, money. For a few decades after World War II, scientific research was sponsored primarily by the government and academic institutions, which let researchers ask and answer questions largely free of commercial or partisan influence (although many academic researchers worked for the military). But in recent years the pool of scientists looking for work has grown while state and federal government research budgets have flattened. Universities themselves face declining revenue and higher costs. Private companies, meanwhile, have found it both cheaper and more prestigious to retain academic, government or commercial researchers than to set up in-house operations that some might suspect of bias. Corporations, litigants, political candidates, trade associations, lobbyists, special interest groups—all can buy research to use as they like. Freedom of the press, the critic A. J. Liebling once said, belongs only to those who own one. In the information business, truth has come to belong to those who commission it.

The commercialization of research means that the number of independent voices in our society is dwindling. Every university professor, researcher or doctor who sells his soul to self-interested sponsors comforts himself with some rationale: "*I* can accept this money without compromising my independence; *my* ethics are intact; *I* won't be biased." But it is never so. "[F]ew doctors accept that they themselves have been corrupted," wrote Michael D. Rawlins in the medical journal *Lancet*. "Most doctors believe that they are quite untouched by the seductive ways of the [drug] industry's marketing men. . . . The degree to which the profession . . . can practise such self-deceit is extraordinary. No drug company gives away its shareholders' money in an act of disinterested generosity. . . . The harsh truth is that not one of us is impervious to the promotional activities of the industry, and that the industry uses its various sales techniques because they are effective."

Without the unpaid voices of these researchers, no one speaks disinterestedly. "Say you're sick and you want to buy some drugs," said David Noble, a historian and author. "The drug industry can provide you with a wealth of information about the drugs. You know what you're reading is part information and part advertisement, and that it's important to distinguish the two. So you try to get an independent evaluation. Where are you going to get it? The universities in theory are the only institutions in our society that supply information on a disinterested basis. But in fact, the universities are bought. If someone comes from Squibb, caveat emptor. But here, you're disarmed, which is precisely what the clients are seeking. The universities are going to lose their credibility, and I think that's tragic."

Others who worry about the overlap between business and academia wonder whether it will change the whole course of scientific inquiry. Will applied research drive out basic research? Will the proprietary needs of the sponsor overwhelm traditions of science like openness? Will the large, powerful and affluent dictate what subjects are researched, and will there be any accountability to anyone else? Will scientists cling to their positions even more defensively than usual, since abandoning them could mean losing not just face but money?

Privately sponsored research also exacerbates the problem of overreporting positive results and underreporting negative ones. In science, positive does not necessarily mean good; it simply means the results are statistically significant; in other words, they could not be attributed to chance alone. Negative means that nothing happened or that whatever happened could have happened by chance alone. Commercial sponsors obviously want to publicize only positive results that make their product look good; results that make their product look bad, or no results at all, they almost never want to talk about. Nor, for the most part, do researchers, journals or the news media. The overemphasis on positive results reaches down to many of today's students, who say, if their hypothesis is not supported by their results, "My research didn't work." Furthermore, the increasing stratification among research scientists means junior and senior scientists are less likely to work shoulder to shoulder in the lab, where the traditions and ethics of science have long been conveyed by example. "There has been a tremendous influx of new people who weren't grounded in the traditions of scientific thinking," lamented Jack Douglas. "It's getting harder to be an honest scientist."

The subject of information has been researched many times, although, as it turns out, none of the research asked the precise questions I have in mind. A batch of studies about newspaper credibility came out in the mid-1980s during one of the regular flare-ups of criticism by political conservatives that the media are liberal. In 1985, the Times Mirror Company sponsored a study on the credibility of thirty-nine news organizations and personalities, from Walter Cronkite (most believable) to the *National Enquirer* (least believable, just edging out *Rolling Stone* magazine). In a 1989 study on public attitudes toward the press, Pope John Paul II was identified as the most believable leader, and Mikhail Gorbachev the least—less believable even than Geraldo Rivera and Donald Trump. Studies have compared the credibility of various categories of media—newspapers, magazines, television. Louis Harris did a study, "The Road After 1984," which showed a population concerned about "information abuse"—primarily technological invasions of privacy. All of these studies share a flaw: People can't be trusted when they say they believe someone.

Studies have also been done on the psychological aspects of credibility, like the "Dr. Fox effect" research of the early 1970s, in which an actor was programmed to teach material he knew nothing about. A majority of the audience of well-educated professionals found the distinguished and authoritative Dr. Fox stimulating and interesting; one member of the audience even claimed to have read something Dr. Fox had written. The researchers concluded that even well-educated audiences cannot necessarily detect propaganda or false information.

"You can't separate the medium from the message," warns Albert E. Gollin, director of research for the Newspaper Advertising Bureau.

I do not want to. I want to ask about credibility across all disciplines, all media, all sources. But I doubt that I have a question worth asking yet.

Asking the right question is the pillar of good science, both social and other, as well as a source of endless debate and despair among researchers. In survey work, the perfect question has become the Holy Grail, forever out of reach. Researchers dedicate themselves to the question, experimenting with words to create the perfect inquiry—a question that does not presume, lead or color. But, as many of the attendees of the 1992 conference of the American Association for Public Opinion Research, a trade organization of survey research, knew, there will never be a truly neutral question.

Researchers know one thing about questions: However precise and neutral they seem to be, they often have unpredictable effects—response effects, researchers call them. Response effects arise from the quirkiness of language and the complexities of human emotion—pride, embarrassment, self-righteousness, contempt or any of the hundreds of other strings that play when one person speaks to another. Even under ideal circumstances, when asked to remember something recent and concrete, recall is often different from fact. What time did you go to bed the night before last? What is your license plate number? What did you do last Sunday? What color shirt is your spouse wearing today?

Because modern polls ask busy adults to answer dozens, sometimes scores, of questions on a variety of topics, respondents often feel they have to give their answers quickly. The respondents reason that the interviewers could not possibly be asking for a precise answer because they are leaving no time to compute it. So they take a guess. Unfortunately, a guess is a guess, and people tend to guess in a self-serving way.

A classic example of the way people's egos distort fact is a poll about television viewing. Two groups of people were asked how much they watched a day. Both groups were given scales from which to choose. One scale started at less than thirty minutes of television a day and ended at more than two and a half hours. The other scale had a much higher minimum—less than two and a half hours—and the maximum was more than four and a half hours. In the first group, only 16.2 percent admitted to watching the greatest amount of television—more than two and a half hours. But in the second group, more than double that number said they watched at least two and a half hours. Whatever the truth, people did not want to be on the high end of the scale.

And that is a question of fact. When there is an emotional or political component—questions about race, religion, abortion, sex—recall is an even faultier connection from the churning stew of the mind.

The imprecision of language exacerbates the problem. Single words that mean the same thing can convey wildly different ideas. Taxes or revenues? MX missile or Peace-keeper? Pro-choice or pro-abortion? Welfare or public assistance? Department of War or Department of Defense? There are "magical qualities" in the phrase "to maintain world peace," one pollster noted; the linguist S. I. Hayakawa called some words "purr-words," and others "snarl-words." A young monk was once rebuffed by his superior when he asked if he could smoke while he prayed. Ask a different question, a friend advised. Ask if you can pray while you smoke.

Responses can also be dramatically different depending on whether people are given options from which to choose or simply say whatever comes to mind. In one survey, respondents were asked what is the most important thing for children to learn to prepare them for life. When given a choice of five options, 62 percent chose "to think for themselves." But when given the open-ended question with no options, only 5 percent gave that answer.

Meanwhile, there is a person asking the questions who may seem, to those being interviewed, as a judge of knowledge or character. That can tempt respondents to sound more sure than they really are or even lie to seem more informed. In 1947, a researcher named Sam Gill asked people their thoughts on the entirely fictitious Metallic Metals Act; some 70 percent opined about it. When the American Jewish Committee studied Americans' attitudes toward various ethnic groups, almost 30 percent of the respondents had an opinion about the fictional Wisians, rating them in social standing above a half-dozen other real groups, including Mexicans, Vietnamese and African blacks.

There are also times when a question written in a remote and sterile office clashes with a complex and ungraspable reality. "You sit in a lady's room, look through cracked, broken-out windows at blocks and blocks of gutted has-been homes," remembered a researcher. "You walk across a sagging creaking floor, and look into narrow eyes peering at you from beneath a dresser. Not a dog, nor a cat—no, a child. Now you ask the big question in the neighborhood problem section: 'Have you had any trouble because of neighbors not keeping up their property?'" Passion, too, is rarely captured by surveys or polls. A cartoon by Lee Lorenz pictures a polltaker standing outside an apartment door, talking to a hefty man. On his T-shirt, in big bold letters, are the words NUKE EM. "Suppose we just put you down as believing eternal vigilance is the price of liberty," the polltaker says.

The growing understanding of the problem with the question has been a setback for survey researchers, but it is not good news for everyone else, either. In one study, researchers asked people to make a hypothetical choice between two treatments for lung cancer—surgery or radiation. Everyone received statistical data on the effectiveness of the two therapies, but the data for one group were stated in terms of survival and for the other in terms of mortality. For example, the "survival" group was told that "Of 100 people having surgery, 90 will live through the surgery, 68 will be alive at the end of the first year, and 34 will be alive after five years. Of 100 people having radiation therapy, all live through the treatment, 77 will be alive at the end of the first year, and 22 will be alive at the end of five years." The "mortality" group was told this: Of 100 people having surgery, 10 will die during the treatment, 32 will have died in a year, and 66 will have died by five years. Of 100 people having radiation therapy, none will die during treatment, 23 will die by one year, and 78 will die by five years.

Presented the first way—in terms of survival—only 18 percent chose radiation therapy over surgery. But presented the second way, in terms of mortality, more than twice as many people—47 percent—chose radiation therapy over surgery. The statement that "none will die during treatment" seemed to loom much larger than long-term survival even to doctors and business students, two groups who should be able to sort out statistics from the words "live" and "die."

If all this was not already discouraging, researchers now know that the order in which questions are asked is as critical as the wording of any of them. Consider these two questions, artifacts of 1950. The first: Do you think the United States should let Russian newspaper reporters come here and send back whatever they want? The second: Do you think Russia should let American newspaper reporters come in and send back whatever they want?

If people were asked the first question first, only 36 percent of them said the U.S. should allow Russian reporters in. But if they were asked about American journalists first, they had to, at least subconsciously, think about fairness, and more than twice as many people—73 percent—said the Russians should be allowed in.

Researchers have tried to reduce this problem, the so-called context effect, by experimenting with "buffer" questions, which are asked between items on the same topic. In one experiment on buffer questions people were asked to say something—anything—about what their U.S. representative had done for his or her district. Then they were asked if they follow politics a lot, some or not that much. If they had not been able to think of much to say about their congressman, it was hard for them to pretend to themselves they followed politics. No number of buffer questions about unrelated topics, up to 101, seemed to let most people off that psychological hook.

But a single buffer question on the same topic did the trick. That intervening question asked people to evaluate the quality of their representative's public relations work. Now people who knew nothing about their representative could blame it on his or her public relations efforts, an alternative explanation for their lack of knowledge.

If any question would seem straightforward, it is a simple comparison: Compare this to that. But even this turns out to be loaded. A German research team has shown that you can get dramatically different answers depending on whether you ask someone if tennis is more or less exciting than soccer or if soccer is more or less exciting than tennis. (This might also hold true if someone is asked whether Clinton would be a better or worse president than Bush or vice versa.) The theory is that when people are asked to compare tennis to soccer, they focus on the features of soccer and then mentally check to see if those features are also in tennis. People would not remember the unique features of tennis, because they are brought to mind by soccer.

The well-known difficulties of asking and answering questions have become opportunities for sponsors of research. The wording of questions, their order, the intonations, the pacing—all are so subtly persuasive that they can look innocent even though they have been consciously manipulated. The pitfalls of the researcher's craft have also become the tools of its corruption.

Activity: RESPONDING TO THE TEXT

1. Do you believe, as Crossen claims, that people tend to see survey results as factual and unbiased?
2. If Crossen is correct that surveys can be misleading, should they be discounted altogether? How should they be used?

Activity: SYNTHESIZING THE TEXTS

1. Relate Thomas's distinction between scientific reductionist observation and observing for complexity to Didion's description of the differences between a diary and a notebook.
2. Thomas, Crossen, and Didion all talk about the problems of using inappropriate information-gathering techniques. Cite examples from each reading and discuss how they're similar.

Writing Assignments

Academic Essays

1. Psychology

In his notes, Darwin mentions that his grandfather "thought the feeling of anger, which rises almost involuntarily when a person is *tired* is akin to insanity." Gather information to support or refute the connection between fatigue and anger. Do you have any experiences that would support one or the other position? Use freewriting, brainstorming, or mapping to explore the connections (or lack of connections) between fatigue and anger. Then use conversations, interviews, or surveys to gather more information.

Write a paper that takes a stand on whether fatigue and anger are often connected. Your thesis should also probably comment on how they are connected or why they are not. Organize the evidence you have gathered from your own experience and the experience of others into a coherent explanation of your conclusion.

2. Psychology/Biology

In "The Tucson Zoo" Thomas claims that altruism may be part of our nature—a primitive and essential component for our survival. Many sociologists, psychologists, and biologists are looking for evidence that altruism is or is not part of human nature. Do you think humans are essentially altruistic or not? Use freewriting, brainstorming, or mapping to gather evidence from your own experience; then use interviews or surveys to find supporting evidence. You might also find a few articles or books which describe the results of research done to try to answer this question. Use the information you have gathered to support your opinions in a four- or five-page essay.

3. Political Science

Working in groups of three or four, design, complete, and report on a survey of people's attitudes on a current political issue. Before you begin working on the survey, think about what you want to find out. Do you want to know what kinds of people have certain attitudes? Do you want to know what affects their attitudes? Do you want to know how strongly they hold these attitudes? How these attitudes affect their behavior?

First, formulate questions about the issue that are as unbiased as possible, and select some follow-up questions to help you characterize the people answering the questions. Then choose a group you want to survey and plan a method that will do the best job of getting a representative sampling of responses from this group. Administer the survey. Collect the data and then report on the results.

Your report should contain three sections. In the first section, discuss the questions asked and the survey method used. This section should be as specific as possible. For example, instead of writing, "I distributed the surveys in my dorm," write, "On March 26, between 6:00 P.M. and 9:00 P.M., I went door-to-door in Miller dorm asking whoever answered the door to fill out the questionnaire." The second section should show the results of the survey and present any relevant calculations like averages or means. The results section should also contain any conclusions you have come to about the data you collected. Finally, you should include a section that suggests the possible sources of bias in the survey. What might have affected the results? Could the survey be changed to avert this bias?

Workplace Writing

A good job application letter can make the difference between getting an interview and having your resumé thrown in the wastebasket. Writing a strong job application letter is difficult because the information you include must be complete but concise, your style must be friendly but professional, and your structure must be conventional but not boring. Besides having to satisfy these conflicting demands, your letter must be perfectly formatted and free of any errors in spelling, grammar, or mechanics.

This writing assignment will give you practice writing a convincing letter. Find an advertisement for a job you would like to apply for now or in the near future. Follow the steps below to write a job application letter.

Step 1: Gather Information

Gather information about the job and/or the company named in the ad. The library or your campus career center should have many reference books and databases containing the information you require. Try to discover what skills, qualities, experience, or education the job or company requires. Then refer to the list of the experience, education, skills, and personal qualities you made in your Writing Log in Chapter 1. Look at the information you have gathered and try to match your profile with that required for the job. Honestly evaluate what you have to offer and plan to emphasize those qualities which most closely match those desired by the employer. You may have no job experience in the field for which you're applying, but you could emphasize that the job experience you do have shows that you have some of the necessary qualities, such as leadership or creativity.

Step 2: Write the Letter

Explain what job you are applying for and where you heard or read about the job. Then describe your qualifications for the job, including some specific evidence to support your claims that you will be a great employee. Include information about how, where, and when you can be reached for an interview.

Step 3: Revise the Content

   A. Review your purpose and audience. What are you trying to do in this letter? Make yourself stand out from other candidates? Communicate your qualifications? Convince the employer to give you an interview? Who will read this letter? What do you imagine is of most interest and concern to the reader? Have you included the information that would be most appealing? If you feel as though everyone who applies will have the same educational qualifications, maybe you should spend more time emphasizing other characteristics that make you unique. If you feel that the employer is most concerned about job experience, perhaps you need to revise your letter to explain your experience in more detail.

   B. Review your evidence. Have you included enough specific evidence to support each of your qualifications? If you say that you are a dependable worker, you should include evidence, such as "During the two years I was employed at my previous job, I never missed a day of work." Keep the evidence short, but specific.

   C. Have you used numbers whenever possible? "I have three years' experience," "I saved my company $2,000.00," "I earned a 4.00 grade average," or "I trained twelve other employees."

   D. Have you included all the relevant information about your qualifications? Do you have skills or experiences you acquired outside of work or school that could be used at this job? Do you possess personality or character traits that would be worth mentioning because they are particularly useful or appealing to the employer?

E. Have you included any irrelevant information? If something you include does not in some way relate to proving you are a great candidate for the job, it should be eliminated, even if it is an outstanding accomplishment. If you were named most valuable player in the state basketball championships, you would not include this information in a letter applying for a job as an accountant, unless you could explain how your achievement helps prove your ability to do the job.

Step 4: Revise Your Structure

A. Are you presenting your qualifications in the best order? Begin with the most important or appealing point so that you can be sure your reader doesn't stop reading before reaching it. Other points should be arranged in order of importance *to the reader*.

B. If you have two or three qualifications grouped together in one paragraph, have you linked them together in some way so the paragraph flows smoothly?

C. Will your last paragraph make the reader take action? Leave the reader with a positive impression and a clear request for action. "I'm looking forward to speaking to you at an interview and becoming part of your team."

Step 5: Revise Your Sentences

A. Do too many of your sentences start with "I"? Although you are writing about yourself and must use "I" frequently, try to vary the sentence structure to keep from sounding too repetitive.

B. Have you used strong verbs? Try to cut down on the use of "to be" and "to have" verbs. Substitute verbs that show you in action. For example, instead of writing, "I am a good manager," write, "I managed five other employees at my last job" or, to eliminate the beginning "I" and provide more positive information, you might write, "As a manager of five employees at my last job, I learned that praise motivated people more than punishment."

C. Do your sentences focus on the reader's concerns rather than on yours? A sentence such as "I would enjoy working in a team-oriented environment such as yours," focuses on your satisfaction, not your reader's. Rewording the sentences shifts the emphasis to how the employer will benefit: "As an enthusiastic team player, I'll fit right in at your company."

D. Are your sentences concise? Eliminate unnecessary words and phrases.

Step 6: Proofread the Letter

Reading the letter backwards, last sentence to first sentence, will help you notice errors in grammar and punctuation. You might also have other people proofread for you. Your goal is a letter free of all errors.

Personal Writing

Using the work you've done in your Writer's Log assignments throughout the chapter, write an essay about a person or event that influenced your life. You should have already gathered a significant amount of information; now you need to think about your purpose and thesis. Why would you want to tell readers about this significant person or event? Why would they want to read about it? What information do they need to have a clear understanding of the person or event? Look over the information you've gathered and think about how you will focus the paper. What information will you include? What will be left out? You may find that you need to do further information gathering to fill in the missing pieces. You may find yourself choosing one particular piece of information around which to build your essay. However you choose to focus and organize your information, the essay should give the reader a clear understanding of why this person or event was so important to you.

POLISHING AND REFLECTING ON TEXTS

Learning from Other Student Writers

Letter of Application
Glen Keesling

Glen Keesling wrote a letter applying for his first teaching job after graduating. He emphasized his practical experience in internships and volunteer work and called his personal qualifications to readers' attention in the fourth paragraph.

March 15, 2000

Dr. Roberto Rodgriguez, Superintendent
Lyndale School District
1243 Oakwood Road
Lyndale, CT

Dear Dr. Rodgriguez:

I am pleased to offer my application for the teaching position in the Special Education Department at Lyndale Elementary School. I believe you will find my qualifications well suited to this position. My selection of Lyndale Elementary is based on its reputation for excellence within its faculty, which accounts for the high success rate among its students.

My qualifications include a B.A. in Liberal Studies, a teaching credential in Multiple-Subject Learning Handicapped Program, and a Master's in Special Education. I received all my degrees from San Jose State. Moreover, I have successfully completed the CBEST Test. My course work encompasses two years of sign language and one year of Spanish.

In order to meet the learning needs of this L.D. population, I have taken course work to acquaint myself with the Orton-Gillingham methodology, which I have used successfully during my internship at the Little

Red School House in San Jose, California. The student population consisted of students from age six through eleven. These students were identified as learning disabled and many were struggling with dyslexia. The Orton-Gillingham strategies I used had a positive effect on the majority of students. Additionally, I have volunteered at my local elementary school, where the master teacher, Miss Smith, shared with me her vast repertoire of multisensory techniques.

My interest in this population emanates from the fact that I, too, have learning disabilities. From early childhood I have experienced learning problems personally. Therefore, I have gained empathy for those of us who learn differently. I believe I have the capacity to be not only a good teacher but also a good mentor because of what I have endured.

I would welcome the chance to discuss with you in person the way in which my experience and background can meet your hiring needs. I can be reached at (404) 659-5517.

Sincerely,

Glen Keesling

Activity: **RESPONDING TO THE TEXT**

1. How would the emphasis and tone of the letter change if the second and third paragraphs were switched? Why do you think Keesling chose the order he did?
2. What can you assume about the expectations of the readers? What do you think they're looking for in a candidate for this position? Where have the writer's choices about content taken the readers' concerns, values, and needs into account?

Activity: **PEER WORKSHOP**

Working with a partner or in a small group, review one of your essays to see if you have communicated a clear point to a reader and included adequate specific evidence. After the workshop, revise your essay to incorporate any suggestions that you think will strengthen your paper.

Writers answer these questions before the workshop:

1. What is the purpose, the point you are making, and the intended audience for your essay?
2. What aspect of your essay are you most satisfied with?
3. What aspect of your essay are you unsure of or dissatisfied with?

4. What information-gathering strategies did you use? Which did you find most useful? Put a ✔ in areas where you've used information-gathering techniques and identify the techniques you used.

Readers respond to these questions:

1. Has the reader included adequate, convincing information in the essay? Mark with a ★ areas that you think use information effectively. Mark with an ✗ areas you think would be improved by adding more information.

2. What has the writer done best?

3. What one change could the writer make to improve the essay?

Activity: PROOFREADING YOUR WORK

When you include specific information from other sources, remember that you must use quotation marks to indicate the exact words you take from the source. Your writing will also be clearer to the reader if you identify the source of the quotations and explain its relationship to the rest of your paper. Punctuation for quotations can also be confusing. You should know the answers to the following questions before reviewing the quotations in your paper:

- When are quotation marks used?
- Do commas, periods, question marks, and exclamation points go inside or outside quotation marks?
- When are single quotations marks used?

Check the quotations you've used in your paper. Can your reader identify who is being quoted? If there is a period or comma at the end of the quotation, is it inside the quotation marks? If there is an exclamation point or question mark at the end of the quotation, is it appropriately placed?

Activity: POSTSCRIPT

1. Which approaches to information gathering presented in this chapter seem most useful to you? What makes these techniques best for your writing? What makes the other techniques less useful or appealing?
2. How will you be able to use some of these techniques in other writing situations? In solving daily problems? In decision making?
3. Do you usually observe in a scientifically reductionist way or with the intention of seeing "complexity"? Which way of observing do you think is more useful at school? At work? In your personal life? Do certain kinds of writing require certain kinds of observation? Why?

PARAGRAPHS AND ESSAYS

P R E V I E W

This chapter's explanations about organizing information into paragraphs, combining paragraphs into essays, and writing effective introductions and conclusions will help answer these common questions:

- What makes a paragraph?
- How are paragraphs used in longer pieces such as essays, memos, and reports?
- How is an essay structured?
- What are some methods of introducing and concluding essays?

L E A R N I N G   A B O U T   T E X T S

Organizing Writing

When we think about a topic, ideas do not appear fully formed in orderly sentences and paragraphs; instead, they often crowd together in a jumble of facts, opinions, judgments, examples, and details. This jumble, like a large heap of clothes in the corner of a room, may seem comfortable and manageable to its owner, but others may view it with confusion or distaste. They may wonder, "Why are all these clothes in one pile? Are they clean or dirty? Do they all belong to one person? Should they be washed together? Can they all fit in one load?" The disorder is disorienting and overwhelming. If the pile of clothes were sorted into neat piles by color and fabric type, an observer would understand how to treat each pile (some with bleach, some in hot water) and the task of laundering the pile would seem more manageable. In a similar way, writers must order their ideas to make them readable; otherwise, relationships between ideas may not be clear, and the task of reading them might seem too difficult. In most academic, professional, and personal writing, paragraphs are the primary tools for ordering ideas. Larger structures, such as essays, memos, and reports, provide order for longer, more complex communications.

Usually, the ideas themselves or the writer's purpose suggests ways of sorting the piles into shorter, clearer units. For example, a writer analyzing different genres of films would most naturally discuss one type at a time. Besides content and purpose, context also contributes to a writer's choices about organization. In college classes, students most commonly organize ideas into essays, and in business settings ideas are communicated through letters and memos. If they are aware of readers' expectations about these forms, writers can use them effectively to communicate clearly.

Putting ideas in order is not always easy, however, because we're not sure exactly what is in the pile, or we haven't really thought about how one item relates to another, or there is just too much to think about. Organizing for a reader forces us to clarify our thoughts for ourselves and make conscious choices about our goals and message. The standard paragraph, essay, and memo forms can make this organizing process easier because they serve as tools for putting thoughts in order. Once our ideas become more organized, they become clearer to us and our readers and, as they become clearer, other possible orders and forms may present themselves.

In this chapter, you will learn about the standard features of common organizing forms—topic paragraphs, essays, and letters and memos. Knowing these forms well allows you the freedom to use them or vary them as your content, purpose, and context require.

Understanding Topic Paragraphs

Although sentences are often referred to as the building blocks of language, in practice we rarely write a text that consists of only one sentence. We usually use words or phrases—to answer questions, fill in blanks, give brief directions—or we group sentences into paragraphs. Think of the last five times you have picked up a pencil or pen to write or sat at a computer keyboard. Did the text you wrote consist of words or phrases, of single sentences, of paragraphs, or perhaps even of numbers, pictures, or symbols? Now try to remember the last time you wrote just one single sentence: You were probably either writing grammar exercises in an English class or answering brief questions in a textbook. In most of our personal, professional, and academic writing, sentences do not convey enough information, so we group them together into paragraphs to communicate effectively. Occasionally, you will write a text that consists of only one paragraph, for example, an e-mail message announcing the time and place of a meeting or a note to your child's teacher. Usually, however, the texts you write, whether at work, at home, or in college, will consist of multiple paragraphs. Many of the paragraphs you will write, whether you are writing a college research paper, a personal letter, or a business proposal, are the type called topic paragraphs.

Constructing Topic Paragraphs

Topic paragraphs are brief discussions of a topic. However, a group of statements on the same topic—for example, seven sentences about the Civil War—would not necessarily constitute an effective paragraph. An effective topic paragraph is unified by one limited subject, makes and supports a point about that subject, and has a logical, coherent organization. This way of grouping sentences works well when ideas need to be orderly and easy to read, as in analytical essays, work reports, newsletters, or articles.

Limiting a paragraph's subject

Topic paragraphs usually present one part of a larger argument or explanation. Once you know what you are trying to communicate in a particular text, you usually find that your overall point or thesis must be broken down into smaller sections so that readers can more easily follow your train of thought. By using limited topic paragraphs, you can fully discuss each reason or piece of evidence. For example, if you wanted to convince your supervisor to change to a flex-time work week, you could not do so in a paragraph, because an effective argument would have to include explanations of all the ways both employees and employers would benefit from the new plan. A complete discussion of all these benefits might go on for pages and pages. Without paragraph breaks, such a long argument would be difficult to follow. Breaking your long argument into a series of topic paragraphs, each discussing one point, increases readability. For example, by limiting the topic of each paragraph to one benefit of the flex-time schedule, you help the readers sort out what all the benefits are and help them to see the evidence you present in support of each one. When a paragraph is limited to one topic, it is unified. Unified topic paragraphs provide the readers with a sense of order because they provide information in manageable and coherent chunks.

FYI: For more on chunking, see the workplace box on p. 277.

Making and supporting a point

A topic paragraph makes a point about the paragraph's subject and supports that point with evidence. The point of the paragraph is usually expressed in one sentence, called the topic sentence. Although topic sentences sometimes come at the end or even in the middle of a paragraph, they most often begin the paragraph. Putting the topic sentence at the beginning of the paragraph helps readers by clarifying the purpose and making ideas easier to follow. For example, if you were writing a paragraph about the cost savings of flex-time for employers, you might begin with a sentence like this: "Employers could save money by allowing a flex-time schedule." This sentence would alert the readers to the point of the paragraph so they would be ready to consider the evidence you present.

A good topic sentence is clearly worded. Precise phrasing that limits the topic to the paragraph's main point helps readers understand the logic and order of the ideas. Your topic sentences may contain transition words and phrases, such as "similarly," "on the other hand," "another," "also," and "secondly," which alert readers to the way this paragraph's topic builds on or differs from the previous paragraph.

Because your readers may not agree with the point you make in a topic sentence, you need to supply convincing supporting evidence. The supporting evidence may come from the following sources:

- personal experience
- library research
- Internet research
- field research (surveys, interviews, experiments, studies)
- logical deductions

Examples to illustrate the point and explanations to expand the readers' understanding of the point can be used as supporting material. For example, the passage below about how flex-time would save employers money contains personal experience about how employees use personal days, logical deductions about how the company would save money, explanations about the hiring of a replacement worker, and examples of occasions that required the writer to take personal days:

> Every time I have to take a personal day, my supervisor has to hire a temporary worker to replace me, so the company ends up paying my wage and my replacement's. I figure they lose $80.00 for each personal day I take. Last year I had to use all three of my personal days so that I could go to doctors' appointments, meet with my kids' teachers, and wait for plumbers. If I had flex-time, I would have been able to do all these things without taking a personal day.

Because the evidence in this passage is specific (including numbers, lists, and details), it is more likely to convince the audience.

A topic paragraph allows you enough space and time to develop each of your ideas using specific evidence. In general, the more specific your evidence, the more convinced your readers will be that the point you make in your paragraph is valid. The paragraph below illustrates a topic paragraph with a limited topic and specific evidence.

FYI: For more information about supporting your points with evidence and examples, see Chapter 6.

> A flexible work schedule would allow me to take fewer personal leave days. My doctor and my dentist work the same nine-to-five schedule that I do, so even a routine event like an annual flu shot or having my teeth cleaned causes me to take a half-day's leave. Furthermore, because I'm a single parent, I often take personal leave time for my daughter's activities. Last Thursday I took the afternoon off to see her school's historical pageant, and the week before that I took the morning off because she missed the bus and I had to drive her to school.

Specific examples and details improve a paragraph because they help readers to form mental pictures of the main point. When you have provided sufficient detailed explanations, evidence, and examples, your paragraph is complete.

Creating coherence

Coherence, which literally means "sticking together," is the logical arrangement of parts. A paragraph is coherent when all the points and examples are connected smoothly so that readers can easily follow the writer's train of thought. Just as on a train, where individual cars are linked together with couplings to create one vehicle moving in one direction, writers create coherence by linking ideas together through their choice of words. A coherent paragraph keeps readers moving in one direction with one destination—the main point of the paragraph. By using transition words and phrases such as "because," "therefore," "for example," and "in addition" to link sentences together, writers help readers see how the ideas in one sentence grow out of or lead to the ideas in the previous or following sentences.

Structure can also help create coherence. A topic sentence alerts readers to the main point and helps them to keep it in mind as they read through the evidence and examples. Presenting ideas in a logical order also keeps the reader on track. A writer can choose an order appropriate for the content and purpose: from beginning to end, from most familiar to least familiar, from most important to least important, from top to bottom, from first to last. If the structure gives readers a sense that an underlying order connects one idea to another, the essay will be coherent.

Activity: WRITER'S LOG

The passage below is really a pile of ideas rather than a good topic paragraph because it touches on too many different, though related, points that aren't presented in an orderly way. Because too many points are included, none is really developed with enough specific evidence or examples. Read the passage and do the following:

1. Pick out one idea that would be a more limited subject for a good topic paragraph.
2. Write a good topic sentence.
3. Take the evidence provided in the passage and improve it by making it more specific. You might give some specific examples as part of the evidence.
4. Arrange the material in a logical, coherent order.

Passage for revision:

> College hasn't changed much since my parents went, but students have changed. A lot of them are older and have families. Twenty years ago, most students were just that—college students. Now many students work while they go to school. Many more minority students and non-native speakers are in college. If college students have changed a lot, why haven't colleges changed much?

Using Topic Paragraphs

Most of the time, topic paragraphs are part of larger pieces of writing such as essays, letters, memos, reports, articles, and books. Writers of these forms use topic paragraphs differently, adjusting length, format, order, style, and content to fit the context. Books, for example, often contain paragraphs that are quite long and complicated because the arguments presented in such long works are often complex, and the readers expect to spend time getting thorough explanations and extensive supporting evidence. On the other hand, shorter forms, such as memos and letters, often contain shorter paragraphs, because readers want to get the point quickly and expect any extensive supporting evidence to be provided in attachments. Learning more about the expectations and conventions of the larger forms allows you to write topic paragraphs appropriate to your form, purpose, and audience.

Constructing Essays

In college courses, the most common form of writing is the essay. Essays are also found in magazines, journals, and newspapers. The essay form is used when the writer wants to explore, explain, or prove an idea, so it's ideal for academic settings where professors often want students to demonstrate their ability to analyze or synthesize ideas learned in the classroom. Essays written for college classes may be brief—a few paragraphs—or lengthy—several pages. Regardless of its length, an essay can be structured using a simple three-part form: (1) an introduction, (2) topic paragraphs that provide supporting evidence, and (3) a conclusion. Like an individual topic paragraph, an essay has a limited topic, makes a point expressed in a thesis statement, supports that point with evidence, and is coherently and logically organized.

Selecting a Limited Topic

Like paragraphs, essays are discussions of topics, and like paragraphs, each essay must have a limited topic. College students frequently choose topics far too large for their papers, in the hopes that they will have plenty to write about. The resultant papers are necessarily unfocused, vague, and unconvincing. No one can write an effective essay of two or three typed pages about a large topic such as the biotechnology industry, propaganda in advertising, or trial law. Almost any topic, however, can be narrowed to produce a suitable subject for an essay. The genetic alteration of one vegetable, one propaganda technique used in three or four current advertisements, the use of DNA evidence in a recent trial—all these would make excellent essay topics. Although you will frequently need to gather information from other sources for your college papers—from books, lectures, conversations, electronic sources—you should still follow the advice in Chapter 1 by considering your role, your knowledge, and your interests when choosing a topic.

Activity: WORKING TOGETHER   DAEDALUS

Below are six large topics. Working in small groups, try to narrow the topics to ones that would be suitable for papers of two or three typed pages. Create at least two topics for each category. The topics you choose could be ones you would use in college, in your personal life, or on the job. When you have finished, compare your group's topics with those of the other groups. The first one has been done for you.

1. Ethnic Groups
   A. Three ways to integrate non-English-speaking children in the neighborhood child care center.
   B. The effects of my Korean heritage on my American spouse.
2. Movies
3. Getting a job

4. Tests and exams
5. Pollution
6. Parents

Writing and Using Thesis Statements

Every essay, like every topic paragraph, makes a point. In paragraphs, the topic sentence states the paragraph's point. As you learned in Chapter 3, the sentence that states the point of the essay is called the thesis. The thesis statement is valuable for readers because it clarifies the point of the paper they are reading. Formulating a working thesis statement before you begin to write is equally valuable for you because it simplifies your work, as you gather information and draft your essay, by providing focus and direction. However, as you draft your essay and gain a different perspective on your topic, you may revise your thesis to make it more precise, to shift the focus, or to add subtleties.

Because the thesis alerts the reader to your purpose, it most often occurs in the first paragraph. If you delay the thesis statement until the middle or end of your paper, your readers may not understand the points you make in support of your main idea. However, thesis statements may be placed in the middle or at the end of essays if that placement furthers the writer's purpose.

Writing specific thesis statements

Effective thesis statements, like effective purposes, are **specific**. The readers will be able to tell **exactly** what you want them to understand, believe, or do if the words in the thesis statement are precise. "Stephen King is a good writer" is not a specific thesis because the wording is not precise enough to ensure that the reader understands the point. Will this text prove that Stephen King writes without errors, that Stephen King writes thrilling books, or that Stephen King is as talented as William Shakespeare? Because "good" can mean different things at different times, it is not a precise word choice. To keep your thesis statement clear, avoid vague words like "interesting," "bad," "exciting," and "boring." Instead, make your intentions clear by choosing precise words so your reader will know what to expect; for example, "Stephen King's novels thrill readers because they exploit common anxieties, yet provide a safe, satisfying conclusion."

Also avoid open-ended statements that lead to no clear conclusion. A thesis like "We should help the homeless" is vague because it could mean any number of things. A more concise thesis might say, "We should give the homeless money when they beg on the street," "We should give the homeless temporary shelter," or "Shelters for the homeless should work systematically to place inhabitants in jobs." These specific interpretations of the vague thesis reflect varying purposes, so the papers based on them would contain completely different information. A vague thesis often indicates a vague purpose; if you are having trouble wording your thesis, go back and define your purpose more carefully.

Writing thesis statements that are neither too broad nor too narrow

Effective thesis statements, like effective purposes, are not too broad or too narrow. If you wanted to convince an audience that "The social security system needs radical revisions," you would probably have to write a book, or at least a very long report.

FYI: For more on tightening your prose, see Chapter 7.

Choosing too broad a thesis for a brief paper, such as an in-class essay, would be dangerous. Because you would end up trying to fit too much information into too few paragraphs, your paper would be vague and unconvincing. On the other hand, if you wanted to convince your readers that fast-food jobs offer college students flexible schedules, you might only have enough information to fill a paragraph, so trying to write an essay about it would be frustrating. You would end up repeating yourself or adding unnecessary explanations in an attempt to fill up the pages.

One way to decide whether your thesis is too broad or too narrow is to list the probable contents of your paper. Imagine what your readers would need to know to understand or believe your thesis. In the case of the thesis about social security, you would have to explain why the social security system needs radical revisions. But in order to convince your readers, you would first have to be certain they understand how the social security system works, what specific problems you believe demand correction, and what you think the reforms should be. Without thinking much longer, you can tell that your paper would need to be far too lengthy. In the case of the fast-food thesis, after you had explained to readers that the work hours can be easily adjusted to mesh with college and family schedules, there isn't much else to add.

If you discover your thesis is too broad or too narrow, you can often narrow or expand it to produce a paper of the required length. For example, instead of discussing all the possible reforms for social security, you could limit yourself to one aspect of the social security system that you find problematic, preferably one you have extensive knowledge about or experience with. The narrow fast-food thesis could be expanded by adding other advantages of fast-food jobs for college students, producing a thesis such as this one: "Despite the lower pay and even lower prestige, jobs in the fast-food industry provide college students with flexible hours, opportunities to relocate to other franchises, training in business practices, and management options." Now you have four topics to write about, so you could easily write a two-page paper.

Supporting the Thesis

You convince your readers of the validity of your thesis by providing supporting evidence. This evidence will be organized into topic paragraphs, each of which will support the thesis. Suppose, for example, you were asked to write an essay about the solution to a problem at home or at work. You decide to write about how students who work while going to school have difficulty keeping up with assignments. Your thesis might be "Students who work while enrolled in college need planning, people skills, support, and perseverance to cope with their difficult schedules." To support the thesis, you must supply topic paragraphs containing evidence and examples. The topic sentences for your support paragraphs might be like these:

1. Planning ahead helps students avoid getting behind in their work.
2. Clearly and respectfully communicating difficulties to bosses and professors helps work out conflicts.
3. The support of family and friends increases working students' chances of success.
4. Working students must persevere to overcome the difficulties inherent in trying to balance two lives.

Having developed a thesis and ideas for supporting paragraphs, writing the rest of the essay is fairly straightforward. Complete each paragraph by supplying the necessary explanations and examples.

Some thesis statements do not contain such a clear list of what supporting material will follow in the essay. A thesis such as "Working students are at greater risk for dropping out of school" doesn't include information about what subtopics readers might expect to find covered in the essay. Such thesis statements can still be effective as long as the writer knows what needs to be covered to support the point and can organize the supporting material into unified, coherent, complete paragraphs.

Activity: WORKING TOGETHER   DAEDALUS ONLINE

Form groups of three to five students who will work together to create a very basic draft of an essay. The general topic of the essay is: _____ is popular because _____. The first blank should be filled in with one of the following:

- type of book (for example, romance, mystery, books by a particular author)
- genre of movie (for example, romantic comedy, science fiction, action, crime)
- type of TV show (for example, police drama, sitcom, daytime talk show, soap)

First, find a topic that all members of the group know something about. Then brainstorm the reasons for the popularity of the subject you chose. Write a thesis and develop your evidence using either reasons or examples. Express each reason or example in one clear topic sentence. Assign one topic sentence to each member of the group for further development. To complete this activity see the instructions below under Computer Workshop. If you can't work on a computer, complete the same steps on paper.

Activity: COMPUTER WORKSHOP

Open a file named for the subject of your paragraph. Develop a paragraph of five to ten sentences, using specific details and examples to explain the topic sentence's point. E-mail your paragraph to the other members of your group. When you get the e-mailed paragraphs from the other group members, follow these steps:

1. Open a new file.
2. Choose an order for the paragraphs.
3. Assemble them and the thesis sentence into an essay draft.
4. Print out copies of your draft, one for each member of your group.
5. Save your document for a further assignment.

Once you have completed the "essays," reassemble as a group, hand out your versions of the essay draft, and discuss the following questions:

- Why did you put the paragraphs in the order you did?
- Could these collections of paragraphs make a good essay? Why or why not?
- What would have to be changed? Added? Deleted?
- Is the process of writing an essay with others different from writing one alone? How?
- What is difficult about collaborating on an essay like this?
- What is the benefit of collaborating on an essay this way?

Special Paragraphs

Although most of the paragraphs you write will be topic paragraphs, there are three other types of paragraphs you need to write in essays. These paragraphs have special functions:

- to introduce a paper
- to conclude a paper
- to provide a transition leading from one topic to another within a paper

Introductory paragraphs

Writers often have difficulty beginning their essays when they try to write the introduction first. They are stymied because until they have written the draft, they do not know what they are trying to introduce. Many writers find it easier to write the introduction to a paper after having completed the topic paragraphs that comprise the body of the paper.

The introductory paragraph of an essay has two purposes:

- to spark the readers' interest
- to clarify the point of the paper

Because the thesis serves the purpose of clarifying the writer's main point, it usually is placed in the introductory paragraph, most often as the last sentence. However, writers sometimes save the thesis for the second paragraph, especially if the introductory material is long or involved, or the transition between the thesis and supporting points is clearer when the thesis is in the second paragraph. The introduction leads the readers to the thesis and creates interest in the topic. Below are five strategies writers frequently use. Although these approaches can occasionally be combined—for example, an anecdote might contain a quotation—writers typically select only one of these techniques.

1. Open with a general statement on your topic; narrow that statement, leading toward the thesis. For example, if you were going to write on Topic B in the Working Together exercise on p. 168, you might start with a general statement like this: "Being Korean colors many aspects of my daily life." You might then continue with a narrower focus: "My preference in food and clothes, my choice of pastimes, my attitudes and reactions to events in the neighborhood or in the news are all affected by my heritage." This sentence could lead to the thesis: "However, in no aspect of my life is my Korean-ness more evident than in my relations with and expectations of

my American wife and our daughter." If you begin your essay with a general statement, avoid being overly general. Sentences such as "People's backgrounds are important" or "Your ethnic background affects your life" are so general that readers don't get any picture at all of the essay's subject, so they might become bored or confused right away.

2. Start with a short anecdote about your topic. Almost everyone finds stories interesting, and most writers have personal experience with their topics, so anecdotes are relatively easy to come by. Make sure the story you use is clearly linked to your thesis. For example, if you were writing about the poor design of your local library, you might begin with a story about your recent visit:

> Our town's new fifty-million-dollar library opened to fanfare, festivities, and ooohs and aaaahs from the local press, so during its first week of operation, I packed up my one-year-old for a much-anticipated expedition to tour the new facility and return some books. After passing through an entryway of stately columns, marble floors, and brass fixtures, we headed for the book return slot. Though it was tucked away in a corner, it wasn't hard to find because a long line of people waited to drop off their books. When we finally reached the return slot, I understood why the line had been so long. Dropping off my books was not easy. I set my bag of books on the floor, then tried to open the flap while holding my baby. I found that instead of opening down to form a shelf, the flap lifted up—but only as long as it was held up. How was I going to hold my baby, pick up the books from the floor, and hold the flap open? I only had two hands. By putting my baby on the floor and pinning him against the wall with my leg while I bent over numerous times to reach for books and put them in the slot, I managed to deposit my returns. However, after performing acrobatics to use the deposit slot, I didn't have the time, energy, or enthusiasm necessary to tour the rest of our magnificent library.

FYI: For more on writing narratives, see Chapter 10.

3. Begin with necessary background information—a statement of a problem, the definition of terms the readers need to understand your paper, a very brief history of the topic. The key to writing introductions that provide background is to include only the information your readers need to know, so the first step is a careful analysis of your intended audience. For example, if you were writing an essay analyzing a short story's *point of view*, you would need to define that term if the audience were unfamiliar with it. The following introduction provides the necessary background for the reader:

> Who's telling the story? When you answer this question, you are identifying the point of view. An author may take the point of view of one of the characters, using the first-person pronoun "I" and describing the action through that character's eyes. For example, Edgar Allan Poe's "The Pit and the Pendulum," which begins, "I was sick—sick unto death with that long agony; when they at length unbound me, and I was permitted to sit, I felt my senses were leaving me," uses a first-person point of view. Alternately, the author may describe the action through a narrator who

is not part of the action, as in Kate Chopin's "The Story of an Hour," which begins, "Knowing that Mrs. Mallard was afflicted with a heart trouble, great care was taken to break to her as gently as possible the news of her husband's death." An author using this kind of narration uses the third-person pronouns (he, she, it, and they). The author may tell the story focusing on one or two characters' lives and feelings or may range widely from one character and place to another. Choice of point of view influences other choices the author makes about content and style. For example, an author using first-person point of view cannot describe the thoughts and feelings of more than one character. Therefore, choosing point of view is one of the most important decisions an author makes, and changing point of view can completely change a story.

When using background information in your introduction, carefully analyze your audience and choose information that fits their needs. If the introduction contains information that is already very familiar to them, they may be bored or offended.

4. Use a quotation on the topic. If, like most people, you cannot remember many quotations, you can use a dictionary of quotations in your library or on the Internet. However, the most effective quotations may not be famous ones. A quotation from an expert on your topic or from someone with relevant, personal experience often makes an effective beginning. A quotation can focus readers on a central issue in your paper. For example, a paper arguing the importance of familiarity with European geography would have a livelier opening line if it quoted your classmate's comment, "Why bother to learn this stuff—it just keeps changing anyway?" than if it opened with a Shakespearean quotation.

5. Start with a question or two to stimulate your readers' thinking. Your thesis can be the proposed answer to the questions. For example, if you are writing a paper about why marijuana should be legalized, you might begin by asking "What is the difference between marijuana and alcohol?" This question would get the readers thinking about your topic without really stating your main point. Avoid beginning with questions that are impossible to answer, uninteresting, or unrelated to your main point. For example, beginning with the question "How many times do you think your doctor has smoked marijuana?" is not effective as an opening because most readers can't answer the question, don't really care how many times their doctor has smoked marijuana, and won't see the connection between this question and any important arguments about legalizing marijuana.

Concluding paragraphs

A conclusion should follow naturally from the preceding paragraphs. If you have already written an introductory paragraph, review it before writing a conclusion. Often you can make the conclusion fit the introduction. For example, you might want to comment on, conclude, or add to your opening—whether you began with a general statement, a story, a quotation, a question, or background information.

If an idea for concluding your paper does not spring to mind, you can try one of these strategies:

1. Restate the thesis and summarize the main points. In academic writing, a summary is probably the most frequent type of conclusion. The strength of a summary is that it reinforces the essay's contents; the drawback of a summary is that it may seem mechanical and uninteresting. In a short essay that makes only a few points, a summary conclusion can usually be brief. If you write a summary, avoid repeating your thesis or topic sentences word for word—a sure way to bore your readers. An essay on the 1997 block-buster movie *Titanic* began with this thesis, "Despite its many strengths, *Titanic* is no masterpiece: the film succeeds because it interweaves two genre films—the disaster film and the love story—with a historic film, thereby appealing to an unusually wide audience." The essay's main points were briefly summarized in this conclusion:

   > *Titanic* was a box office smash for many reasons—including a "hot" cast, phenomenal special effects, and an appealing sound track, but it was a popular film, not a great film. Its box office success resulted from the merger of the disaster film, the love story, and the historical film, which created a film calculated to appeal to men and women as well as to younger and older viewers.

2. Demonstrate the relevance of your thesis to your readers. Readers are more likely to take your thesis seriously if they feel it relates to their lives. The conclusion below is from an essay arguing that user-friendly design should be important to consumers. It points out the relevance and importance of this topic in readers' everyday lives:

   > A poorly designed return book slot may not ruin a library. A dishwasher rack that fails to hold dishes in place may not destroy civilization. However, bad designs lead to waste, injuries, and bad attitudes. Should home and business consumers have to pay the physical, mental, and monetary costs associated with poor design? Consumers who pay close attention to design issues when choosing products will force producers to pay attention as well. Maybe better design of everyday goods won't create utopia, but it may result in fewer broken dishes, sore backs, and empty wallets.

   Avoid overstating the importance of the issues. Conclusions claiming that readers' lives will somehow be ruined if they do not believe in your thesis or follow your advice are not likely to be effective.

3. Conclude with an anecdote or a quotation that illuminates the central idea of your essay. Anecdotes have the advantage of being enjoyable to read and easy to understand. Both quotations and anecdotes can tie an abstract topic to human experience and make readers aware of the topic's relevance to their lives. Remember that the most effective quotation may be from an expert on the topic or from a person with experience or insight on the topic, rather than a famous person or source. Here's an example of an anecdote used as a conclusion for an essay on reorganizing the school day around integrated units of instruction:

"Why do one half-cup and one half-cup make one cup?" Panic set in as I attempted to explain addition of fractions to my son. I was suddenly back in fifth grade, struggling to learn how to add one half and one third. I couldn't figure out why I couldn't add the bottom numbers together as I did with the top numbers. Even after I learned the rules and passed the unit test, I didn't really understand the principle behind adding fractions, so I promptly forgot all the rules I'd learned. Years later, as I was cooking with my son and doubling a recipe for cookies, the rules for adding fractions suddenly made sense. Maybe if I had learned math in a unit on cooking, sewing, building, or gardening, I might have lived a life free of fraction fear. Don't we all deserve to enjoy and understand fractions, spelling, vector analysis, and counterpoint? Integrating units of instruction makes school learning like life learning—relevant and fun.

Notice that the anecdote directly relates to the point made in the essay—that integrated units of instruction are best. The writer presents the anecdote and then explains its significance.

4. Draw an inference based on your evidence. Although your evidence has been organized to support the thesis, you may wish to focus briefly on another issue that also arises from the evidence. The strength of this approach is that it may lead the reader to react thoughtfully to your essay. However, writing a conclusion that draws an inference is more difficult than writing a summary. Your concluding paragraph must still be closely linked to the contents of the previous paragraphs and must follow smoothly and logically from them. Otherwise, your conclusion may seem abrupt and confusing or, even worse, more like the introduction to another essay. In the sample paragraph in strategy #1, the writer concluded the essay about the movie *Titanic* with a brief summary. This alternative ending draws an inference:

FYI: For more on inferences, see p. 55.

Titanic's triple-whammy use of the disaster, love story, and historic film genres yielded huge audiences. But why is the genre film so popular? For one thing, people prefer to know something about a film before they see it, so there's less chance of being disappointed. A viewer who enjoys love stories will be fairly sure of enjoying another one. Also, viewers derive pleasure from having familiar scenes—such as the first kiss of a love story—recast in new forms with new faces, in the same way we enjoy hearing familiar tunes sung by different artists. Whether they understood the reasons for the genre film's popularity or not, the producers of *Titanic* were able to cash in on its appeal.

Activity: WORKING TOGETHER

Get back into the groups that wrote the "essay" about the popularity of a type of book, movie, or TV show. Now each member will write an introductory and a concluding paragraph. Compare the introductions and conclusions produced in your group and discuss the strengths and weaknesses of each.

Transition paragraphs

A transition leads from one section to another. Words or phrases like "next," "the final reason," or "most important" are usually enough to lead the reader from one sentence or one topic to another in an essay of two or three typed pages. Occasionally, you may want to add a transition sentence to show the reader that you have concluded one topic and are beginning another. For example, in the essay on *Titanic*, this sentence led to the third part of the discussion of genres: "In addition to the appeal of the disaster film and the love story, *Titanic* also offers moviegoers an accurate historical account of the ill-fated luxury liner."

In long or complicated papers, brief transition paragraphs may help the reader move from one topic to another. A transition paragraph does not need a topic sentence, nor does it usually add new information. Since its function is to form a bridge between two topics, a transition paragraph usually has a simple two-part form: The writer first summarizes the last section of the paper and then introduces the new topic. In a research paper on genetically altered produce, the writer might signal to readers that a new topic is beginning with a brief paragraph like this:

> A tomato can be genetically altered to have a perfect shape, an appealing bright red color, and a skin and flesh tough enough to withstand long shipment undamaged. What lurks behind this apparent perfection? What is the real cost to consumers?

Activity: BUILDING AN ESSAY

Consult the information you generated about your topic in Chapter 4. Keeping your working thesis and purpose in mind, organize the information into paragraphs. Write a clear topic sentence for each paragraph. Review the drafts of the paragraphs, deleting extraneous information and adding relevant information, examples, and details. When you are satisfied with the content of your topic paragraphs, write an introductory and a concluding paragraph.

For advice on all phases of essay writing, including discovering ideas for writing, developing a thesis, drafting and revising an essay, consult the *Paradigm Online Writing Assistant* at

☞   http://www.powa.org/

The Workplace

FYI: For samples of letters and memos, see Chapter 23.

ORGANIZING LETTERS AND MEMOS

In the workplace, brief written communication usually takes place through letters (intended for readers outside the workplace) and memos (intended for readers inside the workplace). Like other kinds of texts, letters and memos have different patterns of organization, depending on their purpose. The following are four common types of letters and memos:

1. A **request for information or action** usually follows this pattern:
   - A polite request for information or action
   - The reason for the request with pertinent explanations and details
   - A courteous request for a specific response, a statement of appreciation, and information on how to be contacted

2. A **positive reply** usually follows this pattern:
   - A statement of the main idea or positive response
   - An explanation of the action that will be taken
   - Any information, details, or explanations the reader needs
   - A positive statement, often about future actions, and a courteous close

A **negative reply** usually takes one of two forms, an indirect plan or a direct plan.

3. The **indirect plan** usually follows this pattern:
   - A buffer—a neutral statement closely related to the message's main point
   - The reasons for the negative reply
   - A clear statement of the negative reply
   - A courteous, helpful closing

4. The **direct** plan usually follows this pattern:
   - A clear statement of the negative reply
   - The reasons for the negative reply
   - A courteous closing

Remember that all letters and memos, regardless of their purpose, should adhere to readers' expectations for workplace communication (see p. 12).

READING AND WRITING TEXTS

Readings

In this chapter, you learned how to form effective paragraphs and essays. The following three essays discuss neurology, biology, film, and engineering. Even though the topics of the essays vary widely, the writers' discussions of how form relates to function are relevant to decisions writers make when constructing their paragraphs and essays. As you read these selections, compare the importance of form—whether in a brain, a Western, or a water faucet—with form in written texts. The fourth reading, "The Lottery," is a fictional account of a ritual, which is a form of social behavior. Identify the ritual's function in the community. Does the form of the ritual fit its function? Also think about the story's function. What was the writer trying to do? How does "The Lottery"'s form fit its function?

Activity: PREREADING

Working Together:
In small groups, discuss the following topics:

1. Look at the room you are in. How does the room's design fit its purposes? How does it not ? List each feature of the room and the purpose it does or doesn't fit. Now discuss what the room's design reveals about people's assumptions regarding what and how students learn in classrooms.
2. Brainstorm some ideas for technological devices or systems that don't exist that you would like to see developed. Why don't they exist? How could the obstacles to their development be overcome?
3. List all the types of movies you can identify. Which genres do you like best? Why?
4. Would you follow the traditions and rules of behavior of a country you were visiting even if they seemed unfamiliar or strange?

A Proper Form for Everything

Richard Restak

"A Proper Form for Everything," from The Brain Has a Mind of Its Own, *has implications for the structure of any written text. The author, Richard Restak, torn between two career choices—medicine and writing fiction—first chose medicine but eventually also became an author. In the "Introduction" to* The Brain Has a Mind of Its Own, *Restak explains that these seemingly disparate fields, neurology and fiction, are united in their exploration of "why people do the unpredictable, amazing, and sometimes just plain crazy things that they do." Both neurology and writing allow one to explore "the forces that motivate the con man, the serial killer, and the saint."*

My t'ai chi instructor emphasizes "form" in his teaching of this ancient Chinese martial art. Feet must be exactly shoulder width apart and no wider. Hands must move as if through water. Stiffness, rigidness, and clumsiness of any sort are greeted with horror.

One day while performing these relaxing but demanding exercises, I realized that there is a proper form for everything: fairly narrow parameters within which activities and structures must be accommodated lest chaos ensue.

Severe penalties are exacted for bad form in chess, tennis, and boxing. An inelegant chess move can lose the match. The tennis ball must be struck at just the right moment and with just the right amount of force, or the ball is lost in the net or perhaps missed altogether. If a punch is off target because of a slight lack of technique, a chance for a knockout has been missed. What's worse, it may have opened the way for a counterblow that could end the fight.

Form is also preeminent in the arts and determined by our biology, the way nature has constructed us. The time between beats is only between 0.63 seconds and 0.29 seconds in the range of tempos from adagio and andante to allegro and presto. If the cymbals come a fiftieth of a second too late, the audience winces. Form has been violated.

Carried to an extreme, form turns back on itself, becomes parody. The anorexic, believing that "thin is beautiful," goes too far, ends up a freak. Some weight lifters become so overdeveloped that their arms no longer move freely as they walk. The pursuit of the "perfect" form has led to the grotesque.

In biology good form is strictly and inexorably defined. Consider an animal's weight. Are there absolute limits to an animal's size, or could one exist weighing as much as one hundred tons? Bone artifacts from the dinosaur, the biggest land animal that ever lived, indicate that it may have weighed about eighty tons.

So why not a hundred-ton gargantuan? The answer is that the animal would require such a profound alteration of form, it could not survive. There are limits to the strength of bones and the power of muscles. Bone strength is proportional to cross-sectional area (a two-dimensional measure), whereas body weight is proportional to volume (a three-dimensional measure). Accordingly, the bone cross-sectional area must increase faster than body weight. Indeed, an animal weighing more than eighty tons would have to be composed *entirely* of bones frozen into immobility, because the creature's muscles would be unable to function. If the animal were to lie down—or, more likely, fall down of its own weight—its muscular system would be too weak to enable it to get up.

Form is also important to the human brain. As it turns out, just having a big brain is no guarantee of great intelligence. If it were, all six-foot-four men and women would be smarter than their five-foot-four counterparts. It's the brain-to-body ratio that's important, not brain size alone.

The size of the female pelvis imposes limitations on the brain's form. If the brain continued to expand, it would eventually get so big that the head couldn't pass through the birth canal. Nature has solved this problem of proper brain form in two ways. First, the greatest increase in brain size takes place *after* birth. Second, increased surface area is achieved without increasing brain volume by a process similar to what happens if you take a handkerchief and spread it out on a table, then roll it into a ball and put it into your pocket. The surface area remains the same, but the volume is greatly reduced. The same thing happens in the human brain. A fetus's hemispheres are smooth and unwrinkled. But an adult's looks like a gnarled walnut, because of billions of nerve cells sequestered deep below the surface. Just as in the handkerchief, a large surface area has been confined in a limited volume.

As the brain ages or is afflicted with disease, a person's walk, speech, and posture change. The form of the brain can be understood by those skilled in decoding such messages. But one does not have to be a neurologist to make such observations. Individuals who are clumsy, retarded, schizophrenic, or autistic: dancers, martial artists—often these people can be identified by the way they walk, which, basically, is form in motion.

On the whole, I think my t'ai chi teacher is right. The form must be exactly right. Excellence ultimately involves a preoccupation with form. Indeed, at the most basic level, structure, function, and form are inseparable. Or, as my t'ai chi teacher puts it: "After you do the form often enough, something marvelous happens: You and the form become one. Finally it begins to do you."

Activity: RESPONDING TO THE TEXT

1. What is the thesis statement?
2. Sometimes Restak uses two paragraphs to support one topic sentence, so not every paragraph has a topic sentence. What are the topic sentences?
3. What kind of evidence does Restak include to support his topic sentences?
4. Review the section on introductory and concluding paragraphs on pp. 172–176. What technique does Restak use to introduce his essay? How does he tie the conclusion to the introduction?

Genre Films
Thomas Sobchack

In "Genre Films," Thomas Sobchack argues that all genre films, whether they are westerns, romances, horror films, or any of the other genres, rely on established, recognizable forms. According to Sobchack, the success of a genre film depends on predictable plots, recognizable characters, and adherence to previous films of the same genre.

Long the staple product of Hollywood, the genre film such as the western or the gangster film is different from other fiction films in that it follows established narrative structures, uses stereotypical characters, and communicates through certain familiar images (icons). These structures and images are a sort of shorthand, compressing information about the story, characters, and theme into conventional actions and objects such as décor, costume, and topography. In a western, for example, the derringer (a small, easily concealed pistol) indicates its owner's basically underhanded character. Or consider clothing: both cowboys and outlaws wear loose-fitting and practical clothing, indicating a free and open life-style, but people from the town usually wear suits, vests, and ties to indicate their more restricted way of life. The genre film also builds upon preexistent audience expectations: we go to see a thriller, a gangster film. The experience of the genre film is a familiar rather than a new experience and its satisfactions are based on our previous knowledge of the formulas, conventions, and iconography used in the films. . . .

The Definition of Genre

What, precisely, is a genre film? It is a film which belongs to a particular group of films that are extremely similar in their subject matter, thematic concerns, characterizations, plot formulas, and visual settings. Such a film somehow depends on these similarities for its very existence and for the satisfactions it brings the viewer. Some genres, such as the western, are easily recognizable; many points of similarity exist between films, linking them firmly into a group.

For a movie to be considered part of a genre, or of a generic tradition, then, it need not include *all* the conventions of that genre, but it should include *enough* generic elements to cause the viewer to associate it clearly and consciously with other films containing similar elements. These similarities of theme, plot, and characterization should also be quite specific. There are countless films built on the relationships between men and women, yet all these films do not constitute a genre because the details, characterizations, and themes of the films may have no other points of resemblance whatsoever.

Primarily then, the genre film is part of a system of well-known narratives, sets of stories, prepackaged and familiar, like breakfast cereals, which have proved popular in the past. Film producers and film audiences (in sum—the culture) together have defined (and continue to redefine) the shape and form of these narratives and the meanings they convey in response to the culture's changing and unchanging desires and needs.

FORMULA

Genre films are constructed from formula plots. The basic conflict of the story is familiar, and we know from past viewing experiences more or less how the story will be resolved. Thus, what happens in a particular genre film is predictable; we do not get *surprise* so much as *suspense* generated by small variations. We can relax and only pretend anxiety about whether the protagonist will live or die at the end of the movie. Different genres, however, tend to concentrate on different basic conflicts. From one genre to another, then, we get different episodes in the plot and different characters.

Consider, for example, the adventure film. One of the basic conflicts presented in certain kinds of adventure films—whether it is a film about a wild animal hunt like Howard Hawks's *Hatari!* (1962), a war movie like *Bat-*

tleground (William Wellman, 1949), or a survival movie like *The Poseidon Adventure* (Ronald Neame, 1972)—is the formation, from a random group of people, of a functioning minisociety, which can accomplish a given task successfully. Because this is the central issue, all these films tend to concentrate on delineating different stereotypical characters (the coward, the braggart, the lover) and on the process whereby these individuals are tested and found to be useful or useless to the group and its single goal. Thus, the formula situations (a shipwreck, a jet plane in trouble, a platoon cut off behind enemy lines, a search for hidden treasure) provide a way to isolate and estrange the characters from civilized society so that their true natures may come to the surface. The characters represent a cross section of society, sometimes ethnically and geographically (the Italian-American from New York, the black, the Texan), sometimes occupationally (the banker, the laborer, the farmer), and always morally (the sniveler, the stoic, the sentimentalist) to indicate the democratic nature of group action.

In such adventure films, certain formula scenes seem almost obligatory. When we see war movies or disaster movies, we recognize fairly early on which characters will do what, which will die early in the film, which will selfishly betray or desert the group, which will survive. We know that there will be scenes that will individually test the characters. We know that the film will be structured so that it will begin in a normal context in which people take themselves and their social roles for granted. We know that the characters will be in a situation in which a microcosm can be collected on some realistic pretext: on an airplane, in the random unit of an army, on a pleasure ship or railroad train, on a floor of an office building. We also know that after the characters have been shown to us in their civilized guise, a catastrophe will occur that will shut them off from contact with the larger society to which they belong. From that point on in the film, we expect small tests of courage and ingenuity and endurance, and we may even have a fairly good idea of who will fail and who will succeed, and of when and how they will do so—simply by the casting of various familiar actors and actresses in several kinds of roles. [*Airplane!* (Jim Abrahams, 1980) successfully parodies the adventure genre in part by casting Lloyd Bridges and Robert Stack in the same type of roles they played in more serious versions of the airplane disaster film.] We know, because we are familiar with the formula, that in the end there will be survivors of the adventure and that they will rejoin the larger society at the close of the film.

The word formula, of course, denotes a repeated series of activities that result in a predictable end result. Certain formulas underlie specific genres—the natural catastrophe, which tests a minigroup of individuals, is the stuff of the adventure film, and the variations on the theme of opposing groups in the American west (settlers vs. Indians, ranchers vs. sheepmen, cavalry vs. Indians, and so forth) is the stuff of the western. But it is also true that certain formulas tend to be the communal property of all narrative film—in fact, of all narrative. For example, boy-meets-girl, boy-loses-girl, boy-gets-girl is one such formula, and another is that of the falsely accused person who must clear his or her name. Part of the enjoyment of watching traditional narrative films is our familiarity with such basic formulas, our recognition of the basic outline which holds togeth-er the innumerable small, fresh details that make the film different from the previous one with the same basic outline. Thus, when we watch a genre film, a pleasurable tension is created between the expected and pre-dictable and familiar elements of formula and the unexpected variations of the specific film story we are watching.

CONVENTION

Whereas a formula is an entire structure or series of actions that results in a predictable and familiar end, a convention is a small, relatively separate unit of action in genre films. Conventions are the specific ways in which the formula plot (who did what, when and where, to whom) is translat-ed into visualized action in a particular genre. The showdown gunfight be-tween the protagonist and antagonist in the western, or the love duet between the boy and girl in the musical, are examples of such conven-tions. These conventional actions recur from film to film, sometimes even in remarkably similar detail.

Besides the gist of content of the convention—the chief thing that happens—there is also the way in which the content is treated, that is, the way in which the camera photographs it and the editor edits it. These, too, become familiar and predictable. Conventionally, in that shoot-out, there will be clear, sunny weather so that long shadows can dramatically enhance the action. There will seldom be any wind. A long shot of the street, usually from a high angle look-ing down, will give the viewer a clear idea of the spatial relationship be-tween the two characters. This long shot will usually be followed by a series of cuts alternating between each of the men in medium shot and close-up, and these may be followed with a long shot of the townspeople scattering, and a few close-ups of eyes peering from behind windows. Then the cutting of close-ups between the two men will accelerate until the final close-ups show the faces of each, the hands reaching for the hips, the guns being drawn. Then there will usually be a long shot of the villain being struck by the fatal bullet and his fall to the ground. This is customarily followed by a high-angle long shot again revealing the town and letting the viewer see the townspeople and possibly the heroine rejoin the lone hero on the street. Variations, of course, are probable; the street may be larger or smaller, there may be fewer or more witnesses to the showdown, there may or may not be a heroine, there may be shots inserted of the villain's henchman on a hotel roof waiting to gun down the hero before he can fire at the villain. Still, the basic convention in both content and form is clearly recognizable and sat-isfyingly familiar. This convention is almost never violated except purpose-ly, for example, when a filmmaker parodies the genre or makes a consciously antigenre film, which attempts to subvert our expectations. Otherwise, cer-tain aspects of the gunfight are always maintained: the hero never draws first, he never shoots his opponent from ambush, and he always triumphs in the end. . . .

We tend to be more aware of plot conventions than of formal conven-tions, but both are crucial to the genre film and to the pleasure we derive from watching variations on their familiarity.

ICONOGRAPHY

An even smaller unit of the genre film is the icon, from a Greek word meaning "image," "likeness." Whereas formula refers to an entire structure or series of actions upon which an entire film is based (the essential plot and characters), and convention refers to a unit of action or episode within a formula that recurs from film to film, the film icon is a yet smaller element of the genre film. Certain costumes (cowboy clothes, space suits), certain objects (cigarette holders, pistols), certain landscapes (foggy moors, wide-open prairies), and certain performers (John Wayne, Sylvester Stallone) instantly signify—simply by their presence—elements of plot that have not yet occurred, complete psyches and motivations in characters, and complex thematic associations regarding the content of the genre and with the past cinematic experience of the viewer.

An icon get its meaning from its repeated use in many films. . . . The sound of a creaking door, [for example] tends to be iconic, conveying menace, dread, potential horror; it evokes all those moments of terror and all those dreaded figures from past horror films the viewer has seen. . . . The sound of a machine gun with its rapid-fire rat-a-tat and its specific physical appearance in a gangster film signifies not only itself in the one particular film, but also signifies the crudeness of gangsters. . . .

While the iconic significance of objects in genre films is often easily discernible because we notice *things* in movies, the more pervasive yet less noticed background can also function iconically. We expect a certain physical topography in the western (even if it is actually filmed in Spain or Italy), and that landscape conveys more than its physical self; it communicates a way of life with particular hardships, particular demands; it communicates certain unplayed dramas that have taken place in its arena in other movies or will take place in the movie being viewed and in future movies (the ambush in the box canyon, the Indians appearing on the crest of a bluff, the stumbling descent of a horse through badlands). The city is more than a merely physical characteristic of the gangster film; it communicates from film to film a nightmare landscape, a cold, unnatural world, a world full of hiding places where devious transactions can take place in the shadows.

Finally, certain performers are iconic. They communicate not only themselves as recognizable stars, or as the characters they play in the specific film, but they also communicate a kind of character, a whole set of moral values, from film to film simply by their physical appearance in these films. John Wayne, for example, is an actor who is an icon. He need not have very many lines of dialogue in any given western movie for the viewer to understand, to know almost intimately, who and what the character is, what he believes in and how he will act in a given situation. . . .

Genre films can also function as a cultural barometer. The viewer can look at the evolution of a particular genre, say the western, and see reflected in its shifts in attitude, changes that can be likened to shifts of attitude in the contemporary society which made and attended the films. It cannot be dismissed as mere accident that the western hero has changed from a figure like Bronco Billy Anderson, who bore some strong resemblance to his real-life counterpart, to a white-hatted hero on an intelligent horse, like Roy Rogers or

Gene Autry in the 1930s and early 1940s; to the psychologically contemplative or disfigured hero-villains of the 1950s and 1960s; to the corporate hero-villains of the late 1960s and 1970s such as those in *The Wild Bunch* (1969); to those films of the 1970s which presented the hero as septuagenarian and outdated as in *The Shootist* (Don Siegel, 1976) or *Tom Horn* (William Wiard, 1980). Those shifts reflect the contemporary concerns of the culture in which the films were made, and while it may not be useful to assign a one-to-one correspondence between occurrences in the social and political and economic life of movie viewers and occurrences on the screen, it can be productive to examine genre films as a response to social history and contemporary concerns. Surely it is reasonable to see, in the changes in the hero of the western, from the single-minded Gene Autry and Roy Rogers to the pragmatic Bill Holden and Lee Marvin, a shift in the way in which America defines its heroes. In 1981 Michael Cimino tried to make a socially conscious western about labor strife in Wyoming. *Heaven's Gate* cost 50 million dollars to make and was a disaster at the box office. In that same year *The Legend of the Lone Ranger* also failed to make money. Until 1985, no serious westerns were made. This could mean that Hollywood was afraid of losing money on a form the audience no longer wanted. The lukewarm response to *Silverado* and *Pale Rider* in 1985 indicates the traditional value system associated with the western and its lone hero are no longer something the public wants to buy.

Seeing genre films as a barometer of popular and often unconscious tensions and moods can help explain why, for example, certain genres suddenly reestablish their popularity after lying dormant for a period of time, or why certain foreign countries adopt and transform as their own a particular American film genre and have little interest in others. Japan, for example, has made many science fiction films, Italy many westerns. Looking at genre films as a reflection of the culture that produced and responded to them can lead to the contemplation of such questions as whether the popularity of the disaster film was a natural response to contemporary ecological concerns—or whether it was popular because it appealed covertly as a fantasy drama in which contemporary people were the helpless victims of cataclysmic forces beyond their control and for which they could not possibly be held responsible, a cinematic response of sorts to a world already beset with famine, drought, and Watergate.

Activity: RESPONDING TO THE TEXT

1. According to Sobchack, genre films have recognizable plots, characters, and iconography. In what ways is this predictability an advantage to the viewer?
2. How can form in genre films be compared to form in writing? In what ways is the predictability of the typical essay an advantage to the reader? In what ways might it be a disadvantage?
3. Underline all the topic sentences. Do these sentences provide a complete and accurate overview of the article?

The Design of Everyday Things

Donald A. Norman

In this excerpt, Donald A. Norman explains how the design of even a seemingly simple, everyday item like a water faucet is extremely complex, requiring multiple complicated decisions in order to create a functional form.

You might think that a water faucet would be pretty easy to design. After all, you merely want to start or stop the flow of water. But consider some of the problems. Suppose the faucets are for use in public places, where users may fail to turn them off. You can make a spring-operated faucet, which operates only as long as the handle is held. This automatically turns the faucet off; but it is difficult for users to hold the handle while wetting their hands. Ok, so you add a timer; then one push on the faucet handle yields five or ten seconds of water flow. But the extra complexity of the faucet design adds to the cost and lowers the reliability of the faucet. Furthermore, it is difficult to decide how long the water should stay on. Somehow it never seems like long enough for the user.

How about a foot-operated faucet, which overcomes the problems of springs and timers because the water stops as soon as the foot leaves the pedal? This solution requires slightly more elaborate plumbing, again raising the cost. It also makes the control invisible, violating a major design principle and making it difficult for a new user to find the control. How about a high-technology solution, with automatic sensors that turn on the water as soon as a hand is placed in the sink, turning it off as soon as it leaves? This solution has several problems. First, it is expensive. Second, it makes the controls invisible, causing difficulty for new users. And third, it is not easy to see how the user could control either the volume of water or the temperature. More on this faucet later.

Not all faucets are designed under the constraints of public faucets. At home, aesthetic considerations tend to dominate. Styles often reflect the social and economic class of the user. And different kinds of users have different requirements.

The same considerations hold true for most everyday things. The variety of possible solutions to the usual problems is enormous. The range of expression permitted the designer is vast. Moreover, the number of tiny details that must be accounted for is astounding. Pick up almost any manufactured item and examine its details with care. The little wiggly bends on a hairpin are essential in keeping it from slipping out of the hair: someone had to think of that, then design special equipment to create the bends. The felt-tip pen I am examining as I write has six different sizes on the pen body, two different sizes on the cap. The pen changes its taper at numerous spots, each change serving some function. Four different substances comprise the pen body (and I am not counting the ink, the container that holds the ink, or the felt tip). The cap is made of two kinds of plastic and one kind of metal. The inside of the cap has a number of subtle indentations and internal structures that clearly match up with corresponding parts of the pen body, both to hold the cap on firmly and to prevent the felt tip from drying out. There are more parts and variables than I would ever have imagined.

The pen's designer must be aware of hundreds of requirements. Make the pen too thin, and it will not be strong enough to stand up to the hard use of schoolchildren. Make the middle section too thick, and it can neither be grasped properly by the fingers nor controlled with enough precision. Yet people with arthritic hands may need a thick body because they can't close their fingers entirely. Leave out the tiny hole hear the tip, and pressure changes in the atmosphere will cause the ink to leak out. And what of those who use the pen as a measuring device or as a mechanical implement to pry, poke, stab, and twist? For example, the instructions for the clock in my automobile say to set it by depressing the recessed button with the tip of a ballpoint pen. How could the pen designer have known about this? What obligation does the designer have to consider varied and obscure uses?

Activity: RESPONDING TO THE TEXT

1. According to Norman, what factors does a designer have to consider when designing an object for everyday use?
2. In what ways does designing an everyday object correspond to writing an essay? In what ways might deviating from the expectations—whether in design or writing—be problematic? In what ways might it be advantageous?

The Lottery

Shirley Jackson

"The Lottery," a short story by Shirley Jackson, has remained popular since it was written in 1949. Initially, most readers respond to the compelling plot of "The Lottery"; however, the most chilling aspect of the story is not what happens, but what insights the story reveals about traditions and human nature.

The morning of June 27th was clear and sunny, with the fresh warmth of a full-summer day; the flowers were blossoming profusely and the grass was richly green. The people of the village began to gather in the square, between the post office and the bank, around ten o'clock; in some towns there were so many people that the lottery took two days and had to be started on June 26th, but in this village, where there were only about three hundred people, the whole lottery took less than two hours, so it could begin at ten o'clock in the morning and still be through in time to allow the villagers to get home for noon dinner.

The children assembled first, of course. School was recently over for the summer, and the feeling of liberty sat uneasily on most of them; they tended to gather together quietly for a while before they broke into boisterous play, and their talk was still of the classroom and the teacher, of books and reprimands. Bobby Martin had already stuffed his pockets full of stones, and the other boys soon followed his example, selecting the smoothest and roundest stones; Bobby and Harry Jones and Dickie Delacroix—the villagers pronounced this name "Dellacroy"—eventually made a great pile of stones in one corner of the square and guarded it against the raids of the other boys. The girls stood aside, talking among themselves, looking over their shoulders at the boys, and the very small children rolled in the dust or clung to the hands of their older brothers or sisters.

Soon the men began to gather, surveying their own children, speaking of planting and rain, tractors and taxes. They stood together, away from the pile of stones in the corner, and their jokes were quiet and they smiled rather than laughed. The women, wearing faded house dresses and sweaters, came shortly after their menfolk. They greeted one another and exchanged bits of gossip as they went to join their husbands. Soon the women, standing by their husbands, began to call to their children, and the children came reluctantly, having to be called four or five times. Bobby Martin ducked under his mother's grasping hand and ran, laughing, back to the pile of stones. His father spoke up sharply, and Bobby came quickly and took his place between his father and his oldest brother.

The lottery was conducted—as were the square dances, the teenage club, the Halloween program—by Mr. Summers, who had time and energy to devote to civic activities. He was a roundfaced, jovial man and he ran the coal business, and people were sorry for him, because he had no children and his wife was a scold. When he arrived in the square, carrying the black wooden box, there was a murmur of conversation among the villagers and he waved and called, "Little late today, folks." The postmaster, Mr. Graves, followed him, carrying a three-legged stool, and the stool was put in the center of the square and Mr. Summers set the black box down on it. The villagers kept their distance, leaving a space between themselves and the stool, and when Mr. Summers said, "Some of you fellows want to give me a hand?" there was a hesitation before two men, Mr. Martin and his oldest son, Baxter, came forward to hold the box steady on the stool while Mr. Summers stirred up the papers inside it.

The original paraphernalia for the lottery had been lost long ago, and the black box now resting on the stool had been put into use even before Old Man Warner, the oldest man in town, was born. Mr. Summers spoke frequently to the villagers about making a new box, but no one liked to upset even as much tradition as was represented by the black box. There was a story that the present box had been made with some pieces of the box that had preceded it, the one that had been constructed when the first people settled down to make a village here. Every year, after the lottery, Mr. Summers began talking again about a new box, but every year the subject was allowed to fade without anything's being done. The black box grew shabbier each year; by now it was no longer completely black but splintered badly along one side to show the original wood color, and in some places faded or stained.

Mr. Martin and his oldest son, Baxter, held the black box securely on the stool until Mr. Summers had stirred the papers thoroughly with his hand. Because so much of the ritual had been forgotten or discarded, Mr. Summers had been successful in having slips of paper substituted for the chips of wood that had been used for generations. Chips of wood, Mr. Summers had argued, had been all very well when the village was tiny, but now that the population was more than three hundred and likely to keep on growing, it was necessary to use something that would fit more easily into the black box. The night before the lottery, Mr. Summers and Mr. Graves made up the slips of paper and put them in the box, and it was then taken to the safe of Mr. Summers's coal company and locked up until Mr. Summers was ready to take it to the square next morning. The rest of the year, the box was put away, sometimes one place, sometimes another; it had spent one year in Mr. Graves's barn and another year underfoot in the post office, and sometimes it was set on a shelf in the Martin grocery and left there.

There was a great deal of fussing to be done before Mr. Summers declared the lottery open. There were lists to make up—of heads of families, heads of households in each family, members of each household in each family. There was the proper swearing-in of Mr. Summers by the postmaster, as the official of the lottery; at one time, some people remembered, there had been a recital of some sort, performed by the official of the lottery, a perfunctory, tuneless chant that had been rattled off duly each year; some people believed that the official of the lottery used to stand just so when he said or sang it, others believed that he was supposed to walk among the people, but years and years ago this part of the ritual had been allowed to lapse. There had been, also, a ritual salute, which the official of the lottery had had to use in addressing each person who came up to draw from the box, but this also had changed with time, until now it was felt necessary only for the official to speak to each person approaching. Mr. Summers was very good at all this; in his clean white shirt and blue jeans, with one hand resting carelessly on the black box, he seemed very proper and important as he talked interminably to Mr. Graves and the Martins.

Just as Mr. Summers finally left off talking and turned to the assembled villagers, Mrs. Hutchinson came hurriedly along the path to the square, her sweater thrown over her shoulders, and slid into place in the back of the crowd. "Clean forgot what day it was," she said to Mrs. Delacroix, who stood next to her, and they both laughed softly. "Thought my old man was out back stacking wood," Mrs. Hutchinson went on, "and then I looked out the window and the kids were gone, and then I remembered it was the twenty-seventh and came a-running." She dried her hands on her apron, and Mrs. Delacroix said, "You're in time, though. They're still talking away up there."

Mrs. Hutchinson craned her neck to see through the crowd and found her husband and children standing near the front. She tapped Mrs. Delacroix on the arm as a farewell and began to make her way through the crowd. The people separated good-humoredly to let her through; two or three people said, in voices just loud enough to be heard across the crowd, "Here comes your Missus, Hutchinson," and "Bill, she made it after all." Mrs. Hutchinson reached her husband, and Mr. Summers, who had been waiting, said cheerfully, "Thought we were going to have to get on without you, Tessie."

Mrs. Hutchinson said, grinning, "Wouldn't have me leave m'dishes in the sink, now would you, Joe?" and soft laughter ran through the crowd as the people stirred back into position after Mrs. Hutchinson's arrival.

"Well, now," Mr. Summers said soberly, "guess we better get started, get this over with, so's we can go back to work. Anybody ain't here?"

"Dunbar," several people said. "Dunbar, Dunbar."

Mr. Summers consulted his list. "Clyde Dunbar," he said. "That's right. He's broke his leg, hasn't he? Who's drawing for him?"

"Me, I guess," a woman said, and Mr. Summers turned to look at her. "Wife draws for her husband," Mr. Summers said. "Don't you have a grown boy to do it for you, Janey?" Although Mr. Summers and everyone else in the village knew the answer perfectly well, it was the business of the official of the lottery to ask such questions formally. Mr. Summers waited with an expression of polite interest while Mrs. Dunbar answered.

"Horace's not but sixteen yet," Mrs. Dunbar said regretfully. "Guess I gotta fill in for the old man this year."

"Right," Mr. Summers said. He made a note on the list he was holding. Then he asked, "Watson boy drawing this year?"

A tall boy in the crowd raised his hand. "Here," he said. "I'm drawing for m'mother and me." He blinked his eyes nervously and ducked his head as several voices in the crowd said things like "Good fellow, Jack," and "Glad to see your mother's got a man to do it."

"Well," Mr. Summers said, "guess that's everyone. Old Man Warner make it?"

"Here," a voice said, and Mr. Summers nodded.

A sudden hush fell on the crowd as Mr. Summers cleared his throat and looked at the list. "All ready?" he called. "Now, I'll read the names—heads of families first—and the men come up and take a paper out of the box. Keep the paper folded in your hand without looking at it until everyone has had a turn. Everything clear?"

The people had done it so many times that they only half listened to the directions; most of them were quiet, wetting their lips, not looking around. Then Mr. Summers raised one hand high and said, "Adams." A man disengaged himself from the crowd and came forward. "Hi, Steve," Mr. Summers said, and Mr. Adams said, "Hi, Joe." They grinned at one another humorlessly and nervously. Then Mr. Adams reached into the black box and took out a folded paper. He held it firmly by one corner as he turned and went hastily back to his place in the crowd, where he stood a little apart from his family, not looking down at his hand.

"Allen," Mr. Summers said. "Anderson. . . . Bentham."

"Seems like there's no time at all between lotteries any more," Mrs. Delacroix said to Mrs. Graves in the back row. "Seems like we got through with the last one only last week."

"Time sure goes fast," Mrs. Graves said.

"Clark. . . . Delacroix."

"There goes my old man," Mrs. Delacroix said. She held her breath while her husband went forward.

"Dunbar," Mr. Summers said, and Mrs. Dunbar went steadily to the box while one of the women said, "Go on, Janey," and another said, "There she goes."

"We're next," Mrs. Graves said. She watched while Mr. Graves came around from the side of the box, greeted Mr. Summers gravely, and selected a slip of paper from the box. By now, all through the crowd there were men holding the small folded papers in their large hands, turning them over and over nervously. Mrs. Dunbar and her two sons stood together, Mrs. Dunbar holding the slip of paper.

"Harburt. . . . Hutchinson."

"Get up there, Bill," Mrs. Hutchinson said, and the people near her laughed.

"Jones."

"They do say," Mr. Adams said to Old Man Warner, who stood next to him, "that over in the north village they're talking of giving up the lottery."

Old Man Warner snorted. "Pack of crazy fools," he said. "Listening to the young folks, nothing's good enough for *them*. Next thing you know, they'll be wanting to go back to living in caves, nobody work any more, live *that* way for a while. Used to be a saying about 'Lottery in June, corn be heavy soon.' First thing you know, we'd all be eating stewed chickweed and acorns. There's *always* been a lottery," he added petulantly. "Bad enough to see young Joe Summers up there joking with everybody."

"Some places have already quit lotteries," Mrs. Adams said.

"Nothing but trouble in *that*," Old Man Warner said stoutly. "Pack of young fools."

"Martin." And Bobby Martin watched his father go forward. "Overdyke. . . . Percy."

"I wish they'd hurry," Mrs. Dunbar said to her older son. "I wish they'd hurry."

"They're almost through," her son said.

"You get ready to run tell Dad," Mrs. Dunbar said.

Mr. Summers called his own name and then stepped forward precisely and selected a slip from the box. Then he called, "Warner."

"Seventy-seventh year I been in the lottery," Old Man Warner said as he went through the crowd. "Seventy-seventh time."

"Watson." The tall boy came awkwardly through the crowd. Someone said, "Don't be nervous, Jack," and Mr. Summers said, "Take your time, son."

"Zanini."

After that, there was a long pause, a breathless pause, until Mr. Summers, holding his slip of paper in the air, said, "All right, fellows." For a minute, no one moved, and then all the slips of paper were opened. Suddenly, all the women began to speak at once, saying, "Who is it?" "Who's got it?" "Is it the Dunbars?" "Is it the Watsons?" Then the voices began to say, "It's Hutchinson. It's Bill." "Bill Hutchinson's got it."

"Go tell your father," Mrs. Dunbar said to her older son.

People began to look around to see the Hutchinsons. Bill Hutchinson was standing quiet, staring down at the paper in his hand. Suddenly, Tessie Hutchinson shouted to Mr. Summers, "You didn't give him time enough to take any paper he wanted. I saw you. It wasn't fair!"

"Be a good sport, Tessie," Mrs. Delacroix called, and Mrs. Graves said, "All of us took the same chance."

"Shut up, Tessie," Bill Hutchinson said.

"Well, everyone," Mr. Summers said, "that was done pretty fast, and now we've got to be hurrying a little more to get done in time." He consulted his next list. "Bill," he said, "you draw for the Hutchinson family. You got any other households in the Hutchinsons?"

"There's Don and Eva," Mrs. Hutchinson yelled. "Make *them* take their chance!"

"Daughters draw with their husband's families, Tessie," Mr. Summers said gently. "You know that as well as anyone else."

"It wasn't fair," Tessie said.

"I guess not, Joe," Bill Hutchinson said regretfully. "My daughter draws with her husband's family, that's only fair. And I've got no other family except the kids."

"Then, as far as drawing for families is concerned, it's you," Mr. Summers said in explanation, "and as far as drawing for households is concerned, that's you, too. Right?"

"Right," Bill Hutchinson said.

"How many kids, Bill?" Mr. Summers asked formally.

"Three," Bill Hutchinson said. "There's Bill, Jr., and Nancy, and little Dave. And Tessie and me."

"All right, then," Mr. Summers said. "Harry, you got their tickets back?"

Mr. Graves nodded and held up the slips of paper. "Put them in the box, then," Mr. Summers directed. "Take Bill's and put it in."

"I think we ought to start over," Mrs. Hutchinson said, as quietly as she could. "I tell you it wasn't *fair*. You didn't give him time enough to choose. *Every*body saw that."

Mr. Graves had selected the five slips and put them in the box, and he dropped all the papers but those onto the ground, where the breeze caught them and lifted them off.

"Listen, everybody," Mrs. Hutchinson was saying to the people around her.

"Ready, Bill?" Mr. Summers asked, and Bill Hutchinson, with one quick glance around at his wife and children, nodded.

"Remember," Mr. Summers said, "take the slips and keep them folded until each person has taken one. Harry, you help little Dave." Mr. Graves took the hand of the little boy, who came willingly with him up to the box. "Take a paper out of the box, Davy," Mr. Summers said. Davy put his hand into the box and laughed. "Take just *one* paper," Mr. Summers said. "Harry, you hold it for him." Mr. Graves took the child's hand and removed the folded paper from the tight fist and held it while little Dave stood next to him and looked up at him wonderingly.

"Nancy next," Mr. Summers said. Nancy was twelve, and her school friends breathed heavily as she went forward, switching her skirt, and took a slip daintily from the box. "Bill, Jr.," Mr. Summers said, and Billy, his face red and his feet over-large, nearly knocked the box over as he got a paper out. "Tessie," Mr. Summers said. She hesitated for a minute, looking around defiantly, and then set her lips and went up to the box. She snatched a paper out and held it behind her.

"Bill," Mr. Summers said, and Bill Hutchinson reached into the box and felt around, bringing his hand out at last with the slip of paper in it.

The crowd was quiet. A girl whispered, "I hope it's not Nancy," and the sound of the whisper reached the edges of the crowd.

"It's not the way it used to be," Old Man Warner said clearly. "People ain't the way they used to be."

"All right," Mr. Summers said. "Open the papers. Harry, you open little Dave's."

Mr. Graves opened the slip of paper and there was a general sigh through the crowd as he held it up and everyone could see that it was blank. Nancy and Bill, Jr., opened theirs at the same time, and both beamed and laughed, turning around to the crowd and holding their slips of paper above their heads.

"Tessie," Mr. Summers said. There was a pause, and then Mr. Summers looked at Bill Hutchinson, and Bill unfolded his paper and showed it. It was blank.

"It's Tessie," Mr. Summers said, and his voice was hushed. "Show us her paper, Bill."

Bill Hutchinson went over to his wife and forced the slip of paper out of her hand. It had a black spot on it, the black spot Mr. Summers had made the night before with the heavy pencil in the coal-company office. Bill Hutchinson held it up, and there was a stir in the crowd.

"All right, folks," Mr. Summers said, "let's finish quickly."

Although the villagers had forgotten the ritual and lost the original black box, they still remembered to use stones. The pile of stones the boys had made earlier was ready; there were stones on the ground with the blowing scraps of paper that had come out of the box. Mrs. Delacroix selected a stone so large she had to pick it up with both hands and turned to Mrs. Dunbar. "Come on," she said. "Hurry up."

Mrs. Dunbar had small stones in both hands, and she said, gasping for breath, "I can't run at all. You'll have to go ahead and I'll catch up with you."

The children had stones already, and someone gave little Davy Hutchinson a few pebbles.

Tessie Hutchinson was in the center of a cleared space by now, and she held her hands out desperately as the villagers moved in on her. "It isn't fair," she said. A stone hit her on the side of the head.

Old Man Warner was saying, "Come on, come on, everyone." Steve Adams was in the front of the crowd of villagers, with Mrs. Graves beside him.

"It isn't fair, it isn't right," Mrs. Hutchinson screamed, and then they were upon her.

Activity: RESPONDING TO THE TEXT

1. What does the story's title lead you to expect? What other aspects of the story keep you from suspecting the outcome?
2. The characters in the story follow their tradition and adhere to its form without questioning it. Why are the characters so compliant and unquestioning? Why are readers usually appalled?
3. Do you agree with the depiction of human behavior in the story?
4. This story was published four years after the end of World War II. What political relevance might it have had for readers then?

Activity: SYNTHESIZING THE TEXTS

1. Genre films and rituals both appeal to people's desire for order and regularity. Do the readings present any possible explanations for people's desire for predictability? Are there other explanations you can add?

2. These readings have described the forms of several seemingly unrelated objects—a brain, a barbaric ritual, a water faucet, genre films. Identify a few other objects or events in your life that have prescribed forms. Discuss the ways each object or event could be changed without defeating its purpose. What must remain unchanged to keep the object's or event's function intact?

Writing Assignments

Academic Essays

1. Film

Many films (e.g., action/adventure, comedy, romance, detective) follow conventional forms. For example, a romance usually features a young man and woman who meet and are attracted to each other. Complications or forces beyond their control separate them. They overcome the obstacles and are reunited. The film ends with the assumption that they will live "happily ever after."

Choose a film that you think uses a traditional formula but that also varies the form to better fit the filmmaker's purpose. Review the information in Sobchack's article on genre films. List the basic elements of the genre of the film you have chosen. Then watch the film carefully and take notes about how the traditional form has been both preserved and changed. When you write your paper, you will probably need to describe the characteristics of the traditional form before you can begin to discuss how the film you have analyzed fits or does not fit this form. Your paper should also include a discussion of why the filmmaker may have thought that the changes were desirable or necessary.

2. Engineering/Architecture/Design

A basic design principle is that form should fit function. Choose a building, a room, an appliance, or a common household item and write an essay describing the ways its form either does or does not fit its function.

If your essay argues that the design does not fit your object's function, begin by collecting some information about how the design fails. Does the design make the object look like something it isn't? Does the design make it difficult to use? After you have analyzed the problem with the design, divide the information into limited topic paragraphs. In each paragraph, describe one design flaw as specifically as possible.

If your essay argues that the design does fit the function, begin by listing the elements of the design and their functions for each part of your item. Be specific: it might be helpful to review Norman's discussion of the felt-tip pen in the excerpt from *The Design of Everyday Things*. Choose a pattern for organizing your essay. For example, you might describe your object from outside to inside or from top to bottom.

3. Literature

Read "The Lottery" or another short story you enjoy and rewrite it in an entirely different form. You might take a mystery short story and write it as a police report or newspaper account. Or you might rewrite a romantic short story as a poem or a song. You might rewrite a story as a diary or personal log. You will find that you can't change the story's form without making other substantial changes. After you have rewritten the short story, write a brief analysis of how the change in form changed the story.

Workplace Writing

You are the head of a search committee for an opening at your workplace. The committee has interviewed several candidates, narrowed the choice to two finalists, held second interviews, and made its selection. Now you must communicate that decision to the two finalists. Using the advice in the Workplace Box on p. 178, write one "positive" reply letter to the candidate to whom you're offering the position. Write one "negative" reply letter using the indirect plan to the candidate to whom you are not offering the position. For models of business letters, consult Chapter 23.

Personal Writing

Brainstorm about the traditions important to you and your family. Generate as complete a list as possible: Include items like holiday observances and religious rituals, habits like evening walks or Friday night videos, foods or food preparations for special occasions, or the telling of favorite anecdotes. Choose one tradition that seems particularly interesting or revealing. Write a paper identifying the tradition, discussing the form the tradition takes, and exploring why you think that tradition and its form are important to you and your family.

POLISHING AND REFLECTING ON TEXTS

Learning from Other Student Writers

Sherlock Never Had It This Bad

Robert Zornes

To compare a film to the conventions of its genre (see the film assignment, p. 195), Robert Zornes chose X-Files, *a movie based on the popular television series.*

"Full circle" is the simplest and most descriptive term that could be used to explain one of the main differences between the film *X-Files: Fight the Future* and other films of the mystery genre. Having aspects of action/adventure, science-fiction, and horror, *X-Files* is not a typical mystery movie. However, it does closely follow the formula laid down by mystery films of old.

Sherlock Holmes and other mystery films usually begin with a crime, murder, or implausible situation. This being the case, *X-Files* begins as most mysteries do, with a crime. As the film opens, a young boy is mentally taken over by a shadowy creature. The antagonists of the film quickly arrive and kidnap the boy, murdering him to kill the alien inside. They then take the boy's body along with those of several others and disintegrate the evidence in a supposed terrorist bombing. Here you have an example of three things a mystery film could start with and all are presented within the first fifteen minutes of the film.

Fox Mulder and Dana Scully take the place of the typical hero, a position which is usually held by one cop, detective, or investigator. Rather than being called to the scene, Mulder and Scully stumble into the investigation mostly through misfortune and a little instinct. A detective or investigator will usually become aware of a crime and quickly begin to deduce the minuscule clues that had gone unnoticed by others. Much is the same with *X-Files*, the genius of Sherlock Holmes being transferred into Fox Mulder and Dana Scully. He has knowledge of the paranormal, whereas she has a background in medicine, and both are FBI agents. Clues don't come quite so easily for these two as they would for Holmes. Instead of putting all of the clues together with a sudden burst of realization, Mulder and Scully have to systematically go from one clue on to the next, never knowing where they may lead.

When the answers of the mystery have been deduced, the investigator normally would find the mastermind of the scheme. However, with *X-Files*, the audience is made aware of the criminals from the very beginning. In contrast, Mulder and Scully are unaware of the circumstances, or where they may take them, until the middle of the film. This is a break from the normal format, where the detectives would not know who is responsible until the very end of the film, at which point, they would bring those individuals to justice.

Detectives always get their man in the end. This statement doesn't apply to *X-Files*: not only do those responsible escape from justice, but they also go on to return to the same evil deeds from the beginning of the film, effectively closing the circle. This film closely follows the outline of the mystery genre movies that have come before. Although *X-Files* follows the outline, it does deviate from typical mystery guidelines. Our hero becomes heroes, the characters know early on who has committed the crime, and the conspirators escape from justice. In the end, *X-Files* completely goes off the path and has the villains partake in a semi-victory, proving you don't always get your man in a mystery and justice isn't always served.

Activity: RESPONDING TO THE TEXT

1. What is the essay's thesis? Where is the thesis statement located?
2. What topic does each paragraph discuss? Does Zornes use topic sentences? What kind of supporting evidence does he use in the paragraphs? Is his evidence convincing?
3. Where do you learn what Zornes means by the first words in the essay, "Full circle"? What type of conclusion does Zornes use? Is it effective for his purposes?

Activity: PEER WORKSHOP   DAEDALUS ONLINE

Using one of the essays written for this chapter, writers will first examine their own papers, answering the questions below. Then a partner will read the paper, following the specific directions below. When reviewing the comments your partner wrote about your paper, compare them to your own responses. Did the reader find the same strengths and weaknesses you did? If not, why not?

Writers respond to these questions before the workshop:
- What is your essay's main point?
- What is the point of each of the body paragraphs?
- Which paragraph do you think is the strongest? Why?
- Which paragraph needs improvement? What are the difficulties with this paragraph?

Readers respond to the following questions:
1. What is the essay's main point? Write "Delete?" next to any paragraphs or sections that don't seem to add information useful for explaining or proving the main point.
2. Look at each paragraph:
   - If it doesn't have a topic sentence, put "TS?" next to it.
   - Underline any information in the paragraph that does not seem necessary to making the point.
   - Is the paragraph missing any necessary information, evidence, or examples? Make suggestions about additions in the margin.
3. How does the writer catch the readers' attention in the introduction? Does the introduction contain any of the following weaknesses:
   - overly general opening statement
   - an anecdote that is not clearly linked to the main point
   - background information inappropriate for the intended readers
   - uninteresting, unrelated, or unanswerable questions
   If so, identify the problem next to the introductory paragraph.

4. How does the conclusion cause the readers to remember and reconsider the points made in the essay? Does the conclusion contain any of the following weaknesses?

- a summary that too mechanically repeats the thesis and topic sentences
- an overstatement of the importance of the issue
- a quotation or anecdote unrelated to the main point
- an inference or judgment that doesn't follow smoothly and logically from the rest of the essay

If so, identify the problem next to the concluding paragraph.

Activity: PROOFREADING YOUR WORK

Learning to use commas correctly can be confusing. Review a few of the most common uses of commas, by finding answers to the following questions:

- What is a compound sentence?
- Where is a comma placed in a compound sentence?
- What is an introductory phrase or clause?
- When are commas used to separate introductory phases or clauses from the main clause?

Now read your paper carefully, underlining introductory phrases and clauses and putting brackets around compound sentences. Place commas where they are necessary.

Activity: POSTSCRIPT

1. Which of the introduction strategies presented in this chapter seems most appealing to you as a reader? Which would be easiest for you to use as a writer?
2. Review the readings from this chapter and the explanations in the text itself, noticing how the writers use topic sentences. Does the use of topic sentences make the paragraphs clearer or easier to read?
3. What features of the form of this chapter helped you as a reader?

SUPPORTING EVIDENCE

P R E V I E W

This chapter's explanation about how to strengthen your writing by including specific facts, details, and examples will answer these questions:

- Why do you need to include facts and examples in your papers?
- How can you make your writing more convincing?
- How can you make your papers longer?

L E A R N I N G   A B O U T   T E X T S

Understanding Details and Examples

Memories, ideas, and plans are often stored in our minds as pictures or stories. When we remember first grade, we probably can reconstruct a fairly detailed image of our teacher, the classroom, and the other children. When we "look" into the future to plan a dinner menu, a career move, or a vacation, we visualize our actions and their outcomes. Many of our thoughts are "seen" in our mind's eye as if we are looking at photographs or movies.

Writers use words to recreate their mental images. The writer's goal is to produce a word picture that recreates a mental image so vividly and accurately that the readers "see" the exact image in their own minds. In that way, the readers will understand the writer's message clearly.

To create a clear, accurate image, writers use details and examples. Otherwise the readers will not be able to picture—to understand—the writer's ideas. As you learned in Chapter 1, all texts must be completed by readers. If the writer leaves gaps that are too wide, the reader may misinterpret the text. When we have trouble understanding something we read, it is often because the writer has not provided us with enough details or examples. For example, if you receive a note that says, "Order food for tomorrow's conference, and meet me at the hotel at 8:00, so we can take care

Using Examples

You can help your readers visualize your message by using examples, sometimes called "illustrations." If you were reading a magazine article about the use of animals in medical research in which the authors claim that researchers treat animals cruelly, you might have trouble understanding the nature and extent of that mistreatment; however, if the article were accompanied by a photo of a monkey in a small cage, you would have a better understanding of what the authors mean by cruel treatment. If the authors could not include a photograph, they might have to use a verbal illustration instead, using words to describe a particular lab's facilities for housing its research animals. This example would help clarify the readers' understanding of the authors' ideas.

General statements leave readers with questions that might be answered by examples. For instance, a statement in a training manual that says, "Be helpful to customers," might leave the trainees with questions such as "How can I be helpful?" or "What kind of help is appropriate?" If the general statement were followed by some examples, these questions would be answered. The manual might add an illustration such as "Assist customers in finding the correct size or color," or "Offer to hold purchases at the desk until the customer is ready to buy." These examples give the trainees a clearer picture of the helpful behavior the employer is encouraging.

An example can be a word or a short phrase, or it can be as long as a paragraph. The length of the example depends on the context. Read the following statements:

1. Many jobs require more writing than you might expect.
2. Your body language can reveal your mood or attitude.
3. "Entire cultures operate on elaborate systems of indirectness." (Deborah Tannen, *You Just Don't Understand*)

Because the above statements don't contain any examples to create images for the readers, they may be boring or unclear. Now read the revised versions of those passages, in which the examples clarify the meaning:

1. Many jobs, such as nursing and engineering, require more writing than you might expect.
2. Your body language can reveal your mood or attitude. Crossing your arms across your chest, for instance, may signal a defensive or insecure attitude.
3. "Entire cultures operate on elaborate systems of indirectness. For example, I discovered in a small research project that most Greeks assumed that a wife who asked, 'Would you like to go to the party?' was hinting that she wanted to go. They felt that she wouldn't bring it up if she didn't want to go. Furthermore, they felt, she would not state her preference outright because that would sound like a demand. Indirectness was the appropriate means for communicating her preference." (Deborah Tannen, *You Just Don't Understand*)

FYI: For more on writing illustrations, see pp. 327–328.

Activity: WRITER'S LOG

Find three instances where examples are used in this chapter. Read the paragraphs without the examples and notice how much meaning is lost. Next find one instance where an example could have been added to this chapter to clarify the message. Think of a good example to add to the passage.

Understanding Evidence

Often when we think of evidence, we think of the proof of guilt or innocence presented during trials. In court cases, the attorneys try to convince the judges or jurors that their clients' statements are true by presenting corroborating witnesses, physical evidence, or expert testimony. The lawyers hope that by supplying enough evidence in their clients' interest, they will persuade the courts to decide in their favor.

When you are writing for the purpose of convincing someone that your ideas are reasonable, you need to provide evidence for your conclusions or opinions, just as attorneys do in trials. Evidence can be

- facts
- examples
- information or quotations from experts.

FYI: For more on the distinction between facts and opinions, see p. 55.

The kind and amount of evidence you use depends on your paper's purpose, context, and audience. If you were writing a persuasive paper convincing readers to change their behavior or beliefs, you would use more rigorous evidence than if you were writing an informational memo or essay. If you were writing in a formal setting, such as a professional journal or published report, you would include more complete and factual evidence than if you were writing an informal essay. Writing to your supervisor or professor requires more rigorous evidence than writing to friends and family. For instance, if you were writing a letter to a friend about your experiences at college and you concluded that professors are less helpful than high-school teachers, you probably would be giving enough evidence if you recounted a few of your own experiences with professors at your school. However, if you were writing a formal report on a study done by your university's administration of the faculty's effectiveness, and you concluded that the professors are less helpful than high-school teachers, you

Activity: BUILDING AN ESSAY

Read what you wrote for the "Building an Essay" assignment in Chapter 5. Can you think of any examples that would support your ideas or clarify your explanations? Add them to your essay in appropriate paragraphs or create new paragraphs for the examples.

would need more rigorous evidence. Statistical results of surveys, interviews, and observations completed in the study would be included along with some specific examples. A convincing paper contains evidence of an appropriate quality and quantity.

Using Facts as Evidence

An attorney trying to convince jurors of a client's innocence will not merely state, "My client is innocent." A lawyer would present facts to support that claim (e.g., Witnesses say the perpetrator was blond, but my client is brunette; the crime took place at 9:00 A.M. when my client was getting a haircut). Facts are statements that can be proven objectively. To be relevant, a fact must help to prove your point.

Opinions and conclusions are more convincing when they are backed up with a sufficient number of appropriate facts. A writer arguing that local public schools do not adequately prepare students for college mathematics might cite his own placement in a developmental mathematics course. Although this information might be factual, it is not sufficient. To prove the thesis, the writer would have to supply data about the placement in mathematics courses of all students from the local public schools over a period of years.

In some cases, personal facts can be relevant and appropriate. For example, a writer trying to prove that it is difficult to break a bad habit might include the fact that she spent three years trying to quit smoking. As long as this personal fact was just one of a number of supporting facts and examples, its use would be justified.

Using Examples as Evidence

Examples provide excellent support for opinions and conclusions. To be relevant, the examples, like factual evidence, must help to prove the writer's point, as in the following paragraph:

> People are not always aware of how much they are influenced by their peers. How many people who get tattoos have friends who have them? Would someone decide to start skateboarding without following the example set by peers? My friend recently got her nose pierced. She said she did it because she thought it looked good, but I know she never would have thought of a ring in her nose as looking good before she started hanging out with a group of friends who also had pierced various parts of their bodies. Many times we think we do things to please ourselves, and maybe that's partially true, but what pleases us is often shaped by those around us.

To find facts to support your ideas, you can use an online almanac. For comprehensive information on a variety of topics, consult Infoplease at

☞   http://www.infoplease.com

If you want to find listings of online almanacs, go to the Internet Public Library at

☞   http://www.ipl.org/ref/RR/static/ref0500.html

Writers must also supply enough examples to fulfill their purpose. If you are trying to inform your audience, one or two short examples might be sufficient to explain your point. But if you are trying to persuade readers about a controversial point, you need a number of powerful examples to be convincing.

When using examples as evidence, develop each example in detail, and always make a clear connection between the example and the point you are supporting.

Using Expert Testimony as Evidence

Lawyers often call in expert witnesses to support their claims. A lawyer claiming that a client cannot be held responsible for a crime because the client is insane supplies testimony from psychiatrists to prove the point. To be convincing, writers—like lawyers—use the best expert testimony possible. Usually, in court cases and in writing, experts are considered more reliable if

- they are objective
- they are respected in their field
- their knowledge is up-to-date.

Although in most cases experts are people with degrees, publications, or credentials in the relevant field of study, sometimes the best expert is someone who has some personal experience with the issue. For example, a victim of crime might be considered an expert on the mental state of crime victims.

Sometimes you will use quotations taken directly from interviews with experts, but more frequently your expert testimony will be derived from sources you read. When you quote evidence from books or periodicals, you are using expert witnesses secondhand. Just as in courts of law, supporting evidence from books or periodicals should be

- from an objective source
- credible
- up-to-date.

For example, information about a company's environmental record found in its annual report might be less objective than information obtained through a governmental agency or nonprofit foundation. The most convincing evidence will come from sources that are respected by people who work in the field. Articles about illnesses in *The New England Journal of Medicine* would be recognized by health professionals as more reliable than those in a popular magazine. Finally, evidence should be up-to-date. If you are writing a paper about the depletion of the ozone layer, evidence from studies done five years ago would be out-of-date.

FYI: For information on citing and documenting evidence from sources, see Chapter 21.

Activity: WORKING TOGETHER

Read "Why Schools Flunk Biology" on pp. 000–000. Mark all the places where the article presents facts, examples, or expert testimony. Then try to estimate what percentage of the article is supporting evidence. In small groups, compare your results.

Activity: BUILDING AN ESSAY

Once again, read the essay you are writing for this assignment, and consider whether there are any facts or expert testimony that could be added to strengthen your paper. You may need to do some research or interviewing to gather the information you need. Then add the facts or expert testimony to the appropriate paragraphs in your essay.

Activity: COMPUTER WORKSHOP

Write a paragraph persuading someone to take some action about her or his personal life, health, or politics. As you draft your paper, mark areas you need to develop by underlining or boldfacing them. Use brackets to enclose comments to yourself. Highlight, boldface, or capitalize the comments so they'll stand out. At the end of the draft, list the facts or information you need to gather or the examples you want to develop. As you gather the necessary information, insert it into your document and delete the notes you made to yourself.

The Workplace

USING EVIDENCE IN WORKPLACE DOCUMENTS

Workplace readers also value evidence and examples, but they may look for them in different places in the document. Short examples and directly relevant evidence may go directly into a memo or letter, but more extensive evidence may be added in attachments.

Writing Succinctly

Like college texts, workplace documents, whether their purpose is to record, inform, or persuade, are strengthened by the inclusion of specific evidence. In college writing, lively, interesting details that pique a reader's interest are appreciated. Effective workplace texts, however, are almost always succinct. Because employees often have to read, absorb, and act on information from many texts, they are understandably impatient with unnecessarily long texts. In workplace writing, brief, clear, easy-to-read documents containing all the pertinent evidence are highly valued.

Using Attachments

In academic and personal writing, evidence is included in the text. In workplace writing, texts are often too brief to include all the relevant supporting evidence. Writers usually place long or complicated evidence in attachments to the text so that readers can read the text quickly and refer to documentation.

READING AND WRITING TEXTS

Readings

These readings all discuss school, particularly high school, using details, examples, and evidence to support the authors' points. As you read these selections, pay attention to the type of evidence each author uses, and decide whether the evidence seems convincing.

Activity: PREREADING

In your Writer's Log, respond to these questions:

1. What do you think high schools do well? What do they do poorly?
2. How well did your high school meet your educational and social needs?
3. What do you imagine would have been the attitude most students had toward their high school in their senior year?

What High School Is

Theodore R. Sizer

Theodore R. Sizer's report "What High School Is," part of a study done for the National Association of Independent Schools, is from a 1984 book titled Horace's Compromise: The Dilemma of the American High School. *Sizer describes one student's day in detail. Based on his observations, Sizer draws several conclusions about American high-school education.*

Mark, sixteen and a genial eleventh-grader, rides a bus to Franklin High School, arriving at 7:45. It is an Assembly Day, so the schedule is adapted to allow for a meeting of the entire school. He hangs out with his friends, first outside school and then inside, by his locker. He carries a pile of textbooks and notebooks; in all, it weighs eight and a half pounds.

From 7:30 to 8:19, with nineteen other students, he is in Room 304 for English class. The Shakespeare play being read this year by the eleventh grade is *Romeo and Juliet*. The teacher, Ms. Viola, has various students in turn take parts and read out loud. Periodically, she interrupts the (usually halting) recitations to ask whether the thread of the conversation in the play is clear. Mark is entertained by the stumbling readings of some of his classmates. He hopes he will not be asked to be Romeo, particularly if his current steady, Sally, is Juliet. There is a good deal of giggling in class, and much attention paid to who may be called on next. Ms. Viola reminds the class of a test on this part of the play to be given next week.

The bell rings at 8:19. Mark goes to the boys' room, where he sees a classmate who he thinks is a wimp but who constantly tries to be a buddy. Mark avoids the leech by rushing off. On the way, he notices two boys engaged in some sort of transaction, probably over marijuana. He pays them no attention. 8:24. Typing class. The rows of desks that embrace big office machines are almost filled before the bell. Mark is uncomfortable here: typing class is girl country. The teacher constantly threatens what to Mark is a humiliatingly female future: "Your employer won't like these erasures." The minutes during the period are spent copying a letter from a handbook onto business stationery. Mark struggles to keep from looking at his work; the teacher wants him to watch only the material from which he is copying. Mark is frustrated, uncomfortable, and scared that he will not complete his letter by the class's end, which would be embarrassing.

Nine tenths of the students present at school that day are assembled in the auditorium by the 9:18 bell. The dilatory tenth still stumble in, running down aisles. Annoyed class deans try to get the mob settled. The curtains part; the program is a concert by a student rock group. Their electronic gear flashes under the lights, and the five boys and one girl in the group work hard at being casual. Their movements on stage are studiously at three-quarter time, and they chat with one another as though the tumultuous screaming of their schoolmates were totally inaudible. The girl balances on a stool; the boys crank up the music. It is very soft rock, the sanitized lyrics surely cleared with the assistant principal. The girl sings, holding the mike close to her mouth, but can scarcely be heard. Her light voice is tentative, and the lyrics indecipherable. The guitars, amplified, are tuneful, however, and the drums are played with energy.

The students around Mark—all juniors, since they are seated by class—alternately slouch in their upholstered, hinged seats, talking to one another, or sit forward, leaning on the chair backs in front of them, watching the band. A boy near Mark shouts noisily at the microphone-fondling singer, "Bite it . . . ohhh," and the area around Mark explodes in vulgar male laughter, but quickly subsides. A teacher walks down the aisle. Songs continue, to great applause. Assembly is over at 9:46, two minutes early.

9:53 and biology class. Mark was at a different high school last year and did not take this course there as a tenth-grader. He is in it now, and all but one of his classmates are a year younger than he. He sits on the side, not taking part in the chatter that goes on after the bell. At 9:57, the public address system goes on, with the announcements of the day. After a few words from the principal ("Here's today's cheers and jeers . . ." with a cheer for the winning basketball team and a jeer for the spectators who made a ruckus at the gymnasium), the task is taken over by officers of ASB (Associated Student Bodies). There is an appeal for "bat bunnies." Carnations are for sale by the Girls' League. Miss Indian American is coming. Students are auctioning off their services (background catcalls are heard) to earn money for the prom. Nominees are needed for the ballot for school bachelor and school bachelorette. The announcements end with a "thought for the day. When you throw a little mud, you lose a little ground."

At 10:04 the biology class finally turns to science. The teacher, Mr. Robbins, has placed one of several labeled laboratory specimens—some are pinned in frames, others swim in formaldehyde—on each of the classroom's eight laboratory tables. The three or so students whose chairs circle each of these benches are to study the specimen and make notes about it or drawings of it. After a few minutes each group of three will move to another table. The teacher points out that these specimens are of organisms already studied in previous classes. He says that the period-long test set for the following day will involve observing some of these specimens—then to be without labels—and writing an identifying paragraph on each. Mr. Robbins points out that some of the printed labels ascribe the specimens names different from those given in the textbook. He explains that biologists often give several names to the same organism.

The class now falls to peering, writing, and quiet talking. Mr. Robbins comes over to Mark, and in whispered words asks him to carry a requisition form for science department materials to the business office. Mark, because of his "older" status, is usually chosen by Robbins for this kind of errand. Robbins gives Mark the form and a green hall pass to show to any teacher who might challenge him, on his way to the office, for being out of a classroom. The errand takes Mark four minutes. Meanwhile Mark's group is hard at work but gets to only three of the specimens before the bell rings at 10:42. As the students surge out, Robbins shouts a reminder about a "double" laboratory period on Thursday.

Between classes one of the seniors asks Mark whether he plans to be a candidate for schoolwide office next year. Mark says no. He starts to explain. The 10:47 bell rings, meaning that he is late for French class.

There are fifteen students in Monsieur Bates's language class. He hands out tests taken the day before: "*C'est bien fait, Etienne . . . c'est mieux, Marie . . . Tch, tch, Robert . . .*" Mark notes his C+ and peeks at the A– in front of Susanna, next to him. The class has been assigned seats by M. Bates: Mark resents sitting next to prissy, brainy Susanna. Bates starts by asking a student to read a question and give the correct answer. "*James, question un.*" James haltingly reads the question and gives the answer that Bates, now speaking English, says is incomplete. In due course: "*Mark, question cinq.*" Mark does his bit, and the sequence goes on, the eight quiz questions and answers filling about twenty minutes of time.

"Turn to page forty-nine. *Maintenant, lisez après moi . . .*" and Bates reads a sentence and has the class echo it. Mark is embarrassed by this and mumbles with a barely audible sound. Others, like Susanna, keep the decibel count up, so Mark can hide. This I-say-you-repeat drill is interrupted once by the public address system, with an announcement about a meeting for the cheerleaders. Bates finishes the class, almost precisely at the bell, with a homework assignment. The students are to review these sentences for a brief quiz the following day. Mark takes note of the assignment, because he knows that tomorrow will be a day of busy-work in French class. Much though he dislikes oral drills, they are better than the workbook stuff that Bates hands out. Write, write, write, for Bates to throw away, Mark thinks.

11:36. Down to the cafeteria, talking noisily, hanging, munching. Getting to room 104 by 12:17: U.S. history. The teacher is sitting cross-legged on his desk when Mark comes in, heatedly arguing with three students over the fracas that had followed the previous night's basketball game. The teacher, Mr. Suslovic, while agreeing that the spectators from their school certainly were provoked, argues that they should neither have been so obviously obscene in yelling at the opposing cheerleaders nor have allowed Coke cans to be rolled out on the floor. The three students keep saying that "it isn't fair." Apparently they and some others had been assigned "Saturday mornings" (detentions) by the principal for the ruckus.

At 12:34, the argument appears to subside. The uninvolved students, including Mark, are in their seats, chatting amiably. Mr. Suslovic climbs off his desk and starts talking: "We've almost finished this unit, chapters nine and ten . . ." The students stop chattering among themselves and turn toward Suslovic. Several slouch down in their chairs. Some open notebooks. Most have the five-pound textbook on their desks.

Suslovic lectures on the cattle drives, from north Texas to railroads west of St. Louis. He breaks up this narrative with questions ("Why were the railroad lines laid largely east to west?"), directed at nobody in particular and eventually answered by Suslovic himself. Some students take notes. Mark doesn't. A student walks in the open door, hands Mr. Suslovic a list, and starts whispering with him. Suslovic turns from the class and hears out this messenger. He then asks, "Does anyone know where Maggie Sharp is?" Someone answers, "Sick at home," someone else says, "I thought I saw her at lunch." Genial consternation. Finally Suslovic tells the messenger, "Sorry, we can't help you," and returns to the class: "Now, where were we?" He goes on for some minutes. The bell rings. Suslovic forgets to give the homework assignment.

1:11 and Algebra II. There is a commotion in the hallway: someone's locker is rumored to have been opened by the assistant principal and a narcotics agent. In the five-minute passing time, Mark hears the story three times and three ways. A locker had been broken into by another student. It was Mr. Gregory and a narc. It was the cops, and they did it without Gregory's knowing. Mrs. Ames, the mathematics teacher, has not heard anything about it. Several of the nineteen students try to tell her and start arguing among themselves. "O.K., that's enough." She hands out the day's problem, one sheet to each student. Mark sees with dismay that it is a single, complicated "word" problem about some train that, while traveling at 84 mph, due west, passes a car that was going due east at 55 mph. Mark struggles: Is it $d = rt$ or $t = rd$? The class becomes quiet, writing, while Mrs. Ames writes some additional, short problems on the blackboard. "Time's up." A sigh; most students still writing. A muffled "Shit." Mrs. Ames frowns. "Come on, now." She collects papers, but it takes four minutes for her to corral them all.

"Copy down the problems from the board." A minute passes. "William, try number one." William suggests an approach. Mrs. Ames corrects and cajoles, and William finally gets it right. Mark watches two kids to his right passing notes; he tries to read them, but the handwriting is illegible from his distance. He hopes he is not called on, and he isn't. Only three students are asked to puzzle out an answer. The bell rings at 2:00. Mrs. Ames shouts a homework assignment over the resulting hubbub.

Mark leaves his books in his locker. He remembers he has homework, but figures that he can do it during English class the next day. He knows that there will be an in-class presentation of one of the *Romeo and Juliet* scenes and that he will not be in it. The teacher will not notice his homework writing, or won't do anything about it if she does.

Mark passes various friends heading toward the gym, members of the basketball teams. Like most students, Mark isn't an active school athlete. However, he is associated with the yearbook staff. Although he is not taking "Yearbook" for credit as an English course, he is contributing photographs. Mark takes twenty minutes checking into the yearbook staff's headquarters (the classroom of its faculty adviser) and getting some assignments of pictures from his boss, the senior who is the photography editor. Mark knows that if he pleases his boss and the faculty adviser, he'll take that editor's post for the next year. He'll get English credit for his work then.

After gossiping a bit with the yearbook staff, Mark will leave school by 2:35 and go home. His grocery market bagger's job is from 4:45 to 8:00, the rush hour for the store. He'll have a snack at 4:30, and his mother will save him some supper to eat at 8:30. She will ask whether he has any homework, and he'll tell her no. Tomorrow, and virtually every other tomorrow, will be the same for Mark, save for the lack of the assembly: each period then will be five minutes longer.

Most Americans have an uncomplicated vision of what secondary education should be. Their conception of high school is remarkably uniform across the country, a striking fact, given the size and diversity of the United States and the politically decentralized character of the schools. This uniformity is of several generations' standing. It has, however, two appearances, each quite different from the other, one of words and the other of practice, a world of political rhetoric and Mark's world.

A California high school's general goals, set out in 1979, could serve equally well most of America's high schools, public and private. This school had as its ends:

- Fundamental scholastic achievement . . . to acquire knowledge and share in the traditionally academic fundamentals . . . to develop the ability to make decisions, to solve problems, to reason independently, and to accept responsibility for self-evaluation and continuing self-improvement.
- Career and economic competence . . .
- Citizenship and civil responsibility . . .
- Competence in human and social relations . . .

- Moral and ethical values . . .
- Self-realization and mental and physical health . . .
- Aesthetic awareness . . .
- Cultural diversity . . .[1]

In addition to its optimistic rhetoric, what distinguishes this list is its comprehensiveness. The high school is to touch most aspects of an adolescent's existence—mind, body, morals, values, career. No one of these areas is given especial prominence. School people arrogate to themselves an obligation to all.

An example of the wide acceptability of these goals is found in the courts. Forced to present a detailed definition of "thorough and efficient education," elementary as well as secondary, a West Virginia judge sampled the best of conventional wisdom and concluded that

> there are eight general elements of a thorough and efficient system of education: (a) Literacy, (b) The ability to add, subtract, multiply, and divide numbers, (c) Knowledge of government to the extent the child will be equipped as a citizen to make informed choices among persons and issues that affect his own governance, (d) Self-knowledge and knowledge of his or her total environment to allow the child to intelligently choose life works—to know his or her options, (e) Work-training and advanced academic training as the child may intelligently choose, (f) Recreational pursuit, (g) Interests in all creative arts such as music, theater, literature, and the visual arts, and (h) Social ethics, both behavioral and abstract, to facilitate compatibility with others in this society.[2]

That these eight—now powerfully part of the debate over the purpose and practice of education in West Virginia—are reminiscent of the influential list, "The Seven Cardinal Principles of Secondary Education," promulgated in 1918 by the National Education Association, is no surprise.[3] The rhetoric of high school purpose has been uniform and consistent for decades. Americans agree on the goals for their high schools.

That agreement is convenient, but it masks the fact that virtually all the words in these goal statements beg definition. Some schools have labored long to identify specific criteria beyond them; the result has been lists of daunting pseudospecificity and numbing earnestness. However, most leave the words undefined

---

[1] Shasta High School, Redding, California. An eloquent and analogous statement, "The Essentials of Education," one stressing explicitly the "interdependence of skills and content" that is implicit in the Shasta High School statement, was issued in 1980 by a coalition of educational associations. Organizations for the Essentials of Education (Urbana, Illinois).

[2] Judge Arthur M. Recht, in his order resulting from *Pauley v. Kelly,* 1979, as reprinted in *Education Week,* May 26, 1982, p. 10. See also, in *Education Week,* January 16, 1983, pp. 21, 24, Jonathan P. Sher, "The Struggle to Fulfill a Judicial Mandate: How Not to 'Reconstruct' Education in W. Va."

[3] Bureau of Education, Department of the Interior, "Cardinal Principles of Secondary Education: A Report of the Commission on the Reorganization of Secondary Education, appointed by the National Education Association," *Bulletin,* no. 35 (Washington: U.S. Government Printing Office, 1918).

and let the momentum of traditional practice speak for itself. That is why analyzing how Mark spends his time is important: from watching him one uncovers the important purposes of education, the ones that shape practice. Mark's day is similar to that of other high school students across the country, as similar as the rhetoric of one goal statement to others'. Of course, there are variations, but the extent of consistency in the shape of school routine for a large and diverse adolescent population is extraordinary, indicating more graphically than any rhetoric the measure of agreement in America about what one does in high school, and, by implication, what it is for.

The basic organizing structures in schools are familiar. Above all, students are grouped by age (that is, freshman, sophomore, junior, senior), and all are expected to take precisely the same time—around 720 school days over four years, to be precise—to meet the requirements for a diploma. When one is out of his grade level, he can feel odd, as Mark did in his biology class. The goals are the same for all, and the means to achieve them are also similar.

Young males and females are treated remarkably alike; the schools' goals are the same for each gender. In execution, there are differences, as those pressing sex discrimination suits have made educators intensely aware. The students in metalworking classes are mostly male; those in home economics, mostly female. But it is revealing how much less sex discrimination there is in high schools than in other American institutions. For many young women, the most liberated hours of their week are in school.

School is to be like a job: you start in the morning and end in the afternoon, five days a week. You don't get much of a lunch hour, so you go home early, unless you are an athlete or are involved in some special school or extracurricular activity. School is conceived of as the children's workplace, and it takes young people off parents' hands and out of the labor market during prime-time work hours. Not surprisingly, many students see going to school as little more than a dogged necessity. They perceive the day-to-day routine, a Minnesota study reports, as one of "boredom and lethargy." One of the students summarizes: School is "boring, restless, tiresome, puts ya to sleep, tedious, monotonous, pain in the neck."[4]

The school schedule is a series of units of time: the clock is king. The base time block is about fifty minutes in length. Some schools, on what they call modular scheduling, split that fifty-minute block into two or even three pieces. Most schools have double periods for laboratory work, especially in the sciences, or four-hour units for the small numbers of students involved in intensive vocational or other work-study programs. The flow of all school activity arises from or is blocked by these time units. "How much time do I have with my kids" is the teacher's key question.

Because there are many claims for those fifty-minute blocks, there is little time set aside for rest between them, usually no more than three to ten minutes, depending on how big the school is and, consequently, how far students and teachers have to walk from class to class. As a result, there is a frenetic quality to the school day, a sense of sustained restlessness. For the adolescents, there are frequent

---

[4]Diane Hedin, Paula Simon, and Michael Robin, *Minnesota Youth Poll: Youth's Views on School and School Discipline.* Minnesota Report 184 (1983), Agricultural Experiment Station, University of Minnesota, p. 13.

changes of room and fellow students, each change giving tempting opportunities for distraction, which are stoutly resisted by teachers. Some schools play soft music during these "passing times," to quiet the multitude, one principal told me.

Many teachers have a chance for a coffee break. Few students do. In some city schools where security is a problem, students must be in class for seven consecutive periods, interrupted by a heavily monitored twenty-minute lunch period for small groups, starting as early as 10:30 A.M. and running to after 1:00 P.M. A high premium is placed on punctuality and on "being where you're supposed to be." Obviously, a low premium is placed on reflection and repose. The students rush from class to class to collect knowledge. Savoring it, it is implied, is not to be done much in school, nor is such meditation really much admired. The picture that these familiar patterns yield is that of an academic supermarket. The purpose of going to school is to pick things up, in an organized and predictable way, the faster the better.

What is supposed to be picked up is remarkably consistent among all sorts of high schools. Most schools specifically mandate three out of every five courses a student selects. Nearly all of these mandates fall into five areas—English, social studies, mathematics, science, and physical education. On the average, English is required to be taken each year, social studies and physical education three out of the four high school years, and mathematics and science one or two years. Trends indicate that in the mid-eighties there is likely to be an increase in the time allocated to these last two subjects. Most students take classes in these four major academic areas beyond the minimum requirements, sometimes in such special areas as journalism and "yearbook," offshoots of English departments.[5]

Press most adults about what high school is for, and you hear these subjects listed. *High school? That's where you learn English and math and that sort of thing.* Ask students, and you get the same answer. High school is to "teach" these "subjects."

What is often absent is any definition of these subjects or any rationale for them. They are just there, labels. Under those labels lie a multitude of things. A great deal of material is supposed to be "covered"; most of these courses are surveys, great sweeps of the stuff of their parent disciplines.

While there is often a sequence *within* subjects—algebra before trigonometry, "first-year" French before "second-year" French—there is rarely a coherent relationship or sequence *across* subjects. Even the most logically related matters—reading ability as a precondition for the reading of history books, and certain mathematical concepts or skills before the study of some physics—are only loosely coordinated, if at all. There is little demand for a synthesis of it all; English, mathematics, and the rest are discrete items, to be picked up individually. The incentive for picking them up is largely through tests and, with success at these, in credits earned.

Coverage within subjects is the key priority. If some imaginative teacher makes a proposal to force the marriage of, say, mathematics and physics or to require some culminating challenges to students to use several objects in the solution of a complex problem, and if this proposal will take "time" away from other things, opposition is usually phrased in terms of what may be thus for-

---

[5]I am indebted to Harold F. Sizer and Lyde E. Sizer for a survey of the diploma requirements of fifty representative secondary schools, completed for *A Study of High Schools*.

gone. If we do that, we'll have to give up colonial history. We won't be able to get to programming. We'll not be able to read *Death of a Salesman*. There isn't time. The protesters usually win out.

The subjects come at a student like Mark in random order, a kaleidoscope of worlds: algebraic formulae to poetry to French verbs to Ping-Pong to the War of the Spanish Succession, all before lunch. Pupils are to pick up these things. Tests measure whether the picking up has been successful.

The lack of connection between stated goals, such as those of the California high school cited earlier, and the goals inherent in school practice is obvious and, curiously, tolerated. Most striking is the gap between statements about "self-realization and mental and physical growth" or "moral and ethical values"—common rhetoric in school documents—and practice. Most physical education programs have neither the time nor the focus really to ensure fitness. Mental health is rarely defined. Neither are ethical values, save at the negative extremes, such as opposition to assault or dishonesty. Nothing in the regimen of a day like Mark's signals direct or implicit teaching in this area. The "school boy code" (not ratting on a fellow student) protects the marijuana pusher, and a leechlike associate is shrugged off without concern. The issue of the locker search was pushed aside, as not appropriate for class time.

Most students, like Mark, go to class in groups of twenty to twenty-seven students. The expected attendance in some schools, particularly those in low-income areas, is usually higher, often thirty-five students per class, but high absentee rates push the actual numbers down. About twenty-five per class is an average figure for expected attendance, and the actual numbers are somewhat lower. There are remarkably few students who go to class in groups much larger or smaller than twenty-five.[6]

A student such as Mark sees five or six teachers per day; their differing styles and expectations are part of his kaleidoscope. High school staffs are highly specialized: guidance counselors rarely teach mathematics, mathematics teachers rarely teach English, principals rarely do any classroom instruction. Mark, then, is known a little bit by a number of people, each of whom sees him in one specialized situation. No one may know him as a "whole person"—unless he becomes a special problem or has special needs.

Save in extracurricular or coaching situations, such as in athletics, drama, or shop classes, there is little opportunity for sustained conversation between student and teacher. The mode is a one-sentence or two-sentence exchange: *Mark, when was Grover Cleveland president?* Let's see, was 1890 . . . or something . . . wasn't he the one . . . he was elected twice, wasn't he . . . *Yes . . . Gloria, can you get the dates right?* Dialogue is strikingly absent, and as a result the opportunity of teachers to challenge students' ideas in a systematic and logical way is limited. Given the rushed, full quality of the school day, it can seldom happen. One must infer that careful probing of students' thinking is not a high priority. How one gains (to quote the California school's statement of goals again) "the ability to make decisions, to solve problems, to reason independently, and to accept responsibility for self-evaluation and continuing self-improvement" without being challenged is difficult to imagine. One certainly doesn't learn these things merely from lectures and textbooks.

---

[6]Education Research Service, Inc., *Class Size: A Summary of Research* (Arlington, Virginia, 1978), and *Class Size Research: A Critique of Recent Meta-Analyses* (Arlington, Virginia, 1980).

Most schools are nice places. Mark and his friends enjoy being in theirs. The adults who work in school generally like adolescents. The academic pressures are limited, and the accommodations to students are substantial. For example, if many members of an English class have jobs after school, the English teacher's expectations for them are adjusted, downward. In a word, school is sensitively accommodating, as long as students are punctual, where they are supposed to be, and minimally dutiful about picking things up from the clutch of courses in which they enroll.

This characterization is not pretty, but it is accurate, and it serves to describe the vast majority of American secondary schools. "Taking subjects" in a systematized, conveyer-belt way is what one does in high school. That this process is, in substantial respects, not related to the rhetorical purposes of education is tolerated by most people, perhaps because they do not really either believe in those ill-defined goals or, in their heart of hearts, believe that schools can or should even try to achieve them. The students are happy taking subjects. The parents are happy, because that's what they did in high school. The rituals, the most important of which is graduation, remain intact. The adolescents are supervised safely and constructively most of the time, during the morning and afternoon hours, and they are off the labor market. That is what high school is all about.

Activity: RESPONDING TO THE TEXT

1. The first half of "What High School Is" is an extremely detailed description of one day of one student in one high school. Do you think Sizer includes too many details? Why might he have thought it useful to include all these details about one student?

2. In the second half of "What High School Is" Sizer draws some conclusions about high school. What kind of evidence and examples does he use to support his conclusions? Pick out two and explain in what ways these examples or pieces of evidence are appropriate or inappropriate.

3. Are Sizer's conclusions convincing? Why or why not?

The Seven-Lesson Schoolteacher

John Taylor Gatto

"The Seven-Lesson Schoolteacher" is an excerpt from John Gatto's 1992 book Dumbing Us Down: The Hidden Curriculum of Compulsory Schooling. *Gatto, an award-winning New York City English teacher argues that, despite the intentions of curricula, schools actually teach negative lessons like dependency, confusion, and indifference.*

I

Call me Mr. Gatto, please. Twenty-six years ago, having nothing better to do with myself at the time, I tried my hand at schoolteaching. The license I have certifies that I am an instructor of English language and English literature, but that isn't what I do at all. I don't teach English, I teach school— and I win awards doing it.

Teaching means different things in different places, but seven lessons are universally taught from Harlem to Hollywood Hills. They constitute a national curriculum you pay for in more ways than you can imagine, so you might as well know what it is. You are at liberty, of course, to regard these lessons any way you like, but believe me when I say I intend no irony in this presentation. These are the things I teach, these are the things you pay me to teach. Make of them what you will.

1. Confusion

A lady named Kathy wrote this to me from Dubois, Indiana the other day:

> What big ideas are important to little kids? Well, the biggest idea
> I think they need is that what they are learning isn't idiosyncratic—
> that there is some system to it all and it's not just raining down on
> them as they helplessly absorb. That's the task, to understand, to
> make coherent.

Kathy has it wrong. *The first lesson I teach is confusion. Everything* I teach is out of context. I teach the un-relating of everything. I teach disconnections. I teach too much: the orbiting of planets, the law of large numbers, slavery, adjectives, architectural drawing, dance, gymnasium, choral singing, assemblies, surprise guests, fire drills, computer languages, parents' nights, staff-development days, pull-out programs, guidance with strangers my students may never see again, standardized tests, age-segregation unlike anything seen in the outside world. . . . What do any of these things have to do with each other?

Even in the best schools a close examination of curriculum and its sequences turns up a lack of coherence, full of internal contradictions. Fortunately the children have no words to define the panic and anger they feel *at constant violations of natural order and sequence* fobbed off on them as quality in education. The logic of the school-mind is that it is better to leave school with a tool kit of superficial jargon derived from economics, sociology, natural science, and so on, than with one genuine enthusiasm. But quality in education entails learning about something in depth. Confusion is thrust upon kids by too many strange adults, each working alone with only the thinnest relationship with each other, pretending, for the most part, to an expertise they do not possess.

Meaning, not disconnected facts, is what sane human beings seek, and education is a set of codes for processing raw data into meaning. Behind the patchwork quilt of school sequences and the school obsession with facts and theories, the age-old human search for meaning lies well concealed. This is harder to see in elementary school where the hierarchy of school experience seems to make better sense because the good-natured simple relationship between "let's do this" and "let's do that" is just assumed to mean something and the clientele has not yet consciously discerned how little substance is behind the play and pretense.

Think of the great natural sequences—like learning to walk and learning to talk; the progression of light from sunrise to sunset; the ancient procedures of a farmer, a smithy, or a shoemaker; or the preparation of a Thanksgiving feast—all of the parts are in perfect harmony with each other, each action justifies itself and illuminates the past and the future. School sequences aren't like that, not inside a single class and not among the total menu of daily classes. School sequences are crazy. There is no particular reason for any of them, nothing that bears close scrutiny. Few teachers would dare to teach the tools whereby dogmas of a school or a teacher could be criticized, since everything must be accepted. School subjects are learned, if they *can* be learned, like children learn the catechism or memorize the Thirty-nine Articles of Anglicanism.

I teach the un-relating of everything, an infinite fragmentation the opposite of cohesion; what I do is more related to television programming than to making a scheme of order. In a world where home is only a ghost, because both parents work, or because of too many moves or too many job changes or too much ambition, or because something else has left everybody too confused to maintain a family relation, I teach you how to accept confusion as your destiny. That's the first lesson I teach.

2.   *Class Position*

The second lesson I teach is class position. I teach that students must stay in the class where they belong. I don't know who decides my kids belong there but that's not my business. The children are numbered so that if any get away they can be returned to the right class. Over the years the variety of ways children are numbered by schools has increased dramatically, until it is hard to see the human beings plainly under the weight of numbers they carry. Numbering children is a big and very profitable undertaking, though what the strategy is designed to accomplish is elusive. I don't even know why parents would, without a fight, allow it to be done to their kids.

In any case, that's not my business. My job is to make them like being locked together with children who bear numbers like their own. Or at the least to endure it like good sports. If I do my job well, the kids can't even *imagine* themselves somewhere else, because I've shown them how to envy and fear the better classes and how to have contempt for the dumb classes. Under this efficient discipline the class mostly polices itself into good marching order. That's the real lesson of any rigged competition like school. You come to know your place.

In spite of the overall class blueprint, which assumes that ninety-nine percent of the kids are in their class to stay, I nevertheless make a public effort to exhort children to higher levels of test success, hinting at eventual transfer from the lower class as a reward. I frequently insinuate the day will come when an employer will hire them on the basis of test scores and grades, even though my own experience is that employers are rightly indifferent to such things. I never lie outright, but I've come to see that truth and school-teaching are, at bottom, incompatible, just as Socrates said thousands of years ago. The lesson of numbered classes is that everyone has a proper place in the pyramid and there is no way out of your class except by number magic. Failing that, you must stay where you are put.

3.   *Indifference*

The third lesson I teach is indifference. I teach children not to care too much about anything, even though they want to make it appear that they do. How I do this is very subtle. I do it by demanding that they become totally involved in my lessons, jumping up and down in their seats with anticipation, competing vigorously with each other for my favor. It's heartwarming when they do that; it impresses everyone, even me. When I'm at my best I plan lessons very carefully in order to produce this show of enthusiasm. But when the bell rings I insist they drop whatever it is we have been doing and proceed quickly to the next work station. They must turn on and off like a light switch. Nothing important is ever finished in my class nor in any class I know of. Students never have a complete experience except on the installment plan.

Indeed, the lesson of bells is that no work is worth finishing, so why care too deeply about anything? Years of bells will condition all but the strongest to a world that can no longer offer important work to do. Bells are the secret logic of schooltime; their logic is inexorable. Bells destroy the past and future, rendering every interval the same as any other, as the abstraction of a map renders every living mountain and river the same, even though they are not. Bells inoculate each undertaking with indifference.

4.   *Emotional Dependency*

The fourth lesson I teach is emotional dependency. By stars and red checks, smiles and frowns, prizes, honors, and disgraces, I teach kids to surrender their will to the predestined chain of command. Rights may be granted or withheld by any authority without appeal, because rights do not exist inside a school—not even the right of free speech, as the Supreme Court has ruled—unless school authorities say they do. As a schoolteacher, I intervene in many personal decisions, issuing a pass for those I deem legitimate, or initiating a disciplinary confrontation for behavior that threatens my control. Individuality is constantly trying to assert itself among children and teenagers, so my judgments come thick and fast. Individuality is a contradiction of class theory, a curse to all systems of classification.

Here are some common ways it shows up: children sneak away for a private moment in the toilet on the pretext of moving their bowels, or they steal a private instant in the hallway on the grounds they need water. I know they don't, but I allow them to "deceive" me because this conditions them to depend on my favors. Sometimes free will appears right in front of me in pockets of children angry, depressed, or unhappy about things outside my ken; rights in such matters cannot be recognized by schoolteachers, only privileges that can be withdrawn, hostages to good behavior.

5. *Intellectual Dependency*

The fifth lesson I teach is intellectual dependency. Good students wait for a teacher to tell them what to do. It is the most important lesson, that we must wait for other people, better trained than ourselves, to make the meanings of our lives. The expert makes all the important choices: only I, the teacher, can determine what my kids must study, or rather, only the people who pay me can make those decisions, which I then enforce. If I'm told that evolution is a fact instead of a theory, I transmit that as ordered, punishing deviants who resist what I have been told to tell them to think. This power to control what children will think lets me separate successful students from failures very easily.

Successful children do the thinking I assign them with a minimum of resistance and a decent show of enthusiasm. Of the millions of things of value to study, I decide what few we have time for, or actually it is decided by my faceless employers. The choices are theirs, why should I argue? Curiosity has no important place in my work, only conformity.

Bad kids fight this, of course, even though they lack the concepts to know what they are fighting, struggling to make decisions for themselves about what they will learn and when they will learn it. How can we allow that and survive as schoolteachers? Fortunately there are tested procedures to break the will of those who resist; it is more difficult, naturally, if the kids have respectable parents who come to their aid, but that happens less and less in spite of the bad reputation of schools. No middle-class parents I have ever met actually believe that *their* kid's school is one of the bad ones. Not one single parent in twenty-six years of teaching. That's amazing, and probably the best testimony to what happens to families when mother and father have been well-schooled themselves, learning the seven lessons.

Good people wait for an expert to tell them what to do. It is hardly an exaggeration to say that our entire economy depends upon this lesson being learned. Think of what might fall apart if children weren't trained to be dependent: the social services could hardly survive; they would vanish, I think, into the recent historical limbo out of which they arose. Counselors and therapists would look on in horror as the supply of psychic invalids vanished. Commercial entertainment of all sorts, including television, would wither as people learned again how to make their own fun. Restaurants, the prepared-food industry, and a whole host of other assorted food services would be drastically down-sized if people returned to making their own meals rather than depending on strangers to plant, pick, chop, and cook for them. Much of modern law, medicine, and engineering would go too, the clothing business and schoolteaching as well, unless a guaranteed supply of helpless people continued to pour out of our schools each year.

Don't be too quick to vote for radical school reform if you want to continue getting a paycheck. We've built a way of life that depends on people doing what they are told because they don't know how to tell *themselves* what to do. It's one of the biggest lessons I teach.

6. *Provisional Self-Esteem*

The sixth lesson I teach is provisional self-esteem. If you've ever tried to wrestle into line kids whose parents have convinced them to believe they'll be loved in spite of anything, you know how impossible it is to make self-confident spirits conform. Our world wouldn't survive a flood of confident people very long, so I teach that a kid's self-respect should depend on expert opinion. My kids are constantly evaluated and judged.

A monthly report, impressive in its provision, is sent into a student's home to elicit approval or mark exactly, down to a single percentage point, how dissatisfied with the child a parent should be. The ecology of "good" schooling depends on perpetuating dissatisfaction, just as the commercial economy depends on the same fertilizer. Although some people might be surprised how little time or reflection goes into making up these mathematical records, the cumulative weight of these objective-seeming documents establishes a profile that compels children to arrive at certain decisions about themselves and their futures based on the casual judgment of strangers. Self-evaluation, the staple of every major philosophical system that ever appeared on the planet, is never considered a factor. The lesson of report cards, grades, and tests is that children should not trust themselves or their parents but should instead rely on the evaluation of certified officials. People need to be told what they are worth.

7. One Can't Hide

The seventh lesson I teach is that one can't hide. I teach students they are always watched, that each is under constant surveillance by myself and my colleagues. There are no private spaces for children, there is no private time. Class change lasts exactly three hundred seconds to keep promiscuous fraternization at low levels. Students are encouraged to tattle on each other or even to tattle on their own parents. Of course, I encourage parents to file reports about their own child's waywardness too. A family trained to snitch on itself isn't likely to conceal any dangerous secrets.

I assign a type of extended schooling called "homework," so that the effect of surveillance, if not that surveillance itself, travels into private households, where students might otherwise use free time to learn something unauthorized from a father or mother, by exploration, or by apprenticing to some wise person in the neighborhood. Disloyalty to the idea of schooling is a devil always ready to find work for idle hands.

The meaning of constant surveillance and denial of privacy is that no one can be trusted, that privacy is not legitimate. Surveillance is an ancient imperative, espoused by certain influential thinkers, a central prescription set down in *The Republic,* in *The City of God,* in the *Institutes of the Christian Religion,* in *New Atlantis,* in *Leviathan,*[1] and in a host of other places. All these childless men who wrote these books discovered the same thing: children must be closely watched if you want to keep a society under tight central control. Children will follow a private drummer if you can't get them into a uniformed marching band.

---

[1] *The Republic,* in *The City of God . . . Leviathan:* Famous political and philosophical writings by authors like Plato, St. Augustine, and Thomas Hobbes.

II

It is the great triumph of compulsory government monopoly mass-schooling that among even the best of my fellow teachers, and among even the best of my students' parents, only a small number can imagine a different way to do things. "The kids have to know how to read and write, don't they?" "They have to know how to add and subtract, don't they?" "They have to learn to follow orders if they ever expect to keep a job."

Only a few lifetimes ago things were very different in the United States. Originality and variety were common currency; our freedom from regimentation made us the miracle of the world; social-class boundaries were relatively easy to cross; our citizenry was marvelously confident, inventive, and able to do much for themselves independently, and to think for themselves. We were something special, we Americans, all by ourselves, without government sticking its nose into and measuring every aspect of our lives, without institutions and social agencies telling us how to think and feel. We were something special, as individuals, as Americans.

But we've had a society essentially under central control in the United States since just before the Civil War, and such a society requires compulsory schooling, government monopoly schooling, to maintain itself. Before this development schooling wasn't very important anywhere. We had it, but not too much of it, and only as much as an individual *wanted*. People learned to read, write, and do arithmetic just fine anyway; there are some studies that suggest literacy at the time of the American Revolution, at least for non-slaves on the Eastern seaboard, was close to total. Thomas Paine's *Common Sense*[2] sold 600,000 copies to a population of 3,000,000, twenty percent of whom were slaves, and fifty percent indentured servants.

Were the colonists geniuses? No, the truth is that reading, writing, and arithmetic only take about one hundred hours to transmit as long as the audience is eager and willing to learn. The trick is to wait until someone asks and then move fast while the mood is on. Millions of people teach themselves these things, it really isn't very hard. Pick up a fifth-grade math or rhetoric textbook from 1850 and you'll see that the texts were pitched then on what would today be considered college level. The continuing cry for "basic skills" practice is a smoke screen behind which schools preempt the time of children for twelve years and teach them the seven lessons I've just described to you.

The society that has come increasingly under central control since just before the Civil War shows itself in the lives we lead, the clothes we wear, the food we eat, and the green highway signs we drive by from coast to coast, all of which are the products of this control. So too, I think, are the epidemics of drugs, suicide, divorce, violence, cruelty, and hardening of class into caste in the United States, products of the dehumanization of our lives, the lessening of individual, family, and community importance, a diminishment that proceeds from central control. The character of large

---

[2]*Common Sense:* Paine's fifty-page pamphlet, published January 10, 1776, was recognized as the war-cry of the American revolutionary movement.

compulsory institutions is inevitable; they want more and more until there isn't any more to give. School takes our children away from any possibility of an active role in community life—in fact it destroys communities by relegating the training of children to the hands of certified experts—and by doing so it ensures our children cannot grow up fully human. Aristotle taught that without a fully active role in community life one could not hope to become a healthy human being. Surely he was right. Look around you the next time you are near a school or an old people's reservation if you wish a demonstration.

School as it was built is an essential support system for a model of social engineering that condemns most people to be subordinate stones in a pyramid that narrows as it ascends to a terminal of control. School is an artifice that makes such a pyramidical social order seem inevitable, although such a premise is a fundamental betrayal of the American Revolution. From Colonial days through the period of the Republic we had no schools to speak of—read Benjamin Franklin's *Autobiography* for an example of a man who had no time to waste in school—and yet the promise of democracy was beginning to be realized. We turned our backs on this promise by bringing to life the ancient pharaonic dream of Egypt: compulsory subordination for all. That was the secret Plato reluctantly transmitted in *The Republic* when Glaucon and Adeimantus extort from Socrates the plan for total state control of human life, a plan necessary to maintain a society where some people take more than their share. "I will show you," says Socrates, "how to bring about such a feverish city, but you will not like what I am going to say." And so the blueprint of the seven-lesson school was first sketched.

The current debate about whether we should have a national curriculum is phony. We already have a national curriculum locked up in the seven lessons I have just outlined. Such a curriculum produces physical, moral, and intellectual paralysis, and no curriculum of content will be sufficient to reverse its hideous effects. What is currently under discussion in our national hysteria about failing academic performance misses the point. Schools teach exactly what they are intended to teach and they do it well: how to be a good Egyptian and remain in your place in the pyramid.

Activity: RESPONDING TO THE TEXT

1. What kind of evidence does Gatto use to support his argument? Are Gatto's conclusions convincing?
2. Do you think most teachers would agree with Gatto's conclusions? Why or why not?
3. Based on your experience in high school, do you agree with Gatto's conclusions? What evidence can you supply to support or refute Gatto's conclusions?

From "I Just Wanna Be Average"

Mike Rose

"I Just Wanna Be Average" is an excerpt from Mike Rose's book, Lives on the Boundary: The Struggles and Achievements of America's Underprepared. *Rose uses his own personal history to illustrate problems faced by all underprepared students.*

Students will float to the mark you set. I and the others in the vocational classes were bobbing in pretty shallow water. Vocational education was aimed at increasing the economic opportunities of students who do not do well in our schools. Some serious programs succeed in doing that, and through exceptional teachers—like Mr. Gross in *Horace's Compromise*—students learn to develop hypotheses and troubleshoot, reason through a problem, and communicate effectively—the true job skills. The vocational track, however, is most often a place for those who are just not making it, a dumping ground for the disaffected. There were a few teachers who worked hard at education: young Brother Slattery, for example, combined a stern voice with weekly quizzes to try to pass along to us a skeletal outline of world history. But mostly the teachers had no idea of how to engage the imaginations of us kids who were scuttling along at the bottom of the pond.

And the teachers would have needed some inventiveness, for none of us was groomed for the classroom. It wasn't just that I didn't know things—didn't know how to simplify algebraic fractions, couldn't identify different kinds of clauses, bungled Spanish translations—but that I had developed various faulty and inadequate ways of doing algebra and making sense of Spanish. Worse yet, the years of defensive tuning out in elementary school had given me a way to escape quickly while seeming at least half alert. During my time in Voc. Ed., I developed further into a mediocre student and a somnambulant problem solver, and that affected the subjects I did have the wherewithal to handle: I detested Shakespeare; I got bored with history. My attention flitted here and there. I fooled around in class and read my books indifferently—the intellectual equivalent of playing with your food. I did what I had to do to get by, and I did it with half a mind.

But I did learn things about people and eventually came into my own socially. I liked the guys in Voc. Ed. Growing up where I did, I understood and admired physical prowess, and there was an abundance of muscle here. There was Dave Snyder, a sprinter and halfback of true quality. Dave's ability and his quick wit gave him a natural appeal, and he was welcome in any clique, though he always kept a little independent. He enjoyed acting the fool and could care less about studies, but he possessed a certain maturity and never caused the faculty much trouble. It was a testament to his independence that he included me among his friends—I eventually went out for track, but I was no jock. Owing to the Latin alphabet and a dearth of *R*s and *S*s, Snyder sat behind Rose, and we started exchanging one-liners and became friends.

There was Ted Richard, a much-touted Little League pitcher. He was chunky and had a baby face and came to Our Lady of Mercy as a seasoned street fighter. Ted was quick to laugh and he had a loud, jolly laugh, but when he got angry he'd smile a little smile, the kind that simply raises the corner of the mouth a quarter of an inch. For those who knew, it was an eerie signal. Those who didn't found themselves in big trouble, for Ted was very quick. He loved to carry on what we would come to call philosophical discussions: What is courage? Does God exist? He also loved words, enjoyed picking up big one like *salubrious* and *equivocal* and using them in our conversations—laughing at himself as the word hit a chuckhole rolling off his tongue. Ted didn't do all that well in school—baseball and parties and testing the courage he'd speculated about took up his time. His textbooks were *Argosy* and *Field and Stream,* whatever newspapers he'd find on the bus stop—from the *Daily Worker* to pornography—conversations with uncles or hobos or businessmen he'd meet in a coffee shop. *The Old Man and the Sea*. With hindsight, I can see that Ted was developing into one of those rough-hewn intellectuals whose sources are a mix of the learned and the apocryphal, whose discussions are both assured and sad.

And then there was Ken Harvey. Ken was good-looking in a puffy way and had a full and oily ducktail and was a car enthusiast . . . a hodad. One day in religion class, he said the sentence that turned out to be one of the most memorable of the hundreds of thousands I heard in those Voc. Ed. years. We were talking about the parable of the talents, about achievement, working hard, doing the best you can do, blah-blah-blah, when the teacher called on the restive Ken Harvey for an opinion. Ken thought about it, but just for a second, and said (with studied, minimal affect), "I just wanna be average." That woke me up. Average?! Who wants to be average? Then the athletes chimed in with the clichés that make you want to laryngectomize them, and the exchange became a platitudinous melee. At the time, I thought Ken's assertion was stupid, and I wrote him off. But his sentence has stayed with me all these years, and I think I am finally coming to understand it.

Ken Harvey was gasping for air. School can be a tremendously disorienting place. No matter how bad the school, you're going to encounter notions that don't fit with the assumptions and beliefs that you grew up with—maybe you'll hear these dissonant notions from teachers, maybe from the other students, and maybe you'll read them. You'll also be thrown in with all kinds of kids from all kinds of backgrounds, and that can be unsettling— this is especially true in places of rich ethnic and linguistic mix, like the L.A. basin. You'll see a handful of students far excel you in courses that sound exotic and that are only in the curriculum of the elite: French, physics, trigonometry. And all this is happening while you're trying to shape an identity, your body is changing, and your emotions are running wild. If you're a working-class kid in the vocational track, the options you'll have to deal with this will be constrained in certain ways: You're defined by your school as "slow"; you're placed in a curriculum that isn't designed to liberate you but to occupy you, or, if you're lucky, train you, though the training is for work the society does not esteem; other students are picking up the cues from your school and your curriculum and interacting with you in particular ways. If you're a kid like Ted Richard, you turn your back on all this and let your mind roam where it may. But youngsters like Ted are rare. What Ken and so many others do is protect themselves from such suffocating madness by taking on with a vengeance the identity implied in the vocational track. Reject the confusion and frustration by openly defining yourself as the Common Joe. Champion the average. Rely on your own good sense. Fuck this bullshit. Bullshit, of course, is everything you—and the others—fear is beyond you: books, essays, tests, academic scrambling, complexity, scientific reasoning, philosophical inquiry.

The tragedy is that you have to twist the knife in your own gray matter to make this defense work. You'll have to shut down, have to reject intellectual stimuli or diffuse them with sarcasm, have to cultivate stupidity, have to convert boredom from a malady into a way of confronting the world. Keep your vocabulary simple, act stoned when you're not or act more stoned than you are, flaunt ignorance, materialize your dreams. It is a powerful and effective defense—it neutralizes the insult and the frustration of being a vocational kid and, when perfected, it drives teachers up the wall, a delightful secondary effect. But like all strong magic, it exacts a price.

Activity: RESPONDING TO THE TEXT

1. Mike Rose's examples and descriptions all come from his personal experience. Why does he tell us about the students he knew in high school? What point do these examples support?
2. Is Rose's evidence convincing? Why or why not?
3. Based on your experience in high school, do you agree with Rose's conclusions? What evidence can you supply to support or refute Rose's conclusions?

Why Do Schools Flunk Biology?

Lynnell Hancock

The following article, published in the February 19, 1996 edition of Newsweek, *summarizes scientific findings on the correlation between biology and learning. In it, Lynnell Hancock describes how schools fail to consider students' biology in their planning of curricula and schedules. Because this article is a survey of research, its evidence comes mainly from scientific studies.*

Biology is a staple at most American high schools. Yet when it comes to the biology of the students themselves—how their brains develop and retain knowledge—school officials would rather not pay attention to the lessons. Can first graders handle French? What time should school start? Should music be cut? Biologists have some important evidence to offer. But not only are they ignored, their findings are often turned upside down.

Force of habit rules the hallways and classrooms. Neither brain science nor education research has been able to free the majority of America's schools from their 19th-century roots. If more administrators were tuned into brain research, scientists argue, not only would schedules change, but subjects such as foreign language and geometry would be offered to much younger children. Music and gym would be daily requirements. Lectures, work sheets and rote memorization would be replaced by hands-on materials, drama and project work. And teachers would pay greater attention to children's emotional connections to subjects. "We do more education research than anyone else in the world," says Frank Vellutino, a professor of educational psychology at State University of New York at Albany, "and we ignore more as well."

Plato once said that music "is a more potent instrument than any other for education." Now scientists know why. Music, they believe, trains the brain for higher forms of thinking. Researchers at the University of California, Irvine, studied the power of music by observing two groups of preschoolers. One group took piano lessons and sang daily in chorus. The other did not. After eight months the musical 3-year-olds were expert puzzlemasters, scoring 80 percent higher than their playmates did in spatial intelligence—the ability to visualize the world accurately.

This skill later translates into complex math and engineering skills. "Early music training can enhance a child's ability to reason," says Irvine physicist Gordon Shaw. Yet music education is often the first "frill" to be cut when school budgets shrink. Schools on average have only one music teacher for every 500 children, according to the National Commission on Music Education.

Then there's gym—another expendable hour by most school standards. Only 36 percent of schoolchildren today are required to participate in daily physical education. Yet researchers now know that exercise is good not only for the heart. It also juices up the brain, feeding it nutrients in the form of glucose and increasing nerve connections—all of which make it easier for kids of all ages to learn. Neuroscientist William Greenough confirmed this by watching rats at his University of Illinois at Urbana-Champaign lab. One group did nothing. A second exercised on an automatic treadmill. A third was set loose in a Barnum & Bailey obstacle course requiring the rats to perform acrobatic feats. These "supersmart" rats grew "an enormous amount of gray matter" compared with their sedentary partners, says Greenough.

Of course, children don't ordinarily run such gantlets; still, Greenough believes, the results are significant. Numerous studies, he says, show that children who exercise regularly do better in school.

The implication for schools goes beyond simple exercise. Children also need to be more physically active in the classroom, not sitting quietly in their seats memorizing subtraction tables. Knowledge is retained longer if children connect not only aurally but emotionally and physically to the material, says University of Oregon education professor Robert Sylwester in "A Celebration of Neurons."

Good teachers know that lecturing on the American Revolution is far less effective than acting out a battle. Angles and dimensions are better understood if children chuck their work sheets and build a complex model to scale. The smell of the glue enters memory through one sensory system, the touch of the wood blocks another, the sight of the finished model still another. The brain then creates a multidimensional mental model of the experience—one easier to retrieve. "Explaining a smell," says Sylwester, "is not as good as actually smelling it."

Scientists argue that children are capable of far more at younger ages than schools generally realize. People obviously continue learning their whole lives, but the optimum "windows of opportunity for learning" last until about the age of 10 or 12, says Harry Chugani of Wayne State University's Children's Hospital of Michigan. Chugani determined this by measuring the brain's consumption of its chief energy source, glucose. (The more glucose it uses, the more active the brain.) Children's brains, he observes, gobble up glucose at twice the adult rate from the age of 4 to puberty. So young brains are as primed as they'll ever be to process new information. Complex subjects such as trigonometry or foreign language shouldn't wait for puberty to be introduced. In fact, Chugani says, it's far easier for an elementary-school child to hear and process a second language—and even speak it without an accent. Yet most U.S. districts wait until junior high to introduce Spanish or French—after the "windows" are closed.

Reform could begin at the beginning. Many sleep researchers now believe that most teens' biological clocks are set later than those of their fellow humans. But high school starts at 7:30 A.M., usually to accommodate bus schedules. The result can be wasted class time for whole groups of kids. Making matters worse, many kids have trouble readjusting their natural sleep rhythm. Dr. Richard Allen of Johns Hopkins University found that teens went to sleep at the same time whether they had to be at school by 7:30 A.M., or 9:30 A.M. The later-to-rise teens not only get more sleep, he says: they also get better grades. The obvious solution would be to start school later when kids hit puberty. But at school, there's what's obvious, and then there's tradition.

Why is this body of research rarely used in most American classrooms? Not many administrators or school-board members know it exists, says Linda Darling-Hammond, professor of education at Columbia University's Teachers College. In most states, neither teachers nor administrators are required to know much about how children learn in order to be certified. What's worse, she says, decisions to cut music or gym are often made by noneducators, whose concerns are more often monetary than educational. "Our school system was invented in the late 1800s, and little has changed," she says. "Can you imagine if the medical profession ran this way?"

Activity: RESPONDING TO THE TEXT

1. "Why Do Schools Flunk Biology?" suggests that schools do not take the realities of students' biological characteristics into account when planning curricula and schedules. Can you add any evidence of ways that schools' organization, curricula, schedule, and physical surroundings ignore students' physical needs?
2. What kind of evidence is used most in this article? Is this evidence convincing?
3. Would the evidence be convincing to school officials? Why or why not?

Activity: SYNTHESIZING THE TEXTS

1. Compare Sizer's and Gatto's criticism of high schools. What kind of evidence are each author's conclusions based on? To what extent do their conclusions conflict? To what extent do they agree? To what extent do they agree or conflict with your experience?
2. All four of the readings in this chapter are critical of high-school education. What do high schools do well?

Writing Assignments

Academic Essays

1. Psychology

Rose states that "Students will float to the mark you set." This idea that children behave according to the expectations parents and teachers have for them is one that is commonly held by child psychologists. Do you think this is true? Write a paper that uses facts, examples, and/or expert testimony as evidence to prove your point.

2. Sociology

Sociologists and anthropologists often give detailed descriptions of cultural institutions or activities, just as Sizer does in "What High School Is." Choose some other institution to describe in detail. You might write about a public institution, such as a courtroom or a library, or you might write about a private institution, such as a fraternity or a grocery store. The key to a good description is careful observation. Go to the institution and take specific notes about what you see. Sizer chooses to describe high school from the point of view of one student, and he organizes his description chronologically, following through one student's day. When you write your description, you should also choose a point of view. Through whose eyes are you observing this institution? You must also decide how you are going to organize your observations. After describing the institution, list some conclusions that you have come to about the institution's purpose in the society.

3. Film/Literature

Choose a recent film or novel in which a substantial part of the story is set in a high school. Discuss whether the film is a realistic portrayal of high school. Support your thesis with specific examples from the movie or novel.

Workplace Writing

In most businesses, agencies, and institutions, employees are evaluated annually. These evaluations, called performance reviews or merit appraisals, usually rate employees in several categories, such as

- quality of work
- quantity of work
- institutional commitment
- initiative
- problem-solving ability
- accountability
- human relations

In each category, supervisors give employees ratings like "needs improvement," "satisfactory," "superior," or "outstanding." To justify the ratings, supervisors must supply facts, details, and examples as supporting evidence.

Many institutions also require that employees evaluate themselves. Write a self-evaluation for your current job. If you are not currently employed, you can evaluate your performance on a previous job, or you can evaluate yourself as a student. Use either the evaluation categories of your workplace or some of the categories in the list above. Give yourself a rating in each category and support your choice with specific facts, details, and examples. The evidence for each category should form one well-developed paragraph.

Personal Writing

Choose one aspect of your high school experience that you think could have prepared you better personally, professionally, or academically for adult life. You can select one limited area, such as the school's attitude toward coping with conflict or its approach to bilingual education, or a large academic area, such as the relevance of the social studies curriculum. Write a paper that describes your experience and then makes recommendations for improvement. Be sure to use specific details and examples to describe both your experience and your recommendations.

POLISHING AND REFLECTING ON TEXTS

Learning From Other Student Writers

Do Students Float to the Mark We Set?
David Wright

David Wright, the writer of the following essay, read Mike Rose's "I Just Wanna Be Average," discussed it in class, and wrote this response in class in two hours for his mid-term exam. Because of the limited time available, Wright used a simple five-paragraph form to organize his paper. He did not spend much time working on his introduction or conclusion or on revising sentences. Instead, he focused on providing a variety of detailed, relevant examples so that readers would be convinced that "students will float to the mark you set."

In "I Just Wanna Be Average" Mike Rose states that "Students will float to the mark you set." I have found through the experiences of others and myself that students do, in fact, float to the standards that are imposed on them. In this essay I will show several cases in which the students rose to or exceeded the expectations placed on them.

When I was in high school, I had a teacher, Mr. Parker, who recognized my full potential and set expectations for me that, at the time, I thought were unreachable. Mr. Parker, my electronics teacher, constantly challenged me not only to answer questions but to prove why my answers were right. At times, I felt that his demands were excessive and pondered why he was picking on me. By the end of the year, I had exceeded my classmates and was given permission to work on further studies rather than the normal class work. Even though I felt they were unfair, I was able to surpass the expectations placed on me by Mr. Parker. His confidence and ability to see my potential led me to where I am today, working in electronics.

My mom, a grade-school teacher, had a student in her class with mental and physical disabilities. In school, he was treated differently than the other kids his age. The teachers never expected him to play dodge ball or to do well on tests. My mom set her standards for this student equal to that of the other children. By the end of the year, this child was playing dodge ball and receiving better grades on his homework and tests than ever before. Because my mom had set a goal for this student that was higher than anyone had placed on him before, he was able to rise to her challenge.

Many nights I would sit and listen to my brother complain about how hard his class was and how the teacher was expecting too much of the students in a class he was taking. Every night he would come home, sit at the table, and study for hours. He despised the teacher for expecting so much and therefore making his life difficult. Frustrated every night, he would sit there and study. By the end of the semester, he had passed his class with a 98% grade, even though the teacher placed such high standards on his class.

I believe that students can and will "float to the mark you set." In this essay we have seen three separate people in three separate circumstances meet the goals and expectations placed upon them by their teachers. It is in human nature for people to meet or surpass the expectations put on them.

Activity: **RESPONDING TO THE TEXT**

1. Which example is the strongest? Why? Would adding more examples make the paper more convincing?
2. If Wright had had more time, what other kind of supporting material could he have added to prove his point?
3. Wright might have chosen to begin his paper with an example instead of with a general discussion of Mike Rose's idea. Would the essay be improved and/or weakened if Wright switched his first and second paragraphs so that the essay began with an example?

Activity: **PEER WORKSHOP**   DAEDALUS

Work in pairs to review the use of evidence and examples in one paper each of you has written. First, writers will evaluate their own papers. Then readers will do a detailed and thorough analysis of the quality and quantity of the evidence and examples. Finally, writers and readers will compare their analyses.

Writers:

Before the workshop, list the facts, examples, and expert testimony you used. Do you think your evidence is sufficient and appropriate for your paper's audience and purpose?

Readers:

1. Put an **F**, **E**, or **T** in the margin wherever the writer used Facts, Examples, or expert Testimony as evidence, and answer these questions:
   • Does the essay contain enough evidence?
   • Are there places where evidence should be deleted?
   • Is the evidence credible?

- Is the evidence appropriate for the writer's purpose?
- Should there be more of one kind of evidence?

2. Write **ADD** in the margin wherever you think adding evidence would clarify or strengthen the text.

Writers and Readers:

Compare your reactions to the paper's evidence. Make suggestions for revisions.

Activity: PROOFREADING YOUR WORK

If readers are to understand your ideas and evidence, you must use pronouns clearly. Ambiguous pronouns and pronouns that don't agree with their antecedents can make your reading difficult to understand and can undermine your credibility as a writer. To refresh your knowledge of pronoun use, find answers to the following questions:

- What is a pronoun?
- What is an antecedent?
- What is an ambiguous or vague pronoun?
- What does it mean when a pronoun and antecedent don't agree?
- How do you correct pronoun-agreement problems without using gender-biased language?

To review pronouns in your essay, do the following:

1. Underline the pronouns "it," "this," and "which." Draw a line to the word each pronoun replaces. If the pronoun is vague, rewrite the sentence to eliminate the problem.
2. Underline the pronoun "they" and draw a line to the antecedent. The word that "they" refers to should be plural. If the pronoun and antecedent do not agree, revise the sentence. Remember to use language that is not gender-biased.

Activity: POSTSCRIPT

1. When you read, what kind of details, examples, or evidence do you find most interesting and convincing? Why?
2. Do you ever have difficulty coming up with details, examples, or evidence to include in your writing? What could you do to overcome those difficulties?
3. Would the texts you find frustrating or difficult to read in college or at work be improved by the addition of facts or examples?

APPROPRIATE WORDS AND STYLE

P R E V I E W

This chapter's explanations about ways you can improve or adapt your style by choosing specific words, varying sentences, and being more concise will help answer these questions:

- How can you make your papers sound more professional?
- How can you make your style more appealing?
- What do teachers mean when they say your word choice could be improved?

L E A R N I N G   A B O U T   T E X T S

Understanding Style

If you look around at the students in your class, you will see a variety of clothing styles. One student may be wearing cotton slacks, a button-down shirt, and loafers; another may be wearing ragged jeans, a tie-dyed shirt, and sandals; a third may be wearing a tailored suit with a silk shirt and expensive leather shoes. Most of us assume that choice of style reflects one's personality or social situation. Based on your observations of clothing styles, you may make certain assumptions about each classmate's personality, interests, and values. These assumptions may cause you to react differently to the student in the tie-dyed shirt than to the student in the tailored suit. You may decide to strike up a conversation with one classmate and avoid the other. Though clothing style may not give you a complete or accurate understanding of a person's character, it makes a powerful first impression.

A person's writing style can have a similar effect on a reader. If you go to a library to choose a book to take on your summer vacation, you may read a few passages to get a feel for the writer's style. Usually, this brief reading will be enough for you to determine whether you will take the book or not. You may find that the author uses too many long, complicated sentences and big words—not the kind of prose that you want to read at the beach. Or you may discover that the author's tone is light and humorous—just the thing for vacation reading.

You could probably identify a piece of writing by a favorite author based on the style alone. Magazine and newspaper columnists, sports writers, and novelists all use distinctive styles. You would not confuse a paragraph by Stephen King with a paragraph by Mary Higgins Clark, even if they were describing a similar event—a love scene or death scene, for example. Two sports writers describing the same football game will not sound exactly the same, not just because they choose different facts to report, but because they choose different styles.

A writer's style is characterized by many elements, including choice of words and phrases, use of slang, length and type of sentence structure, number of details and examples included, use of figurative language (metaphors and similes), punctuation preferences, and paragraph structure and length. Writing style results from unconscious preferences and conscious choices. One author may naturally prefer to use long sentences because they "sound" more pleasing to him or her. Without consciously thinking about sentence length, that author will compose paragraphs made up of three- or four-line sentences. However, that same author, when writing a children's book, could consciously choose to use shorter sentences to make the prose easier for children to understand. Good writers adjust style to fit their purpose and context.

The following passages all discuss the same topic, women's work and its connection to mothering. Each writer has something different to say about the topic, and each writer has her own style. In the first excerpt by Charlotte Perkins Gilman from *Women and Economics*, notice the use of long, complex sentences and words such as "contingency" and "extinguish" which give the passage a formal sound:

> It seems almost unnecessary to suggest that women as economic producers will naturally choose those professions which are compatible with motherhood, and there are many professions much more in harmony with that function than the household service. Motherhood is not a remote contingency, but the common duty and the common glory of womanhood. If women did choose professions unsuitable to maternity, Nature would quietly extinguish them by her unvarying process. Those mothers who persisted in being acrobats, horse-breakers, or sailors before the mast, would probably not produce vigorous and numerous children. If they did, it would simply prove that such work did not hurt them. There is no fear to be wasted on the danger of women's choosing wrong professions, when they are free to choose.

In the second passage from *Women's Work*, Elizabeth Wayland Barber's style is characterized by the use of side comments in parentheses and a number of sentences using colons and semicolons:

> Twenty years ago Judith Brown wrote a little five-page "Note on the Division of Labor by Sex" that holds a simple key to these questions. She was interested in how much women contributed to obtaining the food for a preindustrial community. But in answering that question, she came upon a model of much wider applicability. She found that the issue of whether

or not the community *relies* upon women as the chief providers of a given type of labor depends upon "the compatibility of this pursuit with the demands of child care." If only because of the exigencies of breast feeding (which until recently was typically continued for two or three years per child), "nowhere in the world is the rearing of children primarily the responsibility of men . . . ." Thus, if the productive labor of women is not to be lost to the society during the childbearing years, the jobs regularly assigned to women must be carefully chosen to be "compatible with simultaneous child watching." From empirical observation Brown gleans that "such activities have the following characteristics: they do not require rapt concentration and are relatively dull and repetitive; they are easily interruptable [I see a rueful smile on every care giver's face!] and easily resumed once interrupted; they do not place the child in potential danger; and they do not require the participant to range very far from home."[1]

Just such are the crafts of spinning, weaving, and sewing: repetitive, easy to pick up at any point, reasonably child-safe, and easily done at home. (Contrast the idea of swinging a pick in a dark, cramped, and dusty mine shaft with a baby on one's back or being interrupted by a child's crisis while trying to pour molten metal into a set of molds.) The only other occupation that fits the criteria even half so well is that of preparing the daily food. Food and clothing: These are what societies worldwide have come to see as the core of women's work (although other tasks may be added to the load, depending upon the circumstances of the particular society).

The final example, from *Fruitful* by Anne Roiphe, has an entirely different style, using vivid images such as the phrases "munched on our salad" and "the little boy looking out over the audience." The writer uses a more conversational style, giving certain statements emotional emphasis by using short, striking sentences:

> But I would have been hurt very badly if I had not had children. To care for a child was not an alien duty imposed on me by a hostile culture, it was rather the core, the emotional wellspring, the gravity that held my soul in place. I was having lunch with a feminist writer friend who told me that her oldest son was competing in an interschool spelling bee right then as we munched on our salad. "Why aren't you there?" I asked. She shrugged. "I'm not going to follow little boys around," she said. I thought she was right. I thought she was wrong. I thought of the little boy looking out over the audience of students and parents, searching the seats for his own mother's face. I wished she had gone to the spelling bee. I understood perfectly why she had not.

---

[1]Notice Brown's stipulation that this particular division of labor revolves around reliance, not around ability (other than the ability to breast-feed), within a community in which specialization is desirable. Thus females are quite able to hunt, and often do (as she points out); males are quite able to cook and sew, and often do, among cultures of the world. The question is whether the society can afford to rely on the women as a group for all of the hunting or all of the sewing. The answer to "hunting" (and smithing, and deep-sea fishing) is no. The answer to "sewing" (and cooking, and weaving) is yes.

FYI: for more on writers' roles, context, and text, see Chapter 1.

These writers have different backgrounds, experiences, purposes, and audiences, all of which influence their styles in these passages.

All writers, including you, use a variety of styles. We learn these styles through what we read, how much and what kind of writing we do, and the style of talking we hear in our families and in the media. Most of us have one style, our "voice," that predominates in much of our writing. This may be the style we are most comfortable with in most situations; however, we may also be able to adopt different styles for special circumstances. For example, when we write an application for a scholarship, we use a more formal style than we might use when we write in our journals or send e-mail messages to friends, because we are aware that different writing situations require different styles.

Writing at work and at school usually requires a more formal style than personal writing. Many people have difficulty switching to this more formal style because it is not "natural" to them; it is not the way they talk or hear others talking. They have trouble forming sentences or choosing words that say what they mean in this more formal setting. Very experienced writers learn to combine elements of their own conversational voice with the requirements of a more formal style, but achieving that level of stylistic confidence requires practice, experimentation, and an awareness of the stylistic possibilities. By noticing the components of other writers' styles and by paying more attention to the elements that make up your own style, you will gradually develop a formal style that works for you.

Choosing Words That Reflect Your Style

Your choice of words is one of the most important elements of your style. The paper's context and purpose help determine the style, which, in turn, determines word choice. If the paper is intended for a formal setting—a classroom or office, for example—select words appropriate for the formal tone and avoid slang. If the purpose of your paper is to describe a process, select specific words that help the reader to visualize the process. Being aware of the context and purpose of your writing helps you to compose in an appropriate style.

Choosing Specific Words

In most cases, effective writers choose specific words whenever they write. They avoid vague words and empty phrases that might make them sound careless or trite. Writers who settle for vague phrases give readers the impression that they are trying to hide something or that they do not know enough about their topic. Vague words and phrases weaken arguments and explanations because they leave the reader with blurry mental images. To sharpen an image, choose specific words.

For example, an ad that said, "Car for sale, bargain price," would not convey enough information to allow readers to decide whether the car was worth buying because they could not form a mental image of the car or the amount of money they would have to spend. If the writer substituted "1994 Accord" for "car" and "$1,500.00" for "bargain price," readers would have a much clearer mental image. In changing the words, the writer has not increased the length of the description, but has brought it into focus by choosing more specific words.

You should be alert for opportunities to substitute more specific words in your sentences. Adjectives such as "interesting," "good," "large," "exciting," "many," or "pretty" are vague because they do not paint precise pictures of the objects or ideas they describe. Substitute more specific words for these vague modifiers. For example, the vague sentence, "The novel's characters had interesting personalities," could be revised to read, "The novel's characters had eccentric personalities." If we are told that characters are "eccentric," we have a much clearer picture of them than if we are told they are "interesting."

Nouns can also be revised to create clearer pictures. Use proper nouns and names whenever possible. "*The Scarlet Letter*" is more specific than "the novel." Choose specific nouns, which carry more detailed information than general nouns. For example, a general word like "vehicle" does not give us much information, except that the writer is talking about some kind of mechanical conveyance. Because the general noun "vehicle" does not focus the image, the readers cannot tell whether the writer envisioned a bicycle, a car, a truck, a camper, a bus, or a golf-cart. A more specific noun like "car" gives the readers more information about the vehicle; it has four wheels, passenger seats, a roof, two or four doors, and a trunk. To be even more specific, you might choose the proper noun, "Camaro"; then the readers would have even more information about the vehicle. They would be able to create an almost exact mental picture from the information provided by the word "Camaro." Avoid nouns such as "thing," "aspect," and "element," because these words convey little specific information.

By choosing vivid, lively verbs, you can create a moving picture in the readers' minds. Some verbs, such as "is," "was," "were," "have," "has," "had," "make," and "do," create little sense of action. Substitute more active verbs whenever possible. Instead of writing, "Mary is in charge of the project," you might use a more active verb: "Mary directs the project." By substituting "directs" for "is," the writer creates a picture of Mary acting rather than just being. Look at the sample passage below and notice how many weak, vague verbs are used:

> High school grades are not reliable predictors of a student's success in college. Sometimes students' social activities have a disruptive influence on their study habits. They are not responsible about scheduling the time necessary to finish their homework. When these students are in college, they have the realization that the amount of time they study is a determining factor in their final grades. They do more work because they have more motivation.

The sentences in this passage are wordy and vague because they rely on verb forms of "to be" and "to have." Usually, the sentences can be revised quite easily by transforming one of the other words in the sentence into the verb. For example, to revise the first sentence, the writer could substitute the verb "predict" for "are" to make a tighter sentence: "High school grades do not reliably predict a student's success in college." Rewriting the sentences with more active verbs would produce a clearer, shorter, and more effective paragraph.

When trying to improve their style, many students turn to a thesaurus, a book that lists alternate possibilities for a large number of nouns, verbs, adjectives, and adverbs. The thesaurus can be useful for jogging your memory about words that might not come readily to mind when you're composing, but its use has limits—namely, the limits of your vocabulary. If you use an unfamiliar word you've found in a thesaurus, you may be choosing a word that does not have the exact meaning, level of formality, or connotations you think it does. For example, the thesaurus lists "hireling," "employee," "subordinate," and "agent" as synonyms for "workers." However, in the sentence "Workers should be allowed to join unions," none of those choices proposed by the thesaurus could be substituted because they are either too formal or archaic, don't fit the context, or have the wrong connotations. Using a thesaurus can help you think of words that might be appropriate for your sentence, but be wary of substituting unfamiliar words. Remember, your writing should sound like you (you at your best, of course), so your sentences should use vocabulary you know and use.

Activity: **WORKING TOGETHER**

In the passage above about high-school grades, underline all the weak verbs and rewrite the sentences, substituting more active verbs.

Choosing Words According to Their Level of Formality

The words you choose for a letter to friends would probably be different from the words you choose for a job application letter. In the letter to friends, the style is informal, so you can use slang words, perhaps even nonstandard grammar, because you are not trying to impress your friends, and because you know that they share your knowledge of slang. However, the style of your job application letter would be much more formal because your choice of words tells the prospective employer something about your competence, personality, and abilities. If you choose inappropriate words or nonstandard usages, the employer might get the impression that you are not qualified for the job.

Look at the following examples:

Example 1:

I've got a lot of cooking experience at fast-food places. All of my bosses will put in a good word for me. I always showed up and never hassled my boss or the other guys on the job. I think working here would be great. Maybe if you hire me, I can try to do your manager training. I can't wait to hear from you.

Example 2:

I have had extensive experience as a cook at fast-food restaurants. All of my former employers will vouch for the quality of my work. I never missed work and never caused any problems for my employers or the other employees. Working at your restaurant would let me use the skills I have learned during my previous employment. Perhaps if you hire me, I can apply for your management-training program. I look forward to hearing from you.

The first example is very informal. It uses contractions (I've, can't), trite phrases (put in a good word, can't wait), and nonstandard constructions (a lot). In addition, the writer has chosen more informal words such as "bosses," "maybe," and "hassled," which make the writing seem more like speech. Sometimes, as in a letter to friends, this informal word choice would be appropriate because it is friendly and down-to-earth. However, in the classroom and on the job, a more formal style, as illustrated in the second letter, is more appropriate.

Activity: **BUILDING AN ESSAY**

Once again, working on the essay you have been writing through the last six chapters, consider the level of formality of your style. Experiment with one of your middle paragraphs. Rewrite it, making the style more or less formal. Would a more or less formal style be more appropriate? If not, why not?

Varying Sentences for a Smoother Style

Sentences come in a variety of lengths and structures. You must choose sentence structures that convey your ideas clearly and concisely, but you should also keep style in mind. Probably the most common sentence pattern is the short sentence that begins with the main subject and verb. The first sentence of this paragraph is an example of such a sentence; it begins with the subject and verb, "Sentences come." This sentence structure is so common because it is clear and easy to read. Look at the example below from Mona Simpson's novel *Anywhere But Here*:

> Torches flared on both sides of the road that led to the Bel Air Hotel. The path wound in and out of the woods. My mother drove real slow. She parked underneath the awning. I moved to get out but she stopped me and told me to wait. She rested her hands on the steering wheel the way she used to for years on top of my shoulders. The valet came and opened the doors, her door first and then mine. She wasn't shy to relinquish the car now. There was nothing embarrassing in it. It was clean. The leather smelled of Windex.

Go For It!

Webster's Dictionary and the *Oxford English Dictionary* are both available online. The first address will access Merriam-Webster's; the third will access the OED:

☞ http://www.m-w.com/

☞ http://www.digicity.com/eng_0075.htm

☞ http://oed.com

....

To choose the correct word, you may want to consult a thesaurus. *Roget's Thesaurus* is available at:

☞ http://humanities.uchicago.edu/forms_unrest/ROGET.html

....

If you're looking for a quotation, *Bartlett's Familiar Quotations* is available at:

☞ http://www.columbia.edu/acis/bartleby/bartlett

In this example, every sentence begins with the main subject and verb; the ideas are very clear, but using so many sentences with this one basic pattern creates an uneven, uneasy feeling. The feeling is appropriate in this paragraph from the novel, because the novelist's purpose is to convey a girl's uncertainty about what her eccentric mother will do next.

In most of the writing you do for school or for work, increasing your sentence variety will strengthen your writing. By using various sentence patterns in each paragraph, you will improve the flow of your writing and make it sound more sophisticated. In the following example from Joseph Campbell's *Myths to Live By*, notice how many different sentence patterns Campbell used:

> All life is structure. In the biosphere, the more elaborate the structure, the higher the life form. The structure through which the energies of a starfish are inflected is considerably more complex than that of an amoeba; and as we come on up the line, say to the chimpanzee, complexity increases. So likewise in the human cultural sphere: the crude notion that energy and strength can be represented or rendered by abandoning and breaking structures is refuted by all that we know about the evolution and history of life.

The first sentence is short and simple because it makes an important, forceful statement of Campbell's main idea. In the remaining sentences, Campbell uses longer, more complex structures because they allow him to make clear connections between various examples and supporting points.

Often, when we are in a hurry to put ideas down on paper, we rely on short, simple sentence structures, but when we revise our writing to improve the style, we should try to choose a variety of sentence patterns appropriate for the messages we want to convey. The simple sentence, the compound sentence, and the complex sentence are the three basic sentence patterns. Longer, more complex sentences can be built by combining these three patterns in various ways.

Simple Sentences

A simple sentence contains one subject and verb pair, for example, "The student laughed." Although sentences this simple may occasionally be effective, they cannot be overused without making your writing seem simplistic. Simple sentences can be expanded, however, by adding modifiers. These modifiers are words and phrases that provide additional information about the subject or verb. In the following sentence, the five modifiers added to the simple sentence above are enclosed in parentheses: "The student (in the front row) (of the sociology class) (suddenly) laughed (loudly) (at his professor's pun)."

Compound Sentences

A compound sentence consists of two or more simple sentences joined by a comma and one of these seven coordinating conjunctions: *and, but, or, for, nor, so, yet*. The two sentences in a compound sentence should be of equal emphasis, and the conjunction should show the relationship between the two ideas:

AND—The second sentence provides additional information.

BUT and *YET*—The second sentence provides a contrast.

OR and *NOR*—The second sentence offers an option; *nor* is used when the sentences are negative.

SO—The second sentence tells the result of the action of the first sentence.

FOR—The second sentence gives the reason for the action of the first sentence (similar to "because")

For example, the two simple sentences "I despised my boss." and "I quit my job." can be combined with the conjunction "so" to show the cause/effect relationship between them: "I despised my boss, so I quite my job."

Complex Sentences

A complex sentence consists of a simple sentence and a dependent clause. A dependent clause is a group of words that contains a subject and a verb but cannot stand alone as a sentence. A complex sentence can be constructed with the dependent clause at the beginning, the middle, or the end of the sentence. The following examples, in which the dependent clauses are underlined, illustrate and explain the rules for punctuating complex sentences:

1. When the dependent clause begins the sentence, it is followed by a comma.
2. The dependent clause, when it interrupts the sentence, is set off by commas.
3. The dependent clause needs no comma when it is at the end of the sentence.

A compound sentence may also contain a dependent clause; the sentence is sometimes referred to as compound-complex. Here is an example: A dependent word clause may come at the beginning or end of a sentence, but you can also find them in the middle, where they are sometimes set off with commas.

Activity: **WORKING TOGETHER**   DAEDALUS ONLINE

Write a paragraph of about eight sentences describing either your job or the basic objectives of a course you are taking, for a reader considering either applying for your job or enrolling in the course. Your paragraph must contain simple, compound, and complex sentences. The compound sentences should not repeat the same conjunction, and the complex sentences should vary the position of the dependent clause. Include at least one compound-complex sentence. Number your sentences, and provide a key on the back of the page to identify the sentence types. Trade papers with a classmate, and identify the sentence types in each other's papers.

Activity: **COMPUTER WORKSHOP**

Open a file named "sentences" and type in the sentences below. Then open a file named "version1," copy the "sentences" file into "version1," and combine the twelve short sentences into a few compound and complex sentences that communicate the same ideas using substantially the same words. Add conjunctions ("and," "but," "or," "nor," "yet," "so," and "for"), transitions (such as "also," "then," "first of all"), dependent words (such as "although," "because," "if," "while"), and conjunctive adverbs (such as "therefore," "however," "nevertheless") to join sentences. You may alter or delete a few words as necessary. Once you have completed the first version, open a file named "version2," copy the "sentences" file into it, and combine the sentences in a different way to create a new version. Compare the two versions to see which one you like better.

- I want to quit my job.
- The hours are terrible.
- The pay is low.
- My manager is unfair.
- I am worried about getting another job.
- I don't have the specialized job skills employers want.
- My family needs the money I make.
- I must be employed.
- A better job would make me happier.
- I'd like a job that pays at least $10.00 an hour.
- Working 9 to 5 would be great.
- A fair boss might be too much to ask.

Improving Sentence Style by Being Concise

Some writers employ a very wordy style. They do not use five words when they can use ten. They believe the more words, the better. This wordy writing is especially common in specialized fields such as law and government. Although the wordiness sometimes seems impressive, most readers will see it for what it is—unclear writing. To really impress your readers and make your ideas clear, write concise sentences.

Activity: BUILDING AN ESSAY

Choose one of the paragraphs in your essay to use in another experiment with style. Rewrite the paragraph using the same ideas and mostly the same words but combining them into different sentences. You might link two simple sentences to form a compound or complex sentence. You might break a long sentence down into two shorter sentences. Compare your revision with the original. Have you made any improvements? Do you like the original version better?

Concise sentences use only the number of words necessary to convey the message clearly. Read the two sentences below.

Sentence 1:

The actual truth of the matter is that the newspaper reporter who was investigating the story wrote in a way that made it difficult for readers to determine the order in which the sequence of events occurred. (37 words)

Sentence 2:

The reporter wrote so confusingly that readers could not determine the sequence of events. (14 words)

The second sentence conveys the same idea as the first, but with twenty-three fewer words! The more concise sentence is clearer, as well as shorter. To check your style for wordiness, follow these guidelines:

1. Examine the beginnings of your sentences for unnecessary phrases. In Sentence 1, "The actual truth of the matter is that . . ." is an unnecessary phrase.
2. Avoid sentences using "there is" or "there are," and, in general, avoid using weak verbs such as forms of the verbs "to be," "to have," and "to make." Using these constructions almost always leads to wordiness. For example, "There are dumplings that are cooked and eaten in many cultures throughout the world" is more concise when revised to read, "People in many cultures throughout the world cook and eat dumplings."
3. Eliminate redundancies. A word, phrase, or sentence is redundant if it repeats an idea that is already clear. For example, in Sentence 1, "actual truth" is redundant because something that is a truth **is** actual. In the same way, "the order in which the sequence of events occurred" is redundant because "order" and "sequence" convey the same idea.

Activity: WORKING TOGETHER   DAEDALUS ONLINE

Each member of your group should revise the following passage to make it more concise while maintaining the same meaning. Then compare results.

It seems to me that cooking my own food at home is an improvement over the old eating habits I used to have when I was a fast-food junkie. Now I have the option of eating food that is more healthy and better for my body. There are other benefits, including improved taste and decreased amount of money spent on food expenditures. However, in order to gain these benefits, there is a cost. It is much more time-consuming to cook my own meals. I have to admit that it is worth it.

The Workplace

WORKPLACE STYLE

Professional writing should contain all the same elements of good style that academic writing does—a variety of sentences, strong word choice, and concise phrasing. In addition, workplace writers want their documents to exhibit the following characteristics:

- **Courtesy** Whatever your purpose in letters and memos, polite phrasing will increase the readers' goodwill toward you and your organization. Using "please" and "thank you," phrasing your needs as requests rather than demands, and taking readers' feelings into consideration will make readers more likely to respond positively to your message.

- **Friendly but Businesslike Tone** Business writers must sound friendly without seeming too familiar and professional without seeming aloof. Choose an appropriate level of formality by assessing your reader's background, relationship to you, corporate or national culture, and/or position in the company's hierarchy. A conversational style which might be appropriate in a memo to a colleague might not be appropriate for a proposal to a client overseas. In any case, avoid humor and personal comments about the reader, as these often lead to embarrassing misinterpretation.

- **Positive Emphasis** Accentuate the positive elements of the message and deemphasize the negative. Focus on the glass being half full instead of half empty. You can create positive emphasis through your phrasing—say what is instead of what isn't, use words with positive connotations rather than negative ones. For example, instead of saying, "We cannot deliver your order until July 25," say, "We will deliver your order by July 25." Revise "We are sorry the confusing ordering system caused you difficulties," to eliminate negative words such as "sorry," "confusing," and "difficulties." Instead, write, "Our new system will make ordering easy."

- **"You" Attitude** Keep the focus on the audience's needs and concerns. This may mean that you revise sentences that use the words "I" or "we" to use the word "you" instead. For example, instead of saying, "We sent the package on Thursday," say, "You will receive the package on Friday," because the reader is more interested in when the package will arrive than in when it was sent. If you put yourself in the reader's place as you write and revise, you'll be able to present information in the style that is most useful and pleasing to your audience.

Activity: WRITER'S LOG

Look through three or four of the papers you've written at work or in college. For each paper, analyze your style by answering these questions:

- Have you chosen specific nouns, verbs, adjectives, and adverbs?
- Is your style formal or informal?
- What kinds of sentence structures do you use?
- Are your sentences concise?
- Is your style appropriate for your role as a writer?
- What do you like about your style?
- What would you like to change about your style?

READING AND WRITING TEXTS

Readings

The readings in this chapter are written in a variety of styles and address a number of work-related issues. As you read, focus on the authors' variations in style. Consider word choice, level of formality, and sentence variety.

Activity: PREREADING

In your Writer's Log, respond to these questions:

1. What jobs have you had? What were your experiences on these jobs with your supervisors, coworkers, hours, salary, and job satisfaction? Do you expect your work experiences to be different after you complete your studies? In what ways?
2. Do you think it's important for people to work? Why or why not?

My Young Men Shall Never Work

Chief Smohalla (as told by Herbert Spinden)

"My Young Men Shall Never Work" is a response by Chief Smohalla of the Nez Percé tribe of the Pacific Northwest to the incursion of settlers and farmers into his people's traditional land and way of life. Smohalla's description is poetic and metaphoric, giving it an elegant style that is not usually found in day-to-day writing.

My young men shall never work. Men who work cannot dream and wisdom comes in dreams.

You ask me to plow the ground. Shall I take a knife and tear my mother's breast? Then when I die she will not take me to her bosom to rest.

You ask me to dig for stone. Shall I dig under her skin for bones? Then when I die I cannot enter her body to be born again.

You ask me to cut grass and make hay and sell it and be rich like white men. But how dare I cut off my mother's hair?

It is a bad law and my people cannot obey it. I want my people to stay with me here. All the dead men will come to life again. We must wait here in the house of our fathers and be ready to meet them in the body of our mother.

Activity: **RESPONDING TO THE TEXT**

1. What word choices, sentence structures, or details establish the level of formality in this piece?
2. Chief Smohalla uses questions throughout the passage. Is this effective for his purpose? Why or why not? How does it affect his style?

From *The Communist Manifesto*

Karl Marx

Karl Marx's ideas about socialism, as expressed in The Communist Manifesto, *changed the world. In the following excerpt Marx explains how the owners of capital (the bourgeoisie) exploit workers (the proletariat). Marx believes that this exploitation will eventually be intolerable; workers will unite against the bourgeoisie and will overthrow capitalism.*

In proportion as the bourgeoisie, i.e., capital, is developed, in the same proportion is the proletariat, the modern working class, developed, a class of laborers who live only so long as they find work, and who find work only so long as their labor increases capital. These laborers, who must sell themselves piecemeal, are a commodity, like every other article of commerce, and are consequently exposed to all the vicissitudes of competition, to all the fluctuations of the market.

Owing to the extensive use of machinery and to division of labor, the work of the proletarians has lost all individual character, and, consequently, all charm for the workman. He becomes an appendage of the machine, and it is only the most simple, most monotonous and most easily acquired knack that is required of him. Hence, the cost of production of a workman is restricted almost entirely to the means of subsistence that he requires for his maintenance, and for the propagation of his race. But the price of a commodity, and also of labor, is equal to its cost of production. In proportion, therefore, as the repulsiveness of the work increases the wage decreases. Nay more, in proportion as the use of machinery and division of labor increases, in the same proportion the burden of toil increases, whether by prolongation of the working hours, by increase of the work enacted in a given time, or by increased speed of the machinery, etc.

Modern industry has converted the little workshop of the patriarchal master into the great factory of the industrial capitalist. Masses of laborers, crowded into factories, are organized like soldiers. As privates of the industrial army they are placed under the command of a perfect hierarchy of officers and sergeants. Not only are they the slaves of the bourgeois class and of the bourgeois state, they are daily and hourly enslaved by the machine, by the overlooker, and, above all, by the individual bourgeois manufacturer himself. The more openly this despotism proclaims gain to be its end and aim, the more petty, the more hateful and the more embittering it is. . . .

Hitherto every form of society has been based, as we have already seen, on the antagonism of oppressing and oppressed classes. But in order to oppress a class, certain conditions must be assured to it under which it can, at least, continue its slavish existence. The serf, in the period of serfdom, raised himself to membership in the commune, just as the petty bourgeois, under the yoke of feudal absolutism, managed to develop into a bourgeois. The modern laborer, on the contrary, instead of rising with the progress of industry, sinks deeper and deeper below the conditions of existence of his own class. He becomes a pauper, and pauperism develops more rapidly than population and wealth. And here it becomes evident that the bourgeoisie is unfit any longer to be the ruling class in society, and to impose its conditions of existence upon society as an overriding law. It is unfit to rule, because it is incompetent to assure an existence to its slave within his slavery, because it cannot help letting him sink into such a state that it has to feed him, instead of being fed by him. Society can no longer live under this bourgeoisie; in other words, its existence is no longer compatible with society.

The essential condition for the existence, and for the sway of the bourgeois class, is the formation and augmentation of capital; the condition for capital is wage labor. Wage labor rests exclusively on competition between the laborers. The advance of industry, whose involuntary promoter is the bourgeoisie, replaces the isolation of the laborers, due to competition, by their involuntary combination, due to association. The development of Modern Industry, therefore, cuts from under its feet the very foundation on which the bourgeoisie produces and appropriates products. What the bourgeoisie therefore produces, above all, are its own grave diggers. Its fall and the victory of the proletariat are equally inevitable.

Activity: RESPONDING TO THE TEXT

1. Marx uses repetition of words and phrases to connect his ideas and create emphasis. Find a few passages that use repetition.
2. Make a list of the words Marx uses to refer to the proletarians. Then make a list of the words he uses to refer to the bourgeois. Compare these lists. Do they reflect Marx's attitude toward these groups? How do you think members of these groups would respond if they saw themselves described in these terms?

Year of the Blue-Collar Guy
Steve Olson

"Year of the Blue-Collar Guy" discusses the position of the laborer in society. Steve Olson writes in a contemporary style and medium (Newsweek *magazine*) *about how blue-collar workers deserve more respect for their contributions to society and their superior abilities.*

While the learned are attaching appropriate labels to the 1980s and speculating on what the 1990s will bring, I would like to steal 1989 for my own much maligned group and declare it "the year of the blue-collar guy (BCG)." BCGs have been portrayed as beer-drinking, big-bellied, bigoted rednecks who dress badly. Wearing a suit to a cement-finishing job wouldn't be too bright. Watching my tie go around a motor shaft followed by my neck is not the last thing I want to see in this world. But, more to the point, our necks are too big and our arms and shoulders are too awesome to fit suits well without expensive tailoring. Suits are made for white-collar guys.

But we need big bellies as ballast to stay on the bar stool while we're drinking beer. And our necks are red from the sun and we are somewhat bigoted. But aren't we all? At least our bigotry is open and honest and worn out front like a tattoo. White-collar people are bigoted, too. But it's disguised as the pat on the back that holds you back: "You're not good enough so you need affirmative action." BCGs aren't smart enough to be that cynical. I never met a BCG who didn't respect an honest day's work and a job well done—no matter who did it.

True enough, BCGs aren't perfect. But, I believe this: we are America's last true romantic heroes. When some 21st-century Louis L'Amour writes about this era he won't eulogize the greedy Wall Street insider. He won't commend the narrow-shouldered, wide-hipped lawyers with six-digit unearned incomes doing the same work women can do. His wide-shouldered heroes will be plucked from the ranks of the blue-collar guy. They are the last vestige of the manly world where strength, skill and hard work are still valued.

To some extent our negative ratings are our own fault. While we were building the world we live in, white-collar types were sitting on their ever-widening butts redefining the values we live by. One symbol of America's opulent wealth is the number of people who can sit and ponder and comment and write without producing a usable product or skill. Hey, get a real job—make something—then talk. These talkers are the guys we drove from the playgrounds into the libraries when we were young and now for 20 years or more we have endured the revenge of the nerds.

BCGs fidgeted our way out of the classroom and into jobs where, it seemed, the only limit to our income was the limit of our physical strength and energy. A co-worker described a BCG as "a guy who is always doing things that end in the letter 'n'—you know—huntin', fishin', workin' . . ." My wise friend is talking energy! I have seen men on the job hand-nail 20 square of shingles (that's 6,480 nails) or more a day, day after day, for weeks. At the same time, they were remodeling their houses, raising children, and coaching Little League. I've seen crews frame entire houses in a day—day after day. I've seen guys finish concrete until 11 P.M., go out on a date, then get up at 6 A.M. and do it all over again the next day.

These are amazing feats of strength. There should be stadiums full of screaming fans for these guys. I saw a 40-year-old man neatly fold a 350-pound piece of rubber roofing, put it on his shoulder and, alone, carry it up a ladder and deposit it on a roof. Nobody acknowledged it because the event was too common. One day at noon this same fellow wrestled a 22-year-old college summer worker. In the prime of his life, the college kid was a 6-foot-3, 190-pound body-builder and he was out of his league. He was on his back to stay in 90 seconds flat.

Great Skilled Work Force

Mondays are tough on any job. But in our world this pain is eased by stories of weekend adventure. While white-collar types are debating the value of reading over watching TV, BCGs are doing stuff. I have honest to God heard these things on Monday mornings about BCG weekends: "I tore out a wall and added a room," "I built a garage," "I went walleye fishing Saturday and pheasant hunting Sunday," "I played touch football both days" (in January), "I went skydiving," "I went to the sports show and wrestled the bear." Pack a good novel into these weekends.

My purpose is not so much to put down white-collar people as to stress the importance of blue-collar people to this country. Lawyers, politicians, and bureaucrats are necessary parts of the process, but this great skilled work force is so taken for granted it is rarely seen as the luxury it truly is. Our plumbing works, our phones work and repairs are made as quickly as humanly possible. I don't think this is true in all parts of the world. But this blue-collar resource is becoming endangered. Being a tradesman is viewed with such disdain these days that most young people I know treat the trades like a temporary summer job. I've seen young guys take minimum-wage jobs just so they can wear suits. It is as if any job without a dress code is a dead-end job. This is partly our own fault. We even tell our own sons, "Don't be like me, get a job people respect." Blue-collar guys ought to brag more, even swagger a little. We should drive our families past the latest job site and say "That house was a piece of junk, and now it's the best one on the block. I did that." Nobody will respect us if we don't respect ourselves.

Our work is hard, hot, wet, cold, and always dirty. It is also often very satisfying. Entailing the use of both brain and body there is a product—a physical result of which to be proud. We have fallen from your roofs, died under heavy equipment and been entombed in your dams. We have done honest, dangerous work. Our skills and energy and strength have transformed lines on paper into physical reality. We are this century's Renaissance men. America could do worse than to honor us. We still do things the old-fashioned way, and we have earned the honor.

Activity: RESPONDING TO THE TEXT

1. Identify words in Steve Olson's essay that sound as though they were written by a "blue-collar guy." Are there words that might have more of a "white-collar" tone to them?
2. Olson argues, "There should be stadiums full of screaming fans for these guys." Does his evidence convince you that blue-collar guys deserve such admiration? Why do you think they don't get as much respect as Olson thinks they deserve?

Los Pobres

Richard Rodriguez

Richard Rodriguez is most famous for his autobiography, Hunger of Memory: The Education of Richard Rodriguez, *but he also writes frequently about issues involving education, affirmative action, and bilingualism. In this story about a summer construction job, Rodriguez conveys the complexities of his relationships with other laborers and the contractor.*

It was at Stanford, one day near the end of my senior year, that a friend told me about a summer construction job he knew was available. I was quickly alert. Desire uncoiled within me. My friend said that he knew I had been looking for summer employment. He knew I needed some money. Almost apologetically he explained: It was something I probably wouldn't be interested in, but a friend of his, a contractor, needed someone for the summer to do menial jobs. There would be lots of shoveling and raking and sweeping. Nothing too hard. But nothing more interesting either. Still, the pay would be good. Did I want it? Or did I know someone who did?

I did. Yes, I said, surprised to hear myself say it.

In the weeks following, friends cautioned that I had no idea how hard physical labor really is. ("You only *think* you know what it is like to shovel for eight hours straight.") Their objections seemed to me challenges. They resolved the issue. I became happy with my plan. I decided, however, not to tell my parents. I wouldn't tell my mother because I could guess her worried reaction. I would tell my father only after the summer was over, when I could announce that, after all, I did know what "real work" is like.

The day I met the contractor (a Princeton graduate, it turned out), he asked me whether I had done any physical labor before. "In high school, during the summer," I lied. And although he seemed to regard me with skepticism, he decided to give me a try. Several days later, expectant, I arrived at my first construction site. I would take off my shirt to the sun. And at last grasp desired sensation. No longer afraid. At last become like a *bracero*. "We need those tree strumps out of here by tomorrow," the contractor said. I started to work.

I labored with excitement that first morning—and all the days after. The work was harder than I could have expected. But it was never as tedious as my friends had warned me it would be. There was too much physical pleasure in the labor. Especially early in the day, I would be most alert to the sensations of movement and straining. Beginning around seven each morning (when the air was still damp but the scent of weeds and dry earth anticipated the heat of the sun), I would feel my body resist the first thrusts of the shovel. My arms, tightened by sleep, would gradually loosen; after only several minutes, sweat would gather in beads on my forehead and then—a short while later—I would feel my chest silky with sweat in the breeze. I would return to my work. A nervous spark of pain would fly up my arm and settle to burn like an ember in the thick of my shoulder. An hour, two passed. Three. My whole body would assume regular movements. Even later in the day, my enthusiasm for primitive sensation would survive the heat and the dust and the insects pricking my back. I would strain wildly for sensation as the day came to a close. At three-thirty, quitting time, I would stand upright and slowly let my head fall back, luxuriating in the feeling of tightness relieved.

Some of the men working nearby would watch me and laugh. Two or three of the older men took the trouble to teach me the right way to use a pick, the correct way to shovel. "You're doing it wrong, too fucking hard," one man scolded. Then proceeded to show me—what persons who work with their bodies all their lives quickly learn—the most economical way to use one's body in labor.

"Don't make your back do so much work," he instructed. I stood impatiently listening, vaguely watching, then noticed his work-thickened fingers clutching the shovel. I was annoyed. I wanted to tell him that I enjoyed shoveling the wrong way. And I didn't want to learn the right way. I wasn't afraid of back pain. I liked the way my body felt sore at the end of the day.

I was about to, but, as it turned out, I didn't say a thing. Rather it was at that moment I realized that I was fooling myself if I expected a few weeks of labor to gain me admission to the world of the laborer. I would not learn in three months what my father had meant by "real work." I was not bound to this job; I could imagine its rapid conclusion. For me the sensations of exertion and fatigue could be savored. For my father or uncle, working at comparable jobs when they were my age, such sensations were to be feared. Fatigue took a different toll on their bodies—and minds.

It was, I know, a simple insight. But it was with this realization that I took my first step that summer toward realizing something even more important about the "worker." In the company of carpenters, electricians, plumbers, and painters at lunch, I would often sit quietly, observant. I was not shy in such company. I felt easy, pleased by the knowledge that I was casually accepted, my presence taken for granted by men (exotics) who worked with their hands. Some days the younger men would talk and talk about sex, and they would howl at women who drove by in cars. Other days the talk at lunchtime was subdued; men gathered in separate groups. It depended on who was around. There were rough, good-natured workers. Others were quiet. The more I remember that summer, the more I realize that there was no single *type* of worker. I am embarrassed to say I had not expected such diversity. I certainly had not expected to meet, for example, a plumber who was an abstract painter in his off hours and admired the work of Mark Rothko. Nor did I expect to meet so many workers with college diplomas. (They were the ones who were not surprised that I intended to enter graduate school in the fall.) I suppose what I really want to say here is painfully obvious, but I must say it nevertheless: The men of that summer were middle-class Americans. They certainly didn't constitute an oppressed society. Carefully completing their work sheets; talking about the fortunes of local football teams; planning Las Vegas vacations; comparing the gas mileage of various makes of campers—they were not *los pobres* my mother had spoken about.

On two occasions, the contractor hired a group of Mexican aliens. They were employed to cut down some trees and haul off debris. In all, there were six men of varying age. The youngest in his late twenties; the oldest (his father?) perhaps sixty years old. They came and they left in a single old truck. Anonymous men. They were never introduced to the other men at the site. Immediately upon their arrival, they would follow the contractor's directions, start working—rarely resting—seemingly driven by a fatalistic sense that work which had to be done was best done as quickly as possible.

I watched them sometimes. Perhaps they watched me. The only time I saw them pay me much notice was one day at lunchtime when I was laughing with the other men. The Mexicans sat apart when they ate, just as they worked by themselves. Quiet. I rarely heard them say much to each other. All I could hear were their voices calling out sharply to one another, giving directions. Otherwise, when they stood briefly resting, they talked among themselves in voices too hard to overhear.

The contractor knew enough Spanish, and the Mexicans—or at least the oldest of them, their spokesman—seemed to know enough English to communicate. But because I was around, the contractor decided one day to make me his translator. (He assumed I could speak Spanish.) I did what I was told. Shyly I went over to tell the Mexicans that the patron wanted them to do something else before they left for the day. As I started to speak, I was afraid with my old fear that I would be unable to pronounce the Spanish words. But it was a simple instruction I had to convey. I could say it in phrases.

The dark sweating faces turned toward me as I spoke. They stopped their work to hear me. Each nodded in response. I stood there. I wanted to say something more. But what could I say in Spanish, even if I could have pronounced the words right? Perhaps I just wanted to engage in small talk, to be assured of their confidence, our familiarity. I thought for a moment to ask them where in Mexico they were from. Something like that. And maybe I wanted to tell them (a lie, if need be) that my parents were from the same part of Mexico.

I stood there.

Their faces watched me. The eyes of the man directly in front of me moved slowly over my shoulder, and I turned to follow his glance toward *el patrón* some distance away. For a moment I felt swept up by that glance into the Mexicans' company. But then I heard one of them returning to work. And then the others went back to work. I left them without saying anything more.

When they had finished, the contractor went over to pay them in cash. (He later told me that he paid them collectively—"for the job," though he wouldn't tell me their wages. He said something quickly about the good rate of exchange "in their own country.") I can still hear the loudly confident voice he used with the Mexicans. It was the sound of the *gringo* I had heard as a very young boy. And I can still hear the quiet, indistinct sounds of the Mexican, the oldest, who replied. At hearing that voice I was sad for the Mexicans. Depressed by their vulnerability. Angry at myself. The adventure of the summer seemed suddenly ludicrous. I would not shorten the distance I felt from *los pobres* with a few weeks of physical labor. I would not become like them. They were different from me. . . .

In the end, my father was right—though perhaps he did not know how right or why—to say that I would never know what real work is. I will never know what he felt at his last factory job. If tomorrow I worked at some kind of factory, it would go differently for me. My long education would favor me. I could act as a public person—able to defend my interests, to unionize, to petition, to speak up—to challenge and demand. (I will never know what real work is.) I will never know what the Mexicans knew, gathering their shovels and ladders and saws.

Their silence stays with me now. The wages those Mexicans received for their labor were only a measure of their disadvantaged condition. Their silence is more telling. They lack a public identity. They remain profoundly alien. Persons apart. People lacking a union obviously, people without grounds. They depend upon the relative good will or fairness of their employers each day. For such people, lacking a better alternative, it is not such an unreasonable risk.

Their silence stays with me. I have taken these many words to describe its impact. Only: the quiet. Something uncanny about it. Its compliance. Vulnerability. Pathos. As I heard their truck rumbling away, I shuddered, my face mirrored with sweat. I had finally come face to face with *los pobres*.

Activity: RESPONDING TO THE TEXT

1. Notice instances when Rodriguez uses short sentences. What effect do they have on the tone of the writing?
2. How are the carpenters, electricians, plumbers, and painters Rodriguez meets that summer different than he expected? How are they different from him? How are they different from the Mexican laborers the contractor hires?

Activity: SYNTHESIZING THE TEXTS

1. Would Rodriguez agree with Olson about blue-collar workers? If so, why didn't Rodriguez want to be a laborer? Would Olson have the same respect for the Mexican workers that he had for the workers he describes in his own essay? Would Marx consider Rodriguez and Olson proletarians?

2. All of the readings consider the relative value of the work of various people. Summarize each writer's opinion of what makes some work more valuable than others. Is it the worker's skill? Demands of the market? Cultural values? Political or social power? What do you think of as the most valuable type of work? Why?

Writing Assignments

Academic Essays

1. Psychology

Chief Smohalla and Marx both talk about the effect of work on a person's character and identity. They see work as doing violence to a person's sense of self, reducing them to cogs in a materialistic wheel. Many psychologists, such as Freud and Maslow, have explored the connection between work and people's mental and spiritual health. Both Freud and Maslow believe that meaningful work is essential to mental health and that oppressive work can deaden the spirit. Other psychologists believe that any work, even boring or menial work, can be beneficial because it allows people to feel useful and gives structure to their lives. Do you think that meaningful work is necessary to mental health? Can someone be happy and well adjusted and not work? Support your position by giving examples from your own life, from history, or from current events. Pay particular attention to the style of your sentences when you write this paper.

2. Mass Media

Examine how work is portrayed in the media. You can approach this topic in many ways. You could focus on:

- *one book, movie, or television series* and the way work is portrayed throughout—for example, the way work is depicted in *The Simpsons*
- *a particular job*—law enforcement, teaching, accounting—and its portrayal in various TV shows, movies, or books
- *one conclusion about the way jobs are portrayed*—for example, the boring part of the job is never shown—using examples from various media
- *a type of film, TV show, or book*—for example, sitcoms, romance novels, *Star Trek* films.

Narrowing your topic is an important part of this assignment. You'll also need to determine your audience and purpose. Are you trying to persuade your audience to change their behavior? Are you informing them of something they don't know?

The more precise you can be in your thesis, the stronger your paper will be. "*ER* is an unrealistic portrayal of doctors" is less specific than, "The level of excitement depicted in *ER* is not typical of most emergency rooms."

Use specific examples to support your point. Think about how many examples you need to be convincing or informative. Describe the examples in detail so readers can picture them as they read.

3. Policy and Planning

With three or four other students, you will plan, administer, and report on an investigation of college students' expectations about their future jobs. Follow these steps to complete this project:

A. Choose an audience. Decide who will be interested in this information. Who would want to know about students' expectations for their jobs? Future employers? Politicians? Economists? College administrators? Choose one group to be your "clients." List the particular information they might be most interested in. For example, future employers might be most interested in what students expect in terms of compensation, benefits, and working conditions, while politicians might be more interested in people's expectations about job opportunities and job security.

B. Collect some data. You might design a survey to gather some information or you might conduct interviews with a sampling of students. You might even review student publications for hints about students' expectations.

C. Report your findings. Give your clients an overall view of what methods you used and what information you found. Then draw some conclusions about what this data shows and how it might be useful to them.

This report should be fairly formal in sentence structure, word choice, and organization.

Workplace Writing

Write a newsletter article that informs students about an upcoming campus or community event or fellow workers about something new at your company. A newsletter article, like other journalistic writing, follows certain conventions:

- *Leads* The opening sentence contains answers to the questions: who, what, where, when, why, and how. A lead allows readers to immediately know what the article is about and whether they want to read further. As in all other writing, keep your audience in mind when writing the lead. The information that is most essential or interesting to your reader should be in your lead.
- *Inverted Pyramid* The rest of the article supplies information in descending order of importance, saving least important background information for last.
- *Journalistic Style* Use sentences with strong verbs and put the main actor or activity in the subject position of the sentence. Be concise and factual. Do not express personal opinions or use "I." Keep paragraphs short.

Personal Writing

Think about your life ten or fifteen years from now and describe the job you would ideally like to have. Try to be realistic, but still describe the best possible situation for you. Be as specific and complete as possible. Brainstorming or freewriting might help you collect your thoughts. Thinking about these questions might get you started:

1. What sort of job do you have? What kind of company do you work for? How large is the company?
2. Where is your job located? What is your physical working environment like? Describe your immediate surroundings (your work space) and any relevant surrounding spaces (common areas, buildings, campus, cafeteria, meeting rooms, etc.).
3. What are your coworkers like? How many and what kind of people do you deal with daily? What is your relationship with these people? Are you in charge of them, supervised by them, cooperating with them, on a team?
4. What are your daily work activities? How much of your time is spent in each activity? What is an average day like? Is your work challenging? Is it predictable? Is it likely to change?
5. What is your daily and yearly schedule? Is your work fairly consistent, or do you work in spurts? Do you control your work and schedule? Do you have restricted breaks or vacations?
6. How are you compensated for your work? Are you paid a salary? Do you work on commission? How much do you get paid? Are there any other compensations?
7. How do you feel about your work? Is it demanding physically or mentally? What difficulties do you face? What are the rewards and satisfactions of the job?

Write this paper as though you are presently doing the job. For example, write "I am an accountant with a major firm in the Washington area." You can be fairly informal, but try to be specific and clear.

POLISHING AND REFLECTING ON TEXTS

Learning From Other Student Writers

How Are Young Women Portrayed in TV Sitcoms?

Shelly Froehlich

Shelly Froehlich wrote this essay about how young women are portrayed in sitcoms. In one paragraph, she discusses the way work is portrayed in these shows.

Young women in sitcom TV shows such as *Friends, Dharma and Greg*, and *Will and Grace* are portrayed as uncommitted to work, abnormally thin, and dysfunctional in relationships. The characters never have a bad hair day, are never out of style or obese. In fact, each season the young female characters appear to lose more weight. All the women in the programs I've watched—Phoebe, Rachel, Monica, Dharma, and Grace—are abnormally thin and never seem to monitor what they eat. They can eat all they want and don't seem to need to exercise. Their lives continually show chaotic and spontaneous behavior toward work and personal relationships. I have never witnessed a character having a major problem or tragic event happen on these programs. The characters do, however, care about their own social lives, lounging around with the gang all day and drinking coffee or going to lunch or dinner. The characters' lack of commitment to work makes them appear to not need a job to survive. They never care about finances and act as though they can go on living without working and paying bills. The lives of the women in these TV programs are never quite as focused, balanced, or scheduled as typical life tends to be.

Phoebe, Rachel, and Monica are the characters on *Friends*. Phoebe, the queen of flightiness, is very funny, eccentric, and ditzy. She has had a variety of different jobs from masseuse to guitar player to cab driver. Phoebe has a problem keeping a job for more than a month, and I wonder how she pays her rent. Rachel is portrayed as a Barbie doll type of young woman. She tries to hold a job and be respected by her coworkers, but she usually fails. On one episode, Rachel started a new job where everyone smoked. She did not smoke but started because everyone else was smoking at her new work. She was choking, coughing, and gagging, but continued because she wanted to fit in. When the whole group at work decided to quit smoking together, Rachel threw her cigarettes in the trash and started a fire. She was fired, but she stated she didn't care because she didn't like all those smokers anyway. Getting fired from a job is not a good message to be presenting to thirteen- and fourteen-year-old girls who typically watch the show.

Recently, on an episode of *Dharma and Greg*, the couple mapped out plans for Thanksgiving. Dharma planned seven houses to be visited by the two of them for the holiday. She decided that they would not eat at any of the houses, so she made a huge breakfast for the two of them. Of course, as the episode went on, the couple ended up eating at every house. Dharma stated several times that she wouldn't fit into any of her clothes anymore and gave the appearance of throwing up in the back seat of their car on the way to the last house to visit. Throwing up is not a great message to be giving girls who may have an eating disorder. All the characters on these shows are abnormally thin, can eat anything without gaining weight, and never exercise. On *Friends*, Rachel is always eating ice cream, candy, and cake. On one episode she ate a carton of ice cream for dinner every night and never mentioned being worried about her weight. Many young women feel that it is OK to eat whatever they want because these characters do, and they are not fat.

Monica, a character on *Friends*, is portrayed as lacking commitment in relationships. She is always trying to find a boyfriend and her relationships never seem to materialize because she is so demanding and doesn't communicate well. On a recent episode, Monica started to date Chandler, her brother's best friend, and went to Las Vegas for the weekend. For some reason, Monica thought Chandler wanted to get married and vice versa. All weekend long, both were trying to challenge each other for reasons not to get married. They even rolled dice to see if they should get married. Another example of being noncommitted is when Grace, from the program *Will and Grace*, decided to sleep with Greg, the brother of her roommate. This was a very casual relationship. At a dinner party, they both decided that they wanted to spend the night together and went to bed immediately after the party. No bond or feelings were ever mentioned by either party, and after that night, they decided not to see each other because of Will. They thought it would be too difficult on him. This message that "one-night stands" are OK is not a good one to be giving to teenagers who watch the show.

The fact is these TV programs depict a very fantasy type of life that young women think can occur for them if they are pretty or skinny enough. What are the chances of a girl dating a guy and two weeks later they are in Vegas rolling dice to see if they're supposed to get married? The odds are better of winning the lottery. These characters' lives do not make much sense, and their morals are off. However, many young women think their lives could be like these characters' if they just lose that extra weight, get a boob job, and exercise night and day. Reality tells us a different story. Seventy percent of Americans are overweight, according to a recent newscast. Real life is a completely different world than that dramatized on the sitcoms. Working life coming second to social life is a fantasy image conveyed to young women through these TV programs. These images give women false hope that they too could lounge around with friends all day and not need to worry about rent and food. These programs diminish women's self-worth and are still portraying women as inferior.

Activity: RESPONDING TO THE TEXT

1. Shelly's paragraphs are long and detailed. In fact, each of them could be expanded into an essay of its own. Look at Shelly's introductory statements about how working is portrayed in sitcoms and at the paragraph about working. What could Shelly do to expand this paragraph into an essay? Can you think of other examples that could be added? Write an outline of an essay that could be built by expanding her paragraph.

2. Look at her choice of words, length of sentences, sentence variety, use of examples. What could you say about Shelly's style?

3. Rewrite the first paragraph using your own words and sentences to say the same thing Shelly does. How is your style different from Shelly's?

Activity: PEER WORKSHOP

Writers answer these questions before the workshop:

1. Can you describe your style in this essay?
2. Is the level of formality appropriate to your style, purpose, and reader?
3. Are your sentences adequately varied?

Readers respond to the writer's comments. Then do the following:

1. In the margin, mark with a ✔ the places where the writer used specific language.
2. In the margin, mark with an ✘ spots where more concise language would strengthen the essay.

Activity: PROOFREADING YOUR WORK

Parallel structure is one method of forming strong, clear, sentences. Learn how to make words, phrases, and clauses parallel.

Then find all the sentences that contain a series of words, phrases, or clauses. Make sure the items are in parallel form.

Activity: POSTSCRIPT

1. Which aspects of style presented in this chapter are your strengths? Which need more attention?
2. Do you think your style of writing reflects your personality? In what ways?
3. Review the readings in this chapter and note some of the variations in formality and in style. Do any styles appeal to you more than others? Which style appeals most to you? Why?

REVISION

P R E V I E W

This chapter's explanations about improving the content, organization, and style of your papers will help answer these questions:

- Why is revising papers important?
- What should you look for when revising?
- How do you improve the flow of your paper and the sound of your sentences?
- How can you proofread more effectively?

L E A R N I N G   A B O U T   T E X T S

Understanding the Revision Process

Parents often have biased views of their children. When a parent tells us that his or her child is a genius, we are often skeptical because we know that parents tend to exaggerate their children's accomplishments and minimize their shortcomings. Parents' biases toward their children are natural because we are all biased about our creations.

Writers are much like parents when it comes to their texts. They find it difficult to be objective about what they have produced. Writers often look at their writing with pride and have a hard time seeing anything that could be changed or improved. However, unlike parents, writers cannot be blindly satisfied with their work. In order to produce strong papers, writers usually must revise. Because there are so many elements in writing a good essay, letter, memo, or report, it is almost impossible for even the best writer to get everything right the first time.

Most writers revise their work numerous times to improve and refine the content, organization, and style. In fact, most writers probably spend more time revising their work than they spend writing the original draft. In "The Maker's Eye: Revising Your Own Manuscripts," (pp. 283–287) Donald Murray reports on the revising habits of some established writers:

- Business writer Peter Drucker refers to his first effort as the zero draft—the beginning of a lengthy revision process.
- British novelist Anthony Burgess says that he "might revise a page twenty times."
- Children's author Roald Dahl says that he will have read and revised early portions of a story 150 times by the time he reaches the end.

Of all the skills useful in revision, perhaps the most crucial is objectivity. To revise well, you need to view your writing with the detachment of an outsider. Try to react to your paper as if you were an editor; that is, your purpose is not to defend your paper, but to examine it critically to discover areas that need improvement.

Peer editing is a valuable tool because peer editors bring objectivity to the process. Listening to the reactions of your peers enables you to view your writing through the eyes of others. If you are unable to work in a group to revise your writing, you can still get input from others. Give copies of your file on disks to group members, or send it to them online. Your peer editors can insert comments and suggestions within your document, in boldface or in brackets, and return the file to you.

Because it is almost impossible to concentrate on all aspects of a paper simultaneously, writers often review their work several times, each time focusing on a different aspect. In the peer review workshops located at the end of the previous chapters, you have already practiced limited revision. In this chapter you will practice a method of revising your work in stages, each of which focuses on a different aspect of writing.

First, you revise the content, making your paper more complete and unified. Next, you revise for organization, making sure the ideas fit together logically and smoothly. Finally, you revise your sentences to make the style more appealing and to correct errors. When you have finished all these steps, your paper is likely to be substantially different—and substantially better—than your first draft.

Revising for Completeness and Unity

Completeness

You have already been using strategies to ensure that your paper is complete by considering your reader, purpose, and thesis in the planning stages of writing. In revising for completeness, you check your paper to be sure you have included all the informa-

Online Writing Labs, called OWLs, can help you with many phases of your writing. Many colleges provide OWLs for students. One well-established OWL is at Purdue University:

☞   http://owl.english.purdue.edu/

tion your readers need. The least efficient way is to merely reread your draft—which will almost inevitably look just fine to you the way it is. Because you wrote it, you understand what you are trying to communicate, so it is difficult to notice what information may be missing. Start with a blank sheet of paper on which to make some brief lists.

First, list your topic and your intended reader. Do you have a specific reader—e.g., people debating which computer to buy, Civil War history buffs, students new to your campus, coworkers training on new software? If not, you are probably writing for what is referred to as the general reader, an educated person with wide interests and general knowledge, but without specialized background in any particular area.

Next, list your purpose. Elaborate on your purpose by adding either an explanation or your thesis statement. Your page should now look roughly like one of these two examples:

Example 1:

TOPIC:	divorce
READER:	divorcing parents of school-aged children
PURPOSE:	to inform
EXPLANATION:	I want divorcing parents to know how to minimize the negative effects of divorce on their children.

Example 2:

TOPIC:	adjusting to college
READER:	students entering college just after high school
PURPOSE:	to persuade
THESIS:	College offers much more freedom than high school; therefore, to be successful, college students have to supply the discipline, organization, and time management which are built into the high-school system.

If you cannot list a topic, a reader, and a thesis or a purpose which you can explain, your paper is probably unfocused, and before you can proceed, you need to clarify your reader and purpose.

When you are satisfied with your reader and purpose, continue to the next step: List all the information your reader needs in order to fulfill your purpose. Since you are revising for completeness, you need not worry about the order of your ideas. Just jot down everything you think readers need to know, including main points, definitions, evidence, details and examples, and reasons. In the previous example about divorce, you would have to explain what negative impact divorce could have on school-aged children and what specific steps parents can take to minimize those effects. To be interesting, you would have to give specific examples of behaviors and actions that would benefit the children; to be convincing, you would have to give solid evidence that those behaviors and actions are effective.

When you have completed your list, turn to your draft. Check off the items on your list when you locate them in your paper. Look at the items left on your list and decide whether they should be added to your paper.

Because revising for completeness is a demanding task, you might want to ask friends, colleagues, or other students in your class for help. Ask them to read your list, your draft, or both, as if they were the intended readers. They should then ask you questions. For example, they might ask you to clarify information, provide definitions, expand explanations, or add examples. When revising your paper, add information that answers their questions and addresses their concerns.

In writing this textbook, the authors went through many drafts. Here is an example of a section from Chapter 5 that was revised because the content was weak; it did not supply enough specific information for students unfamiliar with topic sentences. The original version said this:

> Putting the topic sentence at the beginning of the paragraph helps readers by clarifying your purpose and making your ideas easier to follow.

This sentence makes a general statement that might not be clear, so the authors added an example to clarify their point:

> For example, if you were writing a paragraph about the cost savings of flex-time for employers, you might begin with a sentence like this: "Employers could save money by allowing a flex-time schedule." This sentence would alert the readers to the point of the paragraph so they would be ready to consider the evidence you present.

To revise for completeness, answer the questions in this checklist.

Checklist—Revising for Completeness

1. What is the topic of your paper?
2. Who is your intended reader?
3. What is the purpose of your paper?
4. What is your thesis? If you don't yet have a thesis, what specific goals do you want your paper to accomplish?
5. What main topics will you need to discuss to accomplish your purpose?
6. Will you need to define any terms or give any background information?
7. What evidence (e.g., reasons, examples, details) will you give to support each main topic?
8. Show your draft to two or three friends, colleagues, or family members. What information do they think you need to add to accomplish your purpose?

Activity: BUILDING AN ESSAY

Working in groups of three, discuss the essays you drafted in Chapter 5 by answering the questions in the checklist and deciding what revisions would improve each paper's contents. Make any appropriate revisions.

Unity

When a paper is unified, it contains no irrelevancies: Every topic paragraph supports the thesis, and the information within each paragraph supports the topic sentence. A unified paper does not ramble on about topics that do not relate directly to the thesis. Read your paper once more, checking to be sure that everything—every fact, detail, piece of evidence, anecdote—is consistent with your purpose. The most interesting or amusing anecdote or quotation must be eliminated or changed if it does not help you fulfill the purpose of your paper. When you discover an irrelevant element in your paper, you can

- eliminate it,
- alter it so it is appropriate, or
- replace it with relevant information.

When writing this textbook, the authors often had to cut out sentences or whole sections that seemed like valuable information when they wrote the first draft, but that ended up being unnecessary or distracting. Here is an example of a section in Chapter 1 that was revised to eliminate unnecessary information.

Original:

> Everyone is constantly responding to texts, when they notice the style of an outfit, glance at a billboard advertisement, or watch a movie. However, college courses focus primarily on written texts. In college, students are expected to respond to written texts through reading and to create texts through writing. The purpose of this book, then, is to help you become a better reader and writer of texts. Because written texts have many features in common, improving your ability to read and write texts will also help you become a more successful writer in your personal life and on the job.

Revised:

> However, college courses focus primarily on written texts. Students must read and write texts especially suited in style, format, and content to their professors' interests and expectations. Although you are already fairly accomplished at reading and writing, this book will help you become a better reader and writer of academic texts. Because all written texts have many features in common, improving your ability to read and write college texts will also help you become a more successful writer in your personal life and on the job.

In the revised version, the first sentence of the original has been completely eliminated because, although it may be an interesting point, it seemed unnecessary for the understanding of the rest of the paragraph. Do you think anything important was lost by eliminating this information? The phrase "in college" has been dropped from the second sentence in the revised version because it is unnecessary; readers will know the students are college students.

One of the difficulties in revising for unity is remaining objective and focused on the task of eliminating extraneous material. Eliminating sections that we find especially interesting, insightful, or clever is difficult to do. If you are writing on a computer, try pasting the information you eliminate from your paper into a separate file. That way you can easily add the information in a revised form if appropriate, or you can save it for possible inclusion in another paper.

To revise a paper for unity, answer the questions in the checklist below.

Checklist—Revising for Unity

1. Read each topic sentence. Does each topic sentence directly support the thesis?
2. Check each topic paragraph. Does all the information in the paragraph support the topic sentence?
3. Have you eliminated, revised, or replaced every element of your paper that does not help fulfill the purpose of a topic sentence or of the thesis?

Revising Organization for Order and Coherence

Logical Order

Having revised for completeness and unity, you can be confident that your paper contains the information your reader needs. In revising for organization, you decide whether the contents of your paper are arranged logically and smoothly.

In Chapters 9–18 you will learn several patterns of organization frequently used in academic and workplace writing. However, common sense will usually provide you with a logical way to organize your material.

You know, of course, that college essays and reports have introductory paragraphs and concluding paragraphs. In between, you make several points, each of which is discussed briefly, usually in a paragraph. These topic paragraphs contain evidence supporting your thesis. To revise for organization, first check to see that each of the topic paragraphs clearly supports the thesis or helps fulfill your paper's purpose.

Activity: BUILDING AN ESSAY

Using the papers you drafted in Chapter 5, work in small groups answering the questions in the Revising for Unity Checklist. Decide what revisions would improve each paper's unity and make appropriate revisions.

Next, be sure that each topic paragraph in your draft is restricted to only one topic. For example, if you were writing the paper on adjusting to college described in the second example on p. 267, you would have to write three sections—one on self-discipline, one on organization, and one on time management. If you find a paragraph that discusses more than one topic or meanders from idea to idea, you will need to subdivide the paragraph, provide a topic sentence for each new paragraph, and add sufficient supporting evidence for each paragraph.

The next step is to decide whether you have found a logical order for your paragraphs. If your readers need background information or definitions in order to understand your paper, those paragraphs should come first. If you are telling a story, explaining a process, or giving any information that naturally breaks into steps or stages, then a chronological order makes sense, and your description of the events should be in the order in which they happen.

If, however, your paper consists of information, examples, or reasons in support of your thesis, you might consider arranging your paragraphs in emphatic order. In the emphatic order, writers arrange their evidence from the least to the most significant. The emphatic order is convincing because your evidence builds gradually and your readers are left with the most powerful evidence as their final impression. Sometimes finding the emphatic order is easy. For example, if you were persuading readers not to smoke, you might give them four broad reasons—the unattractiveness of smokers, the inconvenience for smokers of smoke-free environments, the cost of smoking, and the health hazards. When you developed your topic paragraphs, clearly the evidence about the unattractiveness of smokers—stained teeth, stale odor on hair and clothes—would be less significant than the health hazards—the risk of chronic bronchitis, emphysema, or lung cancer. Sometimes the emphatic order is less obvious. In the example about adjusting to college, you might have trouble ranking the factors—organization, self-discipline, and time management—in an emphatic order. When they have difficulty finding an appropriate order, writers usually choose as most emphatic the topic for which they have the most powerful evidence or examples.

In Chapter 1 of this textbook, the authors list the characteristics of all texts. The original order for this list was as follows:

1. Texts have power.
2. Because texts have more than one meaning, they are open to interpretation and criticism.
3. Texts are not written or read in a vacuum.
4. All writers make choices, including how to organize their texts, what information to include, and what format to use.
5. Texts are completed by readers who interpret the meaning.

The revised order is below:

1. Texts have power.
2. All writers make choices, including how to organize their texts, what information to include, and what formats to use.
3. Writers' choices about their texts are influenced by many factors, including historical events, social and personal circumstances, time, distance, and other texts.
4. Texts are completed by readers who interpret the meaning according to their own information, experience, and expectations.

In making this revision, the authors first decided to eliminate the third item in their original list because it overlapped with the fourth and fifth items. Then they decided that a change in the order would make the progression of ideas more logical. Notice that the wording of Number 3 was also changed to make it clearer.

When you revise on a computer, you can view only a portion of your document on the screen. Be careful not to restrict your revisions to what you can see. If your document is short, you may be able to scroll up and down to keep the entire text in mind; however, most writers prefer to check organization by printing a hard copy to consult.

Revising for organization on a computer enables you to experiment with different patterns of development. You can cut and paste in order to move sentences, paragraphs, or sections of your paper. Because you may be unsure about some of the changes, you should save each version in a separate file. You can move back and forth among files or print copies to compare the effects of the different versions.

To spot any problems your paper may have in organization, answer the questions in the checklist below.

Checklist—Revision for Organization

1. Does your paper have an introductory paragraph or section?
2. Does the introduction contain a clear thesis statement? If there is no thesis, is the purpose of the paper made clear to the reader?
3. Are the contents of your paper divided logically into paragraphs, each of which discusses only one topic?
4. Does each support paragraph have a topic sentence? Does each topic sentence clearly support the thesis or help fulfill the purpose of the paper?
5. Does the information in each paragraph support the topic sentence by offering details, evidence, or examples?
6. Are the supporting paragraphs in a logical order?
7. Does your paper have a concluding paragraph or section?

Activity: BUILDING AN ESSAY

Using the paper you drafted in Chapter 5, work in groups to answer the questions on the checklist for organization. Decide whether the organizational pattern each group member used is appropriate for the purpose and contents of the paper. Make any necessary changes.

Coherence

When you revised for completeness, you improved your paper's coherence by adding any missing information. When you revised for unity, you improved the coherence of your paper by eliminating distracting irrelevancies. When you revised for organization, you made your paper more coherent by providing a clear, easily followed pattern. At this stage in your revision, you need to revise only the language of your paper, adding transitions to make the relationship of the parts clearer to your reader.

Transitions, as you learned in Chapter 5, are used to show the relationships between ideas. Although these relationships may seem perfectly clear to you, adding transitions throughout your paper makes your ideas easier for the reader to follow and makes your writing seem more polished.

Transitions can be words, phrases, sentences, or even brief paragraphs. Be sure that your final draft contains transitions that make the relationship of ideas clear to your readers.

The following words and phrases are common transitions:

words		phrases
after	however	at the same time
also	nevertheless	for example
consequently	next	in addition
finally	similarly	on the other hand
first	therefore	the third reason

Transitions lead the reader through your paragraphs, like road signs showing how one idea relates to another. Look at the following passage from the first paragraph of Chapter 4. It uses transitions (highlighted) to guide the readers:

> When you cook or bake, you usually gather your ingredients in one place before you begin. When you make a repair on your house or car, you usually make sure you have the right tools before you begin the project. **In the same way**, gathering the materials for your paper before you begin writing makes drafting much easier. **Once** you have determined your purpose, you have a general idea of what must be included in your text. **However**, you will need to spend some time finding the exact facts, arguments, examples, and details necessary to write the paper.

Now look at the passage with the transitions removed:

> When you cook or bake, you usually gather your ingredients in one place before you begin. When you make a repair on your house or car, you usually make sure you have the right tools before you begin the project. Gathering the materials for your paper before you begin writing makes drafting much easier. You have determined your purpose, and you have a general idea of what must be included in your text. You will need to spend some time finding the exact facts, arguments, examples, and details necessary to write the paper.

Without **In the same way**, the transition between the second and third sentences is abrupt and confusing. Eliminating **Once** makes it difficult to see the sequence of events. **However** signals that the last sentence reverses the idea of the one before; without it, readers aren't prepared for the shift.

Sentence transitions, although they often contain transition words and phrases, are written to fit the exact context of your paper. For example, in a paper on painting drywall, you might have this transition sentence: "Having completed all the preparations, you are finally ready to begin to paint." In a paper on the dangers of smoking, you might move from a paragraph on cost to a paragraph on health with a transition sentence like this: "Even wasting a thousand or more dollars a year is insignificant compared to the enormous risks to your health." Look at the example of the revised passage from Chapter 1 of this textbook on p. 269. Not only was the passage made more coherent by improving its unity, but its coherence was also improved by beginning with a transition sentence.

Remember that you already improved your paper's coherence when you revised for completeness, unity, and organization. Answering the questions in the following checklist will ensure a coherent text that is easy to follow.

Checklist—Revising for Coherence

1. Are there transitions between the paragraphs?
2. Are there sufficient transition words and phrases within each paragraph to make it flow smoothly?

Revising Words and Sentences

Revising for Sentence Structure

This stage of revision polishes your paper by strengthening sentences. Chapter 7 discusses style thoroughly, but you can improve your paper substantially by using more specific words, improving sentences' clarity, being concise, and varying sentence structure.

Activity: BUILDING AN ESSAY

Use the same paper that you have already revised for completeness, unity, and logical order. Now revise your paper for coherence. First, circle all transition words and phrases. Then, in your group, decide where you could improve the flow of ideas by adding more. Underline all transition sentences. Are they sufficient to link the paragraphs together? Make any appropriate changes.

- Use more specific words. Substitute specific adjectives, nouns, and verbs for vague ones. Instead of writing, "That is a good car," write, "That Prelude handles like a racing car."

FYI: For more on specific word choice, see pp. 240–242.

- Make your meaning clear. Eliminate awkward or confusing wording. Make sure subjects, verbs, and objects make sense together. For example, if you said, "Tamales are an old Mexican custom," the subject and object would not match because a food isn't a custom. Be careful where you place modifiers. For example, the sentence "The store has clothes for kids that are inexpensive" is confusing because it sounds as though the kids may be inexpensive.

- Be concise. Pay special attention to sentences beginning with "There is," "There are," "It is," and similar constructions. Revising these sentences is often an easy way to strengthen the overall style of your paper. Try to eliminate redundancies—words that repeat an idea that has already been stated or implied in another word or phrase. For example, in the sentence "The bear has animal instincts which tell it to hibernate," "animal" is redundant because we know a bear is an animal. Shortening wordy sentences also improves clarity.

FYI: For help writing more concise sentences, see pp. 246–247.

- Notice each sentence's structure. Are you using short, simple sentences over and over? If so, you might want to combine some into more complex sentences. On the other hand, if you use only long, complex sentences, you may need to vary this pattern by breaking some of the longer sentences into shorter, simpler ones.

FYI: For more on varying sentence structures, see pp. 243–245.

Activity: COMPUTER WORKSHOP

Open a file titled "one" and write a paragraph describing typical activities of a group to which you belong. After saving your first file, open a second file titled "two" and write another paragraph describing the same typical activities of the same group but using different words and sentences. Don't look at the first paragraph while you're writing the second. Open a third file titled "three" and write a third version of the same material. Then merge all three versions into one file titled "compare." Examine the word choice and sentence structure in the three versions, take the best of each, and compose a fourth paragraph that is better than all the others.

Proofreading Your Paper

In Chapter 1, you learned that academic and workplace readers expect your writing to have very few errors in spelling, grammar, and mechanics. After revising your paper for style, you should proofread your paper carefully to eliminate any minor errors. By now you probably know your trouble spots. Although you want to be alert for any type of mistake in your paper, you should be especially careful in proofreading your paper to find and eliminate the errors you typically make.

Among the boons of computer-assisted writing are the programs that check spelling and grammar. During the final stages of revision, you should use the spellchecker to help you locate spelling and typographical errors. Be careful, however, not to rely too much on these computer tools.

- <u>Spell-checker</u>. Although a spell-checker will recognize misspelled words, it will also ignore correctly spelled words that are not the words you intended. A spell-checker will ignore common typographical errors, such as "or" instead of "of," and it will not distinguish between commonly confused words such as "it's" and "its."
- <u>Grammar checker</u>. Grammar checkers are even more problematic. While they will point out errors or weaknesses in structure, their advice is often confusing or misleading.
- <u>Thesaurus</u>. The electronic thesaurus, just like its print counterpart, will list vocabulary options, but won't give any indication of which word is more appropriate in the circumstances.

The following checklist contains questions to help you polish your paper. To make the checklist more helpful, add several questions to help you check for the errors you frequently make.

Checklist—Polishing Your Paper

1. Check each sentence for appropriate word choice. Have you used specific words whenever possible? Have you used words that the reader will understand?
2. Are there any unnecessary words in your sentences? Check especially for sentences that begin with "there is" or "there are" structures. Also look for redundancies.
3. Check for sentence clarity. Is the meaning of each sentence clear? If you are unsure about a sentence, read it to someone and see whether the listener can restate your sentence in his or her own words.
4. Do you vary your sentence structures? If not, try to increase the sentence variety by combining short sentences or breaking down long ones.
5. Check for errors in sentence structure by looking for fragments and run-ons. Starting at the end of your paper, read every word group that begins with a capital. Is each a complete sentence?
6. Check carefully for errors in pronoun use, subject-verb agreement, use of modifiers, and punctuation. Pay particular attention to those errors you know you make frequently.
7. Have you spelled all words correctly? Pay particular attention to sound-alike words such as "they're," "there," and "their."

Add a few more items to help you proofread for the errors you frequently make.

8. _____
   _____
9. _____
   _____
10. _____
    _____

Activity: BUILDING AN ESSAY

Review your revised paper one final time. Exchange papers with other members of your group, using the checklist above to help you identify problems. Suggest some revisions.

DESIGNING A VISUALLY EFFECTIVE DOCUMENT

The Workplace

In this chapter you learned to revise writing. However, the effectiveness of workplace documents depends on design as well as on content and organization. Writers use visual elements to make their documents easier to read, understand, and remember. When creating a workplace document, you need a clear visual design that incorporates the features listed below. When revising workplace documents, you need to evaluate completeness, unity, organization, and coherence. In addition, you need to evaluate the effectiveness of the document's design.

To design an effective workplace document

- **Chunk information.** Break information into units that are easy to identify, read, and remember. Set off the material by using white space between lines and in the margins. Add boxes, shading, or columns.

- **Show relationships between ideas.** Bulleted lists show readers that the items are similar. Numbered lists show that items have a specific sequence or hierarchy. Headings in the same typeface (ALL CAPS, **Boldface**, Underlined) are on the same organizational level (for example, MAIN REASONS, **Supporting Evidence**, Examples). Columns establish a relationship between items above, below, and across from each other.

- **Emphasize material.** Italicized, underlined, boldfaced, colored, or capitalized text draws a reader's attention to important material. Use these devices in headings or within the text to help readers locate and remember the information they need. Icons, shading, and boxes also emphasize chunks of material.

Good design of visual elements aids readers in skimming, understanding, and recalling information. Clearly designed documents save readers time. Striking a balance between too many visual elements, which make the document seem cluttered, and too few, which make the document appear intimidating and dull, requires an understanding of your own material and an awareness of your readers' needs.

READING AND WRITING TEXTS

Readings

This chapter contains four readings on revision—three commentaries by professional writers and the revisions made in the drafting of a portion of The Declaration of Independence. As you read the writers' comments on revision, compare their remarks to your own revision process. As you review the changes made in The Declaration of Independence, consider the reasons for the alterations.

Activity: PREREADING

In small groups, explore these topics:

1. Do you usually spend more time writing or revising your papers?
2. What do you typically focus on when you revise?

Shitty First Drafts

Anne Lamott

Anne Lamott writes fiction and nonfiction. Her latest books are a novel, Crooked Little Heart, *and* Tender Mercies: Some Thoughts on Faith. *This reading is a chapter from* Bird by Bird: Some Instructions on Writing and Life *which Lamott claims contains "almost every single thing I know about writing."*

Now, practically even better news than that of short assignments is the idea of shitty first drafts. All good writers write them. This is how they end up with good second drafts and terrific third drafts. People tend to look at successful writers, writers who are getting their books published and maybe even doing well financially, and think that they sit down at their desks every morning feeling like a million dollars, feeling great about who they are and how much talent they have and what a great story they have to tell; that they take in a few deep breaths, push back their sleeves, roll their necks a few times to get all the cricks out, and dive in, typing fully formed passages as fast as a court reporter. But this is just the fantasy of the uninitiated. I know some very great writers, writers you love who write beautifully and have made a great deal of money, and not *one* of them sits down routinely feeling wildly enthusiastic and confident. Not one of them writes elegant first drafts. All right, one of them does, but we do not like her very much. We do not think that she has a rich inner life or that God likes her or can even stand her. (Although when I mentioned this to my priest friend Tom, he said you can safely assume you've created God in your own image when it turns out that God hates all the same people you do.)

Very few writers really know what they are doing until they've done it. Nor do they go about their business feeling dewy and thrilled. They do not type a few stiff warm-up sentences and then find themselves bounding along like huskies across the snow. One writer I know tells me that he sits down every morning and says to himself nicely, "It's not like you don't have a choice, because you do—you can either type or kill yourself." We all often feel like we are pulling teeth, even those writers whose prose ends up being the most natural and fluid. The right words and sentences just do not come pouring out like ticker tape most of the time. Now, Muriel Spark is said to have felt that she was taking dictation from God every morning—sitting there, one supposes, plugged into a Dictaphone, typing away, humming. But this is a very hostile and aggressive position. One might hope for bad things to rain down on a person like this.

For me and most of the other writers I know, writing is not rapturous. In fact, the only way I can get anything written at all is to write really, really shitty first drafts.

The first draft is the child's draft, where you let it all pour out and then let it romp all over the place, knowing that no one is going to see it and that you can shape it later. You just let this childlike part of you channel whatever voices and visions come through and onto the page. If one of the characters wants to say, "Well, so what, Mr. Poopy Pants?" you let her. No one is going to see it. If the kid wants to get into really sentimental, weepy, emotional territory, you let him. Just get it all down on paper, because there may be something great in those six crazy pages that you would never have gotten to by more rational, grown-up means. There may be something in the very last line of the very last paragraph on page six that you just love, that is so beautiful or wild that you now know what you're supposed to be writing about, more or less, or in what direction you might go—but there was no way to get to this without first getting through the first five-and-a-half pages.

I used to write food reviews for *California* magazine before it folded. (My writing food reviews had nothing to do with the magazine folding, although every single review did cause a couple of canceled subscriptions. Some readers took umbrage at my comparing mounds of vegetable puree with various ex-presidents' brains.) These reviews always took two days to write. First I'd go to a restaurant several times with a few opinionated, articulate friends in tow. I'd sit there writing down everything anyone said that was at all interesting or funny. Then on the following Monday I'd sit down at my desk with my notes, and try to write the review. Even after I'd been doing this for years, panic would set in. I'd try to write a lead, but instead I'd write a couple of dreadful sentences, xx them out, try again, xx everything out, and then feel despair and worry settle on my chest like an x-ray apron. It's over, I'd think, calmly. I'm not going to be able to get the magic to work this time. I'm ruined. I'm through. I'm toast. Maybe, I'd think, I can get my old job back as a clerk-typist. But probably not. I'd get up and study my teeth in the mirror for a while. Then I'd stop, remember to breathe, make a few phone calls, hit the kitchen and chow down. Eventually I'd go back and sit down at my desk, and sigh for the next ten minutes. Finally I would pick up my one-inch picture frame, stare into it as if for the answer, and every time the answer would come: all I had to do was to write a really shitty first draft of, say, the opening paragraph. And no one was going to see it.

So I'd start writing without reining myself in. It was almost just typing, just making my fingers move. And the writing would be *terrible*. I'd write a lead paragraph that was a whole page, even though the entire review could only be three pages long, and then I'd start writing up descriptions of the food, one dish at a time, bird by bird, and the critics would be sitting on my shoulders, commenting like cartoon characters. They'd be pretending to snore, or rolling their eyes at my overwrought descriptions, no matter how hard I tried to tone those descriptions down, no matter how conscious I was of what a friend said to me gently in my early days of restaurant reviewing. "Annie," she said, "it is just a piece of *chick*en. It is just a bit of *cake*."

But because by then I had been writing for so long, I would eventually let myself trust the process—sort of, more or less. I'd write a first draft that was maybe twice as long as it should be, with a self-indulgent and boring beginning, stupefying descriptions of the meal, lots of quotes from my black-humored friends that made them sound more like the Manson girls than food lovers, and no ending to speak of. The whole thing would be so long and incoherent and hideous that for the rest of the day I'd obsess about getting creamed by a car before I could write a decent second draft. I'd worry that people would read what I'd written and believe that the accident had really been a suicide, that I had panicked because my talent was waning and my mind was shot.

The next day, though, I'd sit down, go through it all with a colored pen, take out everything I possibly could, find a new lead somewhere on the second page, figure out a kicky place to end it, and then write a second draft. It always turned out fine, sometimes even funny and weird and helpful. I'd go over it one more time and mail it in.

Then, a month later, when it was time for another review, the whole process would start again, complete with the fears that people would find my first draft before I could rewrite it.

Almost all good writing begins with terrible first efforts. You need to start somewhere. Start by getting something—anything—down on paper. A friend of mine says that the first draft is the down draft—you just get it down. The second draft is the up draft—you fix it up. You try to say what you have to say more accurately. And the third draft is the dental draft, where you check every tooth, to see if it's loose or cramped or decayed, or even, God help us, healthy.

What I've learned to do when I sit down to work on a shitty first draft is to quiet the voices in my head. First there's the vinegar-lipped Reader Lady, who says primly, "Well, *that's* not very interesting, is it?" And there's the emaciated German male who writes these Orwellian memos detailing your thought crimes. And there are your parents, agonizing over your lack of loyalty and discretion; and there's William Burroughs, dozing off or shooting up because he finds you as bold and articulate as a houseplant; and so on. And there are also the dogs: let's not forget the dogs, the dogs in their pen who will surely hurtle and snarl their way out if you ever *stop* writing, because writing is, for some of us, the latch that keeps the door of the pen closed, keeps those crazy ravenous dogs contained.

Quieting these voices is at least half the battle I fight daily. But this is better than it used to be. It used to be 87 percent. Left to its own devices, my mind spends much of its time having conversations with people who aren't there. I walk along defending myself to people, or exchanging repartee with them, or rationalizing my behavior, or seducing them with gossip, or pretending I'm on their TV talk show or whatever. I speed or run an aging yellow light or don't come to a full stop, and one nanosecond later am explaining to imaginary cops exactly why I had to do what I did, or insisting that I did not in fact do it.

I happened to mention this to a hypnotist I saw many years ago, and he looked at me very nicely. At first I thought he was feeling around on the floor for the silent alarm button, but then he gave me the following exercise, which I still use to this day.

Close your eyes and get quiet for a minute, until the chatter starts up. Then isolate one of the voices and imagine the person speaking as a mouse. Pick it up by the tail and drop it into a mason jar. Then isolate another voice, pick it up by the tail, drop it in the jar. And so on. Drop in any high-maintenance parental units, drop in any contractors, lawyers, colleagues, children, anyone who is whining in your head. Then put the lid on, and watch all these mouse people clawing at the glass, jabbering away, trying to make you feel like shit because you won't do what they want—won't give them more money, won't be more successful, won't see them more often. Then imagine that there is a volume-control button on the bottle. Turn it all the way up for a minute, and listen to the stream of angry, neglected, guilt-mongering voices. Then turn it all the way down and watch the frantic mice lunge at the glass, trying to get to you. Leave it down, and get back to your shitty first draft.

A writer friend of mine suggests opening the jar and shooting them all in the head. But I think he's a little angry, and I'm sure nothing like this would ever occur to you.

Activity: RESPONDING TO THE TEXT

1. Why does Lamott have difficulties writing a first draft? Lamott claims that all the writers she knows (except one) have problems writing first drafts. Do most of the people you know have difficulties writing? Why? Have you had a similar experience? What are the voices in your head that make writing difficult?

2. What are some things Lamott does to overcome the difficulties of writing a first draft? Why do you think these work? Would they work for you?

From *On the Teaching of Creative Writing:
Responses to a Series of Questions*

Wallace Stegner

This excerpt is from a response to a series of questions about writing posed at Dartmouth in 1980 to Wallace Stegner, a noted and prolific author of fiction and essays. Published in 1988 as On the Teaching of Creative Writing: Responses to a Series of Questions, *the book covers many aspects of talent and teaching in creative writing. The question Stegner responds to in this excerpt is on the importance of correctness in language.*

What about the creative-writing teacher's concerns centering upon grammar and syntax and the like?—

W.S. There are two kinds of teaching at issue here. One of them is the plain instruction—often the corrective instruction—in the communication of meaning through language. That goes on in "Freshman English" classes and in the kind of exposition courses often offered to engineers and other professional trainees.

It is absolutely essential . . . and it is never done well enough. It has its basis in grammar and syntax, which are simply the logic of the language. (No two languages have quite the same logic, but each within itself is consistent.)

Inevitably, that kind of teaching has a certain place in a creative-writing course. I take it as a basic principle that anyone who aspires to use his native tongue professionally and publicly had better know it. I have spent a lot of time going over manuscripts with students, in the way an editor might go over them, to clean them up and make them presentable, and keep the author from appearing in public with his shirt tail out and egg on his tie.

That is not the truly important matter, but it is one of the things that can be taught, and it is not trivial—though young writers, full of fire and the will to unbridled originality, sometimes think it is.

Grammar and syntax are more important in fiction than in poetry, which can proceed by daring leaps. When a fiction writer dissolves grammar, syntax, and logic, he is in grave danger of dissolving everything he is trying to communicate. If he cannot be restrained or directed, he must be permitted to go his way, but he had better know what he is risking. If he tells me, "Don't try to figure it out, just groove on it," I am at least going to make it difficult for him to get away with it, without an argument.

So, whether dismembered syntax has sprung from ignorance or from the lust after originality, I believe it should be questioned. After all, all a reader knows is the marks on the printed page. Those marks have to contribute meaning—every meaning the story or poem is going to have.

We are dealing with a complicated symbolic system, and every element of that system, down to the conventional signs for pauses and nuances, has had a long testing. Its function is to help reproduce in cold print what was a human voice speaking for human ears. The system can be challenged—and, even, cracked—but it is challenged at the writer's peril, and he had better know it before he undertakes to change it. A good writing class can help him discover what works and what does not.

Activity: RESPONDING TO THE TEXT

1. Why does Stegner say that correct grammar, syntax, and mechanics are crucial to good fiction writing? What reasons does Stegner have beyond his concern with the effectiveness of writing?
2. Elsewhere in *On the Teaching of Creative Writing*, Stegner says that "Writing is a social act, an act of communication both intellectual and emotional. It is also, at its best, an act of affirmation—a way of joining the human race." How does this comment reflect his belief in the importance of correctness in language?

The Maker's Eye: Revising Your Own Manuscripts
Donald Murray

Donald Murray, a writer and teacher of writing, explains the value and difficulties of revision. "Making something right," he explains, "is immensely satisfying." According to Murray, "A piece of writing is never finished." Murray voices what most writers experience—that writing is a process that begins before the first word is put on paper and that never really ends.

When students complete a first draft, they consider the job of writing done—and their teachers too often agree. When professional writers complete a first draft, they usually feel that they are at the start of the writing process. When a draft is completed, the job of writing can begin.

That difference in attitude is the difference between amateur and professional, inexperience and experience, journeyman and craftsman. Peter F. Drucker, the prolific business writer, calls his first draft "the zero draft"—after that he can start counting. Most writers share the feeling that the first draft, and all of those which follow, are opportunities to discover what they have to say and how best they can say it.

To produce a progression of drafts, each of which says more and says it more clearly, the writer has to develop a special kind of reading skill. In school we are taught to decode what appears on the page as finished writing. Writers, however, face a different category of possibility and responsibility when they read their own drafts. To them the words on the page are never finished. Each can be changed and rearranged, can set off a chain reaction of confusion or clarified meaning. This is a different kind of reading which is possibly more difficult and certainly more exciting.

Writers must learn to be their own best enemy. They must accept the criticism of others and be suspicious of it; they must accept the praise of others and be even more suspicious of it. Writers cannot depend on others. They must detach themselves from their own pages so that they can apply both their caring and their craft to their own work.

Such detachment is not easy. Science fiction writer Ray Bradbury supposedly puts each manuscript away for a year to the day and then rereads it as a stranger. Not many writers have the discipline or the time to do this. We must read when our judgment may be at its worst, when we are close to the euphoric moment of creation.

Then the writer, counsels novelist Nancy Hale, "should be critical of everything that seems to him most delightful in his style. He should excise what he most admires, because he wouldn't thus admire it if he weren't . . . in a sense protecting it from criticism." John Ciardi, the poet, adds, "The last act of the writing must be to become one's own reader. It is, I suppose, a schizophrenic process, to begin passionately and to end critically; to begin hot and to end cold; and, more important, to be passion-hot and critic-cold at the same time."

Most people think that the principal problem is that writers are too proud of what they have written. Actually, a greater problem for most professional writers is one shared by the majority of students. They are overly critical, think everything is dreadful, tear up page after page, never complete a draft, see the task as hopeless.

The writer must learn to read critically but constructively, to cut what is bad, to reveal what is good. Eleanor Estes, the children's book author, explains: "The writer must survey his work critically, coolly, as though he were a stranger to it. He must be willing to prune, expertly and hard-heartedly. At the end of each revision, a manuscript may look . . . worked over, torn apart, pinned together, added to, deleted from, words changed and words changed back. Yet the book must maintain its original freshness and spontaneity."

Most readers underestimate the amount of rewriting it usually takes to produce spontaneous reading. This is a great disadvantage to the student writer, who sees only a finished product and never watches the craftsman who takes the necessary step back, studies the work carefully, returns to the task, steps back, returns, steps back, again and again. Anthony Burgess, one of the most prolific writers in the English-speaking world, admits, "I might revise a page twenty times." Roald Dahl, the popular children's writer, states, "By the time I'm nearing the end of a story, the first part will have been reread and altered and corrected at least 150 times. . . . Good writing is essentially rewriting. I am positive of this."

Rewriting isn't virtuous. It isn't something that ought to be done. It is simply something that most writers find they have to do to discover what they have to say and how to say it. It is a condition of the writer's life.

There are, however, a few writers who do little formal rewriting, primarily because they have the capacity and experience to create and review a large number of invisible drafts in their minds before they approach the page. And some writers slowly produce finished pages, performing all the tasks of revision simultaneously, page by page, rather than draft by draft. But it is still possible to see the sequence followed by most writers most of the time in rereading their own work.

Most writers scan their drafts first, reading as quickly as possible to catch the larger problems of subject and form, then move in closer and closer as they read and write, reread and rewrite.

The first thing writers look for in their drafts is *information*. They know that a good piece of writing is built from specific, accurate, and interesting information. The writer must have an abundance of information from which to construct a readable piece of writing.

Next writers look for *meaning* in the information. The specifics must build to a pattern of significance. Each piece of specific information must carry the reader toward meaning.

Writers reading their own drafts are aware of *audience*. They put themselves in the reader's situation and make sure that they deliver information which a reader wants to know or needs to know in a manner which is easily digested. Writers try to be sure that they anticipate and answer the questions a critical reader will ask when reading the piece of writing.

Writers make sure that the *form* is appropriate to the subject and the audience. Form, or genre, is the vehicle which carries meaning to the reader, but form cannot be selected until the writer has adequate information to discover its significance and an audience which needs or wants that meaning.

Once writers are sure the form is appropriate, they must then look at the *structure*, the order of what they have written. Good writing is built on a solid framework of logic, argument, narrative, or motivation which runs through the entire piece of writing and holds it together. This is the time when many writers find it most effective to outline as a way of visualizing the hidden spine by which the piece of writing is supported.

The element on which writers may spend a majority of their time is *development*. Each section of a piece of writing must be adequately developed. It must give readers enough information so that they are satisfied. How much information is enough? That's as difficult as asking how much garlic belongs in a salad. It must be done to taste, but most beginning writers underdevelop, underestimating the reader's hunger for information.

As writers solve development problems, they often have to consider questions of *dimension*. There must be a pleasing and effective proportion among all the parts of the piece of writing. There is a continual process of subtracting and adding to keep the piece of writing in balance.

Finally, writers have to listen to their own voices. *Voice* is the force which drives a piece of writing forward. It is an expression of the writer's authority and concern. It is what is between the words on the page, what glues the piece of writing together. A good piece of writing is always marked by a consistent, individual voice.

As writers read and reread, write and rewrite, they move closer and closer to the page until they are doing line-by-line editing. Writers read their own pages with infinite care. Each sentence, each line, each clause, each phrase, each word, each mark of punctuation, each section of white space between the type has to contribute to the clarification of meaning.

Slowly the writer moves from word to word, looking through language to see the subject. As a word is changed, cut, or added, as a construction is rearranged, all the words used before that moment and all those that follow that moment must be considered and reconsidered.

Writers often read aloud at this stage of the editing process, muttering or whispering to themselves, calling on the ear's experience with language. Does this sound right—or that? Writers edit, shifting back and forth from eye to page to ear to page. I find I must do this careful editing in short runs, no more than fifteen or twenty minutes at a stretch, or I become too kind with myself. I begin to see what I hope is on the page, not what actually is on the page.

This sounds tedious if you haven't done it, but actually it is fun. Making something right is immensely satisfying, for writers begin to learn what they are writing about by writing. Language leads them to meaning, and there is the joy of discovery, of understanding, of making meaning clear as the writer employs the technical skills of language.

Words have double meanings, even triple and quadruple meanings. Each word has its own potential for connotation and denotation. And when writers rub one word against the other, they are often rewarded with a sudden insight, an unexpected clarification.

The maker's eye moves back and forth from word to phrase to sentence to paragraph to sentence to phrase to word. The maker's eye sees the need for variety and balance, for a firmer structure, for a more appropriate form. It peers into the interior of the paragraph, looking for coherence, unity, and emphasis, which make meaning clear.

I learned something about this process when my first bifocals were prescribed. I had ordered a larger section of the reading portion of the glass because of my work, but even so, I could not contain my eyes within this new limit of vision. And I still find myself taking off my glasses and bending my nose towards the page, for my eyes unconsciously flick back and forth across the page, back to another page, forward to still another, as I try to see each evolving line in relation to every other line.

When does this process end? Most writers agree with the great Russian writer Tolstoy, who said, "I scarcely ever reread my published writings, if by chance I come across a page, it always strikes me: all this must be rewritten; this is how I should have written it."

The maker's eye is never satisfied, for each word has the potential to ignite new meaning. This article has been twice written all the way through the writing process, and it was published four years ago. Now it is to be republished in a book. The editors make a few small suggestions, and then I read it with my maker's eye. Now it has been re-edited, re-revised, re-read, re-re-edited, for each piece of writing to the writer is full of potential and alternatives.

A piece of writing is never finished. It is delivered to a deadline, torn out of the typewriter on demand, sent off with a sense of accomplishment and shame and pride and frustration. If only there were a couple more days, time for just another run at it, perhaps then . . .

Activity: RESPONDING TO THE TEXT

1. What are the eight things writers look for in their drafts when they revise? Which of these areas do you think you need to pay the most attention to when you revise?
2. Murray explains that writers must "develop a special kind of reading skill" to produce good revisions. What attitudes and behaviors are involved in this special kind of reading for revision? What makes reading for revision difficult?

Revision of "The Declaration of Independence" from *American Scripture*

Pauline Maier

Although we assume that the memos, papers, and reports we write could be improved by revision, we also tend to assume that other documents spring from their creators in a finished form. This reading shows the revisions The Declaration of Independence underwent from its first draft by Thomas Jefferson to its acceptance by Congress.

A Declaration by the Representatives of the UNITED STATES OF AMERICA in General Congress assembled.

When in the course of human events it becomes necessary for one people to dissolve the political bands which have connected them with another, and to assume among the powers of the earth the separate and equal station to which the laws of nature and of nature's god entitle them, a decent respect to the opinions of mankind requires that they should declare the causes which impel them to the separation.

We hold these truths to be self-evident; that all men are created equal; that they are endowed by their Creator with ~~inherent and~~ _{certain} inalienable[1] rights; that among these are life, liberty, and the pursuit of happiness; that to secure these rights, governments are instituted among men, deriving their just powers from the consent of the governed; that whenever any form of government becomes destructive of these ends, it is the right of the people to alter or to abolish it, and to institute new government, laying it's foundation on such principles, and organising it's powers in such form as to them shall seem most likely to effect their safety and happiness. Prudence indeed will dictate that governments long established should not be changed for light & transient causes. and accordingly all experience hath shewn that mankind are more disposed to suffer, while evils are sufferable, than to right themselves by abolishing the forms to which they are accustomed. but when a long train of abuses and usurpations, ~~begun at a distinguished period, &~~ pursuing invariably the same object, evinces a design to reduce them under absolute despotism, it is their right, it is their duty, to throw off such government, & to provide new guards for their future security. such has been the patient sufferance of these colonies; & such is now the necessity which constrains them to ~~expunge~~ alter their former systems of government. the history of the present king of Great Britain, is a history of ~~unremitting~~ repeated injuries and usurpations, ~~among which appears no solitary fact to contradict the uniform tenor of the rest; but~~ all having in direct object the establishment of an absolute tyranny over these states. to prove this let facts be submitted to a candid world~~, for the truth of which we pledge a faith yet unsullied by falsehood~~.

He has refused his assent to laws the most wholesome and necessary for the public good.

he has forbidden his governors to pass laws of immediate & pressing importance, unless suspended in their operation till his assent should be obtained; and when so suspended, he has neglected ~~utterly~~ utterly to attend to them.

he has refused to pass other laws for the accomodation of large districts of people, unless those people would relinguish the right of representation in the legislature; a right inestimable to them, & formidable to tyrants only.

---

[1]In the printed version, "inalienable" became "unalienable." Becker, n. 1 at p. 175, suggests that "unalienable" might have been "the more customary form in the eighteenth century."

he has called together legislative bodies at places unusual, uncomfortable, & distant from the depository of their public records, for the sole purpose of fatiguing them into compliance with his measures.

he has dissolved Representative houses repeatedly ~~& continually,~~ for opposing with manly firmness his invasions on the rights of the people.

he has refused for a long time after such dissolutions to cause others to be elected whereby the legislative powers, incapable of annihilation, have returned to the people at large for their exercise, the state remaining in the meantime exposed to all the dangers of invasion from without, & convulsions within.

he has endeavored to prevent the population of these states; for that purpose obstructing the laws for naturalization of foreigners; refusing to pass others to encourage their migrations hither; & raising the conditions of new appropriations of lands.

he has ~~suffered~~ obstructed the administration of justice ~~totally to cease in some of these states,~~ by refusing his assent to laws for establishing judiciary powers.

he has made ~~our~~ judges dependent on his will alone, for the tenure of their offices, and the amount & paiment of their salaries.

he has erected a multitude of new offices ~~by a self assumed power,~~ & sent hither swarms of officers to harrass our people, and eat out their substance.

he has kept among us, in time of peace, standing armies ~~and ships of war,~~ without the consent of our legislatures.

he has affected to render the military independant of, & superior to, the civil power.

he has combined with others to subject us to a jurisdiction foreign to our constitutions and unacknoleged by our laws; giving his assent to their acts of pretended legislation

for quartering large bodies of armed troops among us;

for protecting them by a mock-trial from punishment for any murders which they should commit on the inhabitants of these states;

for cutting off our trade with all parts of the world;

for imposing taxes on us without our consent;

for depriving us in many cases of the benefits of trial by jury;

for transporting us beyond seas to be tried for pretended offences;

for abolishing the free system of English laws in a neighboring province, establishing therein an arbitrary government and enlarging it's boundaries so as to render it at once an example & fit instrument for introducing the same absolute rule into these states.[2]

for taking away our charters abolishing our most valuable laws, and altering fundamentally the forms of our governments;

for suspending our own legislatures, & declaring themselves invested with power to legislate for us in all cases whatsoever.

he has abdicated government here~~, withdrawing his governors, &~~ by declaring us out of his ~~allegiance and~~ protection and waging war against us.

he has plundered our seas, ravaged our coasts, burnt our towns, & destroyed the lives of our people.

he is at this time transporting large armies of foreign mercenaries, to compleat the works of death, desolation & tyranny, already begun with circumstances of cruelty & perfidy scarcely paralleled in the most barbarous ages and totally unworthy the head of a civilized nation.

he has excited domestic insurrections amongst us and has endeavored to bring on the inhabitants of our frontiers the merciless Indian savages, whose known rule of warfare is an undistinguished destruction of all ages, sexes & conditions ~~of existence~~.

~~he has incited treasonable insurrections of our fellow citizens, with the allurements of forfeiture & confiscation of property.~~

he has constrained our fellow citizens ~~others,~~[3] taken captives on the high seas to bear arms against their country, to become the executioners of their friends & brethren, or to fall themselves by their hands.

~~he has waged cruel war against human nature itself, violating it's most sacred rights of life & liberty in the persons of a distant people, who never offended him, captivating and carrying them into slavery in an-~~

---

[2] Boyd, in *The Declaration of Independence: The Evolution of the Text* . . . (revised edition, Princeton, N.J., 1945), argues that Congress substituted "states" for "colonies," and so restored Jefferson's original wording, which had been changed either by Jefferson or the drafting Committee (p. 30 and n. 57, p. 33 and n. 61). Becker did not include this among Congress's changes, nor have I, since the Lee copy says "states."

[3] Boyd, *Declaration of Independence*, 33, does not seem to include this among Congress's changes. I have followed Becker, who explained his position in n. 2 at p. 166. The change is clearly shown on the Lee draft. The Lee copy is now in the possession of the American Philosophical Society, which published it, with background information on the manuscript by I. Minis Hays, in its *Proceedings*, Vol. XXXVII (1898), pp. 88–107 (mss. on 103–107).

~~other hemisphere, or to incur miserable death in their transportation thither. this piratical warfare, the opprobrium of *infidel* powers, is the warfare of the *Christian* king of Great Britain. determined to keep open a market where MEN should be bought & sold, he has prostituted his negative for suppressing every legislative attempt to prohibit or to restrain this execrable commerce: and that this assemblage of horrors might want no fact of distinguished die, he now is now exciting those very people to rise in arms among us, and to purchase that liberty of which *he* has deprived them, by murdering the people upon whom *he* also obtruded them: thus paying off former crimes committed against the *liberties* of one people, with crimes which he urges them to commit against the *lives* of another.~~

In every stage of these oppressions, we have petitioned for redress in the most humble terms; our repeated petitions have been answered only by repeated injury. a prince whose character is thus marked by every act which may define a tyrant, is unfit to be the ruler of a people ^free^ ~~who mean to be free. future ages will scarce believe that the hardiness of one man adventured within the short compass of twelve years only, to build a foundation, so broad and undisguised, for tyranny over a people fostered and fixed in principles of freedom~~.

Nor have we been wanting in attentions to our British brethren. we have warned them from time to time of attempts by their legislature to extend ^an unwarrantable^ a jurisdiction over ^us^ ~~these our states.~~ we have reminded them of the circumstances of our emigration and settlement here, ~~no one of which could warrant so strange a pretension: that these were effected at the expence of our own blood and treasure, unassisted by the wealth or the strength of Great Britain: that in constituting indeed our several forms of government, we had adopted one common king, thereby laying a foundation for perpetual league and amity with them: but that submission to their parliament was no part of our constitution, or ever in idea, if history may be credited: and~~ we ^have^ appealed to their native justice & magnanimity, ~~as well as to~~ ^and we have conjured them by^ the tyes of our common kindred, to disavow these usurpations, which ~~were likely to~~ ^would inevitably^ interrupt our connection^s^ & correspondence. they too have been deaf to the voice of justice and of consanguinity; ~~and when occasions have been given them, by the regular course of their laws, of removing from their councils the disturbers of our harmony, they have by their free election re-established~~

~~them in power. at this very time too, they are permitting their chief magis-~~
~~trate to send over not only soldiers of our common blood, but Scotch and~~
~~foreign mercenaries to invade and destroy us. these facts have given the last~~
~~stab to agonizing affection; and manly spirit bids us to renouce forever these~~
~~unfeeling brethren.~~ we must ^therefore^ ~~endeavor to forget our former love for them,~~
~~and to hold them, as we hold the rest of mankind, enemies in war, in peace~~
~~friends. we might have been a free & a great people together; but a com-~~
~~munication of grandeur and of freedom, it seems, is below their dignity. be~~
~~it so, since they will have it. the road to happiness and to glory is open to~~
~~us too; we will climb it apart from them and~~ acquiesce in the necessity which
^and hold them, as we hold the rest of mankind, enemies in war, in peace friends.^
denounces our ~~eternal~~ separation!

We therefore the Representatives of the United states of America, in Gen-
^appealing to the supreme judge of the world for the rectitude of our intentions,^
eral Congress assembled, do, in the name and by authority of the good peo-
^colonies, solemnly publish and declare, that these united colonies are and of right ought to be free^
ple of these ~~states, reject and renounce all allegiance and subjection to the~~
^and independent states; that they are absolved from all allegiance to the British Crown, and that^
~~kings of Great Britain, & all others who may hereafter claim by, through,~~
~~or under them; we utterly dissolve~~ all political connection ~~which may hereto-~~
~~fore have subsisted~~ between ~~us~~ ^them^ and the ~~parliament or people~~ ^state^ of Great Britain;
^is & ought to be totally dissolved;^
^and finally we do assert~~ [and declare]⁴ ~~these colonies to be free and inde-~~
~~pendant states,~~ & that as free & independant states, they have full power to
levy war, conclude peace, contract alliances, establish commerce, & to do all
other acts and things which independant states may of right do. And for
^with a firm reliance on the protection of divine providence,^
the support of this declaration, we mutually pledge to each other our lives,
our fortunes, and our sacred honor.

Activity: RESPONDING TO THE TEXT

1. Look at the revision of the The Declaration of Independence. The
   changes were made to Jefferson's draft by the Continental Congress. Locate some specific alterations, and decide why Thomas Jefferson, his committee members, or Congress might have decided on the changes. What
   changes seem to have been prompted by consideration of the readers? Do
   any changes seem to have been prompted by political motivations?

---

⁴Becker added the words "and declare" from Jefferson's "Rough Draft," assuming
that Jefferson had mistakenly left it out of the Lee copy. Becker also reversed "parliament or people" in conformance with the Rough Draft. There I chose to remain
consistent with the Lee copy. See Becker 170, n.1.

2. The paragraph that begins "he has waged cruel war against human nature itself. . . ." was eliminated by Congress from the draft presented to them by the committee working with Jefferson. What is this paragraph about? Why might Congress have decided to make this revision?

3. Language is always in flux. When Jefferson wrote this document, he was using the clear, correct language of the educated people of his day, yet several elements would be considered incorrect or nonstandard today. Judging from the passage reprinted above, what are some of the changes in the conventions of written American English?

Activity: SYNTHESIZING THE TEXTS

1. Compare Lamott's, Murray's, and Stegner's attitudes and ideas about revision.

2. Place each of the changes made in The Declaration of Independence in one of the eight categories Murray identifies as the things writers look for when revising.

Writing Assignments

Academic Essays

1. Journalism

Choose an article from a local paper on a topic you know something about. For example, your local paper might contain an article about a tutoring program you're volunteering in, or the campus paper might have an article about a sports team you participate in. You are going to rewrite the article, checking facts, adding information, reorganizing and rephrasing, in order to make the article appropriate for an audience unfamiliar with your town or campus.

1. Analyze your audience—answer the following questions to identify changes that will need to be made.

   A. What will the new audience need to know that isn't in the current version of the article? Think about adding background information, more explanations about local situations, and identifications of names or places that would not be familiar to a larger audience.

   B. How might their interests and concerns be different from those of the local audience? For example, while a local audience might be concerned about whether a sports team won or lost, a wider audience might be more interested in coaching techniques used or the personalities of the players or some other unique aspect of the team.

   C. How will you make this local event relevant to a larger audience? What makes this news from your town or campus significant for a larger audience? For example, a report about a graduate-student

strike on your campus might be the basis for an exploration of issues about fair employment practices in academia, a topic of interest to many people.

    D. What changes should be made in content and organization? For exam-
ple, if the campus article on the sports team starts with the score of the
last game, you might want to shift that information to later in the article or omit it entirely. An article about a local tutoring program may contain information about whom to contact to volunteer, information which
would be irrelevant to a larger audience. You might need to rearrange or
add information to give unfamiliar readers necessary background.

  2. Check facts. Make sure that all the facts in the article are true. Checking
facts may involve consulting people, agencies, or other publications.

  3. Plan the new organization and content. You might want to outline your
revision.

  4. Rewrite the article for the new audience. Make the style and tone consistent throughout. The revised article should not contain some sentences that sound like the writer of the original article and some that
sound like you. Make appropriate adjustments in word choice and sentence structure to ensure a smooth style.

2. Sciences

Look through recent issues of *Science, Science News,* or *Scientific American.* Although these publications are written for a general audience, they assume that readers have a high-school or college level of scientific knowledge and are generally
educated and interested enough to understand scientific information that might
be unfamiliar to them.

    Choose an article on a topic of interest to you and rewrite that article for a less
scientifically knowledgeable audience. Your rewritten version should explain all the
main points that the original did, and you may need to add further explanations of
unfamiliar concepts, definitions of important terms, or examples. At the same time,
you may be able to delete some fine points that are beyond the audience's interest
or knowledge level. You may also need to simplify word choice and sentence structure as you rewrite the article.

3. Sociology

Every group has behaviors, beliefs, or characteristics that help define it. Choose a small
group that you belong to. It could be a circle of close friends, your coworkers, a group
of students in your academic program, or any other relatively small group. Write a
paper defining that group by their behaviors, beliefs, or characteristics. You might consider physical characteristics like clothes and hair style, common activities, language
characteristics, political or religious beliefs, interests, attitudes, or any other shared characteristics. After you have defined your group, discuss what deviations from the group's
norms would cause a person to seem like Stegner's writer "with egg on his tie."

Workplace Writing

Select a document from your workplace that uses one or more of the strategies discussed in Designing a Visually Effective Document on pp. 000–000. You might, for
example, choose a memo from the human resources department comparing new and

old benefits, instructions for changing the toner in the copier, or an organization chart classifying departments. Rewrite the document using the guidelines in this chapter. Add bullets, graphics, shading, and other visual elements, as appropriate, to make the document easier to read and understand.

Personal Writing

Each individual's life is constantly undergoing revision. Most people change some of their actions, beliefs, or attitudes whenever they make a major change in their lives. Choose one major change in your life, such as entering college, moving away from your family, or having a child. Use freewriting, brainstorming, or talking with others to gather information about how you have changed as a result of this event.

1. Write to someone who knows you well—a friend, parent, spouse, or sibling—to explain how you have changed. Before you begin, review the information you have gathered and decide what would be most interesting to your audience. What would someone who cares about you and has known you for a long time want to know? Would some items be too obvious (e.g. you got less sleep after you had a child)? Would some be uninteresting to your readers (e.g. entering college changed your TV viewing habits)? Also keep in mind that these people may already know a great deal about the changes you have experienced because they are close to you. What are you going to write about that they don't already know?
2. Rewrite the description of an event that changed your life. This time, write to a more general audience, a group of people who will be going through this life change in the near future and would like some insight into what is ahead. How will your content, organization, and style change? Do you need to add or delete information? Present your ideas in a different order? Begin with a different introduction? Write in a more or less formal style?

POLISHING AND REFLECTING ON TEXTS

Learning From Other Student Writers

My Group of Friends
Adam Ruiz

Adam Ruiz wrote this essay in response to the assignment in this chapter that asks students to describe the behavior of a group to which they belong. As he revised the paper, he added details to help readers to understand his group, and he unified his paragraphs to make his description easier to follow.

Society seems to misunderstand my group of friends. They stereotype us as a gang instead of just a group of friends who grew up together. We are far from a gang. We don't fight over colors or numbers, and we don't go out to start trouble. We just like to have fun. But along with the fun there are negative sides to the activities we participate in. Such activities usually put us in bad situations. Being thrown in jail, getting stabbed, shot, or beaten up are the bad situations we get into. Through all the bad times we face, we still manage to stick together. We have learned to take the good in with the bad.

When we go out, we usually travel in a group of eight. Our physical characteristics make us stand out. Our pants are never worn waist high; they sag about three-to-four inches below the normal waist line. We are usually wearing the top-of-the-line, overpriced running shoes to convey a high-status lifestyle. We avoid hair spray, gel and mousse because we are all bald, not because we are losing our hair, but because we choose to shave our hair off. We are not into hairstyles because we are too lazy to fix our hair and we believe that hairstyles are for pretty boys. Tattoos help define our circle because they give us a rugged look. The most common tattoo in my group is a dragon. Some of us have tattoos that say our last names, the city we are from, samurai warriors, tribal designs, and tigers. We don't always put tattoos on the same body part or on the same spot as the next person in our group. I have friends who have tattoos on their neck, chest, forearms, back, calves, and the most popular place is the shoulder.

I think our attitudes make society think we are a gang, even though we are far from that. We don't claim colors, and we don't go out looking for trouble. We go out, drink, and just have fun. We all have this attitude that whatever happens, happens. We don't act tough, but we fear no man. We show respect to everybody who shows respect to us. Sometimes our attitudes change after we have consumed alcohol. The respect we have towards everybody seems to diminish with every beer guzzled down our throats. Being intoxicated and in a public area is a bad combination for us. It usually ends in fighting or getting thrown in jail.

We stick together for so many different reasons. Some of us share the same interests. Rap music is a common shared interest in my group. Rap is a very influential part of our lives. Tupac Shakur is my group's most influential rapper. We listen to his music and feel his rage because we relate to topics he talks about. In his song called "War Stories," he sings:

Can your mind picture,
a thug figure,
drinking hard liquor
This ghetto life has got me catching up to god quicker.
Who would figure,
that all I needed was a chrome trigger,
semi-automatic mac-11,
to scare somebody bigger.

These lyrics describe my group's mentality. Topics such as living an unhappy life are described in another song called "Who Do You Believe In?" where Tupac says:

All the Hennessy and weed can't hide,
the pain I feel inside,
I know I'm living just to die.
I fall on my knees and beg for mercy.
Not knowing if I'm worthy,
Living life thinking no man can hurt me.
So I'm asking before I lay me down to sleep,
Before you judge me look at all the shit he did to me, my misery,
I arose up from the slums.
Made it out of the flames.
In my search for fame will I change.

I choose to stick with my circle of friends because of the guilt of leaving. Since I was working and going to school, I barely had enough time to hang around with all of my friends. I felt guilty because it seemed that I was starting to do good in my life, and at the same time, I was leaving my friends in the gutter. I began to think that my friends were developing a feeling of hate towards me because I left them behind. Leaving my circle of friends and maintaining the respect they have or had for me is difficult because I feel paranoid that my friends are out to get me. In some cases if a person were to leave our circle of friends on bad terms, the result would usually end in a violent beating. Now, if a person were to leave on good terms, the result usually ends in a violent beating, but that person would still maintain everybody's respect.

The main reason we stick together is the family factor. We spend more time together than we do with our families. When a group member is down, we take him out, get him drunk, and cheer him up. Our families were absent during the hard times. We had nobody to turn to for support, except each other. There is nothing to come between my friends and me. We have three rules:

1. Never fight over a girl.
2. Never fight a friend.
3. Never disrespect a friend.

These three rules are important because they keep us together as a family unit and help us avoid conflicts.

Not just anybody can share moments with my circle of friends. Even though we are from the same neighborhood, the other people who live nearby choose not to hang around with us. That's okay, they are exactly who we don't want around us anyway. We refer to those people as "squares." Spending time with us is not for everybody. Squares seem to think the life we live is negative. It is easy for a square to pass judgment upon my group of friends because squares have everything going right for them. Squares have a lot to lose. They do not take the chances we would take in certain situations. Being in my group requires taking chances such as public intoxication, scuffles, run-ins with authorities, marijuana use, and even driving drunk. We do not take pride in these activities, but we have programmed ourselves to take the good with the bad. Taking chances like these is not for squares. It's for people like us who have nothing to lose. The negative things we do have become second nature to us. Sometimes we don't even know when we are doing something wrong because we don't think about it. The bottom line is, squares think twice, and we don't think at all.

The friends in my circle see each other as an alternative to family. Our families don't see eye-to-eye with us on how we view and live life. Our attitudes were never learned; they were developed over the years of growing up together. We don't choose to live life negative. We just don't see things positive. The lack of positive energy in our lives helped develop the mentality that we have nothing to lose.

Activity: RESPONDING TO THE TEXT

1. In the second paragraph of his essay, Ruiz uses many details, so readers are able to picture his group. Identify instances in other paragraphs where Ruiz uses detailed lists or descriptions to enhance his writing.
2. Ruiz added the song lyrics to his paper when he wrote his third draft. Why do you think he didn't have them in the first draft? Why do you think he added them? What do they contribute to the essay as a whole?
3. What can you say about Ruiz's style? What kinds of sentences and words does he choose? Do you think this style is appropriate?

Activity: PEER WORKSHOP

By this time, you have had quite a bit of experience answering workshop questions. To become a more masterful reviser of your own writing, you should practice coming up with your own questions about your writing. By questioning your own writing, you distance yourself somewhat, so that you can look at your writing with fresh eyes. For this peer workshop, you will write questions, following the guidelines below.

Compose two questions about *each* of the following:
- the paper's purpose, thesis, and/or audience
- the paper's content
- the paper's paragraph structure

After you have finished, examine your own paper and answer the questions you created. Then your partner will read your paper and answer the same questions on a separate sheet of paper. Compare and discuss the answers when you are both finished.

Activity: PROOFREADING YOUR WORK

You have already reviewed the rules for using commas with introductory clauses and in compound sentences. Now find out about using commas around interrupters by finding answers to the following questions:

- What is an interrupter?
- How can you identify interrupters in your sentences?
- Where are commas placed when the interrupter is at the beginning of the sentence? At the end? In the middle?

Now review the commas in your paper. Underline any word or phrase you think is an interrupter. Make sure it possesses the two characteristics: 1) It interrupts the flow of the sentence, and 2) deleting it does not alter the sentence's main idea.

Activity: POSTSCRIPT

1. Which part of the revision process was easiest for you? Most difficult or frustrating? Why? What would make revising easier or more satisfying?
2. Do you revise differently for different types of documents and papers?
3. How many drafts do you usually write? Do you revise as you write your draft or after you complete it or both?
4. What have you learned about revising that you might incorporate into your writing process?

RHETORICAL STRATEGIES

PREVIEW

This chapter's introduction to some of the conventional ways of organizing information—narrating a story, describing a person, place, object, or action, illustrating a point, defining a word or concept, explaining a process, examining cause and effect, comparing and contrasting, classifying and arguing—will help answer these questions:

- What are rhetorical strategies?
- Why do writers use them in papers, letters, memos, and reports?

LEARNING ABOUT TEXTS

Pizzas are usually round, angel food cakes are made in tube-shaped pans, and apple turnovers are triangular. The forms these foods take are patterns we recognize and expect. These patterns developed for practical reasons (for example, it is easier to flatten and spread pizza dough in a circular pattern than in a square one), but because they are used so frequently, they become part of the nature of the food, part of the convention of making it. Patterns like these can be found in many everyday objects, such as cars, houses, dishes, clothes, and appliances. These conventional forms often result because the purpose of the object and the materials used make certain patterns most effective. Cars, for example, have a conventional shape because it provides the least air resistance and the most passenger and cargo space.

In the same way, people use conventional patterns of thinking that grow out of the various ways they examine the world and try to make sense of it. When you look at the list below, you will see that you use these patterns every day when you talk with friends and family, do your job or schoolwork, make decisions, and evaluate and appreciate the world around you:

- **Narration** (telling a story)
- **Description** (creating a verbal picture of something)
- **Illustration** (giving examples)
- **Process Analysis** (describing or explaining "how to")
- **Causal Analysis** (analyzing why something happens or what will result)
- **Comparison and Contrast** (examining similarities and differences)
- **Classification** (grouping things)
- **Definition** (explaining the nature of something)
- **Argument** (justifying your ideas)

Activity: WORKING TOGETHER   DAEDALUS ONLINE

In small groups, list all the ways you have used the nine thinking patterns list-ed above in your daily life in the last couple of days. Think about your ac-tivities at home, at work, and at school. You might have used these patterns to guide your thinking (in making decisions or judgments), to help you speak (in conversations with friends, dealings with coworkers, encounters with ser-vice people or professionals), or to help you write (school papers, memos, let-ters, reports, or forms). Which patterns were used most frequently? Why?

Using Rhetorical Strategies

When these patterns of thinking are used by writers, they are called rhetorical strategies because something is "rhetorical" when it relates to effective writing or speaking, and a "strategy" is a way to approach a problem. Much of the time, a rhetorical strategy grows naturally out of the writer's choice of content and pur-pose. For example, a writer who starts out with the general topic of tamales might think about the paper's purpose and content and begin drafting, describing how tamales are made (process analysis), what they are (description or definition), their history (narration or causal analysis), or how they relate to similar dishes (classifi-cation or comparison/contrast). The writer uses these patterns of development unconsciously because they are part of the way people think. However, at some point in the writing process, it might be useful to use the rhetorical strategies in a more conscious, systematic way to help you determine what information readers need and what organization would help them understand the material. Some writ-ers use rhetorical strategies to help them brainstorm, some to help plan or outline material, some to revise drafts and refine organization and content. They are ben-eficial as a guide to facilitate the construction of a piece of writing. A clear rhetor-ical structure also benefits the readers because once they recognize the pattern, they know what to expect and will more easily follow and understand the writer's ideas.

Rhetorical strategies are not employed only in college English papers. Because they are primarily patterns for developing ideas, they are equally effective in personal and professional writing. Establishing your topic and your purpose often leads you to rhetorical strategies appropriate for use as tools for developing your material. Once you've chosen a rhetorical strategy, decisions about content and organization become less complicated. For example, a letter describing your decision to seek a new job could be expressed using the causal analysis pattern—to explain why you decided to change jobs (the causes) or to discuss the advantages of the new job (the effects). A memo recommending a new software package for your office could be convincing if you used the comparison/contrast method to show the advantages of one software package over the competitors'. A report on absenteeism at work could use the classification pattern to demonstrate the various reasons people miss work.

Modifying and Mixing Rhetorical Strategies

Although the rhetorical strategies are described and practiced separately in the following chapters, writers usually combine these strategies to accomplish their purpose. For example, a memo may begin by using the cause-and-effect pattern to describe a problem, then may conclude with a comparison/contrast of two possible solutions. Sometimes students are asked to write papers using just one of these strategies so they can practice the patterns. However, even when you are asked to write a paper using a particular rhetorical strategy, such as comparison/contrast, you will usually use other strategies, such as definition, description, and illustration, as well because these patterns are so much a part of the way people think. Being aware of the various patterns you are using in a piece of writing will enable you to exert more control over your composition.

Writers also sometimes vary the conventional rhetorical strategies if their purposes require that they do so. Just as some pizza outlets make square pizza, a writer may sometimes write a process paper that does not follow chronological order or a comparison/contrast paper that doesn't consistently compare the two items in the same order. These variations can be effective if the writer has a clear reason for them. If you know how to use the rhetorical strategies, you will have more choices for organizing your papers.

Activity: WRITER'S LOG

Look over the readings in one of the first eight chapters. Note places where the authors have used rhetorical strategies. Are there sections where strategies have been combined? Where they have been modified? Select an example of the use of rhetorical strategies and comment on why the strategy is or is not effective for the purpose.

Activity: WORKING TOGETHER   DAEDALUS ONLINE

Before you come to class, find an example of each of the rhetorical strategies listed in this chapter by looking through the following texts from your personal, professional, and academic life:

- Personal letters, advertising, and junk mail you receive
- Books, magazines, and newspapers you read
- Memos, letters, and reports you receive or that are posted at work
- Textbooks, reading assignments, course handouts, syllabi, exams, and other materials used in your college classes

List each rhetorical strategy you found, the source, and a brief summary or description of the example.

Working in small groups, compare your list with those of others. Try to decide which patterns of organization are used frequently in specific types of texts; for example, textbooks include numerous definitions and classifications. Compile a list of texts that typically employ specific strategies. Discuss reasons some strategies would be more common in certain types of writing.

READING AND WRITING TEXTS

Activity: PREREADING

In your Writer's Log

Describe a food that you associate with your childhood or that triggers a memory of a childhood event. Now that you're an adult, how do you respond to this food?

Reading

Pie

Judith Moore

"Pie" is the first chapter of Never Eat Your Heart Out, *a memoir by Judith Moore. In each chapter of her book, Moore describes her memories of the people, events, feelings, and food of a particular period of her life.*

Its filling sequestered beneath a canopy of top crust, hidden from the eye (if not the nose), a pie (not unlike the body) offers itself for reverie on the enigma of inside and out.

Even when I was a child, a pre-school toddler, I adored concocting for my dolls mud-crust pies in doll-size pie tins. I filled them with pansies or nasturtiums or marigolds or yellow chinaberries picked off bushes that grew along the back alley, or with pea gravel culled from our driveway. With Belinda, my rag doll, snuggled in the crook of my arm, I would curl up in bed at naptime or at night, engrossed—transported, really— in figuring out what ingredients I could fill pies with next. In my mind I would roll out mud circles, and more daintily in thought than ever in fact I would tuck these crusts in pans. In my mind's eye I would see my- self, in passionate imitation of adult pie-makers, layering in flowers or pebbles, dribbling over them my sandbox sand for sugar, and adding daubs of wet mud butter. Then, carefully, with an enormous sigh of sat- isfaction that comes as one nears a task's completion, I spread a top crust over my pie's filling, and with the stubby dimpled fingers I see now in my photographs at that age, I pinched together, around the pie's entire cir- cumference, the edges of the top and bottom mud crusts. What was in the pie was a secret only I knew.

I so heartily believed in my mud and sand ingredients that falling asleep I smelled my pie baking (it would be a doubled make-believe, because I did not smell mud, I smelled apples, cherries, apricots). While my body gave off that last shudder as tensed muscle let go, I began to arrange in my mind's eye all the dolls on chairs around my playhouse table, even in- continent Betsy-Wetsy, who left wet spots wherever she sat, the cloth rabbit, the woolen Pooh bear come across the ocean from what my fa- ther called "war-torn England."

Next to pie, what pleasure cake offers, whether looked at or eaten, seems meager. To wonder about a cake's interior, given a well-made cake's un- varying, uniform web and constant all-chocolate or all-"white" taste (even when lemon or raspberry filling or dark chocolate glistens silkily between its layers) is to have the mind taken nowhere. The simplest breakfast muffin, aclutter with plump raisins and walnuts, seems more a marvel, inciting cu- riosity in the mind, bonanza for the mouth.

Another person might see this pie-cake distinction in an entirely opposite fashion, and consider cake, leavened as it is by baking powder and by the air- retaining foam of whipped egg whites or whole eggs and baking powder— which means that its volume is significantly increased by internal gas expansion—is far more the miracle. But it seems to me that mere chemistry can explain what makes a cake, while pie demands metaphysics. The oppo- sition between a pie's inside and out, the dialectic, if you will, between crust and filling, can't but set minds wondering. As children and as adults we never lose interest in it. Confronted with turtle or snail shell, high fence, blank wall, lid, door, veil, or wrapping past which the eye cannot go (think of egg rolls, turnovers, pocket bread), the mind proceeds at once to ask, "What's in there?" or, more suspiciously, "What is being hidden?" and, of course, "Why?" If one is in an elegiac mood, this consideration of outside and in may steer one to certain qualities of innerness: tenderness, vulnerability. One may then find oneself filled with emotions similar to the poet Rilke's, in which "the imagination sympathizes with the being that inhabits the protected space."

In my mud-pie days I had a tiny wooden rolling pin equipped with handles lacquered bright red. I had to ask permission, but once having done so, I was allowed to dust the wide lower step of the back stoop with sand from my sandbox and then I'd plop down my mud mix on top of the sand, pat my mud flat, and roll out my crusts on the concrete.

How did I bake my mud pies? Next to my sandbox I built an oven from red bricks left over from some project of my father's. Four bricks made the oven floor, four bricks stood on end made its sides, and for the oven roof I used a piece of corrugated tin. I had more bricks that I stood up against the oven for its door. As my pies (I could fit two in the oven) baked, I would conjure drawings in my mind like the ones in my picture books: pies cooling on wide wooden windowsills, steam rising up out of vents cut in the pies' top crusts and floating in chimney-smoke whorls across blue skies above fairy-tale villages, and I could work myself up into a fret of fear by imagining that the sweet, fruity aroma drifting off my pie had attracted a sharp-toothed wolf. I would remember the nursery rhyme that began:

> *Sing a song of sixpence,*
> *A pocket full of rye;*
> *Four and twenty blackbirds,*
> *Baked in a pie.*

I asked permission to use the back stoop for my mud-pie making from Black Mary, so called to distinguish her from my father's aunt, whom, I guess, we would have called White Mary, had things been equal. Black Mary lived with us, kept our house, washed and ironed our clothes, and cooked our food. She had raised my father and his younger brother from the day they were born, and after their mother died, when my father was six, she became all the mother my father had left. He adored her. Black Mary had what my father called a Queen Mary bosom, by which he meant a breastline carried well forward, like a ship's prow. She was better to me than anybody, better than my maternal grandmother or paternal stepgrandmother, better than my mother, and better even than my father, if only because she, unlike my father and mother, was always home. I loved to bury my nose deep down in the cleft between her breasts, where her smooth skin gave off the fragrance of spices and breakfast bacon and furniture oil and the flowery talcum she dusted her brown skin with, spotting it white. I loved to lay my cheek along the bodice of Mary's print dresses and hear her heart beat. Its thump reverberated through her huge body into my ear, her flesh quivered and hummed, and I would begin to breathe with her. I felt lulled and narcotized, and I wondered if, like Sleeping Beauty or Rip Van Winkle, I might not fall asleep there forever.

I remember a springtime afternoon when a storm came up; bright lightning strokes and a series of thunderclaps—not rolling thunder, but sharp, harsh cracks—woke me from my nap. It was not long after lunch, but outside, the sky looked dark as evening. My mother was at school and my father at work. Mary set me at the kitchen table. Our dog, a black Scottie like President Roosevelt's Fala, lay under the table and whimpered every time another thunderbolt crashed. Mary had her little Bakelite radio turned on to one of her stories about romance, which did not interest me. I touched the dog with my bare toes and he growled.

My father loved Mary's chicken pie, and she was fixing us one for dinner. To make the pie she had to start by stewing what she called an old hen. I remember old hens coming to us (but don't remember from where, or how they got to the kitchen). The hens arrived headless and plucked, with their skinny yellow scaly legs and feet still attached.

That afternoon Mary stood by the stove and held the old hen over a gas flame, singeing off bluish pinfeathers that poked out from the hen's naked body the same way my father's weekend beard poked from his chin. The remains of the hen's broken neck drooped downward, and a long empty sleeve of loose skin hung off it, bobbing. Every time a flame caught at a pinfeather, the burning feather set off a *psst* sound. The feathers burning smelled the same as hair burning.

The storm didn't let up and rain came down so hard onto our roof that I couldn't even hear the voices on Mary's radio anymore. Mary had water boiling by then in her black iron stew pot and had put the hen in the bubbling water and then turned down the flame and covered the pot with a lid. Right away, the glass in the kitchen windows began to steam up, and soon I couldn't see out the window, and then my father called from his office to make sure we were all right in the storm. Mary let me talk to him for a minute. He said if I couldn't see out the kitchen windows I should get in the dining-room window seat and watch the storm from there, and then the line crackled and I could barely hear him and gave the phone, back to Mary.

I knelt on the window-seat cushions, which were covered with rough monk's cloth and scratched my bare knees. I pulled back the curtain and looked through the glass Mary kept spotless with ammonia, out into the unnaturally dark side yard. Lightning flared across the sky, leaving behind an eerie radiance. Rain hit the grass and beat yellow blossoms off the forsythia canes and knocked petals off the red Darwin tulips. Low spots in the yard were drowning.

In no time rain turned to hail, and Mary came and stood by me, hand on my shoulder and dog whimpering right behind her, and Mary said that with so much hail hitting the roof so hard she felt as if we were stuck inside a drum that was being rat-a-tat-tatted with about a hundred drumsticks. She said she hoped the hail didn't ruin our roof or break her windshield, which had happened before, or beat down the lettuce and spinach that had been up just a few weeks out in the garden.

Mary said come along into the kitchen, which by then was hot and smelled of good chicken steam. I helped by shelling peas while Mary chopped onion and carrot and potato to go into the chicken pie. The dog went to sleep, and when I had all the peas shelled and a bowl on the table half full of bright green peas and a pan heaped up with empty pods, I looked up and the storm was over. Sun was shining down in a twinkly brightness onto the yard. I squinted because I had gotten used to the dark. Mary brushed flour off her hands, which had made them all white, and helped me into my shoes and tied them and, telling me not to fall on slick grass or get in puddles, allowed me out the back door to go play.

Right away of course I went out to the sidewalk to see if my friend Janet from across the street was out, but she wasn't. I started looking around to see what had happened in the storm. Hailstones, big as mothballs and as white, littered the lawn, and my father's spinach and lettuce had been beaten down in the rows he'd planted them in, and dirt was on the lettuce leaves. The poplars that stood in a line between our lot and the one next door had their leaves knocked off, and the apple trees along the back fence, too. My foot touched something soft, and I looked down. My foot had touched a dead baby robin.

Maybe wind had blown the bird from its nest; maybe rain had drowned the bird in its nest, or maybe hailstones had killed it. It had no real feathers yet, only fuzzy down, and the down was soaked. Its bluish-pink skin was wrinkled all over its body, and its wings had hardly formed and were more like flippers. Its feet were needle-like and not strong enough to have held it up if it had tried to stand. Its head looked too big for its body and its eyes too big for its head. Its beak was halfway open, as if maybe it had struggled for breath. There was no life left in it.

I wasn't supposed to touch it and I knew I wasn't. It was cold to touch. I felt voracious guilt, the quality of which returns to me even now. I was disobeying Mary and my parents—"Do not touch wild birds; they're dirty, crawling with filthy diseases and nasty lice."

I knew what I should do. I should call for Mary and say, "Come quick, there's a dead baby bird out here." Against my better judgment, against what I knew was right, I felt my will move the other way. I felt myself slide down into the desire to make this dead bird into a pretend-chicken pie. I ran to the door and knocked, and Mary stuck out her head. The smell of chicken pie baking came out. Mary looked up in the sky and wondered out loud if I needed my sweater, and I said no and asked permission to make mud pies and got it, as long as I didn't come in and out and track her clean linoleum. She said soon my father and mother would be home.

So I gathered my pots and pans and used water from a puddle and dug with my old tablespoon in the back flower bed, where my father let me dig, and I got two mud balls, one for the top crust and one for the bottom, just right, not too wet and not too dry, and I put some sand on the stoop and took the red lacquered handles of the rolling pin, one handle in each hand, and rolled and rolled the mud balls out flat, and I fitted the bottom crust into the little pie pan and then looked up at the kitchen window with its blue-checkered curtains and the window in the back door to see if Mary was looking out and she wasn't, and I hurried over with my pie pan to the fruit trees where the bird was lying with its beak half open and its feet up in the air and I picked it up and tucked it on its side in the pie shell and it just fit and then I put some soft apple-tree leaves over it for vegetables and then I carried the pie pan back to the back stoop and when I looked up Mary was still not looking out, her big face wasn't smiling in the window, so I put the pie pan down on the stoop and carefully picked up the top crust and laid it over the leaves and pinched the two crusts together all around and carried it to my oven and put it in and piled up the bricks and sat down on the corner of my sandbox to wait for it to be done. I never told anyone this until now.

Of course I knew I couldn't feed the pie to my dolls, because it didn't seem right, and I wasn't happy, sitting there, with all the robins by then singing and out in the yard pulling worms from the wet ground, and I thought that one of them was the one whose baby was dead and she would fly up to her nest and her nest would be empty. I undid the door bricks and took the pie out of the oven and walked to the far corner of the garden and gently turned the pie over at the back of a flower bed and tipped all of it onto the ground and covered it up with the dead leaves that my father stacked there in the fall.

By the time I got my mess cleaned up off the stoop, my mother and father were home. My father first thing checked his garden for damage, and Mary let the dog out and he yipped and ran in circles around my father and got muddy paw prints on his trousers. My father and mother asked Mary and me if we'd been scared during the storm, and we said no. For dinner, we had the chicken pie, served in the high-sided Pyrex pie pan in which Mary had baked it. I am sure that it tasted as it always did and does now when I make it: chunks of white breast meat, green peas, squares of potato, carrot, celery, the rich chicken gravy, which, mixed together, is like tasting an old-fashioned farm landscape. But I didn't eat much and Mary said maybe I was tired because the storm woke me from my nap.

After that I didn't make mud pies anymore. Not for a long time, or not for what seemed, at that age, like a long time, probably only a week or two. And then I went to nursery school and then my parents broke up, and then we moved and I started grade school. All that was a long time ago. But it stayed with me.

As a child rolling out mud crusts I felt much as I feel now, wearing an apron in my kitchen—that making a pie I'm handmaiden to a miracle. I will begin, let's say, with pale green and ruby rhubarb stalks, sour red pie cherries, McIntosh apples, butter, sugar, flour, salt, and shortening. I peel the coarse strings off the outer blades of the rhubarb, pit cherries, peel and core apples. I spoon the raw fruit into the bottom pie shell, daub the fruit with chunks of butter, dribble sugar and strew flour, the latter for thickening. I sprinkle all this with no more cinnamon than will lightly freckle the fruit. I fold the second round of pie dough in half and gently lift it onto the heaped high fruit with the fold in the pie's center. One half of the pie's fruit, then, is covered. Last, ever so painstakingly, I unfold the top crust across the pie's other half and crimp the edges of the top and bottom crusts together. With a fork I prick the top crust in several places so that while the pie bakes steam can escape.

A transformation that is almost sorcery begins when the pie is set on a middle rack in the heated oven. While I wash the bowl and knives and dust flour off the pastry board, the baking fruit's aroma begins to perfume the house. Thirty, forty minutes later, I open the oven door a few inches and peer in. The oven's radiating heat rises around the pie in indistinct waves, like the contours of a dream. The heat is insinuating itself into the pie's interior, creating between the sealed crusts its own steamy, primordial climate, a site (to use the French postman-philosopher Gaston Bachelard's translated-into-English words) of "thermal sympathy" and "calorific happiness," in which apple and rhubarb and cherry cell walls break down and sugar crystals alter and butter melts.

Another half hour passes and I lean over, open the oven door. Heat rushes out onto my cheeks. What I take out from the oven (my hands protected by potholders) seems precisely like those childhood pies: born rather than made.

If the weather's right I'll set the pie to cool on the windowsill. I have no trouble, all these years later, imagining that heat floats off the pie's browned crust out the window and sails in stylized whorls out into the courtyard and over the fence into the neighborhood. If I happen to be anxious, I may fear that the pie's aroma may tempt a distant wolf. The wolf will appear decidedly older, leaner, and more vicious than the wolves from my childhood.

As a child with mud and as an adult with crust and apples, in the moment before the first cut is taken into a pie, I often have felt uncomfortable, as if I were about to violate a taboo. Someone has suggested to me that cutting into a pie is not all that different from cutting into a body. So I think it is good to make something of a ceremony of cutting a pie. The table can be laid with a pretty cloth and napkins and the best silver and your favorite plates.

Once the pie is brought to the table, I like to take a moment to admire it. I like to give the pie a chance to wet the mouth with anticipation of its tastes (the mouth's imagination at work). I like to contemplate the lustrous lightly browned crust. I like to think one more time about inside and out. Because the moment the pie is cut, outside will have no more meaning. A new dimension, the dimension of this pie's delectable interiority, opens up.

Gathered around the table, those about to eat will say "Ahhh" and "Mmmmm, doesn't that look delicious." They will lean forward, noses alert. Sometimes you can hear them breathing in.

The first bite rises toward the opening mouth. The sentinel nose having anticipated pie's arrival, a tide of saliva crests in the mouth, pools in the tongue's center, washes over the several thousand taste buds. The teeth bite through flaky, slightly salty crust and then into tart cherries and rhubarb and apple. The fruits' sweet and buttery juices, in a total immersion baptism of the mouth, flood tongue, teeth, cheeks. There is no more outside. Everything is in.

Activity: RESPONDING TO THE TEXT

1. Which rhetorical strategies does Moore use in "Pie"? How does each strategy suit Moore's purpose?
2. Most of "Pie" recounts a very early childhood memory. Does Moore's discussion of pie and cake seem out of place? Why or why not? Could there be something appropriate about this discussion being included in the first chapter of Moore's memoir?

Writing Assignments

Interview someone who is at least twenty years older than you about their past experiences with food selection, preparation, and habits. You might want to focus on a particular period of this person's life. For example, you might ask your grandmother about the food she prepared and ate when she was first married. Or you might ask your uncle about the food he ate when he was a child. Make a list of questions that will give you a sense of how the selection, purchase, preparation, consumption, storage, and presentation of food were different in the past than they are today. You might ask about what foods were eaten then that are not eaten now, how food was cooked, who cooked it, when certain foods were eaten, where food was eaten, how changes in technology have affected food, what foods were unavailable or uncommon then, which changes are beneficial and which regrettable. Use some of the rhetorical strategies to think about the information you gathered in the interview. For example, you might use

- comparison/contrast to compare/contrast food practices from the past to the present.
- classification to divide food from past and/or present into categories.
- process analysis to explain how certain foods are/were grown, processed, or cooked.
- causal analysis to analyze the causes and/or effects of certain changes that have occurred.
- illustration to give examples that make a point about food practices.
- narration to tell a story about an experience your interviewee had relating to food.
- description to create a picture of food or food practices from past or present.
- definition to clarify an unfamiliar term or idea about food.

Write a paper using what you learned in the interview to make a point about the changes in food and food practices in the last twenty years. Instead of trying to cover everything you learned in the interview, narrow your focus so that you develop your point about the changes in sufficient depth. For example, you could focus on changes in the way food is prepared or served on special occasions, or what was served at particular meals, or who was responsible for food preparation. Your purpose might be informative (for example, "Refrigeration changed my grandmother's cooking and eating habits—and her lifestyle") or it might be persuasive ("The food my grandfather ate when he was young was healthier than today's food"). You will probably use the comparison/contrast strategy, but you may also use others such as description, narration, and illustration. Depending on your thesis, you may also develop your ideas using classification ("If we use the traditional four food groups to examine changes in food consumption over the last twenty years, it's clear that the typical eater has shifted away from fruits and vegetables and toward proteins and grains"), causal analysis ("Changes in technology have changed family eating patterns"), or process analysis ("Although it is easier to can food today than it was in my grandmother's time, fewer people do it because our values and needs have changed"). You may use a number of different rhetorical strategies to fulfill the purpose of your paper.

NARRATION

P R E V I E W

This chapter's explanation about the effective use of narration will help answer the following questions:

- When is narration used?
- What is the best way to organize narrative writing?
- How do you choose which incidents and details to include in your narrative?
- How do you ensure that the narrative fulfills the purpose of your writing?

LEARNING ABOUT TEXTS

A narrative is another term for a story. People naturally love to listen to stories, whether they are children's bedtime stories, the stories families repeat when they gather together at holidays, or the stories told on their favorite television programs. People also naturally love to tell stories: After a horrible day, a pleasant surprise, or an unusual experience, the first impulse most people have is to tell a close friend or family member what happened.

Narratives are also written on many occasions. If you keep a journal or diary, your entries probably consist mostly of narratives, and when you e-mail a friend, you narrate your recent activities. If you are in an accident or witness a crime, you are asked to narrate precisely what happened. At work you may have to write reports that document events, such as incident reports, or that evaluate yourself or your employees by telling what tasks have been done well or poorly. In college, you will be asked to write essay exams that contain narratives. For example, an economics professor might ask you to narrate the events that preceded the Great Depression, or a history professor might ask you to tell about Reconstruction in the South.

Writing a Narrative

Whether you are writing an academic, professional, or personal narrative, you can make the task easier and the results better by following these guidelines:

1. <u>Consider your purpose.</u> Are you writing to record, to inform, or to persuade? If you are describing an accident to persuade inexperienced drivers to be more cautious, your narrative will have a different purpose than if you are explaining to a police officer how the accident occurred.
2. <u>Consider the reader.</u> What background information does the reader need? For example, members of your family would need less background information to understand a personal narrative than strangers would, and people you work with daily would need less information than people who hold different positions in your company.
3. <u>Make the significance of your story clear.</u> If you are trying to convince drivers to be more cautious, you might include a sentence like "My accident taught me that a light rain after a dry spell can create dangerously slippery conditions." Some writers state the narrative's point at the conclusion as a way of summing up or closing the story; on the other hand, stating the story's point in the introduction lets the readers know what to expect, so they may find your narrative easier to read.
4. <u>Briefly establish the setting and the characters.</u> To decide how much information to include, consider your readers' backgrounds. Include all the information they need to understand your narrative and its point, but do not provide any unnecessary or irrelevant data.
5. <u>Tell events in the order they happened.</u> Sometimes films, television shows, and books use flashbacks, flash forwards, or other changes in the sequence of events. While these devices can be both interesting and effective, they are more difficult to understand than straightforward chronology. Using a simple chronological order makes your narrative clearer and easier to read.
6. <u>Add vivid, specific details.</u> Details and, if appropriate, dialogue make your narrative lively and interesting. Be sure, however, that the details are relevant: Every detail should contribute to the story.
7. <u>Make your narrative complete and unified.</u> Include all the information readers need to understand and appreciate your story. Eliminate any unnecessary or irrelevant information.
8. <u>Add transitions.</u> To be sure the readers can easily understand the sequence of events, use expressions such as "first," "next," "at the same time," or "two hours later."

FYI: For more about using specific details see p. 202–203 in Chapter 6.

Activity: WRITER'S LOG

Think about experiences in your life involving food—memorable meals, pleasant or unpleasant childhood memories, unusual experiences with cooking or eating, holiday food, experiences with fasting or hunger, growing or buying food. Write a paragraph that narrates this experience.

READING AND WRITING TEXTS

Activity: PREREADING

In your Writer's Log

Describe a food that connects you with your family, with your ancestors, or with your ethnic group. How would you feel if you could no longer eat this food?

Reading

Lefsa, A Traditional Norwegian Holiday Bread
Chelsie Levin

The following essay was written by Chelsie Levin in response to an assignment asking for a description of a food which is important to a family or ethnic group. The writer uses narration along with description and process analysis to create a vivid picture of the role this holiday food plays in her family life today and in the past.

3 cups mashed boiled potatoes
1 tablespoon shortening
A dash of salt
A dash of sugar
3 cups sifted flour

Mix ingredients together in a metal bowl until firm and dough-like texture. Heat lefsa griddle to 450 degrees. Roll dough into small balls and flatten into round thin pancakes. Place on griddle and allow to bubble. Turn over until bubbles appear on the other side. Allow to cool, butter, and roll into cigar shape. Serve hot or cold with holiday meal.

When I was a child, holidays spent at my Great Aunt Thelma's were the most magical. Traditional and fun, my aunt would decorate the house to suit the occasion and have small surprises for all the children. A table of delicacies would be put out around mid-afternoon, and my sister and I patiently waited until everyone had taken their turn piling their plates full of food. As soon as the last people took their trips around the table and settled in the living room to eat, my sister and I would run and fill our plates with the most wonderful food in the world—lefsa!

Lefsa, a simple holiday bread made from potatoes, was a tradition brought over on the *Mayflower* by my great-great-great-grandmother Besta Johnson. Originally from Norway, this recipe made its way through generations of our family. Aunt Thelma was the last of her generation to be able to produce this wonderful bread and made sure it appeared at every holiday meal. Unfortunately, my aunt had a stroke before I ever learned from her the secret of making this scrumptious food.

Years after my aunt passed away, I was cleaning out boxes of recipes and came across a small book of Norwegian traditional breads. A smile came to my face as I found the recipe for lefsa in the table of contents. Opening the book that was published in Norway in 1832, I scrambled through its contents. Along with the recipe for lefsa, I also found notes scribbled on the page from generations past. A piece of paper that fell from the book also contained notes from my Aunt Thelma, updating the recipe to include techniques for making this traditional bread with an electrical lefsa cooking grill instead of a frying pan. Running to the phone, I eagerly called my mom and told her of my find.

Unfortunately, my mother had no use for the grill my Aunt Thelma had used to make this bread and had sold it at a garage sale. It took many phone calls and a few Internet searches to finally purchase a real lefsa grill of my own. On a mission to reproduce this bread of my family's heritage, I prepared my kitchen, cleared my busy schedule, and made way for a day of lefsa making.

Setting the new grill in the middle of my counter top and preparing it as the directions stated, I waited as the heat cooked off the water and oil I had applied. Leaving it at the heat of 300 degrees for the thirty minutes stated in my aunt's worn page of notes, I pulled out a big metal bowl and started filling it with flour. Remembering a trick my aunt used when I had once observed her in the kitchen, I melted a cup of shortening and mixed a tablespoon of the hot liquid with the flour. Spreading a little salt and a little sugar over this mixture, I then added the three cups of mashed boiled potatoes, a small amount at a time. Using a wooden spoon, as my aunt clearly stated in her notes, I smoothed and scraped the mixture until it became a full, white, doughy ball of fluff. Letting it sit for a few minutes, I then washed my hands with flour and proceeded to form small balls about the size of a golf ball out of the dough. I must say that this part was fairly easy and fun. The memories of holidays spent with my aunt filled my mind as I worked. When I finally produced about thirty small balls of fluffy texture, I flipped the heat on the grill up to 450 degrees to make it ready to start the next step.

For the average first-time lefsa maker, shaping the balls into thin flat pancakes is the hardest part of the process. Fortunately, I had learned to make tortillas when I lived with a girlfriend and her traditional Mexican family years ago. The lefsa dough, not quite as firm as tortilla dough, was not as easy to manipulate, so it took me several tries to produce a pancake. Finally reaching perfection, I placed the round pancake on the grill. As directed by my aunt, I waited for the bubbles to appear. I smelled the dough as it cooked, filling my kitchen with a nostalgic air. Turning the lefsa over is also a work of art and took me several attempts. Out of the first batch of thirty small balls, only ten made it through the entire process. I repeated the recipe three more times until I had produced a stack of sixty pancakes.

With the hard work finished, I took time to clean the kitchen before I buttered and rolled the fruits of my labor. Using a small frosting knife, I placed a gob of whipped real butter upon every pancake one at a time. Making sure the butter covered the entire surface, I then started at the edges and rolled the cooked dough firmly into a cigar-shaped object. Cutting any ragged edges from the form, I sliced each cigar into four smaller pieces and made five small packages with sixty lefsa rolls in each. Decorating each package with ribbon and colored cellophane, I placed them in my refrigerator, refusing to taste any leftovers. Wanting to surprise my family and enjoy the bread in a traditional way, I forced myself not to eat any scraps and fed them to my Cocker Spaniel, Carrie.

Placing the four individually wrapped packages under my mom's tree on Christmas Day gave me a special feeling. Making everyone wait until the other presents were opened, I finally handed my sister, brother, mom and dad their finished gifts. The tears that rolled from my mother's eyes as she saw what I had produced tugged at my heart and brought tears to my own eyes. Turning to look at the rest of my family, I saw the packages opened and their contents being greedily devoured as I laughed and hugged my mom, knowing I brought her happy memories from long ago.

Lefsa now graces every holiday meal in our family. One Christmas I also sent the recipe and copies of my aunt's notes to all her relatives, hoping the tradition will carry on through further generations. I can now produce a batch of lefsa in less than two hours (which I think is quite a remarkable feat!). My sister and I still consume it before we eat anything else and fight over the last piece. And every time I place the lefsa on the table, I feel my Aunt Thelma smiling as she watches over me.

Activity: RESPONDING TO THE TEXT

1. Why does the writer include the recipe at the beginning when the complete process of making lefsa is described in the body of the essay? How would the readers' experience be different if the recipe were removed?
2. Where else could the writer have put the recipe? How would moving the recipe affect the essay? Why do you think she chose to put it where she did?
3. How would the essay be different if the writer had left out the first paragraph and begun with the second? What does the first paragraph add to the essay?
4. What else do you learn about in this essay besides how to make lefsa? Does anything in the essay relate to your own experiences, concerns, or interests?

Writing Assignment

The Writer's Log assignment on p. 314 asked you to:

> Think about experiences in your life involving food—memorable meals, pleasant or unpleasant childhood memories, unusual experiences with cooking or eating, holiday food, experiences with fasting or hunger, growing or buying food. Write a paragraph that narrates this experience.

Turn this or a similar experience into a narrative essay. Think about why you would want to tell someone about your experience or why someone would want to read about it. What is it about this experience that makes it memorable, significant? What purpose could you have for this narrative? Does it illustrate some point? Do you want to compare your experience to some other experience? Did your experience cause something or was it the effect of something? In your essay, use your experience to make a larger point about something—food, family, traditions, values, society. Try to compose a narrow, specific thesis. In narrative essays, the thesis may not be at the beginning, but there should be some point and purpose guiding your decisions about content, organization, and style.

DESCRIPTION

11

PREVIEW

This chapter's explanation about description will answer the following questions:

- When should description be used?
- What makes a description effective?

LEARNING ABOUT TEXTS

At work, nurses, police officers, engineers, and countless other professionals must be able to observe carefully and describe accurately both people and circumstances. In college, students write lab reports, research projects, and many types of assignments that require careful observing and recording of information. Description may be a small part of your paper—a paragraph or two—or your entire paper may be one long description of an event, person, or object. To determine how extensive and detailed a description should be and to avoid being boring or unclear, writers of descriptions must focus on their readers' needs and their purposes.

Writing A Description

To write an effective description, follow these guidelines:

1. <u>Consider your reader.</u> If you are describing the results of a lab experiment, persuading a friend to try a new restaurant, or informing your employers of a hazard at work, you will write very different descriptions, not only because your topics are different, but also because your readers are different. However, in all descriptions, you will keep this question in mind: What do the readers need to know? If you choose information that exactly fits the readers' needs, your description will be clear and interesting. Briefly analyze your audience before you begin, and remember the readers as you brainstorm, draft, and revise.

2. <u>Clarify your purpose.</u> If you are describing a vegetarian diet, you should know whether you are trying to inform readers about what vegetarians eat or trying to persuade them to eat vegetarian meals. Different purposes will result in different choices about what information to include. Most of the time, your description will be easier to read if your purpose is clear to readers as well.

3. <u>Observe closely, using all the senses.</u> Before you begin to write, list all the details you can observe. Even though you may not include them all in your paper, you might uncover some original insights or impressions. Remember that not all your observations will be visual details. Use all your senses, and record smells, tastes, sounds, and textures.

4. <u>Identify the dominant impression.</u> If you listed every detail about a movie, a restaurant, or a vacation spot, your readers would be more confused than enlightened. To find the dominant impression, review the list of details you made. Some details will seem more significant than others because they most effectively convey the impression you want the readers to have.

5. <u>Organize your description logically.</u> For example, if you were writing a review of a new restaurant for a local newspaper, you might have two or three paragraphs describing food and prices (entrees, appetizers, side dishes, and desserts), a paragraph describing decor and atmosphere, and a paragraph describing clientele (whether the restaurant caters to families, college students, or professionals).

Activity: WRITER'S LOG

Write a one-paragraph description of a restaurant or food market with which you are familiar. Your description should convince the readers to become customers of the place you describe. Now write a description of the same place, this time describing it in such a way that readers would not want to become customers.

READING AND WRITING TEXTS

Activity: PREREADING

In your Writer's Log
Describe your favorite food, including the details readers need in order to understand why it is your favorite.

Reading

From "Spaghetti"

Robert Girardi

This excerpt from Robert Girardi's essay contains descriptions of his childhood home, his parents, his father's hometown, his parents' wedding, and—of course— spaghetti. His careful choice of details in these descriptions conveys his thoughts and feelings about the things he describes.

In the den of our old house in Springfield, I remember an ancient black Naugahyde reclining chair, taped and tattered, the works so broken it wouldn't recline anymore; a fraying oval of Oriental carpet around whose whorls and arabesques I pushed Matchbox cars encrusted from the dirt pile out back; an ominous couch covered in green, itchy fabric, flanked by two rather funereal lamps; and in the far corner beside the window always kept shuttered, a huge dusty television with a very small screen, outdated even then. This last item, of German manufacture—a Telefunken, I think—had been acquired by my parents in occupied Vienna in the '50s. The cabinetry was beautiful, inlaid wood and marquetry, but the black-and-white picture was always too bright or too dark, the sound intermittent at best.

One evening in the early '60s—I was no more than two or three—I sat cross-legged on the carpet, my face tipped up toward the glowing screen. A slow countdown vibrated from the speakers and then a silver projectile— probably one of the Mercury rockets—blasted into the sky above Cape Canaveral, trailing smoke like white feathers. I don't know now why I sat in the den alone watching this monumental event: the rest of the family was in the kitchen, just settling down to dinner. But moments after the rocket passed the low clouds and became a silver glint in the gray sky of the television, my mother called me to the table. The spaghetti was ready.

I tottered across the living room into the kitchen's yellow light just as my father lifted the long strands of wheat-colored spaghetti from the steel pot. Another pot contained thick, fragrant red sauce swimming with meatballs large as my fist. Plates were passed across the turquoise Formica counter and returned heaping to the white tablecloth. Rich, red sauce covered every plate except for mine and my mother's. She ate her spaghetti plain, with salt and butter, a perversity that bears some explaining. I was too young to know better. The steely side of the pot of spaghetti on the stove showed the same silver glint of the rocket on its way into space as my mother bowed her head for the blessing.

This is probably my first memory.

My parents made their strange bargain in the late 1940s in Washington, D.C., in the exuberant days just after the war. The bargain itself was of the usual sort: that they would marry, raise children, make a life together. It was only strange because they had nothing in common. Not blood, perspective, culture, cuisine. The hardest part of the bargain encompassed the understanding that my father would abandon his culture as an ethnic Italian American to become an unhyphenated American in what was then the American century, and that my mother would leave her people behind to facilitate this transformation.

He was short, fond of dancing, good food, wine; a solid, first-generation Italian from a small coal-mining town just outside of Pittsburgh. She was tall, American, grave, dignified, never danced, and was partial to plain roast beef, strong opinions, and nights at home; an eccentric white Anglo-Saxon Catholic from a line of eccentric white Anglo-Saxon Catholics who dated their presence on these shores back to 1634. Her ancestors had come over on the *Arc* and *Dove*, two famous ships that brought the first and last English Catholic settlers across the Atlantic to establish the colony that later became the state of Maryland.

Of course, my mother's parents were opposed to her marriage from the beginning. They would not tolerate their daughter marrying a foreigner, they said, and threatened to disown her if she did. Pointing out that my father was a Pennsylvanian who had served honorably in the U.S. Army during the war did nothing to sway their resolve. At twenty-five my mother still lived with her parents, on the dormer floor of a well-kept, spacious Victorian house on Kanawah Street in northwest Washington. There were some stiff, ugly scenes, then she packed her things secretly one night in November 1946 and took a Greyhound bus to Pennsylvania with the remains of her savings hidden in a white leather cosmetics bag in her suitcase.

Even at its most prosperous, there was something baroque and foreboding about my father's hometown, folded into the hills above the brown sluice of the Allegheny River. Now it is abandoned, empty, a maze of broken factories and rusting corrugated iron, as if in fulfillment of an evil promise. But in those days the air above its row houses and steep streets hung thick with the fires of the great smelters, and trucks full of plate steel roared up and down the highway through town; Pittsburgh blossomed, a black smudge of coal smoke on the horizon.

My mother stayed at the YWCA on Main Street downtown near the Alhambra movie theater, now closed, while last preparations went forward with the inevitability of an execution. My father's mother and his sisters cooked for three days straight for the wedding feast. His uncle, a wizened little Italian man who rarely spoke, dug up the last precious homemade wine laid in the ground during Prohibition; wine made from secret black grapes grown somewhere in the hills overlooking the town.

The wedding reception took place in the Knights of Columbus hall across from the Catholic church on a rainy afternoon. The rain, full of coal soot, spotted my mother's white satin dress. Friends of my father still talk about the food: A mighty spread of antipasti covered three trestle tables; five more tables sagged beneath the weight of fifteen different kinds of pasta—including baked ziti, cannelloni, stuffed shells, lasagna; even *timpano*, which is a sort of pie of pasta, cheese, ham, onions, and sweetbreads—baked suckling pig Calabrian-style, chicken cacciatore, a half-dozen rich desserts. My mother wouldn't touch a bite. She didn't like Italian food. Italian food was for Italians. It was as simple as that. And she would have no wine. She didn't drink, either.

I can imagine my Italian relatives sadly shaking their heads. My Italian grandfather and grandmother, both of whom died long before I was born, must have been disappointed. I imagine them like Indians in a grade-B Western, puzzled over the mysterious ways of white people. What sort of creature could fail to be tempted by so much good food? And I can see her there, my mother, resplendent in her spotted white satin, superior, dignified, not eating, not drinking. She is like Persephone in Hades, pale as an apparition as the *tarantella* plays, as the feast whirls around her in all its vulgar color. Wine flows and my cousins cram ziti into their mouths, the *timpano* is cut, releasing a cloud of aromatic steam—but she is dreaming of overdone Anglo-Saxon pot roast and Jell-O molds, of limp string beans and parsleyed potatoes, of unsauced chicken, of dry turkey on a bed of plain iceberg lettuce.

Her revenge for this single evening of Italian culinary excess was a slow and subtle torment that lasted through forty-five years of married life: Six days a week, she inflicted the food she had dreamed of the night of her wedding on her husband and family. Only on Sunday were we allowed a respite from the bland English fare of her forefathers. On that day she would condescend to make spaghetti from the recipe handed down in my father's family. But this, too, as it turned out, was part of her revenge—the pasta on her plate, gleaming, unadorned, bare of sauce, reproached us with every swallow.

My Italian Aunt Philomena in her retirement kept a little house in St. Petersburg, Florida, where we spent summer vacation once or twice during the turbulent years between the Kennedy assassination and Kent State. There, as traveller palms swayed outside the aluminum frame window, she patiently taught my mother how to make the sauce. The preparation had a ritualistic quality that colored Sundays in my youth every bit as much as Mass: The meatballs were started in the morning and lowered into the sauce to cook all day. By afternoon the fragrance of simmering meat, tomatoes, and spices filled our tepid suburban bungalow as piazzas in towns in Italy are full of golden light in the hour before the sun goes down. The fragrance of the sauce cooking was no mere odor; it was family history in a smell.

Activity: RESPONDING TO THE TEXT

1. Look at all the passages where Girardi describes his mother. What impression do you get of her?
2. What is Girardi's point in describing spaghetti? What is his purpose?
3. Notice Girardi's descriptions of spaghetti and other Italian foods. What does he focus on when he describes them? In what way are these details appropriate to his purpose?

Writing Assignment

Describe what you consider to be the perfect meal. Your purpose is to make readers understand why this meal is perfect. Consider all aspects of the meal—food, location, time, and people. You might describe a meal you've had already or one you would like to have. You may even describe a fantasy meal, one you could experience only in your imagination. Use details that fit your purpose and that appeal to the senses.

ILLUSTRATION

12

P R E V I E W

This chapter's explanation of illustration will answer the following questions:

- When is illustration an effective rhetorical strategy?
- How do you choose illustrations that are interesting and convincing?
- What is the best way to organize an illustration essay?

L E A R N I N G   A B O U T   T E X T S

An illustration is a picture that offers some clarification or insight. Newspapers use illustrations to make their stories seem more immediate or more human; magazines use illustrations to attract the readers' attention, create an atmosphere, or provide information; textbooks use illustrations to add information or clarify the concepts. However, not all illustrations are visual; in writing, an illustration is an example, a "verbal picture" that "illustrates" the point the writer is making.

Written illustrations can be brief, a word or a phrase, or they can be extended, one to several paragraphs in length. Writing an extended illustration often requires using techniques for narration or description.

Writing an Illustration

To use illustration to support a thesis, follow these guidelines:

1. <u>Select relevant examples.</u> Be sure your examples support the point you want to make and are not merely interesting anecdotes on the topic. Unless your thesis highlights the unusual ("Some truly bizarre customers shop

at Sam's Surplus"), your examples should focus on the typical, not the unusual. For example, if you intend to demonstrate that your workplace has too many barriers for the disabled, you would be more persuasive if you described typical obstructions, such as heavy doors, rather than obstacles only rarely encountered.

2. <u>Describe examples using specific details.</u> Your examples will be more interesting and more convincing if you include specific details. "My Aunt Doris" is more specific, and more interesting, than "a relative of mine." Explaining that "last week three customers in wheelchairs were unable to maneuver their chairs through the aisles because the displays of sale items were crowded in the middle of the store" is more persuasive than saying that "the store is hard for disabled people to move through."

3. <u>Make your examples appropriate in length.</u> Although you need to add enough detail to make your examples clear, be sure you do not add irrelevant details that might mislead or bore the readers.

Activity: WORKING TOGETHER

1. Each group member will write a one-paragraph example to support this thesis: "Americans acquire status by conspicuous consumption of material goods."

2. Read each other's paragraphs and discuss them together. Are they all relevant to the thesis? Are they all appropriate in length? Do they all include specific details?

3. Compare the examples. Which are the most effective? Why?

READING AND WRITING TEXTS

Activity: PREREADING

In small groups, discuss the following questions:

- What foods do you think you wouldn't eat, even if you were hungry?
- Why wouldn't you eat them?

Reading

What's Cooking?: Eating in America
Bill Bryson

The following excerpt is from a book by Bill Bryson called Made in America: An Informal History of the English Language in the United States. *In this chapter, Bryson describes the new words that came into English as the settlers from Europe learned to eat the foods available in the New World. He uses many short examples in each paragraph to illustrate his points about the settlers' ideas and behavior.*

To the first Pilgrims, the gustatory possibilities of the New World were slow in revealing themselves. Though the woods of New England abounded in hearty sustenance—wild duck and turkey, partridge, venison, wild plums and cherries, mushrooms, every manner of nuts and berries—and though the waters teemed with fish, they showed a grim reluctance to eat anything that did not come from their dwindling stockpile of salt pork (which they called *salt horse*), salt fish, and salt beef, hardtack (a kind of biscuit baked so hard that it became more or less impervious to mold, weevils, and human teeth), and dried peas and dried beans, "almost preferring," in the words of one historian, "to starve in the midst of plenty rather than experiment with the strange but kindly fruits of the earth." Or as another put it: "The first settlers had come upon a land of plenty. They nearly starved in it."

    Lobster was so plentiful that "the least boy in the Plantation may both catch and eat what he will of them," but hardly any did. John Winthrop lamented in a letter home that he could not have his beloved mutton but only such impoverished fare as oysters, duck, salmon, and scallops. Clams and mussels they did not eat at all, but fed to their pigs. To their chagrin the colonists discovered that English wheat was unsuited to the soil and climate of New England. The crops were repeatedly devastated by a disease called smut. For the better part of two centuries, wheat would remain a luxury in the colonies. Even their first crop of peas failed, a consequence not so much of the challenges of the New England climate as of their own inexperience as farmers. With their foodstocks dwindling and their aptitude as hunter-gatherers sorely taxed, the outlook for this small group of blundering, inexperienced, hopelessly underprepared immigrants was bleak indeed.

    Fortunately, there were Indians to save them. The Indians of the New World were already eating better than any European. Native Americans enjoyed some two thousand different foods, a number that even the

wealthiest denizen of the Old World would have found unimaginably varied. Among the delicacies unique to the New World were the white and
sweet potatoes, the peanut, the pumpkin and its cousin the squash, the per-
simmon (or *putchamin,* as the first colonists recorded it), the avocado,
the pineapple, chocolate and vanilla, cassava (the source of tapioca), chili
peppers, sunflowers, and the tomato—though of course not all of these
were known everywhere. Even those plants that already existed in Europe
were often of a superior variety in the New World. American green beans
were far plumper and richer, and soon displaced the fibrous, chewy variety previously grown in Europe. Likewise, once Europeans got sight and
taste of the fat, sumptuous strawberries that grew wild in Virginia, they
gladly forsook the mushy little button strawberries that had theretofore
been all they had known. The Indians' diet was healthier, too. At a time
when even well-heeled Europeans routinely fell prey to scurvy and watched
helplessly as their teeth fell from spongy gums, the Indians knew that a
health body required a well-balanced diet.

But above all, their agriculture had a sophistication that European husbandry could not begin to compete with. They had learned empirically to
plant beans among the corn, which not only permitted a greater yield from
the same amount of land but also replenished the nitrogen the corn took
away. As a result, while Europeans struggled even in good years to scrape a
living from the soil, the Indians of the New World enjoyed a constant boun-
ty. That a single tribe in New England had sufficient surpluses to support a
hundred helpless, unexpected visitors for the better part of a year is eloquent testimony of that. . . .

The Indians introduced the colonists not only to new foods, but to
more interesting ways of preparing them. Succotash, clam chowder,
hominy, corn pone, cranberry sauce, johnnycakes, even Boston baked
beans and Brunswick stew were all Indian dishes. In Virginia it was the Indians, not the white settlers, who invented Smithfield ham. Even with the
constant advice and intervention of the Indians, the Puritans stuck to a diet
that was for the most part resolutely bland. Meat and vegetables were
boiled without pity, deprived of seasonings, and served lukewarm. Peas,
once they got the hang of growing them, were eaten at almost every meal,
and often served cold. The principal repast was taken at midday and called
dinner. *Supper,* a word related to *soup* (and indeed at the time still often
spelled *souper*), was often just that—a little soup with perhaps a piece of
bread—and was consumed in the evening shortly before retiring. Lunch
was a concept yet unknown, as was the idea of a snack. To the early
colonists, *snack* meant the bite of a dog. . . .

As time moved on, the diet of the average American became earti-
er if not a great deal more appealing. In an environment where women
devoted their lives to an endless, exhausting round of activity, from
weaving and making soap and candles to salting and pickling anything
that could be preserved, it is hardly surprising that quality cooking
was at a premium and that most people were, in the words of Thomas
Jefferson, "illy fed." Nonetheless, by the late eighteenth century,
portions for almost everyone were abundant, and visitors from the

Old World commonly remarked on the size of meals in even the humblest households. For the wealthier families, dishes were varied and, by earlier standards, exotic. The cookbook kept at Mount Vernon, written by George Washington's mother, tells us much about both the variety of foods eaten and their sometimes curious spelling and pronunciation, notably *mushrumps, hartichocke pie, fryckecy of chicken,* and *lettice tart.*

By the time of the Revolution, the main meal was taken between 2 and 4 P.M. A typical meal might consist of salted beef with potatoes and peas, followed by baked or fried eggs, fish, and salad, with a variety of sweets, puddings, cheeses, and pastries to finish, all washed down with quantities of alcohol that would leave most of us today unable to rise from the table—or at least to rise and stay risen. Meat was consumed in quantities that left European observers slack-jawed with astonishment. By the early 1800s the average American was eating almost 180 pounds of meat a year, 48 pounds more than people would consume a century later, but fresh meat remained largely unknown because of the difficulty of keeping it fresh. Even city people often had chickens in the yard and a hog or two left to scavenge in the street. Until well into the nineteenth century, visitors to New York remarked on the hazard to traffic presented by wandering hogs along Broadway. Even in the more temperate North, beef and pork would go bad in a day in summer, chicken even quicker, and milk would curdle in as little as an hour. And even among the better classes, spoiled food was a daily hazard. One guest at a dinner party given by the Washingtons noted with a certain vicious relish that the General discreetly pushed his plate of sherry trifle to one side when he discovered that the cream was distinctly iffy but that the less discerning Martha continued shoveling it in with gusto. Ice cream was a safer option. It was first mentioned in America in the 1740s when a guest at a banquet given by the governor of Maryland wrote about this novelty, which, he noted, "eat most deliciously." . . .

As the nineteenth century progressed, diet evolved into two camps—the few who ate well and the many who did not—and class antagonisms were not long in emerging. The patrician New Yorker Martin Van Buren was ousted from the presidency in 1840 in part because one of his Whig opponents made a celebrated speech attacking him for serving such delicate and unmanly fare in the White House as strawberries, cauliflower, and celery. (Van Buren gained a sort of vicarious revenge when, at the subsequent inauguration, the crusty William Henry Harrison refused to don an overcoat, contracted pneumonia, and with alarming haste expired; his tenure as President was just thirty days, much of that spent unconscious.) Gradually even poorer Americans became acquainted with a wider variety of fruits and vegetables, though the linguistic evidence shows that they weren't always quite sure what to make of them. For the potato alone, the *Dictionary of American English on Historical Principles* records such arresting nineteenth-century concoctions as potato custard, potato chowder, potato pone, potato pudding, and even potato coffee. We can assume that most of these were consumed in a spirit of either experimentation or desperation and didn't survive long in the native diet.

Activity: RESPONDING TO THE TEXT

1. Bryson uses many lists of examples to support his points. What is the effect of these lists on the readers?
2. Bryson uses one or two longer examples. Why do you think he decided to develop these examples in more detail?

Writing Assignment

Write an essay that makes a general point about food, eating, cooking, or some related topic. If you can't think of your own point, choose one of the following statements, narrowing or modifying it to suit your interests. Use illustration to support the main point. Your examples may come from your own life, the lives of people you know, from history, books or articles you've read, or from the news. Select examples that are the most relevant to your point and most interesting to readers.

- Eating at home is not always cheaper than eating out.
- Families who eat dinner together almost every night have stronger relationships than families who don't share meals.
- In this country, much food is wasted.
- Children's food preferences are influenced by their peers.

PROCESS
ANALYSIS

13

P R E V I E W

This chapter's explanation of process analysis will answer the following questions:

- What can you do to make your process analysis perfectly clear to readers?
- How does your purpose affect your writing of a process analysis?
- When should process analysis be used?

L E A R N I N G   A B O U T   T E X T S

When you analyze a process, you break it down into separate steps and present those steps to your reader in one of two ways. You can either instruct the reader on how to do something (for example, how to change the oil in a car) or explain how something happens (how coins are minted). Both types of process analysis will present steps chronologically, but otherwise the resulting papers will be quite different because the purposes of the papers differ fundamentally. The purpose of instructions is to enable the readers to repeat the process successfully: Having read the paper on changing oil in a car, readers should be able to change the oil in their car correctly. The purpose of an explanation is to inform readers about the process: Having read the paper on the minting of coins, readers should understand the basic procedure, but would certainly not be capable of minting their own money.

To give you practice in process analysis, college composition instructors may ask you to write about a process you know well. In such a case, select and limit your topic carefully. If a topic is too complex (such as rewiring an old house), you cannot discuss it fully in the space of a typical writing-course paper. On the other hand, if a topic is too simple (making a sandwich), no instructions are required. An appropriate topic would meet all four of these criteria:

- The process should be one you do well and often, such as a procedure you do daily in school, on the job, or at home.

- The process should be suitable for its intended audience. For example, instructions on tying shoelaces would be inappropriate for children too young to follow written instructions.
- The process should be one whose instructions are not easily found elsewhere. For example, instructions on making Jell-O or baking a cake mix would be useless because readers could follow the instructions on the box more easily than they could read a paper on the process.
- The process should be one that can be discussed fully in the required length of the paper.

To find a suitable topic, refer to the lists of roles and interests you made in Chapter 1 or use an information-gathering technique, such as brainstorming or mapping, to review all the things you do during a typical week. You will probably be able to find several appropriate topics.

You may also be asked to write instructions or explain a process at work. Instructions for a simple process, such as accessing the Internet, might well be provided in an e-mail message to employees with Internet access. A more complex process, such as submitting annual budget requests, may need to be explained in a section of your company's fiscal policies manual. As in most writing tasks, considering your purpose and your reader will help you determine what information to include and which process analysis strategy to employ.

Writing Instructions Using Process Analysis

When writing instructions, follow these guidelines:

1. Use the second person (you). Since you are speaking directly to the readers, telling them what to do, use the imperative verb form (e.g., prepare the surface by sanding it lightly; mix the ingredients thoroughly) and the pronoun *you* (e.g., you should allow at least two hours for the paint to dry).
2. Divide the process into separate actions. Almost any undertaking, even a relatively complex one, can be followed if the instructions separate the process into clear steps that the reader can follow one at a time.
3. Make the sequence clear. Use plenty of transitions to indicate the chronological sequence of steps: Every step should have expressions like "first," "second," "next," "at the same time," or "fifteen minutes later." The readers should never have to guess when, or in what order, the steps should be followed.
4. Give complete instructions. Remember that your readers do not know how to perform the task; that's why they are reading the instructions. Include all steps, no matter how obvious they seem to you, and include necessary background information. Also consider the errors readers might make, and add any appropriate cautions or warnings.
5. Be specific. For example, telling the readers to "remove the old oil filter" is inadequate; they might not know where to locate the oil filter or how to remove it. To be specific, you may want to go through the process (or better yet, convince a friend to go through it), taking notes on exactly what you do and when you do it.

6. <u>Avoid the telegraphic style.</u> To ensure that readers will be able to understand the instructions, do not omit words like "the" and "a," and do not rely on abbreviations. For example, instead of writing, "Add 1 lb flour to dough," write, "Add one pound of flour to the dough."

Writing Explanations Using Process Analysis

When explaining a process, follow these guidelines:

1. <u>Use the third person (he, she, it, they).</u> When writing instructions, speak directly to the reader, using the pronoun *you.* However, when explaining a process, speak about the people performing the process, using the third-person pronouns *he, she,* and *they.* You can avoid the problem of referring to both genders with the masculine pronoun *he* by using the plural whenever possible; e.g., "Cannibals usually eat only their enemies," not "A cannibal usually eats only his enemy."

2. <u>Divide the process into steps and make the sequence clear.</u> As in instructions, you must add enough transitions to make sure the sequence is clear. Because the reader will not try to duplicate the process, the steps can be less detailed than in instructions.

3. <u>Be sure the explanation is complete.</u> Your purpose is to inform interested readers; if your explanation is incomplete, their curiosity will not be satisfied, and they will not be adequately informed about the process.

4. <u>Make your explanation lively and interesting.</u> We all remember learning experiences that were fascinating—as well as those that were deadly dull. The difference between information that interests us and information that bores us often lies not in the subject matter itself, but in the presentation of the subject. Make your explanation lively and interesting by adding relevant details, insights, or anecdotes.

Activity: COMPUTER WORKSHOP

Choose a task you do at work (operate a cash register, schedule employee hours) or at home (raise tomatoes, pay bills, remove wallpaper). Compose two brief papers using multiple screens on your computer. The first paper will instruct your reader on the process; the second will explain the same process. To see this difference, try the following:

1. Open a file, titled "Brainstorm Process," and rapidly list the steps in the process.

2. Open another file titled "Instructions." Now switch back to "Brainstorm Process," copy your list, and paste it into "Instructions." Quickly revise the first three steps so a reader could follow them as instructions.

3. Open another file titled "Explanation." Paste the original list of steps into this file. Quickly draft two paragraphs that explain the first few steps in the process.

4. Take a moment to analyze the differences between your instructions and explanations.

Even though the subject is the same, your final papers should have significant differences because of their different purposes.

READING AND WRITING TEXTS

Activity: PREREADING

In your Writer's Log
Write a one- or two-paragraph process analysis of a ritual that is part of your daily life. Does writing about the ritual make you notice details that you don't normally notice as you perform it?

Reading

The Way of Iced Coffee
Donald W. George

Donald W. George uses a detailed process analysis to turn an everyday event into a meditation on the idea that "pleasure can sometimes be savored in such simple things." The lyrical language and philosophical tone keep this detailed description of a familiar process from becoming dull.

Three months ago I was sitting in a Tokyo coffee shop, lingering over a glass of iced coffee and watching the world go by. I was smiling at everything and nothing, sipping my iced coffee, watching the people passing outside and the people sipping inside, and suddenly it struck me that one reason for my sense of well-being was the little ritual I was enacting—a ritual I had been enacting ever since my first sip of iced coffee ten years before.

As I reflected on this, I realized that I had seen variations of this ritual enacted—unconsciously—in countless Japanese coffee shops by countless people, and that in fact the preparation and drinking of iced coffee had become one of those delightful little rites that unify and enrich Japanese life.

To my knowledge, however, no one had recognized it as such, so I decided to order another iced coffee and to set down my own modest version of *aisu kohido,* "the way of iced coffee."

To enjoy this simple rite, you need first to install yourself in a comfortable coffee shop, then order by saying, "*Aisu kohi, kudasai.*" What follows probably won't reveal any profound truths, but it may make you feel more intimately a part of the mesh of modern Japan—and it will certainly provide a welcome chance to relax and reflect in the middle of a hard sightseeing day.

When your iced coffee is placed before you, study it for a while: the dark, rich liquid glistens with ice cubes whose curves and cracks hold and reflect and refract the liquid.

Notice the thin silver streaks and peaks in the ice cubes, and the beads of water on the outside of the glass—a cooling sight on a hot day. Then take up the tiny silver pitcher of sugar syrup that has been set just beside the glass and pour it into the part of the glass that is nearest to you. The syrupy stream courses through the coffee like a tiny waterfall, then quickly disperses and dissolves, like the dream of a rain shower on a summer afternoon.

After that, pick up the tiny white pitcher of cream that was placed just beyond the silver pitcher and pour it into the middle of the glass. Watch it disperse into countless cream-colored swirls and whirls and streams, which hang suspended in the middle of the coffee like a frozen breeze. Notice how the cream is pure white in some parts and a thin brownish hue in others. Notice also that a little trace stays on the surface, spiraling down into the middle of the glass.

Then unwrap the straw that has been set beyond the glass and place it in the middle of the glass. This sends out ripples that reconfigure the cream's liquid breeze, creating new waves and textures and layers of iced coffee.

Finally, after appreciating this effect to your satisfaction, stir the coffee vigorously with your straw—the ice cubes clinking like wind chimes in a seaside breeze—until the coffee is a uniform sand-colored hue.

Then sip the coffee through the straw, tasting its coolness and complex mix of bitter coffee and sweet sugar and cream.

Now sit back, sip, and watch the world go by—smiling and serene that pleasure can sometimes be savored in such simple things.

Activity: RESPONDING TO THE TEXT

1. Why do you think George decided to write instructions for the process rather than an explanation of the process?
2. What does George focus on in his description and details? What does this focus tell you about his purpose?

Writing Assignment

Write a process paper describing a food that is associated with or important to an ethnic group you belong to or are familiar with. Decide whether the purpose of your discussion is to explain to your readers how the food is prepared or to write instructions enabling the reader to prepare the food. Make sure your process includes enough details to fulfill your purpose. In your introduction or conclusion, include additional information such as your attitude toward the food, its traditional place in the ethnic culture, what variations the food may take, or where the food can be purchased locally.

CAUSAL ANALYSIS

14

PREVIEW

This chapter's explanation of causal analysis will answer the following questions:

- What is the purpose of causal analysis?
- What information should be included in a causal analysis?
- How should a causal analysis be organized?

LEARNING ABOUT TEXTS

Every time you ask "why," you are wondering about the causes of an event, and every time you ask "what would happen if . . . ," you are wondering about the effects. At work, psychologists explore the causes of their clients' behavior, mechanics seek the causes of malfunctioning machines, and physicians try to find the causes of their patients' symptoms. Every time you decide to make a change in your life, whether to enroll in college, to get married, or just to skip lunch, you are reacting to causes. In college courses, you will frequently write papers describing the causes or the effects of an event, e.g., what events led to American involvement in the Spanish-American War, what effects the glaciers had on the land forms in the Northern Hemisphere.

Writing Causal Analysis

When writing about causes and effects, follow these guidelines:

1. <u>Analyze the relationships among causes and effects carefully.</u> Avoid the following logical errors when analyzing causes and effects:
   - ***Post hoc*** is a logical error described in Chapter 18. Do not assume that because one event comes after another, the first is the cause of the second. If you eat out and then get sick that evening, you cannot automatically assume that what you ate made you sick.

FYI: For more on logical fallacies, see pp. 379–381 in Chapter 18.

- **Oversimplifying multiple causes** is an error that occurs when you pinpoint one thing as a cause when, in fact, there are many causes. For example, if you wanted to talk about why HIV is spreading so rapidly in southern Africa, you couldn't just say that people are having too much unprotected sex. You would have to examine the economic, social, religious, and medical conditions that lead to higher rates of infection.
- **Mistaking a correlation for a cause** results when you see two things occur together and assume that one causes the other. For example, for many years, scientists have believed that high cholesterol causes heart disease because people with heart disease often have high cholesterol. They assumed that the correlation between cholesterol and heart disease showed that one caused the other. But some recent research is raising the possibility that the scientists' assumption about cause is false. In fact, both high cholesterol and heart disease may be caused by a third factor, namely, high levels of a certain amino acid.

2. Qualify your assertions. In many instances it is impossible to prove that one event caused another. When you write about a correlation or a cause that you cannot definitively prove, do not overstate your case by writing as if what you say is always true. Instead, qualify your evidence with words and phrases like "often," "frequently," "likely," or "probably." Then your readers will realize that you understand the limitations of your argument.

3. Find a limited focus. You may not be able to write about every cause and effect. Choose one or a few that seem most interesting, most unusual, or most significant and explain the limitations of your focus to your readers.

4. Word the thesis carefully. Your thesis should be clear and limited. For example, "divorce has many effects" is far too broad and vague. A more limited thesis— for example, "Of all the psychological effects of divorce, the pervasive feeling of failure is often one of the most devastating"—provides a clearer focus for both the writer and the reader. Once the thesis has been limited, the writer can then use the techniques of narration, description, or illustration to provide evidence for the thesis.

5. Organize the causes and/or effects to suit your purpose. Four basic organization patterns are available for writing causal analysis:

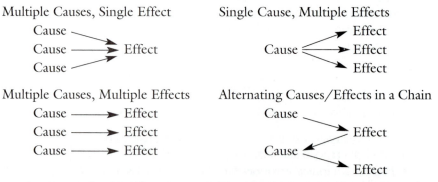

Multiple Causes, Single Effect

Single Cause, Multiple Effects

Multiple Causes, Multiple Effects

Alternating Causes/Effects in a Chain

Choose the pattern that best fits your material and your purpose. You can organize the causes or the effects either chronologically (in the order in which the events occurred) or emphatically (from least to most important).

Activity: **COMPUTER WORKSHOP**

Think about a recent decision you made in your life or at work. Brainstorm all your reasons for making that decision (the causes) and all the results of your decision (the effects). Now explore the different ways you could arrange this information if you were to write a paper or memo explaining why the decision was either good or bad. Write informal outlines using all four strategies illustrated above on p. 342. Now open a file titled "graphics" and experiment with different ways to use your word processor's graphics tools to display the different organizing options in visually clear and appealing ways. Could you draw lines? Use boxes? Use different colors or fonts? Be creative and adventuresome with the tools you have.

READING AND WRITING TEXTS

Activity: **PREREADING**

In small groups
Make a list of the foods you ate today. Then, as a group, go through each person's list and discuss what ingredients were used, where the ingredients came from, under what conditions they were grown and processed, and how they were stored and shipped.

In your Writer's Log
1. Briefly describe what, when, where, and with whom you eat on a typical day.
2. Briefly explain why you eat the way you do.
3. List the consequences of your eating habits. How do your eating habits affect you, your friends and family, your neighborhood, your country, the world?

Reading

The Pleasures of Eating
Wendell Berry

In "The Pleasures of Eating," Wendell Berry—a writer and environmentalist—discusses the politics of food and considers the causes and effects of the urban dweller's failure to recognize that "eating is an agricultural act." He concludes his essay with the description of a process by which the reader can be a more responsible preparer and consumer of food.

Many times, after I have finished a lecture on the decline of American farming and rural life, someone in the audience has asked, "What can city people do?"

"Eat responsibly," I have usually answered. Of course, I have tried to explain what I meant by that, but afterwards I have invariably felt that there was more to be said than I had been able to say. Now I would like to attempt a better explanation.

I begin with the proposition that eating is an agricultural act. Eating ends the annual drama of the food economy that begins with planting and birth. Most eaters, however, are no longer aware that this is true. They think of food as an agricultural product, perhaps, but they do not think of themselves as participants in agriculture. They think of themselves as "consumers." If they think beyond that, they recognize that they are passive consumers. They buy what they want—or what they have been persuaded to want—within the limits of what they can get. They pay, mostly without protest, what they are charged. And they mostly ignore certain critical questions about the quality and the cost of what they are sold: How fresh is it? How pure or clean is it, how free of dangerous chemicals? How far was it transported, and what did transportation add to the cost? How much did manufacturing or packaging or advertising add to the cost? When the food product has been manufactured or "processed" or "precooked," how has that affected its quality or price or nutritional value?

Most urban shoppers would tell you that food is produced on farms. But most of them do not know what farms, or what kinds of farms, or where the farms are, or what knowledge or skills are involved in farming. They apparently have little doubt that farms will continue to produce, but they do not know how or over what obstacles. For them, then, food is pretty much an abstract idea—something they do not know or imagine—until it appears on the grocery shelf or on the table.

The specialization of production induces specialization of consumption. Patrons of the entertainment industry, for example, entertain themselves less and less and have become more and more passively dependent on commercial suppliers. This is certainly true also of patrons of the food industry, who have tended more and more to be *mere* consumers—passive, uncritical, and dependent. Indeed, this sort of consumption may be said to be one of the chief goals of industrial production. The food industrialists have by now persuaded millions of consumers to prefer food that is already prepared. They will grow, deliver, and cook your food for you and (just like your mother) beg you to eat it. That they do not yet offer to insert it, prechewed, into your mouth is only because they have found no profitable way to do so. We may rest assured that they would be glad to find such a way. The ideal industrial food consumer would be strapped to a table with a tube running from the food factory directly into his or her stomach.

Perhaps I exaggerate, but not by much. The industrial eater is, in fact, one who does not know that eating is an agricultural act, who no longer knows or imagines the connections between eating and the land, and who is therefore necessarily passive and uncritical—in short, a victim. When food, in the minds of eaters, is no longer associated with farming and with the land, then the eaters are suffering a kind of cultural amnesia that is misleading and dangerous. The current version of the "dream home" of the future involves "effortless" shopping from a list of available goods on a television monitor and heating precooked food by remote control. Of course, this implies, and depends on, a perfect ignorance of the history of the food that is consumed. It requires that the citizenry should give up their hereditary and sensible aversion to buying a pig in a poke. It wishes to make the selling of pigs in pokes an honorable and glamorous activity. The dreamer in this dream home will perforce know nothing about the kind or quality of this food, or where it came from, or how it was produced and prepared, or what ingredients, additives, and residues it contains—unless, that is, the dreamer undertakes a close and constant study of the food industry, in which case he or she might as well wake up and play an active and responsible part in the economy of food.

There is, then, a politics of food that, like any politics, involves our freedom. We still (sometimes) remember that we cannot be free if our minds and voices are controlled by someone else. But we have neglected to understand that we cannot be free if our food and its sources are controlled by someone else. The condition of the passive consumer of food is not a democratic condition. One reason to eat responsibly is to live free.

But if there is a food politics, there are also a food esthetics and a food ethics, neither of which is dissociated from politics. Like industrial sex, industrial eating has become a degraded, poor, and paltry thing. Our kitchens and other eating places more and more resemble filling stations, as our homes more and more resemble motels. "Life is not very interesting," we seem to have decided. "Let its satisfactions be minimal, perfunctory, and fast." We hurry through our meals to go to work and hurry through our work in order to "recreate" ourselves in the evenings and on weekends and vacations. And then we hurry, with the greatest possible speed and noise and violence, through our recreation—for what? To eat the billionth hamburger at some fast-food joint hellbent on increasing the "quality" of our life? And all this is carried out in a remarkable obliviousness to the causes and effects, the possibilities and the purposes, of the life of the body in this world.

One will find this obliviousness represented in virgin purity in the advertisements of the food industry, in which food wears as much makeup as the actors. If one gained one's whole knowledge of food from these advertisements (as some presumably do), one would not know that the various edibles were ever living creatures, or that they all come from the soil, or that they were produced by work. The passive American consumer, sitting down to a meal of pre-prepared or fast food, confronts a platter covered with inert, anonymous substances that have been processed, dyed, breaded, sauced, gravied, ground, pulped, strained, blended, prettified, and sanitized beyond resemblance to any part of any creature that ever lived. The products of nature and agriculture have been made, to all appearances, the products of industry. Both eater and eaten are thus in exile from biological reality. And the result is a kind of solitude, unprecedented in human experience, in which the eater may think of eating as, first, a purely commercial transaction between him and a supplier and then as a purely appetitive transaction between him and his food.

And this peculiar specialization of the act of eating is, again, of obvious benefit to the food industry, which has good reasons to obscure the connection between food and farming. It would not do for the consumer to know that the hamburger she is eating came from a steer who spent much of his life standing deep in his own excrement in a feedlot, helping to pollute the local streams, or that the calf that yielded the veal cutlet on her plate spent its life in a box in which it did not have room to turn around. And, though her sympathy for the slaw might be less tender, she should not be encouraged to meditate on the hygienic and biological implications of mile-square fields of cabbage, for vegetables grown in huge monocultures are dependent on toxic chemicals—just as animals in close confinement are dependent on antibiotics and other drugs.

The consumer, that is to say, must be kept from discovering that, in the food industry—as in any other industry—the overriding concerns are not quality and health, but volume and price. For decades now the entire industrial food economy, from the large farms and feedlots to the chains of supermarkets and fast-food restaurants, has been obsessed with volume. It has relentlessly increased scale in order to increase volume in order (presumably) to reduce costs. But as scale increases, diversity declines; as diversity declines, so does health; as health declines, the dependence on drugs and chemicals necessarily increases. As capital replaces labor, it does so by substituting machines, drugs, and chemicals for human workers and for the natural health and fertility of the soil. The food is produced by any means or any shortcut that will increase profits. And the business of the costmeticians of advertising is to persuade the consumer that food so produced is good, tasty, healthful, and a guarantee of marital fidelity and long life.

It is possible, then, to be liberated from the husbandry and wifery of the old household food economy. But one can be thus liberated only by entering a trap (unless one sees ignorance and helplessness as the signs of privilege, as many people apparently do). The trap is the ideal of industrialism: a walled city surrounded by valves that let merchandise in but no consciousness out. How does one escape this trap? Only voluntarily, the same way that one went in: by restoring one's consciousness of what is involved in eating; by reclaiming responsibility for one's own part in the food economy. One might begin with the illuminating principle of Sir Albert Howard's *The Soil and Health*, that we should understand "the whole problem of health in soil, plant, animal, and man as one great subject." Eaters, that is, must understand that eating takes place inescapably in the world, that it is inescapably an agricultural act, and that how we eat determines, to a considerable extent, how the world is used. This is a simple way of describing a relationship that is inexpressibly complex. To eat responsibly is to understand and enact, so far as one can, this complex relationship. What can one do? Here is a list, probably not definitive:

1. Participate in food production to the extent that you can. If you have a yard or even just a porch box or a pot in a sunny window, grow something to eat in it. Make a little compost of your kitchen scraps and use it for fertilizer. Only by growing some food for yourself can you become acquainted with the beautiful energy cycle that revolves from soil to seed to flower to fruit to food to offal to decay,

and around again. You will be fully responsible for any food that you grow for yourself, and you will know all about it. You will appreciate it fully, having known it all its life.

2. Prepare your own food. This means reviving in your own mind and life the arts of kitchen and household. This should enable you to eat more cheaply, and it will give you a measure of "quality control": you will have some reliable knowledge of what has been added to the food you eat.

3. Learn the origins of the food you buy, and buy the food that is produced closest to your home. The idea that every locality should be, as much as possible, the source of its own food makes several kinds of sense. The locally produced food supply is the most secure, the freshest, and the easiest for local consumers to know about and to influence.

4. Whenever possible, deal directly with a local farmer, gardener, or orchardist. All the reasons listed for the previous suggestion apply here. In addition, by such dealing you eliminate the whole pack of merchants, transporters, processors, packagers, and advertisers who thrive at the expense of both producers and consumers.

5. Learn, in self-defense, as much as you can of the economy and technology of industrial food production. What is added to food that is not food, and what do you pay for these additions?

6. Learn what is involved in the *best* farming and gardening.

7. Learn as much as you can, by direct observation and experience if possible, of the life histories of the food species.

The last suggestion seems particularly important to me. Many people are now as much estranged from the lives of domestic plants and animals (except for flowers and dogs and cats) as they are from the lives of the wild ones. This is regrettable, for these domestic creatures are in diverse ways attractive; there is much pleasure in knowing them. And farming, animal husbandry, horticulture, and gardening, at their best, are complex and comely arts; there is much pleasure in knowing them, too.

It follows that there is great *dis*pleasure in knowing about a food economy that degrades and abuses those arts and those plants and animals and the soil from which they come. For anyone who does know something of the modern history of food, eating away from home can be a chore. My own inclination is to eat seafood instead of red meat or poultry when I am traveling. Though I am by no means a vegetarian, I dislike the thought that some animal has been made miserable in order to feed me. If I am going to eat meat, I want it to be from an animal that has lived a pleasant, uncrowded life outdoors, on bountiful pasture, with good water nearby and trees for shade. And I am getting almost as fussy about food plants. I like to eat vegetables and fruits that I know have lived happily and healthily in good soil, not the products of the huge, bechemicaled factory-fields that I have seen, for example, in the Central Valley of California. The industrial farm is said to have been patterned on the factory production line. In practice, it looks more like a concentration camp.

The pleasure of eating should be an *extensive* pleasure, not that of the mere gourmet. People who know the garden in which their vegetables have grown and know that the garden is healthy will remember the beauty of the growing plants, perhaps in the dewy first light of morning when gardens are at their best. Such a memory involves itself with the food and is one of the pleasures of eating. The knowledge of the good health of the garden relieves and frees and comforts the eater. The same goes for eating meat. The thought of the good pasture and of the calf contentedly grazing flavors the steak. Some, I know, will think it bloodthirsty or worse to eat a fellow creature you have known all its life. On the contrary, I think it means that you eat with understanding and with gratitude. A significant part of the pleasure of eating is in one's accurate consciousness of the lives and the world from which food comes. The pleasure of eating, then, may be the best available standard of our health. And this pleasure, I think, is pretty fully available to the urban consumer who will make the necessary effort.

I mentioned earlier the politics, esthetics, and ethics of food. But to speak of the pleasure of eating is to go beyond those categories. Eating with the fullest pleasure—pleasure, that is, that does not depend on ignorance—is perhaps the profoundest enactment of our connection with the world. In this pleasure we experience and celebrate our dependence and our gratitude, for we are living from mystery, from creatures we did not make and powers we cannot comprehend. When I think of the meaning of food, I always remember these lines by the poet William Carlos Williams, which seem to me merely honest:

> There is nothing to eat,
>   seek it where you will,
>   but the body of the Lord.
> The blessed plants
>   and the sea, yield it
>   to the imagination
> intact.

Activity: RESPONDING TO THE TEXT

1. Berry focuses on the effects of urban dwellers' failure to recognize that "eating is an agricultural act." List the effects he identifies. Does he mention the causes?
2. What is the purpose of Berry's essay? Does his choice of causal analysis suit his purpose?
3. How does Berry organize his causal analysis? Why does he choose to present the effects in the order he does?

Writing Assignments

1. Choose a food that you purchase regularly. Do research to discover the path this food took from its origin to your kitchen. Analyze each step in the process to determine what resources (including labor, energy, and materials) are used in the production of this food. Write an essay that 1) describes the process of

the food's production, 2) classifies the resources used in its production, and 3) identifies changes in the process or resources that would affect the cost of the food. Chapter 20 will help you research your topic.

2. Keep a record of all the food you eat for a week. Identify all the times that you made unhealthy choices about food. What was unhealthy about the food you ate? Did you realize you were making an unhealthy choice when you ate it? If so, why did you eat it anyway? Write an essay that describes the causes of unhealthy eating. For each reason, supply some illustrations from your own eating habits. What would be the best order for the list of causes?

COMPARISON AND CONTRAST

15

PREVIEW

This chapter's explanation of comparison and contrast will answer the following questions:

- What is the purpose of comparing and contrasting?
- What are the conventional patterns for organizing a comparison/contrast?
- What information needs to be included to make a comparison/contrast complete and clear?

LEARNING ABOUT TEXTS

When you decide which restaurant to eat at, what candidate to vote for, which job to apply for, or what academic area to major in, you are comparing and contrasting. At work, when supervisors decide to promote employees or to purchase new equipment, they make comparisons. In college courses you will frequently be asked to compare (to look for similarities) or to contrast (to look for differences), whether you are comparing characters in short stories, economic policies of American presidents, styles of business management, or political theories.

Writing Comparison and Contrast

When comparing and contrasting, follow these guidelines:

1. <u>Compare two subjects that have some similarities.</u> We've all heard the saying, "Don't compare apples with oranges," meaning you can't fairly compare two things that are in different categories. There must be some basis for comparison.

Therefore, you might compare television advertising to radio advertising, but you usually would not compare television advertising to radio talk shows. However, in some cases, you may see some basis for comparison that isn't obvious. For example, you may want to compare eggs and evergreen trees—two objects which might seem to have nothing in common; however, you can establish a basis for comparison by explaining that they're both symbols of Christian holidays.

2. Establish a clear purpose that fits the readers and the context. Be sure your readers understand your reason for discussing the two topics. Your purpose might be to record data on the behavior of two or three groups taking part in a psychology study, to inform the readers about a new management strategy by comparing it to the old strategy, or to persuade readers that one candidate is a stronger supporter of environmental protection than another. To keep your comparison interesting, make sure it informs the readers about an interesting or valuable topic. For example, comparing high school to college to inform readers that they are different types of educational institutions would be boring because readers already know they are different. On the other hand, explaining some of the differences to high-school seniors so that they can adjust more easily to college could be a useful comparison. You can also write an effective paper by choosing two subjects frequently thought to be quite different and demonstrating how they are actually much more alike than people might think.

3. Use specific wording in your thesis. A vague thesis, such as "There are many similarities and differences between Korean and Japanese food," leaves readers confused and bored. They won't know what your purpose is or how it relates to them. A more specific thesis, such as "Korean and Japanese cuisine reflects the two nations' shared history which was marked by useful exchanges and intense conflicts," gives readers a better idea of why you are writing the comparison (to show how the two nations' food reflects their shared history) and some clues as to what points will be discussed (exchanges and conflicts). Crafting a specific thesis is difficult because it requires many decisions about audience, purpose, and content, so you may find your thesis evolving as you go through the pre-writing and drafting stages of your writing. However, the time and attention you spend on constructing a strong thesis will result in a comparison/contrast that is more interesting and easier to write.

4. Choose points to compare and contrast. The process of choosing points of comparison begins as you settle on your topic. The two subjects you compare and your purpose naturally lead to some points of comparison. For example, if you are writing about your grandmother's memories of cooking and eating and comparing them to your own, you immediately know you will talk about food—what kind, how much, how it was prepared, etc. However, other less obvious points may arise as you brainstorm: What were children's roles in food preparation, where did families get their food, how was food preserved? The points you choose should reflect the purpose of the comparison and the overall purpose of the paper.

5. Organize your information. When you compare and contrast, you can organize your information in one of three basic patterns: 1) point by point, 2) similarities and differences, or 3) one subject at a time. To see how each method works, imagine you are comparing two job candidates:

Point-by-Point Organization

Using the point-by-point method, decide which aspects of the two candidates to compare, and discuss them one by one. In the paragraphs supporting your thesis, you might discuss the candidates' 1) educational qualifications, 2) work experience, and 3) personal characteristics. Your concluding paragraph might provide a summary and a statement of which candidate, based on the information in the supporting paragraphs, would best fill your company's needs. An outline of the body of such a comparison/contrast might look like this:

¶2—Support paragraph 1:　　{ Education, Candidate A
　　　　　　　　　　　　　{ Education, Candidate B

¶3—Support paragraph 2:　　{ Work Experience, Candidate A
　　　　　　　　　　　　　{ Work Experience, Candidate B

¶4—Support paragraph 3:　　{ Personal Characteristics, Candidate A
　　　　　　　　　　　　　{ Personal Characteristics, Candidate B

Similarities and Differences Organization

Using the similarities and differences pattern, first discuss the ways in which the two candidates are similar. Then in the next section discuss how the two candidates are different. The number of paragraphs in the discussion of similarities and the discussion of differences depends on the amount of information in each area.

A sample outline of the body paragraphs might look like this:

Similarities:　¶2—Support Paragraph 1—education
　　　　　　　¶3—Support Paragraph 2—work experience
Differences:　¶4—Support Paragraph 3—personal characteristics

Topic A/Topic B Organization

In the third pattern, discuss one subject (in this case, one candidate) at a time. Again, the number of paragraphs you devote to the discussion of each subject depends on how much information you want to include. A sample outline of the body paragraphs might look like this:

Candidate A:　¶2—education
　　　　　　　¶3—work experience
　　　　　　　¶4—personal characteristics
Candidate B:　¶5—education
　　　　　　　¶6—work experience
　　　　　　　¶7—personal characteristics

No matter which pattern of organization you choose, arrange the points in emphatic order; that is, organize your points from the least to the most significant. For example, in the point-by-point outline, the author considered personal characteristics the most important and therefore put this topic last.

Comparison/contrast essays have introductions which present the two subjects to be compared. The paper's thesis may map out the points of comparison in the order in which they will appear in the body of the essay. In most comparison/contrast essays, the last paragraph plays an important role because it presents conclusions about which is better, why the comparison is useful or significant, or how the comparison explains a crucial concept. The conclusion is especially important when you use the Topic A/Topic B pattern of organization. Since each topic was discussed individually in the body of the essay, the conclusion is your only opportunity to draw the two topics together for examination and synthesis. Without a strong conclusion, the readers may not understand why you are comparing the two topics.

6. <u>Use transitions.</u> Even if your paper is well organized, readers can become confused. State clearly which subject you are discussing. Show comparisons by using terms such as "also," "similarly," and "in the same way," and show contrasts by using terms like "on the other hand," "however," and "although."

Activity: WRITER'S LOG

Choose two or three brands of an item that you either frequently buy (for example, orange juice, dog food, athletic shoes) or an item you would like to purchase (a CD player, an answering machine). Decide what points of comparison you should make in order to decide which would be the best brand to buy. Create outlines using each of the three organizational patterns.

READING AND WRITING TEXTS

Activity: PREREADING

In a small group

1. Each member lists what she or he eats on a typical day.
2. Compare the lists. Make one group list of the similarities among people's food choices and a second group list of the differences among people's food choices. What would account for the similarities? The differences?

Reading

Meat and Gender Hierarchies
Jeremy Rifkin

Jeremy Rifkin is a writer/activist/environmentalist whose books include The Biotech Century: Harnessing the Gene and Remaking the World, *which warns readers about the dangers of biotechnology, and* Beyond Beef: The Rise and Fall of the Cattle Culture, *an indictment of the meat industry. One chapter from that book, "Meat and Gender Hierarchies," argues that in meat-eating cultures, beef is associated with masculinity.*

Despite the vast differences in context and consciousness that exist between various cattle cultures, most share certain core values. An examination of those values can shed some much-needed light on what needs to be done to move beyond the beef culture in the coming century.

Joseph Campbell describes the essential characteristics that distinguish cultivator cultures from hunting cultures. The former are concerned with growth and regeneration, the latter with slaughter and death. These very different approaches to "eating the earth" require very different worldviews.

The cultivation of plants necessitates tending and nurturing as opposed to stalking and sequestering. Plants are viewed less as prey and property and more as an endowment or gift bestowed from the living earth. Generativity is a prevailing ethos in a strictly agricultural society. While the plant world provides food, clothing, and shelter for people just as the animal world does, the relationship between human beings and their source of food stems from a different cosmological model, one based on the great cycle of nature—what anthropologist Mircea Eliade calls "the eternal return." Because agricultural societies are wedded to the life cycle of nature, regeneration—the life instinct—is always at the cosmological core of their worldview.

Premodern cultures that rely primarily on meat to supply their dietary needs, clothing, and building materials are always closer to the act of killing than cereal grain cultures. In beef-eating cultures, says Joseph Campbell:

> The paramount object of experience is the beast. Killed and slaughtered it yields to people its flesh to become our substance, teeth to become our ornaments, hides for clothing and tents, sinews for ropes, bones for tools. The animal life is translated into human life entirely through the medium of death, slaughter, and the arts of cooking, tanning, sewing.

Bloodletting permeates these societies. Few boundaries exist between nature and culture. Nowhere is this more apparent than in the cooking of food.

French anthropologist Claude Lévi-Strauss points out that cooking is the primary mediator between culture and nature. Only the human species cooks its meat, creating an essential boundary between civilization and the natural world. Cooking is also the universal means "by which nature is transformed into culture, and categories of cooking are always appropriate for use as symbols of differentiation."

Food, says Lévi-Strauss, can be separated into three categories, the raw, the cooked, and the rotten. Cooking transforms the raw into a food, temporarily holding at bay the natural process of decay. The manner in which the meat is cooked, in turn, provides a useful clue to the nature of the people, their values, institutions, and worldviews. Beef-oriented cultures prefer "roasting" over "boiling," as it is closer to the rawness of slaughter. Mixed agricultural societies that both herd and plant also both roast and boil meat. Plant-based cultures rarely prepare meat and boil much of their plant food.

Lévi-Strauss explains the psychological difference between roasting and boiling. He points out that roasting is closer to raw, the meat being exposed directly to the fire. Boiled food, on the other hand, requires a twofold process of mediation. It is placed in a pot of water, and then placed over a fire. The receptacle and the water mediate between the meat and the fire, creating greater boundaries between the culture and nature. Roasting, says Lévi-Strauss, maintains only a thin wall between civilization and the natural world. The meat is usually burned on the outside and red or even blood-raw on the inside, making the food as close to raw as to cooked. "Roast meat which is burned on one side and raw on the other, or grilled on the outside and red inside, embodies the ambiguity of the raw and the cooked, of nature and culture." Among many American Indian tribes and other hunter-gatherer societies, roasting is a male-dominated activity while boiling is given over to the females. Roasting is associated with masculinity, prowess, the hunt, and the cult of the warrior.

Boiling, Strauss points out, is more economical and less wasteful than roasting:

> Boiling provides a method of preserving all the meats and its juices, whereas roasting involves destruction or loss. . . . Boiled food is life, roast food death. . . . One suggests economy, the other waste; the second is aristocratic, the first plebeian.

Roasting has always been associated with power, privilege, and celebration, while boiling has always been associated with curative and regenerative values and frugality. In medieval Europe, the roasting of an ox and other animals was commonplace among the warlords and feudal aristocracy, whereas the boiling of meat was standard among the peasants, farmers, and freemen of the cities. Roasting, in most cultures, is reserved for special occasions—Sunday dinner, feast days, banquets, and weddings. Stewing is more routine and mundane, conferring little status and arousing less anticipation and excitement. Roasting is associated with the robust, with valor and virility. By contrast, Edwardian cookery books recommend "steamed and coddled foods as appropriately bland for the sick."

It is not surprising that the dominant beef-eating cultures of Europe, the Americas, and Australia have preferred roasting to boiling. The warlords of medieval Europe, the landed gentry of early modern times, the explorers and discoverers of new worlds, the frontiersmen of the Appalachian Trail, the cowboys of the great plains—all used roasting to mediate their relationship to their prey. One never thinks of cowboys and boiled beef. Even today, in postindustrial America, the image of the cattle culture, with its scenes of cowboys roasting beef over an open fire, is reenacted in countless suburban backyards on summer weekends, as the "man" of the household lights up the charcoal and slaps the raw beef patties on the sizzling metal grill.

Of all foods, beef confers the most status. In virtually every meat-eating culture, red meat, especially beef, is ensconced atop the food pyramid, followed in descending order by chicken and fish and then by animal products—eggs and cheese. Red meat and beef are especially prized because of the qualities ascribed to them. It has long been held in myth and tradition that the blood flowing through red meat confers "strength, aggression, passion and sexuality," all virtues coveted among beef-eating people.

Blood is the vital "living force" of the animal. It is imbued with spirit or manna. The mounted horsemen of the Eurasian steppes, often unable to stop long enough to kill and roast a steer, would cut a small incision in the animal and use a thin hollow reed to suck out its blood to gain nourishment and strength, especially during long and protracted military campaigns. Today, in parts of southern Spain, it is still common for women to go to the local butcher shop after a bullfight to "buy a steak from the bravest bull for her husband's supper, thus ensuring his continued strength and manliness."

Blood is also viewed in traditional cultures as the carrier of inheritance. Bloodlines have been the most convenient way of establishing social hierarchies. As we have already noted, the British aristocracy was obsessed with the breeding of superior stock and took every effort to maintain "pure bloodlines" in their herds. By consuming their "aristocratic" beasts, they ensured that the animal's pedigreed bloodline would meld with their own, keeping them strong in body and pure in spirit.

The blood flowing through red meat has been thought of as conferring passion. Blood conjures up notions of aggression and violence—valued emotions among warriors, sportsmen, and lovers. Soldiers have always been favored with beef before battle. So too have athletes before entering the arena. Consuming blood-rare beef has long been thought to excite the sexual passions. John Newton, the captain of a slave ship, wrote how he gave up meat on one voyage after having a religious conversion experience. He hoped that his change in diet would prevent him from "lusting after the female slaves." In the nineteenth century, educators often recommended eliminating red meat for adolescent males and substituting a vegetarian diet as the "greatest aid we can give boys in the fight against self-abuse."

Red meats, especially beef, have been associated with maleness and male qualities while the "bloodless" white meats have been associated with femaleness and feminine qualities. During the Victorian era and in the early years of the twentieth century, health journals "often suggested a reduction in [red] meat intake for pregnant and lactating women, putting the emphasis instead on delicate, light dishes like chicken, fish or eggs. The prescribed dishes not only mirrored the women's own delicate 'feminine' condition but avoided any of the stimulation of those qualities of red-bloodedness that seemed inappropriate to those fulfilling the nurturing role." Invalids were treated in a similar way, "being fed on the classic 'low' diets of steamed fish, boiled chicken, poached eggs." Red meat was even considered "too strong" to be consumed by the more bookish types, men of letters, accountants, and clerks.

A meat hierarchy exists in virtually every meat-eating culture, separating people by gender. In this respect, meat cultures differ fundamentally from many traditional plant-based agricultural societies. The latter seldom develop a highly stratified food hierarchy. While gender hierarchies exist in plant-based cultures, the rigid food pyramids so characteristic of meat-eating societies are less in evidence. There is a greater egalitarianism in food consumption habits.

In a survey of over a hundred nontechnological cultures, anthropologist Peggy Sanday found, not unexpectedly, that animal-based economies were male-dominated and male-driven while plant-based economies were far more oriented toward the feminine pole. The animal-based economies were characterized by male gods, patrilineality, and a gender hierarchy with men at the top of the social pyramid. Women performed the lion's share of the work and virtually all of the "less valued" menial tasks. By contrast, in plant-based cultures, characterized by female deities and matrilineality, the economies were "more likely to be egalitarian." Because women performed the critical role of food gathering, they were able to achieve relative equality with men in their social relationships. Sanday also found that contrary to animal-based cultures in which meat was almost always used as a means of separating the genders and establishing rank and hierarchy, in plant-based cultures "women do not discriminate as a consequence of distributing the staple."

Even today, in our modern world of high technology and postindustrial sensibilities, the primordial divisions between animal and plant, male and female, continue to haunt the body politic. The ancient cattle complexes of Western civilization have imprinted a near indelible stamp on the consciousness of much of our species. Hegel once remarked that

> the difference between men and women is like that between animals and plants. Men correspond to animals, while women correspond to plants because their development is more placid.

The same system of stratification that places men and meat atop the social pyramid continues to place women and plants on the bottom. In her book *The Sexual Politics of Meat,* Carol J. Adams reminds us of how far these ancient food and gender biases have penetrated the psychological landscape. Meat, for example, has come to signify far more than a food. So coveted is meat in Western culture, that we now use the term metaphorically to represent the essence of something. "Thus we have the 'meat of the matter,' 'a meaty question.' To 'beef up' something is to improve it."

Vegetables, on the other hand, have come to represent dullness. In our highly transient society, where success is equated with speed and mobility, we disparage those who seem to lead a vegetative existence. When a person has been declared brain-dead, we refer to him or her as a vegetable. Plants conjure up the notion of passivity in most people's minds, a value little regarded in an aggressive market-driven society that rewards initiative and risk-taking. In the past century, women have described men as "hunks," "beefcakes," or "animals," and men have referred to women as "hot tomatoes," "shrinking violets," or "wallflowers." By often equating men with meat and women with plants, the social order is able to perpetuate a system of social stratification in which the food hierarchy continually reinforces the gender hierarchy and vice versa.

Despite the inroads made by the modern feminist movement, the ancient biases and practices surrounding the beef culture continue to reinforce food and gender discrimination. The French anthropologist Bourdieu says that among Frenchmen the beef and gender myth still prevails:

> It behooves a man to eat and drink strong things. . . . [Men] leave the tidbits to the children and the women. . . . The charcuterie is more for the men . . . whereas the crudités (raw vegetables) are more for the women, like the salad. . . .

The subtleties that bind men and meat together atop the food chain and the social order are varied and complex. For example, in the beef-eating cultures, men come to believe that eating red meat, especially beef, is inherently more manly and masculine than eating white meats, especially fish. Again, according to Bourdieu:

> Fish tends to be regarded as an unsuitable food for men, not only because it is a light food, insufficiently "filling" . . . but also because like fruit it is one of the "fiddly" things which a man's hands cannot cope with and which make him appear childlike. . . . Above all, it is because fish has to be eaten in a way which totally contradicts the masculine way of eating, that is, with restraint, in small mouthfuls, chewed gently, with the front of the mouth, on the tips of the teeth (because of the bones). . . . The whole masculine identity—what is called virility—is involved in these two ways of eating, nibbling and picking as befits women or with whole-hearted male gulps.

Bourdieu concludes that "[red] meat, the nourishing food par excellence, strong and strong-making, giving vigor, blood, and health, is the dish for men."

Men have long used meat as a weapon of social control, a means of conditioning women to accept a subservient status in society. In Indonesia, for example,

> flesh food is viewed as the property of the men. At feasts . . . it is distributed to households according to the men in them. . . . The system of distribution thus reinforces the prestige of the men in society.

Nowhere is the meat hierarchy more in evidence than in England. In the first national survey of British dietary habits, conducted in 1863, investigators were told that in rural communities the women and children "eat the potatoes and look at the meat." Among the urban working class and poor, women reported that they "saved" the meat for their husbands, believing that the men had to have it to properly perform their role as provider. According to the survey, women ate meat on the order of once a week while men consumed meat "almost daily."

Little has changed in the dietary habits of the rural poor and urban working class over the past one hundred or so years. Where meat is too costly or scarce, it is almost always apportioned first to the male head of the household. In a survey conducted in the late 1970s of over 200 working-class women in a small town in northern England, researchers found that the male "breadwinners" were always favored with the most meat and the choicest cuts. Of all the meats, the highest status

> was attributed primarily to a joint of meat but also extended to steak and chops. Mince dishes and stews and casseroles occupied an intermediate position with meats like liver and bacon.

Interestingly enough, researchers discovered that when the male head of the household lost his job, he also was "less likely to be privileged in food consumption." His ration of meat was often reduced in proportion to his loss of income-producing capability, no doubt partially to save on expenses, but also to let him know, in no uncertain terms, that he was no longer worthy of his formerly privileged position in the family hierarchy. Reviewing the data, Marion Kerr and Nicola Charles conclude that "meat undoubtedly provides the most striking instances of adult male privilege."

Even in countries like the United States, where beef has been abundant and cheap, the prevailing norm has always favored men atop the food hierarchy. Adams conducted a random survey of American cookbooks and found the authors reinforcing many, if not most, of the ancient biases and myths. Readers are told to include London broil on the menu for Father's Day because "a steak dinner has unfailing popularity with fathers." In one chapter of a popular cookbook entitled "Feminine Hospitality," women were advised "to serve vegetables, salads, and soups" when hosting ladies' luncheons.

Ironically, but perhaps understandably, as our modern high-tech culture becomes further removed from the kind of bodily labor and pursuits that placed a premium on brute strength and physicality, many men seem more determined than ever to perpetuate the male meat myth. Nutritionist Jean Mayer suggests that the reason may have something to do with the fact that "the more men sit at their desks all day, the more they want to be reassured about their maleness in eating those large slabs of bleeding meat which are the last symbol of machismo."

If there were any lingering doubt as to the powerful symbolism Western cultures still attach to meat and machismo, the statistics linking domestic violence and quarrels over beef are both revealing and compelling. Authorities report that many men use "the absence of meat as a pretext for violence against women." Believing that they are being denied their maleness by being denied their meat, husbands often lash out at their spouses. Their rage is sometimes violent and uncontrollable. Said one battered wife, "It would start off with him being angry over a trivial little thing like cheese instead of meat on a sandwich." Another woman reported,

> A month ago, he threw scalding water over me, leaving a scar on my right arm, all because I gave him a pie with potatoes and vegetables for his dinner, instead of fresh meat.

The identification of raw meat with power, male dominance, and privilege is among the oldest and most archaic cultural symbols still visible in contemporary civilization. The fact that meat, and especially beef, is still widely used as a tool of gender discrimination is a testimonial to the tenacity of prehistoric dietary practices and myths and the influence that food and diet have on the politics of society.

Activity: RESPONDING TO THE TEXT

1. What is Rifkin's thesis in "Meat and Gender Hierarchies"? Do you agree with his thesis? Does he provide enough supporting evidence to be convincing?
2. How does he use comparison/contrast to fulfill his purpose?
3. What other rhetorical strategies does he use?

Writing Assignment

Rifkin's essay claims that beef is considered a male food, and other meats, such as chicken and fish, are considered female foods. Do you think that people in our culture associate certain foods with males or females? Do men and women eat different foods or eat them differently? If there are differences, what causes them? Write a comparison/contrast essay describing different attitudes men and women have toward foods and beverages. Use one of the three methods described in this chapter for organizing comparison/contrast papers.

CLASSIFICATION

PREVIEW

This chapter's explanation of classification will answer the following questions:

- How do you organize a classification?
- What makes a classification useful to readers?

LEARNING ABOUT TEXTS

Classification, the division of a group of items into categories, simplifies our lives by providing order, helping us to understand complex subjects. Imagine walking into a supermarket where all the items were put on shelves wherever there was space for them. Coffee might be next to potatoes, milk with shoe polish. Bread might be in seven different spots, according to where space was available when the daily shipment arrived. Such a method for stocking a store certainly would create confusion. Instead, items are classified, divided according to their type, as bakery goods, dairy products, produce, and so on, and similar items are shelved together.

All of us automatically classify: We sort our laundry and our bills, and we also mentally sort our friends, our college courses, and our supervisors according to types. Because classifying makes information clearer and more meaningful, both businesses and academic areas rely on classification to make sense of subjects. For example, literature anthologies may be divided into genre (poetry, fiction, drama), into era (medieval, Renaissance), into nationality (British, African-American, Chinese), or in numerous other ways. Businesses or trades classify workers by the way they are paid (salary, hourly wage, contract), by their role in the company (administrative, managerial, technical), or by their experience (apprentice, journeyman, master).

Writing Classification

When you classify, follow these guidelines:

1. <u>Select a ruling principle that fits your purpose.</u> The ruling principle is applied to sort your subject into smaller groups. In the example above, literature texts were classified by three ruling principles—genre, era, and nationality; jobs were classified by two ruling principles—role in the company and experience. Although most groups could be divided according to several ruling principles, restrict your classification to the one that best fits your purpose. For example, if you were in charge of a team fixing all the bugs customers found in your company's computer game, you could use several ruling principles to break down the large group of bugs into smaller, more comprehensible units. You might divide them by type, so you could assign each category to the team member with the most expertise to fix it. You might divide them by priority, so you knew which bugs absolutely needed to be fixed and which could wait until you had more time. You might divide them by difficulty, so that work could begin right away on bugs that needed the most time.

2. <u>Make sure the ruling principle is complete and avoids overlapping categories</u>. When a classification is complete, each item in the larger group will be included in one of the subdivisions. The diagram below illustrates a ruling principle that is incomplete:

Diagram A

Group to Be Classified: Toys
Ruling Principle: Age Groups

Incomplete Classification

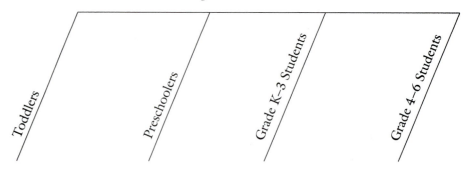

The classification is incomplete because toys for babies, high-school-aged kids and adults would be left out. A ruling principle with overlap results in items fitting into more than one category, making the classification invalid. The diagram below illustrates a ruling principle with overlapping categories:

Diagram B

Group to Be Classified: Toys
Ruling Principle: Type of Toy

Overlapping Categories

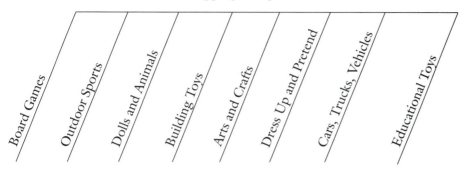

In this classification system, some toys might fit into more than one category: for instance, the game Scrabble could fit into the "board games" or the "educational" categories.

3. <u>Organize your classification.</u> Discuss one category at a time, describing each one completely. The order you choose for presenting the categories depends on your purpose and content. Some categories might lend themselves to chronological order (for example, customer complaints divided by months they were received in, or literature divided by era); some might lend themselves to spatial ordering (for example, sales trends categorized by region might be ordered north to south or east to west); some might use emphatic order (for example, categories of computer bugs might be ordered from least to most important). Other possibilities will present themselves depending on the material, but you should choose an order that will make reading and understanding easy for your audience.

4. <u>Order each category consistently</u>. Discuss comparable points within each category. For example, if your topic is management styles, and you discuss decision making, communication, and delegation in the first category, you should cover the same three areas in the same order in the remaining categories. The diagram below illustrates a consistent organization:

Diagram C

Management Styles

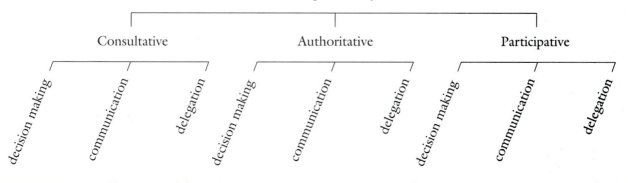

Activity: **WRITER'S LOG**

Consider a group of people you know well—the students in your class, your teammates, your coworkers, the members of an organization in which you are active. Use one of the following ruling principles to classify the people in your chosen group: their attitudes, their habits, or their characteristics. For example, you might classify your teammates according to their attitude toward the sport, your classmates according to their methods of revising, or your coworkers according to their attitude toward the paperwork they must do. Be sure your initial group is divided into subgroups; for example, if you discuss three classmates, instead of three types of classmates, you are comparing and contrasting, not classifying.

READING AND WRITING TEXTS

Activity: **PREREADING**

In a small group

1. Each member lists what she or he eats on a typical day.
2. Make a giant list of all the food all the members eat and divide the list into as many different categories as the group can come up with. For example, you could divide it into groups according to the food pyramid. What other ways can you think of? Compare your list of categories with those of other groups in your class.

Reading

From "Understanding Society and Culture Through Eating"
Peter Farb

The following is an excerpt from "Understanding Society and Culture Through Eating," the prologue to Peter Farb's book, The Anthropology of Eating. *In his prologue, Farb supports most of his assertions through examples; however, he concludes with a classification of the explanations given for the variety of food customs.*

How can the multiplicity of unusual food customs around the world be accounted for? The many attempts to do so can be placed into a few categories: the fortuitous, the mentalist, the ecological, the innate, and the cultural. The fortuitous can be quickly dismissed. Any explanation of human behavior based on the assumption that it "just happened" obviously explains nothing. It furthermore postulates a world in which human behavior is meaningless, accidental, capricious—things which the science of anthropology long ago showed to be untrue.

The mentalist view regards eating behavior as part of a cultural code that expresses the world view of each society. To the French structuralist Claude Lévi-Strauss, for example, food taboos become explicable once they have been interpreted in terms of mythology. He observes that the species of animals tabooed for food are those that in some way deviate from the norm in anatomy, behavior, or habitat—anomalies which render them "unclean" and therefore inedible. His categorization is inadequate for at least three reasons: It does not explain how the members of particular societies arrived at their world view in the first place; it offers no logical explanation for why animals that people regard as unusual must necessarily also be unclean and inedible; and it ignores more obvious explanations, such as that the prohibited animals are dangerous, scarce, or notably vulnerable to overhunting.

The ecological explanation, on the other hand, does attempt to account for the differences and similarities in eating behavior of various peoples by way of a detailed analysis of environments and the potential foods within them. This approach, though, is flawed in that it reduces the problem to the environment alone, whereas human behavior is demonstrably influenced by a considerable number of other variables.

The innate explanation, which has long been fashionable, can be found in the statement by Dr. Benjamin Spock that very young children possess an "instinctive knowledge" about their dietary needs. This belief seemed to be given scientific validity by an experiment more than half a century ago in which three very young children were allowed for six months to select from foods offered to them. Although the day-to-day variations in the nutritive value of what the children selected were substantial, the total of all the foods selected added up to a healthful diet. But these experiments were so naively conceived that they are scientifically inadmissible. The array of highly nutritious foods presented—meat, fish, eggs, milk, cereals, fruits, and vegetables—was such that the children could not possibly have selected an unwholesome diet. The experiments included none of the junk foods that make up a large part of what children eat: candy, soda pop, high-fat cookies, jams and jellies, and potato chips. Until a similar study is made that incorporates junk foods as well as nutritious ones, and in which a large number rather than just a few children take part, the claim that children instinctively select the foods they need cannot be sustained.

Perhaps the most common explanation for the variety of eating customs is enculturation—that through the learning experience members of the younger generation come to accept the traditional ways of their society.

Proponents of enculturation theories would say that Chinese children eat with chopsticks instead of with forks, and consider milkshakes inedible, simply because they have been enculturated into Chinese rather than North American society. But things are by no means as simple as that. Enculturation can account for only a portion of the eating behavior found in different societies—and in fact that of the older generation is never duplicated exactly, or there would be no "generation gap."

Rather than attempting to pin down eating customs as fortuitous, mentalist, ecological, innate, or due to enculturation, this book will approach the subject from a broader perspective, taking account of the cultural system as a whole. Any such system is composed of three interlocked sectors; first, the techno-environmental (the way in which the cultural system is adapted to its habitat in extracting, transforming, and distributing food and other forms of energy); second, the social structure (the maintenance of orderly relations among individual members of the society who obtain the energy and also produce the next generation); and third, the ideology (the way the members of the society view the world, their techno-environmental adaptation, and their social structure).

Activity: RESPONDING TO THE TEXT

1. Peter Farb uses classification to present the various anthropological theories about food and cultures. Why might classification be an appropriate rhetorical strategy for a prologue? What is the ruling principle for his classification? Does he discuss comparable points within each category? Does he link the categories with transitions?
2. Which other rhetorical strategies does Farb use?

Writing Assignment

Look into someone's refrigerator, food cupboard, or pantry. List all the foods you find there. Then write an essay that uses classification to describe the contents on the list. Your essay's purpose will be to examine what the food you found reveals about the food's owner or the culture in general. Divide the items on the list into categories based on a ruling principle that fits your purpose. Try to choose a ruling principle that allows you to include most, if not all, of the foods you listed. You might classify them by length of time in storage, function, source, value, texture, food group, time of day they're used, or any other principle that will yield interesting results.

DEFINITION

PREVIEW

This chapter's explanation of definition will answer the following questions:

- When is definition necessary?
- What makes a definition effective for readers?

LEARNING ABOUT TEXTS

Defining, explaining what terms mean or what their essential characteristics are, is central to learning, whether at home, work, or school. On the job, employees need to be familiar with the terms used at their place of employment and in their career field. In college courses, textbooks contain numerous definitions, and students frequently demonstrate their understanding of course material on tests by recognizing or writing definitions. In college, you will be asked to write two types of definitions: 1) sentence definitions and 2) expanded definitions, in which you elaborate on a term by adding further explanation.

Writing Sentence Definitions

Sentence definitions have a traditional form that makes them easy to write. To write a clear, effective sentence definition follow these guidelines:

1. <u>Use the conventional, three-part form.</u> A sentence definition consists of three sections: 1) the term being defined, 2) the general category to which the term belongs, and 3) the special characteristics that make the term distinct from others in its class. In the following two examples, the term, category, and characteristics are underlined and labeled.

    A <u>buteo</u> (term) is a <u>type of hawk</u> (category) with a <u>heavy body and a short, wide tail</u> (characteristics).

The <u>Haida</u> (term) are <u>several Native American tribes</u> (category) who <u>speak the Haida language and who live in Alaska, British Columbia, Prince of Wales Island, and the Queen Charlotte Islands</u> (characteristics).

2. <u>Be clear and simple.</u> Ask yourself whether your definition will be clear to readers who are unfamiliar with the term and are depending on you to help them understand. Never use a form of the word you are defining in your definition: To say that "fibrinolysis is the breakdown of fibrin by the action of fibrinolysin" is not helpful. Never use terms more complicated than the term you are defining: To define the femur as "the proximal bone of the lower or hind leg in vertebrates" is less helpful than calling it the thigh bone.

3. <u>Do not quote a dictionary</u>. If your readers wanted a dictionary definition, they could easily find one. However, definitions in dictionaries, due to the limitations of space, are often unclear and confusing.

Writing Expanded Definitions

Although a sentence definition provides the meaning of a term, it may be inadequate to give your reader a complete understanding of the term. These three guidelines will help you write an extended definition:

1. <u>Focus on your purpose.</u> Occasionally writers make the mistake of rambling on aimlessly about the term they're defining, so their definitions are unfocused and disorganized. Keep in mind that your purpose is to define the term for your readers, so you should include only information that clarifies the meaning of your term.

2. <u>Consider your audience.</u> If you are writing for coworkers, avoid defining terms they already know, but be careful to define all terms they may be unfamiliar with. In college writing, choose topics about which you have some personal experience, insight, or knowledge, so that you will be able to say something original and interesting. Avoid writing about large abstractions, such as "love" or "liberty." Although these abstractions may seem easy to talk about, they are difficult to define; in fact, entire books are devoted to the effort.

3. <u>Use rhetorical strategies.</u> Any of the rhetorical strategies discussed in this section may be helpful in writing an expanded definition. For example, you may clarify a term by describing it, giving examples, telling a story, or explaining its causes or effects. In addition, you may also be able to define by negation, that is, by telling what your term is not. Defining by negation may be especially helpful as a starting point because it allows you to distinguish your term from other similar terms and therefore eliminates confusion.

Activity: WORKING TOGETHER

In a small group, decide on a term to define. Each group member will write a sentence definition and a one-paragraph expanded definition. Now compare your definitions. Are they similar? How are they different? Which rhetorical strategies did your group use? Do you think readers would clearly understand the term if they read the definitions?

READING AND WRITING TEXTS

Activity: PREREADING

In small groups

Discuss what a "party" is. What does it take to make a party? How do you know when you're at a party?

Reading

How to Give a Party

Laurie Colwin

In this excerpt from "How to Give a Party," from her book Home Cooking, *Laurie Colwin uses definition to develop her ideas about party-giving. Colwin's essay incorporates other rhetorical strategies to enlighten readers about the best way to give parties.*

I have never thought of myself as much of a party-giver, but it turns out I have given my share over the years.

By "party" I mean a gathering of more than eight whose eventual destination is not the dining room table: in short, there are parties, and there are dinner parties. And while I know there are such things as large parties which feature an evening meal, in my household this is called "having people over for dinner" and the number, except for Christmas Eve or Thanksgiving, is usually six or under.

A party by its nature is free-floating. People are free to float about your rooms grinding cake crumbs into your rugs, scattering cigarette ash on your wood floors, scaring your cat and leaving their glass to make rings on your furniture. This sort of thing is enthralling to some potential hosts and hostesses, horrific to others. Most people feel a combination of these things: the idea of a party fills them half with horror, half with excitement.

But no matter how you dread them, parties must be given because events must be celebrated: birthdays, book publications, engagements, homecomings and so on. Birthdays, especially, come year after year and one must know what to do about them. Those of us who have no servants like to keep things simple and still show people a good time. This is easier to do than one might think. . . .

Low tea, taken at four, may be as humble as bread and butter and a pot of tea with a plate of biscuits, or it may be as elaborate as a large iced cake, a plate of strawberries and a heap of tea sandwiches. For inspiration, it is useful to read *Mary Poppins* by P. L. Travers or the early novels of Iris Murdoch, in which tea menus are elaborately described.

The great advantage of a tea party is that everything can be done in advance and the hostess gets to put her feet up and sit around for a little while before the thundering herds appear. Furthermore, the menu should resemble a crazy quilt or set of unmatched china. The chocolate cake sits next to the cheese buns, and the cucumber and anchovy sandwiches commingle with the shortbread. In short, you can serve four or five (or two or three) of your favorite things and a pot of tea (with coffee or wine for those who do not drink tea).

There are times when the tea party will not do: Christmas Eve and the Fourth of July. Christmas Eve requires a sit-down dinner with a big bird or large fish. Our Christmas Eve menu is not fixed. One year we had goose, a magnificent-looking creature sitting majestically on a huge platter. When this enormous bird was carved, each person received a wisp of meat, since that is about all you get from a goose, and my husband had an allergic reaction to it and had to be put to bed with two Benadryl tablets. We have had capon, ducks, turkey and last year we had salmon which was enjoyed by all except for one of the guests who confessed at the table to being highly allergic to fish.

A festival meal requires one big item, some elegant side dishes and a wonderful dessert. Then everyone leaves the table and sits in the living room drinking decaffeinated espresso, eating pistachio nuts, oranges and chocolates, leaving your floor littered with pistachio shells and little shreds of the colored paper from the chocolates.

The Fourth of July was always taken seriously in my family when I was a child, and I have maintained this tradition. Each year the menu is always the same: fried chicken, potato salad and cole slaw, with something down home for dessert: peaches and ice cream or gingerbread.

But when birthdays come around, I always revert to the tea party. This began with a tea party to celebrate my husband's birthday. It was neither high nor low, but a combination. Twenty-five people consumed a large platter of ham sandwiches, another of cucumber sandwiches, a tower of brownies, a ginger cake, an enormous Latvian birthday cake (a coffee cake made of saffron-flavored yeast dough spiked with yellow raisins and formed in the shape of a figure eight), a basket of cheese straws, two pots of baked beans, a basin of strawberries and a samovar of tea. . . .

Activity: RESPONDING TO THE TEXT

1. Identify passages where Colwin is defining "party." What techniques does she use to develop her definition?

2. Why did Colwin need to define "party" before she gave advice about how to give one?
3. What other rhetorical strategies does Colwin use in this essay? How do these other strategies fit her purpose?

Writing Assignment

What does "party" mean to you? Write an essay, similar to Colwin's, in which you define what a party is and give advice about how to create a great party.

ARGUMENT

18

P R E V I E W

This chapter's explanation of argument will answer the following questions:

- What makes an argument effective in convincing the readers?
- How should an argument be organized?
- How is evidence used in argument?

LEARNING ABOUT TEXTS

Any time you take a stand on an issue, you are arguing. When you write to an employer stating that you are the best candidate for a job, when you explain to your parents why you want to attend a particular college, when you suggest a change in your child's school, you are arguing. In arguments, you take a position and present reasons supported by evidence to convince others that your claim is valid. We argue many times during a day: in our conversations with friends and family, collaborations with coworkers, or discussions with classmates. In our everyday lives, arguments are usually friendly and reasonable explorations of our opinions and beliefs about ordinary experiences.

Writers also often find that they are arguing—making claims—about their topics. In fact, many comparison/contrast, causal analysis, illustration, or classification papers also are arguments: A comparison/contrast may claim that one motorcycle is better than another; a causal analysis may claim that poor marketing analysis led to low sales; an illustration may give examples of children hurt by skateboards to justify the ban of skateboards from city streets; a classification may claim that community college students belong in a different category from students at four-year liberal arts colleges and universities. Like the other rhetorical strategies discussed in this section, argument can be part of a larger piece of writing or can stand alone.

Writing an Argument

An effective argument rests on accurate audience analysis, sound logical reasoning, strong evidence, and precisely worded sentences. The following guidelines will help you construct an argument:

- *Carefully consider your claim.* What exactly do you want to assert? Writing an argument requires you to question yourself repeatedly throughout the writing process to make certain that you are claiming what you really think about the topic. For example, on the topic of required courses you may begin with a claim: "Colleges should not force students to take required courses." But as you analyze your audience, assemble your evidence, and evaluate the opposing claims, you may realize that your claim is too vague and broad. Should no courses be required? What is reasonable for colleges to require? Should students graduate taking only art courses? You may revise your claim to state, "College degree requirements should be few and flexible." Careful writing and rewriting of your claim will prevent you from trying to prove something you don't believe or can't support.

- *Analyze your audience.* In order to convince your readers, you need to understand them. What do they believe about your topic? Will they be more convinced by statistics, facts, examples, experts, appeals to emotion? Do they need definitions or explanations? Will they have objections to your reasons? Will they share your assumptions? You will make your choices about your argument's content, organization, and tone based on answers to questions like these.

- *Present logical reasons for your claim.* Logical reasons are based on induction or deduction. Inductive reasons rest on a proliferation of evidence. If three out of four children who watch five hours of TV a day show antisocial behavior, you may infer that extensive TV viewing can cause antisocial behavior. The specific evidence leads to the conclusion. On the other hand, deductive reasons follow from widely held assumptions of truth. For example, the claim that beginning drivers should not drive after midnight is based on the assumptions that beginning drivers are less competent than experienced ones and that driving after midnight is more challenging for drivers. Notice that when you use deductive reasoning, you assume that readers agree with your assumptions; otherwise, your assumptions must be defended before your argument can be considered valid.

- *Provide evidence.* Facts can be the strongest pieces of evidence in a logical argument because they cannot be challenged. However, supporting facts can be hard to come by because if there were sufficient facts, there would be no argument; everyone would agree with your claim. Other evidence includes statistics, expert opinions, and personal experiences. You must provide enough evidence to be convincing. How much is enough depends on context—the readers' expectations, your purpose, and the requirement of the writing situation. In professional situations, you will probably need more and stronger evidence than in arguments with friends.

- *Refute the opposition.* To make an argument complete, you must recognize and refute opposing arguments. Realize that opposing arguments may be varied. There are usually more than two sides to an issue. Some people may agree with some parts of your claim but not others. Some may disagree entirely. The more you know about other points of view on your topic, the more clearly and honestly you can understand and present your argument. Your goal is not to defeat the "other side" but to take differing facts, assumptions, and logical conclusions into account in your presentation of your own claim. If you ignore these opposing arguments, you are undermining your own credibility by failing to be honest about your claim.

- *Maintain a reasonable tone.* In real life, when arguments become mean or aggressive, neither side is likely to listen to the other. The same is true in writing. To keep your audience attentive and open-minded, you need to maintain a reasonable tone. You must assume the stance of someone having a reasonable, even friendly, discussion with another reasonable person. If you present your argument with confidence and authority, you will be more effective than if you sound strident or superior.

Recognizing Logical Fallacies

Reading critically requires you to detect possible biases and errors in logic. Some errors in reasoning result from careless, shoddy thinking, while others are deliberate attempts to mislead or manipulate the reader. In either case, a familiarity with some relatively common errors in reasoning will enable you to recognize them in others' writing and avoid them in your own.

Ad hominem—*Ad hominem* is a Latin phrase meaning "to the person." The *ad hominem* fallacy is one which attacks an individual instead of evaluating the merits of the person's argument:

> "Don't take Dr. McMann's advice on your relationship. She's been divorced twice, so she cannot possibly be a good marriage counselor."

While it's fair to infer that Dr. McMann must have learned a great deal about marriage through experience, it's unfair to conclude that she is not competent in her profession.

Ad populum—An *ad populum* fallacy is an appeal "to the people" that distracts readers from the issues by using language that arouses emotions and exploits prejudices. *Ad populum* arguments are often used in political campaigns. Saying that a candidate upholds "family values" or is "soft on crime" is an *ad populum* appeal intended to create powerful positive or negative reactions to a candidate without giving specific evidence about the candidate's beliefs or actions. *Ad populum* arguments also exploit readers by flattering them. Appeals for charitable and political organizations often begin with flattery: Because the readers are intelligent, compassionate, and right-thinking, they will support the cause.

Bandwagon appeal—The bandwagon appeal exploits people's fear of being left out by attempting to convince the audience that everyone already agrees with a position or uses a product. Advertising relies heavily on the bandwagon appeal:

Toyota's slogan "everyday people" implies that there is something unusual about people who do not choose Toyotas, and Domino's slogan, "delivering a million smiles a day," suggests that their pizza is the popular choice.

Begging the question and circular argument—In both of these fallacies, writers assume that what they are trying to prove is true. A circular statement repeats its evidence as proof:

> "Barbara Kingsolver is a first-rate novelist because she writes powerful, fascinating best-sellers."

In begging the question, the writer makes a similar assumption:

> "The United States' inadequate welfare program has failed to rescue too many people from poverty."

By labeling the welfare program as "inadequate," the writer has assumed that the "program has failed."

Either/or—The either/or approach reduces a complex issue to two possibilities, so the reader's two options are to agree with the writer or choose the other alternative, usually a catastrophic one:

> "You can either raise taxes to expand library services in our county, or you can accept a generation of illiterate schoolchildren."

While a good library undoubtedly contributes to literacy in a community, inadequate library services could never make all the children in one generation illiterate. The two choices offered the reader, raising taxes or making children illiterate, is not only an either/or fallacy, but also an *ad populum* argument.

False analogy—An analogy is a comparison between two items that contain an essential similarity. A false analogy assumes that because the items resemble each other in some ways, an identical conclusion can be drawn about them:

> "Sending American troops into Vietnam plunged this nation into a decade-long crisis: We should never again allow our soldiers to become involved in foreign wars."

This analogy is false because it assumes that sending troops abroad will have the same results every time. It also ignores other conflicts and wars in which American troops were sent to foreign lands.

False authority—This fallacy appeals to an authority to support an argument; however, the authority's expertise is in a different field. Most advertisements featuring celebrities endorsing products are appeals to false authority. For example, Jerry Seinfeld is a successful stand-up comedian, but that does not make him an authority on which credit cards viewers should use.

Hasty generalization—A hasty generalization is a conclusion based on inadequate evidence. The evidence may be inadequate because it's based on too small a sample or because it's not typical. Suppose you conclude that seat belts are unsafe because you know someone who was saved by being thrown free of a crash and another who was severely injured while wearing a seat belt. You would be generalizing on too small a sample and your evidence would be atypical. Examination of a larger sample would provide overwhelming evidence of the safety of seat belts.

Non sequitur—*Non sequitur*, a Latin phrase, means "it does not follow." Arguing that Phoenix is an unhealthy place to live because it has a higher death rate than most major American cities is a *non sequitur*. The higher death rate is more likely to be because many retirees move to Phoenix, which, as a result, has an older population.

Post hoc—The Latin phrase *post hoc, ergo propter hoc* means "after this, therefore because of this." The *post hoc* fallacy assumes that if one event follows another, the first event must have caused the second. Nearly everyone has heard someone say, "Every time I get into the shower, the phone rings" or "Whenever I wash my car, it rains." Obviously, taking a shower does not cause a phone to ring, and washing a car doesn't cause rainy weather.

Red herring—In hunting, a red herring is a strong scent that distracts dogs from the scent they are following, and in mystery stories, a red herring is a false clue that distracts readers from recognizing the true villain. As a logical fallacy, a red herring distracts the reader from the central issue, usually by inserting a highly emotional, irrelevant element:

> "Providing public elementary education for non-native speakers is a complex, expensive undertaking. And the children's parents, who are often illegal immigrants, may be taking jobs from local people."

Because job security is an issue that worries many people, the red herring ignites negative emotions and distracts readers from the real issue—public education for non-native speakers.

Slippery slope—The slippery slope fallacy assumes that one action will lead uncontrollably to a disastrous sequence of events:

> If the bypass is built, no one will come to our town. Restaurants, hotels, and stores will go out of business, and soon Danville will become a ghost town.

The construction of a bypass would undoubtedly have both positive and negative consequences; however, the string of catastrophes predicted in the slippery slope is exaggerated and highly unlikely.

Arguing With Integrity

Writers face numerous temptations when they write arguments—especially when they stand to gain something by persuasion. When writing an argument, be sure to

- acknowledge other viewpoints
- avoid using logical fallacies that would manipulate your readers, such as the *ad hominem, ad populum,* or bandwagon arguments
- represent information fairly and accurately, without omitting or skewing material.

Many of the logical fallacies—especially the *ad populum*, bandwagon, red herring, and slippery slope—have the power to sway readers. As a reader, recognizing these fallacies protects you against manipulation by unprincipled writers. As a writer, you want to sway readers by presenting information logically, factually, and fairly, not by resorting to the use of logical fallacies.

Activity: **WORKING TOGETHER**

Your group will choose one of the claims listed below:

- *The American diet is not very healthy.*
- *The food you eat reveals your personality.*
- *Children should not be forced to eat anything they do not want to eat.*
- *The United States should ensure that everybody in the world has enough food to eat.*

Then discuss the following questions:

1. Would the claim be easier to defend if it were narrower? How could it be narrowed?
2. What logical reasons could be presented to defend this claim?
3. Can you think of any evidence to support this claim?
4. What would the opposition say against this claim?

The Workplace

BUSINESS PROPOSALS

When you write a proposal, you are convincing the audience to take action. A grant proposal might ask a government agency to fund your neighborhood school's art program. An internal proposal, written to your managers, might suggest an action they should take to solve a problem with which you're familiar. A solicited proposal might be a response to an announcement that a company, agency, or organization is seeking certain products or services. In each proposal, you are writing an argument. You are trying to convince your audience that you are qualified to give them what they want or need. Because a proposal is meant to convince the readers, careful audience analysis is important to its success. You must know what the readers want and present convincing evidence that you know how they can get it.

The format for proposals, like the format for rhetorical modes, is somewhat conventional, but is varied to meet the context. Essentially, a proposal presents a problem and a solution. You will usually find the following sections:

1. Summary or overview—very brief presentation of the essential information
2. Problem or need—statement of why action needs to be taken
3. Solution or plan—fairly complete description of the action being proposed to address the need
4. Personnel—description of the people involved in the plan and their qualifications
5. Time line or schedule—explanation of how much time action will take and how that time will be used
6. Costs or budget—breakdown of all expenses involved in the action and totals costs

Depending on the situation, these sections might be combined or rearranged, but each of these issues should be addressed in the proposal.

Successful proposals closely follow any guidelines that are provided by the reader or that are standard in your company. Most important, your plan should (like all arguments) be logical, specific, and supported with evidence.

READING AND WRITING TEXTS

Activity: **PREREADING**

In your Writer's Log, answer the following question:
Why do you eat (or not eat) meat? List logical reasons to defend your decision.

Reading

"All Things Are Connected"
John Robbins

In his book, Diet for a New America, *John Robbins argues that meat consumption is unhealthy, environmentally unsound, and unjust. He provides facts, statistics, studies, and examples to back up his argument. In this excerpt, Robbins focuses on the wastefulness of beef production and consumption.*

There is an old story which tells of a man who lived a long and worthy life. When he died, the Lord said to him: "Come, I will show you hell." He was taken to a room where a group of people sat around a huge pot of stew. Each held a spoon that reached the pot, but had a handle so long it couldn't be used to reach their mouths. Everyone was famished and desperate; the suffering was terrible.

After awhile, the Lord said: "Come, now I will show you heaven." They came to another room. To the man's surprise, it was identical to the first room—a group of people sat around a huge pot of stew, and each held the same long-handled spoons. But here everyone was nourished and happy and the room was full of joy and laughter.

"I don't understand," said the man. "Everything is the same, yet they are so happy here, and they were so miserable in the other place.

"What's going on?"

The Lord smiled. "Ah, but don't you see—here they have learned to feed each other."

WASTING THE FOOD WE HAVE

The livestock population of the United States today consumes enough grain and soybeans to feed over five times the entire human population of the country. We feed these animals over 80% of the corn we grow, and over 95% of the oats.

It is hard to grasp how immensely wasteful is a meat-oriented diet-style. By cycling our grain through livestock, we end up with only 10% as many calories available to feed human mouths as would be available if we ate the grain directly.

Less than half the harvested agricultural acreage in the United States is used to grow food for people. Most of it is used to grow livestock feed. This is a drastically inefficient use of our acreage. For every sixteen pounds of grain and soybeans fed to beef cattle, we get back only one pound as meat on our plates. The other fifteen are inaccessible to us. Most of it is turned into manure.

The developing nations are copying us. They associate meat-eating with the economic status of the developed nations, and strive to emulate it. The tiny minority who can afford meat in those countries eats it, even while many of their people go to bed hungry at night, and mothers watch their children starve.

To supply one person with a meat habit food for a year requires three-and-a-quarter acres. To supply one lacto-ovo vegetarian with food for a year requires one-half acre. To supply one pure vegetarian requires only one-sixth of an acre. In other words, a given acreage can feed twenty times as many people eating a pure vegetarian diet-style as it could people eating the standard American diet-style.

Lester Brown of the Overseas Development Council has estimated that if Americans were to reduce their meat consumption by only 10 percent, it would free over 12 million tons of grain annually for human consumption. That, all by itself, would be enough to adequately feed every one of the 60 million human beings who will starve to death on the planet this year.

By cycling our grain through livestock, we not only waste 90 percent of its protein; in addition, we sadly waste 96 percent of its calories, 100 percent of its fiber, and 100 percent of its carbohydrates.

Meanwhile, malnutrition is the principle cause of infant and child mortality in developing nations. In many of them, over 25 percent of the population die before reaching the age of four. In Guatemala, 75 percent of the children under five years of age are undernourished. Yet, every year Guatemala exports 40 million pounds of meat to the United States. It borders on the criminal!

Many of us believe that hunger exists because there's not enough food to go around. But as Frances Moore Lappe and the anti-hunger organization Food First have shown, the real cause of hunger is a scarcity of justice, not a scarcity of food. Enough grain is squandered every day in raising American livestock for meat to provide every human being on earth with two loaves of bread.

Hunger is really a social disease caused by the unjust, inefficient and wasteful control of food. In Costa Rica, beef production quadrupled between 1960 and 1980. But almost all this beef is exported to the United States, and what does stay in the country is eaten by a tiny minority. Though more and more Costa Rican land is being turned over to meat production, the population is not eating more meat for the change. The average family in Costa Rica eats less meat than the average American housecat.

The world's cattle alone, not to mention pigs and chickens, consume a quantity of food equal to the caloric needs of 8.7 billion people—nearly double the entire human population of the planet.

According to Department of Agriculture statistics, one acre of land can grow 20,000 pounds of potatoes. That same acre of land, if used to grow cattlefeed, can produce less than 165 pounds of beef.

In a world in which a child dies of starvation every two seconds, an agricultural system designed to feed our meat habit is a blasphemy. Yet it continues, because we continue to support it. Those who profit from this system do not need us to condone what they are doing. The only support they need from us is our money. As long as enough people continue to purchase their products they will have the resources to fight reforms, pump millions of dollars of "educational" propaganda into our schools, and defend themselves against medical and ethical truths.

A rapidly growing number of Americans are withdrawing support from this insane system by refusing to consume meat. For them, this new direction in diet-style is a way of joining hands with others and saying we will not support a system which wastes such vast amounts of food while people in this world do not have enough to eat.

Activity: RESPONDING TO THE TEXT

1. Robbins provides many statistics to support his claim. Where does he include emotional appeals? Is it fair to include such emotional appeals? Is it effective?
2. Can you find any logical fallacies in Robbins' argument?
3. What might the opposition say about Robbins' argument?

Writing Assignment

Robbins is arguing that overconsumption of meat is wrong because it is wasteful. Think of a common activity or behavior that wastes time, energy, or material resources. Write an argument that convinces people to stop this wasteful activity. Present logical reasons for your claim and include supporting evidence. You may present your argument in the form of an essay or a business proposal.

RESEARCH PAPERS

P R E V I E W

This chapter's explanations about strategies for writing a research paper
will help answer these questions:

- How do you generate a topic or thesis?
- How do you correctly incorporate source material into your draft?

L E A R N I N G   A B O U T   T E X T S

Understanding Research Writing

Although you might think of research as something done by scientists and
scholars, you do research frequently. When you want to buy a car, you go online or to various dealers to find out what models are available with what features at what cost. When you ask your grandparents what their childhoods were
like, you are doing historical research. The research done at universities is different
from the research you do every day only because it is more rigorous (more attention
is paid to accuracy and completeness) and more formal (methods of research and
formats for communicating that research follow commonly accepted patterns). Researchers usually begin with a question or questions—often ones that are suggested
by previous research or by observation of unusual situations or problems. They then
devise methods for finding answers to the questions; experiments, surveys, and analysis of historical or literary documents are all examples of research methods. Researchers then synthesize the results of their investigation and come to conclusions.
These conclusions are usually reported to colleagues and the public in written form.

Although writing research papers may seem like a daunting task, it doesn't need
to be because the process is very similar to that of writing other papers: You consider your topic and purpose, generate ideas, draft the paper, and revise repeatedly.
The research paper is different only in that much of the supporting information
you generate, instead of coming from your own brain, comes from research done

at the library or on the Internet, or from other media sources. For example, you could write an essay about the way families' structures are changing by giving examples of people you know, or you could develop your ideas by including research on family structures done by experts. In either case, you would construct a paper with a thesis and supporting evidence organized to suit your purpose. The process of writing a research paper is almost identical to writing an essay, except that you must be able to gather relevant material from sources. If you have a clear research strategy and an understanding of how to use the library and Internet resources, you will be able to write a research paper or report for college classes or on the job.

When writing research papers, many people make going to the library their first step. Having a general topic in mind, they search out some seemingly relevant sources, go home, and try to write a paper. Often, they become frustrated because they don't know what to do with the material they've gathered—How does it fit together? Which sources should they use? What point are they trying to make? Their research wasn't done with a purpose in mind, so they have difficulty producing a coherent text. To avoid the frustrations of researching without context, prepare to write a research paper just as you would any other paper: Think about context, determine purpose, and generate some ideas for organization and content. To gather the necessary material to fulfill your purpose, you will usually need a number of research sessions: First of all, you do research to become familiar with and narrow the topic; then you must do research to gather necessary supporting evidence for your thesis; finally, you may need to go back and "fill in the blanks" as you develop your paper and see gaps in your argument or explanations.

Like all other writing, a research paper or report is a text created by you to communicate your ideas, reactions, and conclusions on a topic. Your goal is not to paste researched material into a one-stop summary of other people's thoughts on the topic; your goal is to present your point of view on a topic using research to support or explain your conclusions.

Approaching a Research Writing Task

The first phase of writing a research paper involves analyzing the assignment, creating a schedule, choosing a topic, and generating a working thesis. This phase is crucial, but often neglected as students rush ahead to start their research. Taking time to think and plan carefully will make the process of research writing progress more smoothly.

Analyzing the Assignment

Chapter 1 discussed how context affects writing, and this is especially true in research writing. Because usually you are investing more time and effort in a research paper than in an essay, you want to be as efficient as possible. Knowing as much as you can about the audience, purpose, and constraints of the writing task will allow you to make intelligent choices about your topic, thesis, content, organization, and style so you won't waste time on unnecessary research or unusable drafts. Before you begin choosing, refining, or researching your topic, you should know the criteria for the assignment. Look at the assignment sheet, ask the instructor or manager, or consult with colleagues to find accurate answers to the following questions:

- Does the assignment specify a purpose (to report, to inform, to persuade)?
- How broad and deep should the research be?
- Are you required to use particular kinds of sources or search strategies?
- Is there a length requirement?
- What are the due dates?

FYI: For more on how context affects writing choices, see Chapter 1.

Try to answer these questions in as much detail as possible to make determining your topic, thesis, and research schedule as easy as possible.

Planning Your Time

Once you know the parameters of your writing and researching tasks, you can establish a schedule for completion of your paper. Breaking your work down into smaller tasks will make the process more manageable, will make it less likely that you will get bogged down or sidetracked, and will make you more confident and more relaxed about completing the assignment. As a general rule, you should probably look at the amount of time you have until the due date and divide the time into four segments:

1. *Approaching the research writing task*
   A. analyze assignment
   B. choose topic and determine purpose
   C. create working thesis
2. *Locating sources and taking notes*
   A. search campus library and Internet
   B. refine or revise thesis as research progresses
   C. evaluate sources
   D. take notes
   E. gather additional material at other locations or through interviews
3. *Incorporating source material into a coherent draft*
   A. write rough draft using sources found so far
   B. return to library to find additional evidence or information to fill gaps
   C. revise organization or thesis as necessary in light of new research
   D. write complete draft with all relevant sources properly documented
4. *Revising and polishing a draft*
   A. revise for completeness, unity, order, and coherence
   B. proofread for errors in grammar, spelling, and punctuation
   C. check all citations for accuracy and correctness

You can figure that the first and last segments will take a little less than a quarter of the time you have (usually, you will need at least a week for each segment). The middle two segments will take a little more than a quarter each. Of course, the schedule will vary depending on the topic and the kind of research you plan to do. If you need to do a lot of research off campus, you may need to allow extra time to locate material, or if you know that the drafting process always takes you a long time, you may need to factor that into your schedule. On the other hand, if your research assignment is so narrow that you have little choice of thesis or research material, you may be able to go through the first segment in a day or two. If you can make good estimates of the amount of time each segment will take, you'll be able to stay on schedule and reduce last-minute panic.

Generating a Workable Topic

To generate a workable topic, you can use many of the same techniques you practiced in Chapter 4. Usually, whatever topics you have in mind need to be focused before they are workable. If you have an idea for a topic, you might use freewriting, brainstorming, or mapping to produce some possibilities for further examination and clarification. For example, you might decide that you want to write about global warming, a big topic that could be approached from many perspectives. You need to focus the topic and determine your purpose, so you might freewrite to find out what you already know about it, what questions you have, and what readers might want to know about it. Often, a writer generates a list of questions about the topic. One (or more) of these questions then becomes the focus of the research. If your topic were global warming, you might come up with a long list of questions:

FYI: For more on generating ideas, see Chapter 4.

- What are the effects of global warming?
- What evidence is there that global warming exists?
- What are the causes of global warming?
- What prevents governments from taking action against global warming?
- What can be done about global warming?

Choosing a more focused topic and determining your purpose at this point in your research writing process will save you time when you gather source material. If you write to inform readers about solutions to global warming, you won't have to look at any source material that discusses only the causes. Further along in the process you may decide to narrow your focus even more, for example, by concentrating on persuading readers that one proposed solution to global warming would be ineffective.

When choosing your topic, keep the following criteria in mind. Your topic should:

- interest you
- not be too broad or too narrow
- lend itself to research given the resources you have
- fit the assignment

Choosing a strong topic is the foundation of the research process, so be patient and allow enough time to determine that the topic is workable and interesting. You may want to consult with your instructor or manager at this point to make sure that your ideas about the paper's focus are appropriate.

Many writers go to the library at this early stage to verify that there is some material available on the topic and to alert themselves to possible subtopics. Sometimes new questions or possibilities will present themselves as you survey the topic. However, if you decide to do some preliminary research, don't become overwhelmed with possibilities and forget what really interested you to begin with. If you use information-gathering techniques to generate your own questions and opinions, you'll usually find that you can adequately narrow your topic.

FYI: For more on purpose and thesis, see Chapter 3.

Writing a Working Thesis

Once you have a topic, you can write a working thesis. However, especially in research writing, the thesis you generate at this point in the process will be very provisional. You will most likely narrow it, change it, and refine it as you research, draft, and revise your paper. Nevertheless, it helps to have a working thesis as you begin your research, so you can test each source to see whether it's relevant to the paper's purpose.

Doing Research to Gather Supporting Evidence

Once you have a working thesis, you will begin the research process, which is discussed in detail in the next chapter. As you research, always keep your thesis and purpose in mind. Remember that you are not just collecting information on a broad topic; you are trying to find examples, evidence, and explanations to support the ideas you already have. In the course of your research, you may refine, narrow, revise, or totally change your ideas as you learn more about your topic. During the research process, you will probably have to return to your working thesis again and again to revise it in light of the new information you are discovering. For example, you may begin with a working thesis "Genetically engineered crops should be banned." But as you research your topic, you may modify your views several times. Your thesis might evolve as you become more informed. Your thesis might become narrower: "Genetically engineered corn presents clear danger to the monarch butterfly population." You might change your purpose from being persuasive to being informative: "The research on genetically engineered crops is complicated and inconclusive." You may change your opinion about the topic altogether: "Genetically engineered crops are one safe and efficient solution to the world's food shortage."

To be a good researcher, you should begin with a purpose and thesis in mind; at the same time, you should remain curious and open-minded so you can objectively evaluate your position and your research. You cannot write a strong research paper if you stay with an idea for which there is no supporting evidence.

Being a good researcher also means being persistent and thorough. If you can't find the evidence you want in the library, look on the Internet. If you find what looks like great information on the Internet, find corroborating evidence in books and journals. You may have found what looks like adequate supporting evidence in the first book you looked through, but gathering evidence from more than one book or journal or website will help to ensure that you've found the best and most complete evidence, resulting in a stronger, more interesting paper.

Writing a Coherent Draft

Once you have found and taken notes on the sources relevant to your topic, you need to write a draft that uses these sources to explain and support the ideas you want to communicate. Instead of letting the sources determine what your paper will cover, take time to think about and organize your ideas by mapping or outlining the points you want to discuss. Then determine which sources will fit in particular sections to support your points. It is tempting, but not necessary, to include all the relevant, interesting source material you've found; instead, you need to choose the material that best conveys your ideas completely and clearly.

The paper should be a coherent expression of your best thinking about the topic. It should sound like your writing, have one voice; it should not sound like a panel of experts patching together a summary of their various views. For this

For more on your style
and voice, see Chapter 7.

reason, paraphrasing source material is preferable to direct quotation whenever possible. If it is not necessary to use the author's exact words, paraphrase the material so that your paper is more unified and has a consistent style and tone.

When you use information from your notes in the text of your paper, there are two requirements: 1) The information must be smoothly integrated so that source information does not seem to be abruptly or illogically inserted into your own thoughts; and 2) the information needs to be labeled (in more precise terms, documented) to identify its source. The integration of source material into your draft will be discussed in this chapter and rules for documentation of sources will be presented in more detail in Chapter 21.

Smooth Integration of Source Material

When leading up to a quote or paraphrase, make sure the reader understands the information's purpose. To provide the reader with a context for the quote, paraphrase, or summary, you usually need to begin with a brief introduction to the source material. If the quote supports your argument, you might introduce it by saying, "This opinion is supported by one of the prominent researchers in the field, who says, . . ." If the paraphrase provides an example of a situation you have just described, you might introduce the paraphrase by saying, "One example is . . ." By using explanatory introductions—sometimes called tags—which describe the significance of the upcoming quote, paraphrase, or summary, you make a smooth transition between your writing and the source material used to support your ideas. Your introduction to the quote or paraphrase may do the following things:

- give readers information about the author's qualifications or relationship to other experts
- identify the source of the information (author, title of book, name of organization which did the research)
- evaluate the significance or credibility of the source material
- show the relationship between the source material and the rest of the paragraph

You should realize that your introduction to the source will reveal your evaluation of it. If you identify the author as an "expert," you automatically lend it credibility. If you introduce a quote by saying, "Rifkin claims . . ." your use of the word "claims" implies that his statement might not be true, thereby undermining Rifkin's credibility. Choose words carefully when characterizing a source as you introduce it.

It may sometimes be useful to explain the source material's significance further in a sentence following it. The brief explanation may provide a bridge from the source material to your next point or next example. The sample research paper included at the end of this chapter illustrates how quotations and paraphrases might be integrated smoothly into your own prose.

Revising Your Draft

When you write an essay, you revise to make the organization consistent, to strengthen the supporting evidence, or to improve the style. In the same way, once you have completed the draft of your research paper, you should work on revising it. First of all, look carefully at your thesis to make sure it fits your ideas about the topic and the purpose of your paper. Because research papers are usually longer and more complex than essays, it is important to read your draft carefully to make sure you are not straying from your topic and purpose. Eliminate any source material that is not relevant to your thesis and purpose, even if the information is interesting in its own right. When you revise, you should also read your draft critically, asking yourself whether the evidence you've included is sufficient and of high quality. You may find that some sections of your paper lack strong evidence; if so, you will need to do more research to find the material you need. Because you are incorporating many different voices into your research paper—your own, along with those of all the various sources—you must pay close attention to the style of your paper. Although the paper may contain quotes or paraphrases, the bulk of the paper should present your ideas and should be written in your words using an appropriate style. Make sure that each quote or paraphrase is introduced with a tag that reflects your impression of the material or its author. Each piece of evidence should be connected to your thesis and purpose by some explanation of how the quote or paraphrase supports your position.

Revision Checklist for Research Papers:

- *Thesis and Purpose*
  1. Does the thesis reflect your current, more informed understanding and position on the topic?
  2. Should the thesis be narrower? Can you provide complete and thorough evidence for your thesis and still stay within the required length?
  3. Can you make the wording of the thesis more precise or accurate?

- *Content and Organization*
  1. Do you have enough supporting evidence for each part of your paper?
  2. Is the evidence of good quality—up-to-date and from reliable sources?
  3. Does your evidence present a fair picture of what you found when you researched the topic, or is it a one-sided view?
  4. Is any source material irrelevant to your thesis and purpose?
  5. Does the paper present your own ideas and argument clearly, using sources as supporting material, or does the source material dominate, making the paper a string of sources without a controlling idea to link them together?

- *Style*
  1. Is each quote or paraphrase introduced in a way that allows readers to see the relationship of this source to the paper as a whole?
  2. Have you carefully chosen tag words to introduce each quote or paraphrase?
  3. Do you maintain a consistent style throughout the paper?

Activity: **WORKING TOGETHER**

Read the research paper on pp. 394–395 and use the revision checklist above to produce a list of suggestions for improving the paper.

READING AND WRITING TEXTS

Activity: **PREREADING**

In your Writer's Log

Answer the following questions:

- What do you know about genetically altered foods?
- What questions do you have about genetically altered food?
- Have you eaten any genetically altered food that you know of?
- Would you want to know if the food you ate was genetically altered?

Reading

The writer of this paper started out thinking that she was going to write about biotechnology and eventually narrowed her topic to the safety of genetically engineered food. Her paper contains a variety of sources which all work to support the conclusion she came to after researching the topic.

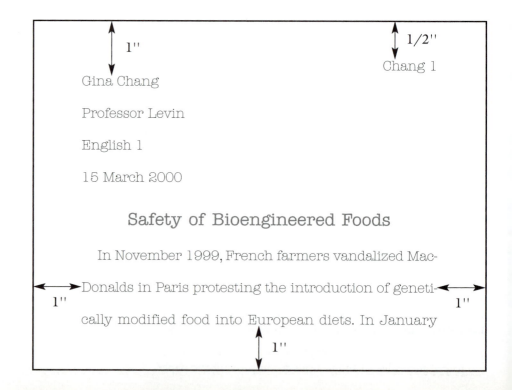

1"

1/2"

Chang 1

Gina Chang

Professor Levin

English 1

15 March 2000

Safety of Bioengineered Foods

In November 1999, French farmers vandalized Mac-Donalds in Paris protesting the introduction of genetically modified food into European diets. In January

1"

1"

1"

Chang 2

2000, an international conference convened to negotiate whether genetically modified crops could be exported to Europe. Both Gerber and Heinz have
announced that they will not use genetically modified
ingredients in their baby food. Two national grocery
chains have stopped using genetically modified ingredients in their store brands. What are all these people
upset about? What harm is done if scientists splice a
gene into a tomato to make it resist spoilage or into a
corn plant so it can produce its own pesticide? Should-
n't we be glad that through genetic engineering farmers can produce healthier, cheaper food?

Most people don't even know they're eating genetically altered food, though, in truth, they are. One estimate is that "60 percent of all processed foods—from
candy bars and tortilla chips to tofu dogs and infant
formula—contain at least one genetically engineered
component" and "nearly half of all soybeans and a third
of all corn in the United States" is grown from genetically altered seeds (Luoma 54). Consumers don't know
the extent of their consumption of genetically modified
(GM) food because the FDA does not require labeling

to indicate when ingredients have been genetically altered. As a result, very few of us know or care whether the corn used to make our cooking oil produced its own pesticide or had pesticide sprayed on it. If we've been eating genetically altered food with no ill effects and without noticing a difference in the product, why worry about whether genetically modified foods are safe to eat?

Until recently, most Americans didn't worry. However, Europeans have been concerned for years about the safety of their food supply and have been pushing for greater regulation and labeling. A poll done in the United Kingdom in 1998 "found 77% of people want genetically modified crops banned, while 61% do not want to eat genetically modified food" (Williams 768). More recently, in January of 2000, 130 nations gathered in Montreal to work out a biosafety treaty which "allows countries to bar imports of genetically altered seeds, microbes, animals and crops that they deem a threat to their environment" (Pollack). Increased publicity regarding European fears and protests has heightened Americans' wariness about GM products. But are the concerns about the genetic engineering of our food justified?

Chang 4

Answering this question is not easy because experts disagree about the long-term effects of genetically engineering crops and because the process is so new and so complex that the effects cannot yet be adequately evaluated.

When scientists genetically alter a plant, they take a gene from one organism and insert it into another to create a new plant that exhibits some desired trait, such as drought resistance, pest resistance, or increased nutritional value. Often, the inserted gene comes from a related species or even a mutation of the same species, but sometimes genes from totally unrelated organisms—even fish or bacteria—are chosen for their valuable properties. For example, scientists have introduced a gene from a soil bacterium into a pear tree to create trees that produce the same amount of fruit in a smaller amount of space (Gugliotta). In most cases of such transgenic plants, since only one gene is added, the plant appears to be exactly as it was before—both to the naked eye and under chemical analysis—except that it now exhibits the beneficial trait.

However, as critics point out, switching genes is not as straightforward as switching a piece of your wardrobe because each known characteristic that is changed may affect the organism in unknown ways. Dr. Richard Lacey, an expert on food safety quoted in <u>Mother Jones</u> magazine, explains the dangers of gene splicing this way:

> Its risks are in large part due to the complexity and interdependency of the parts of a living system, including its DNA. Wedging foreign genetic material in an essentially random manner into an organism's genome necessarily causes some degree of disruption, and the disruption could be multifaceted. . . . It is impossible to predict what specific problems could result in the case of any particular genetically engineered organism. (Luoma 57)

Adding a gene to make corn produce its own pesticide may also change other fundamental chemical features of the plant in ways that are not obvious, but that may have adverse effects on people who consume these plants. Until recently, scientists had not identified any cases of such harm caused by genetically altered food

Chang 6

and saw no research to suggest such harm would occur, so most food processors and consumers felt GM food was safe.

Recently, however, one researcher seemed to find disturbing evidence of health problems associated with genetically altered food. Arpad Pusztai, a prominent British researcher, announced the results of his study of rats fed potatoes genetically altered to contain a naturally occurring pesticide. Pusztai claimed that the rats "suffered damaged immune systems and stunted growth of vital organs" (Firth 21). This study immediately caused a furor among British scientists, resulting in Pusztai's suspension from his position due to claims that the study was "muddled" and the results "erroneous" (Firth 21). Reputable scientists are still debating the validity of Pusztai's study and its implications for the safety of genetically engineered food. Even if this research is incomplete and unreliable, it raises concerns because it points out the potential dangers that might be slipped onto consumers' plates without careful testing and regulation.

Chang 7

Another alarming incident involved the use of a gene from the Brazil nut in genetically modified soybeans. In his book <u>The Biotech Century</u>, anti-biotech activist Jeremy Rifkin describes a 1996 study by scientists at the University of Nebraska showing that blood serum from people allergic to Brazil nuts reacted positively when exposed to the extract of the soybeans containing the single Brazil nut gene. Rifkin says, "The biotech industry had long dismissed critics who warned of the potential allergenic effects of introducing foreign genes into conventional food crops. The Nebraska study gave added weight to critics' concerns" (Rifkin 104). However, as one newspaper pointed out, this example "hardly seems like a strong argument against genetic engineering, given that the problem was detected by tests on the new beans' safety long before they might have reached the market" ("The Year"). Once again, though the problem was caught during testing and no people were harmed by the product, such an incident makes the public skeptical about the safety of GM food.

Chang 8

Some people are concerned because in the process of creating genetically modified plants, scientists sometimes introduce another gene that could possibly result in antibiotic resistance in people:

> When scientists splice a foreign gene into a plant or microbe, they often link it to another gene, called a marker, that helps determine if the first gene was successfully taken up. Most markers code for resistance to antibiotics. Some researchers warn that these genes might be passed onto disease-causing microbes in the guts of people who eat altered food, contributing to the growing public-health problem of antibiotic resistance. (Tangley 40)

In response to this possibility, The Economist newspaper points out that "a host of experiments has failed to detect a single case of a gene jumping from a plant to a bacterium. . . . Even if such a thing could happen, it would add only marginally to a danger that already exists in nature. Thousands of naturally occurring antibiotic-resistance genes are known to be carried by bacteria" ("The Year").

The critics of GM food often say that they don't want to abandon the development of GM foods entirely; they just want to slow the process down enough so that more rigorous and thorough testing can be done before products are released to the general public. In an article in <u>Mother Jones</u> magazine, one expert claims that the way genetically engineered foods are now regulated is "like playing Russian roulette with public health" (Luoma 54). Critics such as this take the attitude "better safe than sorry." They prefer to err on the side of caution to avoid any possibility of harm.

Supporters, on the other hand, claim that current testing and regulations are adequate to assure the safety of GM foods for human consumption. For example, when Monsanto developed a genetically modified soybean that could withstand the application of a powerful herbicide, the company put the new plant through extensive testing in order to prove that it met the FDA regulations, which state that producers of genetically modified food must "ensure that all safety and regulatory questions have been fully addressed" (FDA). "It did 1,800 analyses comparing the two types, looking at fatty

Chang 10

acids, proteins, and hundreds of other substances. The

results: The normal and genetically engineered plants

are indistinguishable" (Carey 72).

In an interview, FDA Commissioner Jane E. Henney

describes the FDA's regulatory process regarding ge-

netically modified food:

> Under the Food, Drug, and Cosmetic Act, compa-
>
> nies have a legal obligation to ensure that any
>
> food they sell meets the safety standards of the
>
> law. . . . In the specific case of foods developed uti-
>
> lizing the tools of biotechnology, FDA set up a con-
>
> sultation process to help companies meet the
>
> requirements. While the consultation is voluntary,
>
> the legal requirements that the foods have to meet
>
> are not. (Thompson)

Henney goes on to explain that a bioengineered food

does not need to be labeled because it does not vary in

any "significantly different way from its conventional

counterpart." If the food does contain any modification

in nutritional value or if it contains any known allergy-

causing component, the FDA would require labeling

(Thompson). Critics, such as Consumers Union, point

out that the regulatory system is "largely run on the honor system" ("Seeds" 45), and they call for mandatory federal safety review of all genetically engineered foods before they are allowed on the market ("Seeds" 46).

In the end, the question does not seem to be whether GM food is safe, but whether it is safe enough. After all, toxins occur naturally in plants, such as potatoes. All the food we eat carries some danger of contamination from bacteria such as E coli. Even traditional breeding of plants can produce dangerous new varieties. For example, one conventionally cross-bred potato was taken off the market in 1970 because it contained dangerously high levels of a toxin. Additionally, much of the non-GM food we eat now is filled with pesticides and processed with chemicals that consumers have accepted as safe enough, even though no researcher can prove that these chemicals will never harm anyone's health. All they can prove is that the small risks of using such chemicals are worth the benefits in higher quality, cheaper food. Finally, though scientists cannot say for sure that GM foods present no risk, even critics concede that no harm has been done by genetically engi-

Chang 12

neered food so far. An article in <u>Consumer Reports</u>, a publication which is not especially supportive of genetically engineered foods, states, "There's no evidence that genetically engineered foods on the market are unsafe to eat" ("Seeds" 44). No food we produce is totally safe. Therefore, we must evaluate whether the current potential benefits of GM food outweigh the risks.

Then the question becomes who makes the decision about whether the food is safe enough. Currently, the companies make that decision as they do the testing advised by the FDA, but there is no agency that requires such testing or certifies the food's safety. Many people do not trust such voluntary testing and believe consumers should have the right to exclude such food from their diet, just as people can now choose to eat only organic food because such food is regulated and labeled. Up until now, the industry has resisted labeling, fearing that consumers would construe the label as a warning that GM food was inferior or dangerous. However, the food industry is now responding to consumers' growing awareness and uneasiness by considering some kind of labeling—perhaps labels that designate some food as GM free.

Chang 13

But putting labels on GM food does not really resolve the issue of whether consumers should buy and consume GM food. Perhaps most consumers will decide that GM food seems too dangerous and may side with critics who say, "Why take the risk on modified corn when normal corn was just fine?" We might conclude that genetic engineering is a technology that is not worth the risk to most people. However, as many supporters point out, halting the development of genetically modified food now may have large costs in human health in the future. Recently researchers have used genetically engineered crops to address some staggering health issues facing the Third World. One example is "yellow rice," a modified strain of rice containing large quantities of Vitamin A, which could prevent death and blindness caused by dietary deficiency. The World Health Organization says that a quarter of a million children in Southeast Asia go blind each year because of Vitamin A deficiency (Hotz 4). <u>Science</u> magazine describes work being done to develop other transgenic plants that would improve human health throughout the developing world: a high protein sweet potato for use in re-

Chang 14

gions where other protein sources are lacking; plants that would produce edible vaccines for easier distribution; and plants that could produce disease-fighting weapons such as insulin for diabetics and monoclonal antibodies for fighting infections (Moffat 2177).

If consumers in America and Europe do not buy GM foods, large companies such as Monsanto and Novartis that invest in genetic engineering research to improve the technology will not continue to do so. Efforts to develop health-enhancing transgenic plants may falter. So while individual health of consumers in America and Europe will be assured against the slightest risk by the abandonment of genetically altered foods, millions of people in the Third World may suffer and die due to lack of development of potentially beneficial genetically modified plants.

The decision about whether to eat genetically modified food is further complicated by the presence of problems other than danger to human health. Critics have warned that GM crops will cause environmental damage as well. In light of these difficulties, the safest decision might be to stop the use of genet-

ically modified crops altogether. Critics compare genetic engineering to nuclear energy, warning that a
technology that once seemed to be the solution to dire
global problems could end up being a long-term
health, environmental, and economic disaster itself.
Our decision about genetically modified food must be
a decision based on an evaluation of the risks versus
the benefits. We can only make such a decision if we
know the facts about the dangers and promises of
this new technology.

Works Cited

Carey, John, Ellen Licking and Amy Barrett. "Are Bio-Foods Safe?"

    Business Week 20 Dec. 1999: 70-76.

Firth, Peta. "Leaving a Bad Taste." Scientific American May 1999:

    34-35.

Food and Drug Administration. "Bioengineered Foods." 15 Feb. 2000.

    Department of Health and Human Services. 26 Mar. 2000.

    http://www.fda.gov/oc/biotech/default.htm

Gugliotta, Guy. "At USDA Unit, Seeds of Many Ideas." The Wash-

    ington Post 27 Dec. 1999. ProQuest. DeAnza College Lib.,

    Cupertino, CA. 12 Feb. 2000.

    http://www.proquest.com

Hotz, Robert Lee. "Bioengineered Rice May Ease Deadly Problem."

    The Los Angeles Times 14 Jan. 2000, home ed.: A1-4.

Luoma, Jon. "Pandora's Pantry." Mother Jones Jan. 2000: 52-59.

Moffat, Anne Simon. "Toting Up the Early Harvest of Transgenic

    Plants." Science 282 (1998): 2176-2177.

Pollack, Andrew. "130 Nations Agree on Safety Rules for Biotech

    Food." The New York Times 30 Jan. 2000, late ed.: A1.

Rifkin, Jeremy. The Biotech Century. New York: Penguin Put-

    nam, 1998.

"Seeds of Change." Consumer Reports September 1999: 41-46.

Tangley, Laura. "How Safe Is Genetically Modified Food?" U.S. News & World Report 26 July 1999: 40.

Thompson, Larry. "Are Bioengineered Foods Safe?" FDA Consumer January/February 2000. 1 Jan. 2000. Food and Drug Administration. 26 Mar. 2000.

http://www.fda.gov/fdac/features/2000/100_bio.html

Williams, Nigel. "Agricultural Biotech Faces Backlash in Europe." Science 281 (1998): 768-771.

"The Year of the Triffids: Genetic Engineering." The Economist 26 April 1997: 80-83. Infotrac. Newton Public Library, Newton, N.M. 5 Feb. 2000.

http://www.infotrac.galegroup.com

Activity: RESPONDING TO THE TEXT

1. How would the paper be different without the introductory and concluding paragraphs? What do they contribute to the paper?
2. Which section makes the strongest argument that eating genetically altered food might be unsafe? Why is that the strongest?
3. Chang touches on some topics that she doesn't develop because they are not directly relevant to her main point. Do you see any ideas contained in this paper that might be the basis for another complete research paper?
4. Are there any relevant questions readers might have about this topic that have not been answered in the paper? What information could be added to strengthen the paper's evidence?

Writing Assignments

After choosing one of the following assignments for your research paper, complete Steps 1–5.

1. Before you begin your research, analyze the question, create a timetable for the paper's completion, generate a workable topic, and write a working thesis.
2. After doing your research, write a draft. Be careful to maintain your own point of view and voice throughout the paper and to use sources as support rather than allow them to dominate the paper.
3. Revise the paper using the checklist on p. 393.
4. Proofread your paper to make sure the documentation was done properly. Use the checklist on p. 450.
5. Write a paragraph or two answering the following questions:
   - What was most enjoyable about the research writing process? What was least enjoyable? What do you think will be easier the next time? What will you do differently the next time?
   - Did you choose a good topic for your paper? Did the topic hold your interest throughout the research and writing process? Why do you think readers might be interested in the topic? What might have made it more interesting or significant?
   - What advice would you give someone just starting a research paper?

Academic Writing

Journalism

Although newspapers and magazines often seem to be reporting the news objectively, as "Consider the Sources" on pages 423–425 points out, they sometimes exhibit biases in their stories and articles. A writer's selection of facts, choice of words, and pattern of organization can all influence a reader's opinion about an issue. Choose an issue that is currently controversial, and survey five newspapers, news magazines, or general interest magazines to determine whether any of them are presenting the issue in a biased way. You may be able to find enough evidence by looking at issues from the past year, or you may have to read the periodicals for the last few years. After you have read the articles and determined whether they are biased in any way, organize your findings into a research paper.

Your paper will have a thesis which states your findings. Then the report will prove your thesis by providing evidence from the articles in the periodicals. Quotations, paraphrases, and summaries from particular biased (or unbiased) articles can be used to support your thesis. Use Modern Language Association (MLA) documentation.

Medicine and Science

At the beginning of her article, "The Egg and the Sperm," on pp. 425–431 Martin says, "I am intrigued by the possibility that culture shapes how biological scientists describe what they discover about the natural world." She believes that the political, economic, social, and artistic climate of a culture may make scientists see and describe their data in a particular way. Someone from another time or place might notice different parts of the data, give different parts more or less significance, and describe the data in different terms. In Martin's example, she shows how researchers' cultural assumptions about male and female relationships have affected the things they notice about the sperm and the egg, the conclusions they come to about what they see, and the way they describe those findings.

Choose one of the following medical and scientific topics:

agriculture	embryology
AIDS	genetic research
biotechnology	global warming
breast cancer	nuclear energy
diet and nutrition	space exploration

Once you have chosen a topic, you may need to narrow it to make it more manageable or interesting. Look at research that was done on your chosen topic ten to twenty years ago. Then find the most recent research in the field. First, report on what has changed in the knowledge about or approach to the topic. Then try to find some relationship between that change and economic, political, social, or artistic changes. Have there been breakthroughs in the field because more money is available for research? Why is more money available? Have changes in society (aging population, shifts in gender roles or family structures) caused researchers to look at the problem differently? Have there been books, plays, or music that might have changed researchers' outlook on the problem? You might find answers to these questions in the sources themselves, or you may have to draw conclusions from your own experiences or knowledge or from the research you do. Use American Psychological Association (APA) format to report your findings.

History

Examine some aspect of your life, such as education, recreation, work, or child rearing. Then think about how someone in a similar social situation years ago might have experienced this same aspect of life. For example, if you are a middle-class, twenty-year-old man, you might try to discover how the education of a middle-class, twenty-year-old man who lived in 1840 would have differed from your education. You can gather your information from books or from personal interviews. You might choose to compare one aspect of your life with that same aspect of your parents' or grandparents' lives when they were your age. In this case, you might be able to use more personal interviews.

At the conclusion of the paper, make note of the kinds of information or facts that did not seem to be available. What questions were left unanswered or what information was left out of all the sources you consulted? Draw some conclusions about why this information may have been unavailable or difficult to find.

Remember that you will not need to document facts that are common knowledge, but you will need to document statistics, findings, discoveries, and opinions of the historians you read. Search both books and periodicals for information, and remember that videotapes, personal interviews, and television shows may provide you with valuable information. You might want to review the explanation of a comparison/contrast organization pattern in Chapter 15. Use MLA documentation format.

Workplace Writing

Using your college, workplace, or a local business or agency as a topic, investigate the technological changes that have occurred during the last five years and their effects on the institution. If the workplace is small, consider the whole institution; if it is large or complex, limit your investigation to one office or division.

First, determine what technological changes have taken place. To gather information, interview relevant people and examine documents such as job descriptions, training manuals, and administrative handbooks.

Next, investigate what secondary changes have taken place directly or indirectly due to technological changes. For example, the institution may have shifts in budgeting to provide for technology. It may hire more people with technological training to support new systems. It may have "downsized" because fewer people can fulfill the institution's functions. You will probably need to conduct more interviews to gather information. You will probably also need to gather print and electronic information about institutions' incorporation of technology and about current trends in business administration.

Finally, incorporate your research into a paper focusing on the effects of the electronic revolution on your institution. Use APA documentation style.

Personal Writing

Do some research on a problem in your college, home, family, or neighborhood. Then write an essay explaining how your research changed your understanding of the problem or suggested a solution. Use the source material to help explain your change in point of view or your proposed solution.

INTERNET AND LIBRARY RESEARCH

PREVIEW

This chapter's explanation of research in the library and on the Internet will answer the following questions:

- How do you find the supporting evidence you need in libraries?
- What are the best ways to access Internet information?
- How can you evaluate the sources you find?
- How can you keep track of this evidence in notes?

LEARNING ABOUT TEXTS

When you do research for class assignments or on the job, you may use many methods such as experiments, surveys, and observations; however, since you do not have the financial support that scientists and scholars do, you will usually not be able to mount your own direct investigations of the topics you are studying. If, for example, you want to study the effects of domestic violence on children, you will probably not be able to do extensive surveys of victims of domestic violence. Instead, you will rely on the research of others, research you will find in books and periodicals in the library or on the Internet. The library will also allow you to find documents that you can analyze and interpret, just as many researchers do. You may read diaries, editorials, statistics, and/or eyewitness reports that you can use to draw your own conclusions about a particular research question. Whether you are using the research of others—called secondary sources—or documents from which you draw your own conclusions—called primary sources—the library provides you with a wealth of information. All you have to do is find the right information to answer your question, connect that information together in a logical way, and communicate your conclusions in an accepted format.

To research your topic, you will probably use a library which may house books, periodicals, sound and video recordings, databases (online or on CD-ROM), government documents, and various other resources. You may also use a computer (in the library or at your home or office) to search the Internet for relevant websites, read e-mail from experts, or participate in newsgroups. In some cases, your research may include interviews with experts or witnesses or visits to museums, historical societies, company archives. No matter where or how you do your research, you must gather relevant information, record it accurately, and evaluate its credibility.

You do research to gather information for two reasons: 1) to survey a large body of information on one general topic to get an overview of the issues and knowledge in the field, and 2) to find particular facts, statistics, or expert opinions to support an argument. Sometimes these two purposes overlap, as is the case when you write a research paper in a college class. In the process, you might read a large body of information on a topic, then narrow your focus and choose a thesis, then go back and identify particular pieces of information that support your thesis. Some resources and research tools are better suited to giving you an overview, and some are better for finding specific pieces of information. As you become a more experienced and efficient researcher, you will learn where to go for particular kinds of information.

Library Research

The library is a good place to start your research because it has such a wide variety of resources, including reference librarians. If you want to make the best use of the library's resources, do as much as possible to familiarize yourself with its layout and services. The time you invest in learning about your library will pay off as you become a more effective and efficient researcher.

Familiarizing Yourself with Your Library

Though a library contains vast amounts of information, this information is useless unless you can retrieve it efficiently. Though most libraries contain similar basic resources—such as books, periodicals (magazines, journals, newspapers), and media (sound and video recordings, CDs and CD-ROMs)—the details of how you access these holdings vary from library to library. Many libraries' catalogs of books and indexes of periodicals are accessed on computer terminals or on CD-ROMs, some use bound copies of indexes, and a few have card catalogs. Sometimes this information can be accessed on the Internet; sometimes you can also access catalogs and indexes from other libraries that share a system with yours. This chapter will introduce you to the various research materials and tools found in most libraries, but you should become acquainted with the particular resources and modes of access of your local library and your college library.

The first step is to familiarize yourself with the physical layout of the library. Find answers to the following questions about the location of resources and tools by looking at library maps, reading instructions posted near computer terminals or electronic information centers, or consulting the reference librarian, who can direct you to the resources you need:

- Does the library staff give tours or orientations to the library or offer other research workshops?
- Where and how can you locate books by title, author, or subject?
- Where are the books stored and how do you find them?
- How do you find periodical listings for your subject?
- How can you find and read these periodicals?
- Where is the reference section of the library? What does it contain?
- Are there any electronic resources? How are they accessed?
- Where are the reference librarians? What services do they provide and during what hours?
- Can you access the library holdings over the Internet from home or from other locations on campus? How?
- Can you access the holdings of other libraries? How?
- Can you do Internet searches from library terminals? Are there any restrictions?

At the very minimum, you will need to find the reference section of the library, the catalog, and the periodical indexes. These are the three major access points for information.

Using the Reference Section

The reference section contains books that provide condensed information on a variety of subjects (such as encyclopedias and almanacs) and books that list sources of further information (such as indexes and bibliographies, both of which are lists of books or other documents relating to a certain topic). Because these books are valuable to so many people, they usually do not circulate. You cannot take them out of the library. Many writers begin their search by reading encyclopedia entries on their topics. The entries are usually useful only for background information because they do not contain sufficient facts, figures, and expert opinions to support a thesis. However, encyclopedia entries often provide clues for further research. An entry may include a list of books on its topic or may refer to prominent researchers in the field. These references will point you in the right direction for the rest of your search.

One of the most valuable types of reference works is a bibliography; it lists most of the books (and sometimes also the periodicals) written in a certain field or on a certain topic. The entries are usually listed by subtopics, so you can look for headings that relate to your search and browse through the list of entries for titles that appear relevant. For example, if you are doing research on how television violence affects children, you might consult the *Mass Media Bibliography* and look in the subject index under "Children and Mass Media." If you browse through the other headings, you may find additional relevant titles such as "Action for Children's Television" and "Violence and the Mass Media."

Using Online Catalogs and Indexes

A few libraries still keep their catalogs in large rows of cabinets with drawers full of index cards, but this method of cataloging is becoming rare in college and community libraries. In most libraries, you will use an online catalog accessible from computer terminals to identify all the library's holdings related to your subject. You usually have to do separate searches for books (and other media) and for periodicals. To begin your online search, go to the terminals located in the library and read any instructions posted near the terminals regarding how to search for materials. If you have never done an online search before or if you feel uncomfortable working on your own, you might seek out an orientation workshop or the help of a library aide or reference librarian. Most catalogs are easy to use, once you go through the search process a few times. Here is an example of what an online catalog's search page looks like:

| CATALOG | GATEWAYS | RESERVE DESK | INFO. DESK | USER SERVICES |

GO BACK   HELP   PREFS   EXIT

Search the Library Catalog

| QUICK SEARCH | COMPLEX SEARCH | CALL NO. BROWSE |

◆ Keyword ◆ Browse ◆ Exact

```
I
```

SEARCH EVERYTHING   AUTHOR   TITLE   SUBJECT   SERIES   PERIODICAL TITLE

1. Enter the word(s) you want to find.
Keyword returns records *containing* the word(s) entered.
Browse returns catalog headings *beginning* with the first word entered.
Exact returns records that *exactly* match the word(s) entered.
2. Choose a target search field.
Search Everything targets all indexed fields within a record.
All other choices target specified fields within a record.

Web*Cat*®
a f % product by **SIRSI**
Copyright ©1995 – 1998
Sirsi Corporation

TOP

| CATALOG | GATEWAYS | RESERVE DESK | INFO. DESK | USER SERVICES |

Decide whether you are going to search for books or for periodicals. Searches for books and periodicals use the same kinds of strategies, but you may have to go to different online locations. You can search the library catalogs and indexes in the following ways:

- *Title Search* If you know the title of a book, periodical, or media item related to your search, doing a title search will tell you whether the library owns the book, whether it's available, and where to find it.
- *Author Search* If you want to find what the library owns written by a particular author, do an author search.

- *Subject Search* If you want a list of all the library's holdings on your topic, do a subject search. The drawback of doing such a search is that the list of holdings is often so long that it is overwhelming.
- *Keyword Search* Keyword searches are similar to subject searches because they list all holdings that contain whatever keyword you enter. Like subject searches, keyword searches can yield lists that are of unmanageable length.

Author and Title Searches

To search for a work using the author or title, just type the author's name (usually last name first, but check your catalog's instructions) or the book's title in the search box and click on the SEARCH button or press ENTER. If the search says no items were found that matched the author or title you entered, check your spelling of title words and names. If your author or title is found and listed for you, click on the appropriate line and you will see a screen that contains information about the book, author, call number, current status, and other bibliographic information. You can jot this information down or print it.

Subject and Keyword Searches

Each item in the library's holdings is cataloged by standard subject terms that were established by the Library of Congress. You can look up these Library of Congress Subject Headings (LCSH; in a book in the reference section or online or on CD-ROM) to find the ones relevant to your search. Begin by looking up subjects that seem obvious to you. Each subject is cross-referenced, so you can find other related subjects. Below is an example of a page from the LCSH that lists other search terms for global warming:

Global Temperature Changes
  (Not Subd Geog)
   [QC903]
    UF   Temperature changes, Global
          World temperature changes
    BT   Climatic changes
          Global environmental change
    RT   Atmospheric temperature
    NT   Global warming
Global trade
    USE   International trade
Global Warming *(Not Subd Geog)*
   [QC981.8 G56]
    UF   Warming, Global
    BT   Global temperature changes
    RT   Greenhouse effect, Atmospheric
    NT   Plants, Effect of global warming on
   —**Law and legislation** *(May Subd Geog)*
          BT Environmental law
   —**Research** *(May Subd Geog)*
   ——**Law and legislation**
          (May Subd Geog)

Global Weather Experiment Project
     BT   Meteorology—Research
           Weather
Globalism (Education)
     USE   Global method of teaching
Globe artichoke
     USE   Artichokes

Once you have a list of all relevant topics, you can enter these subject headings in the subject search box of the online catalog for a list of the library's holdings with that subject heading.

A keyword search is similar to a subject search, but instead of using Library of Congress Subject Headings, you enter a word or phrase that seems to be a "key" word for the topic. For example, if you were doing a paper on global warming, you might try keywords "global warming" or "ozone layer." Find keywords by thinking of words and phrases relating to your topic. You might try looking at a thesaurus or using subject heading terms as keywords. In a keyword search, the computer will find any holding that uses these words in the title or in the body of the entry, so keyword searches may result in even longer lists than subject searches.

Both subject searches and keyword searches are great tools, but learning to use them efficiently takes some practice and persistence. If you try a subject or keyword search and get no results, you may need to find a different term. Each relevant item you find can give you clues about other places to search because each will contain subject heading terms and keywords you can try as search words. Look below at an example of a book found in a search using "global warming" as a keyword:

Search Result –– Quick Search

Viewing record **2** of **14** from catalog.

☐ Check here to mark this record for Print/Capture

QC981.8 .G56 G45 1997
The heat is on : the high stakes battle over Earth's threatened climate / Ross Gelbspan.
Gelbspan, Ross.

Personal author:	Gelbspan, Ross.
Title:	The heat is on : the high stakes battle over Earth's threatened climate / Ross Gelbspan.
Publication info:	Reading, Mass : Addison-Wesley Pub. Co., c1997.
Physical description:	viii, 278 p. ; 24 cm.
Subject:	Global warming--Government policy.
Subject:	Energy industries--Political activity.
Subject:	Greenhouse effect, Atmospheric--Government policy.
Subject:	Global warming--Government policy--United States.
Subject:	Energy industries--Political activity--United States.
Subject:	Greenhouse effect, Atmospheric--Government policy--United States.

CALL NUMBER	COPY	MATERIAL	LOCATION
1) QC981.8 .G56 G45 1997	1	BOOK	CHECKED OUT

Once you have found this item, you can see that "greenhouse effect" and "energy industry" are other possibilities for subject or keyword searches.

When your subject or keyword search returns a list that is very long, you need to narrow the search; if your list is very short, you may need to expand your search. In most catalogs, you can narrow or expand your search by using what are called "Boolean logic terms," which are listed below:

- AND Use this between two terms if you only want to see items that contain both subjects or keywords. For example, if you are using "climate" as a keyword, you may want to narrow your search by adding another term such as "change": climate AND change.
- OR Use this between terms to search for any item using either of the terms: climate OR weather.
- NOT Use this if you want all items that use a term, but not if the items also contain another term. For example, if you are searching for items on global warming, and you use the word "climate," you may end up with a long list that includes entries about global warming, but also entries about air conditioning, which is also known as "climate control." Use NOT to avoid those irrelevant entries: climate NOT control.

Notice that these Boolean terms are always in full capitals. You can string these terms together, so you might end up with a search that looks like this: climate OR weather AND change NOT control. Using Boolean logic terms takes practice. If your library offers workshops on advanced search strategies, use of these terms will probably be explained in more detail.

Locating Books and Periodicals

Once you have found a relevant entry on the computer, you will want to locate that item in the library. For books, copy the title, author, and "call number," which is a combination of letters and numbers so identified on the terminal screen. Make sure you copy down all the letters and numbers because they pinpoint the book's exact location in the library. Each book in the library has the call number on a label on its spine. The books are arranged on the shelves with the call numbers in numerical and alphabetical order. The first three digits of the call number indicate the book's general location. Find a library map that shows the location of the first three digits of the book you are looking for or look at the labels on the sides of the stacks. Once you have found the general location, continue looking through the shelves until you find the number that corresponds to your call number.

To find periodicals, you need the article title, author, periodical title, publication date, and page number. Periodicals are housed differently in different libraries. Some have all holdings online, so that you can find the complete text of the article on your computer screen and can print it out and carry it home. Others have periodicals on microfilm or microfiche, so you have to locate the film, read it on a microfilm/fiche reading machine, and take notes or print it from the machine. In some libraries, recent holdings are kept in open stacks on periodical shelves or are bound into larger volumes kept in the periodical section. Sometimes, periodicals are kept in a back room, so you must request the issue you want from the staff. Until you become familiar with the library's system, you may need some help when looking for periodicals. Do not be afraid to consult the reference or periodical librarian, who is there to help you.

Using Periodical Indexes

In some libraries, periodical indexes are not online, but on CD-ROM or in bound volumes. These indexes are found in the reference section. The most popular periodical index is *The Reader's Guide to Periodical Literature*, which lists all articles published in general interest magazines, but there are more specialized periodical indexes such as *The New York Times Index*, *The Humanities Index*, *The Book Review Index*, and *The Social Science Index*. To find information about a particular topic, just find an appropriate heading in the index and browse through the entries to see which of the listed articles seem to be relevant to your search. If you looked under "global warming" in the *Reader's Guide*, you'd see a note that refers you to relevant articles listed under "greenhouse effect" instead. The example below shows a list of articles as you might find them in the *Reader's Guide*:

GREENFELD, LIAH
Non-partisan reflections on the president's affair. *Society* V36 no3 p18–21 Mr/Ap '99
GREENGRASS, PAUL
about
The theory of flight [film] Reviews
People Weekly il v51 no1 p73–4+ Ja 11 '99. D. Jewel
People Weekly v51 no5 p32 F 8 '99. L. Rozen
GREENHOUSE EFFECT
America, the beautiful carbon sink. P. W. Huber. il *Forbes* v163 no7 p126 Ap 5 '99
Anthropogenic influence on the autocorrelation structure of hemispheric-mean temperatures. T. M. L. Wigley and others. bibl f il *Science* v282 no5394 p1676–9 N 27 '98
Biomass energy versus carbon sinks: trees and the Kyoto Protocol D. O. Hall. bibl f *Environment* v41 no1 p5+ Ja/F '99
Blame it on El Niño [global warming] S. Beers. il *E: the Environmental Magazine* v9 no5 p22–3+ S/O '98
Climate treaty talks mark some progress. J. Raloff. il *Science News* v154 no21 p325 N 21 '98
Fossil fuels without CO_2 emissions. E. A. Parson and D. W. Keith, bibl f *Science* v282 no5391 p1053–4 N 6 '98
Global warming: worse than we thought. P. Brown. *World Press Review* v46 no2 p44 F '99
Greening transportation: toward a sustainable future: addressing the long-term effects of motor vehicle transportation on climate and ecology. M. Fergusson and I. Skinner. Bibl f *Environment* v41 no1 p24–7 Ja/F '99
How warm weather threatens our society [global warming and Y2K concerns in Canada] C. Gordon. il *Maclean's* v111 no52 p11 D 28 '98-Ja 4 '99
The incredible shrinking atmosphere. F. Saunders. *Discover* v20 no1 p68 Ja '99
Mankind is possible cause of earth's warm weather trend: experts. *Jet* v95 no6 p55 Ja 11 '99

On the global warming front. il *The Wilson Quarterly* v23 no1 p132–4 Wint '99

Possibly vast greenhouse gas sponge ignites controversy. J. Kaiser. il map *Science* v282 no5388 p386–7 O 16 '98

Spring's sprung early. W. J. Cook. il *U.S. News & World Report* v126 no10 p60 Mr 15 '99

Stars in their eyes [interview with S. Baliunas] V. I. Postrel and S. Postrel. il pors *Reason* v30 no5 p42–50 O '98

Where has all the carbon gone? R. Monastersky. *Science News* v154 no21 p332 N 21 '98

Wild weather [Canada; cover story] C. Wood. il *Maclean's* v112 no4 p16–19 Ja 25 '99

Economic aspects

The greenhouse gas trade. A. Agarwal and S. Narain. il *The Unesco Courier* v51 no10 p10–13 O '98

S. Boukhari. *The Unesco Courier* v51 no10 p12–13 O '98

Pollution permits for greenhouse gases? J. Kaiser. *Science* v282 no5391 p1025 N 6 '98

You may find many entries under one heading, a few under another, and none under another. Each entry contains information about the article's title, author, magazine or journal it appeared in, date and volume number of the issue, and page numbers. This information allows you to locate the periodical in the library and the article within the publication.

Internet Research

The Internet is a vast network of thousands (maybe millions) of computers linked electronically. Anyone who wants to make information (their writing, products, research data, pictures, movies, music—anything that can be turned into digital data) available on the Internet, can set up a Web page containing the material they wish to make public. Each Web page has an "address," a string of letters, symbols, and numbers, which identifies its location on the Internet the way your house number and street name, city, state, and zip code identify your location in the world. This address is called the URL (Uniform Resource Locator) and each element in it has meaning, just as the elements of your address have meaning. You can access information on the Internet through a "browser" such as Netscape or Internet Explorer. You can find information on the Internet in two ways: If you want to visit a particular website, just enter the URL in the appropriate box on the browser screen; if you want to search for information about a particular topic without knowing the URLs of any relevant websites, do a search using a search engine or directory such as Alta Vista, Yahoo, Hotbot, Google, or Infoseek. These search engines and directories respond to search terms, just like the ones you used to search your library's catalog. In fact, the Internet is like one big library of websites, and search engines and directories are just big catalogs. To make your Internet searching more efficient, you should find a few search engines or directories that you like and use them until they become familiar. Though they are all similar, each one has particularities that can be frustrating if you're not familiar with them. The search engine will display a list of websites that it thinks are relevant to your topic, based on the terms you entered. Just as in your library research, you may need to narrow your search by refining, combining, or expanding your search term. Learning to search the Internet efficiently takes time and practice, but you can gather large quantities of information with the basic search skills described in this chapter. If you used the search term "global warming" on Alta Vista, you would find a list of sources that included the one shown below:

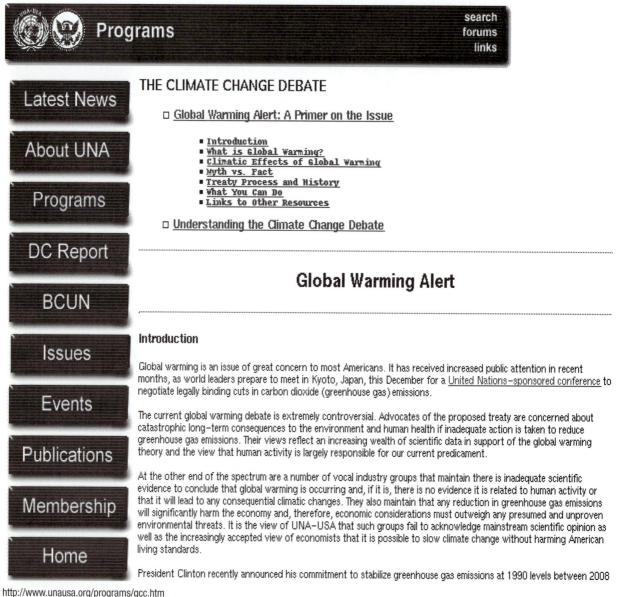

Programs

search
forums
links

THE CLIMATE CHANGE DEBATE

☐ Global Warming Alert: A Primer on the Issue

- Introduction
- What is Global Warming?
- Climatic Effects of Global Warming
- Myth vs. Fact
- Treaty Process and History
- What You Can Do
- Links to Other Resources

☐ Understanding the Climate Change Debate

Global Warming Alert

Latest News

About UNA

Programs

DC Report

BCUN

Issues

Events

Publications

Membership

Home

Introduction

Global warming is an issue of great concern to most Americans. It has received increased public attention in recent months, as world leaders prepare to meet in Kyoto, Japan, this December for a United Nations-sponsored conference to negotiate legally binding cuts in carbon dioxide (greenhouse gas) emissions.

The current global warming debate is extremely controversial. Advocates of the proposed treaty are concerned about catastrophic long-term consequences to the environment and human health if inadequate action is taken to reduce greenhouse gas emissions. Their views reflect an increasing wealth of scientific data in support of the global warming theory and the view that human activity is largely responsible for our current predicament.

At the other end of the spectrum are a number of vocal industry groups that maintain there is inadequate scientific evidence to conclude that global warming is occurring and, if it is, there is no evidence it is related to human activity or that it will lead to any consequential climatic changes. They also maintain that any reduction in greenhouse gas emissions will significantly harm the economy and, therefore, economic considerations must outweigh any presumed and unproven environmental threats. It is the view of UNA-USA that such groups fail to acknowledge mainstream scientific opinion as well as the increasingly accepted view of economists that it is possible to slow climate change without harming American living standards.

President Clinton recently announced his commitment to stabilize greenhouse gas emissions at 1990 levels between 2008

http://www.unausa.org/programs/gcc.htm
7/23/1999

Notice that the Web page not only provides information about global warming, it contains "Links to Other Resources." You can click on these links and you will be automatically transferred to other Web pages that contain relevant information.

If you are using the Internet for research, remember to bookmark sites that you may want to view again at another session. To review the sites you've already seen in the current session, use the "Back" button or "History."

Using the Internet to research your topic has many advantages. Since many writers can access the Internet from their homes, offices, or colleges, it is frequently more convenient for researching than traditional print sources. Furthermore, you may find information that is more up-to-date, more on the "fringe" of the field, or more complete than that in libraries. You may also be able to find multimedia resources, such as a site that shows real-time pictures from an orbiting satellite. Because websites are linked to other sites, you may be led through links to information that you wouldn't have found in a library search. The chief appeal of Internet research is the amount of readily available information.

On the other hand, Internet searching can lead to many dead ends, and you can spend a lot of time reading irrelevant or unusable information. Many people get so wrapped up in all the interesting information they find that they have trouble focusing on their research task. Finally, if you don't have easy access to an Internet-linked computer, Web research can mean more inconvenience than library research.

Evaluating Sources

The source material you find in books and periodicals and on the Internet will be of varying quality and usefulness. You need to read the sources critically and evaluate them carefully for their relevance to your purpose, their currentness, their credibility, their biases, and their accuracy.

Evaluating the Relevance of Sources to Your Purpose

Some sources may be authoritative and interesting, but they may not be relevant to the point you are trying to prove. For example, if you are writing a paper about the relative merits of various treatments for eating disorders, an article that explains how eating disorders affect the patients' siblings will probably not be an appropriate source, even if it is interesting, informative, and authoritative. You need to evaluate each source to determine whether it is useful for fulfilling your paper's purpose.

Evaluating the Timeliness of Sources

Most research writing requires that you include the most up-to-date material on your topic. If you are discussing savings rates in the United States, your statistics must be as recent as possible. If you are exploring a scientific topic, research from more than a year or two ago is probably out-of-date, especially in rapidly changing fields such as genetic research. Older research may be included in your paper, as long as the latest material is also provided. Finding out the age of material is usually as easy as looking at the publication dates of books and periodicals. The currentness of information found on websites is sometimes harder to discover, though often websites contain the most up-to-date information.

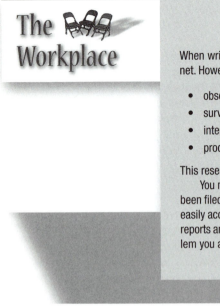

RESEARCH ON THE JOB

When writing reports on the job, you may use source material from libraries or from the Internet. However, you may need to do more of your own research by gathering information through:

- observation of employees, facilities, or procedures
- surveys
- interviews
- product trials or experiments with equipment

This research should be done carefully to avoid inaccuracies or inadvertent biases.

You may also research primary documents such as letters, memos, and reports which have been filed throughout the years. Sometimes these records are cataloged and stored, so they are easily accessible in the company archives. Sometimes you may have to track down the relevant reports and correspondence by contacting people and departments involved in the issue or problem you are investigating.

Look for references within the text. Most reputable sites also list the date the site was last updated, which can give you some idea about the currentness of the information it contains.

Evaluating Sources' Credibility

You want your research to come from credible sources. If the information comes from an expert in the field, a reputable research institution, or a respected publishing body, it is considered credible. You determine the reputations of authors or publications by the way they are regarded by others in the field. For example, if you find that *The New England Journal of Medicine* is cited with respect in many authoritative sources, you can assume that it is reputable. On the other hand, material published by an organization that is never cited in any reputable articles is probably suspect. Juried publications are the most respected and reliable.

Information in print sources such as books and periodicals is referred to as "juried." A juried publication is one that has been reviewed and selected for publication by professional editors or by experts in the field. A juried publication may still, of course, be flawed. Its author may have been biased, the data may be dated, or the conclusions erroneous. Still, some system of safeguards governed its original publication. That is why material printed by reputable publishers of books and periodicals is considered credible.

Publications on the Internet, however, are not usually juried: Anyone can post anything. While this freedom allows for the dissemination of a wealth of information and opinions, it also allows for the dissemination of information that is biased, incomplete, and inaccurate. The document you discover on the Internet may have been written by a world-renowned scholar; however, it may have been written by an uninformed amateur using inaccurate data and drawing unsupported conclusions. Internet documents may even be spurious; for example, in the late spring in

1998, a commencement address by Kurt Vonnegut, posted on the Internet, was widely quoted—until Vonnegut denied having given the address. The speech attributed to him had been a hoax.

In evaluating the credibility of Internet documents, the first step is to discover and evaluate the document's author. If the author is identified, look for biographical data, such as academic affiliations or other publications, within the document. Headers or footers may reveal whether the document is associated with a university or is part of an established scholarly association. You can gain additional information by searching for the author's name on the Web or using an e-mail address, if one is provided, to contact the author directly.

Evaluating Sources for Bias

To evaluate the fairness of print and Internet sources, begin by reading the contents critically. If the author does not back up assertions with adequate evidence, then you should be skeptical about the value of the source. You should be equally skeptical if the tone of the document seems either unreasonably pessimistic or enthusiastic. Reliable authors acknowledge alternative views and strive to represent other sources and opinions fairly. If the author of your source seems biased against other viewpoints, then perhaps his approach to his own material is equally biased.

When evaluating an Internet source for possible bias, you should consider the website's origin. A website sponsored by a political party, social or political action group, religious group, or corporation will be presenting information and opinions that reflect their political, social, religious, or corporate stance. Although you may choose to use these sources in your research, you should be aware of their possible bias and acknowledge in your writing that the source is an advocate for a specific viewpoint or product.

Evaluating Sources for Accuracy

Reliable authors, whether their publications are in print or online, will state the source of their information. When using Internet documents, check hyperlinks and look for additional sites to validate the content of a source. If you are unsure about the accuracy of some of the data, you should consult more print and electronic sources to confirm the information.

FYI: For more on evaluating sources for credibility, bias, and accuracy, see the "Reading Critically" section on pp. 54-56 in Chapter 2.

 Activity: **WORKING TOGETHER**

Choose one of the following topics and find two Internet sources and three print sources—a book, an article, and one reference work—with information on the topic.

1. wind-powered energy
2. fiction by Latino writers
3. Jungian psychology
4. particle accelerators
5. community-based policing

For valuable tips on evaluating Internet information, try these websites:

1. Alastair Smith, "Evaluation of Internet Sources":
☞   http://www.vuw.ac.nz/~agsmith/evaln/evaln.htm

2. Alexander, Janet, and Marsha Tate, "Evaluating Web Resources":
☞   http://www2.widener.edu/wolfgram-Memorial-Library/webeval.htm

3. Kirk, Elizabeth, "Evaluating Information Found on the Internet":
☞   http://milton.mse.jhu.edu:8001/research/education/net.html

Taking Research Notes

When you gather information from your own head, you jot down your ideas by freewriting, brainstorming, outlining, or mapping. By recording your ideas, you can more easily organize them into a coherent paper. When you gather information from written sources, you also need to record your findings so that you can organize them coherently, but there are three other important reasons that notetaking for a research paper is extremely important. First of all, the information from outside sources must be carefully recorded in notes because it is not always possible to carry around the books or periodicals. If a book you are using for research is recalled to the library, or if a periodical cannot be removed from the library, you must have a complete record of the source's relevant information if you are going to use it in your paper. Secondly, when you do research on a large scale, your written sources will yield many important pieces of information. It will be impossible to sort through all of this information to find what you need when you need it unless you have developed an efficient notetaking system. Thirdly, and most importantly, when you write a research paper using print or electronic sources, you must give credit to the people who wrote those books, periodicals, and documents. You will not be able to give proper credit unless you have taken careful notes about what information came from which source.

Note Cards, Notebooks, and Computer Files

Researchers take notes in a variety of ways. Some people make copies of periodical articles and highlight useful information. This technique will work if the scope of your research is very limited. Otherwise, finding the material you need to write your draft will mean flipping through pages and pages of articles each time you want to include some relevant research. For longer research-writing projects, you need a system that lets you group related information from various sources together easily, so that when you draft your paper, all the relevant information will be readily available. You can set up a notetaking system using notebooks, computer files, or index cards. Most people doing large research projects take notes on index cards because they are efficient, flexible, and portable. However, in today's technological age, people with portable computers may prefer to put notes directly into computer files to save themselves a lot of copying of material.

If you use an index card system, each card contains only ONE piece of information—one quote, one statistic, one anecdote, one opinion or judgment by an expert, one fact. Each card also contains the author's last name, the page number from which the information was taken, and a heading which identifies the note's topic or how the note might be used in the paper. This is all you need to find the source information quickly when you are writing the paper and to give credit to the author in your paper. An example of a note card is shown below:

Fear of death as cause of war

Kübler-Ross 13

"Groups of people from street gangs to nations may use their group identity to express their fear of being destroyed by attacking and destroying others. Is war perhaps nothing else but a need to face death, to conquer and master it, to come out of it alive—a peculiar form of denial of our own mortality?"

Along with the note cards, you will need to create bibliography cards, one for each book, article, or document that you use for research. The bibliography card contains the author's name, title of the book or article, and publication information. For books, list the place of publication, publisher, and date of publication. For articles, list the title of the periodical, volume and/or date of the issue, and page numbers. When you use Internet sources, record the author, document title, date of publication or last revision, address of the website and URL (full path to locate the source), and the date you accessed the source. To be able to retrieve the source efficiently, you should bookmark each source you access. Because Internet sources change frequently, you should also print copies of the sources you might use in your paper. You will need this information later when you give credit to your sources. Below is an example of the bibliography card corresponding to the note card illustrated earlier:

Kübler-Ross, Elisabeth. *On Death and Dying.*
   New York: Macmillan, 1969.

If you use a notebook or computer file to take notes, your first step is to establish certain categories of information. For example, if you are writing a paper about the use of drugs throughout history, one section of your notes would contain references to drug use in ancient times, one to drug use in the Middle Ages, and so on. Just as in note cards, each piece of information from a source must be clearly identified so that you know where the material came from. You will also need to create bibliography entries, just as if you had bibliography cards.

You can set up a similar system using computer files. When you use computer files, you will be able to transfer URLs directly to your bibliography, thereby eliminating copying errors.

Quoting, Paraphrasing, and Summarizing

When you find a useful piece of information in a book or article, you will want to put it on a note card for later use in your paper. When transferring information from the source to your notecard, you have three choices: You can quote the information, paraphrase it, or summarize it. You usually choose to quote when

- the exact wording is important for the reader's understanding of the idea
- the author's wording is particularly moving or striking
- the exact wording reflects the author's attitude or personality

When you take a quote from a source, you must copy the phrase, sentence, or paragraph **exactly** as it is in the original, including all punctuation and capitalization. You must also put quotation marks at the beginning and end of the quoted material.

If you omit any words or phrases from a quotation, indicate the omission by using ellipsis marks, three spaced periods. If the ellipsis is at the end of a sentence, they follow a period. Use brackets to indicate where you have inserted an explanatory word into a quotation or have changed a word in the quotation. Look at the following example: "[The Jinghpaws] would no doubt consider it trivial that an aged American male bothers to make a distinction between his grandson and his grandnephew. . . ." The ellipsis marks indicate that an unnecessary phrase has been omitted from the original text, and the brackets indicate that the writer, to clarify the meaning of the sentence, has substituted "The Jinghpaws" for the "They" which appeared in the original.

If there is no reason to preserve the exact wording, take your note as a paraphrase of the original text. When you paraphrase, you put the author's idea, conclusion, finding, or judgment into your own words. Make sure that your wording is not similar to the author's, but that the ideas you convey are essentially the same.

A summary is similar to a paraphrase in that you are putting information from the source into your own words, but in a summary you will be "boiling down" a long passage to its most important points. Summaries and paraphrases are the most efficient ways to transfer information from sources onto your note cards and ultimately into your paper.

To clarify the uses of quotes, paraphrases, and summaries, we will look at some notes that could have been taken from the following passage from Peter Farb's book *Word Play*, which contains information that might be useful in a paper about the connection between culture and language:

> Speakers of Jinghpaw, a language of northern Burma, are interested in making much different distinctions about relatives than speakers of English make. The Jinghpaw language offers eighteen basic terms for kin, not one of which can be translated into an equivalent English word. For example, the Jinghpaw word **nu** refers not only to the person called **moth-**

er in English but also to any female relative, such as a maternal aunt, who belongs to the mother's family and is in her approximate age group. **Hpu** can be one's older brother and also the older son of the father's brother; **nau** might be a younger brother, a sister, or even a child of the father's brother. English often seems preoccupied with giving labels to differences between the sexes and to generational-genealogical relationships, but Jinghpaw kinship is concerned with the social order. Jinghpaw's vocabulary emphasizes who belongs to the family unit, who has an obligation to help whom, who can marry. The Jinghpaw system seems very strange to speakers of English, but of course to the Jinghpaws it functions very well in their kind of culture. They would no doubt consider it trivial that an aged American male bothers to make a distinction between his grandson and his grandnephew, since both of them would be equally obliged to help the old man.

It would be appropriate to quote sentences from this passage if they revealed the author's attitudes or personality, as in the following example: "The Jinghpaw system seems very strange to speakers of English, but of course to the Jinghpaws it functions very well in their kind of culture." By using words like "very strange" and "very well in their kind of culture," the author reveals a certain attitude or opinion that you might want to capture by quoting.

However, if you just wanted to use his ideas without conveying the tone of the passage, you might paraphrase an idea, as in the following example:

> Peter Farb explains that in the Jinghpaw language, the word for "mother" would also be used for any female relative who was in the mother's family and about the mother's age.

This paraphrase communicates the same idea and is about the same length as the original.

In the same way, if you wanted to summarize the passage, conveying Farb's main ideas in your own words, you might write something like this:

> Farb uses examples from the Jinghpaw language to show that relatives are labeled according to a completely different system than that used by English-speakers. Because the Jinghpaw are more concerned with who is obligated to whom than who is in which generation or family line (as English speakers are) they group relatives differently. For example, a Jinghpaw speaker makes no distinction between a maternal aunt and a mother (both are called **nu**) because the obligation to both women is the same.

This summary has communicated Farb's basic points, but is shorter and is in the writer's own words.

If your paraphrase or summary does not use your own words, but instead borrows heavily from the source's vocabulary or sentence structure, you will be plagiarizing. It is not sufficient to substitute a few synonyms in a sentence and claim that you have paraphrased the ideas. You must be communicating the idea without imitating the author's prose. Look at the following examples of plagiarized sentences:

1. English often appears to be obsessed with labeling gender differences and generational-genealogical associations, but Jinghpaw's family relations emphasize the social hierarchy.
2. Jinghpaws would probably consider it trivial that an elderly American man makes a distinction between his grandson and his grandnephew, because they both would be required to aid the older man.

Notice that the writer has changed some words, but the sentence structure is essentially the same. Also key words like "trivial," which convey the author's tone and style, have been used. This transference of the source's language and style is considered plagiarism.

Activity: WORKING TOGETHER

Read the first four paragraphs of "Consider the Sources" on the following pages and practice taking notes in the forms of quotes, paraphrases, and summaries. Write one note card with a quote, one with a paraphrase, and one with a summary.

READING AND WRITING TEXTS

Activity: PREREADING

In small groups, discuss the following questions:
- In what ways are you biased as a reader or writer?
- What factors in writers' lives create biases in their writing?

Readings

In Chapter 4 you read an excerpt from Deborah Crossen's book *Tainted Truth* in which Crossen reveals how surveys can be biased, thereby leading to inaccurate conclusions. This chapter contains three readings on ways in which the information we receive may be biased. As you read them, consider the choices and the biases that may affect the information you receive. For instance, how did your local television station decide what story to air first on this evening's news? What biases by the authors of this text may have influenced their selection of this chapter's topic or of the specific readings? What biases affect your choices of writing and reading topics, your perceptions, or your interpretation of information?

"Consider the Sources"

Martin A. Lee and Norman Solomon

"Consider the Sources," from Martin A. Lee and Norman Solomon's book Unreliable Sources: A Guide to Detecting Bias in News Media, *gives an overview of the process by which reporters create stories and reveals some factors that contribute to the stale, repetitive nature of much reporting.*

"The news" usually comes to us as a finished product—smooth and tidy, neatly fitting within printed pages, a TV program or a radio slot. We're likely to assume that well-reasoned logic determines what we will see and hear. And it's true that a lot of professional criteria are at work in selecting what to report as news. Every journalist, facing blank paper or an empty computer screen, constantly makes choices about what to put in and what to leave out. We might wonder why the results tend to be so homogenized.

After all is said and done, the world according to American mass media is carefully screened for our eyes and ears. Spanning the globe with far-flung news gatherers, our country's most pervasive media nevertheless manage to be remarkably insular. Clichés, timeworn or instant, spin like wildfire through the crackly timber of the nation's press. As *Los Angeles Times* journalist David Shaw admitted, "A reporter sitting in his office or in a hotel room can watch Cable News Network and, simultaneously, call up on his computer screen several wire service reports of an event, even as he sits writing his own version. The tendency to conformity can be all but irresistible." Shaw added: "There are far fewer *enfants terribles* than *enfants timids* in the contemporary press corps," working in an environment that has become "both more corporate and more conformist."

Aspiring journalists get started by imitating established journalists, and most of the careers that follow consist largely of echoing others in the profession. The criteria that determined yesterday's coverage are being used to put together today's news, in a self-referencing—and self-perpetuating—process. A newsroom ritual is to spread out a set of clippings from "the morgue"—a collection of past articles on the subject. These days the files may be computerized, but the meaning is the same: Journalists draw heavily on previous stories by reporters who, in turn, probably relied on still earlier stories . . .

All too often, the media circle is unbroken. Facts pass into circulation swiftly—but so do inaccuracies, distortions, skewed frames of reference, and outright lies. Once published or broadcast, they are much more likely to be repeated than corrected.

Erroneous data may be the least of our worries. Many reporters keep their facts straight with admirable regularity. But piled-up facts do not ensure insight: a key omission can make an entire story misleading.

A phone book, or a list of yesterday's stock market closings, or a newspaper's front page might contain lots of factual information—but perhaps no significant truth.

Lacking direct contact with the events and people prominent on the evening news or in the daily papers, we depend on media to enable us to "experience" them. But the supervisors with authority to decide what goes over the Associated Press national wires tonight, or into *Time* magazine next week, are ordinarily far-removed from the scene of events. Firsthand observations by reporters may have little to do with the final copy. In New York suites, editors are slashing and rewriting stories filed from Moscow or Addis Ababa or Managua or Bonn. Reporters in the field are apt to take into account the proclivities of higher-ups back home.

In theory, objective journalism—unaffected by favoritism or prejudice—informs the public about relevant facts, so that citizens can make up their own minds about current issues. Yet value judgments infuse everything in the news media. Ben Bagdikian lays out some of the subjective choices that go into a daily newspaper: "Which of the infinite number of events in the environment will be assigned for coverage and which ignored? Which of the infinite observations confronting the reporter will be noted? Which of the facts noted will be included in the story? Which of the reported events will become the first paragraph? Which story will be prominently displayed on page 1 and which buried inside or discarded? None of these is a truly objective decision." Mass media not only report the news—they also literally *make* the news. Familiar types of coverage can come across as "objective" precisely because they're so ubiquitous, blending in with the customary media landscape.

Like any other human being, a reporter has personal biases, whether or not they affect media products. Many news-media professionals claim to perform impartially. Connie Chung went a step further when she spoke with an interviewer in June 1989, while upheaval raged in Beijing. "Because she feels so strongly about what's going on in China, Chung said she feels the desire to 'take sides' for the first time in her journalistic career. She said it would create a serious 'inner struggle' for her to cover the story objectively." Imagine covering thousands of news stories without ever having felt a desire to "take sides." Either such self-portrayals of internal neutrality are disingenuous, or requisite career pretenses have been creating genuine moral ciphers within the media industry.

Activity: RESPONDING TO THE TEXT

1. In "Consider the Sources," Lee and Solomon give reasons that news stories are so "homogenized." How do they explain the similarity of news stories? Can you think of any other reasons that reporters might all report the same event in similar ways?

2. Have you ever had the problem of having your opinion or view influenced by previous reporting or expert opinion?

From The Egg and the Sperm: How Science Has Constructed a Romance Based on Stereotypical Male-Female Roles

Emily Martin

In this reading, Emily Martin explores how, even in a relatively objective realm like science, cultural stereotypes about gender affect our perceptions of events and therefore our conclusions about them.

The theory of the human body is always a part of a world-picture. . . . The theory of the human body is always a part of a fantasy.
James Hillman. *The Myth of Analysis*[1]

As an anthropologist, I am intrigued by the possibility that culture shapes how biological scientists describe what they discover about the natural world. If this were so, we would be learning about more than the natural world in high school biology class: we would be learning about cultural beliefs and practices as if they were part of nature. In the course of my research I realized that the picture of egg and sperm drawn in popular as well as scientific accounts of reproductive biology relies on stereotypes central to our cultural definitions of male and female. The stereotypes imply not only that female biological processes are less worthy than their male counterparts but also that women are less worthy than men. Part of my goal in writing this article is to shine a bright light on the gender stereotypes hidden within the scientific language of biology. Exposed in such a light, I hope they will lose much of their power to harm us.

At a fundamental level, all major scientific textbooks depict male and female reproductive organs as systems for the production of valuable substances, such as eggs and sperm.[2] In the case of women, the monthly cycle is described as being designed to produce eggs and prepare a suitable place for them to be fertilized and grown—all to the end of making babies. But

[*]Portions of this article were presented as the 1987 Becker Lecture, Cornell University. I am grateful for the many suggestions and ideas I received on this occasion. For especially pertinent help with my arguments and data I thank Richard Cone, Kevin Whaley, Sharon Stephens, Barbara Duden, Susanne Kuechler, Lorna Rhodes, and Scott Gilbert. The article was strengthened and clarified by the comments of the anonymous *Signs* reviewers as well as the superb editorial skills of Amy Gage.
[1]James Hillman, *The Myth of Analysis* (Evanston, Ill.: Northwestern University Press, 1972), 220.
[2]Five textbooks I consulted are the main ones used in classes for undergraduate premedical students or medical students (or those held on reserve in the library for these classes) during the past few years at Johns Hopkins University. These texts are widely used at other universities in the country as well.

the enthusiasm ends there. By extolling the female cycle as a productive enterprise, menstruation must necessarily be viewed as a failure. Medical texts describe menstruation as the "debris" of the uterine lining, the result of necrosis, or death of tissue. The descriptions imply that a system has gone awry, making products of no use, not to specification, unsalable, wasted, scrap. An illustration in a widely used medical text shows menstruation as a chaotic disintegration of form, complementing the many texts that describe it as "ceasing," "dying," "losing," denuding," expelling."[3]

Male reproductive physiology is evaluated quite differently. One of the texts that sees menstruation as failed production employs a sort of breathless prose when it describes the maturation of sperm: "The mechanisms which guide the remarkable cellular transformation from spermatid to mature sperm remain uncertain. . . . Perhaps the most amazing characteristic of spermatogenesis is its sheer magnitude: the normal human male may manufacture several hundred million sperm per day."[4] In the classic text *Medical Physiology*, edited by Vernon Mountcastle, the male/female, productive/destructive comparison is more explicit: "Whereas the female *sheds* only a single gamete each month, the seminiferous tubules *produce* hundreds of millions of sperm each day" (emphasis mine).[5] The female author of another text marvels at the length of the microscopic seminiferous tubules, which, if uncoiled and placed end to end, "would span almost one-third of a mile!" She writes, "In an adult male these structures produce millions of sperm cells each day." Later she asks, "How is this feat accomplished?"[6] None of these texts expresses such intense enthusiasm for any female processes. It is surely no accident that the "remarkable" process of making sperm involves precisely what, in the medical view, menstruation does not: production of something deemed valuable.[7]

One could argue that menstruation and spermatogenesis are not analogous processes and, therefore, should not be expected to elicit the same kind of response. The proper female analogy to spermatogenesis, biologically, is ovulation. Yet ovulation does not merit enthusiasm in these texts either. Textbook descriptions stress that all of the ovarian follicles containing ova are already present at birth. Far from being *produced*, as sperm are, they merely sit on the shelf, slowly degenerating and aging like overstocked inventory: "At birth, normal human ovaries contain an estimated one million follicles [each], and no new ones appear after birth. Thus, in marked contrast to the male, the newborn female already has all the germ cells she will ever have. Only a few, perhaps 400, are des-

---

[3]Arthur C. Guyton, *Physiology of the Human Body*, 6th ed. (Philadelphia: Saunders College Publishing, 1984), 624.

[4]Arthur J. Vander, James H. Sherman, and Dorothy S. Luciano, *Human Physiology: The Mechanisms of Body Function,* 3d ed. (New York: McGraw Hill, 1980, 483–84.

[5]Vernon B. Mountcastle, *Medical Physiology*, 14th ed. (London: Mosby, 1980), 2:1624.

[6]Eldra Pearl Solomon, *Human Anatomy and Physiology* (New York: CBS College Publishing, 1983), 678.

[7]For elaboration, see Emily Martin, *The Woman in the Body: A Cultural Analysis of Reproduction* (Boston: Beacon, 1987), 27–53.

tined to reach full maturity during her active productive life. All the others degenerate at some point in their development so that few, if any, remain by the time she reaches menopause at approximately 50 years of age."[8] Note the "marked contrast" that this description sets up between male and female: the male, who continuously produces fresh germ cells, and the female, who has stockpiled germ cells by birth and is faced with their degeneration.

Nor are the female organs spared such vivid descriptions. One scientist writes in a newspaper article that a woman's ovaries become old and worn out from ripening eggs every month, even though the woman herself is still relatively young: "When you look through a laparoscope . . . at an ovary that has been through hundreds of cycles, even in a superbly healthy American female, you see a scarred, battered organ."[9]

To avoid the negative connotations that some people associate with the female reproductive system, scientists could begin to describe male and female processes as homologous. They might credit females with "producing" mature ova one at a time, as they're needed each month, and describe males as having to face problems of degenerating germ cells. This degeneration would occur throughout life among spermatogonia, the undifferentiated germ cells in the testes that are the long-lived, dormant precursors of sperm.

But the texts have an almost dogged insistence on casting female processes in a negative light. The texts celebrate sperm production because it is continuous from puberty to senescence, while they portray egg production as inferior because it is finished at birth. This makes the female seem unproductive, but some texts will also insist that it is she who is wasteful.[10] In a section heading for *Molecular Biology of the Cell,* a best-selling text, we are told that "Oogenesis is wasteful." The text goes on to emphasize that of the seven million oogonia, or egg germ cells, in the female embryo, most degenerate in the ovary. Of those that do go on to become oocytes, or eggs, many also degenerate, so that at birth only two million eggs remain in the ovaries. Degeneration continues throughout a woman's life: by puberty 300,000 eggs remain, and only a few are present by menopause. "During the 40 or so years of a woman's reproductive life, only 400 to 500 eggs will

---

[8]Vander, Sherman, and Luciano, 568.

[9]Melvin Konner, "Childbearing and Age," *New York Times Magazine* (December 27, 1987), 22–23, esp. 22.

[10]I have found but one exception to the opinion that the female is wasteful: "Smallpox being the nasty disease it is, one might expect nature to have designed antibody molecules with combining sites that specifically recognize the epitopes on smallpox virus. Nature differs from technology, however: it thinks nothing of wastefulness. (For example, rather than improving the chance that a spermatozoon will meet an egg cell, nature finds it easier to produce millions of spermatozoa.)" (Niels Kaj Jerne, "The Immune System," *Scientific American* 229, no. 1 [July 1973]: 53). Thanks to a *Signs* reviewer for bringing this reference to my attention.

have been released," the authors write. "All the rest will have degenerated. It is still a mystery why so many eggs are formed only to die in the ovaries."[11]

The real mystery is why the male's vast production of sperm is not seen as wasteful.[12] Assuming that a man "produces" 100 million (10^8) sperm per day (a conservative estimate) during an average reproductive life of sixty years, he would produce well over two trillion sperm in his lifetime. Assuming that a woman "ripens" one egg per lunar month, or thirteen per year, over the course of her forty-year reproductive life, she would total five hundred eggs in her lifetime. But the word "waste" implies an excess, too much produced. Assuming two or three offspring, for every baby a woman produces, she wastes only around two hundred eggs. For every baby a man produces, he wastes more than one trillion (10^{12}) sperm.

How is it the positive images are denied to the bodies of women? A look at language—in this case, scientific language—provides the first clue. Take the egg and the sperm.[13] It is remarkable how "femininely" the egg behaves and how "masculinely" the sperm.[14] The egg is seen as large and passive.[15] It does not *move* or *journey*, but passively "is transported," "is swept,"[16] or

---

[11]Bruce Alberts et al., *Molecular Biology of the Cell* (New York: Garland, 1983), 795.

[12]In her essay "Have Only Men Evolved?" (in *Discovering Reality: Feminist Perspectives on Epistemology, Metaphysics, Methodology, and Philosophy of Science*, ed. Sandra Harding and Merrill B. Hintikka [Dordrecht, The Netherlands: Reidel, 1983], 45–69, esp. 60–61), Ruth Hubbard points out that sociobiologists have said the female invests more energy than the male in the production of her large gametes, claiming that this explains why the female provides parental care. Hubbard questions whether it "really takes more 'energy' to generate the one or relatively few eggs than the large excess of sperms required to achieve fertilization." For further critique of how the greater size of eggs is interpreted in sociobiology, see Donna Haraway, "Investment Strategies for the Evolving Portfolio of Primate Females," in *Body/Politics*, ed. Mary Jacobus, Evelyn Fox Keller, and Sally Shuttleworth (New York: Routledge, 1990), 155–56.

[13]The sources I used for this article provide compelling information on interactions among sperm. Lack of space prevents me from taking up this theme here, but the elements include competition, hierarchy, and sacrifice. For a newspaper report, see Malcolm W. Browne, "Some Thoughts on Self Sacrifice," *New York Times* (July 5, 1988), C6. For a literary rendition, see John Barth, "Night-Sea Journey," in his *Lost in the Funhouse* (Garden City, N.Y.: Doubleday, 1968), 3–13.

[14]See Carol Delaney, "The Meaning of Paternity and the Virgin Birth Debate," *Man* 21, no. 3 (September 1986): 494–513. She discusses the difference between this scientific view that women contribute genetic material to the fetus and the claim of long-standing Western folk theories that the origin and identity of the fetus comes from the male, as in the metaphor of planting a seed in soil.

[15]For a suggested direct link between human behavior and purportedly passive eggs and active sperm, see Erik H. Erikson, "Inner and Outer Space: Reflections on Womanhood," *Daedalus* 93, no. 2 (Spring 1964): 582–606, esp. 591.

[16]Guyton (n. 3), 619; and Mountcastle (n. 5), 1609.

even "drifts"[17] along the fallopian tube. In utter contrast, sperm are small, "streamlined,"[18] and invariably active. They "deliver" their genes to the egg, "activate the developmental program of the egg,"[19] and have a "velocity" that is often remarked upon.[20] Their tails are "strong" and efficiently powered.[21] Together with the forces of ejaculation, they can "propel the semen into the deepest recesses of the vagina."[22] For this they need "energy," "fuel,"[23] so that with a "whiplash-like motion and strong lurches"[24] they can "burrow through the egg coat"[25] and "penetrate" it.[26]

At its extreme, the age-old relationship of the egg and the sperm takes on a royal or religious patina. The egg coat, its protective barrier, is sometimes called its "vestments," a term usually reserved for sacred, religious dress. The egg is said to have a "corona,"[27] a crown, and to be accompanied by "attendant cells."[28] It is holy, set apart and above, the queen to the sperm's king. The egg is also passive, which means it must depend on sperm for rescue. Gerald Schatten and Helen Schatten liken the egg's role to that of Sleeping Beauty: "a dormant bride awaiting her mate's magic kiss, which instills the spirit that brings her to life."[29] Sperm, by contrast, have a "mission,"[30] which is to "move through the female genital tract in quest of the ovum."[31] One popular account has it that the sperm carry out a "perilous journey" into the "warm darkness," where some fall away "exhausted." "Survivors" "assault" the egg, the successful candidates "surrounding the prize."[32] Part of the urgency of this journey, in more scientific terms, is that "once released from the supportive environment of the ovary, an egg will die within hours unless rescued by a sperm."[33] The wording stresses the fragility and dependency of the egg, even though the same text acknowledges elsewhere that sperm also live for only a few hours.[34]

---

[17]Jonathan Miller and David Pelham, *The Facts of Life* (New York: Viking Penguin, 1984), 5.

[18]Alberts et al., 796.

[19]Ibid., 796.

[20]See, e.g., William F. Ganong, *Review of Medical Physiology*, 7th ed. (Los Altos, Calif.: Lange Medical Publications, 1975), 322.

[21]Alberts et al. (n. 11), 796.

[22]Guyton, 615.

[23]Solomon (n. 6), 683.

[24]Vander, Sherman, and Luciano (n. 4), 4th ed. (1985), 580.

[25]Alberts et al., 796.

[26]All biology texts quoted use the word "penetrate."

[27]Solomon, 700.

[28]A. Beldecos et al., "The Importance of Feminist Critique for Contemporary Cell Biology," *Hypatia* 3, no. 1 (Spring 1988): 61–76.

[29]Gerald Schatten and Helen Schatten, "The Energetic Egg," *Medical World News* 23 (January 23, 1984): 51–53, esp. 51.

[30]Alberts et al., 796.

[31]Guyton (n. 3), 613.

[32]Miller and Pelham (n. 17), 7.

[33]Alberts et al. (n. 11), 804.

[34]Ibid., 801.

In 1948, in a book remarkable for its early insights into these matters, Ruth Herschberger argued that female reproductive organs are seen as biologically interdependent, while male organs are viewed as autonomous, operating independently and in isolation:

> At present the functional is stressed only in connection with women: it is in them that ovaries, tubes, uterus, and vagina have endless interdependence. In the male, reproduction would seem to involve "organs" only.
>
> Yet the sperm, just as much as the egg, is dependent on a great many related processes. There are secretions which mitigate the urine in the urethra before ejaculation, to protect the sperm. There is the reflex shutting off of the bladder connection, the provision of prostatic secretions, and various types of muscular propulsion. The sperm is no more independent of its milieu than the egg, and yet from a wish that it were, biologists have lent their support to the notion that the human female, beginning with the egg, is congenitally more dependent than the male.[35]

Bringing out another aspect of the sperm's autonomy, an article in the journal *Cell* has the sperm making an "existential decision" to penetrate the egg: "Sperm are cells with a limited behavioral repertoire, one that is directed toward fertilizing eggs. To execute the decision to abandon the haploid state, sperm swim to an egg and there acquire the ability to effect membrane fusion."[36] Is this a corporate manager's version of the sperm's activities—"executing decisions" while fraught with dismay over difficult options that bring with them very high risk?

There is another way that sperm, despite their small size, can be made to loom in importance over the egg. In a collection of scientific papers, an electron micrograph of an enormous egg and tiny sperm is titled "A Portrait of the Sperm."[37] This is a little like showing a photo of a dog and calling it a picture of the fleas. Granted, microscopic sperm are harder to photograph than eggs, which are just large enough to see with the naked eye. But surely the use of the term "portrait," a word associated with the powerful and wealthy, is significant. Eggs have only micrographs or pictures, not portraits.

One depiction of sperm as weak and timid, instead of strong and powerful—the only such representation in western civilization, so far as I know—occurs in Woody Allen's movie *Everything You Always Wanted To Know About Sex* *But Were Afraid to Ask*. Allen, playing the part of an apprehensive sperm inside a man's testicles, is scared of the man's

---

[35]Ruth Herschberger, *Adam's Rib* (New York: Pelligrini & Cudaby, 1948), esp. 84. I am indebted to Ruth Hubbard for telling me about Herschberger's work, although at a point when this paper was already in draft form.

[36]Bennett M. Shapiro, "The Existential Decision of a Sperm," *Cell* 49, no. 3 (May 1987: 293–94, esp. 293.

[37]Lennart Nilsson, "A Portrait of the Sperm," in *The Functional Anatomy of the Spermatozoan*, ed. Bjorn A. Afzelius (New York: Pergamon, 1975), 79–82.

approaching orgasm. He is reluctant to launch himself into the darkness, afraid of contraceptive devices, afraid of winding up on the ceiling if the man masturbates.

The more common picture—egg as damsel in distress, shielded only by her sacred garments; sperm as heroic warrior to the rescue—cannot be proved to be dictated by the biology of these events. While the "facts" of biology may not *always* be constructed in cultural terms, I would argue that in this case they are. The degree of metaphorical content in these descriptions, the extent to which differences between egg and sperm are emphasized, and the parallels between cultural stereotypes of male and female behavior and the character of egg and sperm all point to this conclusion.

Activity: RESPONDING TO THE TEXT

1. What kind of evidence does Martin use in "The Egg and the Sperm"? Do you think she provides enough strong evidence to make her point convincing? If not, in what ways do you think her evidence is weak? In what ways is it strong?
2. What other biases besides gender stereotypes may affect scientists' views of their research?

The Historian and His Facts
Edward Hallet Carr

Historian Edward Hallet Carr discusses how a piece of information becomes "a historical fact" and how historians interpret facts to create "history."

What is history? Lest anyone think the question meaningless or superfluous, I will take as my text two passages relating respectively to the first and second incarnations of *The Cambridge Modern History*. Here is Acton in his report of October 1896 to the Syndics of the Cambridge University Press on the work which he had undertaken to edit.[1]

> It is a unique opportunity of recording, in the way most useful to the greatest number, the fullness of the knowledge which the nineteenth century is about to bequeath. . . . By the judicious

---

[1]John Dalberg Acton (1834–1902): British historian and editor of the first *Cambridge Modern History*. [Eds.]

division of labour we should be able to do it, and to bring home to every man the last document, and the ripest conclusions of international research.

Ultimate history we cannot have in this generation; but we can dispose of conventional history, and show the point we have reached on the road from one to the other, now that all information is within reach, and every problem has become capable of solution.[2]

And almost exactly sixty years later Professor Sir George Clark, in his general introduction to the second *Cambridge Modern History,* commented on this belief of Acton and his collaborators that it would one day be possible to produce "ultimate history," and went on:

Historians of a later generation do not look forward to any such prospect. They expect their work to be superseded again and again. They consider that knowledge of the past has come down through one or more human minds, has been "processed" by them, and therefore cannot consist of elemental and impersonal atoms which nothing can alter. . . . The exploration seems to be endless, and some impatient scholars take refuge in scepticism, or at least in the doctrine that, since all historical judgments involve persons and points of view, one is as good as another and there is no "objective" historical truth.[3]

Where the pundits contradict each other so flagrantly the field is open to enquiry. I hope that I am sufficiently up-to-date to recognize that anything written in the 1890's must be nonsense. But I am not yet advanced enough to be committed to the view that anything written in the 1950's necessarily makes sense. Indeed, it may already have occurred to you that this enquiry is liable to stray into something even broader than the nature of history. The clash between Acton and Sir George Clark is a reflection of the change in our total outlook on society over the interval between these two pronouncements. Acton speaks out of the positive belief, the clear-eyed self-confidence of the later Victorian age; Sir George Clark echoes the bewilderment and distracted scepticism of the beat generation. When we attempt to answer the question, What is history?, our answer, consciously or unconsciously, reflects our own position in time, and forms part of our answer to the broader question, what view we take of the society in which we live. I have no fear that my subject may, on closer inspection, seem trivial. I am afraid only that I may seem presumptuous to have broached a question so vast and so important.

The nineteenth century was a great age for facts. "What I want," said Mr. Gradgrind in *Hard Times,*[4] "is Facts. . . . Facts alone are wanted in life." Nineteenth-century historians on the whole agreed with him. When Ranke in

---

[2] *The Cambridge Modern History: Its Origin, Authorship and Production* (Cambridge University Press; 1907), pp. 10–12.

[3] *The New Cambridge Modern History,* I (Cambridge University Press; 1957), pp. xxiv–xxv.

[4] *Hard Times:* a novel by Charles Dickens. [Eds.]

the 1830s,[5] in legitimate protest against moralizing history, remarked that the task of the historian was "simply to show how it really was (*wie es eigentlich gewesen*)" this not very profound aphorism had an astonishing success. Three generations of German, British, and even French historians marched into battle intoning the magic words, "*Wie es eigentlich gewesen*" like an incantation—designed, like most incantations, to save them from the tiresome obligation to think for themselves. The Positivists, anxious to stake out their claim for history as a science, contributed the weight of their influence to this cult of facts. First ascertain the facts, said the positivists, then draw your conclusions from them. In Great Britain, this view of history fitted in perfectly with the empiricist tradition which was the dominant strain in British philosophy from Locke to Bertrand Russell.[6] The empirical theory of knowledge presupposes a complete separation between subject and object. Facts, like sense-impressions, impinge on the observer from outside, and are independent of his consciousness. The process of reception is passive: having received the data, he then acts on them. *The Shorter Oxford English Dictionary*, a useful but tendentious work of the empirical school, clearly marks the separateness of the two processes by defining a fact as "a datum of experience as distinct from conclusions." This is what may be called the common-sense view of history. History consists of a corpus of ascertained facts. The facts are available to the historian in documents, inscriptions, and so on, like fish on the fishmonger's slab. The historian collects them, takes them home, and cooks and serves them in whatever style appeals to him. Acton, whose culinary tastes were austere, wanted them served plain. In his letter of instructions to contributors to the first *Cambridge Modern History* he announced the requirement "that our Waterloo must be one that satisfies French and English, German and Dutch alike; that nobody can tell, without examining the list of authors, where the Bishop of Oxford laid down the pen, and whether Fairbairn or Gasquet, Liebermann or Harrison took it up."[7] Even Sir George Clark, critical as he was of Acton's attitude, himself contrasted the "hard core of facts" in history with the "surrounding pulp of disputable interpretation"[8]—forgetting perhaps that the pulpy part of the fruit is more rewarding than the hard core. First get your facts straight, then plunge at your peril into the shifting sands of interpretation—that is the ultimate wisdom of the empirical, common-sense school of history. It recalls the favorite dictum of the great liberal journalist C. P. Scott: "Facts are sacred, opinion is free."

Now this clearly will not do. I shall not embark on a philosophical discussion of the nature of our knowledge of the past. Let us assume for present purposes that the fact that Caesar crossed the Rubicon and the fact that there is a table in the middle of the room are facts of the same or of a comparable order, that both these facts enter our consciousness in the same or in a comparable manner, and that both have the same objective character in relation to the

---

[5]Leopold von Ranke (1795–1886): German historian. [Eds.]
[6]John Locke (1632–1704): English philosopher; Bertrand Russell (1872–1970): English philosopher and mathematician. [Eds.]
[7]Acton: *Lectures on Modern History* (London: Macmillan & Co.; 1906), p. 318.
[8]Quoted in *The Listener* (June 19, 1952), p. 992.

person who knows them. But, even on this bold and not very plausible assumption, our argument at once runs into the difficulty that not all facts about the past are historical facts, or are treated as such by the historian. What is the criterion which distinguishes the facts of history from other facts about the past?

What is a historical fact? This is a crucial question into which we must look a little more closely. According to the common-sense view, there are certain basic facts which are the same for all historians and which form, so to speak, the backbone of history—the fact, for example, that the Battle of Hastings was fought in 1066. But this view calls for two observations. In the first place, it is not with facts like these that the historian is primarily concerned. It is no doubt important to know that the great battle was fought in 1066 and not in 1065 or 1067, and that it was fought at Hastings and not at Eastbourne or Brighton. The historian must not get these things wrong. But when points of this kind are raised, I am reminded of Housman's remark that "accuracy is a duty, not a virtue."[9] To praise a historian for his accuracy is like praising an architect for using well-seasoned timber or properly mixed concrete in his building. It is a necessary condition of his work, but not his essential function. It is precisely for matters of this kind that the historian is entitled to rely on what have been called the "auxiliary sciences" of history—archaeology, epigraphy, numismatics, chronology, and so forth. The historian is not required to have the special skills which enable the expert to determine the origin and period of a fragment of pottery or marble, to decipher an obscure inscription, or to make the elaborate astronomical calculations necessary to establish a precise date. These so-called basic facts which are the same for all historians commonly belong to the category of the raw materials of the historian rather than of history itself. The second observation is that the necessity to establish these basic facts rests not on any quality in the facts themselves, but on an *a priori* decision of the historian. In spite of C. P. Scott's motto, every journalist knows today that the most effective way to influence opinion is by the selection and arrangement of the appropriate facts. It used to be said that facts speak for themselves. This is, of course, untrue. The facts speak only when the historian calls on them: it is he who decides to which facts to give the floor, and in what order or context. It was, I think, one of Pirandello's characters who said that a fact is like a sack[10]—it won't stand up till you've put something in it. The only reason why we are interested to know that the battle was fought at Hastings in 1066 is that historians regard it as a major historical event. It is the historian who has decided for his own reasons that Caesar's crossing of that petty stream, the Rubicon, is a fact of history, whereas the crossing of the Rubicon by millions of other people before or since interests nobody at all. The fact that you arrived in this building half an hour ago on foot, or on a bicycle, or in a car, is just as much a fact about the past as the fact that Caesar crossed the Rubicon. But it will probably be ignored by historians. Professor Talcott Parsons once called science "a

---

[9]M. Manilius: *Astronomicon: Liber Primus*, 2nd ed. (Cambridge University Press; 1937), p. 87. (A. E. Housman [1859–1936]: poet and classical scholar who edited Manilius. [Eds.])

[10]Luigi Pirandello (1867–1936): Italian playwright. [Eds.]

selective system of cognitive orientations to reality."[11] It might perhaps have been put more simply. But history is, among other things, that. The historian is necessarily selective. The belief in a hard core of historical facts existing objectively and independently of the interpretation of the historian is a preposterous fallacy, but one which it is very hard to eradicate.

Let us take a look at the process by which a mere fact about the past is transformed into a fact of history. At Stalybridge Wakes in 1850, a vendor of gingerbread, as the result of some petty dispute, was deliberately kicked to death by an angry mob. Is this a fact of history? A year ago I should unhesitatingly have said "no." It was recorded by an eyewitness in some little-known memoirs;[12] but I had never seen it judged worthy of mention by any historian. A year ago Dr. Kitson Clark cited it in his Ford lectures in Oxford.[13] Does this make it into a historical fact? Not, I think, yet. Its present status, I suggest, is that it has been proposed for membership of the select club of historical facts. It now awaits a seconder and sponsors. It may be that in the course of the next few years we shall see this fact appearing first in footnotes, then in the text, of articles and books about nineteenth-century England, and that in twenty or thirty years' time it may be a well established historical fact. Alternatively, nobody may take it up, in which case it will relapse into the limbo of unhistorical facts about the past from which Dr. Kitson Clark has gallantly attempted to rescue it. What will decide which of these two things will happen? It will depend, I think, on whether the thesis or interpretation in support of which Dr. Kitson Clark cited this incident is accepted by other historians as valid and significant. Its status as a historical fact will turn on a question of interpretation. This element of interpretation enters into every fact of history.

May I be allowed a personal reminiscence? When I studied ancient history in this university many years ago, I had as a special subject "Greece in the period of the Persian Wars." I collected fifteen or twenty volumes on my shelves and took it for granted that there, recorded in these volumes, I had all the facts relating to my subject. Let us assume—it was very nearly true—that those volumes contained all the facts about it that were then known, or could be known. It never occurred to me to enquire by what accident or process of attrition that minute selection of facts, out of all the myriad facts that must have once been known to somebody, had survived to become *the* facts of history. I suspect that even today one of the fascinations of ancient and mediaeval history is that it gives us the illusion of having all the facts at our disposal within a manageable compass: the nagging distinction between the facts of history and other facts about the past vanishes because the few known facts are all facts of history. As Bury, who had worked in both periods, said, "the records of ancient and mediaeval history are starred with

---

[11]Talcott Parsons and Edward A. Shils: *Toward a General Theory of Action*, 3rd ed. (Cambridge, Mass.: Harvard University Press; 1954), p. 167.

[12]Lord George Sanger: *Seventy Years a Showman* (London: J. M. Dent & Sons; 1962), pp. 188–9.

[13]These will shortly be published under the title *The Making of Victorian England*.

DOCUMENTATION

P R E V I E W

This chapter's explanation of MLA and APA documentation styles will answer the following questions:

- What information needs to be documented?
- What is required for proper documentation?
- How do MLA and APA styles differ?

LEARNING ABOUT TEXTS

When you document information, you are letting the readers of your paper know that the information is the work of someone else; it is not based on your own research or study, nor is it your opinion or conclusion. Documentation serves two functions: It gives credit to the person whose time, energy, money, and/or reputation led to the creation of the idea or data, and it lets your readers identify the source of a quotation, paraphrase, or summary so that they can find the information for themselves and evaluate its importance.

When to Document Sources

If you do not document sources accurately and completely, your readers may assume you are taking credit for others' information and ideas. Incorrect or inadequate documentation is considered a form of plagiarism—a serious type of academic dishonesty—so it's important to know when to document sources.

You must document the following kinds of source material: 1) direct quotations; 2) paraphrases or summaries of information, research results, statistics, opinions, judgments, insights, or examples; and 3) illustrations, graphs, tables, or charts borrowed from a source.

You do not need to document information that is "common knowledge." Something is common knowledge if 1) you would expect most educated readers to know it, 2) it appears as standard information in several sources, or 3) it is a widely known fact generally accepted by those who are knowledgeable in the field. Remember that a piece of information may be common knowledge even if **you** did not know it before doing your research, as long as it is a commonly known fact. Look at the following examples:

1. The Chesapeake Bay is the largest and longest in the United States.
2. The poet John Gower was a contemporary of Chaucer.
3. Charles Darwin developed his theory of natural selection based on variations he observed in the plants and animals he encountered on his journey along the South American coast aboard the *Beagle*.

Although you may not have known these facts, they are commonly known by people who are familiar with these areas of study, so they need not be documented.

Documentation Styles

Various professional organizations have set standards for how documentation should be done in their particular fields. In the humanities, the Modern Language Association, or MLA, documentation style is used; in the social sciences, the American Psychological Association, or APA, style is used. Various styles are used in the different science and technical fields. Every style has the same basic features and purpose. They all provide the reader with enough information about the source so that it can be located in a bookstore or library and so its currentness and quality can be determined. This means that the styles all provide readers with the author's name, the work's title, and publication information. Because you will use either the MLA or APA style of documentation in most college classes, both are explained below.

MLA Documentation

MLA documentation has two parts: One part, called the parenthetical reference or in-text citation, is embedded in the text of the paper immediately following the quotation, paraphrase, or summary; the second part, called the works-cited page, is included at the end of the research paper or report.

Parenthetical Reference

The purpose of parenthetical reference is to provide a clear link between the reference to an outside source and a work in the list of works cited. When the outside source is a print document, the information, whether a quote, paraphrase, or summary, is followed by parentheses containing the author's last name and the page number from which the information was taken. For example,

> One definition of **utility** is "the pleasure or satisfaction obtained from a good or service" (Schiller 448).

Because Internet sources rarely include page numbers, the parenthetical reference often includes only the author's name. If the Internet source includes internal divisions (such as chapters, parts headings, sections) include that information after the author's name.

> The main difference between this journal [*Kairos*] (with frames) and other journals, both printed and online, is that you can simultaneously view information cited in the article you are reading or information that you have found on the web yourself, while still keeping the original article on screen. (Teague, "What you See . . .")

If the author's last name has been identified in the material leading up to the quotation, paraphrase, or summary, the parentheses will only contain the page number. For example,

> Noonan concludes that the modern Catholic Church's regulations regarding birth control were shaped by changes in society and in theological perspectives (476).

If you are using more than one work by the same author in your paper, the parentheses will contain the author's name, an abbreviation of the title of the work from which this quotation, paraphrase, or summary was taken, and the page number. For example,

> When we ask as to the future of the modern Metropolis, we are asking about the future of the modern industrial society . . . (Galbraith, *Age* 318).

Notice that in most quotations and paraphrases, the terminal sentence punctuation (a period, exclamation point, or question mark) appears after the parentheses. The only exception to this rule is when you use the block format for quotations that are more than four lines long; such quotations are set off from the text by a ten-space indention as is illustrated below:

> Throughout the seventeenth century a girl might well have been forced into a marriage against her will, by parental pressure, or even by outright violence from a stranger, and have found herself thereby robbed of her freedom and her money. (Fraser 12)

In that case, notice that the sentence punctuation is followed by two spaces and then, finally, the parentheses.

This basic format for parenthetical references will change in some special circumstances, which are listed below:

Works by more than one author
Edmond Halley was instrumental in improving the work and stature of the Royal Society (Sagan and Druyan 49).

Works without a listed author—A shortened version of the title is used instead of the author's name.

Newsweek reported that the Russians had delivered missiles to Cuba ("Cuba's").

Works that are only one page long—In these cases, the page number is omitted as in the example above.

Indirect sources
Aaron Copland said that film composers can only "make potent through music the film's dramatic and emotional value" (qtd. in Prendergast 201). "Qtd." stands for "quoted." Prendergast is the author of the source in which the quote appeared, so a citation for his book will appear in "Works Cited."

Works-Cited Page

The last page of your paper or report will contain an alphabetically arranged list of the sources cited in the paper. The heading of this page will be "Works Cited." There will be an entry (called a citation) for each source. On the "Works Cited" page, each entry's first line is placed against the margin and succeeding lines are indented five spaces. All the entries are double-spaced. The following examples show a typical citation and some formats for special cases:

Entries for books

In entries for books, you will include the following elements in this order:

1) Author's name, last name first, followed by a period and two spaces
2) Title, which is underlined or in italics, followed by a period and two spaces
3) City of publication, followed by a colon
4) Shortened name of the publisher, followed by a comma
5) Year of publication, followed by a period

A book by one author

Montagu, Ashley. *Man Observed*. New York: Putnam, 1968.

A book by two or three authors—Put the second and third authors' names in normal order.

McMahon, Thomas A., and John Tyler Bonner. *On Size and Life*. New York: Scientific American, 1983.

A book by more than three authors—Use the first author's name followed by et al.

Belenky, Mary Field, et al. *Women's Ways of Knowing*. New York: Basic Books, 1986.

An edited book or a translation—List the author's name first with the editor's or translator's name following the title.

James, Henry. *The American*. Ed. James Tuttleton. New York: Norton, 1978.

García Marquez, Gabriel. *Love in the Time of Cholera*. Trans. Edith Grossman. New York: Penguin, 1988.

An essay or short story appearing in an anthology

Calisher, Hortense. "Heartburn." *American Short Stories Since 1945*. Ed. John Hollander. New York: Harper, 1968. 73–84.

An unsigned article in an encyclopedia—If the encyclopedia is a standard work, do not list full publication information. If it is not a commonly used reference, add information about the publisher and city of publication.

"Teutonic Order." *Encyclopaedia Brittanica: Micropaedia*. 1986 ed.

A signed article in an encyclopedia

Rosenblum, Charles. "Isotope Tracers." *Collier's Encyclopedia*. 1987 ed.

A short story or poem in a collection

> O'Connor, Flannery. "A Good Man Is Hard to Find." *The Complete Stories*. New York: Farrar, 1986.

Entries for articles

In entries for articles, you will include the following information in this order:

1) Author's name, last name first, followed by a period and two spaces
2) Title of the article, enclosed within quotation marks, followed by a period and two spaces
3) Title of the magazine or journal, underlined or in italics
4) Volume number
5) Date of publication, enclosed within parentheses, followed by a colon
6) Inclusive pagination of the full article, followed by a period

Below are examples of entries for various types of periodicals.

An article in a scholarly journal with continuous pagination

> Silberman, Laurence H. "Toward Presidential Control of the State Department." *Foreign Affairs* 57 (1979): 872–893.

An article in a scholarly journal that has separate pagination—Include the volume number followed by a period and then the issue number.

> Tashiro, Charles Shiro. "Videophilia: What Happens When You Wait for It on Video." *Film Quarterly* 45.1 (1991): 7–17.

An article in a weekly or biweekly magazine—Delete the volume and issue number and use the complete date.

> Jenkins, Sally. "Glory and Gloom." *Sports Illustrated* 24 Feb. 1992: 18–19.

An unsigned article in a weekly or biweekly magazine

> "Bluesman Memphis Slim 1915–1988." *Rolling Stone* 5 May 1988: 22.

An article in a monthly or bimonthly magazine

> Morgan, James. "Adventures in the Food Chain." *The Atlantic* June 1992: 30–40.

An article in a daily newspaper—Include the edition and section number or letter.

> O'Brian, Bridget. "American Air Launches New Price Sortie." *Wall Street Journal* 21 Apr. 1992, western ed.: B1.

A review—List the reviewer's name first, followed by the title of the work reviewed.

> Goellnicht, Donald C. Rev. of *Romantic Medicine and John Keats,* by Hermione de Almeida. *Nineteenth-Century Literature* 46 (1992): 550–555.

Entries for nonprint sources

Sometimes you will take information from nonprint sources such as videos, interviews, lectures, or films. Examples of appropriate citations for these sources are listed below:

A lecture—Include the name of the lecturer, the title of the lecture, the location and date, and sponsoring organization. If the lecture did not have a title, supply one that describes the content accurately.

> Brinkman, Alexander R. "Computer-Graphic Tools for Music Analysis." International Computer Music Conference. McGill University, 16 Oct. 1991.

A personal interview

> Babbitt, Milton. Personal interview. 20 May 1998.
> Boxer, Ellen. Telephone interview. 8 Nov. 1999.

A film—Include the film's title, director, distributor, year of release, and any other important information.

> *Dr. Strangelove*. Dir. Stanley Kubrick. With Peter Sellers and George C. Scott. Based on the novel *Red Alert* by Peter George. Columbia Pictures, 1964.

A television or radio program—Include the title of the program, the network, local station, city, date of broadcast, and any other important information. If the program is part of a series, put the individual program's title in quotation marks and italicize the series' title.

> "The Art of Living/Touching the Timeless." *Millennium*. Narr. David Maybury-Lewis. PBS. KCET, Los Angeles 25 May 1992.

Entries for online sources

When you do research on the Internet, you will probably gather material from on-line books, government publications, electronic journals and magazines, and web-sites. You may also want to cite e-mail messages, personal home pages, listserv or newsgroup messages, as well as other electronic sources. Because these sources and their citation formats are evolving rapidly, determining the correct format is sometimes tricky. Refer to the MLA Handbook or website for more detailed information. Here are some examples of formats for the most commonly cited electronic sources.

Website—Include the following information in this order:
1) Author's name, if known
2) Title of the document in quotation marks
3) Title of the complete work, underlined or in italics (if applicable)
4) Date of publication or last revision (if available)
5) Name of institution or organization sponsoring the website (if applicable)
6) Date of access
7) URL (electronic address) in angle brackets.

> McGuire, Patrick A. "Wanted: Workers with Flexibility for 21st-Century Jobs." *The APA Monitor*. July 1998. American Psychological Association. 10 July 1998.
> <http://apa.org/monitor/jul98/factor.html>

Article in an electronic journal or magazine—Include the following information in this order:

1) Author's name
2) Title of the article in quotation marks
3) Title of the journal, in italics or underlined
4) Date of publication:
   - for a journal, the volume number followed by the year in parentheses
   - for a magazine, the date and year of the issue
5) Date of access
6) Name of the sponsoring institution or organization (if applicable)
7) URL (electronic address) in angle brackets.

> Kirschenbaum, Matthew. "Intellectual Property Online: The Case of Student Writing." *Kairos: A Journal for Teachers of Writing in Webbed Environments* 3.1 (1998). Texas Tech University 10 July 1998 <http://www.english.ttu.edu/kairos/3.1/index_f.html>.

Article or other work from a subscription service—If you access periodicals such as magazines, newspapers, and journals through a subscription service (e.g. Electronic library, Infotrac, ProQuest) at a library or other site, include the following information in this order.

1) Author's name
2) Title of the article in quotation marks
3) Title of the periodical, in italics or underlined
4) Publication information for any print version of the work
5) Name of the subscription service.
6) Name, city, and state abbreviation of the library where the service was accessed
7) Date of access
8) URL address in angle brackets.

> Barrett, William P. "Food-Label Follies." *Forbes* 27 Dec. 1999, 30. Infotrac. Mountain View Public Library, CA. 5 February 2000. <http://www.infotrac.galegroup.com>.

Home page—List the author, the term Home Page, the date of posting or last revision, the date of access, and the URL.

> Harrington, Josephine. Home Page. 16 Dec. 1997. 23 June 1998. <www.charles.cc.md.us>

E-mail message—List the author (if known), the e-mail address in angle brackets, the subject line in quotation marks, the type of e-mail (personal, office, distribution list), the date of publication, and the date of access.

> Smithson, Jonas. <jsmithson@juno.com> "Policy Revisions." Personal e-mail. 22 July 1988. 4 Aug. 1998.

Web discussion forum posting—The format is the same as for an e-mail message, except that you add the URL in angle brackets at the end of the citation.

Newsgroup or listserv message—The format is the same as for the e-mail message, except for two elements: 1) eliminate the type of communication, and 2) add the name of the newsgroup or listserv in angle brackets at the end of the citation.

Go For It!

For additional information on MLA documentation, contact the MLA website at
☞ <http://www.mla.org>

APA Documentation

Parenthetical References

Like MLA format, the APA documentation style uses parenthetical references within the text of the paper, then contains a list of sources at the end of the paper. However, in the APA format, the parenthetical reference includes the author's last name, followed by a comma, and the year the work was published instead of the author's last name and the page number. If the parenthetical reference follows a quote or paraphrase of a specific section of the source, the page number is added. The following examples will acquaint you with the format:

If the author and date are included in the citation, the sentence looks like this:

> A recent study (Ferguson, 1992) suggests that the savagery of indigenous North American tribes increased as a result of the invasion of their territory and culture by Europeans.

If the author's name is used in the text, only the year is included in the parentheses:

> Ferguson (1992) recently suggested that . . .

If the name and date are included in the text, no parenthetical reference is necessary:

> In his 1992 study, Ferguson suggested that . . .

If you are quoting from the source or paraphrasing a specific section, the parentheses includes the page number as illustrated below (notice that APA style uses a "p." before the number, unlike the MLA style):

> "Many, perhaps most, recorded wars involving tribal peoples can be directly attributed to the circumstances of Western contact" (Ferguson, 1992, p. 109).

If you have a source with more than one author, more than one source by the same author, a source with no author, or other special cases, refer to the *Publication Manual of the American Psychological Association*.

References

At the end of the paper, you will list all the works cited in the text on a separate page headed "References." For each entry, list the author's last name, initials, date of publication in parentheses, title of the work (capitalize first word only), publication information (city and publisher for books, title of journal, volume, and page number for articles). Look at the examples below and compare them to the corresponding examples in the MLA documentation style:

Entries for books

A book by one author

Montagu, A. (1968). *Man observed*. New York: Putnam.

A book by two or three authors

Goldstein, M. J., & Palmer, J. O. (1963). The experience of anxiety. New York: Oxford University Press.

An edited book

Nichols, B. (Ed.). (1976). *Movies and methods*. Berkeley: University of California Press.

Entries for periodicals

A journal article with one author

Silberman, L. H. (1979). Toward presidential control of the State Department. *Foreign Affairs, 57*, 872–893.

A journal article with two authors

Moss-Morris, R., & Petrie, K. J. (1999). Link between psychiatric dysfunction and dizziness. *Journal of the American Medical Association, 281*, 594.

A journal article with three or more authors

Bejjani, B., Damier, P., Arnulf, I, Thivard, L., Bonnet, A., Dormont, D., Cornu, P., Ridoux, B., Samson, Y., & Agid, Y. (1999). Transient acute depression induced by high-frequency deep-brain stimulation. *New England Journal of Medicine, 340*, 1476–1481.

An article in a magazine

Lemley, B. (1999, August). Alternative medicine man. *Discover*, 56–63.

An article in a newspaper

Scheinin, R. (1999, July 24). Preaching hatred. San Jose Mercury News. pp. E1–2.

Nonprint and electronic sources

A film

Kubrick, S. (Director). (1964). Dr. Strangelove [Film]. Hollywood: Columbia Pictures.

An article from a print source found on a website—References begin with the same information that would be used for a printed source with the website information placed at the end.

McGuire, P. A. (1998, July). Wanted: Workers with flexibility for 21st century jobs. *APA Monitor, 29*. Retrieved May 7, 2000 from the World Wide Web: http://www.apa.org/monitor/jul98/factor.html

For additional information on documenting electronic sources using the APA system, contact one of these two sources:

☞   http://www.apa.org/journals/webref.html

☞   http://www.columbia.edu/cu/cup/cgos/idx_basic.html

<u>An article from an electronic database</u> (e.g., SIRS, Electric Library, Infotrac)—Add name of database to the citation.

> Kuiper, H. A., Noteborn, H. P. J. M., & Peijnenburg, A. A. C. M. (1999, October 16). Adequacy of methods for testing the safety of genetically modified foods. *The Lancet, 354*, 1315. Retrieved February 5, 2000 from Infotrac database on the World Wide Web: http://www.infotrac.galegroup.com

For a more complete explanation of the American Psychological Association documentation style, consult its *Publication Manual*.

Proofreading Documentation

Because the rules for documenting sources require close attention to the details of punctuation and word order, proofreading your documentation is an important part of the research writing process. The following checklist will help you focus on one detail at a time as you proofread.

Proofreading Checklist for Documentation

Parenthetical Documentation

1. Is each quote or paraphrase followed by appropriate parenthetical documentation?
2. Does each parenthetical documentation contain the correct information
   - Author's name and page number OR
   - Page number only OR
   - Author's name only

   as required by the circumstances?
3. Have you included (or not included) the comma between author's name and page number, as required by the documentation style you are using?
4. Is the sentence punctuation (period, semicolon, question mark, exclamation point, or comma) in the correct place for each documented sentence?

Works Cited

1. Is every documented source included in the works-cited or reference list?
2. Does each entry follow the correct format according to the documentation style you chose? Check each element of the entry (author's name, title, and publication information).
3. Are the entries in the correct order?
4. Have you formatted the page correctly according to the documentation style you chose?

Activity: **WRITER'S LOG**

Write a paragraph on the topic you researched in the Working Together assignment in Chapter 20. Your paragraph will use at least one quote AND one paraphrase from the article you found. The paragraph should have a topic sentence, should integrate the information into your paragraph smoothly, and should be documented properly in either MLA or APA style.

READING AND WRITING TEXTS

Activity: **PREREADING**

In your Writer's Log, answer the following question:

When reading researched writing, what makes you feel confident about the writer's ideas? What makes the writing seem credible and authoritative?

Reading

Gina Chang's paper on the safety of genetically engineered food has been revised so it now takes a strong position against bioengineered food instead of the more balanced position in the original paper. As you read the revision, note changes that have been made in the evidence used, the evidence deleted, the way the evidence is presented to the readers, the organization of the material, and the introduction and conclusion. This paper uses APA rather than MLA style of documentation. Notice the differences as you read.

1"

Dangers of Bioengineered Food

Gina Chang

Environmental Studies 100, Section 3

Professor Levin

March 25, 2000

Dangers of Bioengineered Foods

1"

In November 1999, French farmers staged a public protest to alert consumers to the dangers of genetically modified food in European diets. At an international conference in January 2000, a block of nations from Europe and the developing world succeeded in forcing exporters to label shipments that contain genetically engineered food. In response to consumer concern about the dangers of bioengineered food to human health, both Gerber and Heinz have announced that they will not use genetically modified ingredients in their baby food. Two national grocery chains have stopped using genetically modified in-

1"

gredients in their store brands. These actions indicate that many responsible, reasonable people have grave doubts about food made from bioengineered crops, believing they pose a safety hazard to human health. Studies by scientists support their doubts. To ensure the safety of our food supply, bioengineered food should be eliminated from our diets.

Most people don't even know they're eating genetically altered food, though, in truth, they are. One estimate is that "60 percent of all processed foods—from candy bars and tortilla chips to tofu dogs and infant formula—contain at least one genetically engineered component" and "nearly half of all soybeans and a third of all corn in the United States" is grown from genetically altered seeds (Luoma, 2000, p. 54). Consumers don't know the extent of their consumption of genetically modified (GM) food because the FDA does not require labeling to indicate when ingredients have been genetically altered. As a result, very few of us know whether the corn used to make our cooking oil was developed naturally or had its DNA manipulated to include genes from foreign species, such as bacteria or even fish. Producers insist that there is no danger, so there is no need to know. They claim that adding labels will just lead to unnecessary worry.

Until recently, most Americans didn't worry. However, Europeans have been concerned for years about the safety of their food supply and have been pushing for greater regulation and labeling. A poll done in the United Kingdom in 1998 "found 77% of people want genetically modified crops banned, while 61% do not want to eat genetically modified food". (Williams, 1998, p. 768). More recently, in January of 2000, 130 nations gathered in Montreal to push through a biosafety treaty which "allows countries to bar imports of genetically altered seeds, microbes, animals and crops that they deem a threat to their environment" (Pollack, 2000, p. 1). Increased publicity regarding European fears and protests finally has heightened Americans' wariness about genetically modified products. This skepticism seems justified because the process of genetically modifying food crops presents many potential hazards.

When scientists genetically alter a plant, they take a gene from one organism and insert it into another to create a new plant that exhibits some desired trait, such as drought resistance, pest resistance, or increased nutritional value. Often, the inserted gene comes from a totally unrelated organism, such as animals or bacteria, which are chosen for their valuable properties. For example, scientists have introduced a gene from a soil bacterium into a pear tree to create trees that produce the same amount of fruit in a smaller amount of space (Gugliotta, 1999, p. A11). In most cases of such transgenic plants, since only one gene is added, the plant appears unchanged except that it now exhibits the beneficial trait.

However, as critics point out, switching genes is not as straightforward as switching a piece of your wardrobe because each known characteristic that is changed may affect the organism in unknown ways. Dr. Richard Lacey, a highly regarded expert on food safety quoted in Mother Jones magazine, explained the dangers of gene splicing this way:

> Its risks are in large part due to the complexity and interdependency of the parts of a living system, including its DNA. Wedging foreign genetic material in an essentially random manner into an organ-

When scientists splice a foreign gene into a plant or microbe, they often link it to another gene, called a marker, that helps determine if the first gene was successfully taken up. Most markers code for resistance to antibiotics. Some researchers warn that these genes might be passed onto disease-causing microbes in the guts of people who eat altered food, contributing to the growing public-health problem of antibiotic resistance. (Tangley, 1999, p. 40)

In response to this disturbing possibility, reputable consumer groups such as Consumers Union have called for researchers to stop using antibiotic markers in the development of genetically engineered crops ("Seeds," 1999, p. 46).

The critics of GM food often say that they don't want to abandon the development of GM foods entirely; they just want to slow the process down enough so that more rigorous and thorough testing can be done before products are released to the general public. In an article in <u>Mother Jones</u> magazine, one expert claimed that the way genetically engineered foods are now regulated is "like playing Russian roulette with public health. . . . If it continues along this path, some of these foods are eventually going to hurt somebody" (Luoma, 2000, p. 54). Critics such as this believe that human safety requires a greater degree of caution than is currently being applied to the research and development of genetically modified food. They advocate more stringent regulation and oversight by agencies such as the FDA.

In an interview, FDA Commissioner Jane E. Henney described the FDA's regulatory process regarding genetically modified food:

> In the specific case of foods developed utilizing the tools of biotechnology, the FDA set up a consultation process to help companies meet the requirements. While the consultation is voluntary, the legal requirements that the foods have to meet are not. (Thompson, 2000)

Henney went on to explain that a bioengineered food does not need to be labeled because she claims it does not vary in any "significantly different way from its conventional counterpart" (Thompson). Critics, such as Consumers Union, point out that the regulatory system is "largely run on the honor system" ("Seeds," 1999, p. 45), and they call for mandatory federal safety review of all genetically engineered foods before they are allowed on the market (p. 46). So many aspects of our food and drug consumption are closely regulated by the FDA, it seems irresponsible to allow something so new and potentially dangerous to be so loosely regulated. Currently, the companies decide whether the product is safe as they do the testing advised by the FDA, but there is no agency that requires such testing or certifies the food's safety.

Many people do not trust such voluntary testing and believe consumers should have the right to exclude such food from their diet, just as people can now choose to eat only organic food because such food is regulated and labeled. Up until now, the industry has resisted labeling, fearing that consumers would construe the label as a warning that GM food is inferior or dangerous. However, the food industry is now responding to consumers' growing awareness and uneasiness by considering some kind of labeling—perhaps labels that designate some food GM-free.

Another reason to avoid genetically modified food is the presence of problems other than danger to human health. Critics have warned that GM crops will cause environmental damage as well. In light of these difficulties, the safest decision is to stop the use of genetically modified crops altogether. Short of that, genetically modified foods should definitely be labeled so that consumers can make informed decisions and control their own diets. Critics compare genetic engineering to nuclear energy, warning that a technology that once seemed to be the solution to dire global problems could end up being a long-term health, environmental, and economic disaster itself. In both cases it seems clear that the potential risks outweigh any potential benefits. Why put ourselves at risk so that large corporations can make more money by producing larger, cheaper crops. Human health, and perhaps the health of the planet, dictates that we stand on the side of safety when we make our decisions about genetically modified foods.

References

Firth, P. (1999, May). Leaving a bad taste. <u>Scientific American</u>, 34–35.

Gugliotta, G. (1999, December 27). At USDA unit, seeds of many ideas. <u>The Washington Post</u>, A11. Retrieved February 2, 2000 from ProQuest database on the World Wide Web: http://www.proquest.com

Luoma, J. (2000, January). Pandora's pantry. <u>Mother Jones</u>, 52–59.

Pollack, A. (2000, January 30). 130 nations agree on safety rules for biotech food. <u>New York Times</u>, p. 1.

Rifkin, J. (1998). <u>The biotech century</u>. New York: Penguin Putnam.

Seeds of change. (1999, September). <u>Consumer Reports</u>, 41–46.

Tangley, L. (1999, July 26). How safe is genetically modified food? <u>U.S. News & World Report</u>, 40.

Thompson, L. (2000, January/February). Are bioengineered foods safe? <u>FDA Consumer, 43</u>. Retrieved March 26, 2000 from the World Wide Web: http://www.fda.gov/fdac/100_toc.html

Williams, N. (1998, August 7). Agricultural biotech faces backlash in Europe. <u>Science</u>, 768–771.

Activity: RESPONDING TO THE TEXT

1. What evidence has been deleted from the paper? How does this change affect the readers' perception of genetically engineered food?
2. What has changed about the way evidence is presented to the readers? Look at the introductory tags used before quotes and paraphrases and the writer's explanations surrounding the source material.
3. How do the different introduction and conclusion affect the paper?
4. Is the revision better than the original because it takes a more definite stand on the issue?

Writing Assignment

Write an essay comparing the two versions of Chang's paper. Your essay should focus on how changes in the selection and use of evidence, the organization, and the writer's own explanations affect the readers' perceptions of the issue.

ESSAY EXAMS

PREVIEW

This chapter's explanations about writing essay exams will help answer these questions:

- What do professors look for in essay exams?
- How can you prepare for essay exams?
- What techniques will enable you to write an effective essay exam?

Writing Under Pressure

In college and on the job, you will sometimes be confronted with stressful writing tasks. At work you may be given a very short deadline to produce a report or a letter, or be asked to respond in writing to an emerging crisis. When you take tests in college, you will sometimes have to write in-class essays.

Whenever you have to write under pressure, the first rule is, don't panic. As in other writing situations, a good way to start is to focus on a few key aspects: your audience, your purpose, and the information you should include in order to meet the demands of your writing task.

Activity: WRITER'S LOG

Developing self-awareness will help you avoid being caught off-guard. Recall times when you had to write under pressure. What factors hindered you? What factors helped you succeed? What can you do to minimize your weaknesses and maximize your strengths?

Writing Essay Exams

Often professors want students to demonstrate a deeper or broader understanding of the course material than they could by answering true-false, multiple-choice, or fill-in the blank questions. In these instances, professors frequently ask students to write essays on exams. Although the same skills students use in writing essays can be applied to writing essay exams, knowing a few additional techniques can help you be more effective.

Preparing for an Essay Exam

The best way to perform well on an essay test is to be well prepared, which requires gathering information. If your instructor has not told you what the essay questions will cover, your first step is to review material to identify likely topics for essay questions. Most essay questions focus on large or significant issues and ideas. Follow the four steps below, jotting down possible essay questions:

- If your instructor has given you study guides, begin by reviewing them, looking for topics that would make suitable essay questions.
- Next, examine your textbook, focusing on large issues. Refer to chapter summaries or study questions.
- Review your notes, looking for large issues addressed in the course.
- Imagine your instructor's point of view. If you wanted to know how well students understood the large issues in the course, what questions might you ask? If you develop the habit of imagining what your instructor might ask, you'll usually be able to predict the questions accurately.

Once you've reviewed the material and accumulated a list of potential essay questions, you can begin to study. If the same essay topic emerged more than once when you reviewed your study guides, textbook, and notes, review that material first. Next, review information that would help answer several of the potential essay questions on your list. Remember that you're not attempting to write essays at this point, just trying to gain an overview and become comfortable with the material that is likely to be included in the essay questions.

Analyzing the Essay Question

Essay tests almost always allow limited time, and writers usually feel pressured by the time constraints. Explaining the stages of human development or predicting economic trends in thirty minutes is a daunting task under any conditions. Although you may be tempted to begin writing immediately, avoid drafting a response before you've examined the question carefully and organized your thoughts. Taking a few minutes to analyze the questions can speed up the writing process by allowing you to develop an organizational strategy and focus your thoughts so that you avoid wasting time writing about irrelevant material.

Understanding the Question

Keep in mind that the instructor is trying to gauge your knowledge of the topic, so your first task is to understand your instructor's expectations. No matter how knowledgeable you may be on the subject, you won't write an effective essay if you don't understand the question, if your answer does not address the question, or if you ignore part of the question.

First, read the question carefully, looking for key terms and locating all the parts of the question. For example, if you are asked to define three neurological disorders common among the elderly and give examples of the symptoms caused by each, you'll first locate the key terms: *neurological disorders + elderly*. Remember that the instructor asked for three, but don't grasp the first three that come to mind, because the question also stipulated that the disorders be common ones. Then read the question again, focusing on the strategy you should use in answering the question. You are supposed to identify, define, and give examples of symptoms. Often, once you understand the question, a method of organizing your answer becomes clear. In this example, you could open with a statement naming the three common disorders and then devote a paragraph to each, first defining the disorder and then supplying examples of the symptoms.

Choosing a Strategy

Essay questions often include terms that suggest how to approach the assignments. In the example above, the student was asked to identify, define, and supply examples. The following list contains terms frequently found in essay questions and suggests strategies for organizing answers.

- *Analyze*—Break the topic into its main parts. Discuss each part separately and then show how the parts are combined into the whole.
- *Argue*—Give your opinion on a topic and provide evidence to support your viewpoint. (See pp. 377–381.)
- *Cause and Effect*—Explain what led up to an event or situation and then explain what resulted from it. (See pp. 341–342.)
- *Compare*—Demonstrate how the topics are alike. (See pp. 351–354.)
- *Contrast*—Demonstrate how the topics differ. (See pp. 351–354.)
- *Define*—Supply the meaning of the term and then expand the essay by demonstrating how the term fits into a larger context or by providing other relevant information, such as examples or comparisons. (See pp. 371–372.)
- *Discuss*—Unlike most other terms in this list, "discuss" doesn't suggest a clear strategy for the essay. When asked to discuss a topic, ask yourself what is most significant about the topic, and then use one or more of the other strategies on this list.
- *Explain*—Like "discuss," "explain" doesn't indicate clearly what strategy to use. Consider defining the term, providing a larger context, or using one of the other strategies on this list.
- *Identify*—Usually you are expected to define the term and explain how it fits into a larger context. A common essay question asks students to identify a quotation. In this instance, you should identify the speaker and the source of the quotation. Then show how the quotation reveals something fundamental about the speaker, the speaker's theories, or the work the quotation is from.
- *Interpret*—Provide the meaning of the topic. You will frequently have to use additional strategies, such as definition, comparison, or contrast.
- *Respond*—Provide your reaction to the topic, always including supporting evidence. Consider bolstering your response by including expert opinions.
- *Trace*—Show the chronological sequence of events.

Estimating Time

Since finishing the essay within the allotted time is crucial, check your watch, and estimate how much time you have to complete the essay. If you have to respond to two essay questions in one hour, then you'll want to complete the first one within thirty minutes. The amount of time you have for each essay is also a clue to how detailed your instructor expects your answer to be. If you are expected to write one essay in an hour, then your instructor is assessing the depth of your understanding and expects a well-developed, thorough response. However, if you are expected to write four essays in one hour, then your instructor is gauging the breadth of your understanding and expects less detail.

Activity: **WORKING TOGETHER**   DAEDALUS ONLINE

Working in small groups, examine each of the essay questions below. Imagine that you are expected to devote one hour to answering each essay question. Jot down a brief list of the probable contents, organizational strategy, and outline for each essay topic.

1. <u>American History</u>: What was the purpose of Roosevelt's New Deal? Identify the New Deal's three Rs and give an example of each.

2. <u>Computer Science</u>: Define distributed data processing. What are the advantages and disadvantages of DDP?

3. <u>Human Development</u>: Trace normal language development in children from birth to age two. What factors can foster or impede language development?

4. <u>Ornithology</u>: Compare and contrast the three types of hawks—accipiters, buteos, and falcons. Name one of each type found in your area.

5. <u>Classics</u>: How does the structure of architecture in classical Athens reflect the structure of the political community?

Writing the Essay

Once you've decided what the question requires, what strategy will work best, and how much time you should allot to writing the essay, take a minute to jot down a quick outline of the topics and the order in which you'll discuss them. Add any specific supporting evidence that comes to mind. This rough outline will keep you focused as you write.

Unlike traditional college essays, essay exams do not require introductory paragraphs to introduce your topic or interest your reader. Your reader is your professor and your purpose is to demonstrate your knowledge of the subject. Like all readers, your professor will not want to wade through unnecessary material, so begin by stating the point of your essay. Formulate a thesis that clearly reflects the contents of the question.

Although you want to demonstrate your knowledge of the subject by providing specific information, avoid the temptation to throw in extraneous information. Stick to the points you need to make to answer the question thoroughly. When you've completed your discussion of the question, sum up your essay in one succinct sentence.

Most writers cannot focus on all aspects of composition simultaneously. Your primary focus should be on the content—providing the information your professor expects—and your secondary focus should be on the organization—arranging the information in a clear, easy-to-follow form. As you write, don't become distracted by editing and proofreading details. Whether a word is spelled correctly is less important than whether you've included the necessary terms and used them correctly.

When you've finished drafting your essay, you can fix minor errors in the remaining time. An erasable pen is a helpful tool; in the last minutes before handing in a paper, you can correct minor errors without the numerous strike-throughs that might give the impression that you are disorganized or unsure of your information.

Writing Assignments

1. Imagine that you are a professor who wants to assess students' understanding of Chapter 1 of this text. Develop three clear essay questions. Write an "ideal" answer for one of the questions.

2. Reread John Gatto's "The Seven-Lesson Schoolteacher" on pp. 218–225. Select one of Gatto's lessons and, in twenty minutes, write a brief essay supporting or refuting Gatto's argument. Develop your essay with specific examples. In groups of four, read your group members' essays and decide which is best. Pass the essays to another group, read the new essays, and again decide which is best. When all the groups have read all the essays, read the essays that were considered the best. What makes these essays the best? What features do the best essays have in common? In what ways are they distinct from one another?

3. Review the four readings in Chapter 2. All four reveal stark differences in the authors' attitudes toward the value of reading literature. Formulate four essay questions using four of these terms from the list on p. 474: analyze, compare, contrast, argue, respond, trace. For each of the four questions, write a brief paragraph summarizing what organization and contents you would expect in a response to your question. Then write an essay responding to one of your questions.

DOCUMENT DESIGN

PREVIEW

This chapter's explanations about selecting appropriate formats and designs for college and workplace documents will help answer these questions:

- What format do professors expect for college papers?
- How do workplace documents differ from college texts in format and design?
- What factors should you focus on when designing workplace documents?
- What forms are conventional for resumés, memos, and letters?

Distinguishing Between Style and Content

Style matters. When we shop for clothes, we don't consider merely the function of clothing—to cover our bodies and protect us from the elements; we select colors and styles that appeal to us. Restaurants consider not only how food tastes, but also its presentation—how it appears on the plate.

Style, however, must complement, not replace, function. No customer would be satisfied with a stylish ski jacket that didn't protect its wearer against cold and moisture or with an elegantly presented dinner that tasted terrible. The same is true of writing. The best formatting and design will not make a success out of a text that fails to meet the needs and expectations of its readers. Whether you are writing for your department supervisor or for your physics professor, you must create texts that

- fulfill a clear purpose
- supply adequate supporting evidence
- organize and present ideas coherently
- conform to the conventions of Standard American English.

Understanding the Purpose of Format and Design

Format and design determine the way your writing looks on the page. Whether you're writing an essay for an English class or a memo for colleagues, your format and design should fulfill two basic purposes:

- The document should be easy to read and understand.
- The design should be appropriate for its purpose and readers.

As you read in Chapter 1, readers of academic and workplace texts share some expectations of your writing (e.g., clarity and organization), but their expectations also vary. One of the most obvious distinctions between academic and workplace writing is in the readers' expectations of design and format. The colors, graphics, writing, and design of a business's promotional brochure need to look radically different from those of a lab report in a chemistry class.

Formatting and Designing Academic Papers

Because sophisticated software makes complex designs easy to create, writers sometimes load their college papers with color, unusual fonts and sizes, and elaborate graphics in the hopes of creating an interesting, clever paper. All of these elements may enhance a document—depending on the document's purpose and reader. Readers of academic papers, however, usually discourage complicated or colorful designs. An elaborate, complicated design of a college paper may distract from, rather than enhance, the meaning, making the paper more difficult to read. Furthermore, such a design won't

- convey the sense of seriousness appropriate to academic writing
- conform to the conventions of academic writing
- meet the reader's expectations.

Effective writing always depends on meeting readers' expectations. Some professors provide very clear, specific instructions for papers, but others do not. When you are not given specific formatting instructions, adhere to these conventions of academic writing:

- Use good quality 8½-by-11-inch white paper.
- Double-space and type on only one side of the paper.
- Use one-inch margins that are aligned on the left side and ragged on the right.
- Use the Tab key to indent paragraphs.
- Use a 12-point size of a conventional font, such as Times New Roman. Avoid novelty fonts or unnecessary use of italics, boldface, or capitals.
- Title your paper, and provide identifying information—your name, the course, instructor, and date.

Formatting and Designing Workplace Documents

Designing academic documents consists primarily of adhering to well-established conventions. Designing workplace documents is far more complex. The goal of making a paper easy to read is accomplished in academic writing by avoiding irrelevant colors and graphics, by using a conventional font, and by double-spacing. Making a workplace text easy to read may include adding color, headings, boxes, lines, graphics, bullets, or other visual elements, and by replacing standard paragraphs with "chunks" of information.

Making a workplace text meet the readers' expectations is even more complex than making it easy to read. Workplace documents and their readers are so varied that design cannot be reduced to a few general guidelines. A stockholder's report, a company's promotional brochure, an insurance policy statement, a memo, a resumé, an advertisement for a new product—all these typical workplace texts have different readers and purposes and need different formats and designs. However, regardless of the type of workplace document, these elements of design must be considered:

- white space
- headings
- fonts
- bullets
- boxes or lines
- graphics
- color
- chunking

Using White Space

White space, as the name implies, is the area that contains no type or graphics. In an academic paper, white space consists of margins and paragraph indentations. In workplace documents, white space plays a more significant role. In addition to highlighting headings, columns, and blocks of information, white space separates sections, provides visual clues, and directs the reader's eyes, while also allowing the reader's eyes to rest. Without adequate white space, documents are difficult to read. If you examine the statement that accompanies a credit card and explains its terms, you'll notice that the type is small and there is almost no white space: Most readers will have difficulty locating significant information and will tire of reading long before they finish the document. Effective use of white space makes reading and understanding a text easier.

Creating Effective Headings

A brief academic paper typically has a title, and a longer paper may be divided into a few sections. Workplace documents of more than one page typically have headings— short titles that indicate the contents of each section. Headings serve several functions:

- They make documents easier to read by breaking up long segments of text.
- They indicate a movement from one topic to the next.
- They provide visual clues about the relationship and relative importance of sections.
- They allow readers to gain an overview of the entire document by skimming the headings.
- They allow readers to skip over irrelevant information and focus on portions relevant to them.

The form a heading takes indicates its level of importance in a text. Document titles are often centered. Other levels of headings may be centered, aligned on the left, or indented. Because the chapters in this book are long and contain many sections and features, each chapter contains several levels of headings. In Chapters 1 through 8, there are three major headings:

LEARNING ABOUT TEXTS

READING AND WRITING TEXTS

POLISHING AND REFLECTING ON TEXTS

Because these three headings contain similar language and are identical in form, the reader can clearly see the structure of the chapters.

Now look at headings from a portion of Chapter 1. Because the format is identical and the language similar within each level of headings, the reader can easily see the relationship among the chapter's sections.

Understanding Texts

Understanding Context

Context in Written Texts

Cultural Context

Historical Context

Conventions and Context

Understanding the Writer

Discovering Roles for Writing

Discovering Topics for Writing

Understanding the Audience

Because headings are intended to speed up reading, they should be brief. Although they can take other forms, headings are typically words, usually nouns or verbs, or brief phrases. The same grammatical form (parallel structure) indicates to the reader that the headings are of equal significance.

Selecting Fonts

The shape of the letter is called typeface. The term "font," which refers to the combination of typeface and size, describes how letters, numbers, and characters look on the page. Because most word-processing programs contain numerous fonts, writers can create a variety of looks by selecting and changing fonts.

Most fonts fit into two categories: serif and sans serif. Serif fonts have small horizontal bars across the tops and bottoms of vertical letters. "Sans" means "without," so sans serif fonts lack the horizontal bars. Notice the difference:

Times New Roman is a serif font: Note the T, N, R, m, s, w, n, r, and f.
Arial is a sans serif font: Note the lack of horizontal bars on letters.

Serif fonts are usually considered easier to read, so most documents rely on them for the body of the text. Sans serif fonts have a clean, uncluttered look, so they are frequently used in titles or headings.

Selecting a font is a matter of judgment; as in most writing situations, considering your audience and purpose is a starting point. A novelty font might be a good choice for a flier announcing a holiday office party; the same font would be inappropriate, or even offensive, on a memo announcing a decrease in health benefits.

When selecting a font, consider these guidelines:

- Select a serif font for the body of your document; consider a sans serif font for headings.
- Use no more than two fonts in a document, as several fonts may distract and confuse readers.
- Avoid long passages of italics, boldface, or capitals because they are difficult to read.
- Unless they serve a specific purpose, avoid novelty fonts because they may distract or annoy your reader.

Making Lists

Lists are usually marked with bullets, numbers, or squares. Bulleted lists, like the one above, are used if the items are of approximately the same importance and do not constitute a sequence. Although the items in a bulleted list could usually be incorporated into a paragraph, bullets make the items easy to read by separating them and providing additional white space.

If the items in a list form a sequence, number or letter them. In Chapter 2, the instructions for backwards outlining, mapping, and making a double-entry reader's log (pp. 51–52) are given in numbered lists because the steps must be followed in order. Numbered lists are also used to rank items from the most to the least important.

If readers are supposed to select items from a list, the items are often preceded by boxes or blanks. For example, in an application form, gender might be marked with boxes for the applicant to check: ☐ Male
☐ Female

Most word-processing software offers a variety of bullets, symbols, and characters. Although you may occasionally want to use a novelty bullet or symbol—for example, a ✔ by the items in a brief checklist—avoid overusing them, as they may distract readers. Whimsical symbols like ☺ and ❤ are not appropriate in workplace documents.

Using Lines and Boxes

Lines and boxes are effective visual clues that separate portions of text. A horizontal or vertical line can separate portions of text so that the reader immediately understands the distinction between parts of the document. Boxes frame portions of text, setting them off from the body of the document. Sometimes a light shading or color is added to provide a stronger visual clue that the content of the box is distinct from the rest of the text. The chapters of this book begin with boxes: The frame draws the reader's eye and also denotes that the contents, an overview of the entire chapter, do not constitute the first paragraph of the text. The workplace boxes are framed, shaded, and marked with a distinctive icon to indicate that the material, although separate from the surrounding text, is related to the topic of the chapter and germane to the workplace.

Adding Icons and Graphics

An icon is a picture or symbol that denotes the same thing to all viewers. Icons are handy visual shortcuts for communicating simple ideas. At a street corner, pedestrians automatically respond to the red hand or the green silhouette on a traffic light. Users of Macintosh computers or Windows are accustomed to reacting to icons—the printer, the open folder, and scissors are symbols users respond to unconsciously. Icons are convenient: It's quicker to respond to a picture of a printer than to read, "Click here to print a file." However, icons must be used sparingly, and they must always denote the same item or action, or they'll confuse readers.

"Graphics" is a general term that includes all material presented visually, such as clip art, drawings, illustrations, photos, maps, charts, graphs, flowcharts, diagrams, and tables. The purpose of graphics varies widely: The illustration on an advertisement is intended to attract buyers, while the bar chart in a sales report is intended to convey precise statistics to shareholders. Although all types of graphics have their own conventions, a few guidelines govern their use:

- Use graphics for a purpose, not for decoration.
- Allow adequate white space around graphics.
- Refer to graphics such as charts or tables in the text before they appear. Clarify the relationship of the graphic to the text.
- Title and identify graphics, except for illustrations such as icons and logos.
- Check to ensure that the data in statistical representations, such as tables and graphs, is accurate.

Adding Color

Color enlivens documents and makes them more appealing; however, as with all design elements, the color chosen must be appropriate to the purpose. A brochure promoting a singles' resort might choose bright, lively colors; a brochure promoting a bank probably would not.

In general, stick to black-and-white text for easy readability and use color sparingly. Too many colors or too many colored features distract from the text.

Color can provide visual clues that make a document easier to read; it can provide visual interest, focus readers on key elements, provide clues to organization, or highlight areas of special interest. When using color in designing documents, remember these guidelines:

Select colors that

- are appropriate to the document's audience and purpose
- are appropriate to the image of the business or agency
- increase the document's readability
- provide visual clues to the document's organization
- make the document more appealing.

Chunking Information

In academic papers, information is conveyed through paragraphs tied to a thesis. Writers of college papers assume that their readers will start at the beginning and read the entire text. Workplace writing is more pragmatic: Writers assume readers will skim the text and read only relevant portions. To make workplace documents more readable, information is broken into chunks—brief paragraphs restricted to one limited subject each. Relevant supporting information is listed or presented graphically whenever possible. The chunks of information are often made easier to locate by design elements such as headings, lines, and boxes.

Activity: WRITER'S LOG

Flip through the pages of this text. What elements of design have been used? Do they enhance the text? Do any elements seem irrelevant? In what ways might this book differ if its design used the conventions of academic writing?

Using Conventional Workplace Formats

With all the design elements to consider, creating workplace documents can be complicated. Fortunately, many workplace documents have conventional formats, just as academic papers do. Familiarizing yourself with conventional formats for resumés, letters, and memos can simplify workplace writing.

Organizing and Designing Resumés

Job candidates should present their credentials in the most positive light, so although resumés always include the same categories of information, they have different organizational patterns. Every resumé will include the following:

- contact information—name, address, phone number, e-mail address
- career objectives—either general career goals or a specific job title
- education—list of academic degrees, majors or areas of study, institutions, and dates

- work experience—list of jobs with descriptions of positions, places and dates of employment, responsibilities, and highlights of accomplishments
- special skills—computer certifications, foreign languages, relevant skills
- honors, awards, relevant activities—lists of awards, honorary societies, relevant community or academic activities
- references—a list of persons willing to supply references, or a statement that references are available on request.

An effective resumé must have a serious look, so color, novelty fonts, and graphics are usually inappropriate. Resumés are usually printed on good-quality white or off-white paper. Recruiters typically spend less than a minute scanning a resumé, so if a resumé is difficult to read, a prospective employer is likely to set it aside. Choosing an easily read font and a clear organization is crucial. The applicant's name is usually in boldface in a larger point size, and the contact information is often in a different font from the rest of the information. Adequate white space and bulleted lists make information accessible at a glance.

All resumés begin with the contact information and the career objective. The body of the resumé can be organized by chronology, function, or job target to present the job candidate in the most favorable light. The following sections demonstrate methods of organizing resumés and provide examples that Glen Keesling, the student who wrote the letter of application on pp. 377–381, might use at different stages of his career.

Organizing Chronological Resumés

A chronological resumé organizes the information in each category from the most recent to the earliest. Work information is usually included first; however, recent college graduates with limited relevant experience should begin with their stronger selling point, their education.

If Keesling had decided to apply for a teaching position immediately after finishing his bachelor's degree, he might have used a chronological resumé. In this instance, he is applying for only one position, so he names the school. If he were conducting a wider job search, the objective might read, "Special Education Teaching Position, grades K–12," or even "Challenging position using my training in special education." Since his relevant work experience is limited to part-time positions he held while he was an undergraduate, Keesling lists education first. Under skills, he includes both skills relevant to the job he is seeking, such as American Sign Language, and skills frequently sought by employers, such as proficiency with Microsoft Office. Although Keesling is a recent college graduate with no full-time experience, the information on his resumé suggests that he is dedicated, hard-working, and knowledgeable.

Glenn Keesling
7622 Oakmont Drive, Apt. 46
Lyndale, Connecticut 06371
Phone: 860-659-5517 • E-mail: glenk@juno.com

OBJECTIVE: Special education teaching position, Lyndale Elementary School

EDUCATION:
- B.A., Liberal Studies, San Jose State University, San Jose, California, 1997, concentration in educational psychology
- Teaching Credential, Multiple-Subject Learning Handicapped Program, San Jose State University, San Jose, California, 1997

EXPERIENCE:
- Intern, Little Red School House, San Jose, CA, 1997
    Developed lesson plans, taught classes, evaluated students. Applied Orton-Gillingham methodology to classroom situations
- Tutor, developmental studies, Student Learning Laboratory, San Jose State University, 1995–1997
    Worked for the ADA coordinator, tutoring students with learning disabilities, helping them develop study skills and adjust to college
- Volunteer teacher's aide, Bannister Elementary School, San Jose, CA, 1997–1998
    Worked with fourth-grade students, using multisensory techniques to enhance learning

SKILLS:
- Competent in American Sign Language and Signed English
- Speak, read, and write basic Spanish
- Skilled in Microsoft Office: Word, Access, Excel, and PowerPoint

AWARDS:
- Graduated *cum laude*
- Membership, Phi Delta Kappa, professional fraternity in education, 1997
- "Extra-Mile" Award for excellence in tutoring, Division of Learning Assistance, San Jose State University, 1997

REFERENCES: Available on request

Organizing Functional Resumés

A functional resumé opens with the skills and achievements that make a candidate a strong contender, then lists experience and education in later sections. Functional resumés are particularly effective for job candidates who

- are recent college graduates with limited relevant experience
- are changing career fields
- have not worked continuously

Suppose that Glen Keesling had been hired as an elementary special education teacher—the job he applied for with the chronological resumé above. After three years of teaching, he was ready for a change. Keesling decided to apply for a position at the state level in the administration of Connecticut's HARC (Handicapped and Retarded Citizens), a group he has volunteered for during the past two years. Although Keesling's education and experience are relevant to the job he's now seeking, he has no administrative experience. He decides to use a functional resumé to demonstrate that he has the skills for the position. Next, Keesling lists work experience, which he thinks is a stronger selling point than his education.

Glenn Keesling
7622 Oakmont Drive, Apt. 46
Lyndale, Connecticut 06371
Phone: 860-659-5517 • E-mail: glenk@juno.com

OBJECTIVE: Challenging position in Connecticut's HARC administration

AREAS OF EXPERTISE:

Working with People with Disabilities
- Knowledge of the ADA, legal implications, and social and political issues
- Two years' involvement with HARC at county and regional level
- Three years' experience teaching students with disabilities in Connecticut
- ASL interpreter; familiar with Signed English

Personal and Public Communication
- Ability to communicate and work well with people with physical, emotional, and learning disabilities and their families
- Experience conducting meetings and workshops with colleagues, parents, and board of education personnel
- Experience representing people with disabilities to political and community groups

EXPERIENCE:
- Special Education Teacher, Lyndale Elementary School, Lyndale, CT, 1998–2001
  - Provided instruction to classes of ten to fifteen students, aged six to eleven
  - Developed Individual Education Plans
  - Reported student progress to parents, supervisors, and colleagues
  - Provided training workshops for parents and colleagues
  - Presented classroom research at regional conferences
- Intern, Little Red School House, San Jose, CA, 1997
  - Developed lesson plans, taught classes, evaluated students
  - Applied Orton-Gillingham methodology to classroom situations
- Tutor, developmental studies, Student Learning Laboratory, San Jose State University, 1995–1997
  - Worked for the ADA coordinator, tutoring students with learning disabilities, helping them develop study skills and adjust to college
- Volunteer teacher's aide, Bannister Elementary School, San Jose, CA, 1997–1998
  - Worked with fourth-grade students, using multisensory techniques to enhance learning

EDUCATION:
- M.S., Special Education, University of Connecticut, Lyme, CT, degree expected June, 2001
- B.A., Liberal Studies, San Jose State University, San Jose, CA, 1997, concentration in educational psychology
- Teaching Credential, Multiple-Subject Learning Handicapped Program, San Jose State University, San Jose, CA, 1997

SKILLS:
- Interpreter, American Sign Language; familiar with Signed English
- Speak, read, and write Spanish
- Skilled in Photoshop and Microsoft Office (Word, Access, Excel, and PowerPoint)

AWARDS:
- "Teacher of the Year, Special Education," Lyndale Board of Education, 2000
- Graduated *cum laude*
- Membership, Phi Delta Kappa, professional fraternity in education, 1997
- "Extra-Mile" Award for excellence in tutoring, Division of Learning Assistance, San Jose State University, 1997

REFERENCES: Available on request

Organizing Targeted Resumés

A job candidate applying for a specific position may prefer to use a targeted resumé. The goal of a targeted resumé is to demonstrate how well your abilities and experiences qualify you for the position. Suppose Glen Keesling got the job at HARC. After three years as an assistant director, he decided the political and bureaucratic aspects of administration no longer interested him; he missed education. He noticed an advertisement for a supervisor for special education in his old school district of Lyndale. Glen decided to send a targeted resumé to demonstrate how his combination of experience in education and administration made him an ideal candidate.

Glenn Keesling
7622 Oakmont Drive, Apt. 46
Lyndale, Connecticut 06371
Phone: 860-659-5517 • E-mail: glenk@juno.com

Qualifications for the position of Supervisor of Special Education, Lyndale School District, Lyndale, Connecticut

AREAS OF EXPERTISE:

Working with People with Disabilities
- Knowledge of the ADA, legal implications, and social and political issues
- Three years' involvement with HARC at county and regional level
- Three years' experience teaching students with disabilities in Connecticut
- ASL interpreter; familiar with Signed English

Personal and Public Communication
- Ability to communicate and work well with people with physical, emotional, and learning disabilities and their families
- Experience conducting meetings and workshops with colleagues, parents, and board of education personnel
- Experience representing people with disabilities to political and community groups

Administrative Experience
- Established and maintained an agency budget
- Supervised a staff of seven
- Worked with state and local political constituencies to represent issues of importance to HARC
- Provided support to local chapters of HARC

EXPERIENCE:
- Assistant Director, HARC, Connecticut, 2001–2004
- Special Education Teacher, Lyndale Elementary School, Lyndale, CT, 1998–2001
- Intern, Little Red School House, San Jose, CA, 1997

EDUCATION:
- M.S., Special Education, University of Connecticut, Lyme, Connecticut, 2001
- B.A., Liberal Studies, San Jose State University, San Jose, California, 1997, concentration in educational psychology
- Teaching Credential, Multiple-Subject Learning Handicapped Program, San Jose State University, San Jose, California, 1997
- Passed CBEST, 1997

SKILLS:
- Interpreter, American Sign Language; familiar with Signed English
- Speak, read, and write Spanish
- Skilled in Photoshop and Microsoft Office (Word, Access, Excel, and PowerPoint)

AWARDS:
- "Teacher of the Year, Special Education," Lyndale Board of Education, 2000
- Graduated *cum laude*
- Membership, Phi Delta Kappa, professional fraternity in education, 1997
- "Extra-Mile" Award for excellence in tutoring, Division of Learning Assistance, San Jose State University, 1997

REFERENCES: Available on request

Preparing Online Resumés

Many large companies prefer that resumés be submitted online. Resumés are stored in a database and scanned by computers for keywords. To create an online resumé that can be easily scanned, follow these guidelines:

- Begin all lines at the left margin.
- Avoid tabs, bullets, italics, boldface, graphics, or any other font the computer might find difficult to scan.
- Put your name on the first line and add contact information on subsequent lines.
- After the contact information, supply a list of keywords, usually nouns. Use keywords to list skills, job titles, experience, education, and credentials. Use the same words that appeared in the advertisement for the job, since the computer is likely to scan for those terms.

To learn more about preparing resumés, access these websites:

☞ http://www.bridgew.ed.index.htm/ Type "Resumé" in the search box, and then select "Resumé Writing Tips."

☞ http://www1.umn.edu/ohr/ecep/resume/

To search for a job online, try

☞ http://www.monster.com

☞ http://www.headhunters.com

- Use a single column. Since scanners read across the lines from the left to the right margin, they can't distinguish columns.
- To increase the accuracy of scanning, include plenty of white space.

Writing Resumés with Integrity

Although job candidates should present themselves in the most positive light, they should never distort, exaggerate, or falsify information, experience, skills, or achievements. Candidates sometimes exaggerate their academic records or grades, omit references to unsuccessful education or work experience, or overstate their skills. If prospective employers are skeptical about information on a resume, they may suspect that the candidate is unreliable. At many companies, employees who have falsified their resumés will be fired. At best, they will not be trusted and are unlikely to be given opportunities for advancement.

Organizing and Designing Letters and Memos

Letters and memos are the primary forms of written communication in business. Letters are intended for readers outside an institution, and memos are intended for internal readers.

Formatting Letters

Business letters always include the same features in this order, from top to bottom:

1. <u>Heading</u>—the address of the person sending the letter, used only if the letter is not printed on letterhead
2. <u>Date</u>—placed two to six spaces below the heading or letterhead
3. <u>Inside address</u>—the name, title, and mailing address of the person receiving the letter
4. <u>Greeting</u>—("Dear . . .") followed by a colon
5. <u>Body</u>
6. <u>Complimentary Close</u>—(e.g., "Sincerely,")
7. <u>Signature Block</u>—(handwritten signature, followed by typed name)

Although several forms are acceptable for business letters, the most common is the full-block form. Full-block letters are aligned on the left and single-spaced, with a space between paragraphs.

If the letter is short, it is centered slightly above the middle of the page. Because a business letter is intended to convey a serious impression, good-quality white or off-white stationery is used. Novelty fonts or graphics are usually considered inappropriate, unless they fulfill a specific, clear purpose. Because letters are intended to be read quickly, the paragraphs are usually short.

Organizing Letters

As with all texts, the organization of a letter depends on its purpose, its readers, and its contents. Because business letters tend to fall into categories, they have predictable patterns of organization. Chapter 4 contains instructions for writing application letters (see "Workplace Writing," pp. 155–157), and Chapter 5 presents organization patterns for letters or memos requesting information or action and for positive or negative replies to requests (See p. 178).

The following letter, in full-block form, illustrates a typical letter of complaint. The author

1. establishes the relationship between the writer and the reader and the background of the problem
2. clarifies the problem in detail
3. asks that a specific action be taken and requests notification of the resolution of the problem
4. closes cordially, referring to an ongoing relationship.

In letters of complaint, writers must be careful to avoid expressing anger or assigning blame—either of which may elicit a negative response from the reader.

Notice that the writer has created a personal letterhead, so the heading is omitted. Lines added after the signature block indicate that papers are attached.

Georgia L. Lasko
204 E. Logan Street
Danville, Illinois 61832
217-734-2251·glasko@hotmail.com

January 12, 2001

Dr. Maya Gordon
Department of Physical Sciences
Danville Community College
Danville, Illinois 61832

Dear Dr. Gordon:

During the fall 2000 semester I was a student in your section of Astronomy 101 (Mondays and Wednesdays at 2:30 P.M.). According to the course syllabus, final course grades were determined by the grades on the three unit tests, the research paper, and the summaries of news articles. Each of these assignments weighed 20% of the course grade.

When my grades arrived in the mail last week, I was surprised to find I had a C in the course. I was expecting to receive a B. On the three tests I received a 72%, an 86%, and an 89%. I got an 85% on the research paper and a 92% on the news summaries. According to my calculations, my final grade would have been an 85%. Since you returned all the tests and papers, I've attached copies of the front pages.

Would you please recalculate my grade? If there were other factors—such as attendance—determining the final grade, would you please explain them to me? Please phone me at the number above. I'm usually available before 10:00 A.M. and after 5:00 P.M.

I learned a lot in your astronomy course, and I'm eager to begin Astronomy 102 during the spring semester. I hope you enjoy the semester break.

Sincerely

Georgia L. Lasko

Enclosures

Formatting Memos

Like letters, memos have conventional formats. The first line contains the word **Memo** or **Memorandum**, usually in boldface and either aligned at the left margin or centered. Some writers omit this line, since a glance at the document reveals that it's a memo. The next lines contain these headings, often in capitals and boldface and usually aligned at the left margin: **TO, FROM, DATE, SUBJECT**. Each heading is followed by a colon and identifying information. If the memo is being sent to several people, the expression "See Distribution List" follows the heading "To." In this case, each person's name is listed at the bottom of the memo, usually in alphabetical order. Each name is checked or highlighted, to identify the copy, as the memo is distributed.

Most memos use the full-block format: Paragraphs are aligned at the left margin and single-spaced with a space between paragraphs. Unusual fonts, colors, or graphics are used only when they serve a specific purpose. Memos are usually brief; however, if the memo is longer than one page or if it contains complex information, headings are added to increase readability.

Organizing Memos

Many memos are brief, sometimes just one paragraph. Even a brief memo needs

1. An opening—a statement of the memo's purpose
2. A body—the information necessary to fulfill the memo's purpose
3. A closing—often a request for action or an explanation of the follow-up

A memo requesting action or information, giving a positive or negative response, or stating a complaint can be organized like a letter.

MEMORANDUM

TO: Sarah Learner, Technical Support

FROM: Guy Roubidoux, Office Manager
Journalism Department

DATE: December 8, 2000

SUBJECT: Computer Inventory

The recent inventory of computers in faculty offices is inconsistent with the inventory tags on faculty computers in our department. The inventory tags on faculty computers in the Journalism Department all begin with the digit 7. The inventory lists the numbers as beginning with a 1. All other information on the inventory is correct. Would you please resolve this discrepancy? I can supply a list of faculty names and computer inventory tag numbers if it would simplify your task.

Using E-Mail for Letters and Memos

E-mail is replacing letters and memos because it is quicker, more efficient, and less expensive. E-mail has different conventions than traditional business letters and memos: It is less formal, more apt to use abbreviations and symbols, and less concerned with grammar, mechanics, and spelling. When writing to friends, an informal style and casual approach to correctness are acceptable. When writing a business letter or memo, the writer must choose a style and tone appropriate to the reader and purpose. A formal e-mail letter written to someone the sender does not know personally should usually include all the elements of a traditional business letter. A letter written to someone the sender knows or written as part of an ongoing business exchange may be less formal.

E-mail is frequently used for memos. Because e-mail systems provide headings, the writer needs to fill in only the address and subject line before adding a message. However, even a one-sentence message should reflect a tone and style appropriate to the business situation.

Writing Assignments

1. Review your career goals, education, and experience. Then write a chronological, functional, or targeted resumé. Incorporate some of the elements of design listed on pp. 478–483 of this chapter.

   When your resumé is completed, show it to three people who do not know you personally. Ask them to respond to these questions:

   A. Based on the resumé, what is your initial impression of the job candidate?
   B. Does the candidate seem qualified for the position?
   C. Would you be likely to want to interview the candidate? Why or why not?
   D. What aspects of the resumé impressed you? What aspects could be improved?
   Based on the responses, revise your resumé.

2. You are the head of a student committee trying to increase security measures on campus. To begin with, you need to gather data about current security measures. Draft these three documents:

   A. A letter to the head of security at another college requesting information about their campus security. The college you write to should have approximately the same student population, be located in a similar area (e.g., urban, suburban, or rural), and have a similar crime rate.
   B. A memo to the person in charge of security at your college requesting data about campus crime and current security measures.
   C. An e-mail message to an acquaintance on campus who works in security, requesting the same data.

   Working in small groups, examine the drafts. Compare the letters, memos, and e-mails to see if each type of document contains appropriate formatting, organization, and content and if each is written in an appropriate style.

3. Imagine that you recently purchased a CD player or other small appliance that you are dissatisfied with. Write a letter of complaint to the store you purchased it from or to the manufacturer. Then write two replies, one negative and one positive, to your letter. Be sure to use an appropriate format, tone, and style in each of the three letters.

ORAL PRESENTATIONS

P R E V I E W

This chapter's explanations about giving oral presentations in college and at work will help answer these questions:

- How can you become less nervous about speaking?
- What expectations do professors have of classroom presentations?
- How do college and workplace presentations differ?
- How can you best prepare and deliver an oral presentation?

Combating Communication Apprehension

Do you feel nervous when you have to give a report in class? Get tense before presenting your opinions in a committee meeting? Become jittery when you have to make a presentation at work? If so, you suffer from a condition called "communication apprehension." Fortunately, communication apprehension is normal. Almost everyone experiences anxiety—ranging from mild uneasiness to terror—before speaking in public. In fact, some nervousness probably helps most people perform better.

No one can avoid public communication. In college, students are expected to enter into classroom discussions, present information orally, read papers, and make formal presentations. At work, people are expected to present information at meetings, report to committees, respond to customers, colleagues, and supervisors, and make formal presentations. Since people can't avoid speaking, finding ways to cope with anxiety is an important aspect of effective oral communication. Two simple techniques can help reduce communication apprehension and improve effectiveness: adjusting expectations and visualizing success.

Adjusting Expectations

One reason people are anxious about speaking publicly is that they expect themselves to be flawless. They worry that they will stumble over a word, say something that sounds foolish, or lose their concentration or their place in a script. They are afraid that if they are less than perfect, their audience will become bored, annoyed, or even contemptuous.

A first step toward combating communication anxiety is to adjust your expectations of the audience. Think of times when you are part of the audience. In college classes, you are probably curious to hear what your professor or other presenters have to say. At work, you are probably intent on gaining information relevant to your job. In neither case are you interested in judging the speakers or finding flaws in their presentation. Your requirements are simple: A speaker should give you information that is clear, accurate, and easy to understand. As a speaker, you need to remember that the audience are neither your enemy nor your judge. When you make an oral presentation, you are providing them with information that either interests them or is important to them. In either case, your failure would interfere with their needs: They prefer that you do well.

A second step is to adjust your expectations of yourself. Your audience doesn't expect you to be perfect, so you shouldn't expect yourself to be perfect either. Everyone has seen an outtake of a movie or television scene in which a professional actor couldn't manage to deliver a line correctly, even after repeated attempts. A nonprofessional speaker is bound to make an occasional mistake. In fact, worrying about making a mistake will have two negative outcomes—1) distracting the speaker from focusing on important aspects, such as audience needs, purpose, and organization, and 2) increasing the likeliness of making mistakes by focusing on the possibility.

Visualizing Success

In addition to adjusting your expectations of your audience and yourself, you can practice another technique for combating communication apprehension—positive visualization. Positive visualization is used by many people, including speakers, performers, athletes, musicians, and teachers. A person who has a positive self-image tends to perform well. In fact, studies have demonstrated that athletes who practice positive visualization improve their performance.

To practice positive visualization, simply imagine yourself performing a task well and enjoying your success. For example, if you are presenting a brief report at a committee meeting, imagine standing up, looking and feeling confident. Imagine people seated at your conference table turning toward you, expecting a clear, helpful, well-organized report. Imagine yourself presenting your report clearly and confidently. Finally, imagine the committee's appreciation of your work. Your positive image of yourself will help reduce your anxiety and improve your performance.

Understanding Expectations of Oral Presentations in College

Professors frequently require students to make oral presentations. They may ask them to present their research, join in panel discussions, read their papers, or explain topics germane to the course. In any case, the purpose of the presentation is almost always to share information with classmates. When you are asked to make an oral presentation for a class, follow these simple guidelines:

- Clarify any specific expectations of the assignment, for example, a minimum time limit or a required outline of contents.
- Organize your ideas so that they're easy for your classmates to follow.
- Speak clearly, slowly, and loudly enough for everyone in the room to hear you.

Most professors evaluate your presentation on its contents and its value to other students. While you will want to apply any insights or techniques you have learned about oral communication, the emphasis is almost certainly on your content, not on the style of your presentation.

Understanding Expectations of Oral Presentations at Work

Expectations of both the style and the content of workplace presentations are more complex than the expectations of college presentations. College presentations usually focus on sharing opinions and information. Although workplace presentations may have the same goal, they frequently have other purposes—training coworkers, reporting on projects or committee outcomes, conducting negotiations. In each of these cases, a specific outcome is expected—coworkers are able to perform new duties or operate new equipment, projects are approved, policies are developed or revised, and decisions are made. Because oral presentations often lead to decisions, actions, and changes in the workplace, their accuracy and clarity are crucial. Although content is valued far more than style, the ability to make an effective presentation is important. The higher employees are in an organization, the more presentations they are likely to make; the more effective the presentations, the more likely the employees are to rise in the organization.

Activity: **WRITER'S LOG**

Jot down a list of at least five recent occasions on which you've listened to speakers, for example, in class and at meetings. In what ways were the speakers effective? In what ways were they ineffective? In each instance, were you able to grasp the purpose and follow the speaker's ideas? Did you feel the speakers were clear or convincing? Were they easy or difficult to listen to? Why?

Planning a Presentation

Planning an oral presentation is similar to preparing to write. You will begin by developing a clear purpose, analyzing your audience, gathering information, organizing your material, and drafting your presentation.

Clarifying Your Purpose

Most oral presentations, whether in college or at work, are intended to inform, to persuade, or both. However, in order to plan your presentation, you'll need to focus and clarify your purpose. Ask yourself what the specific outcome of your presentation should be: Should coworkers be able to understand and use the new features of their upgraded e-mail? Should committee members reach a consensus on the contents of a final report? Should colleagues understand the terms of a new

FYI: For more on purpose, see Chapter 3.

health benefit? Should potential clients decide to use your company's services? Once you've decided what outcome you want, you have a good start on deciding what you need to include in your presentation.

Analyzing Your Audience

In Chapter 1, you learned about the expectations workplace readers have of writing. The audience for an oral presentation will have the same expectations. Applying the seven Cs, the principles of workplace writing, on p. 12, to your presentation will help you set the right tone for your audience. As you think about your audience, answer these questions:

- How large is my audience? What traits do the members share? How similar or diverse are they?
- What does my audience need to know about the topic? What do they already know about the topic? Do they need any background information?
- What attitude is my audience likely to have? How have they previously responded to this topic?
- Approximately how long should the presentation be to fulfill its purpose?
- How formal or informal should the presentation be?

Preparing the Presentation

Perhaps the first decision to be made is whether your presentation will be delivered extemporaneously, with notes, or from a script. If the situation is informal and your presentation is brief—for example, a one-minute report from a committee—you can probably speak without notes. If your presentation is longer or more complex or contains specific facts or statistics, you will probably want to use notes. If you are presenting a long report in a formal situation, you may prefer to speak from a script. Electronic presentation software offers advantages to both the speaker and the audience. The electronic presentation serves the function of notes to guide the speaker while simultaneously enabling the audience to follow the presentation easily.

Because your audience won't have the advantage of being able to look at a printed text, a clear structure is crucial if they are to follow your ideas. The introduction, body, and conclusion of your presentation should be clear to your audience.

You can begin your presentation by using any of the techniques listed in Chapter 5 (pp. 172–174) for introducing a paper. In addition, however, be sure to accomplish these three goals:

- Clarify the purpose of your presentation.
- Clarify the relevance of your presentation to the audience.
- Clarify the major points you will make or the major topics you will cover.

In the body of your presentation, you make and support your main points, just as you do in writing. To enable your listeners to follow your ideas, enumerate your main points and include adequate examples, details, and facts to explain and support each point. To be clear to the audience, oral presentations need more transitions than written texts do. Be sure to number your main points (e.g., "the first reason") and include plenty of oral clues (e.g., another example of . . .") to the structure.

In the conclusion of your presentation, summarize the main points. You may want to thank the audience for their attendance. If appropriate, remind them of any further action they need to take, for example, signing up for additional training sessions or submitting evaluations.

The style of an oral presentation differs from its written counterpart in several ways. An audience, unlike readers, cannot stop to review material, alter their pace, or pause to absorb information. As a result, oral presentations have to be simpler in structure and language. When preparing an oral presentation, remember that you want to use simple words and short sentences. Use language that your audience will be comfortable with—including contractions and colloquialisms that might be too informal for a written text.

When you incorporate material from other sources in your writing, you provide information about the source in parentheses and on a "Works Cited" page. When you incorporate quotations or information from sources in oral presentations, you need to provide your audience with the source through "oral footnotes" in which you mention the speaker or author and the source of your information.

Preparing the Room

Preparation is not limited to organizing and preparing the contents of your presentation. You also need to check the room you'll be in and the equipment you'll need. To help you prepare, consider the items in this checklist:

- Is the room the right size for your audience? If the room is too large, your audience may have more difficulty focusing on the presentation; if it's too small, they may feel uncomfortably crowded. Is there adequate comfortable seating? Are the lighting and heating or cooling adequate? If the answer to any of these questions is "no," see if you can change either the room or the room's conditions.
- Will you need to use a microphone? Do you know how to turn it on and off? Adjust its height? Practice using the microphone with someone to listen to you so you can learn to judge your distance from the microphone and your volume.
- Do you need a podium to speak from? A space for material or handouts?
- What equipment do you need? If you need an overhead projector, a screen, a laptop, or projection equipment, be sure it will be available and that you know how to operate it. If you are using electronic presentation software, be sure to bring a copy of your presentation on a backup disk with you. Finally, check to be sure the room is arranged so that power cords can reach outlets.

Rehearsing the Presentation

Unless you are an experienced speaker, you should probably rehearse your presentation. If possible, rehearse in the room where your presentation will take place, so you can become comfortable with the surroundings. Ask a friend or colleague to be your audience and give you feedback. If possible, videotape your rehearsal and review it for additional feedback. When you view the videotape, you'll know whether you should speak more quickly or slowly, whether your delivery is too monotonous, or whether you have distracting nervous gestures. View the videotape a second time to focus on content and organization. Decide whether you need to clarify any points, add more supporting information, or reorganize your ideas to make them easier to understand. Finally, ask yourself whether, based on the videotape, you will have fulfilled the purpose of your presentation.

Delivering the Presentation

Keeping your audience in mind is a key to planning and preparing your presentation; it's also the key to effective delivery. Audiences respond more positively to speakers who maintain eye contact and seem relaxed and approachable. Before you begin, take a few deep breaths and make a conscious effort to relax and enjoy the experience. Look at the audience and smile. Look pleasant and sound confident. Many speakers like to memorize the first sentence of their presentation so they get off to a smooth start. If you are nervous, remember to focus on your audience and your message, not on yourself. Focusing on your audience will help you maintain an appropriate pace and volume: Avoid speaking too quickly for them to follow or too softly for them to hear without straining.

No matter how thorough your preparations have been, mistakes occur. You may lose your place, drop your notes, stumble over a powercord, or mispronounce a word. Remember that no one expects perfection. However, audiences do admire people who maintain their poise. Find your place, pick up your notes (or yourself), correct any misunderstandings, and go on with your presentation.

Most presentations offer the audience an opportunity to ask questions. Just as no one expects your presentation to be flawless, no one expects you to know the answer to every conceivable question. In general, try to answer briefly and clearly. Audiences sometimes become restless by the end of a presentation and may be impatient with long answers that seem like further discussions of the topic. The following suggestions will help in these situations:

- <u>If you don't know the answer</u>—Say so, and then promise to find and provide the information by a specified deadline. Be sure to follow up on questions you can't answer on the spot. In some instances, if the presentation is informal, you can ask other members of the audience if they can supply the information.
- <u>If you can't understand the question</u>—If you didn't hear the question, ask the speaker to repeat it. If you're not sure you understood the question, ask a question to clarify it, or rephrase it before answering, so you are confident your answer is appropriate.
- <u>If the questioner seems hostile</u>—Ignore the speaker's attitude and respond as if the question were a neutral request for information. The audience will be impressed with your poise. If you answer in an angry tone, you may lose sympathy.
- <u>If the question is long and complicated</u>—Break the question into small components and answer one part at a time. When you're finished, check with the person who asked the question to be sure your answer is complete.
- <u>If there are no questions or too many questions for the time period</u>—Offer to remain after the presentation to speak informally with anyone who has questions.

Assignments

1. Select one of the papers you've written for this course to present to the class. Follow these steps:

   A. Analyze the audience. In what ways does the class as an audience differ from the audience for whom you wrote the original paper?

   B. Decide how you can make the contents relevant to the new audience. You may need to alter your introduction to establish the relevance of your topic to the audience. Decide whether you need to alter the contents in other ways to make it suitable for the new audience.

   C. Revise the style of the paper. Sentences should be shorter, words simpler, the organization clearer. Add transitions to make the ideas easier to follow.

   D. Decide whether to use notes or a script. Unless the paper is long or complicated or contains extensive specific data, you should speak from notes.

   E. Deliver the paper and ask the class for feedback.

   F. In your Writer's Log, answer these questions:
   - What do you think are your strengths as a speaker?
   - What could you do to improve as a speaker?
   - In your next oral presentation, what aspects of preparation or presentation should you focus on?

2. Compare the presentations of three of your professors by answering these questions:
   - Is the speaker responsive to the audience?
   - Is the presentation well organized?
   - Does the speaker provide enough background information?
   - Are the contents of the presentation and their relevance to the course clear?
   - Did you feel motivated to listen to the speaker? To understand the material?
   - What differences in style are there among the three?

   Based on your responses, answer these questions in your Writer's Log:

   A. What characteristics do you like best in a speaker?

   B. What characteristics do you like least?

   C. Do you think your responses are typical of most students' responses? Why or why not?

   D. How can you improve your oral presentations to incorporate what you like best in other speakers?

3. Prepare a formal presentation to your class arguing for one change that affects students in your college. You might call for the addition or elimination of a course requirement, a change in how courses are scheduled or delivered, the addition of support services or activities, or a change in placement policies or graduation requirements. Be sure your change is limited enough to be discussed thoroughly in five minutes. Also be sure it's feasible: No audience would take seriously an argument for abolishing tuition or grades. At the end of your presentation, answer questions from the audience. At the end of the class session, take a poll to discover which speakers were most persuasive and why.

FYI: For more on arguing effectively, see pp. 377–381.

HANDBOOK

P R E V I E W

This handbook's explanations about sentence structure, standard usage, and punctuation will help answer these questions:

- Have you written a fragment or a sentence?
- What form of a word should you use in a sentence?
- How should you punctuate your sentences?

I. SENTENCE STRUCTURE

In order to recognize and write complete sentences, you must be able to recognize the components every sentence has—subjects and verbs.

Recognizing Subjects

The subject of a sentence is the word or words that name what the sentence is about. To find the subject of a sentence, read the sentence and then ask yourself who or what the sentence is about. Since nouns are words that name, the subject of a sentence is usually a noun. Since a pronoun is a word that can replace a noun, a pronoun can be the subject of a sentence. In these two examples, the subject has been underlined.

   A. <u>Agoraphobics</u> (noun) are people who fear open spaces.
   B. <u>They</u> (pronoun) often spend years inside their homes before getting therapy to help them cope with their phobia.

These hints will help you recognize subjects.

1. <u>The subject of the sentence usually comes before the verb</u>, as it does in this sentence and in the two examples above. However, there are exceptions: The verb comes first in questions and in sentences starting with *there*, *here*, and other similar terms. In the following three sentences, the subject is underlined.

      A. Is <u>Juan</u> majoring in prelaw or engineering?

      B. There are two <u>rabbits</u> on the lawn.

      C. Where did <u>you</u> say the restaurant is?

2. <u>The subject can be compound</u>. A compound has two or more parts joined by *and* or *or*. In this example, the compound subjects are underlined: "<u>Fruit</u>, <u>vegetables</u>, and whole <u>grains</u> should be part of your daily diet."

3. <u>The subject cannot be in a prepositional phrase</u>. A prepositional phrase is a group of words that starts with a preposition and is followed by a noun or pronoun. Because prepositional phrases often follow the subject and provide additional information about it, they can be confused with subjects. Prepositional phrases may be easier to recognize if you remember that a preposition usually tells when or gives the position of something. Here are some examples of prepositional phrases:

during the evening	near the apple tree
in the kitchen	behind the red sports car
by the garage	with her
over the fence	at the same time

In the following three sentences, the subject is underlined and the prepositional phrases are in parentheses.

      A. The <u>woman</u> (with Jesse) is a scriptwriter.

      B. The <u>house</u> (on the corner) (near the playground) was sold (to a young couple) (with three children).

      C. <u>One</u> (of the traffic signals) malfunctioned, causing an accident.

4. <u>A possessive noun</u> (indicated by an apostrophe) <u>cannot be the subject</u>; however, the word following the possessive may be the subject. Consider this sentence, "The college's <u>policy</u> on credit for work experience has been substantially revised." Because this sentence is about the policy, not the college, the subject of the sentence is *policy*.

Recognizing Verbs

A verb is the word in a sentence that tells what the subject does. To find the verb, ask yourself what the subject does. For example, in the sentence "The baby threw the toy out of his crib," you would ask what the baby did. The answer, *threw*, is the verb.

Many verbs, like *threw*, show action. However, some verbs, called linking verbs, do not show action; their purpose is to link the subject to other parts of the sentence. The most common linking verb is the verb *to be*, in all its forms (*am, are, is, was, were, had been*). Other common linking verbs are *become, feel, seem, appear*, and *look*. These two sentences contain linking verbs: "Sarah *became* an office manager last month. Although she *seems* satisfied with her new job, she often *feels* overworked."

These hints should help you recognize verbs:

1. <u>The verb of a sentence may contain more than one word</u>.

    • The verb may be compound, as in this sentence: "Maria, a single parent, <u>works</u> twenty hours a week, <u>volunteers</u> at her daughter's school, and <u>takes</u> an evening course in accounting at the local community college."

- The verb may also be a verb phrase, that is, a main verb with helping verbs, as in this sentence: "They <u>will have been working</u> on the proposal for five weeks." Words like *not* and *always* may come within a verb phrase, but they are not part of the verb. In this sentence "The project <u>was</u> not <u>going</u> as planned," the verb is *was going.*

2. <u>Verbs are the only parts of speech that change form to show time (called *tense*)</u>. If you are unsure about the verb, you can change the tense of the sentence to another time, such as the past or future. The only part of the sentence that will change, other than the words that indicate the change in time, will be the verb. Consider the verb *take:*

   "(Yesterday) we <u>took</u> a long walk along the shore."

   "(Tomorrow) we <u>will take</u> a long walk along the shore."

3. <u>Infinitives and -ing forms, two structures formed from verbs, cannot be the verbs of sentences</u>.
   - An infinitive (*to* + a verb) cannot be the verb of a sentence: Alicia <u>wants</u> (to graduate) in January.
   - The *-ing* form of a verb cannot be the verb of a sentence unless it is accompanied by a helping verb: Quoc <u>plans</u> to go (skating) after school.

To recognize a verb, consider its function in the sentence. All of the three sentences below contain some form of the word *swim*. In the first sentence, *swim* is an infinitive; in the second, *swimming* is a noun and the subject of the sentence; in the third, *swimming* has a helping verb and is the verb of the sentence. The verb of each sentence is underlined.

1. Sam <u>loves</u> to swim.
2. Swimming <u>provides</u> excellent exercise without straining ankles and knees as running does.
3. Sam <u>has been swimming</u> for two years to stay fit.

APPLICATION

In the following sentences, underline the subjects once and the verbs twice.

1. Walking through the woods yesterday, I noticed a patch of wild strawberries along the trail.

2. I vaguely remembered an old book called *Stalking the Wild Asparagus* and began to think about other kinds of edible plants.

3. Raspberries and blackberries are obviously edible.

4. Years ago, my mother used to cook morels, tasty mushrooms found in the woods in spring.

5. Mother's recipe—sautéing the mushrooms in butter—was simple but delicious.

6. There were several other types of mushrooms and fungi people in my home town used to cook.

7. Skunk cabbage, the large green plant found by streams and bogs in early spring, can be simmered and used as a vegetable in stews and soups.

8. May apples are often mistakenly thought to be poisonous.

9. They can be found under the two umbrella-like leaves covering the twelve- to eighteen-inch stalk.

10. What would most families think of a meal consisting of skunk cabbage soup, may apple salad, and various fungi for side dishes?

Choosing Verb Forms

Verbs change their form to show tense and also to fit correctly with their subjects, so choosing the correct verb form can sometimes be confusing. Regular verbs follow simple patterns, so these verbs cause few problems; irregular verbs have variations in their patterns and are therefore more problematic.

Regular Verbs

Present Tense

Present tense verbs use the basic verb form, the one found in the dictionary and used in infinitives (*to walk, to hope, to look*). If the subject is *he, she, it*, or a single noun, the verb adds an *-s* or *-es* ending. Occasionally, spelling changes occur when the ending is added; for example, *worry* becomes *worries*.

HOPE		**WATCH**	
I	hope	I	watch
you	hope	you	watch
he	hope<u>s</u>	he	watch<u>es</u>
she	hope<u>s</u>	she	watch<u>es</u>
it	hope<u>s</u>	it	watch<u>es</u>
Jane	hope<u>s</u>	John	watch<u>es</u>
we	hope	we	watch
they	hope	they	watch

Past and Past Participle Tenses

In the past tense, regular verbs add *-d* or *-ed* to the basic verb form; for example, *she walks* becomes *she walked*. The verb form used with the helping verbs *to be* (*am, is, are, was, were*) or *have* (*have, has*) is called a participle. Regular verbs use the same form for the past participle as for the past: She has walked.

I	hope<u>d</u>	I	watch<u>ed</u>
you	hope<u>d</u>	you	watch<u>ed</u>
she	hope<u>d</u>	she	watch<u>ed</u>

he	hope_d_	he	watch_ed_
it	hope_d_	it	watch_ed_
Jane	hope_d_	John	watch_ed_
we	hope_d_	we	watch_ed_
they	hope_d_	they	watch_ed_

Irregular Verbs

Present Tense

The most troublesome verb is *to be* because it has more forms than other verbs.

TO BE

I	_am_
you	_are_
she, he, it	_is_
we	_are_
they	_are_

Two other verbs that students sometimes have difficulty with are *to have* and *to do*. Most errors with *have* and *do* are with the *-s* form, *has* and *does*. These errors can be avoided by remembering that *has* and *does* are never used with any subject except *she*, *he*, *it*, or a singular noun.

TO HAVE		**TO DO**	
I	have	I	do
you	have	you	do
she, he, it	has	she, he, it	does
we	have	we	do
they	have	they	do

Past and Past Participle Tenses

Irregular verbs do not follow the simple patterns of regular verbs. What follows is a list of the present, past, and past participle forms of the most common irregular verbs. Remember that the past form is used without a helping verb, and the past participle form is used with a form of *be* or *have* as a helping verb. When you are unsure of the correct form of a verb, simply consult the list below.

Present Form	Past Form	Past Participle Form
arise	arose	arisen
awake	awoke or awaked	awoke or awakened
be (am, are, is)	was (were)	been
become	became	become
begin	began	begun
bend	bent	bent

bite	bit	bitten
blow	blew	blown
break	broke	broken
bring	brought	brought
build	built	built
burst	burst	burst
buy	bought	bought
catch	caught	caught
choose	chose	chosen
cling	clung	clung
come	came	come
cost	cost	cost
cut	cut	cut
dive	dived or dove	dived
do (does)	did	done
draw	drew	drawn
drink	drank	drunk
drive	drove	driven
eat	ate	eaten
fall	fell	fallen
feed	fed	fed
feel	felt	felt
fight	fought	fought
find	found	found
fly	flew	flown
forget	forgot	forgot or forgotten
forgive	forgave	forgiven
freeze	froze	frozen
get	got	got or gotten
give	gave	given
go (goes)	went	gone
grow	grew	grown
have (has)	had	had
hear	heard	heard
hide	hid	hidden
hold	held	held
hurt	hurt	hurt
keep	kept	kept
know	knew	known
lay [to put]	laid	laid
lead	led	led

leave	left	left
lend	lent	lent
let	let	let
lie [to recline]	lay	lain
lie [to tell untruths]	lied	lied
light	lit	lit
lose	lost	lost
make	made	made
meet	met	met
pay	paid	paid
ride	rode	ridden
ring	rang	rung
run	ran	run
say	said	said
see	saw	seen
sell	sold	sold
send	sent	sent
shake	shook	shaken
shrink	shrank	shrunk or shrunken
shut	shut	shut
sing	sang	sung
sink	sank	sunk
sit	sat	sat
sleep	slept	slept
speak	spoke	spoken
spend	spent	spent
stand	stood	stood
steal	stole	stolen
stick	stuck	stuck
sting	stung	stung
swear	swore	sworn
swim	swam	swum
take	took	taken
teach	taught	taught
tear	tore	torn
tell	told	told
think	thought	thought
wake	woke or waked	woken or waked
wear	wore	worn
win	won	won
write	wrote	written

Making Subjects and Verbs Agree

The verb in a sentence must agree with its subject in number: A singular subject takes a singular verb, and a plural subject takes a plural verb. In most instances, subject-verb agreement is not very complicated; however, sometimes students make mistakes with the -s form of the present tense verb. We write, "My English professor assigns weekly essays" or "My English professors assign weekly essays." The first subject is singular, so the *verb* ends in -s; the second subject is plural, so the *noun* ends in -s. You may find it helpful to imagine that you can use only one -s in the subject-verb pair. If the subject has an -s, then the verb will not; if the verb has an -s, then the subject will not.

Two other areas of possible confusion with subject-verb agreement arise when the subject is an indefinite pronoun or a compound.

Indefinite Pronouns

Most subject pronouns replace specific nouns: *He* may stand for *Roberto*, and *they* may mean *Carline* and *Maria*. An indefinite pronoun does not refer to a specific noun. Notice that most of the indefinite pronouns end with the words *-body*, *-one*, or *-thing*, all singular terms. The following list contains indefinite pronouns that take singular verbs.

anybody	anyone	anything
each	either	neither
everybody	everyone	everything
nobody	no one	nothing
none		
somebody	someone	something

Compound Subjects

If the parts of the compound subject are joined by *and*, use a plural verb: "Leo and Danielle take the SAT test on Saturday." If the parts of the compound subject are joined by *or* or *nor*, make the verb agree with the subject nearer it. In the first example below, the verb is singular because the nearer subject is *dog*, a singular noun; in the second example, the verb is plural because the nearer subject is *cats*, a plural noun:

> Neither our cats nor our dog runs outside unleashed.
> Neither our dog nor our cats run outside unleashed.

APPLICATION

In each sentence of the following passage, underline the subject and fill in the blank with the correct form of the verb.

1. Last year, high-school students across the country _____ (spend) one Saturday taking the SAT or ACT test.

2. Almost everyone _____ (take) a standardized, multiple-choice test at least once before reaching college.

3. The results of the tests then are _____ (send) to colleges.

4. Often neither the student nor the schools receiving the scores _____ (understand) that the tests are biased.

5. Somebody who is a very good student may have _____ (blow) the SAT and be judged to be a poor student.

6. Each of the tests _____ (have) some flaws in design.

7. Frequently, the culture of the test writers _____ (differ) from that of the students who are being tested.

8. A middle-class professor living in New York City may _____ (write) a test question about a subway without realizing that a student living on a ranch in Montana may never have seen one.

9. A Native American student from Alaska and an Asian-American student from Texas _____ (do) not respond to test questions the same way.

10. The culture, background, and personal circumstances of a student _____ (affect) the way he or she responds to a question.

Recognizing and Eliminating Fragments

A fragment is an incomplete sentence. A group of words might be a fragment because it lacks a subject or a verb or because, even with a subject and verb, it does not express a complete thought. For example, "She ran" is a complete sentence; however, "She likes" is incomplete, even though each word group contains a subject and a verb.

Although any incomplete sentence is a fragment, most of the fragments students write fall into two categories: dependent clauses and brief afterthoughts.

Dependent Clauses

A dependent clause begins with one of the words listed below and contains a subject and a verb. Although a dependent clause can come at the beginning, middle, or end of a sentence, it cannot, by itself, be a sentence.

after	once	where
although	since	wherever
as	so that	whether
because	that	which
before	though	whichever
even if	unless	while
even though	until	who
how	what	whoever
if	whatever	whose
	when	

In the following sentences, the dependent clauses are in parentheses:

> (Because movie tickets are becoming so expensive,) viewers are increasingly willing to wait for the videotape to be released. A family of four can easily spend between forty and fifty dollars to see a first-run film (if they

also purchase popcorn and sodas.) A home video, (even though the small screen is a drawback,) can provide both first-rate entertainment and substantial savings.

Notice that the dependent clauses, by themselves, would be fragments. However, if you read the sentences omitting the dependent clauses, you can tell that the sentences are complete. A dependent clause is so named because it cannot stand alone; it must depend on a complete sentence, also called an *independent clause.*

One dependent word that may pose a problem is *that.* Sometimes *that* is understood, but not written, at the beginning of a dependent clause, as in this sentence: "The videos (you rent for under five dollars) may save you hundreds of dollars over a year."

If you tend to write dependent clause fragments, develop the habit of reviewing your papers by circling the dependent words and putting parentheses around each dependent clause. Then examine each sentence. Each sentence that contains a dependent clause must also contain an independent clause; if there is no independent clause, the word group is a fragment.

You can correct almost any dependent clause fragment by attaching it to the sentence that precedes or follows it. If the combination would be too long or too wordy, removing the dependent word will often correct the dependent clause fragment.

Afterthought Fragments

The second type of fragment students occasionally write may take several grammatical forms. Having written a sentence, the student pauses, thinks of additional information, and adds that information, punctuating the word group as if it were a sentence. In the following example, the afterthought fragments are in parentheses:

> Higher education in the United States has been undergoing significant changes. (During the last thirty years.) Over half the freshmen in college are at community colleges. (A percentage likely to rise.) The average age of college students is well over the traditional eighteen to twenty-one. Because of soaring tuition and the belief that education is a life-long process, most students hold jobs. (Causing two- and four-year degrees to take far longer to complete.) Colleges are also competing vigorously for students. (By adding new evening, weekend, and distance learning programs designed for working adults.)

In the passage above, all the fragments could be corrected by being attached to the previous sentence. However, if students frequently write afterthought fragments, their basic problem may be one not of sentence structure, but of planning. As you can see from the passage above, the writer has several interesting ideas worth pursuing; however, the ideas are incompletely thought out and disorganized. Correcting the fragments would make the passage grammatically correct, but the paper would be much stronger if the writer were to reorganize it and provide stronger, more specific supporting evidence.

Recognizing and Eliminating Run-Ons

Recognizing Run-Ons

A run-on sentence is made up of two complete sentences punctuated as if they were one. If no punctuation mark separates the sentences, the word group is referred to as a *fused sentence;* if a comma separates the sentences, the word group is called a *comma splice.* In the following passage, the correct endpoint for each sentence has been marked with a slash.

> Throughout history epilepsy has been misunderstood, / for example, in ancient Greece epileptics were believed to have divine powers, / centuries later, in the Middle Ages epileptics were believed to be demonic, and until recently epileptics were believed to be mentally ill [comma splice]. Only recently have neurologists discovered several important facts about the disease / epilepsy has several causes and takes several forms [fused sentence].

Eliminating Run-Ons

Once you have recognized a run-on sentence in your writing, correcting it is not difficult. There are four ways to correct a run-on sentence.

1. Since run-ons are actually two sentences, the simplest correction is to add end punctuation (a period, question mark, or exclamation point) at the end of the first sentence and capitalize the beginning of the second sentence.
2. Sometimes the sentences seem too closely related to be separated by a period, especially when the second sentence begins with one of the following words or word groups, which show the relationship between the two sentences. In that case, writers often prefer to separate the sentences with a semicolon.

also	in addition	on the other hand
as a result	indeed	otherwise
besides	instead	then
consequently	meanwhile	therefore
furthermore	moreover	thus
however	nevertheless	

3. A third correction for run-ons is to join the sentences with a comma and a coordinating conjunction, creating a compound sentence. Only seven conjunctions can be used to form compound sentences: *and, but, or, for, nor, so, yet.* To join two sentences without using one of these seven conjunctions, link the sentences with a semicolon.
4. The fourth correction for a run-on, called *subordination,* is to revise one of the sentences so it is no longer complete. Often one sentence can be changed into a dependent clause, a correction which serves to clarify the relationship between the sentences. Consider this run-on: "Ming read Amy Tan's novel *The Joy Luck Club,* she understood her relationship with her Chinese mother better." Readers unfamiliar with Tan's fiction might not see any connection between these two

facts about Ming. In the revised sentence, the first sentence has become a dependent clause and the relationship between the ideas is clearer: "After Ming read Amy Tan's novel *The Joy Luck Club*, she understood her relationship with her Chinese mother better."

APPLICATION

In the blanks, label each sentence as C (complete), F (fragment), or R (run-on). Then rewrite the passage, correcting the errors.

The Chesapeake Bay

1. _____ The Chesapeake is the largest bay in the United States.

2. _____ With a length of 195 miles and a width from 4 to 30 miles.

3. _____ The surface area of the bay is 2,500 square miles, including the tributaries, the surface area is 4,400 square miles.

4. _____ The Bay, which H. L. Mencken called an "immense protein factory," produces over 200 million pounds of seafood each year.

5. _____ An output surpassed in the United States only by the Atlantic and Pacific Oceans.

6. _____ The Algonquin Indians, recognizing the vast seafood harvest provided by the Bay, named it "Chesepiooc"; the name means "great seafood bay."

7. _____ The Bay is famous for its shellfish, including crabs, oysters, clams, and mussels, there are also numerous types of fish.

8. _____ Not only does seafood thrive within the Bay, but many varieties of birds and animals also live in the swamps, marshes, beaches, and tidal flats of the surrounding tidewater area.

9. _____ In recent years, pollution has severely damaged the Bay, making its future uncertain.

10. _____ The Chesapeake Bay Foundation being one organization devoted to saving the Bay.

11. _____ If we do not save the Bay, one of the great natural waterways of the world will be lost.

USING A FLOWCHART TO FIND FRAGMENTS AND RUN-ONS

If you are unsure whether a word group is a sentence, a fragment, or a run-on, you can follow the three-step process in the following flowchart. Although it may seem cumbersome at first, after a few tries, you will be able to go through the steps quickly. As long as you correctly identify subjects, verbs, dependent words, and coordinating conjunctions, the flowchart will always identify the word group accurately.

STEP 1. Underline all subjects once and all verbs twice in any group of words ending with a semicolon, a period, or other end punctuation. Does the word group have at least one subject-verb pair?

  If the answer is **NO** $\longrightarrow$ Word group is a **FRAGMENT**

  If the answer is **YES** $\longrightarrow$ Go to **STEP 2**

STEP 2. Circle all dependent words (remember *that* may be unwritten). Cross out all subject-verb pairs following a dependent word. How many subject-verb pairs are left?

If the answer is **0** ⟶ Word group is a **FRAGMENT**

If the answer is **1** ⟶ Word group is a **SENTENCE**

If the answer is **2** or more ⟶ Go to **STEP 3**

STEP 3. Put brackets [ ] around coordinating conjunctions that join subject-verb pairs. Is there a bracket between each subject-verb pair?

If the answer is **NO** ⟶ Word group is a **RUN-ON**

If the answer is **YES** ⟶ Word group is a **SENTENCE**

APPLICATION

Mark each sentence according to the directions in the flowchart. In the blanks on the side, label each sentence as **C** (complete), **F** (fragment), or **R** (run-on). The first three sentences have been marked and the steps provided for you.

1. _____C_____ During the 1950s, the dominant <u>image</u> of the American family <u>was portrayed</u> by such popular television shows as *Father Knows Best*, *The Donna Reed Show*, and *Leave It to Beaver*.

   Answer to question in STEP 1 is ___*yes*___

   Answer to question in STEP 2 is ___1___

   This word group is a ___*sentence*___

2. _____C_____ <u>Each</u> of these families <u>had</u> a father who went off to a white-collar job dressed in a suit.

   Answer to question in STEP 1 is ___*yes*___

   Answer to question in STEP 2 is ___1___

   This word group is a ___*sentence*___

3. _____R_____ The <u>mother</u> <u>was</u> a homemaker, the two or three <u>children</u> <u>were</u> happy, healthy, and well-adjusted.

   Answer to question in STEP 1 is ___*yes*___

   Answer to question in STEP 2 is ___2___

   Answer to question in STEP 3 is ___*no*___

   This word group is a ___*run-on*___

4. _____ The families were all white, and none belonged to any identifiable ethnic group.

5. _____ Furthermore, they had no problem too serious to be happily resolved within the thirty-minute segment.

6. _____ Such families were always more myth than reality, nevertheless, the family structure has changed significantly since the 1960s.

7. _____ The increase in divorce rates has created many single-parent families, and, at the same time, more unmarried women are having children.

8. _____ As a result, almost 30 percent of American children living with only one parent.

9. _____ As life expectancy has increased, so has the number of elderly people in society.

10. _____ Many times, the elderly live with their middle-aged children, who still have their own children at home.

11. _____ Creating three-generation families.

12. _____ The majority of divorced people remarry; therefore, many families include both children and step-children.

13. _____ The children in these blended families sometimes having three sets of biological parents.

14. _____ Over half of the women work outside the home, in families with two wage-earners, roles and responsibilities are usually different than in families with one wage-earner.

15. _____ As social conditions change, family structures will continue to change.

II. USAGE

In the first section of this chapter, you reviewed how to recognize and write complete sentences. This section will review *usage*, the ways in which language is used conventionally. Because the conventions of English usage would fill several volumes, this overview is limited to areas that pose problems for many students: commonly confused words, pronouns, modifiers, parallelism, capitalization, and abbreviations.

Distinguishing Between Commonly Confused Words

Knowing which word to use can eliminate many minor errors from your papers. As you review these commonly confused words, mark those you have misused in previous papers. Then edit your next paper for those specific words. After you have used them correctly several times, choosing the correct word will become almost automatic.

1. **accept** = take (verb)
   except = but (preposition); to exclude (verb)
   > Every club officer <u>except</u> Andre <u>accepted</u> the nomination.

2. **advice** = an opinion (noun)
   advise = offer advice (verb)
   > When I <u>advised</u> him to calm down, he said, "<u>Advice</u> that is not perceived as helpful is not helpful."

3. **affect** = make a change (verb)
   effect = result (noun), or to bring about (verb)
   > When Carlos asked how the new policy would <u>affect</u> us, we said we probably would not know all the <u>effects</u> for at least two months. He is concerned that the policy will <u>effect</u> changes in benefits.

The Elements of Style, William Strunk, Jr.'s reference guide to writing, contains sections on "Elementary Rules of Usage" and "Elementary Principles of Composition" as well as lists of commonly misspelled words and misused words and expressions. *The Elements of Style* can be accessed at

☞   http://www.bartleby.com

Select "Strunk Style" from the Reference pull-down menu and then click on the link labeled "The Elements of Style."

4. **already** = previously (adverb)
   all ready = completely prepared
   > He had <u>already</u> changed the itinerary twice before we were <u>all ready</u> to leave on vacation.

5. **among** = used for three or more
   between = used for two
   > The twins decided to split the remaining birthday cake <u>between</u> them instead of dividing it <u>among</u> their other brothers and sisters.

6. **awhile** = for a period of time, one word when used as an adverb
   a while = two words when used in a prepositional phrase
   > "Stay <u>awhile</u>," Gina said. "You don't have to be at work for two hours, so you can relax for <u>a while</u>."

7. **beside** = next to
   besides = in addition to, or except for
   > The puppy was curled <u>beside</u> Sarah on the sofa; there was no one <u>besides</u> those two in the house.

8. **brake** = stop (verb), or mechanism for stopping a vehicle (noun)
   break = divide or destroy (verb)
   > As he <u>braked</u> to turn the corner, he said casually, "Perhaps we should <u>break</u> up."

9. **complement** = something added to complete
   compliment = an approving comment
   > I think it was a <u>compliment</u> when he said the sauce was very unusual but <u>complemented</u> the fish well.

10. **coarse** = rough, crude
    course = a class
    > The <u>coarse</u> language and behavior of some adolescents was a topic in the <u>course</u> we took on child development.

11. **desert** = arid region (noun); abandon (verb)
    dessert = sweet last course of a meal
    > When my wife began to eat her <u>dessert</u>, my faithful dog <u>deserted</u> me to sit by her side.

12. **everyday** = ordinary (adjective)
    every day = each day
    > Although murder can hardly be called an <u>everyday</u> occurrence, in some of our cities someone is murdered <u>every day</u>.

13. **farther** = used for measurable distances
    further = additional
    > <u>Further</u> decisions will be made when we are <u>farther</u> along in the process.

14. **fewer** = a smaller number, used for items that can be counted
    less = a smaller amount, used for items that cannot easily be counted
    > In this survey, more people reported <u>less</u> satisfaction with the political party system, and <u>fewer</u> people were generally optimistic about government.

15. **hear** = perceive through the ears
    here = in this place
    > Did you <u>hear</u> her when she asked you to come <u>here</u>?

16. **whole** = entire
    hole = opening or cavity
    > He spent the <u>whole</u> evening worrying about the <u>hole</u> in his muffler.

17. **its** = belonging to it, a possessive
    it's = a contraction of <u>it + is</u> or <u>it + has</u>
    > <u>It's</u> not difficult to understand how Ted's car could need to have <u>its</u> brakes relined every year!

18. **knew** = understood clearly, past tense of <u>know</u>
    new = unused, opposite of old
    > Sara <u>knew</u> she would have to buy a <u>new</u> exhaust system before her car would pass inspection.

19. **loose** = not tight
    lose = misplace or fail to keep
    > If your ring is too <u>loose</u>, you may <u>lose</u> it.

20. **maybe** = perhaps
    may be = a verb showing possibility
    > <u>Maybe</u> they have decided not to come; on the other hand, they <u>may be</u> late because of the traffic tie-ups on the interstate.

21. **pair** = two of a kind
    pare = peel
    pear = a fruit
    > When his mother asked him to <u>pare</u> a <u>pair</u> of <u>pears</u>, he looked blank, so she repeated, "Peel two pears."

22. **passed** = went by (past tense of <u>pass</u>); succeeded at a test
    past = time gone by
    > In the <u>past</u>, I would have <u>passed</u> every car going the speed limit.

23. **patience** = calm perseverance
    patient = person undergoing medical treatment; having patience
    > Health care practitioners must always have <u>patience</u> when working with their <u>patients</u>.

24. **peace** = tranquility, the opposite of war
    piece = a portion
    > There can be no <u>peace</u> in this family if the twins get unequal <u>pieces</u> of cake!

25. **plain** = clear; simple; a level, treeless land region
    plane = airplane
    > It was <u>plain</u> to the passengers that the <u>plane</u> was flying through turbulence.

26. **principal** = director of a school; main
    principle = basic law or rule of conduct
    > The <u>principal</u> of Central High School believes that all policies and decisions must be based on sound <u>principles</u> of education.

27. **quiet** = not noisy
    quite = very
    My father always made it <u>quite</u> clear that he wanted <u>quiet</u> while he was watching the evening news.
28. **right** = correct; a direction
    rite = ceremonial act
    write = express in writing
    Was it all <u>right</u> to <u>write</u> about the <u>rites</u> of passage in my sociology paper?
29. **tail** = appendage; bottom; rear part
    tale = story
    The <u>tale</u> involved smugglers concealing treasure in the <u>tail</u> of an airplane.
30. **than** = used to compare
    then = at that time
    I think I was more patient <u>then</u> <u>than</u> I am now.
31. **their** = a possessive
    there = at a place
    they're = a contraction of <u>they + are</u>
    <u>They're</u> over <u>there</u>, standing by <u>their</u> new car.
32. **though** = in spite of
    thought = past tense of <u>think</u>
    Even <u>though</u> John <u>thought</u> he was right, he decided to end the quarrel by being the first to apologize.
33. **threw** = tossed, past tense of <u>throw</u>
    through = finished; in one side and out the other
    When Matt was <u>through</u> with all his finals, he <u>threw</u> all his class notes away.
34. **to** = part of an infinitive; toward
    too = also; excessively
    two = the number
    Did the <u>two</u> of you want <u>to</u> go, <u>too</u>?
35. **weather** = temperature, humidity, and wind conditions affecting the atmosphere
    whether = indicates alternatives
    The <u>weather</u> tomorrow noon will determine <u>whether</u> we can go on the picnic.
36. **wear** = to have on or put on, such as clothes
    were = plural past tense of the verb <u>to be</u>
    where = in what place
    I wanted to <u>wear</u> my new sandals, but they <u>were</u> not in the closet <u>where</u> I left them!
37. **whose** = a possessive form
    who's = a contraction of <u>who + is</u>
    <u>Who's</u> the farmer <u>whose</u> crops were flooded out last June?
38. **your** = a possessive form
    you're = a contraction of <u>you + are</u>
    <u>You're</u> not going to fail <u>your</u> exam!

APPLICATION

Choose the appropriate word from each pair, and fill in the blank. Be sure to make the verb or noun singular or plural, as appropriate.

1. ACCEPT/EXCEPT
   A. They do not _____ criticism graciously!
   B. All my homework is finished, _____ for my lab report.

2. ADVICE/ADVISE
   A. Take my _____ .
   B. My counselor usually _____ me to manage my time more carefully.

3. AFFECT/EFFECT
   A. Adolescents often ignore the _____ of their actions on their families and friends.
   B. His chronic illness _____ both his emotional and physical well-being.

4. ALREADY/ALL READY
   A. I've _____ finished the research for my report.
   B. We can never seem to be _____ to leave for work on time.

5. AMONG/BETWEEN
   A. _____ you and me, I've always thought I could be a film maker.
   B. The group decision was to divide the work equally _____
      the five members instead of working collaboratively.

6. AWHILE/A WHILE
   A. Why don't we read the morning paper for _____
      longer before we start our Saturday chores.
   B. Think about her advice _____ before you begin arguing!

7. BESIDE/BESIDES
   A. Who is that standing _____ the gate?
   B. _____ those four, are there any other suggestions you would like to offer?

8. BRAKE/BREAK
   A. How could you possibly _____ both lamps?
   B. The mechanic said I should replace the _____ on my car.

9. COMPLEMENT/COMPLIMENT
   A. What vegetables do you think would _____ the seafood casserole?
   B. Mark Twain once said he could "live for two months on a good _____ ."

10. COARSE/COURSE
    A. How many _____ will you take next semester?
    B. Everyone in that family has such _____ eating habits!

11. DESERT/DESSERT
    A. What would you like for _____ ?
    B. The type of cactus depicted in most Mexican and American _____
       scenes is *saguaro*.

12. EVERYDAY/EVERY DAY
    A. They always get hysterical about _____ problems!
    B. She gets up at 5:45 _____ , even on the weekends.

13. FARTHER/FURTHER
    A. Joyce hiked _____ into the forest than she had intended.
    B. _____ hiring must be postponed until the new fiscal year.

14. FEWER/LESS
    A. You should use _____ salt when you cook!
    B. _____ students are enrolled in the computer programs this semester.

15. HEAR/HERE
    A. Your notes are _____ on the desk.
    B. I can't _____ you when the music is so loud.

16. WHOLE/HOLE
    A. Surely Sue didn't eat the _____ pizza!
    B. I hope that leak doesn't mean there's a _____ in the roof.

17. ITS/IT'S
    A. Did the dog lose _____ collar again?
    B. _____ humid today.

18. KNEW/NEW
    A. Is he shopping for a _____ or a used car?
    B. The students were nervous because they _____ how difficult the exit exam was.

19. LOOSE/LOSE
    A. My husband is so absent-minded that he _____ his car keys about twice a week.
    B. Since I went on a diet, many of my clothes are too _____ .

20. MAYBE/MAY BE
    A. Dinner _____ late tonight because Tom has errands to run after work.
    B. _____ seeing a counselor would help them sort out their problems.

21. PAIR/PARE/PEAR
    A. _____ those apples with a paring knife, not a steak knife.
    B. There are _____ , apples, and nectarines in the bowl.
    C. Did you lose a _____ of earrings?

22. PASSED/PAST
    A. We all have to balance putting the _____ behind us while still learning from
       _____ experience.
    B. Sheila _____ every exam with an A or B.

23. PATIENCE/PATIENTS
    A. How many _____ does your doctor see every hour?
    B. Infants require a surprising amount of _____ .

24. PEACE/PIECE
    A. Did you want a second _____ of pie?
    B. Many children worldwide grow up without ever knowing _____ .

25. PLAIN/PLANE
    A. The _____ circled O'Hare for nearly an hour before landing.
    B. My calculus professor can make even the most complicated formula _____
       to the class.

26. PRINCIPAL/PRINCIPLE
    A. What was the _____ reason for taking this course?
    B. When people say, "It's the _____ of the thing,"
       that _____ usually coincides with their own advantage.

27. QUIET/QUITE
    A. Some people study best in a _____ place, while others prefer background noise.
    B. She can certainly be _____ annoying when she's right!

28. RIGHT/RITE/WRITE
    A. How many papers do you have to _____ in your business law course?
    B. At the corner, turn _____ .
    C. In anthropology, we studied the fertility _____ of early cultures.

29. TAIL/TALE
   A. Rainbow-hued streamers formed the _____ of the kite
   B. On wintry evenings, my grandfather used to tell me ghost _____.

30. THAN/THEN
   A. What happened _____?
   B. Candice has always been more assertive _____ her brothers and sisters.

31. THEIR/THERE/THEY'RE
   A. Did Stan and Marge show you the video of _____ wedding?
   B. Look over _____!
   C. _____ unlikely to finish by the deadline.

32. THOUGH/THOUGHT
   A. Guido _____ he would be promoted.
   B. _____ he followed the steps in his owner's manual carefully, he was unable to repair the appliance.

33. THREW/THROUGH
   A. He reread the note, crumpled it, and _____ it in the wastebasket.
   B. Are you finally _____ going _____ that mess on your desk?

34. TO/TOO/TWO
   A. Sheila has three brothers and _____ sisters.
   B. They were _____ angry to think clearly.
   C. Does anyone want _____ go to the mall?

35. WEATHER/WHETHER
   A. Will you go to the beach on vacation despite the _____?
   B. Jennifer decided to stay for the evening lecture _____ or not Tracey could stay.

36. WEAR/WERE/WHERE
   A. What are you going to _____ to the party?
   B. _____ was Thorsten going when he passed us?
   C. How many cars _____ in that pile-up on the freeway?

37. WHOSE/WHO'S
   A. _____ idea was that?
   B. _____ giving the first presentation in speech class?

38. YOUR/YOU'RE
   A. Are _____ library books overdue again?
   B. _____ so smug when you think _____ right!

Using Pronouns

Choosing the correct pronoun involves four considerations—making pronouns agree, avoiding gender-biased language, choosing the correct case, and avoiding vague or shifting pronouns.

Making Pronouns Agree

A pronoun is a word that replaces a noun. When you refer to a blueprint as *it* or to architects as *they,* you are using pronouns. The word the pronoun replaces (*blueprint* or *architects*) is called an *antecedent*. Pronoun agreement means that every pronoun must agree with its antecedent in gender (masculine or feminine) and in number (singular or plural).

Making pronouns agree in gender poses no problem: we automatically say *she* when referring to a female and *he* when referring to a male. Making pronouns agree in number is usually equally simple: We unconsciously use *it* when referring to one item and *they* when referring to two or more items. However, deciding whether to use a single or a plural pronoun can be confusing when the antecedent is compound, a collective noun, or an indefinite pronoun. To choose the correct pronoun, follow these guidelines. In the example illustrating each rule, the antecedent is in italics, and the pronoun is underlined.

Compound Antecedents

When the antecedent consists of two or more nouns joined by *and*, *or*, or *nor*, it is said to be compound.

1. If the antecedents are joined by *and*, use a plural pronoun:
   Broccoli and cauliflower are both known for their vitamin content; they are also high in fiber.
2. If the antecedents are joined by *or* or *nor*, use a singular pronoun if both antecedents are singular and a plural pronoun if both antecedents are plural:
   Neither *spinach nor cabbage* is popular with most children, and getting them to eat it takes some creative planning. In general, *salads or vegetables* are also unpopular with children, despite their high nutritional value.
3. If one antecedent is singular and the other plural and they are joined by *or* or *nor*, the pronoun should agree with the antecedent nearer it. In these two examples, notice that reversing the order of the antecedents changes the pronouns.
   Adding milk to the water when simmering *cabbage or Brussels sprouts* will make them taste milder.
   Adding milk to the water when simmering *Brussels sprouts or cabbage* will make it taste milder.

Collective Nouns

A collective noun denotes a group of items or people considered to be one unit. Common collective nouns include *family*, *team*, *committee*, *group*, and *company*. If the collective noun is acting as a single unit, use a singular pronoun; if the collective noun is acting as separate individuals, use a plural pronoun:
   The *family* had its portrait painted by a local artist.
   The *team* took their places on the field.

Indefinite Pronouns

As you learned earlier in this chapter, many indefinite pronouns take singular verbs (see p. 510). Use a singular pronoun to refer to a singular indefinite pronoun:
   The coach told the girls trying out for the field hockey team, "*Everyone* must have her emergency health form submitted by Monday."
   Everything on this list is numbered according to its priority.

A few indefinite pronouns, such as *all*, *both*, and *many*, are plural; refer to a plural indefinite pronoun with a plural pronoun: "*Many* wish they could succeed on their talent instead of on their energy."

Avoiding Gender-Biased Language

Even when writers remember when to use a singular pronoun, indefinite pronouns can still pose problems. Look at the following example: "Everybody should consult with his adviser before registration." Although this sentence is grammatically correct, it should be avoided because using the masculine pronoun to agree with an indefinite pronoun is gender-biased. Avoiding the problem by substituting "his or her" or "her or his" corrects the gender bias but is awkward and wordy if repeated frequently. Two possible revisions may help you avoid the problem:

- Substitute an article (*a, an, the*) for the pronoun *his* ("Everybody should consult an adviser before registration").
- Replace the indefinite pronoun with a plural noun and pronoun ("All students should consult their advisers before registration").

Choosing a Pronoun Case

In English, pronouns have only three cases:

- <u>subjective</u>, used when the pronoun is a subject
- <u>objective</u>, used when the pronoun is an object
- <u>possessive</u>, used to indicate ownership

Subjective	Possessive	Objective
I	my	me
you	your	you
he	his	him
she	her	her
it	its	it
we	our	us
they	their	them
who	whose	whom

<u>Subjective</u> pronouns, as the name suggests, are used as subjects of sentences and clauses: "<u>He</u> and <u>I</u> have been friends for seven years." In formal English, subjective pronouns are also used after linking verbs: "John's opponents in the election were <u>she</u> and <u>I</u>."

<u>Possessive</u> pronouns, which indicate ownership, do not use apostrophes, so be sure to use *its* and *whose*, not the contractions *it's* and *who's*, when you want to indicate possession: "The organization gives its merit award to the person whose work resulted in the greatest good for the whole community."

<u>Objective</u> pronouns are used as objects of prepositions or as direct or indirect objects of verbs:

OBJECT OF PREPOSITION:	Give it to <u>me</u>!
INDIRECT OBJECT:	Alice sent <u>them</u> a memo yesterday.
DIRECT OBJECT:	The committee chose <u>us</u>.

Writers usually choose the correct form of the pronoun automatically. Occasionally, however, choosing a pronoun is more complicated because you may be unsure which pronoun is correct. The following guidelines will help:

1. If the sentence contains a compound subject or object, read the sentence without the compound and then choose the pronoun you would use if there were no compound. Consider these sentences:
   - "My parents always encouraged my brother and me to excel." If you eliminate "my brother and," the sentence would read, "My parents always encouraged me to excel." The pronoun <u>me</u> is correct because you would not say, "My parents always encouraged I to excel."
   - "Richard and I have been asked to apply for the job." If you read the sentence without "Richard and," you would say, "I have been asked to apply for the job." The pronoun <u>I</u> is correct because you would not say, "Me have been asked."

2. When a pronoun precedes a noun that explains its meaning, choose the pronoun you would use if there were no noun. For example, you would say:
   - "We students are frustrated," because you would say, "We are frustrated," not "Us are frustrated."
   - "The instructions given to us students were ambiguous," because you would say, "The instructions given to us were ambiguous," not "The instructions given to we were ambiguous."

3. If the sentence ends with *than* or *as* and a pronoun, choose the pronoun you would use if the comparison were completed. For example, you would say:
   - "I am more accurate at mathematics than he," because the completed comparison would be "than he is."
   - "Lauren doesn't enjoy trout fishing nearly as much as I," because the completed comparison would be "as I do."

4. Use the subjective form of the pronoun after any form of the verb <u>be</u>: "It was she who phoned." This use of the subjective pronoun, although grammatically correct, is not common in everyday conversation. If it sounds too stilted, you can avoid the issue and still be correct by rewriting the sentence: "She phoned."

Avoiding Vague or Shifting Pronouns

Remember that every pronoun needs an antecedent. Your writing will be clear only if readers know what your pronouns refer to. For example, the pronouns *they* and *it* in this sentence are vague: "They say it will rain by evening." Vague pronouns should be replaced: "The Channel 9 meteorologist predicted rain by evening."

Sometimes pronouns are vague because they are ambiguous; that is, they can refer to more than one noun. Consider this example: "Sarah told Katie that she needed to revise her draft." The reader cannot tell who needs to revise the draft—Sarah or Katie. The sentence must be clarified: "Sarah told Katie, 'You need to revise your draft.'"

Shifting pronouns change from one point of view to another unnecessarily. Consider these examples: "I love novels that offer you insights into different cultures." The writer has switched from *I* to *you*; consistent use of pronouns would be "I love novels that offer <u>me</u> insights. . . ."

APPLICATION

One of the following sentences contains no errors in pronoun usage. All the others contain errors in agreement or case or have gender-biased, vague, or shifting pronouns. Correct each error. You can change the form of the pronoun, replace the pronoun with a noun, or revise the sentence.

1. Advertisements do more than promote the sale of products; they also promote certain values and images.

2. Everyone is influenced by the magazines they read and the television they watch.

3. You and me may think that we are not influenced by them, but we certainly are.

4. If someone sees an ad for a jean jacket sold by the Gap and then goes out to buy himself one, he has been influenced by it.

5. I believe that you cannot avoid advertising's power unless you avoid advertisements.

6. No one is more aware of advertising's effects than me, yet I find myself at the grocery store buying "new improved peppermint-flavored toothpaste" even though I hate peppermint.

7. When I choose between a Coke and a generic cola, I always give in to their dazzling ad campaigns and choose the more expensive product.

8. The advertising team wants their ad to make consumers adhere to their values.

9. A successful ad makes the consumer think that they really want or need the product.

10. Considering how many people think they need a particular brand of cola, they seem to be doing a good job.

Using Modifiers

A modifier is a word, phrase, or clause used as an adjective or adverb. Adjectives and adverbs qualify other words by telling more about them. Mistakes can occur when writers are uncertain whether to use an adjective or adverb, when modifiers are misplaced, or when the words modifiers qualify are unclear.

Recognizing Adjectives

An adjective is a word that modifies a noun or a pronoun by describing or adding information about it: e.g., a <u>seven-foot</u> sapling, an <u>old red brick</u> hotel. Although adjectives usually precede the word they describe, they also follow linking verbs. In this sentence the adjectives are underlined, and the words they modify are in boldface: "She bought an <u>expensive chartreuse silk</u> **blouse**, and **she** was <u>furious</u> when her boyfriend told her **it** was <u>ugly</u>."

Phrases and clauses can also function as adjectives. A prepositional phrase or any other phrase that describes a noun or pronoun functions as an adjective. In this sentence, the prepositional phrases are underlined and the nouns they modify are in boldface: "I looked for a parking **place** in the shade so the **groceries** in the back-seat wouldn't get too warm."

Adjective clauses are dependent clauses beginning with *who*, *which*, or *that*. Traditionally, *who* is used to refer to people, and *that* and *which* are used to refer to things. In each of these two examples, the underlined adjective clause refers to the noun that immediately precedes it: "The **man** who works at the local library is an accomplished storyteller; however, many of the **stories** that he tells are too disturbing for young children."

Using Comparative and Superlative Forms of Adjectives

Most adjectives use -er, more, or less to compare *two* things (called the *comparative* form) and -est, most, or least to compare *three or more* (called the *superlative* form):

Adjective	Comparative	Superlative
nice	nicer	nicest
messy	messier	messiest
unusual	more unusual	most unusual
typical	less typical	least typical

The number of syllables in a word determines whether you should use -er and -est or more and most. Most one-syllable adjectives and some two-syllable adjectives use -er and -est: "Alice is shyer than her brother; in fact, she's the shyest person I know." Most two-syllable adjectives and all adjectives of three or more syllables use more to compare two things and most to compare three or more things: "You should be more careful; you make the most ridiculous blunders in your math calculations." When in doubt, consult a dictionary: Most dictionaries list the comparative and superlative forms of adjectives.

A few adjectives have irregular forms:

Adjective	Comparative Form	Superlative Form
good	better	best
bad	worse	worst
little	less	least
many or much	more	most

His idea is good, and yours is better, but the committee's suggestion is probably the best.

Sam carries little cash, Dan has even less, and Anna has the least, so we'd better settle for cheap entertainment!

Recognizing Adverbs

An adverb is a word that modifies a verb, an adjective, or another adverb. Adverbs usually tell *when*, *where*, *why*, or *how* something occurred. Because they frequently end in *-ly*, adverbs are easily recognizable; in fact, all three adverbs in the previous two sentences end in *-ly*. Like adjectives, adverbs can also be phrases or clauses, as in this brief paragraph:

The Wickstroms went on vacation <u>yesterday</u> (word telling *when*). They've never been <u>to Sweden</u> (phrase telling *where*) <u>before</u> (word telling *when*), and they have been <u>eagerly</u> (word telling *how*) planning this trip for months. They left their house <u>at three in the morning</u> (phrase telling *when*) <u>because their flight departed at 6:20 A.M.</u> (clause telling *why*).

Using Comparative and Superlative Forms of Adverbs

Like adjectives, the comparative form of an adverb uses <u>-er</u>, <u>more</u>, or <u>less</u>, the superlative form uses <u>-est</u>, <u>most</u>, or <u>least</u>, and the number of syllables determines which form to use:

I usually leave for work <u>early</u>, but tomorrow I'll have to leave <u>earlier</u>. Because of the weekend traffic, I leave <u>earliest</u> on Friday.

The <u>more convincingly</u> he spoke, the <u>less angrily</u> the crowd reacted.

Two irregular adverbs have irregular comparative and superlative forms: *well* and *badly*.

<u>Adverb</u>	<u>Comparative Form</u>	<u>Superlative Form</u>
well	better	best
badly	worse	worst

I thought I did <u>well</u> on the exam, but Juan did <u>better</u>, and Tina did the <u>best</u>. No matter how <u>badly</u> Tina does on a test, I always do <u>worse</u>! Fortunately, neither of us is likely to be the <u>worst</u> in the class.

Choosing Between Adjectives and Adverbs

Writers sometimes make mistakes by choosing an adjective when they should use an adverb, or vice versa. Most errors occur when using the following pairs of adjectives and adverbs. Notice that, except for *well*, all the adverbs end in *-ly*.

<u>Adjective</u>	<u>Adverb</u>
good	well

(Al is a <u>good</u> student. He does <u>well</u> in his classes.)

bad	badly

(That's a <u>bad</u> injury. His leg was <u>badly</u> broken.)

real	really

(Is that a <u>real</u> diamond? It's <u>really</u> beautiful!)

slow	slowly

(The leak is <u>slow</u>. The water is <u>slowly</u> dripping into the floor.)

quick	quickly

(That was a <u>quick</u> response. She reacted <u>quickly</u>.)

terrible	terribly

(What a <u>terrible</u> movie! You must have been <u>terribly</u> bored.)

Avoiding Misplaced and Dangling Modifiers

Modifiers must be near the words they modify. If they are misplaced, the sentence may be unintentionally funny or confusing. Consider this sentence: "The carnival barker announced the next show through a megaphone wearing a bright plaid suit." According to this sentence, the megaphone is wearing the suit. The modifier, "wearing a bright plaid suit," should be next to the word it modifies, "barker."

Writers need to be especially careful with words like *only*, *nearly*, and *almost*. For example, the sentence "Pete almost worked for thirteen hours without a break" does not say how long Pete worked. Since the sentence says Pete "almost worked," the reader can assume he did not work at all.

A modifier at the beginning of a sentence must modify the word that follows it; otherwise it is said to be dangling. Look at these examples:

> While reading my physics book, my cat curled up in my lap.
> (The sentence implies that the cat is reading the book.)
> When preparing the picnic, a storm arose.
> (The sentence implies that the storm is preparing the lunch.)

One correction for a dangling modifier is to change the subject of the sentence: "While reading my physics book, I sat with my cat curled up in my lap." The other correction is to provide a subject within the modifier: "While I was preparing lunch, a storm arose."

APPLICATION

The following paragraph is confusing because it contains errors in modifiers. Some modifiers are in the wrong form; others are misplaced or dangling. Cross out each incorrect modifier and write the correct form above the line. If the modifier is misplaced, move it to an appropriate location; if it is dangling, make corrections in the sentence.

Linguists believe that many languages are descended from one ancestor language, including Greek, German, and English. Originating somewhere in central Europe or the Middle East, linguists call this ancestor language Indo-European. Although Indo-European is no longer spoken, once linguists know it existed because Indo-European words have nearly remained unchanged in their modern descendants. For example, *matar*, the word for mother in Sanskrit, almost is exactly the same as *mater*, the word for mother in Latin. Knowing the unchanged words to be the ones used most often, the Indo-European language reveals its ancient speakers' most immediate concerns. By examining a list of Indo-European words, the lifestyle of these people can be determined. Containing words such as *snow, wolf, winter,* and *horse*, linguists conclude that Indo-Europeans were seminomadic.

Using Parallelism

Using the same grammatical form for words, phrases, or clauses that express similar ideas is called *parallelism*. Consider this sentence: "Jan's favorite outdoor activities are swimming, hiking, and cycling." Because *swimming, hiking,* and *cycling* are equivalent ideas, they are in the same grammatical form. Look at these examples of parallelism:

<u>Words:</u>   Adult cats prefer to spend their time *eating, sleeping,* and *thinking* about eating and sleeping.

<u>Phrases:</u>   Charlie wanted to *have a quick dinner, read a good novel,* and *forget about the pressures of the workday.*

<u>Clauses:</u>   Kara changed her major to technology because *she would have more job opportunities* and *she would make a higher salary.*

To be sure your structure is parallel, examine each segment of the sentence as if it were complete. The example of parallel phrases could be broken into three sentences:

Charlie wanted to have a quick dinner.

Charlie wanted to read a good novel.

Charlie wanted to forget about the pressures of the workday.

Since all three of these sentences are grammatically correct and in the same form, the combined sentence is parallel.

Writers usually use parallel form when they join words, phrases, or clauses with coordinating conjunctions (*and, but, or, for, nor, so,* or *yet*) or with correlative conjunctions (*either . . . or, neither . . . nor, not only . . . but also*).

Trisha can pick up the groceries, drop clothes off at the cleaners, and return the videos while I'm in class.

The auditor was not only patient but also helpful.

APPLICATION

In the following passage, locate four parallel structures and underline the parallel words, phrases, or clauses. Revise the one sentence that would be improved by parallel structure.

Parallel structure creates a sense of balance, makes sentences easy to understand, and reflects a sophisticated style. In fact, parallelism can be powerful and it can be memorable. Its effectiveness was obvious to Shakespeare, who had Hamlet ask, "To be or not to be," and to Charles Dickens, who opened his novel *A Tale of Two Cities* with "It was the best of times, it was the worst of times. . . ." Throughout time, compelling speakers and writers of powerful texts have made their words more dynamic by using parallel structures.

Using Capitals

The uses of capitals can be reduced to five categories. If you have questions about capitalization when proofreading a paper, check each capital in your draft against the following rules. Any capital for which you can not find a rule should be omitted.

1. **Beginnings**
   A. Capitalize the beginning of every sentence.
   B. Capitalize the beginning of a quotation that is a complete sentence:
   Hearing a knock at the door, he yelled, "Who's there?"

2. **People, places, and things**
   A. Always capitalize the pronoun *I*.
   B. Always capitalize the proper names of people. Capitalize a person's title if it is used as part of the name; e.g., Mr., Ms., President, Doctor, Reverend, Senator, Professor. Do not capitalize the occupation when it is not part of the title.
   I met Dr. Martin Richardson last night. He's a professor at the university my cousin attends.
   C. Capitalize words indicating family relationships when used as proper names, but not when used to indicate the relationship.
   Uncle Howie told us stories of growing up in Poland, but my father, who's five years younger, couldn't remember much about those years.
   D. Capitalize the names of all deities.
   Different cultures depict their deities with various symbols; for example, Buddha is often shown surrounded by clouds, symbols of wisdom.
   E. Capitalize the proper names of places such as countries, states, cities, buildings, and streets, and of land forms such as mountains, oceans, lakes, and rivers.
   This summer they hiked the Appalachian Trail from Maine to Georgia.
   F. Capitalize the names of regions; do not capitalize words used as directions.
   I lived in the Southwest for ten years before moving several hundred miles north to the Midwest.
   G. Capitalize the names of all languages.
   The Swiss speak French, German, and Italian.
   H. Capitalize the brand names of commercial products, but not the name of the type of product.
   A balanced diet does not consist of a Coke, a Wendy's hamburger, and a Hershey candy bar.

3. **Groups**
   A. Capitalize the names of all nationalities, races, and tribes.
   The Navaho once dominated the Southwest.
   B. Capitalize the proper names of organizations, agencies, clubs, associations, unions, schools, religions, and other groups.
   The activities of the Parent-Teacher Association funded many innovative projects at Parks Elementary School.

4. **Times**

    A. Capitalize the names of days, months, and holidays. Do not capitalize the seasons.

        Last fall, I began my first college course on Tuesday, September 8.

    B. Capitalize the names of historic events and periods, but not of centuries.

        The Renaissance is usually dated from the fifteenth century.

5. **Titles**

    A. Capitalize the first and last and all other important words in the titles of the papers you write and the titles of all published or performed works, e.g., books, magazines, articles, poems, songs, movies, plays.

        I wrote an essay called "The Ethics of the Ordinary" based on two essays I found in *Mark Twain on the Damned Human Race*.

    B. Capitalize the first, last, and important words in the titles of documents.

        The Bill of Rights affects our daily lives in myriad ways.

    C. Capitalize the specific titles of particular courses. Do not capitalize academic areas. Capitalize language courses because the names of languages are always capitalized.

        I've registered for French and Contemporary Literary Theory next semester; I may also add a math, English, or science course.

Using Numbers and Abbreviations

Expressing Numbers

When writing papers for college, write out numbers that can be stated in one or two words, e.g., twenty-five, ten thousand. Use numerals for numbers that require three or more words, e.g., 122, 4,690. Never begin a sentence with a numeral: Either write the number out, or revise the sentence so the number is no longer at the beginning. If a sentence contains more than one number, one of which requires a numeral form, then all numbers should be expressed as numerals. Government agencies and many businesses have slightly different rules for the expression of numbers, so writers should be aware of the guidelines at their jobs.

    Numerals are used, academically and professionally, in these instances: dates, addresses, measurements, percentages, page numbers, book sections, times (except with *o'clock*), and exact sums of money.

Abbreviating

The general guideline for college writing is that abbreviations should be avoided because readers may not understand them. At work, writers find it convenient to use the abbreviations familiar to everyone within the organization. Many employers have style sheets containing appropriate work-related abbreviations.

    Acceptable abbreviations include the following categories:

    A. Abbreviations commonly used with proper names, e.g., Mr., Ms., Dr., M.D., Jr., Esq.

    B. Abbreviations of terms or organizations only rarely seen written out, e.g., A.M., P.M., RSVP, IBM, NBC.

APPLICATION

In the following paragraph, locate and correct the errors in the use of capitals, numbers, and abbreviations.

Throughout the Fall, my Professor has been working with Prof. Ramirez on a new curriculum for a History course about how War affects culture. They will include examples from the italian renaissance, from french culture after WWI, and from America after the civil war. To prepare for the course, they have read "French painting between the Wars," have watched *The Civil War* series on TV, and have traveled throughout Europe and the Southern U.S. They expect to teach the course, called War and Culture, in the January term on mondays, wednesdays and fridays. Although they will have only 35 students in their class, the course will be available as an online course next year, so they could reach thousands of students with their ideas.

III. PUNCTUATION

Using Commas

For many writers commas remain a mystery. Following the dictum that commas represent pauses, they may scatter commas erratically over their work. The following seven guidelines for comma usage should demystify the punctuation process.

1. Items in a series

Put a comma after every item in a series of words, phrases, or clauses. The comma before the conjunction is optional, but be consistent throughout each writing.

Words: She is taking physics, aerobics, and English this semester.

Phrases: He looked for his wallet on the dresser, on the floor, and under the sofa cushions.

Clauses: We had no difficulty with customs when we left Italy, when we entered London, or when we returned to New York.

2. Compound sentences

A compound sentence consists of two complete sentences (also called independent clauses) joined by a coordinating conjunction—*and, but, or, for, nor, so,* or *yet.* Use a comma before the conjunction in a compound sentence. The comma may be omitted if both clauses are short. Do not use a comma in a sentence with a compound verb. Compare these two sentences:

Javier entered the museum's ancient civilizations gallery and then began to study the Etruscan artifacts.

Javier entered the museum's ancient civilizations gallery, and then he began to study the Etruscan artifacts.

The first sentence is not compound; it has a simple subject, *Javier*, and a compound verb, *entered* and *began*. Because there are not two complete sentences, no comma is used. The second example is a compound sentence: It consists of two complete sentences, each with a subject and verb, so a comma is necessary.

3. Introductory elements

Use a comma after a phrase or clause that comes at the beginning of a sentence:

When he was only five, he began to compose simple melodies.

Chuckling to himself, Roberto read the letter again.

If the introductory element is a short prepositional phrase, the comma is unnecessary:

At midnight the wolf began to howl.

4. Interrupters

If a word, phrase, or clause interrupts a sentence, put a comma both before and after it. If the interrupting material is at the end of the sentence, as in the last example in the following list, only one comma is necessary.

She agreed, nevertheless, to cooperate.

Her new dress, shriveled from the heat of the dryer, was ruined.

My neighbor, who recently finished her degree, is coming for dinner tonight.

I loaned my car to Joanna, my old high-school friend.

Sometimes a word or phrase in the middle of a sentence does not really interrupt the flow of ideas, so no commas should be used:

The noise that I heard in the night was only the cat.

The man who stopped to help Steve turned out to be a distant relative.

If you are unsure whether the words truly interrupt the sentence, read the sentence aloud; often you can hear the interruption. If you are still unsure, try reading the sentence without the words in question. If the primary meaning of the sentence is unchanged, then the information is not necessary, and you must use commas to set off the interrupters. If removing the words significantly alters the meaning of the sentence, then all the information is essential, and no commas should be inserted.

5. Direct quotations

Use a comma to set off a direct quotation from the rest of the sentence. If the quote is at the beginning of the sentence, the comma must be inside the closing quotation marks.

"You're still angry," he said sadly.

The professor announced, "Pop quiz time!"

6. Coordinate adjectives

When two or more adjectives can be joined by *and* or can be placed in reverse order, they are called *coordinate adjectives*. Consider the phrase, "a filthy, tattered shirt." Because it is equally correct to say "a tattered, filthy shirt" (reverse order) or "a tattered and filthy shirt," (joined by *and*), the adjectives are coordinate, so a comma is used. However, in the phrase, "an old red brick hotel," no commas are necessary. The adjectives cannot be reversed ("a brick old red hotel"), nor can they be joined by *and* ("an old and red and brick hotel"), so the adjectives are not coordinate, and commas are unnecessary.

7. Miscellaneous use

When writing dates, separate the month and day from the year with a comma. If the date is part of a sentence, it is followed by a comma: "June 6, 1955, is my father's birthday." However, no comma is necessary when the date contains only the month and the year: "We adopted our daughter in June 1999."

When writing addresses, separate each element of the address except the zip code with a comma: "My new address will be 34 Huntington Drive, Danville, Illinois 61832."

When writing long numbers, separate each group of three digits with a comma: 1,354,821. If the number contains only four digits, the comma is optional: Either 4000 or 4,000 is correct.

When writing a personal or business letter, use a comma after the closing (e.g., "Sincerely yours,"). When writing a personal letter, use a comma after the opening (e.g., "Dear Kevin,"). When writing a business letter, use a colon after the opening, even if you know the recipient personally (e.g., "Dear Mr. Wade:" "Dear John:").

APPLICATION

The sentences below contain no commas. Add commas where appropriate, and indicate in the blank the number of the rule or rules that apply.

1. _____ Around 3000 B.C. civilizations appeared in the Indus Valley Egypt and Mesopotamia.

2. _____ However the Mesopotamian civilization located between the Tigris and the Euphrates Rivers probably began as early as 5000 B.C. when settlers from the Elamite Mountains descended into the river valley.

3. _____ The people there were known as Sumerians; this term according to E. O. James is a "linguistic designation."

4. _____ The Sumerians learned to control flood waters and they also developed canals to bring water to their crops.

5. _____ In the Sumerians' small villages life centered on the temple.

6. _____ The temple was thought to be the home of the god of the city yet it was also a school where males but not females were educated.

7. _____ In addition to controlling the temples the schools and the lands priests were once power-

   ful enlightened political leaders before the emergence of military leaders.

8. _____ A great flood sometimes considered a prototype of the flood associated with Noah in He-

   brew scripture swept over the Tigris Valley and destroyed numerous Sumerian towns.

9. _____ Mesopotamian civilization after the flood was a more complex urban culture.

10. _____ Fishermen and farmers outside the city sold their surplus to the merchants artisans

   priests officials and rulers who lived inside the city.

Using Apostrophes

Apostrophes have only two uses: to form contractions and to form possessive nouns.

Forming Contractions

Contractions are formed by the combination of two words to create one shorter word; for example, *she will* becomes *she'll*, and *should not* becomes *shouldn't*. The apostrophe indicates that letters are omitted: The *wi* is omitted from *she'll*, and the *o* is omitted from *shouldn't*. There are only two exceptions to this rule: *will + not* becomes *won't*, and *can + not* loses one *n* and an *o* to become *can't*. Below is a list of some common contractions:

I + am = I'm	could + not = couldn't
I + have = I've	have + not = haven't
he + has = he's	who + is = who's
we + had = we'd	it + is = it's
she + will = she'll	they + are = they're
is + not = isn't	you + are = you're

Forming Possessives

A possessive is a noun that shows ownership, e.g., "Carol's Toyota," "the children's preschool." To form the possessive of a word that does not end in *-s*, add an apostrophe and an *s*:

Brian's book	the professor's lecture
my aunt's promotion	the men's gym
each other's notebook	Sherilla's loss

To form the possessive of a word that ends in *-s*, add only an apostrophe:

my sisters' friends	the boss' office
the Smiths' house	James' assignment
the dogs' barking	both books' covers

Notice that you do not need to determine whether the word is singular or plural. *Brian*, a singular noun, adds *'s*, but so does *men*, a plural noun. *James*, a singular noun, adds only an apostrophe, but so does *dogs*, a plural noun.

If you are occasionally uncertain where to place the apostrophe, here is a foolproof solution: Rewrite the possessive as a phrase, and place the apostrophe at the end of the phrase. For example, if you are uncertain where to place the apostrophe in "my sisters friends," change the phrase to "the friends of my sister." Put the apostrophe on the word at the end of the phrase: "My sister's friends" is correct. If you want to refer to the office of James, the apostrophe will be at the end of the word *James*, "James' office."

Remember to distinguish between plural nouns and possessives. An apostrophe is necessary to make a noun—singular or plural—into a possessive. No apostrophe is used to form a plural noun. In this sentence, the first *movies* is a plural noun, the second a possessive: "Both *movies* we saw last weekend were thrillers; however, the second *movie's* plot was far more original." If you are unsure whether the noun is a simple plural or a possessive, try rewriting it as a phrase. Because "the movie's plot" is a possessive form, the phrase could be rewritten as "the plot of the movie." However, "both movies," which is not a possessive form, cannot be restructured as a phrase.

APPLICATION

Add apostrophes to form contractions or possessives in the following paragraph:

Americas shopping habits have been changing. Because of Americas materialistic culture, people have traditionally achieved status by spending large sums for consumer goods. However, high prices and crowded schedules have popularized two shopping trends: online shopping and discount stores. People dont want to shop after work, especially since its now possible to shop at their computer terminals. Online shopping allows buyers to see the product without leaving their homes. People are also flocking to discount chain stores, such as Walmart, and warehouse food stores, such as PACE. Customers claim theyre routinely saving up to 25 percent on top-quality merchandise. Perhaps well eventually see consumers achieving status by saving instead of spending money.

Using Quotation Marks

Quotation marks are used to enclose short titles and to indicate the exact words people say.

Citing Short Titles

When you refer to the title of a short work, whether it is published by itself or as part of a longer work, enclose the title in quotation marks. The titles of poems, songs, stories, essays, chapters in books, and articles in magazines or newspapers are all enclosed in quotation marks. The title of a long work is italicized or underlined. The titles of magazines, newspapers, books, epics, audiotapes, movies, and television series are all italicized or underlined.

> W. D. Snodgrass' poem "Takeoff," from his collection *After Experience* is a love poem that uses a flight metaphor.
> Dr. Roland assigned the chapter called "Editing" in *Making Movies*; she also told us to read two film reviews from *The New York Times*.

When you read published works, you will notice that titles of long works are usually in italics, not underlined. Printed works use italics for titles; however, if you are writing by hand or using a printer that does not produce easy-to-read italics, underline long titles.

Although you use quotation marks or underlining when referring to titles, the titles you put on your essays, reports, or research papers should not be in quotation marks or underlined.

Indicating Direct Quotations

When you are writing the exact words someone has said (referred to as a direct quotation), enclose the words in quotation marks. When you are repeating what someone said without using the exact words (referred to as an indirect quotation), do not use quotation marks. Compare these examples of a direct and an indirect quotation:

> Ian asked, "Is it still raining?"
> Ian asked if it is still raining.

Using Single Quotation Marks

If a quotation contains another quotation within it, the quotation inside is enclosed in single quotation marks. Look at these two examples:

> The new father exclaimed with awe, "She said, 'DaDa.' My daughter actually said, 'DaDa.'"
> Dr. Shah said, "Read, compare, and prepare to write about Baudelaire's poems 'Elevation' and 'L'Invitation au voyage' before Monday's class."

Blocking Long Quotati+25.75/3ns

Long quotations, more than three typed lines, are set off from the rest of the text. To block a long quotation

- begin on a new line
- indent each line one inch
- do not use quotation marks
- place parenthetical documentation after the period at the close of the quotation

Marking Omissions with Ellipses

Often you will want to eliminate a portion of a quotation because it is irrelevant to the point you are making. You can identify the omission for your reader by using an ellipsis, three spaced periods. Notice the blocked quotation by G. M. A. Grube on p. 541; the ellipsis indicates that the final portion of the quotation is omitted. If the ellipsis is at the end of a sentence, a fourth period precedes it. Notice the placement of the ellipses when the omissions are in these positions:

- <u>beginning of sentence</u>:   ". . . quotation."
- <u>middle of sentence</u>:   "quotation . . . quotation."
- <u>end of sentence</u>:   "quotation. . . ."
- <u>end of sentence with parenthetical documentation</u>:   "quotation. . . ." (22).
- <u>end of blocked quotation</u>:   "quotation. . . ." (22)
- <u>one or more sentences within a quotation</u>   "quotation. . . ."

Inserting Brackets

Sometimes you need to add a word or two to a quotation to clarify the meaning or to make the quotation fit seamlessly into your sentence. Any words you insert into a quotation must be enclosed in brackets: "Experts do not yet know how or why it [self-hypnosis] works." Because they are somewhat distracting, brackets should be used sparingly. When you need to add brackets to make a quotation clear, consider replacing the quotation with a paraphrase. In the example above, a paraphrase would be more effective than the quotation.

Occasionally you will find an error in the material you quote. To indicate that the error is in the original document, add the Latin term *sic* in brackets. *Sic*, which means "thus," indicates that you are quoting the material exactly as it is in the original: "Even in a strong economy and a flourishing market, capitol [*sic*] should be invested cautiously."

Punctuating with Quotation Marks

As you may have noticed from the preceding examples, periods and commas are placed inside the closing quotation marks. Colons and semicolons are placed outside closing quotation marks. Exclamation points and question marks are placed inside if the quotation is an exclamation or question; they are placed outside if the entire sentence, but not the quotation, is an exclamation or question.

PERIOD:	Every time I ask my son what he's doing in preschool, he always answers, "Nothing."
COMMA:	"We can never seem to agree about this," Bill said, "but perhaps we can agree to disagree."
SEMICOLON:	It may be true that "Honesty is the best policy"; however, a white lie is sometimes the best policy for preserving harmony among friends.
COLON:	I loved Grace Paley's story "The Loudest Voice": It reminded me of my school days in New York City.

EXCLAMATION:	(A) "Don't!" she gasped.
	(B) I can't believe she calmly told me, "You are so boring"!
QUESTION:	(A) She asked, "What time is it?"
	(B) Did Ben Franklin say, "A penny saved is a penny earned"?

Using Semicolons and Colons

Using Semicolons

Semicolons are used to separate two complete sentences that are closely related in meaning. Often the second sentence begins with a word like *however* or *therefore*. The second sentence is not capitalized.

> I can begin my new job in January; therefore, I plan to take twenty-one credit hours during the fall semester.

Semicolons can also be used to separate items in a series when one or more items in the list contain commas.

> The hiring committee will consist of Patricia Wheelwright, of the Human Resources Department; Dr. Richard Trombetto, professor of English; and Dr. Elaine Chovanes, dean of instruction.

Using Colons

Colons, which indicate that something will follow, are used to introduce lists, long quotations, and explanations. In each case, the colon is placed at the end of the first sentence.

Introducing Lists

When colons precede lists, the introductions must be complete sentences. Compare the following examples:

| CORRECT: | The itinerary included four cities: Rome, Venice, Istanbul, and Athens. |
| INCORRECT: | The itinerary included: Rome, Venice, Istanbul, and Athens. |

Colons are often overused to introduce lists. If the list is brief and the ideas easily understood, a colon is often unnecessary. For example, the incorrect example above could be corrected by removal of the colon. The sentence would then read, "The itinerary included Rome, Venice, Istanbul, and Athens." The only information missing from the first version of the sentence, that these are four cities, is unnecessary because it is supplied by the context.

Introducing Quotations

Colons are sometimes used to introduce long quotations. Usually, but not always, quotations introduced by colons are long enough to be blocked (i.e., four or more typed lines). The colon must follow a complete sentence. If the introduction to the quotation is not a complete sentence, use a comma. Look at the following example:

> According to G.M.A. Grube, the ancient Greek words for god are not equivalent to the English word *God*:
>
>> "Theos" primarily means something that is eternal; it can be freely applied to all that is greater than man because it lasts for ever. A "god" is the personification of any more-than-human power in nature, or any force within the heart of man which is also greater than the individual because it is shared by all individuals. . . . (41-42)

Introducing Explanations

A colon is also used at the end of a complete sentence to indicate that the material that follows offers an explanation of the previous sentence. The material following the colon can be a word, a phrase, or a complete sentence. If the material following the colon is a complete sentence, usage varies. When using Modern Language Association (MLA) style, do not capitalize the second sentence; when using American Psychological Association (APA) style, capitalize the second sentence. In the preceding paragraph a colon was used to introduce the long quotation. Notice that the colon also introduced an explanation; i.e., the quotation explains the statement that the ancient Greek term for god differs from the modern one. Here are two additional examples:

> Marriages are often complicated by two gender differences: Men and women tend to have different styles of communication and different attitudes toward power.
>
> Three traits will make you successful at almost every job: competence, diligence, and loyalty.

APPLICATION

Add quotation marks, semicolons, or colons to the following passage. In the margin jot down the justification for each punctuation mark you add.

Over the past decade, health practitioners and psychologists have been exploring a new relationship the connection between people's attitude and their physical health. Researchers have demonstrated that four psychological factors can affect the immune system stress, anxiety, depression, and a negative outlook. Other researchers, while acknowledging a connection between attitude and immune system, argue that attitude has never been proven to alter the progress of a disease, nor is there evidence that one's state of mind can be powerful enough to

create a disease. In *Blaming the Victim*, Ellen Switzer reminds readers of the centuries-old ten-

dency to ascribe disease to personality In the Middle Ages, those who suffered from epilepsy . . .

were subjected, if they were lucky, to exorcism to banish evil spirits. Other not-so-lucky epileptics

were burned as witches.

The extent of the relationship between one's state of mind and one's ability to avoid or

recover from disease is still unclear however, all researchers would agree that a healthy

lifestyle, an avoidance of stress, a positive attitude, and excellent medical care all promote

good health.

Using Hyphens

A hyphen has only two functions—to divide a word at the end of a line and to join words to form a compound.

Dividing Words

Almost every workplace and college paper is written on a computer that will automatically divide a long word or move it to the next line, so dividing words with hyphens is usually unnecessary. However, when writing by hand, you may need to divide a word at the end of a line to make it fit inside the right margin. Never divide a one-syllable word, and never leave only two letters before or after the hyphen. When you must divide a word, separate it between syllables. If you are unsure of the correct syllable divisions of a word, look it up in the dictionary. When possible, choose the division that will be easiest for your reader; for example, *harden-ing* is easier to read than *hard-ening*. Place the hyphen at the end of the line, not at the beginning of the following line.

Forming Compounds

Hyphens are also used to form compounds. Some nouns, like *father-in-law*, combine two or more words to form one noun. If you are unsure whether a noun is hyphenated, look it up in a dictionary.

Words are also often combined to form adjectives. These compound adjectives are hyphenated only when they come before the noun they modify. Look at the following examples:

He has a ten-year-old son.
His son is ten years old.

She is a high-school student.
She is a student in high school.

If the first part of the compound modifier ends in *-ly*, no hyphen is used ("a newly constructed building").

Sometimes compound adjectives are used in a series. If all the compounds have the same final word, each modifier before the last can end with a hyphen: "Cut out a five-, a ten-, and a twelve-inch square of paper."

Using Dashes

Dashes are used to highlight interruptions or additions to sentences. Interruptions can be set off by commas, enclosed in parentheses, or set off by dashes:

- <u>commas</u> indicate the interruption is not essential to the sentence
- <u>parentheses</u> deemphasize the interruption
- <u>dashes</u> emphasize the interruption.

When you are typing, indicate a dash by two hyphens with no space before or after.

Stacey arrived at midnight—four hours late—with no explanation.
I am determined to finish this novel tonight—no matter what!

APPLICATION

In the following sentences, add hyphens to form compound modifiers where necessary, and replace commas with dashes if appropriate:

Child rearing experts stress developmental stages, so many people would assume that our eleven month old daughter and our eleven year old son would require different parenting skills. However, two basic areas of child care, safety and socialization, don't seem to vary much with the age of the child. My daughter is unsafe in any circumstance; she will insert a moist finger in any outlet, push a switch on any appliance, put any substance in her mouth. My son will do none of these things. However, in his middle school industrial arts class he was stricken with power tool mania, a dangerous disease in young males. Socialization is also an ongoing process. My daughter has recently learned that people dislike being bitten; my son just learned that people dislike squirt gun attacks at picnics, no matter how hot the day. At the same time, my husband and I are learning the truth of my parents' assertion that parenthood has only one requirement, eternal vigilance!

IV. GUIDELINES FOR SPEAKERS OF OTHER LANGUAGES

Learning the conventions of another language is always complex, especially since so many aspects of language reflect culture. One of the best ways to become comfortable with a language is to read widely and to model your writing on the texts you read. However, these guidelines will help you with a few elements of English that many speakers of other languages find troublesome: articles, verbs, prepositions, and adjectives.

Using Articles

English has two articles: *a* and *the*. Each article indicates that a noun (a word that names a person, place, thing, or idea) will follow. Although the rules governing articles are complicated, the guidelines below will familiarize you with their use.

Using Indefinite Articles

A is called an indefinite article. Indefinite articles do not identify specific items, so "*a* computer" does not indicate which computer the speaker is referring to.

Look at the first sentence of this section; you'll notice that *a* also takes the form *an*. If the word that follows *a* begins with a vowel sound, use *an*:

a peach	an orange
a novel	an interesting novel
a horse	an hour

In the last examples, both *horse* and *hour* start with the letter *h*; however, the *h* in *hour* is not aspirated, so that word begins with a vowel sound and therefore takes *an*.

Since *a* means *one*, indefinite articles are used with singular nouns, not with plural nouns: If you bought one orange at the store, you would say,"I bought *an* orange"; however, if you bought several oranges, you would say "I bought oranges" or "I bought some oranges."

Using Definite Articles

The is called a definite article because it refers to a specific item. If you say, "Juan fixed *the* computer," then both you and your listener know the specific computer you are referring to. *The* can be used with both singular and plural nouns, so both of these sentences are correct:

Mila ate the orange.
Mila ate the oranges.

Count and Noncount Nouns

To use articles accurately, you need to distinguish between count and noncount nouns.

Count Nouns

Count nouns name people or things that can be counted: sandwich, desk, professor, theory. Because they can be counted, they can be plural: two sandwiches, five desks, several professors, many theories.

Noncount Nouns

Noncount nouns name things or ideas that cannot be counted. Because they cannot be counted, they cannot be plural. Although noncount nouns are more difficult to recognize, many of them fit into these categories:

- *Abstractions*: courage, happiness, advice, education, knowledge
- *Elements in Nature*: air, water, gold, silver, earth, lightning, fog
- *Materials*: plastic, concrete, wool, cotton
- *Food and Liquids*: rice, cheese, water, milk, meat

One confusing category consists of groups of items: clothing, furniture, money, hair, equipment. Even though a person could count the pieces of furniture or equipment (one chair, five computer keyboards), the general term for the group of items is a noncount noun.

Because distinguishing between count and noncount nouns can sometimes be tricky, consult an ESL dictionary whenever you're uncertain about a noun. Once you have determined whether a noun is a count or a noncount noun, these guidelines will help determine which article to use:

1. Use *a* or *an* with a singular count noun if the specific identify of the item is unknown:
   Hand me *a* section of the newspaper. (The speaker is not specifying which section.)
   Kim wanted to rent *a* room, not *an* apartment. (The writer is not indicating a specific room or apartment.)
2. Do not use *a* or *an* with noncount nouns. You may use *a* or *an* if you are referring to a quantity of a noncount noun.
   Matt has speed and stamina.
   Learning another language requires *a* lot of patience and perseverance. (*A lot* expresses a vague quantity.)
   I prefer to drink tea.
   I'd like a cup of coffee, please. (Although *coffee* is a noncount noun, *cup* expresses a quantity.)
3. Use *the* with count and noncount nouns when the writer and reader know the item referred to, sometimes because it has been referred to before.
   She stared at the furniture. (Both the writer and the reader know which furniture.)

I'll read *a* magazine while I wait. Would you hand me *the* <u>Newsweek</u> on *the* coffee table? (Although "a magazine" is not specific, both speaker and listener understand which <u>Newsweek</u> and which coffee table are being referred to.)

4. Use *the* with superlatives of both count and noncount nouns. Because superlatives indicate one of a kind, they make a noun specific.

Alice is *the* most articulate student in the class. (*Student* is a count noun.)

Jim has *the* most strength of anyone on the football team. (*Strength* is a noncount noun.)

5. Use *the* with unique things (*the* sun, *the* solar system, *the* future)

There is a model of *the* solar system on professor Genz's desk.

6. Use *the* after expressions ending with *of*.

Most of *the* students felt frustrated.

Did you eat any of *the* potato chips?

7. When speaking generally, do not use *the* with noncount nouns. Use *a* or *the* with singular count nouns.

Water is precious and should never be wasted. (*Water* is a noncount noun.)

A dog is said to be man's best friend, but *a* cat also makes *an* excellent house pet. (*Dog*, *cat*, and *housepet* are count nouns.)

The dog and *the* horse were both domesticated in early civilizations. (*Dog* and *horse* are both singular count nouns.)

8. Use *the* with most plural proper nouns (the names of specific people, places, or things); do not use *the* with most singular proper names.

Although *the* Smiths are excellent neighbors, Deborah Smith is very shy and can be difficult to talk with.

Because so many rules govern the use of articles and because there are so many exceptions to the rules, don't hesitate to consult a dictionary or ask a native speaker. As you read, note the placement of articles; use the texts as models for your own writing.

APPLICATIONS

A. Identify each of the following nouns as count [**C**] or noncount [**NC**].

1. _____ oxygen   5. _____ gold
2. _____ desks   6. _____ tea
3. _____ education   7. _____ magazine
4. _____ fish   8. _____ neighbor

B. Fill in each blank with the appropriate definite or indefinite article.

1. My son is _____ tallest child in his kindergarten class.
2. Would you please hand me _____ apple from the fruit bowl on _____ kitchen counter?
3. I read _____ interesting article in today's *Times*.

4. Teachers need _____ lot of patience.
5. Some of _____ computer disks are defective.
6. Did Professor Roget give us _____ reading assignment for next week?
7. _____ hour ago, I finished reading _____ assignment for this week
8. Because some of _____ problems are confusing, I'm working with _____ tutor.

Using Verbs

Earlier (pp. 504–509), you reviewed the basic forms of regular and irregular verbs. This section will focus on aspects of verbs that pose problems for speakers of other languages: idioms, gerunds and infinitives, modals and helping verbs, conditional sentences, and present and present progressive tenses.

Idiomatic Verb Phrases

An idiom is a phrase whose meaning is not a literal translation of its words. For example, the expression "run across" means "to meet unexpectedly," an expression which involves neither running nor crossing. In English, two- and three-word idiomatic verb phrases, each of which consists of a verb and one or two prepositions, are common. The following list includes only a few of these phrases, so when in doubt, consult your ESL dictionary. The idiomatic verb phrases are divided into two lists:

- "Inseparable"—the words in the phrases can never be separated.
- "Separable"—the words in the phrases can be separated (e.g., "He *handed* the report *in*" or "He *handed in* the report").

Phrase	Definition	Example
Inseparable		
break down	stop functioning	The car *broke down* at the corner.
drop in on	visit unexpectedly	I *dropped in on* Cindy yesterday afternoon.
find out	discover	Did you *find out* what happened?
get up	arise	She usually *gets up* at dawn.
go over	review	The professor *went over* the test questions.
look into	investigate	She should *look into* that!
look out for	watch for	*Look out for* mistakes in your addition.
put up with	tolerate	You shouldn't *put up with* his behavior.
run out of	use up	I *ran out* of gas ten miles from home
show up	appear	He *showed up* fifteen minutes late.
take after	resemble	Which parent does the baby *take after*?

<u>Separable</u>

bring up	raise	Who will *bring up* their daughter?
call off	cancel	They *called* the concert *off*.
figure out	find a solution	I can't *figure* this algebra problem *out*!
hand in	submit	I already *handed in* my essay.
pick out	select	Which sweater did you *pick out*?

Using Gerunds and Infinitives with Verbs

An infinitive is formed by *to* + a verb: *to go, to be, to argue*. Some verbs, such as *want* are often followed by infinitives: "She wants *to leave*." A gerund is a verb form ending in *-ing* that functions as a noun: *cooking, thinking, laughing*. Some verbs, such as *quit*, are often followed by gerunds: "They quit *smoking*." Still other verbs, such as *start*, can be followed by either an infinitive or a gerund: "He started *to laugh*" or "He started *laughing*." The lists below will help familiarize you with many of the verbs followed by infinitives and gerunds.

Verbs Followed by Infinitives

The verbs in this list can be followed by infinitives:

afford	consent	hesitate	need	seem
agree	decide	hope	offer	struggle
appear	demand	intend	plan	tend
arrange	deserve	learn	prepare	threaten
ask	expect	like	pretend	wait
attempt	fail	manage	promise	want
claim	have	mean	refuse	wish

> Because she's shy, Kim usually hesitates *to join* the discussion.
> I learned *to ski* last winter.

Verbs Followed by Gerunds

The verbs in this list can be followed by gerunds:

admit	delay	finish	miss	resist
advise	deny	give up	postpone	succeed in
appreciate	discuss	imagine	practice	suggest
avoid	dislike	insist on	quit	talk about
complete	enjoy	keep	recall	tolerate
consider	escape	mention	recollect	understand

> James talked about *going* home.
> My dog cannot resist *chasing* squirrels.

Verbs Followed by Either Infinitives or Gerunds

The verbs in this list can be followed by either infinitives or gerunds with almost no change in meaning:

begin	continue	hate	love	start
can't stand	dislike	like	prefer	try

I like *getting up* at dawn.
I like *to get up* at dawn.
I prefer *sleeping* until noon.
I prefer *to sleep* until noon.

Verbs Followed by Nouns or Pronouns and Infinitives

Each verb in this list may be followed by either a noun or a pronoun and then an infinitive:

advise	command	have	invite	remind
allow	encourage	hire	order	require
cause	force	instruct	persuade	tell

The loud bang caused him *to come* running.
Dr. Ramirez advised his students not *to become* discouraged.
I told John *to wait* for me in front of the library.

Using Modals and Helping Verbs

Modals

The following verbs are called modals: *can, could, may might, must, shall, should, will, would.* Modals precede the base form of the verb (the form found in dictionary entries):

They will leave at noon.
I can swim.
Could I have another cup of coffee, please?

Modals express many conditions. Consider these distinctions:

- I *can* go. *Can* indicates an ability.
- I *could* go. *Could* indicates a possibility or ability.
- I *may* go *May* indicates a possibility or permission.
- I *might* go *Might* indicates a possibility or permission.
- I *must* go. *Must* indicates an obligation or necessity.
- I *shall* go *Shall*, like *will*, indicates an intention. When used with *you, he, she,* or *they, shall* is stronger than *will* and indicates determination or compulsion.
- I *should* go *Should* indicates an obligation.
- I *will* go. *Will* indicates an intention or a certainty.
- I *would* go. *Would* indicates a condition.

Consider this passage:

> Brian *must* go to class this morning (necessity). At noon he *might* meet you at the cafeteria (possibility). He *should* return to the library after lunch (obligation). In the evening, he *will* finish his chemistry assignment (certainty). I know he *would* like to go to Marcia's party, but he probably *won't* (*will* + not) be finished in time (condition).

Helping Verbs

Modals do not change their forms to indicate tense (time), but three other helping verbs—*have, do,* and *be*—do change forms. Below are their forms:

Do

Notice that the forms of *do* are followed by the base form of the verbs.

> *Do* you want to watch a video tonight?
>
> Charlie *doesn't* agree with us.
>
> *Did* Tony say he'd be here by 8:15?

Have

Notice that the forms of *have* are followed by the past participle form of the verbs.

> They *have* spoken of you often.
>
> Alicia *had* argued until she was exhausted.
>
> Liz *has* enjoyed the mystery novels.

Be

Notice that these forms of *be* are followed by the present participle (the *-ing* verb form).

> I *am* watching television now.
>
> Pat *is* thinking about changing jobs.
>
> They *aren't* leaving until noon.
>
> What *was* he doing?
>
> *Were* you reading when I phoned?

Notice that the form *be* is preceded by a modal.

> Mother should *be* delighted by the news.

Notice that the form *been* is preceded by a form of *have*.

> She has *been* working for twelve hours.

Forming Conditional Sentences

A conditional sentence has two parts—an independent clause and a dependant clause beginning with *if, when, whenever,* or *unless.* Remember that a dependent clause can begin, interrupt, or end a sentence. A conditional sentence may express a factual relationship, state a predication, or speculate about a possibility.

Conditionals Stating Facts

A factual conditional states a factual relationship or a habitual action. A factual conditional uses the same verb tense in both clauses.

> When Betsy *buys* groceries, she *purchases* enough for the entire week.
>
> Whenever his professor *offered* help, he *took* advantage of the opportunity.
>
> People *are* healthier if they *exercise* regularly.

Conditionals Stating Predictions

A conditional stating a prediction is used to predict the future or suggest future possibilities. This type of conditional contains a dependent clause that begins with *if*, *unless* or *when* and uses the present tense of the verb. The independent clause uses a modal and the base form of the verb.

> Unless Shawn *leaves* work early, he *can't watch* his daughter's soccer game.
> If you *study* hard, you *will succeed*.

Conditionals Speculating About Possibilities

A conditional speculating about a possibility contains a dependent clause starting with *if* and uses the past tense. The independent clause uses the modals *could*, *would*, or *might* and uses the base form or a past tense form of the verb.

> If I *had* more time, I *would* exercise every day.
> If we *had left* earlier, we *would* have missed the rush hour.

When the *if* clause expresses something untrue, use the verb form *were* instead of *was*. In the independent clause, use the modal *would*, *could*, or *might* and the base form of the verb.

> If I *were* a millionaire, I *would* support several children's charities.
> If George *were* here, he *would* be furious.

Choosing Between the Present and the Present Progressive Tenses

English has several verb tenses with complicated rules governing their use. The most common problems, however, occur in distinguishing between the present and the present progressive tenses.

The present tense in English indicates a habitual action. The present progressive indicates an action in progress.

Present:	He usually *walks* the dog before he leaves for work. (a habit)
Present progressive:	Pete *is walking* the dog now, but he should be home soon. (an action in progress)

The present progressive tense is common in English, especially in conversation; however, several verbs do not use the present progressive form to describe an action in progress because they describe states of being, not actions:

appear	contain	feel	know	own	smell
be	correspond	forget	like	possess	suppose
believe	deserve	hate	love	prefer	understand
belong	desire	have	mean	recognize	want
consist	differ from	hear	need	see	wish
constitute	exist	involve	owe	seem	

> She *appears* to be upset.
> They *need* to buy a new battery for their car.

APPLICATIONS

A. Fill in the blank in each sentence with the infinitive or the gerund form of the verb in parentheses.

1. Ulli wants _____ (GO) to the concert with us.
2. Did Roger mention _____ (WIN) the essay contest?
3. I keep _____ (FORGET) my password!
4. Can you manage _____ (FINISH) the project by the deadline?
5. I avoid _____ (DRIVE) in rush hour whenever I can.

B. Fill in the blanks with one of these modals or helping verbs: *can, could, do, must, should, will, would.*

_____ you want to rent a videotape tonight? I _____ stop on the way home from work to

choose one. I _____ enjoy a horror film, but you _____ probably prefer a comedy. Since I

_____ get up tomorrow by 6:30, we _____ start right after dinner. In fact, instead of

cooking, I _____ order a pizza; that way we _____ eat dinner and watch a movie at the

same time.

C. Fill in the blank with a correct form of the verb in parentheses in each of these conditional sentences.

1. If I _____ (BE) the team leader, I would organize the project differently.
2. Whenever Marcie worked too long at the computer, she _____ (GET) a headache.
3. If I have time this evening, I _____ (WATCH) the game.
4. Unless you hurry, you _____ not _____ (FINISH) today.
5. When Georgia disagrees with her professors, she always _____ (BECOME) angry.

D. Use the present or the present progressive tense of the verb in parentheses.

1. Sara usually _____ (GO) to bed before midnight.
2. He always _____ (READ) the newspaper while he _____ (EAT) breakfast.
3. I _____ (LEAVE) in ten minutes.
4. José usually _____ (WORK) from nine to five,
    but this afternoon he _____ (WORK) late.
5. The telephone _____ (RING); can you answer it?

Using Prepositions

Prepositions can be difficult to master because their use is idiomatic; for example, we might say *at* night, *in* the morning and *during* the day. Four common prepositions are used to indicate time and place—*at, in, on,* and *by.*

<u>At</u> is used with
- general locations—*at* home, *at* work, *at* the mall
- specific locations—*at* Lee's house, *at* 31 E. Church Street
- specific times and with *night*—*at* noon, *at* 11:15, *at* night

<u>In</u> is used with
- enclosed spaces—*in* the kitchen, *in* the box
- geographic locations—*in* Senegal, *in* Chicago
- printed texts—*in* a newspaper, *in* a book
- seasons, months, years, and *morning, afternoon,* and *evening*—*in* the spring, *in* March, *in* 2001, *in* the evening

<u>On</u> is used with
- surfaces—*on* a desk, *on* the floor, *on* the street
- electronic media—*on* the radio, *on* television, *on* the Internet
- transportation—*on* a train, *on* a plane, *on* a subway, *on* a bicycle (but *in* a car)
- specific days or dates—*on* Monday, *on* November 12

<u>By</u> is used with
- times or dates—*by* August, *by* 10:00 A.M.
- near a place—*by* the table, *by* the door

Many prepositions are idiomatic, so you may sometimes need to ask native speakers which preposition to use. The following list contains a few common prepositions in idiomatic expressions:

by accident	irritated *by*
according *to*	*at* least
apologize *for* (something)	many or most *of*
apologize *to* (someone)	*on* purpose
belief *in*	satisfied *with*
different *from*	similar *to*
frightened *by*	think *about* (ponder)
interested *in*	think *of* (remember or have an idea)

APPLICATION

Fill in each blank with an appropriate preposition.

1. I have an interview _____ Sondheim Enterprises _____ Danville _____ 9:30 this morning.
2. Think _____ what she said, and decide what you're interested _____ doing _____ the problem.
3. Look for your keys _____ your desk, _____ the car, and _____ your coat pockets.
4. She saw the preview _____ television and read a review _____ the newspaper.
5. Put the report _____ your supervisor's desk _____ the end _____ the day.

Using Adjectives

Adjectives are words describing nouns: a *red* truck, a *difficult* concept, an *amusing* story. As you can see in these examples, adjectives usually precede the noun they describe. However, they can also follow linking verbs: The children were *happy*. Sarah is *busy*.

Using Verb Forms as Adjectives

The present participle (the *-ing* form) and the past participle (the *-ed* form) of verbs can both be used as adjectives. Often, the *-ing* form precedes a noun and the *-ed* form follows a linking verb:

> The circus act included a *dancing* bear.
> Kevin is *frustrated*.

Distinguishing between the *-ing* and the *-ed* forms of some adjectives is troublesome. For the adjectives in the following list, use the *-ing* form when the adjective describes a person or thing which causes a condition (a *boring* lecture) and use the *-ed* form when describing the person or thing affected (being *bored* by the lecture):

amusing	&	amused	fascinating	&	fascinated
annoying	&	annoyed	frustrating	&	frustrated
boring	&	bored	interesting	&	interested
confusing	&	confused	irritating	&	irritated
disappointing	&	disappointed	satisfying	&	satisfied
embarrassing	&	embarrassed	surprising	&	surprised
exciting	&	excited	terrifying	&	terrified
exhausting	&	exhausted	tiring	&	tired

> What an *amusing* story. He was *amused* by it.
> Sheila has an *annoying* habit. Several of her friends have said they're *annoyed*.
> The test results were *surprising*. Jorge was pleasantly *surprised* by the results.

Placing Adjectives in Order

If you are using more than one adjective to modify a noun, you will have to arrange the adjectives in an appropriate order:

1. Article (*a, an, the*), demonstrative pronoun (*this, that, these, those*), possessive noun or pronoun (*Eva's, his*)
2. Number giving order (*first, fifth, next, last*)
3. Number giving quantity (*three, nine, some*)
4. Evaluation (*attractive, shocking, lucky, wonderful, repulsive*)
5. Size (*little, enormous, tall*)
6. Shape (*rectangular, circular, square*)
7. Age (*young, ancient, new, elderly*)
8. Color (*green, black, blue, scarlet*)
9. Nationality or religion (*Mexican, Thai, Buddhist, Jewish*)

10. Material (*brick*, *silk*, *plaster*, *granite*)
11. Noun used as adjective (*computer* disk, *dining room* chairs)
    those small green leaves
    (1) (5) (8)
    an ancient Chinese herbal remedy
    (1) (7) (9) (10)
    seven large square cardboard boxes
    (3) (5) (6) (10)

APPLICATIONS

A. Use the present participle (-*ing* form) or the past participle (-*ed* form) of the verb to form an adjective.

1. What a _____ (DISAPPOINT) experience;
    you must feel very _____ (FRUSTRATE).

2. The students were all _____ (IRRITATE) by the
    professor's _____ (CONFUSE) explanations.

3. Everyone was _____ (FASCINATE) by the
    movie's _____ (COMPLICATE) ending.

4. At first I thought the book would be _____ (BORE),
    but it was more _____ (INTEREST) than I expected.

B. Arrange the adjectives in these sentences.

1. Danielle bought (silk new three) blouses.

2. On the table lay (picture large rectangular two) books, (ceramic Italian one blue) candlestick, and (glass several unusual) paperweights.

3. (Chinese the elderly four) ladies stood in front of (granite enormous the white) monument.

4. (oak a fallen) tree blocked the entrance to (red the brick abandoned) house.

This website offers advice, information, and practice to speakers of other languages:
☛   http://owl.english.purdue.edu/Files/25.html

CREDITS

ELIZABETH WAYLAND BARBER, excerpt from *Women's Work: The First 20,000 Years*. Copyright © 1994 by Elizabeth Wayland Barber. Reprinted with the permission of W. W. Norton & Company, Inc.

DOUG BATES, "Fighting Teen Pregnancy" from *San Jose Mercury News* (July 6, 1996). Copyright © 1996 by Religion News Service. Reprinted with permission.

WENDELL BERRY, "The Pleasures of Eating" from *What Are People For?: Essays*. Copyright © 1990 by Wendell Berry. Reprinted with the permission of Farrar, Straus & Giroux, LLC.

WILLIAM CARLOS WILLIAMS, excerpt [7 lines] from "The Host" from *The Collected Poems of William Carlos Williams, Volume II, 1939-1962*, edited by Christopher MacGowan. Copyright 1948, © 1962 by William Carlos Williams. Reprinted with the permission of New Directions Publishing Corporation.

J. E. MANSON, W. C. WILLET, M. J. STAMPFER, G. A. COLDITZ, D. J. HUNTER, S. E. HAWLINSON, C. H. HENNEKENS, and F. E. SPEIZER, "Body Weight and Mortality Among Women" (excerpt) from *The New England Journal of Medicine* (September 14, 1995). Copyright © 1995 by the Massachusetts Medical Society. Reprinted with the permission of *The New England Journal of Medicine*. All rights reserved.

BILL BRYSON, excerpt from "What's Cooking" from *Made in America: An Informal History of the English Language in the United States*. Copyright © 1994 by Bill Bryson. Reprinted with the permission of HarperCollins Publishers, Inc.

JOSEPH CAMPBELL, excerpt from *Myths to Live By*. Copyright © 1972 by Joseph Campbell. Reprinted with the permission of Viking Penguin, a division of Penguin Putnam Inc.

EDWARD HALLET CARR, "The Historian and His Facts" from *What is History?* Copyright © 1961 by Edward Hallet Carr. Reprinted with the permission of Alfred A. Knopf, Inc.

LAURIE COLWIN, excerpt from "How to Give a Party" from *Home Cooking*. Copyright © 1988 by Laurie Colwin. Reprinted with the permission of Alfred A. Knopf, a division of Random House, Inc.

CYNTHIA CROSSEN, excerpts from *Tainted Truth: The Manipulation of Fact in America*. Copyright © 1994 by Cynthia Crossen. Reprinted with the permission of Simon & Schuster, Inc.

CHARLES DARWIN, excerpts from *Charles Darwin's Notebooks 1836-1844, Geology, Transmutation of Species, Metaphysical Inquiries*, transcribed and edited by Paul H. Barrett, Peter J. Gautrey, Sandra Herbert, David Kohn and Sydney Smith. Copyright © 1987 by Paul H. Barrett, Peter J. Gautrey, Sandra Herbert, David Kohn, Sydney Smith. Reprinted with the permission of Cornell University Press.

JOAN DIDION, "On Keeping a Notebook" from *Slouching Toward Bethlehem*. Copyright © 1966, 1968 by Joan Didion. Reprinted with the permission of Farrar, Straus & Giroux, LLC.

PETER FARB and GEORGE J. ARMELAGOS, "Understanding Society and Culture Through Eating" from *Consuming Passions: The Anthropology of Eating*. Copyright © 1980 by The Estate of Peter Farb. Reprinted with the permission of Houghton Mifflin Company. All rights reserved.

CONNIE MAY FOWLER, "No Snapshots in the Attic: A Granddaughter's Search for a Cherokee Past" from *The New York Times Book Review* (May 22, 1994). Copyright © 1994 by Connie May Fowler. Reprinted with the permission of The Joy Harris Literary Agency.

JOHN GATTO, "The Seven-Lesson Schoolteacher" from *Dumbing Us Down: The Hidden Curriculum of Compulsory Schooling*, pp. 166-173. Copyright © 1992. Reprinted with the permission of New Society Publishers, Gabriola, B.C.

DONALD W. GEORGE, "The Way of Iced Coffee" from *The San Francisco Examiner*. Copyright © by *The San Francisco Examiner*. Reprinted with the permission of *The San Francisco Examiner*.

INDEX